CAMBRIDGE READINGS IN

THE HISTORY OF POLITICAL THOUGHT

Cambridge Readings in the History of Political Thought is an authoritative new series of anthologies, intended for students of politics, history and philosophy at all levels from introductory undergraduate upwards. Designed to cover major historical themes like the Enlightenment, or the impact of the French Revolution, each volume of Cambridge Readings will contain extracts from the principal political texts of the period, together with substantial editorial commentary and apparatus. The textual extracts are extensive but manageable for the beginning student, and well-known canonical writings are complemented by less familiar texts. The texts themselves are generally taken from the acclaimed editions published in the series of Cambridge Texts in the History of Political Thought, with authoritative new translations where necessary. There is an accessible introduction to each volume, and further guidance is offered by biographies of each writer and carefully selected bibliographies. These volumes enable the student to engage in depth with the intellectual context of particular periods, and to encounter at first hand some of the most influential and profound political thinking in the western tradition.

CAMBRIDGE READINGS IN
THE HISTORY OF POLITICAL THOUGHT

The Enlightenment

EDITED BY

DAVID WILLIAMS

University of Sheffield

CAMBRIDGE
UNIVERSITY PRESS

CAMBRIDGE
UNIVERSITY PRESS

University Printing House, Cambridge CB2 8BS, United Kingdom

One Liberty Plaza, 20th Floor, New York, NY 10006, USA

477 Williamstown Road, Port Melbourne, VIC 3207, Australia

4843/24, 2nd Floor, Ansari Road, Daryaganj, Delhi - 110002, India

79 Anson Road, #06-04/06, Singapore 079906

Cambridge University Press is part of the University of Cambridge.

It furthers the University's mission by disseminating knowledge in the pursuit of
education, learning and research at the highest international levels of excellence.

www.cambridge.org
Information on this title: www.cambridge.org/9780521564908

First published 1999

A catalogue record for this publication is available from the British Library

Library of Congress Cataloging in Publication data
The Enlightenment / edited by David Williams.
    p.   cm. – (Cambridge readings in the history of political thought)
    Includes bibliographical references and index.
    ISBN 0 521 56373 9 (hb). – ISBN 0 521 56490 5 (pb)
    1. Political science – History – 18th century. 2. Enlightenment.
I. Williams, David, 1938–   . II. Series.
JA83.E66   1999
320´.01–dc21   98-43695 CIP

ISBN 978-0-521-56373-4 Hardback
ISBN 978-0-521-56490-8 Paperback

CONTENTS

Contents

THE NATION STATE

CRIME AND PUNISHMENT

REVOLUTION

INTRODUCTION

The Enlightenment

Many ages can be described as ages of enlightenment, and any definition of the eighteenth-century Enlightenment that seeks to isolate this particular period from its links with other centuries of intellectual upheaval and reorientation would be misleading. The eighteenth century reflects continuities as well as the discontinuities with which it tends to be more often identified. It was an age deeply conscious of its debt to the past, yet aware at the same time of the uniqueness of its own historical moment as an age of light, and also as an age of crisis, transition and reassessment (Gay 1969, pp. 98–125).

Within only eight decades, from the death of the Sun King, Louis XIV, in 1715 to the American Declaration of Independence in 1776 and the birth of the First French Republic in 1792, Enlightenment Europe was to witness more political and social transformation than had been seen within any single previous lifetime. The semi-divine status of royalty, already undermined in England with the Glorious Revolution of 1688, was to be terminated almost exactly a century later with an act of regicide in France that would shake the foundations of autocratic political authority throughout Europe. It is with the eighteenth-century Enlightenment, a unique product of various national Enlightenments, that the birth pangs of a political modernity, in which the realities and problems of our own world, 'staring at us in embryo' (Plumb 1972, p. 31), can be detected, and for which the England of the post-1688 Settlement, the France of Louis XV and Louis XVI, and the American and French Revolutions provide the dramatic backdrop.

No eighteenth-century thinker defined the Enlightenment better in contemporary terms than Kant in his seminal essay, dated 30 September 1784, entitled *An answer to the question: what is Enlightenment?* Looking back on the achievements of his time, Kant defined the Enlightenment as an intellectual coming of age, achieved slowly and painfully, and the flowering of which was still incomplete:

Enlightenment is man's emergence from his self-incurred immaturity. Immaturity is the inability to use one's own understanding without the guidance of another. This immaturity is *self-incurred* if its cause is not lack of understanding, but lack of resolution and courage to use it without the guidance of another. The motto of the Enlightenment is therefore: *Sapere aude!* Have courage to use your own understanding!

Echoing the terms of Pierre Bayle's analysis of the irrational a century earlier in the *Thoughts on the comet* (1682), Kant pointed to laziness and cowardice as the reasons why 'it is so convenient to be immature!'. The shackles of past dogmas were often too familiar and comfortable to simply shake off:

> Thus only a few, by cultivating their own minds, have succeeded in freeing themselves, even among those appointed as guardians of the common mass ... Thus a public can only achieve enlightenment slowly. A revolution may well put an end to autocratic despotism and to rapacious or power-seeking oppression, but it will never produce a true reform in ways of thinking. Instead, new prejudices, like the ones they replaced, will serve as a leash to control the great unthinking mass ... For enlightenment of this kind, all that is needed is *freedom*. And the freedom in question is the most innocuous form of all – freedom to make *public use* of one's reason in all matters ... If it is now asked whether we at present live in an *enlightened* age, the answer is: no, but we do live in an age of *enlightenment*. As things are at present, we still have a long way to go before men as a whole can be in a position (or can even be put into a position) of using their own understanding confidently and well in religious matters, without outside guidance. But we do have distinct indications that the way is now being cleared for them to work freely in this direction, and that the obstacles to universal enlightenment, to man's emergence from his self-incurred immaturity, are gradually becoming fewer. (Reiss and Nisbet 1991, pp. 54, 55, 59–60)

Freedom to think and to express thought, freedom to act, the casting-off of external controls (often self-imposed) in the use of the human mind, were all identified by Kant as key components of the spirit of the times. Illumination of the nature of the Enlightenment's mission had also been the purpose of an earlier defining essay, Jean d'Alembert's *Preliminary discourse* (1751), written as the preface to one of the great French monuments to the Enlightenment, Denis Diderot's multi-volumed *The Encyclopedia, or rational dictionary of the sciences, arts and crafts* (see below, pp. 32–3), where tolerance and the right to free, untrammelled enquiry had been asserted in equally memorable terms.

The political thought of the Enlightenment can be traced back to the Renaissance and the sceptical tradition of Montaigne and Charron, and of course beyond that to the ancient world (Sabine and Thorson 1973; Skinner 1980; Waddicor 1970). The more immediately influential authorities shaping the terms of eighteenth-century political discourse are, however, to be found among seventeenth-century theorists and philosophers, often vulgarised in translation from the original Latin, or German or English. Some were not to have an impact on Europe until many decades after the initial publication of their works. Many early eighteenth-century political treatises, and some later ones, are essentially responses to, and expanded commentaries upon, ideas emanating from this earlier period. The 'delayed reaction' effect is equally apparent in the eighteenth century. Hume noted, for example, that his *Treatise of human nature* 'came unnoticed and unobserved into the world', and even the tremors from an earthquake of a work like Rousseau's *Social contract*, little read in the author's lifetime, with only one new edition between 1763 and 1790, had to wait almost three decades before being widely felt. This hiatus between publication and impact in an age in which the dissemination of ideas was still a difficult and dangerous enterprise inevitably complicates modern attempts to assess the historical significance of individual treatises as *Enlightenment* texts.

For this reason, writers whose work reflects specific features of Enlightenment political thought, but whose influence was largely confined to their times, are included among the more familiar names of writers whose impact transcended their times, and whose ideas continue to have potency. Moreover, not all the writers included in this volume are theorists or philosophers operating uniquely in the world of ideas, like Kant or Mandeville or Barbeyrac. Several texts reflect the professional experience of men holding public office at different times in their lives and who, like Siéyès or Moser, Condorcet or Burke, were professionally involved in the practice of government. Others, like Smith, Montesquieu and Rousseau (if we count his brief period as an embassy official in Venice), moved between both worlds.

In any consideration of the period's political thought, modern readers must also engage with the earlier ideas of Locke, Hobbes, Descartes, Boyle, Bayle, Selden and others, as well as with natural law theorists, such as Hugo de Groot (Grotius),

Samuel Pufendorf and Richard Cumberland. Politics and theology remained closely interlinked in the Enlightenment, and what earlier schools of thought had to say on human nature, God's laws and man's laws, the authority of sovereigns, the relationship between rulers and the ruled, the social contract, property, trade, taxation, war, morality and rights remained indispensable points of reference for most Enlightenment political theorists. Locke's *Letters concerning toleration* (1689–92), the *Two treatises of government* (1690) and above all the *Essay concerning human understanding* (1690), Hobbes' *Of the citizen* (1642) and the *Leviathan* (1651), Grotius' *On the law of war and peace* (1625) and Pufendorf's *On the law of nature and nations* (1672) and *On the duty of man and citizen according to natural law* (1673) are all examples of seminal texts in this regard.

Written mainly in the form of substantial, heavily annotated, densely argued and often rebarbative treatises, many spilling over into theology and metaphysics, this rich seam of seventeenth-century political scholarship was accessible only to a relatively small and intellectually sophisticated readership, well versed in ancient and modern sources and languages. Seventeenth-century political thought evolved, moreover, in the aftermath of the Thirty Years War, of which most of Europe still carried the scars and memories, and against a background of continuing civil unrest and conflict. However, the greatest political commentators of the period bequeathed to the Enlightenment works that transcended their particular experience of historical processes, and touched upon enduring principles and dilemmas. Part of the Enlightenment's achievement was to vulgarise and clarify the arcane language and rhetorical formulations of the seventeenth-century academic treatise, and provide a much wider public access to the ideas it contained, and to an understanding of their contemporary relevance. The language of political analysis in the Enlightenment would grow increasingly secular and polite, and the modes of dissemination more varied and flexible. This is the period in which the elegant, attractively written essay would come of age, largely in response to the rise of the middle classes, and a bourgeois culture which gradually replaced that of the court. Writers like Hume (see below, pp. 26–8, 217–18) had to take increasing account of changes in taste and style, and the need to appeal to a broader and very different readership to that of the narrow circles addressed by the learned treatise-writers of the previous century. However, the old questions about the nature of man and the organisation of the civil order would continue to be posed, but answered in terms of new political and social realities, and in the language of polite society rather than that of Latin discourse. If the format and language of political argument changed, however, its substance and frame of reference continued to be shaped and nourished by the work of this earlier generation.

Locke's *Essay concerning human understanding*, his *Letters on toleration* and, in a rather more diffuse and ambiguous way, his *Two treatises of government*, received much attention from Enlightenment thinkers, for example. There were twenty editions of the *Essay* alone between 1700 and 1800, and countless reprints. Locke demonstrated how freedom was limited by the very nature of the civil order, and in his philosophical writings he revealed the ways in which human knowledge was limited to the world revealed by the senses, exposing the inadequacy of innate ideas as a principle of understanding. In the second of the *Two treatises* contemporary acceptance of biblical, patriarchalist accounts of the origins of political power, exemplified in civil war tracts like Robert Filmer's defence of royalism in *Patriarcha* (1680), had been rejected, thereby marking out new paths of political debate for the next generation of thinkers in England and elsewhere (Hampsher-Monk 1992, pp. 76–88). In politics as well as philosophy, it was the Lockean revolution in the understanding of the sources and boundaries of knowledge that marked the true beginnings of the Enlightenment. His impact on the eighteenth century was immeasurable, and is still being assessed.

Hobbes' *Leviathan, or the matter, form and power of a commonwealth ecclesiastical and civil*, published two years after the execution of Charles I, offered a political analysis based on a view of the natural order which 'is a condition of war of everyone against everyone' (1, 14). Only the fear of death and 'desire of such things as are necessary to commodious living' could incline men to peace, the social order being maintained, and deliverance from the chaos of nature ensured, by a combination of fear and the calculation of self-interest. For Hobbes the state of nature was simply the condition of man deprived of the restraints of sovereign authority, and the political obligations of contract. Hobbes aroused much opposition and vilification, particularly in view of his contempt for religion, but for the Enlightenment much of his importance lay in the way in which he discarded traditional orthodoxies in favour of a doctrine that cut through any notion of the civil order as being the outcome of natural processes, or of instinctive sociability: 'Men have no pleasure in keeping company, where there is no power able to over-awe them all' (1, 13). Echoes, often dissenting, of Hobbes' views on the role of the calculation of self-interest in persuading men to accept the dictates of natural and civil law, and his defence of the absolute power of the sovereign to compel order, without whose iron fist society would swiftly revert to the lethal anarchy of the state of nature, can be heard in countless Enlightenment debates on the authority of rulers, the nature–society controversies, rights, freedoms, duties and moral enquiries into the nature of man (Taylor 1989, p. 20; Hampsher-Monk 1992, pp. 29–36).

In the establishment of the 'modern' natural law school of thought the work of Grotius was also influential (Haakonssen 1985). In his *On the law of war and peace* Grotius had mapped out the frontiers between divine and natural law, thereby severing the links between theology and natural law. Grotius' formulation of the concept of subjective right in his discussion of the origin of political authority was also destined to bear substantial fruits in the later years of his own century and in the next. His successor in natural law theory, Samuel Pufendorf, perhaps the most influential natural law theorist of the whole period, widened this new distance between laws, metaphysics and theological precepts in *On the law of nature and nations* (1672) and *On the duty of man and citizen according to natural law* (1673). The treatises of Grotius and Pufendorf were translated into several European languages, and constituted the basis for key text books for the study of natural and civil law in European universities and law-schools throughout the Enlightenment. Pufendorf, in particular, helped to shape the ideas of eighteenth-century natural law theorists and philosophers like Burlamaqui (see below, pp. 10–14, 85–6), Barbeyrac (see below, pp. 44–6, 364) and Johann Jakob Brucker in the first half of the eighteenth century, as well as political thinkers like Montesquieu, Rousseau and Hume (see below, pp. 15–19, 26–30, 105–6, 217–18, 245–6), to whose principles natural law theory was, in differing ways, a central point of reference. Pufendorf's influence extended even to the nineteenth century with the work of Johann Gottlieb Buhle (Tuck 1987, pp. 99–119).

In addition to these major sources of influence, it should be noted also that it was in the late seventeenth century that streams of translations of other key works from even earlier periods became widely available for the first time in countries other than the country of origin. Machiavelli's *Prince* (1513) was translated into French in 1683, followed by the *Discourses* in 1691, and the works of other Italians such as Paolo Sarpi, Gregorio Leti and Gian Paolo Marana were all widely read in translation in England and France in the late seventeenth and early eighteenth centuries. The major texts of the English seventeenth-century Enlightenment had started to flood into France and other European countries at the turn of the century, possibly as a consequence of the industry of Huguenot refugees from religious persecution living in London and Amsterdam. Among these one of the most influential figures was the Protestant theologian and dissenter, Pierre Bayle, whose attacks on intolerance in France in the wake of Louis XIV's revocation in 1685 of the Edict of Nantes, which Henri IV had enacted in 1598 granting Protestants liberty of conscience, were widely disseminated. It was with Bayle that religious, moral and political controversy started to merge with more public forms of discourse than the academic treatise. His exchanges with contemporary scholars and theologians heralded in fact the emergence of a letter-exchanging Republic of Letters, as well as the rise of the journal and the periodical that would eventually characterise so much of the Enlightenment's publishing trade, and the way in which it was organised.

Political thought in the European Enlightenment fed continuously on this pre-Enlightenment mentality of empirical interrogation of past dogma and theory, of rational challenge to authority and tradition, of scepticism, scientific enquiry, increasing secularism and humanitarianism. The result was the creation of an intellectual environment in which a new-found confidence in the ability of man to understand his past, improve his present and establish a blueprint for his future was the key to unlock a vision of indefinite perfectibility, reflected in the last decade of the century most eloquently in the positivism of Condorcet's tenth *époque* in his remarkable *Historical sketch of the progress of the human mind* of 1795 (Williams 1993, pp. 165–6).

Inevitably, the range of writers who feature in the present volume, some more familiar than others, will appear to be arbitrary and incomplete. What constitutes an Enlightenment text is not always clear-cut, for the ideological, as well as the temporal, boundaries of the Enlightenment are fluid, and notoriously difficult to pinpoint accurately, the historical frame changing according to whether the angle of perception is primarily philosophical, aesthetic, scientific, moral, theological or political. The political perspective, in particular, requires location within the 'long' Enlightenment. Much of the political thought of the early and mid-eighteenth century reflects an assimilation, application and reformulation of concepts that crystallised in the seventeenth century, much as political thinking after the French Revolution reflects a maturation of ideas that first took shape in the closing years of the *ancien régime*. The Enlightenment did not dawn in 1700, nor did it set in 1789, or even 1800.

The frame of reference will thus span the period dating from the 1670s to the 1790s. The texts themselves were written and published for the most part in the middle and later years of the century, but seven belong to the pre-1750 period, and five post-date the French Revolution. Moreover, the Enlightenment was not confined to the activities of a group of mid-eighteenth-century Parisian *philosophes*, important as their role was, and in this volume no less than seven European countries are represented: England, Scotland, Ireland, France, Germany, Italy and Switzerland. One text relates to America. From the standpoint of subject matter, extracts have been arranged under nine thematic headings that interlock, and in many cases overlap: natural law, the civil order, the nation state, government, civil rights, war and international relations, trade and economics, crime and punishment, revolution. Within each grouping, texts are arranged in a chronological order determined by the date of the first edition.

Natural law

Natural law doctrines have their origins in the thought of the earliest ancient Greek philosophers of the sixth to fifth centuries BC. Ancient Greek and Roman currents of speculative thought about the operations of a transcendent intelligence in the natural world and in the world of human affairs gradually coalesced into the theory of a natural law of justice that was separate from, and sometimes in conflict with, society's own laws and conventions. Post-Renaissance interpretations of natural law owe much to the *jus gentium* (or 'law of nations') of the Romans systemised as a code of civil laws under Justinian, of which the *Institutes* and the *Pandects* were the most important from the standpoint of natural law theory (Waddicor 1970, pp. 1–4; Finnis 1980; Tuck 1987).

The ancient tradition of natural law as it came down through the work of the Stoics and the Roman jurists, via Aristotle and Cicero in particular, was developed further by the medieval Church, and in the thirteenth century the *Summa theologica* of St Thomas Aquinas emerged as the orthodox interpretation by which natural law was assimilated into Christian theology, and made subordinate to the principle of divine law. Subordination of natural law to divine law was resisted by secular theorists, and the move to redefine the links between natural and divine law culminated in the seventeenth century with the work of Grotius, Selden, Hobbes, Cumberland, Boyle, Domat, Locke and above all Pufendorf. In the Enlightenment the foundations of a rational, secular school of natural law doctrine that increasingly eroded the medieval understanding of the relationship of God's law to natural law were reinforced with the contributions of jurists and philosophers such as Burlamaqui, Gravina, Vattel, Montesquieu and especially Barbey-rac, editor and translator of treatises by Grotius, Pufendorf, Richard Cumberland and Archbishop Tillotson.

Both Grotius and Pufendorf related natural law to the rules governing self-survival and the individual's drive for self-preservation, although Pufendorf was to depart from Grotius on the issue of moral obligation (Tully and Silverthorne 1991, pp. xxiv–xxix). Grotius envisaged two primary laws of nature, namely the right to self-defence and the right to acquire the means and possessions that facilitate life and well-being. His break with past theorists arose with the celebrated statement in *On the law of war and peace* (*De jure belli ac pacis*) of 1625 that the laws of nature would bind men 'though we should even grant, what without the greatest wickedness cannot be granted, that there is no God, or that He takes no care of human affairs' (Tuck 1987, p. 112).

One of the early models of political analysis, Pufendorf made a significant contribution to the evolution of natural law theory, as well as to concepts of authority and social organisation (Tully and Silverthorne 1991, p. xx). Pufendorf's work was widely referred to, especially in the early decades of the eighteenth century, although later thinkers, such as Rousseau, found much to disagree with. His two seminal treatises, *On the law of nature and nations* (*De jure naturae et gentium*) of 1672 and *On the duty of man and citizen according to natural law* (*De officio hominis et civis juxta legem naturalem*) of 1673, translated into French by Barbeyrac in 1707, systemised and modified the ideas of Grotius, particularly with respect to the latter's integration of natural law into the drive for self-preservation. Pufendorf saw natural law manifesting itself primarily in sociability rather than in self-interest. Moreover, sociability, and the duty to God, to others and to self that this implied, had 'clear utility'. This meant that the drive to obey the raw instincts of self-interest and self-preservation could be over-ridden by the duties of sociability, which were in his view commensurate with long-term interests of the individual (Tully and Silverthorn 1991, p. xxvii).

Pufendorf's thought reflects his experience of life following the 1648 Peace of Westphalia, marking the end of the Thirty Years War, and the emergence of modern nation states in Europe. This experience taught him to see the state as the only true guarantor of order, stability and progress and, bearing in mind the irreconcilable religious conflicts at the heart of the Thirty Years War, he sought, like his French translator Jean Barbeyrac, to reconstruct natural law and develop a new political order on the basis of a scientific theory of politics that was independent of all sectarian religious considerations, yet would tolerate the practice of different religions within a newly defined moral framework (Carr and Seidler 1994, pp. 6–7; Tully and Silverthorne 1991, pp. xviii–xix). In defending the need for the state, however, Pufendorf was equally concerned with the threat to freedom posed by the exercise of sovereign authority, and in *On the duty of man and citizen* he had much to say about the dangers of tyranny, and the restraints on sovereign power that can be provided only by the sovereign's subjects themselves.

In decoupling natural law from institutional religious precept, as well as from other aspects of existing law codes, Pufendorf still retained God as the central legitimising authority for his view of the law, and he sought to align with divine will the needs derived from human nature, to whose features civil law should in his view always respond. For Pufendorf the twin principles of duty and obligation, central to his notion of sociability, lay at the heart of all political dynamics, and involved a close analysis of the benefits of obedience and the conditions of sovereign rule that apply to this. He saw human beings as creatures motivated by the desire to survive, and to advance their well-being. In the pursuit of these two ends, the individual's need for others becomes the key factor in the social equation. In order for men to be secure they must be 'sociable', and sociability becomes the 'common character and condition of mankind'. Pufendorf envisaged the primary role of sociability not simply as an empirically observed, anthropological phenomenon, but more importantly as an expression of natural *and* divine law, and it was in that context that he located its force and authority (see also the 'Fourth dialogue' of Mandeville's *Fable of the bees*, Kaye 1966, II, pp. 177–91). Pufendorf presented the Enlightenment, and modernity, with urgent issues of power and political legitimacy (Krieger 1965; Laurent 1982). He set an agenda that inspired and illuminated European attitudes towards natural law and its role in the legal machinery of civil society, in power relationships, in the understanding of rights and duties, and above all in the promotion of sociability as a basic natural law principle.

Building on the work of Grotius, Pufendorf, Hobbes (and also Barbeyrac), Jean-Jacques Burlamaqui (see below, p. 85) represents a position on self-love, duty, rights, happiness, freedom, virtue, religion, civil society, civil authority and civil obligation typical of the orthodox, Protestant school of Enlightenment natural law doctrine (Rosenblatt 1997, pp. 96–9). In the *Principles of natural right* [*and natural law*] (1747) he reassessed the role of moral theology as part of the defence and definition of natural right and natural law, and in this he reflected elements of Pufendorf's thinking on sociability. God remained the ultimate authorising principle for order and the authority of rulers, but society itself comes about as the consequence of those 'natural inclinations' of association and communal interdependency, including self-love, with which God originally endowed man. Insistence on the essential benevolence of God's dispensation, and on the harmony that flows from obedience to the natural laws governing man's conduct, marks Burlamaqui out as a Leibnizian optimist, or providentialist, who envisaged happiness, virtue, duty to self and duty to others as being compatible elements in a pre-ordained plan for human organisation whose purposes and effects, as expressed in natural law, and in turn human law anchored to natural law, coincided with God's will. Divine law in Burlamaqui's system, moreover, was closely aligned with reason itself, a link illuminated, in his view, by the principles of deism and natural theology.

Thus, following Barbeyrac, Burlamaqui envisaged the civil order as a natural phenomenon evolving in accordance with divine design and purpose. This design and purpose related to man's happiness, but happiness in the secular terms of the Enlightenment, not the transcendental terms of the world of Aquinas. This was the only true purpose of the social and political order for Burlamaqui, and of the civil and natural laws that underpinned that order. Happiness and *douceurs*, by which he meant 'the sweet things of life' (Rosenblatt 1997, pp. 98–9), were only made possible by means of man's surrender of part of his natural right to freedom by means of an unqualified acceptance of a natural law requiring in turn the enactment of a code of civil laws. Burlamaqui was not a defender of absolute monarchies in the tradition of earlier natural law theorists. He advocated 'tempered government' in which the people had some rights in the face of sovereign power. In the *Principles* he referred, for example, albeit fleetingly, to 'the sharing of the rights of sovereignty'. On the other hand, despite his reservations about the dangers of concentrating power in the hands of one person, Burlamaqui nevertheless identified the essential defining feature of any natural law-based society as being subordination to sovereign authority, in which the contract between ruler and ruled required submission to the sovereign's will *without appeal*.

The text of the *Principles* is divided into two parts. Part I, containing eleven chapters, is concerned with the concept of *natural right (jus naturale)*. Hobbes had defined natural right in the *Leviathan* as 'the liberty each man hath to use his own power, as he will himself, for the preservation of his own nature; that is to say, of his own life', and he had distinguished natural right carefully from natural

Interestingly, it was at this point that he then elaborated his ideas on natural equality, the associated principles of equity and reciprocity, and his notion of subordination and obligation in the context of the requirements of the primary and secondary categories of natural law. In the concluding chapters he returns to theological issues, including proofs of the immortality of the soul, that have a bearing on the sanctions that would come into effect as a consequence of man's refusal to comply with natural law in the determination of his conduct.

The *Principles* represent a classic, comprehensive reformulation of natural law theory in the seventeenth-century intellectual tradition. It is not an expression of Enlightenment radicalism, but it belongs to an evolving tradition of legal philosophy with explicitly acknowledged roots in the thought of Grotius, Pufendorf and Barbeyrac. Burlamaqui's treatise was widely used as a course book for law students at a number of European universities, including Cambridge, throughout the latter half of the century, and beyond.

The civil order

In their rationalisation of the civil order most Enlightenment thinkers followed earlier commentators in postulating the notion of a 'state of nature' as a mechanism for determining what man was like in abstract terms of equality, virtue, misery or happiness before entering into a formal association. Eighteenth-century theorists of the state of nature, such as Jean-Jacques Rousseau (see below, pp. 105–6), injected into this long-established concept new scientific and anthropological knowledge about primitive societies that started to accumulate in the Enlightenment, but the concept remained an essentially hypothetical projection.

Pre-Enlightenment views of man's emergence from the 'state of nature' had assumed three stages in the evolution of the civil order, namely those of hunter-gathering, shepherding and agriculture. The Enlightenment added a fourth stage, the 'Age of Commerce', best described in Adam Smith's *Inquiry into the nature and causes of the wealth of nations* (Hont 1987, pp. 253–76). The pre-Smithian three-stage theory had been elaborated in an anti-Hobbesian context by Pufendorf in *On the duty of man and citizen*. For Pufendorf the state of nature was envisaged as a state of natural liberty existing among different family groups, and arising from historical processes that had accelerated as nomadic, solitary man moved into relationships with others, advancing from primitive tribalism to the modern nation state. This three-stage concept of human socialisation, with its associations with reason, and its concomitant imposition of duties on all citizens, also included an account of the rise of property and commercial activity, but not yet separately identified as a fourth stage. It was this inferred fourth stage that was to re-emerge in more explicit terms with Smith (Hont 1987, pp. 270–5; Laurent 1982).

Rousseau always had Barbeyrac's translation of Pufendorf's treatise to hand when writing on political matters, and his account of man's transition from the state of nature to society echoes aspects of the widely accepted view that man was naturally social, although he did not accept that man was by nature *politically* social (Gourevitch 1997a, p. xxv). Rousseau concentrated on the notion of contract not as a social but as a political mechanism, and it was in a political context that he discussed the relationship of the contract to such issues as the General Will, the sovereignty of the people, the authority of government and the law. In addition to the general contract establishing the civil order, Pufendorf had also referred to a second contract, or 'pact of submission', through which members of the newly established civil order transferred their power to the government. Rousseau rejected this second contract arguing that there could only be one authentic contract, the general contract of association, to which individuals agreed of their own free will. This was a contract which involved no surrender of inalienable sovereign authority, and could never absolve rulers from their duty of accountability. Rousseau's reaffirmation of the role of the people as the sovereign power in the state, his concept of the General Will in the articulation of legislation, his concept of the state as a *moral* as well as political entity, of the true nature of political freedom as distinct from natural freedom, and above all his views on the regeneration of human nature necessary for the implementation of the reformed pact of association resonate as powerful analyses of the political, social and moral consequences of the transition to the civil order (Gildin 1983; Rosenblatt 1997, pp. 241–68; Strong 1994).

With his trilogy of best-known doctrinal works, the *Discourse on the sciences and the arts*, the *Discourse on the origin and the foundations of inequality among men* and the *Social contract* Rousseau has become arguably one of the most influential political thinkers of the Enlightenment in terms of his impact on events, as well as on the future direction of theory about civil society (Wokler 1995). In the two *Discourses* and in the *Social contract* Rousseau examined the ways in which he believed emergence from the state of nature had alienated man from his true nature, corrupting his virtue and depriving him of happiness and stability. In the

Discourse on the sciences and the arts, he rejected the ethos of progress central to the thought of most other Enlightenment political theorists. In the second *Discourse* he explored the darker consequences for man that his translation from Nature to Society had incurred. He reflects at length in strikingly rhetorical terms on the moral and political implications of the tragic spectacle of modern man's condition, which he compared graphically in the preface to his second *Discourse* to 'the statue of Glaucus which time, sea and storms have so disfigured that it is less like a God than a wild beast'.

In both *Discourses* he expounded a counter-Enlightenment thesis in which he sought to illustrate the processes whereby 'progress' had generated an artificial, vicious social order, enriching and honouring the wealthy, propertied class and further impoverishing those who had nothing. He offered contemporaries a radically different view of the position of the individual in civil society, and of the culture conditioning individual identity and motivation, and it was a view that presented many of the most cherished premises of the Enlightenment with their most lethal challenge. Rousseau's view of the achievements of civilisation, as well as his diagnosis of man's political and social condition, was uncompromisingly bleak. The first book of his controversial pedagogical treatise, *Emile, or, on education* (1762), contains a memorable statement of his position: 'All our wisdom consists of servile prejudices, all our customs are but enslavement, constraint or bondage. Social man is born, lives and dies enslaved. At birth he is bound up in swaddling clothes; at his death he is nailed down in a coffin. For the whole of his existence as a human being he is chained up by our institutions.'

The second *Discourse* falls into two parts. In Part I Rousseau re-examined traditional concepts of the state of nature from an entirely fresh perspective, rejecting the view that natural law, understood as *moral* law, could explain the origins of the civil order (Gourevitch 1997a, p. xvi). Unlike many natural law theorists, Rousseau could not grant the concept genuine historical status, although in his description of what life must have been like for primitive man he does incorporate as much contemporary knowledge about human pre-social history as was available to him (Grimsley 1972, pp. 5–12). In practice, he accepted the state of nature only as a working hypothesis to throw light on our understanding of man's modern condition and experience rather than to present historical actualities. The state of nature for Rousseau meant little more than possession of the instincts necessary for survival, and he did not accept the Hobbesian account of the state of nature as being a state of war of 'every man against every man'. He accepted Hobbes' view that primitive man was not endowed with moral awareness, but he denied that this meant man was 'naturally wicked', the primal urge to survive being tempered, not by the call of reason, but by another basic instinct that separated man from the animals, which Rousseau called 'natural pity'. Man in the state of nature was good (i.e. self-sufficient rather than virtuous), free and equal (Gourevitch 1997a, pp. xix–xx).

Rousseau never at any stage believed that a literal return to a 'state of nature' was either possible or desirable, but he did envisage a utopic Golden Age, a non-politicised phase of social evolution, that offered natural man a number of advantages over modern, political man, including the potential for happiness, harmony with self and with the environment, and self-sufficiency. He located that Golden Age in a period when man had moved out of solitary, nomadic primitiv-ism into a tribal, community-based mode of living. This was a period pre-dating the advent of property, and characterised by a freedom and an equality whose loss was part of the price modern man had paid for his advancement to the civil order.

In the second *Discourse* Rousseau examined the causes of man's loss of his happiness and equality, and of that alienation from self and others that had widened and formalised natural divisions between the strong and the weak, the effects of which an earlier, solitary, nomadic mode of existence had tended to mitigate. As the human tribe grew and formed communities, the arts and sciences developed, and with them the key discovery of metallurgy and agriculture, and the consequential loss of independence and self-sufficiency. A diminishing free-dom was finally destroyed completely with the arrival of the age of agriculture, the division of labour and the ownership of property. With property the natural inequalities between the weak and the strong were formally consolidated in ways that brought the rich and the poor into existence, and the breakdown of natural liberty. Rousseau envisaged as the consequence of these developments the out-break of the perpetual 'war of all against all' that Hobbes had identified, wrongly in Rousseau's view, as being the original condition of pre-political life. This 'war' came to an end with the establishment of a 'social pact', the first civil society, in which the poor 'ran to meet their chains', and exchange freedom for a false prom-ise of security from the rich by means of a specifically determined contractual agreement. This initial attempt to establish the social contract was, in Rousseau's eyes, to prove disastrous for humanity, a fraudulent mechanism that merely sought to legitimise the continuing oppression of the weak by the strong. A 'clever usurpation' by the strong and the powerful had become an established, but not irrevocable, 'right' to rule.

Rousseau's views on the need for a new social contract, whose terms would redefine the nature of true political freedom, involving 'the surrender of all to all', lie at the heart of the *Social contract*, and were eventually to help ignite a revolution. For Rousseau the only true basis for the civil order lay in general consent, expressed through the General Will of the people whose interpretation, safeguarding the people's inalienable sovereignty, would be the responsibility of the supreme 'Legislator'. The realisation of the General Will, the precise role of the Legislator as founder (and educator) of the nation, the position of minorities, the place of religion, the formation of the citizen, the question of rights and freedoms, the function and responsibilities of government, and the central question of how morally to equip citizens to carry out their civic duties under the new contract have all proved to be controversially ambiguous.

Rousseau believed that political society came into existence only as an act of will agreed to by 'contracting' members as a means to terminate a situation in which 'natural' society had come to the point where it was being torn apart by conflict between the rich and the poor. He set aside traditional theories locating the origin of civil society and political authority in power derived from moral law, rights of conquest, historical processes, divinely ordained prescriptions, or in any 'natural' analogy between the authority of sovereigns and that of fathers over children. Rousseau's political philosophy contains many disturbing subversions, and it injected dynamic, moral dimensions into the political equation that were unprecedented (Hampsher-Monk 1992, pp. 153–95; Wokler 1987). His central concern was always the question of freedom, precisely in his view the one inalienable right denied to individuals in modern society: 'Man is born free, but everywhere he is in chains.' Ironically, however, history has since shown that Rousseau's political legacy has been largely a collectivist one that has in practice served only to reinforce those chains.

The political solutions that he offered were destined to be the subject of controversy, re-interpretation and mis-interpretation for the next two hundred years at the hands of ideologues of both the Left and the Right, and they still continue to cause disturbing ripples across the surface of modern political theory (Strong 1994). With the events of 1789 Rousseau became an icon in France, and his name occupied a high place in the pantheon of the Revolution's heroes. Curiously, however, while Rousseau as a cult figure became popular currency, the *Social contract* itself still remained relatively unread, even between 1789 and 1791, and Rousseau's name was often simply invoked in order to lend authority to arguments and ideas for which he was not responsible. There were exceptions, of course, and the works of political commentators such as the Comte d'Antraigues, Paul-Philippe Gudin and of course Siéyès, all published between 1788 and 1791, reflect a serious study of Rousseau's text. However, it was in the later years of the Revolution that the impact of the *Social contract* was to make itself widely felt with the work of admiring exponents such as Claude Fauchet, whose lectures on the *Social contract* to members of the Social Circle of the Friends of Truth in 1790–1 were attended by many, including Siéyès, Condorcet and Tom Paine. After 1791 Rousseau's ideas were much talked about in Paris, although they would continue to be much misunderstood, and much misused as well (McDonald 1965, pp. 66–86, 155–73).

On the other side of the English Channel controversial thinking on the question of society and the authenticity of the civil order is well represented by Rousseau's close contemporary, Joseph Priestley (see below, pp. 143–71). Priestley too was concerned with many of the questions that Rousseau had raised, and he provided equally subversive answers. Unlike Rousseau, however, who was intensely suspicious of reason, Priestley's radicalism was rooted in the scientific rationality of the period, rather than in its denunciation, for he was a firm believer in, and proponent of, Enlightenment progressivist values and aspirations (Hoecker 1987; Miller 1993). At the time of preparing the first edition of *An essay on the first principles of government, and on the nature of political, civil and religious liberty* (1768), his approach to political issues, by way of further contrast to that of Rousseau, was that of an Enlightenment scientist. Priestley was deeply influenced by Newtonian natural philosophy, as mediated through the work of Samuel Clarke (Miller 1993, pp. xv–xvi), a thinker whom Voltaire had described admiringly in the seventh of his *Letters concerning the English nation* (1733) as a 'reasoning machine' (Cronk 1994, p. 31). From Clarke was derived the ideological link between the Newtonian model of the world, ordered by a rational, omniscient and benevolent God, and the moral and political order of the human condition with its built-in premise of man as a free and rational creature with the potential ability to liberate himself from the shackles of the past, rationalise the present, and move with confidence towards an ever-improving future (Graham 1989/90, pp. 14–46). Clarke's view of 'natural liberty' was linked in turn to political notions of self-determination and self-government.

Priestley's radical elaboration of this chain of associated ideas was to expose him to charges of republicanism in his later years. He certainly embraced fully the progressivist spirit of the Enlightenment and, like Condorcet in France, he anticipated in many ways the positivism of the next century. His position on Clarke changed over the years, and these changes are reflected in the additions and amendments made to the second edition of the *Essay* in 1771. By then Priestley's interest in the work of the Newtonian, David Hartley, author of the *Observations on man* (1775), and the age's leading exponent of physiologically based psychology, was growing (Miller 1993, p. xvi). Under Hartley's influence, he inclined increasingly towards a position of materialistic determinism in which the pursuit of freedom became less dependent on human actions and initiatives and more closely associated with providentialist design, although in the 1771 edition of the *Essay* progress and freedom are still seen as being contingent upon the power of man's intellectual and spiritual potential as an active agent of change and improvement.

An essay on the first principles of government was written, Priestley himself informs us, as a continuation of his earlier engagement, not with Clarke, but with Dr John Brown, an advocate of state intervention in, and control of, the education of children, whose *Thoughts on civil liberty, on licenciousness and faction* had appeared in 1765. Priestley rejected Brown's defence of state interventionism. His reactions to Brown's political philosophy are reflected in his approach to liberty, to political decay and in his conviction that government, in seeking to exercise control over areas of civil life such as education, tended always to affect adversely political and civil freedoms (Miller 1993, p. xvii). The debate on the relationship between education and civil liberty in the light of Brown's views constitutes the subject matter of Part IV of the *Essay*. Between the first and second editions, however, the direction of Priestley's thinking on Brown, and on the general question of political freedom and the determination of the boundaries of the authority of the civil order, were to be increasingly affected by external events, and in particular by those unfolding in the American colonies.

Brown (like Rousseau, though for different reasons) was an admirer of Sparta which, in the name of the common good and the security of all, had placed severe limitations on the freedom of the individual, particularly with regard to freedom of thought. This was a view of the priorities shaping the definition of the state's relationship with individual citizens that was widely shared in England in the second half of the eighteenth century, at a time when there was much public anxiety about sedition, and concern to foster a spirit of defensive patriotism. Priestley was deeply opposed to the prevailing political ethos and, while he always remained basically a utilitarian, his political language and disposition are more reminiscent of those of his friend, the Welsh dissenter Richard Price (Hoecker 1987, pp. 36–7), an advocate of minimalist social structures and government, and a powerfully persuasive defender of natural rights. For Priestley, however, the social order was not just about the survival, at whatever cost, of social structures and state prerogatives, but rather the promotion of the individual's welfare and happiness, to make the situation of men in this world 'abundantly more easy and comfortable'. In the *Essay* the ideal of Sparta is replaced by that of Athens.

Society, in Priestley's view, rested on the principle of consent to be governed, a contractual arrangement by which the individual gained protection in exchange for a concession of obligations and duties. To ameliorate the 'inconvenience' of life outside society, individuals 'join their force in enterprises and undertakings calculated for the common good'. Moving closer to the Rousseauist position in this context, Priestley recognised that there must be somewhere in this arrangement a measure of voluntary surrender of 'some part of their natural liberty'. Freedom in society, as opposed to freedom in nature, needs careful redefinition, and in Parts II and III of the *Essay* he offered two analyses relevant to two different categories, political liberty and civil liberty (Canovan 1978). He defined political liberty as 'the right of magistracy, being the claim that any members of the state hath, to have his private opinion or judgment to become that of the public, and thereby control the actions of others'. Civil liberty, on the other hand, 'extends no farther than to a man's own conduct, and signifies the right he has to be exempt from the control of the society, or its agents: that is, the power he has of providing for his own advantage and happiness' (see below, p. 148). In other words, for Priestley civil liberty was what was sacrificed in entering into society, and political liberty was 'what man may or may not acquire' as compensation for that sacrifice.

Priestley's political thought was based essentially on a view of human nature in which the ability to reason freely and to act in accordance with reason was a God-given feature. This was supplemented by a presumption of natural right, subject to minimal interference from the state. Free enquiry and the tolerance of all forms of freedom of thought and expression followed on logically from this as the key to the achievement of a just, well-balanced civil order. His global defence of freedom and toleration was almost Kantian, and some commentators have seen

Hegel. Most of Herder's writings are fragmentary, often unpolished and in some cases unfinished. He wrote on a wide range of subjects, but it was his vividly and lucidly formulated thoughts on nationhood and German identity in the *Ideas for a philosophy of the history of mankind* (1784–91) and the *Letters for the advancement of humanity* (1793–7) that caught the attention of contemporary Europe. At the beginning of the eighteenth century the political and cultural fragmentation of Germany in the aftermath of the 1648 Peace of Westphalia, ending the Thirty Years War and marking also the collapse of the Hanseatic League, still prevailed. German culture, language and commerce were equally fragmented and sectionalist. The aristocracy and the middle classes looked to France for their models. French was the language of German courts, and French art, manners and products, particularly after the accession of Voltaire's friend and correspondent Frederick the Great to the throne of Prussia, were predominant. Feelings of German patriotism, and the consciousness of a German *people*, are almost entirely absent from the German mind in the first half of the century, and often explicitly rejected. There were exceptions, Johann Jakob von Moser and his son Friedrich Karl (see below, pp. 30–2, 277–8) being notable examples, but on the whole the voice of the German national spirit was silent. It started to be heard faintly during the Seven Years War in the work of writers and dramatists such as Lessing and Klopstock, but a systematically argued case for an over-arching national culture and identity was not to be put seriously to the German peoples until the advent of Herder (Hertz 1962; Sheehan 1989).

Herder's relationship with the Enlightenment is complex (Berlin 1965), and the *Ideas* and the *Letters* reflect in many ways his break with Enlightenment rationalism and cosmopolitanism, and above all with the Enlightenment's faith in an ever-rising trajectory of progress. The past was not seen by Herder in terms of unenlightened darkness, but rather as a necessary link in an organic process of evolution culminating in a perfection to which all previous civilisations have contributed in their own way, a past with which the present and the future continue to interact. Progress for Herder was essentially the path from fragmentation and diversity towards unity, and in political and social terms from individualism to the national group. In the *Ideas* he refers to nationality as an organic, dynamic phenomenon, a 'national plant', or 'national animal'. Central to his view of historical causation is the notion of 'becoming', the driving or 'genetic' force behind all living matter being what he termed *Kraft*, that is to say, vigour or energy (Barnard 1965, pp. 38–53; Clarke 1942, pp. 737–52). In the context of the evolution of human society this force crystallised in the form of various cultures, each of which in turn generated a coherent and unique system of ideas, art, music, traditions and beliefs creating a sense of collective identity, most clearly and fundamentally embodied initially in the development of differentiated languages.

Herder saw in the nation state all the characteristics of growth, maturity and decay common to vital organisms living and dying as part of an on-going cycle of human endeavour and aspiration (McCloskey 1963). He saw this as a process in which the old ways and the new did not clash in accordance with traditional Enlightenment scenarios, but on the contrary complemented each other in a positive and vital way. Rousseau's adversarial distinction between nature and society has no place in Herder's theory of national organisms. In the *Letters* he emphasised that every nationality was the product of nature, not an artifact of man. This national organism, moreover, had a 'genius' or 'soul', the group being envisaged as a succession of such organisms, each with its own linguistic, moral and cultural characteristics. Herder's thoughts on government were concerned essentially with an analysis of those political systems that would best respond, not only to the needs of individuals, but also to those of the national collectivities to which he anchored the foundations of the social and political order.

Herder's legacy has been well documented (Ergang 1966, pp. 239–66; Barnard 1969, pp. 4–7), as have the ways in which key components of his thought on the state as organism been subsequently perverted. Herder's nationalism was not the narrow, divisive nationalism of the nineteenth century (Hayes 1927). Nor can Herder be held responsible for the racist extremes to which nationalism has been taken in the twentieth. Herderian nationalism was essentially humanitarian, and his concern was always with the awakening of the German national spirit to an awareness, not only of its obligations to a *people*, but also of its obligations to all humanity (Ergang 1966, pp. 263–6; Beiser 1996; Hahn 1995).

Government

While the Enlightenment was a period indelibly stamped by ideals of a new world of reform and regeneration, in the world of political practice most governments conformed to a primarily catholic model of monarchy inherited from earlier times. The subordination of the Church to secular authority remained in many countries a distant prospect, and ecclesiastical power would continue to play a central role in the exercise of political authority in many parts of Europe. This would have the effect of prolonging royalty's semi-divine status for many decades, and much of the Enlightenment's thinking on rights and responsibilities evolved in paradoxical proximity to the day-to-day realities of autocratic rule.

The British contribution to fresh thinking on government was considerable, and the influence of earlier thinkers continued to grow throughout the period. Among the eighteenth-century successors to Locke and Hobbes, David Hume (see below, pp. 217–18) was among the most outstanding (Whelan 1985; Phillipson 1989). In Hume we see a brilliant exponent of the essay format for political commentary which many Enlightenment theorists preferred, not least because of its appeal to a rising middle-class culture and readership. In his brilliant observations on the post-1688 British model, Hume reflected a keen awareness of the ephemeral nature of all constitutional arrangements. Systems of government emerged by accident rather than by design, always vulnerable to the destructive forces of party conflict, and the drift towards monarchical absolutism on the one hand, or republicanism on the other. Political stability was threatened continuously by the presence of large standing armies and the weight of ever-mounting public debt (Miller 1981, pp. 181–4). Further potential dangers emanated from the ignorance of the people, which made them vulnerable to the dark forces of fanaticism and superstition. The crowd was potentially the rabble, and individual liberty, if taken to extremes, became the fuse that ignited anarchy and social unrest. Governments, and the political systems that generated them, could, in Hume's view, be easily, and fatally, maimed.

Hume's insistence on the precariousness of governments and political systems was closely linked to his view of human nature, in which he modified Hobbes' thesis of the unsociability of man to take account of the position of natural law thinkers like Grotius and Pufendorf, whose view of man's natural relationship with others was less bleak. For Hume self-interest and sympathy were natural dispositions, the latter engendering benevolence and virtue – key factors regulating human behaviour and relationships. The needs and ambitions relating to these dispositions, such as security and justice, could only be satisfied within a framework of what he called 'regular' government. His political philosophy has often been seen, correctly up to a point, as that of a conservative thinker concerned mainly with the defence of *ancien régime* systems and values. Humean advocacy of the merits of all aspects of freedom, economic as well as political and social, was certainly predicated on the maintenance at all costs of the social order, and of a social and political continuity assured by a privileged, land-owning aristocracy (Miller 1981, pp. 192–3; Haakonssen 1994, pp. xxv–xxx). However, Hume's conservatism also combined significant elements of liberalism. He believed in economic and political freedom under the rule of law, while adhering to the defence of the social hierarchy, and of the need for public deference to it. His faith in freedom was admittedly clouded by a fear of the dangerous instability that its exercise entailed. His political writings represent in many ways a sustained attempt to balance this crucial equation between the dangers and advantages of a 'regular', free society (Stewart 1992).

Hume's greatest work remains *A treatise of human nature* (1739–40), and the philosophical principles he developed here, particularly with regard to judgement, imagination, morality, justice, feeling and passion really illuminate everything he was ever to write subsequently on government (Baier 1991). The *Treatise*, inspired by the model of Newtonian physics and the epistemological principles of Locke, was an attempt to offer nothing less than a science of the human mind from which it would be possible to derive practical applications of direct relevance to other human sciences, and particularly the science of government (Forbes 1975, pp. 3–58; Miller 1981, pp. 19–77).

At the start of the *Treatise* Hume had claimed that politics was a scientifically rigorous discipline, capable of deducing from the laws and from particular forms of government 'consequences almost as general and certain . . . as any which the mathematical sciences afford us'. In *That politics may be reduced to a science* (1741), he aimed further to develop the scientific model relating to politics. This essay is a good example of how Hume uses the analogy of mathematics to offer a general analysis of institutions, and to explore and illustrate the differences between one form of government and another. Here he discusses at length matters such as the balance of power within a 'free' government, the role of legislators in a truly representative legislature, liberty and the public good in the context of the principles and 'general truths' of the new science.

In *Of the first principles of government* (1741), Hume proceeded to examine the factors involved in the 'implicit submission' of the ruled to those who rule. In explaining this 'wonder', Hume related the foundation of government to two 'opinions', namely the 'opinion of interest', by which he meant the sense of advantage which the ruled derive from being ruled, and the 'opinion of right', by which he meant the right to power and the right to property. For a definition of what was meant by a 'free' government, we must turn to *Of the origin of government* (1777). Although Hume's position remains rather ambiguous on the question of whether republics are to be preferred to monarchies, in the *Idea of a perfect commonwealth* (1752), he examined how an ideal form of republican government could function. In explaining his notion of devolved rule in a republican context, he advocated a system of elected representatives working in a constitutional framework of county assemblies selecting senators for seats in a national assembly. Hume was clearly very concerned to ensure that mechanisms would be in place to facilitate public political debate for the people, although by 'people' he meant those citizens qualified to vote under the prevailing franchise who were freeholders of property of a specified value. By 'debate' he envisaged little more than the processes of discussion leading to the choice of representatives. This would produce a 'well-tempered democracy', but a democracy still operating within a constitution that would remain 'aristocratic' in nature, in the sense of selecting 'the best'.

His later essay, *Of the origin of government* (1777), is marked by anxieties about 'democracy' that were widely shared in Britain during the half-decade between the American Declaration of Independence and the outbreak of the French Revolution. Here Hume was more concerned with the control of public disorder arising from the 'perpetual intestine struggle' between freedom and authority. The argument in this essay reflects Hume's reservations about the impact of *philosophe* doctrines of resistance to past authority and tradition, with its implied invitation to civil unrest, and possibly even open insurrection. At the same time, Hume warned against the folly of unbridled autocracy, and the allocation to government of uncontrollable powers to constrain freedom.

The *Spirit of the laws* (1748) by Charles-Louis de Secondat, Baron de Montesquieu (see below, pp. 245–6), was published in the same year as Hume's *Enquiry concerning human understanding*. Montesquieu's *Spirit of the laws* (1748) contains one of the most thorough analyses of the nature and purpose of government, and of the defining characteristics of specific constitutional models, and its formative impact on the development of sociological and political perspectives on Enlightenment views on government cannot be overestimated. The *Spirit* is divided into six parts containing a total of thirty-six books, each book further subdivided into 318 chapters. It ranges over a wide spectrum of interconnected matters, including natural law, religion, morals, virtue, freedom, climate, anthropology and constitutional matters. It also embodies a coherent theory of historical causation of decline and fall, the seeds of which can be seen in an earlier work, the *Considerations on the causes of the greatness of the Romans, and of their decline* (1734). The *Spirit* contains no theory about the origins of government, or about the relationship of the social order to the state of nature. Montesquieu's chief interest was in the relationship between political practice and morality, and the factors that affected that relationship.

In the preface to this vast multi-dimensional work Montesquieu states that he drew his principles, not from prejudice, but from 'the nature of things', and that many of the truths that he wished to express would emerge only when 'one sees the chain connecting them with the others'. Given the intricate, mosaic-like structure of the work, this chain is not easy to discern, there being no clearly defined order of subject matter or thematic architecture (Cohler, Miller and Stone 1990, pp. xxi–xxiii). Montesquieu set out first of all to identify three different types of government to which he assigns a distinctive activating force, republics being activated by virtue, monarchy by honour and despotism by fear. In addition to exploring the principles that shape these three basic forms of government, Montesquieu also offered a general study of civil and natural law and their relationship to government, the separation and balance of constitutional powers, the relationship of the laws to freedom, the influence of climate on law codes, and he had much to say also on economics, slavery and the position of women. His views on the separation of powers are perhaps his most enduring and influential legacy to modern theories of government. These were based on his knowledge of the British constitution in which he had discerned a system of checks and balances, achieved by means of a strictly enforced segregation of the legislative, executive and judicial arms of government. Central to his concerns was the way in which government and the laws mutually combine to define the nature and success (or otherwise) of the civil order.

In the second half of the *Spirit*, the laws are treated in historical perspective, and envisaged, not within the traditional metaphysical context of universal, natural law espoused by Grotius and Pufendorf, but rather within empirically verifiable, sociological and anthropological contexts relating to climate, geography, economics, morality, religion and culture. This 'scientific', almost Newtonian, approach to questions of government and law is reflected in the numerous analogies and metaphors in the *Spirit* taken from the world of physics and cosmology. The focus of interest in this part of the treatise for contemporaries was, unsurprisingly, the historical analysis contained in Books 30 and 31 of the evolution of French monarchical government from its Merovingian and Carolingian origins to the reign

appropriate jobs to do. For Moser the quality of government rested on the personal qualities of officials as much as it did on the personal qualities of their masters, and in his detailed analysis of the differing temperaments of public servants, and of the close link between temperament and efficiency, he demonstrated considerable powers of psychological insight as well as political acumen.

Throughout his observations on the art of government and the exercise of power, Moser stressed the centrality of Christian principles to the workings of good government, and the role of conscience informed by Christian principle and scruple as a vital check on the excesses of autocracy. For Moser a prince's greatness did not consist simply in the possession of great armies and the ability to wage great wars, but in the prince's ability and willingness to familiarise himself with his subjects' lives and problems, to choose his servants wisely and above all to listen to the imperatives of his conscience. With Moser government was not so much a political concept as a moral one.

Civil rights

The age of Enlightenment was coincidentally also the age of absolutism and autocratic rule, and in many countries the promise of rights held out by radical thinkers to the ordinary, disenfranchised, and often cruelly tyrannised, individual was to remain an empty one for many decades. However, the dynamics of political evolution, accelerated by ideas of progress and optimism, increasingly secular concepts of government and the state, the ineluctable decline of religious authority coinciding with the growth of potent ideals of tolerance and the pursuit of happiness, were to create gradually a climate favourable to the implementation of social, political, and humanitarian reforms in which equality and freedom would come to be accepted as inalienable rights deriving from the condition of being human. The coming of age of the notion of rights and the transference of a long-standing theoretical concept to the arena of reformist legislation manifested itself most dramatically in the two best-known examples of Enlightenment political upheaval, the American Declaration of Independence and the French Declaration of the Rights of Man and of the Citizen. Together these declarations have come to be seen as the encapsulation of the Enlightenment's political legacy.

Denis Diderot (see below, pp. 291–2), the editor, initially in collaboration with the mathematician Jean Le Rond d'Alembert, of that great sprawling bible of the

Enlightenment, the multi-volumed *Encyclopedia*, was not a systematic political theorist, and much of his political thought arises in a fragmentary and spontaneous way from his reactions to the ideas of others (Wilson 1963), as can be seen in entries that bear his asterisk like 'Political authority', 'City' and 'Citizen', all of which owe much to Hobbes, Pufendorf, Barbeyrac and Montesquieu. 'Natural law' is built around propositions from Plato. 'Political authority', in which Diderot addressed the dangerous theme of the legitimacy of political power from the angle of human rights, was opposed vociferously in Parisian theological circles, obliging him to print in the corrections to the second volume of the *Encyclopedia* a disingenuous affirmation of his acknowledgement of God as the ultimate source of political authority. 'Natural law' also provoked criticism, not only from the usual sources, but also from Rousseau in his own *Encyclopedia* entry, 'Political economy'.

The question of Diderot's influence over Rousseau has been the subject of much debate (Wokler 1975, pp. 55–111), and certainly Diderot's views on the legitimacy of state authority and the rights of citizens within the civil order anticipate, with important differences, certain features of Rousseau's second *Discourse*, and indeed of the *Social contract* itself. Diderot's views also reflect the influence of Pufendorf, Grotius and Hobbes, especially with regard to the question of rights in the context of contract and sovereignty (Strugnell 1973, pp. 7–14). In 'Political authority' he follows Pufendorf's interpretation of the notion of contract as being based on consent derived either from force of arms or free submission, but he parted company with Pufendorf by asserting that in surrendering natural liberty to the ruler the rights of the individual could not be totally alienated, and that the powers of the ruler were always constrained by natural and civil codes of laws. The humanitarian, though politically conservative, stance of much early to mid-Enlightenment thinkers on the question of rights is well illustrated in Diderot's political contributions to the *Encyclopedia*. His priorities lay always with the preservation of political stability and the defence of the indivisibility of sovereign power (Proust 1963, p. 20; Hope Mason and Wokler 1992, pp. xxxi–xxxv). The question of the right to resist and to rebel does not arise.

In 'City' he makes it clear that the notion of insurrection against the sovereign is unacceptable, because the sovereign rules not as a private person but as a moral being or entity embodying the General Will of society, and is as such politically sacrosanct. This essential point is developed further in 'Citizen' where Diderot rejects the Hobbesian theory of human nature, with its emphasis on human self-interest and the pursuit of self-survival and security. Man, for Diderot, was not naturally a solitary creature continuously at war with others. On the contrary, man was a naturally sociable being, and in 'Natural law' he insisted that as a thinking animal man was able to reflect and act rationally and justly in accordance with the General Will. In this entry, which contains an exploration of the notion of the General Will and its expression through the person of the sovereign, Diderot foreshadowed Rousseau in perceiving the General Will to be the only effective mechanism for establishing within the civil order the rights and responsibilities of individuals. However, possibly because he mistrusted the destabilising potential of the masses as much as Voltaire did, Diderot considered the absolute monarch to be the true repository and executor of the General Will, and not, as Rousseau and others would maintain, the people themselves. In 'Political authority' the idealised image of such a monarch was identified historically with Henri IV. Here Diderot advanced a view of rights and freedoms predicated on the harmonisation of civil codes and institutions that ran with the grain of man's nature and natural inclinations. For Diderot, as for Montesquieu, government was the expression of human, moral and physical realities, and the emergence of rights and freedoms was contingent on the degree of compatibility that could be achieved between man's temperament and the laws and institutions he created.

Enlightenment arguments over rights concerned not only questions of definition, but also of entitlement, and this in turn raised issues relating to human as well as civil status. This came to a particularly explosive conjunction in the second half of the century, with Wilberforce in England and Marie-Jean-Antoine-Nicolas de Caritat, Marquis de Condorcet (see below, pp. 307–8) in France, over the slave trade, in which most major European countries engaged, and the contentious question of the abolition of black colonial servitude and the universal applicability of the principle of equality. In England abolitionism was driven by evangelical Christianity. In France it was driven by the secular imperatives of the Declaration of the Rights of Man and of the Citizen. The case of Condorcet, one of the drafters of the 1789 Declaration, is particularly interesting, although his contributions to the anti-slavery campaign are less well known than those of the English abolitionists.

Although slaves existed in the French West Indies prior to the establishment of the plantation system, the slave trade had become central to French commercial and maritime trading life between the mid-seventeenth and late eighteenth century as the processes whereby cane could be made into sugar became more viable and profitable. By the mid-eighteenth century slaves had become indispensable as a source of cheap labour to meet the increasing demand for exotic produce. The French slave trade in the Enlightenment reached a peak of activity between 1780 and 1792. With the declaration of war on England and Holland in 1793, the traffic came to an end effectively, and during the Revolutionary wars it almost disappeared (Stein 1979).

Details of the horrific conditions of transportation, in which the exigencies of profit had always to be calculated against the escalating mortality rate, as well as more openly disseminated information about plantation conditions in the colonies, gradually captured the attention of reformers in England, and subsequently in France. In France liberal, anti-slaving sentiment really started to grow just prior to the outbreak of the Revolution when Brissot, just back from London in 1788/9, proposed to a group of friends, including Condorcet, Siéyès, Lafayette, Boufflers and Mirabeau, to follow Wilberforce's lead and establish a *Société des amis des noirs* (Society for the Friends of Blacks), with a view to mobilising French public opinion, especially in Paris, in favour of abolition. The Society for the Friends of Blacks made little impact at first, and surprisingly, in view of Condorcet's involvement in the new society, the 1789 Declaration of the Rights of Man was to carry no reference to slavery. Slaves were not citizens in the eyes of the Revolution, and non-interference in, and protection of, the colonists' interests were formally decreed by the National Convention in March 1790. Growing problems and unrest in the colonies, however, ensured that by 1794 slavers and merchants were losing ground to the abolitionist tide of opinion. On 4 February 1794 the French government, under pressure particularly from events in Saint-Domingue rather than from the moral case for human rights, officially emancipated the slaves. However, transition to full freedom proved to be slow, and the slave trade recovered intermittently in the early years of Napoleon's rule, not being finally abolished in France until 1848 (Williams 1998).

Published in 1781, still well before any public campaign had gained momentum, and with a timely reprinting in 1788, Condorcet's *Reflections on black slavery* remains all the more remarkable for its prescience and for the boldness of its proposals. The first edition, printed under the pointed pseudonym of 'M. Schwartz' ('Mr Black'), was well ahead of its time in France. Its remarkable tone is set in the dedicatory epistle where Condorcet openly addresses the slaves as his brothers, praising them for their courage, their steadfastness in suffering and their moral fortitude, and recognising in them a full and unreserved equality with their white European masters, and a corresponding entitlement to human rights. His condemnation of the inhumanity and corruption of the slavers and the plantation owners is unequivocal, and is expressed in the name of the right to justice and equality for all men.

In the main body of his treatise, Condorcet writes eloquently and movingly of the relationship between masters and slaves on the plantations, and of the crushing human realities behind the terms of contract. He speculates interestingly on alternative ways of assuring the production of colonial goods without disruption to trade, on the moral issues involved in the buying and selling of human beings, on new methods of controlling plantation conditions from metropolitan France, on a number of practical humanitarian and economic steps that would be necessary in the wake of abolition relating to compensation to slave-owners and slaves, and on the need to phase in carefully any abolitionist legislation to avoid painful problems of adjustment. Condorcet's *Reflections* is the most radical, wide-ranging and closely argued reformist treatise on the justification of abolition, and the need to enact legislation to manage the problems of emancipation, to come out of the French Enlightenment. It is also one of the few Condorcet texts in which the cool logic of the mathematician and the pragmatic spirit of the legislator is accompanied by an open display of feeling and compassion. In this he mirrored many of the tensions inherent in Enlightenment political thought in general.

In the later decades of the eighteenth century the question of civil rights also encompassed the position of women. In France, the dramatist, flamboyant revolutionary activist, and founder-member of the Club of Revolutionary Republican Citizenesses, Marie Olympe Aubry de Gouges (see below, pp. 317–18), was one of the leading champions of women's rights under the freshly minted civil order of the Revolution. The most famous of her many political pamphlets is *The rights of woman*, composed as an appendix to the Declaration of the Rights of Man and of the Citizen, adopted by the National Assembly in August 1789. The *Rights* was published in 1791, and dedicated to Marie-Antoinette. Its appearance was deliberately timed to coincide with Louis XVI's ratification of the new constitution, based on the rights of man. In heavily ironic style, and addressing the reader in the familiar, egalitarian 'tu' form, Gouges proclaimed in this brief, fiery brochure the rights of humanity in general, not just those of the male sex. Together with Condorcet's *On the admission of women to the rights of citizenship* (1790), and Mary Wollstonecraft's *A vindication of the rights of woman* (1792), Gouges' *Rights* completes a trilogy of late eighteenth-century feminist tracts that represent a historical milestone of some importance in the history of the advancement of women to full legal and civil status in Europe (Angenot 1972; Rendall 1985).

'The woman Degouge', as Fouquier-Tinville described her at the time of her imprisonment in March 1793 to await execution, offered a sustained commentary on the relationship between the sexes, and on the pressing social, moral and political problems arising from the failure of the makers of the 1791 constitution to address the problem of female civil rights and responsibilities with the same enthusiasm as they had addressed those of men. It was in protest at this failure, and in the hope that the National Assembly, in validating the new constitution, would remedy the situation, that Gouges wrote the *Rights*. She was not a creator of political models, or a well-versed political writer in any sense, although many of the formulations used in the *Rights* evoke the style and terminology of Rousseau's *Social contract*. She wrote naively, but with refreshing spontaneity and a compulsive sense of urgency, about the issues and realities of her day, as she and women of her class experienced them. Her feminism was radical, and her claims on behalf of women's civil rights have a strikingly modern flavour.

In the *Rights* Gouges maintained a continuous parodic reference to the 1789 Declaration of the Rights of Man and of the Citizen, in which the advantages of egalitarian political doctrines had been confined to men alone. Condemnation of the tyranny of despots over men had not been extended to the question of the tyranny of men over women. Gouges' *Rights* went much further with its explicit replacement of the notion of civil liberty with that of individual liberty. The seventeen articles that follow on from the opening confident challenge to men's presumptions expressed in the preamble are printed under the subtitle, *Declaration of the rights of woman and of the citizeness*. The articles cover an astonishingly wide range of subjects, some of which are clearly drawn from the author's own experience of marriage, child-rearing and the pursuit of an active political career in the aftermath of a Revolution which continued to deny women electoral rights, and prevent them from standing for public office. Anticipating Fourier in many ways, the *Rights* set out the terms of a new social contract between men and women to replace the traditional marriage contract, in which audacious proposals regarding conjugal property rights, the transfer of property to children (including, contentiously, those conceived outside the framework of marriage, as a consequence of 'natural inclinations'), the responsibilities of fathers, divorce settlements, rights for unmarried mothers, the dignity of motherhood, taxation, politics

the new Eloisa (1762) and his educational blueprint for the education of girls contained in *Emile, or, on education* (1762).

She formulated proposals to change school curricula so that girls, that is to say middle-class girls, could be prepared for life, taught how to support themselves, how to achieve a balanced partnership with men within marriage and within the civil order, to extend their skills, pursue useful interests and advance their professional status. She advocated not only civil and political rights for women equal to those of men, but also the right of women to elect their own representatives. Her stance on the issue of women's civil and political rights appears all the more radical when seen against the prevailing conditions of the franchise in eighteenth-century England, whereby only a small minority of male freeholders above a prescribed income level were permitted to vote in elections, and the right to return members to Parliament bore little relationship to the distribution of the population in general. Public concern, moreover, lay not with the issue of universal suffrage for either sex, but rather with issues relating to patronage and the improvement, rather than the reform, of the electoral system.

Explicitly challenging views on the education of girls, as set out in the fifth book of Rousseau's *Emile*, Wollstonecraft rejected the notion that the sexes should be educated separately, and in accordance with different principles and aims. She also had much to say in the *Vindication* about morality, marriage, motherhood, sensibility and sexuality. Both of her vindications attracted a great deal of attention from contemporaries, but modern appreciations of Wollstonecraft rest principally upon her achievement as the author of *A vindication of the rights of woman*, now recognised as one of the most remarkable eighteenth-century examples of influential feminist writing (Sapiro 1992).

War and international relations

International relations in the Enlightenment evolved against a background of increasingly powerful European states possessing unprecedentedly powerful military capabilities. The power of monarchs was more than ever before defined by the strength and technological sophistication of their armies and navies, many commanded by a scientifically trained officer corps. Most of the institutions, conventions and protocols governing relations between states, the conduct of negotiations and the waging of war, established during the reign of Louis XIV in the years of France's seventeenth-century European supremacy, remained in place for many years after the Enlightenment, and some are still operative.

International relations were no longer simply a function of the dynastic ambition of individual sovereigns. The pursuit of power was becoming more closely aligned with the wider interests of the state, which in turn demanded due regard for the pursuit of trade and commercial advantage. Policies of territorial aggrandisement were still pursued vigorously of course, and dynastic as well as religious factors continued to play a role in international relations, and in the justification of war. While the Enlightenment evolved against a background of some of the most horrific wars ever seen on European soil, it also generated new thinking about traditionally vexatious issues such as the balance of powers, the conduct of diplomacy, the waging of war and the negotiation of treaties. The quest for mechanisms to perpetuate international peace without putting the security of individual, and particularly small, nations at risk, was now to become a central priority in the management of diplomacy.

One of the earliest of the Enlightenment's post-Pufendorf thinkers to open new perspectives on international relations was Charles-Irénée Castel de Saint-Pierre (see below, pp. 355–6), a member of the French diplomatic corps negotiating the peace terms that brought the War of the Spanish Succession to an end with the Treaty of Utrecht in 1713. Saint-Pierre's *A plan for perpetual peace in Europe* was first published in 1712, and the proposals it contained received much attention, and much mockery, in France and elsewhere throughout the eighteenth century. In the prefatory remarks Saint-Pierre stated that he was inspired by Sully's celebrated plan, drawn up in the last book of his memoirs (1638), which Henri IV had proposed to Elizabeth I. Sully's plan had envisaged permanent peace in Europe by means of the creation of a federalist system designed primarily to curtail the power of Austria. No doubt Saint-Pierre wished to use the association with Sully as a means to lend more authority to his own peace proposals, which he anticipated correctly would be greeted with some incredulity by contemporaries. Louis XV's prime minister, Cardinal de Fleury, was to comment famously, for example, that the one article missing in Saint-Pierre's *Plan* was the one requiring missionaries to be sent to princes to soften their hearts. Montesquieu, on the other hand, much admired him, but the caricature-image of Saint-Pierre as a simplistic dreamer, a builder of extravagantly naive, though benevolently intended, schemes for the betterment of mankind has endured, and only relatively recently has it been challenged (Perkins 1989, pp. 3–22).

A utilitarian before his time, Saint-Pierre composed his treatise when modern nation states were just beginning to take shape, and when the problems of international relations, and the now familiar facts of European *realpolitik*, were still at an embryonic stage. As a result, much that seems obvious, even banal to modern eyes, in his peace proposals was seen by many of his contemporaries to be simply perverse or eccentric. However, the core proposals of his *Plan* emanated from a rich seam of serious thinking on trade, economics, science, morality, laws, freedom, violence and above all on human nature, and on what drives human beings to behave as they do. His *Plan* thus interacted with themes that recur in his other later writings, and particularly in his *Political annals* (1757), and should be seen in that context. Saint-Pierre had little confidence in views on man and society that relied on the authority of tradition or faith. His view of the endemic phenomenon of war as a direct consequence of the natural ferocity of human nature owes something to his reading of Hobbes, but even more to his own empirical observations. For him peace was not a natural condition of mankind; it would come about only as a consequence of a widely shared, rational calculation of self-interest (Perkins 1959). Once established, it would be sustainable only through a system of international arbitration, reinforced by effective deterrence.

In one of the 'digressions' in his treatise, which is actually central to its underlying rationale, he speculated on 'the unhappy life of savages'. He visualised primitive, pre-social man living in a state of continuous violence and conflict, dependent for survival on the seasons, on wild animals and on those other even wilder animals, his fellow human beings. The violence of primitive life was unchecked by laws, or any retributive system of justice that for Saint-Pierre was essential if the animal passions in man were to be tamed. With the discovery of the need for rules, and a system of punishment and deterrence to reinforce those rules, beasts were transformed into men, though at the cost of their natural liberty. Saint-Pierre relocated the dangers and uncertainties once faced by natural man in the context of modern international relations. In modern societies life was infinitely preferable to the life of primitive peoples because there was *sufficient guarantee* that the law would be obeyed, and that contractual promises would be kept. Individual citizens could no longer act in their own interests freely against the interests of others *with impunity*. While relations between individuals were so ordered, however, relations between sovereigns were still governed by the untrammelled, state-of-nature powers exercised by the strong over the weak. The terms of treaties were thus not worth the paper they were written on simply because they could not be enforced. If the constant surveillance of subjects within the state was necessary for the avoidance of civil conflict, how much more necessary was a system of mutual surveillance and deterrence at the international level. Promises and commitments at this level could only be enforced by the establishment of what Saint-Pierre called presciently a *European Union* having absolute authority and power to implement the decisions of deputed arbitrators in the settlement of disputes, and take joint action against un-cooperative states.

The actual plan consists of twelve 'fundamental' articles, supplemented by other articles that he calls 'useful' or 'important'. Much of the fine detail of the *Plan* is devoted to an analysis of the advantages of such a system of international control, to an examination of early models provided by the German and Swiss confederations, to the framing of specific articles as the basis for peace negotiations, to detailed arrangements for the security of frontiers, the responsibilities of officials and the problem of cost. Auxiliary issues relating to economics, trade, religion and sovereign authority are also examined in considerable detail. After the War of the Spanish Succession, Saint-Pierre believed that Europe had reached a critical stage in international relations, and now had to choose between continual warfare and eventual, inevitable self-destruction on the one hand, and on the other a way forward that would involve the surrender of sovereign rights to pursue individualist policies of unlimited territorial expansion, and the acceptance of a formidable instrument of international control.

The essence of the *Plan* is to be found in Article 8 (referred to indirectly in summary form in the Recapitulation) which aims to prevent sovereigns from taking up arms against another sovereign state, unless that state had been placed under what Saint-Pierre termed a 'ban of Europe' (Lecercle 1993; Le Cour Grandmaison 1994). His views were based to some extent upon a serious misunderstanding of the nature of the seventeenth-century German Empire, as well as upon a flawed analysis of Sully's 1635 *Grand design of Henri IV* (Riley 1983, pp. 123–31). In spite of all the ridicule and opposition, however, Saint-Pierre continued to press hard for acceptance of his proposals for many years after their initial publication.

The debate over whether states, by analogy with man in the state of nature, were naturally at war or at peace with each other can be traced back to the Greek Stoic and Platonic schools of thought. In Part I, chapter 13 of the *Leviathan* ('Of the natural condition of mankind as concerning their felicity, and misery'),

Hobbes had extended his dark view of man's nature to the nature of the state itself, and for Hobbes international relations amounted to little more than a continuous state of war with sovereigns adopting the 'state and posture of gladiators' (Hobbes 1960, p. 83). Enlightenment thinkers tended to modify Hobbes' uncompromisingly stark vision of the realities of war and peace by introducing into international relations the moral constraints of natural law, often called in this context the 'law of nations'. Montesquieu, Barbeyrac and Vattel were among those natural law theorists of the period who saw significant parallels between the operations of natural law, and their expression in civil law codes, which had suspended war between one individual and another.

The suspension of conflict between individual states was achievable through the systematic application of the moral imperatives of natural law. As with individual citizens, states, by virtue of their existence, had the right to survive, and in the interests of self-preservation could wage war, but wars fought in those circumstances would be in accordance with justice and the law of nations. On war and peace, and the principles governing international relations, most Enlightenment thinkers followed Grotius, who had justified war in terms of the right to self-preservation, and had been among the first to systemise the rules for its declaration and conduct. The notion of states as 'moral persons' was of course to receive its most celebrated and philosophically refined formulation at the end of the century with Immanuel Kant (see below, pp. 375–6).

Grotius' *On the law of war and peace* had been first translated into French by Courtelin in 1687, but the treatise came to the attention of many eighteenth-century readers in Europe through Jean Barbeyrac (see below, pp. 364–5). Barbeyrac had already edited Grotius' text in Latin in 1720, and in 1724 he issued a translation, *Le droit de la guerre et de la paix*. In his dedication to George I in the expanded 1729 edition Barbeyrac defined war and peace as 'the science appropriate to kings', but warned that there were lessons to be drawn from this science that would not please every sovereign, especially not those with a false idea of their own grandeur, and of their own true interests, kings who listened only to the language of flattery, 'directly opposed to the maxims set out in this work'.

The translation was published in two volumes containing three main 'books', or sections. In the first book Grotius had dealt with the origins of the law and of war itself, the different forms that war took, and the limits to sovereign power. In the second book he had considered war and the issue of public and private rights, whose violation authorised recourse to arms. In the third he had examined the conduct and conventions of war, together with a number of questions relating to the conclusion of peace treaties. In the context of natural law, Grotius had treated a wide range of subjects in these three areas relating to the causes of war, rights of self-defence, the protection of property, rights of possession, rights over others, oaths, contracts, the notion of a just war, rights of pillage, rights of territorial acquisition, treatment of prisoners of war, the position of neutrals, rights and privileges of ambassadors, diplomatic forms of confrontation and negotiation, and the intricate balancing of interests.

Some of Barbeyrac's notes on Grotius' text are little more than scholarly references to Grotius' sources, or elucidations of the latter's terminology, but many more are lengthy and learned commentaries on specific issues, constituting in effect miniature essays in their own right. Building on Grotius' text, Barbeyrac reviewed, in the light of his own interpretation of natural law requirements, such questions as the right of sovereigns to raise armies, the position of those who dissent from the call to arms, the factors determining a just war, protocols of ambassadorial representation, rules governing the treatment of prisoners, circumstances authorising the killing of enemies, conventions covering the declaration and termination of hostilities, and the relationship between natural law and the 'law of nations' relevant to all of these issues (Hochstrasser 1993, pp. 289–90).

In his view of international relations Barbeyrac followed not only Grotius, but also Pufendorf and Tillotson, in seeing human self-interest and self-love, and the related instinct for self-preservation, as being ultimately compatible with natural law and divine law. He accepted the anti-Hobbesian emphasis that both Grotius and Pufendorf had placed on sociability and the natural inclination of human beings to live in peace with each other, but he also added a corrective to that emphasis, namely the equally important roles played by reason, conscience and Christian principle in the pursuit of security and survival (Rosenblatt 1997, pp. 93–5). It was against this background, elaborated in more detail in his translation of Pufendorf's *On the law of nature and nations*, as well as in the essay prefacing the 1729 edition of this translation, the *Historical and critical account of the science of morality* . . . , that Barbeyrac's comments on Grotius' thoughts on war and peace, together with his finely detailed elaboration of the technicalities involved in practising the science of war, should be understood.

The *Historical account* contains the essence of Barbeyrac's argument about the place of theological considerations in natural law theory, and in the notes to the

dimensions. The coming into existence of such a commonwealth would always depend on the moral progress of man, which was dependent in turn upon man's responsiveness to what was for Kant the essentially rational message of Christianity, a message coinciding with nature's purpose and God's will (Riley 1983, pp. 120–3; Atkinson 1992). He had already defined the nature of these key links between personal, political and international morality in his 1793 essay on *Religion within the limits of reason alone*, in many ways the ideological prelude to *Perpetual peace* that was to appear two years later.

Trade and economics

Economic philosophies in the Enlightenment evolved against a social background in which most of the workforce earned a living from the land, which continued to be cultivated using methods handed down from medieval times. Changes to agricultural practices were taking place, but they were tentative and piecemeal for most of the period, and significant technological innovation only really took place in English agricultural techniques. Trades, crafts, industrial and other non-agrarian service occupations were proliferating, and production processes were becoming increasingly more sophisticated, producing goods for a widening range of consumers. Many of these new processes had been explained and superbly illustrated in the plates of Diderot's *Encyclopedia*, and they set in train changes that would culminate first in England in an Industrial Revolution which would eventually transform not only productivity, but domestic and international trading patterns and volume as well. The implications and dilemmas of this mixture of agrarian conservatism and industrial revolution, of the tensions between the world of cities and the world of rural communities, on the management of fiscal and trading policies, were to weigh heavily with all governments in Enlightenment Europe. The dawn of a new world of commercial realities would also generate a new science of economics to meet its challenges, and a new generation of economic theorists with fresh ideas on free trade, tariffs, mercantilism, land usage, luxury and conspicuous consumption, taxation, colonial development, employment practices, wage levels, the rich and the poor, and the division of labour (Larrère 1992).

One of the most sensational (and scandalous) writings on economic matters to appear in the early years of the century, and whose impact was to prove as endur-

the conduct and conventions of war, together with a number of questions relating to the conclusion of peace treaties. In the context of natural law, Grotius had treated a wide range of subjects in these three areas relating to the causes of war, rights of self-defence, the protection of property, rights of possession, rights over others, oaths, contracts, the notion of a just war, rights of pillage, rights of territorial acquisition, treatment of prisoners of war, the position of neutrals, rights and privileges of ambassadors, diplomatic forms of confrontation and negotiation, and the intricate balancing of interests.

Some of Barbeyrac's notes on Grotius' text are little more than scholarly references to Grotius' sources, or elucidations of the latter's terminology, but many more are lengthy and learned commentaries on specific issues, constituting in effect miniature essays in their own right. Building on Grotius' text, Barbeyrac reviewed, in the light of his own interpretation of natural law requirements, such questions as the right of sovereigns to raise armies, the position of those who dissent from the call to arms, the factors determining a just war, protocols of ambassadorial representation, rules governing the treatment of prisoners, circumstances authorising the killing of enemies, conventions covering the declaration and termination of hostilities, and the relationship between natural law and the 'law of nations' relevant to all of these issues (Hochstrasser 1993, pp. 289–90).

In his view of international relations Barbeyrac followed not only Grotius, but also Pufendorf and Tillotson, in seeing human self-interest and self-love, and the related instinct for self-preservation, as being ultimately compatible with natural law and divine law. He accepted the anti-Hobbesian emphasis that both Grotius and Pufendorf had placed on sociability and the natural inclination of human beings to live in peace with each other, but he also added a corrective to that emphasis, namely the equally important roles played by reason, conscience and Christian principle in the pursuit of security and survival (Rosenblatt 1997, pp. 93–5). It was against this background, elaborated in more detail in his translation of Pufendorf's *On the law of nature and nations,* as well as in the essay prefacing the 1729 edition of this translation, the *Historical and critical account of the science of morality* . . . , that Barbeyrac's comments on Grotius' thoughts on war and peace, together with his finely detailed elaboration of the technicalities involved in practising the science of war, should be understood.

The *Historical account* contains the essence of Barbeyrac's argument about the place of theological considerations in natural law theory, and in the notes to the

Pufendorf translation itself he commented further on morality and religion in relation to legal codes. The Swiss jurist and diplomat, Emmerich de Vattel, was to draw deeply on Barbeyrac's notes on Grotius in his own *Principles of natural law applied to the conduct and affairs of nations and sovereigns* (1758). In Vattel's treatise the theory of natural law was to be applied rigorously and systematically to the science of international relations, and it was through Vattel that the principles of Grotius and Barbeyrac relating to the conduct of states were transmitted to later generations of international law jurists.

In 1795 Immanuel Kant (see below, pp. 375–6) published *Perpetual peace: a philosophical sketch*, in which the application of the famous Kantian principle of the 'categorical imperative' was extended to the conduct of nations. Kant explained what he meant by this in the *Foundations of the metaphysics of morals*, prefacing the *Critique of pure reason* (1781). Here he emphasised the primacy of free will as the pre-requisite to moral decision making and action in accordance with duty rather than desire, the conflict between duty and desire being resolved by the general moral law, also known as the 'principle of right' or the 'categorical imperative'. Like most Enlightenment thinkers, Kant had a general faith in the possibility of progress, and in the eventual triumph of justice and peace.

In *Perpetual peace* states are deemed to be 'moral persons', with moral obligations that paralleled those that existed between individuals. As with men in the state of nature, for Kant nations existed in a Hobbesian state of natural mutual hostility, always either at war or preparing for war. Enlightened self-interest demanded that nations, like individuals, should concede a measure of their natural freedom to a separate political body that would act in the interest of all, this common interest in the case of nations being international peace. As men moved from the state of nature into the civil order, Kant envisaged that nations too could move towards a republic of sovereign powers, an 'ethical commonwealth', slightly reminiscent of Saint-Pierre's 'European Union' proposal. Kant's commonwealth would also be sustained by economic ties, and would bring into existence an international legal system that would protect the rights of nations in ways analogous to those offered to individuals by national law codes – but only in those states in which the moral autonomy of the individual prevailed and was respected (Sullivan 1994, pp. 20–1).

Kant's treatise is now recognised as one of his most important political statements (Riley 1983; H. Williams 1992). It was composed in the form of a peace treaty in two parts, the first part containing six articles relating to pre-conditions for peace, and the second containing three articles setting out conditions for its preservation, together with two supplements and two appendices. The six preliminary articles require countries signing the treaty to relinquish all covert preparations for a future war, to reject the legitimacy of any state's claims to acquire territory belonging to another state, to abolish standing armies, to avoid the financing of foreign policy from the national debt, to cease all interference in the constitutional arrangements and government of other states, and finally (anticipating the Geneva Convention provisions of our own century) to avoid in the case of states already at war with one another the perpetration of atrocities that might jeopardise future peace negotiations through a consequential lack of mutual respect and confidence between former enemies, and engender bitterly contested claims for reparation and compensation. Kant was concerned, above all, to remove the capability of strong states to coerce weaker states, and to assert the importance in the achievement of stable international relations of each state's recognition of the principle of autonomy in the exercise of self-determination. States, should, in other words, relate to each other in much the same way as individuals.

These issues were of course particularly sensitive and critical in the immediate aftermath of the French Revolution at a time when interference in France's internal affairs was an obvious temptation for neighbouring powers such as England, where Burke was calling openly for military intervention. The combustible condition of contemporary Europe in fact suggested to Kant that there was no possibility of guaranteeing immediate peace, even in the unlikely event of an agreement to adopt his plan, and he always saw perpetual peace as a slow, cumulative process. While the recurrence of war was to be expected, given contemporary European realities, he was nevertheless confident that practical steps could be taken to control international violence, and thereby pave the way for the great, and ultimately achievable, goal of international harmony and stability.

Saint-Pierre had proposed in his *Plan for perpetual peace* a formal association of states by means of a treaty signed by all sovereigns with a view to creating a European supra-national federal power capable of imposing peace by force of arms on disruptive rogue states. Kant, like Rousseau, believed that international peace could only come about as a result of a moral transformation, although he did not share Rousseau's pessimism with regard to the possibility of achieving such a transformation in prevailing circumstances (Williams 1983, pp. 257–68). His vision of a world-wide 'ethical commonwealth' had spiritual as well as moral dimensions. The coming into existence of such a commonwealth would always depend on the moral progress of man, which was dependent in turn upon man's responsiveness to what was for Kant the essentially rational message of Christianity, a message coinciding with nature's purpose and God's will (Riley 1983, pp. 120–3; Atkinson 1992). He had already defined the nature of these key links between personal, political and international morality in his 1793 essay on *Religion within the limits of reason alone*, in many ways the ideological prelude to *Perpetual peace* that was to appear two years later.

Trade and economics

Economic philosophies in the Enlightenment evolved against a social background in which most of the workforce earned a living from the land, which continued to be cultivated using methods handed down from medieval times. Changes to agricultural practices were taking place, but they were tentative and piecemeal for most of the period, and significant technological innovation only really took place in English agricultural techniques. Trades, crafts, industrial and other non-agrarian service occupations were proliferating, and production processes were becoming increasingly more sophisticated, producing goods for a widening range of consumers. Many of these new processes had been explained and superbly illustrated in the plates of Diderot's *Encyclopedia*, and they set in train changes that would culminate first in England in an Industrial Revolution which would eventually transform not only productivity, but domestic and international trading patterns and volume as well. The implications and dilemmas of this mixture of agrarian conservatism and industrial revolution, of the tensions between the world of cities and the world of rural communities, on the management of fiscal and trading policies, were to weigh heavily with all governments in Enlightenment Europe. The dawn of a new world of commercial realities would also generate a new science of economics to meet its challenges, and a new generation of economic theorists with fresh ideas on free trade, tariffs, mercantilism, land usage, luxury and conspicuous consumption, taxation, colonial development, employment practices, wage levels, the rich and the poor, and the division of labour (Larrère 1992).

One of the most sensational (and scandalous) writings on economic matters to appear in the early years of the century, and whose impact was to prove as enduring as it was controversial, was *The fable of the bees: or, private vices, publick benefits* (1714) by Bernard Mandeville (see below, pp. 397–8). Mandeville was denounced almost immediately as a cynical defender and champion of vice and luxury, a superficial perception of the purpose of his arrestingly original *Fable* encouraged no doubt by its provocative subtitle. Early signs of Mandeville's distinctively sardonic style that 'pierces and strikes', as well as intimation of his shocking angle of moral vision, can be seen in *Some fables after the easy and familiar method of Monsieur de La Fontaine*, a work containing two of his own fables, *The carp* and *The nightingale and the owl* (Harth 1970, pp. 8–9).

The *Fable* starts with a sardonic, rhymed allegory about a beehive, the lives of whose inhabitants bear a close resemblance to the English in the late seventeenth century (Dickenson 1975, pp. 80–97). The hive flourished in 'Luxury and Ease'. All the bees were guilty of vices of various kinds, whether advancing their interests openly as 'Knaves', or less openly as 'the grave Industrious'. However, instead of condemning the vices of the bees, Mandeville demonstrated paradoxically that the economic prosperity and happiness of the hive was directly dependent on the flourishing existence of vice. Vice and immorality were the key to a buoyant balance of trade, full employment and national security. Crime was in itself an industry like any other, enabling an army of bailiffs, jailors, turnkeys, locksmiths and lawyers to 'squeeze a Living out of Tears'. Luxury, greed, envy and vanity combined to encourage the conspicuous consumption whose 'trickle-down' effects underpinned the hive's commercial and social harmony.

By all this Mandeville did not seek to prove simply that evil was a good thing. The ethical paradox crystallises in his view of virtue. He defined virtuous acts in his *An enquiry into the origin of moral virtue* (forming part of the 1714 edition of the *Fable*) as acts 'by which man, contrary to the impulse of nature, should endeavour the benefit of others, or the conquest of his own passions out of a rational ambition of being good'. In looking at society in the light of this definition, he concluded that virtue did not exist. All actions were vicious in as much as they sprang ultimately from selfish motives, including those actions that benefit society. All the bees were driven by pride, and all sought, and responded to, the benefits of luxury and dishonesty. Mandeville's 'knaves' are punished, but their punishment comes about not as a consequence of their sins, but as a consequence of a mistakenly acquired zeal to be virtuous, i.e. 'knaves turn'd honest'. They affect uneasiness with vice, and make a hypocritical show of wishing for 'a frugal and honest society'. An outraged Jove grants their wish, and vices and crimes disappear, as does the trade they generate. Commercial life stagnates, unemployment grows and prosperity fades away. The lesson is made explicit in *The moral*: 'Then leave Complaints: Fools only strive / To make a great an honest Hive'.

The ethical and economic issues behind the doggerel-like verse are explored in more detail in the accompanying essay, *An enquiry into the origin of moral virtue* and in a series of shorter commentaries, or *Remarks* on key lines of verse relating to the vices that Mandeville considered essential to national prosperity. *Remark L* is one of nine *Remarks* in which he defends luxury, probably the most carefully elaborated area in his economic philosophy, and much despised by contemporary moralists and theologians (see also *Remarks M, N, P, Q, S, T, X* and *Y*; Goldsmith 1987, pp. 225–51). Here, as elsewhere, Mandeville insisted that while luxury might indeed be sinful, it ensured full employment and the creation of national wealth. It was this association of luxury and conspicuous consumption with the national interest, with its concomitant denial of the virtue of national frugality, that probably caused most offence. Mandeville attacked the notion that luxury softened and corrupted a people, and that it was economically wasteful. Luxury was one of the most obvious examples to many contemporaries of a private vice, and was denounced as dangerous by both moralists and economists, particularly mercantilists, who saw the taste for luxury as encouraging frivolous importations from foreign countries at the expense of plain, honest domestic products. Luxury was, in short, unpatriotic as well as depraving, a moral attitude towards conspicuous consumption that had been enshrined in the sumptuary laws against luxury that had governed commercial life in the city state of Geneva since 1558.

In *Remark L* Mandeville exposed the fallacy of the view that 'Luxury is as destructive to the wealth of the whole body politick, as it is to that of every individual person who is guilty of it'. Such a view would, in Mandeville's opinion, lead only to national bankruptcy. In his redefinition of the meaning of luxury, in his outright denial of its 'enervating' and 'effeminating' effects, and in his uncompromising elaboration of its commercial benefits, Mandeville was in effect isolating economic theory from its conventional moral framework, and relocating it in a pragmatic world in which all bees are wicked, in which hard choices have to be made between policies leading to impoverishment and policies leading to prosperity, and in which moral considerations have no real meaning because 'As long as men have the same appetites, the same vices will remain.' In all this Mandeville's *Fable* offers a thoughtful, if provocative, foretaste of *laissez-faire* principles of trading and economic theory, and the formative impact of Mandeville's iconoclasm on later utilitarian schools of economic thinking has been considerable (Kaye 1966, pp. vii–cxlvi).

In France the middle years of the eighteenth century were dominated by the economic philosophy of François Quesnay and the physiocrats (see below, pp. 409–10). Between 1757 and 1758 what would now be called a 'think-tank' began to gather around Quesnay, including Mirabeau, Gournay, Mercier de La Rivière and its most eminent disciple, Turgot. Many of Quesnay's associates were not just economic theorists, but also experienced public officials, many still active in the financial service of the state. The economist Vincent de Gournay, for example, was a provincial official, equivalent in rank today to a Prefect, and Turgot was Controller-General of Finance between 1774 and 1776. Together, this group of French economists constituted the physiocratic movement, of which Quesnay was to remain the undisputed leading proponent and ideologist (Fox-Genovese 1976, pp. 100–33).

In general terms, physiocrats believed that the only true source of national wealth, and the basis to the social order, was land, to which the produce of commerce and industry added nothing. They advocated the principle of a single tax, to be levied on land, legislation defending agriculture and the doctrine of *laissez-faire, laissez-passer*. The *laissez-faire* maxim, attributed to Gournay, denotes disapproval of any government interference in industry, and opposition to all obstacles to free trade within the state, and between states. The impact of physiocratic theory started to be felt particularly after 1767, the year in which the friendship and collaboration between Quesnay and Mirabeau reached its highest point. It was in September of that year that the two friends decided to enlarge their circle by organising a course of instruction in economic science, in collaboration with the *abbé* Chouart (in whose house it was held) and Court de Gébelin. The course was to focus on a detailed explication of Quesnay's *The economic tableau*, fragments of which had been circulating in manuscript form for some years (Kuczynski and Meek 1972, pp. ix–xx).

Quesnay's 1759 *Tableau* consists of the famous 'zig-zag', a graphic representation of Quesnay's view of how net revenue circulates in an agrarian economy (Woog 1958, pp. 153–68). The 'zig-zag' is followed by twelve pages of arithmetical 'Explanation' which greatly baffled contemporaries, and twenty-four maxims entitled 'Extract from M. de Sully's royal maxims on economic government'. Like Saint-Pierre who, in another context, had also invoked the name and authority of Henri IV's prime minister, Quesnay was hoping no doubt to disarm critics.

There is some affinity between Sully's reformist views on agriculture and those of the physiocrats, but Quesnay's maxims never again appeared under this title in subsequent reworkings of the text in the various physiocratic documents across which the work sprawls. Many of the pretended extracts from Sully have their source in fact in the maxims that Quesnay set out in his entry on 'Grain' for Diderot's *Encyclopedia*, and other sections of his text can be traced back to another entry, 'Farmers (political economy)'. The main body of commentary and analysis, and the most interesting part of the *Tableau*, however, is to be found in the very extensive annotations that Quesnay subsequently appended to the maxims, and which more than quadrupled the length of the original text. Quesnay's *Tableau* has attracted much attention, and much division of opinion, among economists. It deeply influenced contemporaries like Le Trosne, Mercier de La Rivière, Morellet, Turgot and Condorcet, and in the following century was praised by Marx. In spite of its many internal contradictions, obfuscations, impenetrable mathematical mechanisms and inelegances of style and expression, it has ensured that eighteenth-century physiocratic doctrine has continued to stimulate, provoke and preoccupy economic historians and economists (Speck 1975, pp. 66–79).

In reading the *Tableau* it is important to keep the historical context in mind. This is a text that predates what we now call social science. In a France largely still tied to its feudal past, where structural political change was still difficult to envisage, it offered one of the first theoretical models for resolving the tensions between traditional structure and values on the one hand, and the increasingly urgent pressures arising from the requirements of an emerging free-market economy on the other. As such, the *Tableau* represents a revolutionary step forward in the science of economics. It reflected specific physiocratic concerns with the political regeneration of society and the restoration of the financial power of the French monarchy, and it marks a significant stage in the evolution of what Condorcet was later to call 'political arithmetic', that is to say, the principles by which human behaviour can be reliably analysed, predicted and ultimately reconciled with the organisational imperatives of a modern nation state (Hecht 1958, pp. 211–93; Noxon 1971, pp. 233–52).

Quesnay had much to say about free internal and external trade and other economic issues, but he always returned to the central principle of physiocracy, that the only source of true wealth was the land. He was convinced that agriculture rather than foreign trade was the most effective way of raising output, and improving national economic well-being. He believed that the quality of the workforce was more important than its size. It was essential to national security in the case of soldiers, and a skilled workforce was equally essential to the nation's prosperity in the case of farm workers and managers. Quesnay was particularly insistent on the abandonment of policies for agriculture that relied on the labour of an impoverished peasantry. Above all, the *Tableau* reflected a growing concern with the damaging effects of a national economy too closely aligned with monopoly interests, privilege and top-heavy government regulation. In this respect, Quesnay's break with the mercantilists was absolute.

He understood the intricacies of capital production and investment, and the workings of the labour market, but he was never able quite to reconcile their implications with the realities of the pre-capitalist economic and political system in which he lived. Only the land could provide the nation with a disposable surplus. The products of artisans and craftsmen may be useful and decorative, but they added little to the nation's stock of wealth, the value of what they produce being absorbed in the payment for their work, from which Voltaire mockingly drew the conclusion that 'we can be poor with taste'. Only work on the land was capable of yielding a net product in Quesnay's system; everything else was 'sterile', and without a market for a product, there was only a subsistence level of existence for producers. For Quesnay trade and commerce had no value or meaning other than a monetary one. As the net product is the only true revenue, it alone should bear the burden of taxation. Tax should be collected at source, and he proposed that a simple direct tax should be levied on land, not exceeding one third of the net product.

To meet this tax, landowners and farmers would raise the price of raw materials so that every consumer would pay a share of the taxation involved, with the costs of tax collection minimised, and the inefficient financial machinery of the state bypassed. People and nations should, in Quesnay's view, direct expenditure only into two 'productive' channels; tax should be levied on land in due proportion to its annual net product; trade and the circulation of wealth should be pursued without restriction. Quesnay's impact on later Enlightenment economists, such as Adam Smith (see below, pp. 421–2), was considerable. He did not live to see the publication of the *Wealth of nations*, which Smith had intended to dedicate to him. Smith was to comment extensively on the *Tableau* in Book IV, chapter 9.

Although Adam Smith's views on political economy were greatly influenced by Quesnay and other physiocrats whom he had met in Paris in 1765, as well as by earlier French economists like Richard Cantillon, author of the influential *Essay on the nature of commerce in general* (1755), the main elements of Smith's economic philosophy were in fact already in place before his encounter with physiocracy. The gestation of the *Wealth* goes back as far as 1752, the year in which he was first exposed to David Hume's *Political discourses* on money, the balance of trade and the errors of mercantilism. The general drift of the *Wealth* is particularly apparent in Smith's 1759 lectures on 'Jurisprudence', as well as in the *Theory of moral sentiments* (1759) which contains analyses of virtue and moral judgement, known also as the doctrines of sympathy and of the impartial spectator, both of which illuminate Hume's perception of the ways in which economic forces interact dynamically with the social and moral world of human relationships (Lindgren 1973, pp. 20–38).

In assessing the philosophical and ethical basis to the *Wealth*, modern commentators have drawn attention to the apparently contrasting position adopted in the earlier treatise (Morrow 1973, pp. 3–11, and also chapter 2). The degree to which the empathetic principle of 'sympathy' in the *Theory*, i.e. the capacity to 'change places in the fancy' with other individuals, and to align one's sentiments with theirs, a principle owing much to Smith's reading of Shaftesbury and Hutcheson, is actually replaced in the *Wealth* by a more Hobbesian–Mandevillian ethical stance, is in fact less clear on closer examination. This becomes apparent when the key terms *sympathy* and *self-interest* are weighed carefully in their respective contexts, and modern interpretations of both treatises tend to stress continuity on this point rather than dislocation (Morrow 1973, p. 4). The *Theory* thus has its place in any interpretation of Smith's later economic thinking. This is particularly true of the *Wealth* which is much more than a treatise concerned exclusively with economics, and forms, like the *Theory*, part of a much larger sociological *opus magnum* that Smith intended to write, but was never able to complete.

Smith's theory of society completed in many ways the steps in human social evolution elaborated by natural law theorists of property and wealth such as Pufendorf (Hont 1987, pp. 253–76). In mapping man's journey from the state of nature to the civil state, Pufendorf and his followers had envisaged a three-stage transition (Stein 1980). Smith added a fourth, namely that of the 'Age of Commerce' (see above, pp. 14–15). The concept of the fourth age was already present in fragmentary form in Pufendorf's analysis of luxury, and the appearance of a system of private property, in the third, 'agricultural' age, as Barbeyrac had noted. The concept of a separate fourth age might well have come to Smith's attention from that source. Smith certainly owned a copy of Barbeyrac's translation of

Pufendorf's *Of the duty of man and citizen*, and he referred to Barbeyrac's notes in the *Theory* (Hont 1987, p. 276; cf. Pocock 1985, pp. 37–50).

Whatever the source, it was in Smith's *Theory of moral sentiments* and in the *Wealth* that the Four-Stages theory received its most complete and sophisticated expression (see Book I, chapter 4). The fourth stage was not for Smith an isolated postscript, but rather a natural evolution of commercial and trading characteristics already at work during the three 'ruder' stages (Hont 1987, pp. 253–6; Hont and Ignatieff 1983; Meek 1976, pp. 227–8). The acceleration of these elements to produce the fourth stage in the human journey to the civil state, that subsumed modern forms of commercial activity and of the division of labour, was ultimately linked to the same historical drives for self-preservation that Hobbes and Pufendorf pre-supposed, but accentuated by new pressures arising from gradually diminishing natural resources, and a rapidly increasing growth in population.

Writing in a pre-Marxist age, Smith employed a terminology startlingly recognisable to modern readers, although his commentaries on labour markets, commodities, wage levels, profits and the employment of capital are always deeply embedded in the Enlightenment's characteristic preoccupation with social, political and moral considerations such as 'nature', 'liberty' and 'sentiment'. The view of human relationships and motivations in the *Theory* remained operative as an organising philosophical principle in his later economic writings, and is particularly relevant to the argumentation of the *Wealth*: 'It is chiefly from this regard to the sentiments of mankind, that we pursue riches and avoid poverty. For to what purpose is all the toil and bustle of this world ? . . . To be observed, to be attended to, to be taken notice of with sympathy, complacency and approbation.' The pursuit of self-approval, and with that the pursuit of self-interested economic goals, had social, as well as financial, implications in Smith's theory. The instinct to sympathise with the other, to abhor the risk of harm to other individuals, informed Smith's views on the evolution of productive energies. Politics affected the distribution of the products of those energies, and the acceptance of legal and political systems that constrained the capacity of individuals to affect adversely the nature of that distribution (Cropsey 1957, pp. 2–10; Skinner 1979, pp. 42–67).

The *Wealth* was published in 1776, initially in two volumes, and is composed of five books. Book I has eleven chapters, and is concerned with 'the causes of improvement in the productive powers of labour, and of the order according to which its produce is naturally distributed among the different ranks of people'. In addition to chapters on the division of labour, this first book also treats the origin and use of money, commodities, wages, profits, inequalities, land, the history of the use of gold and silver, and it includes a historical account of fluctuations in the value of those metals. In Book II Smith devotes five chapters to 'the nature, accumulation and employment of stock'. Book III has four chapters on 'the progress of opulence in different nations', and Book IV, with nine chapters, looks at systems of political economy, and specific instruments of commercial control. There is one chapter on the inadequacies of mercantilism, and two chapters on the 'unreasonableness' of restrictions on imported goods. Book IV also contains a 'Digression concerning the Corn Trade and Corn Laws', and has a long seventh chapter on the colonies. The last two chapters of this book contain Smith's concluding remarks on mercantilism and on land as a nation's principal source of wealth. Book V, 'Of the revenue of the sovereign or commonwealth', is composed of three very substantial chapters, each with formal sub-divisions, treating aspects of public expenditure such as defence, justice, education, the sources of public revenue and the impact of taxation on rents, property, profits, wages and public debt. Surprisingly, there is no reference to that most sensational and radical economic experiment of the century, namely John Law's notorious banking and stockholding schemes that had culminated in France's virtual bankruptcy in 1720, whose repercussions continued to be felt for many decades, and about which Montesquieu and others had so much to say.

In the 'Introduction and plan of the work' Smith defined what he saw as the true nature of a nation's wealth. He saw wealth as being located not in possessions or commodities *per se*, but rather in the purchasing power derived from such possession, the nation's wealth being essentially the total purchasing power of the 'fund' of those commodities and possessions: 'The annual labour of every nation is the fund which originally supplies it with all the necessaries and conveniences of life which it annually consumes.' Smith then examines the ways in which productivity has been improved by the division of labour, and the new production processes, about which he drew heavily on the entries in Diderot's *Encyclopedia*. The account of pin production in 'Of the division of labour' (Book I, chapter 1), for example, is heavily dependent on Delaire's entry 'Pin' in the fifth volume.

Improvement in productivity was also facilitated by money which itself depends on mechanisms and conventions of exchange. Smith examines how prices are determined in the context of wages, profits and rents, the relationship between capital and labour and the methods of deploying capital, the links between the natural progress of opulence and agriculture, industry and foreign markets (and the impact on all this of European economic policies), the harmful absurdities of mercantilist practices, the futility of protectionist legislation and of the levying of prohibitive duties on the international movement of goods. In all this, Smith was seeking to persuade the British government to abandon economic policies and philosophies that he found morally, as well as economically, untenable (Lindgren 1973, pp. 110–14). The *Wealth* was the most challenging analysis of political economy to emerge from this period, a legacy of the Enlightenment that continues to inspire debate on issues that still confront modern industrial nations in the management of their trading policies, and in the formulation of domestic and international economic strategies.

Crime and punishment

In an age of social reforms and political revolutions grotesque examples of inhumanity and cruelty still abounded, even under the most enlightened legal codes. Nowhere was this more evident than in the area of criminal legislation and judicial punishment itself (Ten 1987). In France, *habeas corpus* had no place in due process, and the widespread use of the *lettre de cachet*, the instrument which permitted the crown to issue warrants for the arrest and indefinite detention of suspects without a court hearing, continued until 1789, as did the indiscriminate use of torture against defendants as a means to gain a confession (Weisser 1979, pp. 129–32). Appalling trials of individuals, involving church as well as state, such as the breaking on the wheel of Jean Calas in 1762, and the torture and execution of the young teenager, the chevalier de La Barre, in 1766, became European *causes célèbres*.

In England judicial torture had not been authorised since 1688, although the gallows, the pillory and public floggings remained central to punishment and deterrence, and the death penalty was extended to relatively minor offences by Parliament in 1723 with the notorious Waltham Black Act. Prisons and the treatment of prisoners offended many consciences, as John Howard's reports to Parliamentary committees on prison conditions indicate. In Prussia, Frederick II abolished torture (except for treasonable offences) in 1740. Torture continued to be used in the higher courts in Russia until 1801, and the Spanish Inquisition continued to use it until 1816. Nevertheless, examples of excesses of judicial sentencing were eventually to recede with the growing impact of humanitarianism, as Jeremy Bentham was to note in the *Principles of morals and legislation* (1789).

The demands of Enlightenment thinkers for reform of the criminal law gathered rapid momentum between 1762, the year of the Calas trial, and 1789. The most celebrated reformist statement came from Italy with the publication in 1764 of *On crimes and punishments* by Cesare Beccaria (see below, pp. 439–40). Beccaria's classic treatise, published when he was only twenty-eight, is relatively short, consisting of forty-seven brief chapters, together with a prefatory note 'To the reader' added to the fifth edition (1766), and an 'Introduction'. It was an eloquent appeal for penal reform, elaborated within a broad social, moral and political context, in which Beccaria's purpose was to discredit all systems of government and justice that drew their legitimacy from class privileges and hereditary rights. Such systems were to be replaced by codes of public administration, whether in the realm of taxation or criminal procedures, thereby embodying that central Enlightenment principle of progressive jurisprudence, namely equality before the law.

Beccaria's approach to issues of crime and punishment was firmly anchored to Lockean psychology, and a notable feature of his treatise is its lack of reference to the authority of natural law, metaphysics or theology in the discussion of penal codes. As can be seen in the second chapter on the right to punish, his position remained uncompromisingly secular and humanistic. Later chapters, such as the sixth on the proportion between crimes and punishments, and the sixteenth on torture, show how human action and reaction were derived from the senses, and the experience of pain and pleasure (Bellamy, Davies and Cox 1995, pp. xv–xvi). Accepting the insights of Lockean empiricism, and its subsequent formulations in the thought of French sensualist philosophers like Condillac and Helvétius, Beccaria related all human knowledge, including morality, to the world of the senses. On this basis he proceeded to elaborate a purely secular account of the origins of law and penal codes, and a theory of law incorporating utilitarian, as well as retributive, notions of punishment. In fact, his thought marked a significant stage in the development of utilitarianism well before the advent of d'Holbach and Bentham (Bellamy, Davies and Cox 1995, p. xvi). The celebrated utilitarian slogan, 'the greatest happiness divided among the greatest number' first occurs in the preface to *On crimes.*

In all this, Montesquieu's influence looms large, and is particularly evident in Beccaria's insistence on the supremacy of the rule of law, rigorously, consistently and universally applied, on a system of punishments devised by the law and not by magistrates, on the sovereign primacy of the law over all aspects of court-room practice, and above all in his insistence on the need for the application of a principle of rational proportionality in the judicious adjustment of sentences to the gravity of offences, gravity being measured strictly by criteria relating to the harm done to the state (Bellamy, Davies and Cox 1995, pp. xxxvii–xxxix). Beccaria reversed traditional legal approaches by establishing the key modern notion of the innocence of the accused until proved guilty. In the twelfth chapter of his treatise, on the purpose of punishment, he accepted the retributive principle of punishment. In a later chapter, on the death penalty, he advocated the abolition of capital punishment, and its replacement by custodial sentences clearly pre-scribed for every offence. Sentencing should be prompt and uncompromising, without appeal, applied equally to all classes of criminal, irrespective of moral or personal considerations, and without possibility of recourse to reprieves and pardons.

For Beccaria the state's right to punish had its origins in political rather than moral or theological authority, being a function of the surrender of natural liberty to which individuals had consented when they entered the civil order, and by which security and peace were the principal advantages accruing to them in con-sequence. This essentially political perspective meant that any system of punish-ment and deterrence with regard to individuals who might threaten the security and peace of others must emanate from the state itself. No magistrate could punish an offender on his own authority. Punishments, moreover, were to be prescribed in the light of specific objectives:

> the purpose of punishment is not that of tormenting or afflicting any sentient creature, nor of undoing a crime already committed . . . The purpose there-fore is nothing other than to prevent the offender from doing fresh harm to his fellows, and to deter others from doing likewise . . . If a punishment is to be just, it must be pitched at just that level of intensity which suffices to deter men from crime.

Thus Beccaria was concerned with both effective deterrence and just retribu-tion, and he advocated the introduction of a rational, consistent and systematic set of legal procedures as the most effective way to guarantee both. In seeking to ensure that the criminal law would deter crime, he was at the same time concerned to create a system that would not destroy the still fragile concept of human rights. If it could be demonstrated that severity of punishment did not in fact have the intended deterrent effect, then its maintenance would be contrary to reason, just-ice and to the requirements of the social contract itself. In advocating a less brutal system of punishments with an arguably less effective deterrent impact, Beccaria laid the foundations of post-Enlightenment approaches to questions of individual responsibility for criminal acts, and of equality before the law. The best deterrence was derived, not from the ferocity of the punishment *per se*, but rather from public confidence in the law's impartiality, infallibility and certainty. To ensure this, laws must also be clear, precise and devoid of any ambivalence that might facilitate arbitrariness. If the laws are clear, then they will be more fully and widely understood, and in consequence more widely respected and obeyed. Verdicts must be delivered in public, and justice, based on certainty of proof, must be seen to be done – ideally, in a context in which an accused person is judged by a jury of peers.

Beccaria's ideas were received enthusiastically by enlightened thinkers through-out Europe, although they were strongly resisted by many jurists and theologians. In Italy opposition was led by Ferdinando Facchinei, a Dominican cleric, whose *Notes and observations on the book on crime and punishment* (1765) was written on behalf of the Council of Ten in Venice (Maestro 1973, pp. 63–7). Beccaria's treatise became known in France through Morellet's 1766 translation, which went through seven editions in the space of six months. Jurists such as Muyart de Vouglans, author of the *Refutation of the principles advanced in the treatise on crime and punishment* (1767), expressed astonished disapproval of the notion of equality in legal processes, and defended strongly the use of torture (as, surprisingly, did Diderot). Vouglans' objections were supported by Jousse in his *Treatise on crim-inal justice in France* (1771), who denounced Beccaria's work as an attack on reli-gion, customs and the 'sacred maxims of government'. Beccaria's proposals for reform were still being attacked in France as later as 1786 by Séguier (Maestro 1973, pp. 63–7).

Among Beccaria's supporters was Voltaire, who read the treatise in the original Italian in 1765, a year before the appearance of Morellet's French translation. *On crimes and punishments* made a deep impression on Voltaire, who was at this time still embroiled in public confrontation with the legal authorities in France over the case of the Sirven family who, like Jean Calas, had also been falsely accused of murder, and sentenced to horrific punishment. In 1766 Voltaire was affected even more deeply by a third notorious miscarriage of justice, followed by judicial barbarity, when La Barre was cruelly mutilated and executed in Abbeville for blasphemous conduct. The three cases sharpened Voltaire's interest in the issues of crime and punishment, and in 1766 Voltaire published a lengthy commentary on Beccaria's work (Williams 1994, pp. xxiii–xxvii, 244–79). The appeal voiced at the end of this commentary was for urgent reform of French judicial procedures, and it was to bear fruit rapidly. It was in large measure due to Beccaria, and to Voltaire's promulgation of the principles contained in *On crimes*, that torture ceased to be an official part of due process in France, and that by 1788 the death sentence was becoming relatively rare (Foucault 1977; Mason 1982, chapter 8). The 1670 Criminal Ordinance would be abolished by the Revolution, and the 1791 code, echoing much of Beccaria's thinking, would herald the reforms to be eventually implemented under the Napoleonic codes of the early nineteenth century.

Revolution

There were many revolts and small-scale revolutions in the Enlightenment, such as those that took place in Geneva, the Austrian Netherlands and the Dutch Republic. They were all overshadowed in terms of long-term historical impact by the American War of Independence and the subsequent Declaration of Independence of 4 July 1776, marking the birth of the American Republic, and the French Revolution with its equally resounding affirmation of Enlightenment political ideals, the 1789 Declaration of the Rights of Man and of the Citizen. Developments in France were to culminate in regicide and the founding of the First Republic. Neither of these cataclysmic events were 'democratic' uprisings in any modern sense, although both were about the broader redistribution of power. These two key political upheavals of the Enlightenment were manifestations of middle-class aspirations and ambitions, as the writings of Adams, Jefferson, Washington, Condorcet, Siéyès, Robespierre, Marat and others clearly indicate. The American Revolution created the first modern republic, and in so doing set in train a much wider, and irreversible, process of change elsewhere, not least in France.

It was against the backdrop of the American Revolution that Tom Paine (see below, pp. 471–2), one of the most radically subversive writers of the Enlightenment, started to make his name. Paine's interest in politics was kindled by his encounter with American insurrectionist and republican opinion soon after his arrival in Philadelphia in 1774. His views were shaped by an empirical engagement with a society already in turmoil, rather than by the world of books and treatises, and he quickly associated himself with the rebel cause. In 1776 he published *Common sense: addressed to the inhabitants of America*, the first of a long series of political essays and tracts that was to culminate in 1791 in the publication of the *Rights of man*.

With its persuasive, demotic advocacy of the Americans' right, not only to resist a British government in which they had no direct representation, but also to constitutional independence, *Common sense* was published at a crucial juncture in the unfolding of the American drama, and it touched the raw nerve of republican sensibilities. Paine offered his readers a stirring defence of the principle of insur-rection, conferring a convincing moral and political legitimacy on the colonists' cause. He coupled his attack on the decadence and corruption of the British crown with an inflammatory exposition of the primacy of natural rights, and of the relevance of those rights to the American situation (Aldridge 1984). *Common sense*, of which more than 120,000 copies were in circulation in America within the first year of publication, authorised revolution as a reasonable and justifiable act against oppressive policies, engineered by what Paine saw as an unscrupulous and ruthless monarchy.

Common sense consists of four chapters. In the first, 'On the origin and design of government in general, with concise remarks on the English constitution', Paine defined general differences between society and government, society being the product of 'our wants' and governments that of 'our wickedness'. For Paine, man is naturally free and naturally equal, 'natural' in Paine's lexicon being almost synonymous with 'rational'. Government was a necessary evil because the world cannot be ordered by the power of virtue alone. For Paine, as for Montesquieu and other more theoretical Enlightenment predecessors, the best government was one that ensured 'the least expense and the greatest benefit'. In the second chapter, 'Of monarchy and hereditary succession', he moved on to the more contentious issue of kings and monarchical systems of government, 'unknown to nature', with their origins in heathen practices and idolatrous traditions. The focus of this chapter is naturally upon the evolution of the English monarchy and the self-perpetuating mechanism of hereditary succession, which Paine rejected as an affront to man's natural equality. In some monarchies, he points out, the king is at least either a judge or a general and of some use, whereas in England, 'a man would be puzzled to know what *is* the King's business'. Americans owed no loyalty or ties of affection to a country in which kings came first and laws second. Thus monarchy in *Common sense* is condemned, not simply as a constitutionally false principle, but also as an unnatural violation of human rights and of nature itself.

In the last two chapters, 'Thoughts on the present state of American affairs' and 'Of the present ability of America, with some miscellaneous reflections', Paine stressed that the colonies could wage their war for independence with a clear conscience, knowing that their case had the support of scripture, natural law and virtue (Fennessy 1963, pp. 21–2). 'A government of our own is our natural right.' The restrictions placed on man's natural liberty and equality as a consequence of his entry into society, stressed so frequently as the price for the civil order, were not irrevocable. Like Rousseau, Paine believed that the contract that had ended the war of all against all was fraudulent, and that natural rights could be reclaimed. For Paine this could be achieved by force if necessary, for if the common good did not coincide with individual good then it was simply a cruel deceit.

It was in the third chapter on the present state of American affairs that the call to assert this right of revocation, and cut the ties with Britain, was formulated most explicitly. Here Paine offered his blueprint of the constitutional arrangements for a new republic, in which the only monarch would be the law itself, 'for as in absolute governments the King is the law, so in free countries the law *ought* to be king, and there ought to be no other'. The closing words of *Common sense* addressed the need for action today, rather than tomorrow, 'and until an Independence is declared, the continent will feel itself like a man who continues putting off some unpleasant business from day to day, yet knows it must be done, hates to set about it, wishes it over, and is continually haunted with the thoughts of its necessity'.

Paine was essentially a political agitator and a propagandist, rather than an original thinker, although his impact and influence were none the less widespread for that. Like Voltaire, he could communicate effectively and provocatively with ordinary people, illuminating complex ideas with brilliant clarity and simplicity, and driving forward public debate in easily understood terms. For all his dramatic unconventionality, and his familiar image as a snarling public figure, smouldering with anger and resentment, Paine remains a fully representative child of the Enlightenment, a believer in the deistic, Newtonian scientific model for understanding the world. Like Condorcet, his faith lay in progress and the existence of fundamental truths that could be discovered through the application of man's reason. He believed passionately in equality and natural rights as undeniable and inalienable ingredients of the social contract (Kuklick 1989, pp. x–xi; Keane 1996).

In the *Rights of man* he continued with his campaign against monarchy ('a silly, contemptible thing'), of which *Common sense* had marked the opening shots, and he went on to establish an enduring model of republicanism (Butler 1984). In his eulogy of the virtues of the French Revolution in the *Rights of man* he was to extend the call for action, first sounded in *Common sense*, in the context of the American insurgency, to the European and, in particular, the English, political arena, setting out a programme for political reorganisation that he fervently hoped would ignite the spirit of revolution in his own native country: 'It is time that nations should be rational and not governed like animals for the pleasure of their riders.' The American Revolution and the Declaration of Independence were the prelude to further constitutional tremors in Europe after 1776, as the cracks in the carapace of *ancien régime* political systems widened in the wake of the American insurgency.

It was soon to be France's turn to taste Paine's revolutionary medicine, and in the months immediately preceding the French upheaval, the significance of the role of Emmanuel-Joseph Siéyès (see below, pp. 492–3) has still to be fully measured. More than thirty thousand copies and four editions of *What is the third estate?* appeared within a few months of the work's publication in January 1789. The *Third* was passed from hand to hand, widely discussed in the streets and cafés of Paris, its contents further diffused by numerous public readings. The transparency of its message, and the dynamic forcefulness of its style, mark the *Third* out as something special from the plethora of brochures, essays and lampoons published in the years following Louis XVI's decision to convene the Assembly of Notables in February 1787. These were years marked by unprecented levels of public debate in France, encouraged by the King, on the mounting crises relating to public finances, the tax system and the privileges of the nobility. The debate was fuelled by almost a century of enlightened thinking on dogma, social structures, rights, responsibilities and the need for reform, all of which coalesced during the transient ministries of Turgot, Necker, Calonne and Loménie de Brienne (Doyle 1980; Bredin 1988). Ambitious projects to reform royal administration on the part of the provincial assemblies in the summer of 1787 had been frustrated by the uncompromising opposition of the *parlements* to tax reform. The resulting paralysis led to the decision, taken by Louis XVI, on the advice of Necker, to summon the Estates-General in May 1789. In response to pressure, not least from Siéyès, Necker had obtained the concession through the Royal Council in December 1788 to double representation of the third estate in the Estates-

General. Thus encouraged, third estate essayists and pamphleteers flooded Paris with their publications. Against this background of highly charged public debate and unprecedented political turbulence, Siéyès' *Third*, with its cogent attack on privilege and the privileged orders, was an immediate sensation (Forsyth 1987; Bastid 1970).

In the *Third* Siéyès aligned the political future of France with that of the third estate. Concentrating on the elucidation of systematic principles derived from what he called the 'science of social order', he audaciously proclaimed the third estate to be 'everything', that is to say 'a nation . . . a body of people who join together to live under a common system of laws and to be represented by the same legislative assembly'. The nation and the people were one, their unity to be realised politically in a unicameral legislature. The existence of the nobility was alien to this concept of nationhood, being the embodiment of the irrational principle of class rule, its mission deriving, not from the will of the people, but from private, advantaged interests.

The underlying Rousseauist syllogism is inescapable in the accompanying argumentation. The nation is the only authority that can speak with the voice of the people: the 'complete nation' is the third estate: the third estate is the voice of the people. Their will is therefore the General Will. However, in spite of being in theory 'everything', the third estate has been, and still is, nothing. Its crucial, minimal demand is to be 'something'. This 'something' turns out to be the right to have representatives in equal number to that of the two other orders combined – a demand that Louis XVI had already conceded by the time Siéyès' brochure appeared. In addition, however, Siéyès demanded that votes in the Estates-General be counted on the basis of individual heads, and not that of orders. To block the will of an order representing 25–6 million people by means of the votes of representatives in the two other orders, reflecting the interests of less than 200,000, was an absurdity that could not be allowed to continue. By the 'people', however, Siéyès did not mean to infer the enfranchisement of the whole population any more than *ancien régime* theorists did. His egalitarian language and vision was that of the Enlightenment, and did not extend to the *sans-culottes*, for example. His loyalty was to the propertied middle classes – a class loyalty that produces some inconsistencies in his view on the question of rights (Van Deusen 1932; Campbell 1963, pp. 3–31; Doyle 1980).

The last two chapters of this remarkable tract contain Siéyès' analysis of what should have been done, together with his proposals for future action. Only through representative institutions could the nation authentically express its identity. After assessing the fiscal and judicial failures of the stewardship of France's affairs under Calonne, Brienne and eventually Necker between 1786 and 1788, and in particular the failure of the 1787 Assembly of Notables to justify their tax privileges, Siéyès approached the problem with a series of eye-catching, epigrammatic formulae: the nation, already defined as the third estate, exists before all else; before it and above it, only natural law exists. It was thus up to the nation freely to adopt its preferred constitution and its system of laws, but Siéyès warned that when the Estates-General came to assemble, the third estate could count only on its own resources. It must, therefore, meet in a separate assembly without the nobility and the clergy, and form a National Assembly, to which the other orders could be admitted only on condition of formal abrogation of their privileges. The privileged orders, nothing less than a tumour eating away at the body of the nation, thus faced exclusion from government, unless they became in effect part of the third estate.

No political thinker in France had ever gone so far, and Siéyès was quite aware of the scandal and uproar that such sentiments would provoke. His anticipation of controversy is reflected in the opening words of the treatise, where he sees himself as the philosopher whose job it is 'to mark out the target . . . to think out the path ahead'. If such a philosopher wishes to make progress, he must destroy error without compromise or exception, and in political and social terms, privilege was for Siéyès the worst kind of error, and the privileged orders the worst kind of enemy.

While the *Third* embodied much of the distinctive terminology and progressivist faith of the Enlightenment from which it springs, it also prefigures many features of the style and language of modern political engagement. An original combination of theoretical precept and practical politics, a bridge between thought and action, the *Third* is a work written in the hot cauldron of political events in France with a view to exerting influence over those events, and to initiating action and radical change. Much of that change was to come about in the wake of the *Third*'s publication, and also partly of course as a consequence of its author's rapid transition from political essayist to hands-on statesman. Siéyès forged in this searing essay many of the instruments now at the disposal of modern democratic powers. Some of these can be seen to take shape in his concept of the unity and sovereignty of the nation, and in the premium that he placed on the representation of the whole nation, not of its separate orders, through its elected representatives. Siéyès' enduring legacy remains that of a proselytising ideologist of popular revolution and popular government, many of whose views on the people's role in the ordering of the state were to resurface in the Marxist and Leninist ideologies of the following century.

The French Revolution, which Paine glorified and Siéyès helped to implement, proclaimed the end of the rule of kings in France. Nowhere was the political fall-out more feared than in Britain, and no figure articulated that fear more intensely than Edmund Burke (see below, pp. 508–9). Burke's *Reflections on the Revolution in France, and on the proceedings in certain societies in London relative to that event: in a letter intended to have been sent to a gentleman in Paris*, the work to which Paine's *Rights of man* was a response, appeared on 1 November 1790. According to Burke's preface, the *Reflections* had its origins in earlier corres-pondence in October 1789 with 'a very young gentleman at Paris who did him the honour of desiring his opinion upon the important transactions which then, and ever since, have so much occupied the attention of all men'. The preface states further that this earlier response to the young man's enquiries had been 'kept back upon prudential considerations'. The 1790 version of the *Reflections*, still in the format of a letter addressed to the 'gentleman in Paris', represents 'a more full discussion on the subject'.

Early intimations of the way in which Burke's political philosophy was to develop can be found in his first published essay, the *Vindication of natural society* (1756). Here Burke had revealed his colours with a deeply hostile attack on Rous-seau over the issue of natural man, and the moral and social degeneration that Rousseau had identified with man's translation to the civil order, an act of political fraudulence that Rousseau had exposed in his second *Discourse* (Dreyer 1978, pp. 462–79; see above, pp. 16–18). Burke linked morality and civil government closely to the requirements and conditions of the divine order, and to the providential authority of God. The pre-eminence of God's government of the human condi-tion, with the acceptance of all the inequalities implied in that, was to remain central to Burke's thinking. The Rousseauist condemnation of inequality meant for Burke nothing less than a denial of the civil order, and of God-given natural law that authorised it. He pursued this point in the context of aesthetics in *A philosophical enquiry into the origin of our ideas of the sublime and beautiful* (1757), where he defended inequality, and the consequent generation of the aristocratic order, as natural and progressive concepts, and as the logical manifestations of an order truly founded on nature and divine principle. Aristocratic systems, the prime casualty of the French Revolution, were to remain for Burke the most important and effective guarantee of social stability (O'Gorman 1973, pp. 23–44; Lock 1985, pp. 62–4).

The argument of the *Reflections* moves forward in two stages. In the first stage Burke aimed to demonstrate the merits of a providentially regulated civil order, God's order, with some comment on the ways in which contemporary British radicalism could endanger this. The second stage concentrates on exposing the disastrous effects of a civil order generated by inadequate human will alone, and in particular the will of the third estate in France (Harris 1993, pp. xvi–xxxiii). Burke defended the *ancien régime* in France, and in Europe generally, and he denounced the French model of revolution as a threat to the foundations of civil society for which it could offer no workable alternative.

The *Reflections* were aimed of course at English rather than French readers, and relate to an English set of circumstances in which radicalism was rising in Burke's view to dangerous levels (O'Gorman, 1973, pp. 109–10). Burke feared that the flames of revolution were licking at a volatile situation in England, and the intensity of his fears can be inferred from the emotionally charged style of so many of his statements. The counter-argument to revolution that he offered reflected his consistently held faith in the merits of 'natural' aristocracy, and the hereditary system that characterised the British constitution. Much of his attack on the radicalism that threatened to engulf 'our constitution in its vital parts', and which he saw as being based on a false interpretation of the notion of rights, was directed primarily at the 'metaphysical' abstractions contained in Price's *Discourse on the love of our country*, issued on 4 November 1789 (see above, pp. 21, 38–9). Burke identified Price as the main ideological enemy, who had deliberately distorted the facts about the workings of the British constitution with his 'fulminating bull'. Burke had already attacked Price in 1771 in the *Letter to the sheriffs of Bristol*, and much of the first part of the *Reflections* was devoted to a refutation of Price's sermon. Jacobinism contained for Burke the seeds of the destruction of the natural political and social world, and raised the nightmare prospect of the dawning of a new, un-Christian age of darkness in Europe, dramatised in the *Reflections* in the dramatic account of the arrest and imprisonment of Louis XVI and Marie-Antoinette.

Contrary to what Siéyès and other revolutionary ideologists were proclaiming, in all of his political writings, and particularly in the *Reflections*, Burke insisted that the people had no natural right to exert power, and participate in the processes of

government: 'By these theorists the right of the people is almost always sophistic-
ally confounded with their power . . . Men have no right to what is not reasonable,
and to what is not for their benefit.' Governments must listen to the voice of the
people, but the people must never be allowed to rule governments: 'Government
is not made in virtue of natural rights, which may and do exist in total independence of it . . . Society requires that . . . the inclinations of men should be frequently
thwarted, their will controlled, and their passions brought into subjection. This
can only be done *by a power out of themselves.*'

The French Revolution illustrated perfectly for Burke the excesses to which the
tyranny of the mob could be taken in the name of liberty and equality, and be
given terrifying reality in the moves to abolish religion, property and rank, and
convert the state's rightful exercise of power from a 'holy function' into a 'pitiful
job'. Unlike the liberty gained by the English at the time of the Glorious Revolution of 1688, the liberty claimed by the revolutionaries in France a century later
was a false liberty, a liberty without order, restraint or security, and therefore not
liberty in the real sense at all. In the second part of the *Reflections* Burke took
pains to demonstrate why the French model, embodying 'a barbarous philosophy,
which is the offspring of cold hearts and muddy understandings', should be
rejected, and the case for a more polite, gradualist process of political change and
reform along British lines preferred. The publication of the *Reflections* had an
immediate impact (Lock 1985, pp. 132–65), the tenth edition having been printed
before the end of 1790. Among the numerous replies and refutations, those of
Joseph Priestley, Mary Wollstonecraft, Catherine Macaulay, James Mackintosh
and of course Tom Paine remain the most memorable.

Scientific and technological progress, idealism, rights, universalism, egalitarianism
and bloody revolution are still inextricably linked elements in modern, popular
perceptions of the Enlightenment, and of its complex aftermath in nineteenth-
century Europe. Its political legacy for the twentieth century has proved to be
notoriously ambivalent, moreover. The degree to which Enlightenment ideas on
the one hand, and actual political change on the other, can be seen legitimately
in terms of causes and effects still remains an open question, and traditional views
of what the term Enlightenment itself means have been seriously challenged in the
last three decades. What is clearer in retrospect is the way in which unprecedented
historical events offered unprecedented opportunities to put into practice theories

and principles once safely confined to the dry world of books and treatises. It is this dynamic, unprecedented encounter between political theory and political actuality that marks the eighteenth-century European Enlightenment out from all other Enlightenments. It was an encounter in which the voices of political modernity could be heard for the first time, and at the beginning of the third millennium their echo has not yet entirely faded.

REFERENCES

Aldridge, A., 1984. *Thomas Paine's American ideology* (Delaware: Dover).

Anderson, R. and Lawrence, C. (eds.), 1987. *Science, medicine and dissent: Joseph Priestley (1733–1804)* (London: Wellcome Trust).

Angenot, M., 1972. *Les champions des femmes: examen du discours sur la supériorité des femmes 1400–1800* (Montreal: Presses de l'Université du Québec).

Atkinson, R., 1992. 'Kant's moral and political rigorism', in H. Williams 1992, pp. 228–48.

Ayer, A., 1988. *Thomas Paine* (London: Secker and Warburg).

Baier, A., 1991. *A progress of sentiments: reflections on Hume's treatise* (Cambridge, Mass.: Harvard University Press).

Baker, K., 1975. *Condorcet: from natural history to social mathematics* (Chicago and London: University of Chicago Press).

Barnard, F., 1965. *Herder's social and political thought: from Enlightenment to nationalism* (Oxford: Clarendon Press).

1969. *J. G. Herder on social and political culture* (Cambridge: Cambridge University Press).

Bastid, P., 1970. *Siéyès et sa pensée* (Paris: Hachette).

Beiser, F., 1992. *Enlightenment, revolution and romanticism: the genesis of modern German political thought* (Cambridge, Mass., and London: Harvard University Press).

(ed. and trans.), 1996. *The early political writings of the German romantics* (Cambridge: Cambridge University Press).

Bellamy, R. (ed.) and Davies, R. (trans.), 1995. *Beccaria: 'On crimes and punishments' and other writings* (Cambridge: Cambridge University Press).

Benot, Y., 1981. *Diderot: de l'athéisme à l'anticolonialisme* (Paris: Maspero).

Berlin, I., 1965. 'Herder and the Enlightenment', in Wasserman 1965, pp. 49–53.

Blanc, O. (ed.), 1993. *Olympe de Gouges: écrits politiques 1788–1791* (Paris: Côté-Femmes Editions).

Blondel, M. and Finer, S. (eds. and trans.), 1963. *What is the third estate?* (London: Pall Mall Press).

Bredin, J.-D., 1988. *Siéyès: la clé de la Révolution française* (Paris, Editions de Fallois).

Butler, M. (ed.), 1984. *Burke, Paine, Godwin, and the Revolution controversy* (Cambridge: Cambridge University Press).

Campbell, P., 1963. 'Siéyès and *What is the third estate?*', in Blondel and Finer 1963, pp. 3–31.

Canovan, M., 1978. 'Two concepts of liberty – eighteenth-century style', *The Price–Priestley Newsletter*, 2, pp. 27–43.

Carr, C. and Seidler, M. (eds.), 1994. *The political writings of Samuel Pufendorf* (Oxford: Oxford University Press).

Cerati, M., 1966. *Le club des citoyennes républicaines révolutionnaires* (Paris: Editions Sociales).

Clarke, R., 1942. 'Herder's concept of *Kraft*', *Publications of the Modern Language Association of America*, 55, pp. 737–52.

Cohler, A., Miller, S. and Stone, H. (trans.), 1990. *Montesquieu: the Spirit of the laws* (Cambridge: Cambridge University Press). Reprint.

Crocker, L., 1983. 'Voltaire and the political philosophers', *Studies on Voltaire and the Eighteenth Century*, 219, pp. 1–17.

Cropsey, J., 1957. *Polity and economy: an interpretation of the principles of Adam Smith* (The Hague: Martinus Nijhoff).

Derathé, R., 1970. *Jean-Jacques Rousseau et la science politique de son temps* (Paris: Vrin).

Dickenson, H., 1975. 'The politics of Bernard Mandeville', in Primer 1975, pp. 80–97.

Domenech, J., 1989. *L'éthique des lumières: les fondements de la morale dans la philosophie française du xviii siècle* (Paris: Vrin).

Doyle, W., 1980. *Origins of the French Revolution* (Oxford: Oxford University Press).

Dreyer, F., 1978. 'The genesis of Burke's *Reflections*', *Journal of Modern History*, 50, pp. 462–79.

Dufour, A., 1991. *Droits de l'homme, droit naturel et histoire* (Paris: Presses Universitaires de France).

Durkheim, E., 1965. *Montesquieu and Rousseau: forerunners of sociology* (Ann Arbor, Mich.: University of Michigan Press).

Ergang, R., 1966. *Herder and the foundations of German nationalism* (New York: Octagon Books).

Fennessey, R., 1963. *Burke, Paine and the Rights of man: a difference of opinion* (The Hague: Martinus Nijhoff).

Finnis, J., 1980. *Natural law and natural rights* (Oxford: Clarendon Press).

Forbes, D., 1975. *Hume's philosophical politics* (Cambridge: Cambridge University Press).

Forsyth, M., 1987. *Reason and Revolution: the political thought of the abbé Siéyès* (New York: Leicester University Press).

Foucault, M., 1977. *Discipline and punish: rebirth of the prison* (London: Allen Lane).

Fox-Genovese, E., 1976. *The origins of physiocracy: economic revolution and the social order in eighteenth-century France* (Ithaca and London: Cornell University Press).

Fritz, P. and Williams, D., 1972. *The triumph of culture: eighteenth-century perspectives* (Toronto: A.M. Hakkert).

Gay, P., 1969. *The Enlightenment: an interpretation*, II: *The science of freedom* (New York: Alfred Knopf).

1988. *Voltaire's politics: the poet as realist* (New Haven and London: Yale University Press). Reprint.

Gildin, H., 1983. *Rousseau's Social contract: the design of the argument* (Chicago: University of Chicago Press).

Goldsmith, M., 1987. 'Liberty, luxury and the pursuit of happiness', in Pagden 1987, pp. 225–51.

Gourevitch, V., 1993. *Montesquieu, la nature, les lois, la liberté* (Paris: PUF).

1997a. *Rousseau: 'The discourses' and other early political writings* (Cambridge: Cambridge University Press).

1997b. *Rousseau: 'The social contract' and other later political writings* (Cambridge: Cambridge University Press).

Graham, J., 1989/90. 'Revolutionary philosopher: the political ideas of Joseph Priestley (1733–1804)', *Enlightenment and Dissent*, 8 (1989), pp. 43–68; 9 (1990), pp. 14–46.

Grimsley, R., 1972. *Jean-Jacques Rousseau: Du contrat social* (Oxford: Clarendon Press).

Haakonssen, K., 1985. 'Hugo Grotius and the history of political thought', *Political Theory*, 13, pp. 239–65.

1992. 'Natural law', in *The Garland encyclopedia of ethics*, ed. L. and C. Becker (New York and London: Garland), II.

1993. 'The structure of Hume's political thought', in *The Cambridge companion to Hume*, ed. D. Norton (Cambridge: Cambridge University Press), pp. 182–221.

1994. *Hume: political essays* (Cambridge: Cambridge University Press).

Hahn, H., 1995. *German thought and culture: from the Holy Roman Empire to the present day* (Manchester: Manchester University Press).

Hampsher-Monk, I., 1992. *A history of modern political thought: major political thinkers from Hobbes to Marx* (Oxford: Blackwell).

Harris, I., 1993. *Burke: pre-revolutionary writings* (Cambridge: Cambridge University Press).

Harth, P. (ed.), 1970. *The fable of the bees, or, private vices, publick benefits* (Harmondsworth: Penguin).

Hayes, J., 1927. 'Contributions of Herder to the doctrine of nationalism', *American Historical Review*, 32, pp. 719–36.

Heath, J., 1963. *Eighteenth-century penal theory* (Oxford: Oxford University Press).

Hecht, J., 1958. 'La vie de François Quesnay', in *François Quesnay et la physiocratie*, ed. J. Hecht (Paris: Institut National d'Etudes Démographiques), I, pp. 211–93.

Hertz, F., 1962. *The development of the German public mind: a social history of German political sentiments, aspirations and ideas*, II: *The age of Enlightenment* (London: Allen and Unwin).

Hochstrasser, T., 1993. 'Conscience and reason: the natural law theory of Jean Barbeyrac', *Historical Journal*, 36, pp. 289–308.

Hoecker, J., 1987. *Joseph Priestley and the idea of progress* (New York and London: Garland).

Hont, I., 1987. 'The language of sociability and commerce: Samuel Pufendorf and the theoretical foundations of the "four stages theory"', in Pagden 1987, pp. 253–76.

Hont, I. and Ignatieff, M., 1983. 'Needs and justice in the *Wealth of Nations*', in *Wealth and virtue: the shaping of political economy in the Scottish Enlightenment*, ed. I. Hont and M. Ignatieff (Cambridge: Cambridge University Press), pp. 1–44.

Hughes, P. and Williams, D. (eds.), 1971. *The varied pattern: studies in the eighteenth century* (Toronto: Hakkert).

Kaye, F. (ed.), 1966. *The fable of the bees, or, private vices, publick benefits*, 2 vols. (Oxford: Oxford University Press). Reprint.

Keane, J., 1996. *Tom Paine: a political life* (London: Bloomsbury).

Kelly, G., 1992. *Revolutionary feminism: the mind and career of Mary Wollstonecraft* (Basingstoke: Macmillan).

Krieger, L., 1965. *The politics of discretion: Pufendorf and the acceptance of natural law* (Chicago: Chicago University Press).

Kuczynski, M. and Meek, R. (trans.), 1972. *Quesnay's Tableau économique* (London: Macmillan; New York: Augustus M. Kelly).

Kuklick, B. (ed.), 1989. *Paine: political writings* (Cambridge: Cambridge University Press).

Larrère, C., 1992. *L'invention de l'économie au XVIIIe siècle: du droit naturel à la physiocratie* (Paris: Presses Universitaires de France).

Laurent, P., 1982. *Pufendorf et la loi naturelle* (Paris: Vrin).

Lecercle, J.-L., 1993. 'L'Abbé de Saint-Pierre, Rousseau et l'Europe', *Dix-huitième siècle*, 25, pp. 23–39.

Le Cour Grandmaison, O., 1994. 'Idées d'Europe et paix perpétuelle: note sur l'abbé de Saint-Pierre', *Temps modernes*, 49, pp. 1–21.

Lindgren, J., 1973. *The social philosophy of Adam Smith* (The Hague: Martinus Nijhoff).

Lively, J. and Reeve, A. (eds.), 1989. *Modern political theory from Hobbes to Marx* (London: Routledge).

Lock, F., 1985. *Burke's reflections on the Revolution in France* (London: Allen and Unwin).

Lough, J., 1989. *The Encyclopédie* (Geneva: Slatkine). Reprint.

McCloskey, H., 1963. 'The state as an organism, as a person and as an end in itself', *Philosophical Review*, 72, pp. 309–24.

McDonald, J., 1965. *Rousseau and the French Revolution 1762–1791* (London: Athlone Press).

Maestro, M., 1973. *Cesare Beccaria and the origins of penal reform* (Philadelphia: Temple University Press).

Mason, H., 1982. *French writers and their society 1715–1800* (London: Macmillan).

Mason, J. and Wokler, R. (eds.), 1992. *Diderot: political writings* (Cambridge: Cambridge University Press).

Meek, R., 1976. *Social science and the ignoble savage* (Cambridge: Cambridge University Press).

Miller, D., 1981. *Hume's political thought* (Oxford: Oxford University Press).

Miller, P., 1993. *Priestley: political writings* (Cambridge: Cambridge University Press).

Morrow, G., 1973. *The ethical and economic theories of Adam Smith* (Clifton, N.J.: Augustus M. Kelly). Reprint.

Nisbet, B. (trans.), 1991. *Perpetual peace*, in Reiss and Nisbet 1991, pp. 99–130.

Noak, P., 1992. *Olympe de Gouges 1748–1793: Kurtisane und Kämpferin für die Rechte der Frau* (Munich: Deutscher Taschenbuch Verlag).

Noxon, J., 1971. 'Dr Mandeville: a thinking man', in Hughes and Williams 1971, pp. 233–52.

O'Gorman, F., 1973. *Edmund Burke: his political philosophy* (London: Allen and Unwin).

Pagden, A. (ed.), 1987. *The languages of political theory in early-modern Europe* (Cambridge: Cambridge University Press).

Perkins, M., 1959. *The moral and political philosophy of the abbé de Saint-Pierre* (Paris and Geneva: Droz).

1965. *Voltaire's concept of international order,* in *Studies on Voltaire and the Eighteenth Century,* 36.

1989. 'Six French *philosophes* on human rights, international rivalry and war: their message today', *Studies on Voltaire and the Eighteenth Century,* 260, pp. 1–158.

Phillipson, N., 1989. *Hume* (London: Weidenfeld and Nicolson).

Plumb, J., 1972. 'The public, literature and the arts in the eighteenth century', in Fritz and Williams 1972, pp. 27–48.

Pocock, J., 1985. *Virtue, commerce and history: essays on political thought and history, chiefly in the eighteenth century* (Cambridge: Cambridge University Press).

Porter, R. and Teich, M. (eds.), 1981. *The Enlightenment in national context* (Cambridge: Cambridge University Press).

Primer, I. (ed.), 1975. *Mandeville studies: new explorations in the art and thought of Dr Bernard Mandeville 1670–1733* (The Hague: Martinus Nijhoff).

Proust, J., 1963. 'La contribution de Diderot à l'*Encyclopédie* et les théories du droit naturel', *Annales historiques de la Révolution française,* 35, pp. 257–86.

Reill, P., 1975. *The German Enlightenment and the rise of historicism* (London: University of California Press).

Reiss, H., 1955. *The political thought of the German romantics (1793–1815)* (Oxford: Oxford University Press).

Reiss, H. (ed.) and Nisbet, H. (trans.), 1991. *Kant: political writings* (Cambridge: Cambridge University Press). Second (enlarged) edition.

Rendall, J., 1985. *The origins of modern feminism: women in Britain, France and the United States 1780–1860* (Basingstoke: Macmillan).

Riley, P., 1983. *Kant's political philosophy* (New Jersey: Rowman and Littlefield).

Rosenblatt, H., 1997. *Rousseau and Geneva: from the First discourse to the Social contract 1749–1762* (Cambridge: Cambridge University Press).

Sabine, G. and Thorson, T., 1973. *A history of political theory* (Orlando: Holt, Rinehart and Winston). Reprint.

Sapiro, V., 1992. *Vindication of political virtue: the political theory of Mary Wollstonecraft* (Chicago and London: University of Chicago Press).

Seidler, M., 1990. *Samuel Pufendorf's 'On the natural state of men'* (Lewiston, N.Y.: Edwin Mellor Press).

Sewell, W., 1994. *A rhetoric of bourgeois revolution: the abbé Siéyès and What is the third estate?* ((Durham, N.C.: Duke University Press).

Shackleton, R., 1961. *Montesquieu: a critical biography* (Oxford: Oxford University Press).

Sheehan, J., 1989. *German history 1770–1866* (Oxford: Clarendon Press).

Shklar, J., 1969. *Men and citizens* (Cambridge: Cambridge University Press).

  1987. *Montesquieu* (Oxford: Oxford University Press).

Skinner, A., 1979. *A system of social science: papers relating to Adam Smith* (Oxford: Clarendon Press).

Skinner, Q., 1980. *The foundations of modern political thought,* II: *The age of Reformation* (Cambridge: Cambridge University Press).

  1989. 'The state', in *Political innovation and conceptual change,* ed. T. Ball *et al.* (New York: Cambridge University Press), pp. 90–131.

Speck, W., 1975. 'Mandeville and the eutopia seated in the brain', in Primer 1975, pp. 66–79.

Stein, P., 1980. *Legal evolution: the story of an idea* (Cambridge: Cambridge University Press).

Stein, R., 1979. *The French slave trade in the eighteenth century: an old regime business* (Wisconsin: University of Wisconsin Press).

Stevenson, V. (trans.), 1989. *Olympe de Gouges: The rights of woman* (London: Pythia Press).

Stewart, J., 1992. *Opinion and reform in Hume's political philosophy* (Princeton, N.J.: Princeton University Press).

Strong, T., 1994. *Jean-Jacques Rousseau: the politics of the ordinary* (London: Sage).

Strugnell, A., 1973. *Diderot's politics: a study of the evolution of Diderot's political thought after the Encyclopédie* (The Hague: Martinus Nijhoff).

Sullivan, R., 1994. *Introduction to Kant's ethics* (Cambridge: Cambridge University Press).

Taylor, A., 1989. 'The ethical doctrine of Hobbes', in Lively and Reeve 1989, pp. 19–39.

Taylor, S., 1981. 'The Enlightenment in Switzerland', in Porter and Teich 1981, pp. 72–89.

Ten, C., 1987. *Crime, guilt and punishment* (Oxford: Clarendon Press).

Thomas, D., 1987. 'Progress, liberty and utility: the political philosophy of Joseph Priestley', in Anderson and Lawrence 1987, pp. 73–80.

  1991. *Richard Price: political writings* (Cambridge: Cambridge University Press).

Todd, C., 1980. *Voltaire: Dictionnaire philosophique* (London: Grant and Cutler).

Tomalin, C., 1992. *The life and death of Mary Wollstonecraft* (London: Penguin).

Tomaselli, S., 1995. *Mary Wollstonecraft: A vindication of the rights of men* and *A vindication of the rights of woman and hints* (Cambridge: Cambridge University Press).

Trachtenberg, Z., 1993. *Making citizens* (London and New York: Routledge).

Trapnell, W., 1972. *Voltaire and his portable dictionary* (Frankfurt-am-Main: Analecta Romanica, 32).

Tuck, R., 1987. 'The modern theory of natural law', in Pagden 1987, pp. 99–119.

Tully, J. and Silverthorne, M., 1991. *Pufendorf: On the duty of man and citizen according to natural law* (Cambridge: Cambridge University Press).

Van Deusen, G., 1932. *Siéyès: his life and his nationalism* (New York: Columbia University Press).

Vichert, G., 1971. 'The theory of conspicuous consumption in the eighteenth century' in Hughes and Williams 1971, pp. 253–67.

Waddicor, M., 1970. *Montesquieu and the philosophy of natural law* (The Hague: Martinus Nijhoff).

Warrender, H., 1957. *The political philosophy of Hobbes: his theory of obligation* (Oxford: Clarendon Press).

Wasserman, E. (ed.), 1965. *Aspects of the eighteenth century* (Baltimore and London: Johns Hopkins Press and Oxford University Press).

Weisser, M., 1979. *Crime and punishment in early-modern Europe* (Hassocks: Harvester Press).

Whelan, F., 1985. *Order and artifice in Hume's political philosophy* (Princeton, N.J.: Princeton University Press).

Williams, D., 1971. 'The politics of feminism in the French Enlightenment' in Hughes and Williams 1971, pp. 333–51.

1992. 'Condorcet and natural rights', *Studies on Voltaire and the Eighteenth Century*, 296, pp. 103–21.

1993. 'Condorcet and the English Enlightenment', *British Journal for Eighteenth Century Studies*, 16, pp. 155–69.

1994. *Voltaire: political writings* (Cambridge: Cambridge University Press).

1998. 'Condorcet and the politics of black servitude', in *Making connections*, ed. J. Dolamere (Bern and New York: Peter Lang), pp. 67–80.

Williams, H., 1983. *Kant's political philosophy* (Oxford: Blackwell).

1992. *Essays on Kant's political philosophy* (Cardiff: University of Wales Press).

Wilson, A., 1963. 'The development and scope of Diderot's political thought', *Studies on Voltaire and the Eighteenth Century*, 27, pp. 1871–1900.

1972. *Diderot* (New York: Oxford University Press). Reprint.

Wokler, R., 1975. 'The influence of Diderot on the political theory of Rousseau', *Studies on Voltaire and the Eighteenth Century*, 132, pp. 55–111.

1987. *Rousseau on society, politics, music and language* (New York: Garland).

1995. *Rousseau* (Oxford: Oxford University Press).

Woog, H., 'Le mécanisme du *Tableau économique* de François Quesnay', in *François Quesnay et la physiocratie*, ed. J. Hecht (Paris: Institut National d'Etudes Démographiques), I, pp. 153–68.

EDITORIAL PRINCIPLES AND ACKNOWLEDGEMENTS

This collection of texts reproduces in the case of Beccaria, Diderot, Herder (*Ideas*), Hume, Kant, Montesquieu, Paine, Priestley, Rousseau, Voltaire and Wollstonecraft material extracted from texts and translated texts already in print, and for ease of reference as many of these as possible have been drawn from texts available in the Cambridge Texts in the History of Political Thought series. Full bibliographic details of the relevant editions are appended. Many of these texts have substantial authorial annotation and editorial commentary which have not been reproduced here. With this exception, all other features, including particular styles of presentation, orthography, punctuation, as well as the editorial principles adopted by the translators and editors concerned, have been fully respected. In each case, the base text used by the translator/editor has also been indicated in the prefatory notes to each extract. The publisher and I should like to express our considerable gratitude to all contributors to the Cambridge Texts series whose work we are utilising in this way.

In the case of Barbeyrac, Burke, Burlamaqui, Condorcet, Gouges, Herder (*Letters*), Mandeville, Moser, Quesnay, Saint-Pierre, Siéyès and Smith, the base text for each extract is the most appropriate, authorised contemporary edition. This is usually, but not always, the first edition, and is clearly indicated in the prefatory notes. In certain cases presenting particular difficulties, e.g. Quesnay's *The economic tableau*, I acknowledge a deep debt of gratitude to modern editors and translators, whose ground-breaking work has informed solutions adopted for translation problems of a technical nature. With regard to this new material, translations have been standardised to modern British English spelling and conventions. The original style, format and spelling of the base texts have been retained in the case of English authors such as Burke, Mandeville and Smith. Some essential authorial annotation has been retained in the new material, given the inaccessibility of some of the original texts. The date given in the title heading before each extract is the date of first publication. This does not necessarily correspond to the date of the edition listed under 'Primary texts consulted' (pp. 522–4). Editorial annotation has been kept to a minimum, and is appended only where further clarification of meaning or allusion is essential.

TEXTS USED

Beccaria: 'On crimes and punishments' and other writings (edited by Richard Paul Bellamy, translated by Richard Brian Davies) ISBN 0 521 47982 7

Diderot: political writings (edited by John Hope Mason and Robert Wokler) ISBN 0 521 36911 8

Hume: political essays (edited by Knud Haakonssen) ISBN 0 521 46639 3

Kant: political writings (edited by H. S. Reiss, translated by H. B. Nisbet) ISBN 0 521 39837 1

Montesquieu: the Spirit of the laws (edited by Anne M. Cohler, Basia Carolyn Miller and Harold Samuel Stone) ISBN 0 521 36974 6

Paine: political writings (edited by Bruce Kuklick) ISBN 0 521 36678 X

Priestley: political writings (edited by Peter Miller) ISBN 0 521 42561 1

Rousseau: 'The discourses' and other early political writings (edited by Victor Gourevitch) ISBN 0 521 42445 3

Rousseau: 'The social contract' and other later political writings (edited by Victor Gourevitch) ISBN 0 521 42446 1

Voltaire: political writings (edited by David Williams) ISBN 0 521 43727 X

Wollstonecraft: A vindication of the rights of men and A vindication of the rights of woman and hints (edited by Sylvana Tomaselli) ISBN 0 521 43633 8

JEAN-JACQUES BURLAMAQUI

BIOGRAPHICAL NOTE

Jean-Jacques Burlamaqui (1694–1748) was born and educated in Geneva, where, in 1723, he became a professor of natural and civil law. He travelled widely in France, England and Holland, forging close links with Barbeyrac in Groningen, whose disciple he became. He spent most of his professional life in Geneva, and was prominent in the public life of the city, becoming a member of the Council of Two Hundred in 1740, and subsequently of the Council of Twenty-Five. The *Principles of natural right [and natural law]* (1747) and the *Principles of political law* (1751) were enormously successful and influential, particularly in England and Germany, though his works were less warmly received in France. In both treatises, as is immediately evident from their style and format, he brings together in a systematically pedagogical way lecture notes that he used in the courses that he gave to his students at the Genevan Academy. He tells the reader in the preface to the *Principles of natural right [and natural law]* of his concern that his notes were already circulating in a fragmentary and unauthorised fashion, and states that, encouraged by his colleagues, he was now publishing 'this first piece' as part of a 'complete system' of thought on the subject of natural law that he intended one day to write. This projected work was intended for the young rather than for 'people who are already enlightened'. Ill-health was to prevent him from completing this more encompassing project.

EDITORIAL NOTE

First published in 1747, the *Principles of natural right [and natural law]* was reprinted five times between 1748 and 1771, and again in 1820 and 1821. The first English translation (by Nugent) appeared in 1748, the last edition of the Thomas Nugent translation appearing in 1838. The work was also translated into Spanish in 1825 (reprinted in 1838 and 1874). The base text for the translated extracts is the *Principes du droit naturel . . . Nouvelle édition revue et corrigée* (Geneva and Copenhagen, C. and A. Philibert, 1762). The word *droit* in the title has been translated as *right* rather than *law*, and *natural law* added as an editorial gloss in view of the nature of the structure of this treatise which falls into two separate parts, the first of which deals specifically with *natural right*, and the second with *natural law*.

FURTHER READING

Hampsher-Monk, I., *A history of modern political thought* (Oxford, Blackwell, 1992).

Rosenblatt, H., *Rousseau and Geneva: from the First discourse to the Social contract, 1749–1762* (Cambridge, Cambridge University Press, 1997). See pp. 90–101.

Taylor, S., 'The Enlightenment in Switzerland', in *The Enlightenment in national context*, ed. R. Porter and M. Teich (Cambridge, Cambridge University Press, 1981), pp. 72–89.

Tuck, R., 'The modern theory of natural law', *The languages of political theory in early-modern Europe*, ed. A. Pagden (Cambridge, Cambridge University Press, 1987), pp. 99–119.

Principles of natural right [and natural law] (1747)

The notion of *a right*, and that of a *natural right* more particularly, are clearly notions that relate to the nature of man. It is thus from the very nature of man, from his *constitution* and *condition*, that the principles of this science must be deduced.

Originally the term *right* is derived from the verb *to direct*, meaning *to reach a certain point by the shortest route*. Thus a right, in the broadest, correct meaning of the word, to which all of its other meanings should relate, is *all that directs, or is well directed . . .* [**Principles**, 1, 1]

First of all, a *right* is often taken to mean a *personal quality*, a *power*, an *ability to act*, a *faculty*. Thus it is that people say that every man has the *right* to ensure his survival; that a father has the *right* to bring up his children; that a sovereign has the *right* to conscript soldiers to defend the state, etc.

In this sense we must define a RIGHT as *the ability man has to use his natural freedom and his natural strength in a certain way, either with respect to himself or others, in as much as the exercise of his strength and his freedom is approved by reason.*

Thus when we say that a father has the right to bring up his children, that does not mean anything else but that reason approves that a father should use his freedom and his strength in a way that is appropriate to the protection of his children, and to the education of their minds and hearts. Similarly, as reason gives its approval to a sovereign to do everything necessary for the survival and welfare of the state, it specifically authorises him to conscript soldiers, and raise armies to confront an enemy. And in consequence, people say that he has the right to do it. But conversely, we insist that a prince does not have the right to take ploughmen from the countryside unnecessarily, or to take skilled workers away from their families and their work. Nor that a father has the right to expose his children to the cold, or to put them to death, etc., because reason, far from approving of such things, utterly condemns them.

Thus the *mere power* to do something should not be confused with the *right* to do it. Mere power is a physical attribute; it is the power to take extreme action using all one's natural strength and freedom; but the notion of a right is more restricted. It links a rule to *appropriateness*, which qualifies physical ability, and channels the ways in which this expresses itself towards particular ends. This is why people say that a *right* is a *moral attribute*. It is true that some people rate *power* as well as *right* as moral attributes, but there is nothing in that essentially to contradict the distinction that we are making between them. Those who place these two notions in the category of moral phenomena understand by *power* more or less what we mean by *right*; and usage itself appears to allow for this confusion, as you can say, for example, *paternal power* just as well as you can say *paternal right, etc.* However that may be, we must not argue about words. The essential thing here is to make a distinction between the *physical* and the *moral*, and it appears that the term *right* is in itself more suited to signify a moral concept than the term *power*, as Pufendorf himself implies. In a word, the use of our faculties becomes a *right* only in as much as it has the approval of reason, and is in accordance with that basic rule of human action. And everything that man can do *reasonably* becomes his *right*, because reason is the only way by which he can be guided to his end by the shortest and surest route. So there is nothing arbitrary about these ideas; they are all taken from the very nature of things, and if you apply to them the principles set out above, you will see that they are the necessary consequences of them.

If you then ask on what basis reason approves one way of using our strength and freedom rather than another, the answer is self-evident. The difference between the judgements it makes arises from the nature of things themselves, and from their effects. Every use of our faculties, which in itself inclines towards the perfection and happiness of man, has the approval of reason, which consequently condemns any use which tends towards a contrary result.

What is important about a *right*, understood in the way that has been explained, and considered in the context of their effect on other people, is *obligation* . . . But to get a correct idea of what is involved here, it will be noted that when reason approves of man making a certain use of his strength and freedom or, what amounts to the same thing, when it recognises in him a particular *right*, as a natural consequence, in order to assure a man of that right, reason must at the same time acknowledge that other men should not use their strength and freedom to resist that man's actions, but that on the contrary they must respect his right, and help him to exercise it, rather than seek to do him harm. From that the notion of *obligation* follows naturally. Here this means nothing more than *a restriction on natural freedom brought about by reason, in as much as reason does not permit opposition to those who are exercising their rights, and that on the contrary reason constrains everyone else to favour and help those who are only doing what reason authorises, rather than resist and cross them in the exercise of what they are proposing legitimately to do.*

Right and obligation are therefore two *correlative* terms, as the logicians say; one of these ideas necessarily implies the other, and you cannot conceive of a *right* without conceiving of a corresponding *obligation*. How, for example, could you attribute to a father the right to bring up his children in wisdom and virtue through a good education, without recognising at the same time that the children must submit to paternal guidance? And that not only are they *obliged* not to resist it but, more than that, they must co-operate, through their docility and obedience, in the implementation of the actions that their father proposes to take with respect to them. If the situation was otherwise, reason would no longer be the *rule* of human conduct. It would be self-contradictory, and all the rights it grants to a man would be useless and to no avail. That would amount to taking something away from him with one hand and giving it to him with the other.

Such is the nature of a right, understood as a faculty, and of the corresponding obligation. In general, you could say that man is aware of these two attributes as soon as he begins to experience what it is to be alive and to have feelings. However, we must differentiate here between right and obligation regarding the time at which these two attributes start to develop in man. The obligations that one is under as a man do not reach their full force until a man has reached the age of reason and judgement. For to discharge an obligation, you must be conscious of it, you must know what you know, and be in a position to consider your actions in the light of a particular rule. But as for rights that might benefit someone without his knowing what is happening, these come into existence, and are valid, from the first moment of life, and place other men under the obligation to respect them. For example, the right to require others not to ill-treat us or injure us belongs no less to children, and even to those still in their mother's womb, than it does to adults. It is the basis of the just rule of Roman Law which says that *children still in their mother's womb are assumed to have come into the world whenever it is a question of something to their advantage.* But we cannot say, strictly speaking, that a new-born child, or a child about to be born, is really constrained by any obligation with respect to others. That condition, in the case of a child, does not start properly until he has reached the age of knowledge and discretion.

A number of distinctions can be made between rights and obligations. We will just confine ourselves to the main ones:

1. There are *natural rights and acquired rights.* The first are those *belonging originally and essentially to man, and which are inherent in his nature, by which he experiences the condition of being human, independently of any particular act on his part. Acquired rights are, conversely, those that man does not enjoy naturally, but which he procures for himself through his own action.* Thus the right to ensure his own survival is a right that is natural to man; but sovereignty, or the right to rule over a society of men, is an acquired right.

2. There are *perfect, rigorous rights, and imperfect, unrigorous rights. Perfect rights are those whose implementation can be required to the letter, if necessary going as far as to use force to ensure that they are implemented, or to ensure that they continue to be observed, against those who might want to resist us, or cause us unease.* Thus it is that we can reasonably use force against whoever might unjustly threaten our lives, our property or our freedom. But when reason does not allow us to take the law into our own hands in order to ensure that we enjoy the rights that reason has granted to us, then those rights are just imperfect and unrigorous. Thus, although reason authorises those who by themselves are bereft of the means to survive to ask for help from others, they cannot, if that help is refused, procure it for themselves by force, nor force it out of other men, if they are unwilling [to

and constitution of man, and that in the last analysis it should relate to his happiness, which is what reason necessarily makes him seek . . .

I define the LAW as *a rule prescribed by the sovereign ruler of a society for his subjects, either to impose the obligation on them to do or not do certain things, on threat of some punishment, or to give them the freedom to act or not act with regard to other things as they think fit,* and *to guarantee them full enjoyment of their rights in that respect.*

I say that the LAW is a rule to indicate first of all what the law has in common with *counsel;* for both are rules of behaviour. Secondly, to distinguish the law from *temporary orders* that a superior might give, and which, not being *permanent* rules for the conduct of his subjects, are not, properly speaking, laws. The idea of rule generally involves two things: *universality* and *perpetuity.* These two qualities being in general essential to *rule,* they also serve to distinguish the law from all other private assertions of the sovereign's will.

I would add that the law is a *prescribed* rule because a simple resolution confined to the mind of the sovereign, without being made explicit through some external sign, would never make a law. The public needs to be *notified* of this will in an appropriate way, so that they can know what the sovereign wants of them, and of the need for them to adapt their conduct to this. For the rest, the form that this notification takes, either oral, written or any other, is neither here nor there. It is enough for subjects to be well informed about the will of the legislator.

Let us complete the development of the main ideas that constitute a definition of the law. The law is prescribed by the *sovereign,* this is what distinguishes it from *counsel,* which comes from a *friend,* from an *equal,* who as such has no power over us, and whose advice in consequence does not have the same force, and does not produce the same sense of obligation, as the law which, emanating from the sovereign, is reinforced by the *command* and *authority* of a superior. We follow counsel for reasons drawn from the very nature of the thing; we obey the law, not only for the reasons that constitute its basis, but also because of the authority of the sovereign who prescribes it. The obligation produced by counsel is a purely *internal* obligation; that produced by the law is simultaneously *internal* and *external.*

SOCIETY *is,* as has already been observed, *the union of a number of people for a certain purpose* that provides *some common advantage.* The PURPOSE is *the effect or advantage that intelligent beings have in mind, and that they wish to achieve for themselves.* The UNION of a number of people is *the concurrence of their will to achieve the purpose they hold in common.* But although the idea of society has been introduced into the definition of the law, you must not conclude that society is an absolutely essential and necessary condition for the establishment of laws. At a pinch, strictly speaking, you can conceive of the law perfectly well even if no individual is subject to the sovereign's authority, and it is only to be relevant to the realities of the current situation that we have assumed [the existence of] a sovereign ruling over a society of men. We must, however, observe that the relationship between a sovereign and his subjects creates between them a kind of society, but one of a peculiar kind that we can call a *society of inequality*: the sovereign commands, and the subjects obey.

THE SOVEREIGN *is* therefore *the person who has the right to command without possibility of any appeal against him.* TO COMMAND is *to direct, according to his will and with authority or with the power to constrain, the actions of subordinates;* and I say that the sovereign commands *without possibility of any appeal* to make clear that as he occupies the first rank in society, his will is superior to everyone else's, and that all members of society are subordinate to him. In the end the RIGHT TO COMMAND is nothing more than *the power to direct with authority the actions of others.* And as the power to use one's strength and freedom is only a *right* in as much as reason approves and legitimises it, it is also only on the basis of *without possibility of any appeal* that the right to command is founded on the approval of reason.

This leads us to look more closely into what constitutes the natural *foundations* of *dominion* and *sovereignty* or, what amounts to the same thing, by what authority does one have the right to impose some obligation on another person, and to require him to submit and obey? This question is very important *per se,* and also because of its implications. Because the more people know about the reasons for the establishment of authority on the one hand, and dependence on the other, the more they will be inclined to actually submit with good grace to those on whom they depend. Moreover, the diversity of views about the bases to sovereignty proves that the subject needs to be treated carefully ... [***Principles,* i, 8**]

ON NATURAL LAWS

After having propounded the general principles of rights, it is now a question of applying this specifically to natural laws. Is man, by his nature and constitution, in effect subject to laws, properly speaking? And what are these laws? Who is this superior who imposes them? By what means can we succeed in knowing them? Where does the obligation to observe them come from? What can happen if we fail to obey them? And conversely, what advantage do we get from observing them?

LET US DEFINE our terms first of all. We understand by NATURAL LAW *a law that God imposes on all men, and that they can discover and understand simply by the light of their reason by considering carefully their nature and condition.*

NATURAL RIGHT *is the system, the totality or the corpus of these same laws.*

NATURAL JURISPRUDENCE *is the art of achieving knowledge of the laws of nature, of developing them, and applying them to men's actions.*

BUT do NATURAL LAWS exist in practice? This is the first question that arises, and it must be examined before anything else. To do this, we cannot avoid going back to the principles of NATURAL THEOLOGY as the first, true foundation of natural rights. For when we ask *if there are any natural laws* we can only resolve the question by examining three issues: 1. Is there a God? 2. If there is a God, has he got the right by himself to impose laws on men? and 3. Is God in fact currently making use of his right in this respect by really giving us laws, and by requiring that we should make our actions conform to them? . . .

As soon as we recognise the existence of a God as a creative force, it is very clear that he is a master who possesses inherently the sovereign right to command men, to prescribe rules of conduct for them, and to impose laws on them. And it is no less obvious that men for their part are, through their natural constitution, under the *obligation* to subordinate their actions to the will of this First Being.

We have shown that the true foundation of *sovereignty* in the person of the sovereign is power allied to wisdom and kindness, and that, on the other hand, the weakness and need of his subjects produces naturally *dependence*. So it is a question of seeing whether these qualities in the sovereign are to be found in God, and whether men for their part are in a state of infirmity and need, making them necessarily dependent on Him for their own happiness.

It cannot be doubted that He who exists necessarily and through Himself, and who has created the universe, is endowed with infinite power. As He has given existence to everything through His will alone, He is able also to preserve them, destroy them or change them at will.

But His wisdom is no less great than His power. Having made everything, He must understand everything. He understands the causes, and the effects that ensue. We can see, moreover, the most excellent *purposes* in all His works, and a choice of the most appropriate *means* to achieve them. In a word, everything is, so to speak, stamped with the die of *wisdom*.

Reason teaches us also that God is an essentially *good* Being, His perfection seeming to flow naturally from His wisdom and His power. For how can a Being who by its nature is infinitely wise and infinitely powerful have an inclination to do harm? Nothing inclines Him to do so. Malice, cruelty and injustice are always the outcome of ignorance and weakness. Also, although man pays little heed to what surrounds him, and reflects little on his own constitution, he will recognise, within himself, and in the outside world, the beneficent hand of his creator, who behaves towards him as a father would. We derive life and reason from God; He provides amply for our needs; He has added what is useful to what is necessary, and what is delightful to what is useful. Philosophers observe that everything that is useful for our survival has been decked out with some delight. Food, rest, activity, heat, cold, in a word everything useful to us, pleases us in turn, and for as long as it is useful to us. Should it cease to be so, because things are being taken too far and are becoming dangerous, then an entirely different sentiment gives us a warning, pleasurable feelings of attraction urging us to make use of something when we need it, disgust and lassitude urging us to abstain from it when it might harm us. Such is the gentle, sweet system of nature which attaches pleasure to the enjoyment in moderation of our senses and faculties, and which turns everything that surrounds us into a source of pleasure as soon as we learn how to enjoy ourselves with discretion. What is more magnificent, for example, than this Theatre of the World in which we live, than this brilliant setting of sky and earth before us, presenting us with countless thousands of ever more pleasing and varied tableaux? What satisfaction the mind gets from the sciences which challenge, stretch and perfect it! What goods do we not derive from human industry? What advantages do we not derive from our neighbours' trade? What charm from conversation with them! What sweetness in friendship, and in those other affections of the heart! When one abuses nothing, almost the whole of one's path through life is sprinkled with pleasurable feelings. And if you consider further ... that the laws given to us by God tend to perfect our nature, to avert all abuse, and to make us use in moderation the blessings of life, on which depends the survival of man, the quality of his life, and his happiness, both public and private, what more do we need to recognise that God's goodness is in no way less than his wisdom and power?

Here then is a superior Being endowed undeniably with all the qualities necessary to have the most legitimate and far-reaching right of dominion that can be imagined. And since, for our part, our experience makes us feel well enough that we are weak, and prone to various needs, since we have received everything from Him, and since He can still either increase our needs or remove them from us, it is clear that nothing is missing from the argument demonstrating on the one hand the absolute sovereignty of God, and on the other our absolute dependency ... [*Principles*, II, 1]

If after that you ask what principles reason must use in order to judge what belongs to the province of natural laws, to deduce what these are, and develop them further, I would answer that, generally speaking, all you have to do is pay attention to the nature of man and to his condition and relationships. And as these relationships are different, there might also be various principles that lead us to an understanding of our duties.

But before going as far as that, it will be appropriate to make a few preliminary remarks on what are called the *principles of natural law*. This is to preclude the equivocations that have caused so much confusion on the matter.

When we ask what are the FIRST PRINCIPLES OF NATURAL LAW, we are asking what are *those truths or those basic propositions by which we can in effect know what God's will is in respect of us*, and thereby achieve, by a just sequence of deductions, true knowledge of the specific laws and duties that God imposes on us through plain reason.

Thus it is necessary not to confuse the principles we are talking about here with the efficient and productive cause of natural law, nor with the principle of obligation in those same laws. It is beyond doubt (and everybody is in agreement about this) that the efficient cause of the laws of nature, and of the obligations that they engender, is the will of the Supreme Being. That having been said, we still need to discover how man can achieve knowledge of that will, and how we can discern the principles which, while assuring us about God's intention, enable us to deduce from that all the specific duties that can be known through reason alone. You ask, for example, whether compensation for injury, or keeping contractual commitments, comes into the area of natural rights. If we simply answer that the issue is beyond argument because God wishes it so, it is obvious that you have not received an adequate reply to your question, and that you could still reasonably ask to be shown a principle that would enable you really to understand that this is in effect the will of God, for that is what you seek.

Next let us note that the first principles of natural law must not just be *true*, but also *simple, clear, sufficient* and *appropriate* to that law.

They must be true. That is to say, they must be drawn from nature and from the condition of things. False, or hypothetical, principles would only produce consequences of a similar nature. A solid building will never be constructed on crumbling foundations.

They must be simple and clear in themselves, or at least easy to grasp and develop. For as natural laws are compulsory for all men, their basic principles must be within the reach of everyone, and everyone must be able to learn from them by using their common sense. Thus it is for good cause that people would distrust principles that were far-fetched, subtle or too metaphysical.

I would add that these principles must be sufficient and universal. We must be able to deduce all the laws of nature, and all the duties that they engender, from their immediate and natural consequences, so that the revelation of their details should really just be the explanation of the principles, a bit like the production and growth of a plant is nothing more than the growing of the bud or the seed.

And as most natural laws are subject to various exceptions, it is even more necessary for the principles to be of such a nature that they embody the reasons for the exceptions, and that not only can the ordinary rules of morality be drawn from them, but that they also serve to modify those rules when place, time and occasion demand it.

Finally, these basic principles must be established in such a way as to be in effect the proper, direct foundation of all the duties of natural law, so that whether you start with the principle in order to deduce the consequences, or you trace the principle back from the consequences, the chain of reasoning is always direct, and the thread, as it were, is never broken.

For the rest, generally speaking, it is neither here nor there whether everything is reduced to a single principle, or whether several are established. In this matter we must consult and follow the rules of a judicious and precise method. What you can say about it is that it seems not to be necessary, either to the strength or perfection of the system, for all natural laws to be deduced from a single solitary basic maxim. Perhaps such a thing is not possible. In any case, it is a piece of quite useless intellectual labour to try to bring everything back to a single, uniform principle.

The only way to achieve knowledge of natural laws is to consider closely the nature of man, his constitution, his relationships with other beings around him, and the conditions that follow from that. Indeed, the very term *natural right*, and the notion of this that we have given, show that the principles of this science can only be drawn from nature itself, and from the constitution of man. So here are two general propositions that we put forward as the basis to the whole system of natural law:

1. PROPOSITION. EVERYTHING *that is in the nature of man and in his basic, original constitution, and everything that is a necessary consequence of that nature and constitution, shows us with certainty what the intention or the will of God is with respect to man, and consequently gives us knowledge of natural laws.*

2. PROPOSITION. BUT *to see a complete system of natural laws, we must consider not only the nature of man in itself, we must also pay attention to man's relationships with others, and with the various conditions that result, otherwise it is very clear that we shall only end up with an incomplete and defective system.*

Thus you can say that the general foundation of the system of natural law is the nature of man, together with all the circumstances associated with it, and in which God Himself has placed man for certain purposes, this being the means by which we can know what God's will is. In a word, as man takes from the hand of God Himself everything he is, everything for his existence, with regard to the way he exists, it is man alone, if we study him well, who will instruct us fully on the purposes that God had in giving us life, and consequently on the rules that we must follow to fulfil the creator's intentions . . .

But a human society can neither subsist nor achieve the happy purposes for which God has established it, unless men have feelings of affection and benevolence towards each other, it follows that our creator, and common father, wants everyone to be motivated by these feelings, and He does everything in His power to keep society beneficial and pleasant, and to bind the ties of society closer and closer to ensure mutual benefits and services.

So there you have the true principle of duty which natural law prescribes for us with respect to others. Moralists have given this the name of SOCIABILITY, by which they mean *that disposition to benevolence towards our fellow citizens, to do them every good that it is within our power to do, to reconcile our happiness with*

that of others, and to always subordinate our private advantage to that of the general
community.

The more we study ourselves, the more we will be convinced that sociability coincides in fact with the will of God. For over and above the fact that this principle is necessary, we will also find it engraved in our hearts. If, on the one hand, the Creator has implanted in us love of ourselves, on the other that same hand has implanted a feeling of benevolence towards our fellow citizens. These two inclinations, although quite different from each other, are in no way, however, contradictory, and God, who has given them to us, has intended them to act together for the purpose of mutual support, and not mutual destruction. Thus it is that kind and generous hearts find the purest satisfaction in doing good for others, because in so doing they are simply following an instinct given to them by nature.

From the principle of *sociability* flow, as if from their source, all society's laws and all of our duties towards others, general and specific:

1. This union that God has established between men requires them to have the COMMON GOOD as their supreme rule of conduct in everything connected with society, and that, paying careful attention to counsels of wisdom, they should never seek their own personal advantage at the expense of the public advantage. For that is what their condition demands, and in consequence it is the will of their common father.

2. THE SPIRIT OF SOCIABILITY must be UNIVERSAL. Human society embraces all men with whom it can have some commerce, as it is founded on the relationships that they share together as a consequence of their nature and their condition.

3. Reason then tells us that creatures of the same rank, of the same species, born with the same faculties, have in general equal and common rights so that they can live together, and share the same advantages. We are thus obligated to REGARD OURSELVES AS BEING NATURALLY EQUAL, AND TO TREAT EACH OTHER AS BEING SO. And it would be a betrayal of nature not to recognise this principle of EQUITY (which jurists call *aequabilitas juris*) as being one of the basic foundations of society. The LAW OF RECIPROCITY is founded on that. The same goes for that rule that is so simple, but so widely practised: THAT we must behave towards others as we would wish them to behave towards us, and always treat them in the same way as we would want them to treat us in similar circumstances.

4. As sociability is a mutual obligation between men, those who, through malice or injustice, break the bond of society, cannot reasonably complain if those whom

they offend cannot treat them as friends, or even go so far as to take the law into their own hands against them.

But if we have the right to suspend acts of kindness with regard to an enemy, it is never permissible to snuff out the principle. As *necessity* alone authorises us to resort to force against an unjust aggressor, this same necessity must therefore be the rule and criterion of the harm that we can do to him. And we must always be readily inclined to befriend him again as soon as justice has been done, and we have nothing more to fear from him.

Thus we must distinguish carefully between JUSTIFIED SELF-DEFENCE and VEN-GEANCE. This first only suspends, necessarily and temporarily, the exercise of benevolence, and in no way contradicts the principle of sociability. But the second, by snuffing out the very principle of benevolence, replaces it with a feeling of hatred and animosity, in itself vicious, contrary to the public good, and formally condemned by natural law.

These general rules produce a rich crop of consequences: we must do no harm to others by word or action; we must compensate all injuries, for society could not subsist if injustices were allowed.

We must be sincere in what we say, hold to our commitments, for what confidence could men have in each other, and what security would there be in trade, if deception and the breaking of faith formally given were to be permitted?

We must render to others not only what belongs to them, but also the degree of respect and honour due to them, according to their condition and rank, because subordination is the bond of society, and without it there would be no order, either in families or in civil government.

But if the public good requires inferiors to obey, that same public good requires superiors to preserve the rights of those who are subordinated to them, and rule over them only to make them happy.

There is more. Men come together through their feelings and good deeds, and nothing is more appropriate to humanity, nor more useful to society, than compassion, gentleness, beneficence, generosity . . . So as all feelings and all acts of justice and kindness are the only true bonds linking men together, and making society stable, calm and prosperous, we must look on these virtues as being equivalent to duties imposed by God, by reason of the fact that everything that is necessary to His purpose is for that very reason in accordance with His will.

Thus there are three general principles behind natural laws which relate to the three conditions of man that we have set out: (1) RELIGION; (2) LOVE OF ONESELF; (3) SOCIABILITY OR BENEVOLENCE towards others . . .

But if these three great principles of our duties are linked together in this way, there is also an element of natural *subordination* between them, which will serve to decide to which of these duties we must give priority in those cases or circumstances in which they come into conflict or opposition with each other, and which do not allow them all to be complied with equally.

The general principle for judging this subordination is that *the stronger obligation must take precedence over the weaker*. But then in order to know which is the stronger obligation, we need only look closely at the very nature of our duties, and at the differing degrees of necessity and utility between them, for this is the truest way of then knowing what the will of God is. In accordance with these ideas, here are some general rules for specific cases:

1. THE *duties of man to God take precedence over all others*. For of all obligations, the one that links us to our all-knowing, all-good Creator is undoubtedly the closest and the strongest.

2. IF *our duty to ourselves clashes with our duty to society in general, society must take precedence*. Otherwise, the order of things would be overturned, the foundations of society would be destroyed. And it would be going directly against the will of God who, having subordinated the part to the whole, imposes on us the indispensable obligation never to depart from the supreme law of the common good.

3. BUT *if, all things being equal, there is a conflict between a duty of self-love and a duty of sociability, self-love must take precedence*. Because as everyone is directly and primarily charged with responsibility for survival and happiness, it follows that in cases where all things are absolutely equal, responsibility for ourselves takes precedence over responsibility for someone else.

4. THAT *finally if there is opposition between two duties of sociability, the one associated with the greatest utility must be preferred, as being the most important*.

What we have demonstrated so far is really to do with *obligatory* natural law, that is to say, the law which, being aimed at actions in which you can see a necessary accord or discord with the nature and condition of man, consequently places us under an indispensable obligation to act, or not act, in a certain way. But . . . it must be recognised that there is also a natural law *of simple permission*, which in certain cases gives us complete freedom to act or not act, and which, by requiring others not to importune us, assures us of the exercise of our freedom in this respect, and of its consequences.

The general principle of this law of permission is THAT *we can reasonably, and in accordance with our judgement, do or not do anything that is not in absolute and essential accordance with nature and with the condition of man, provided that such actions are not specifically ordained or forbidden by a positive law, to which we are in other respects subject.*

The truth of this principle is self-evident. The Creator having given men a number of faculties, among which being the ability to modify their actions as they think appropriate, it is certain that in all those areas where He has not restricted the use of these faculties by an explicit commandment or by a positive interdiction, He leaves men to be their own masters in using [these faculties] in accordance with their own wisdom. It is on this law of permission that all those rights of the sort that can be exercised or not exercised, retained or given up wholly or in part, are founded. And it is a consequence of renunciation that it sometimes happens that actions that are in themselves permissible might be ordered or forbidden on the authority of the sovereign, and become thereby obligatory.

THAT is what plain reason discovers in man's nature, in his constitution and in his basic, original condition. But as man can himself bring about different changes in his basic condition, and enter into a number of adventitious and accessory conditions, consideration of these new conditions also forms part of the objectives of natural law in its broadest sense, and the principles that we have set out must serve as the guiding rules for those conditions in which man finds himself as a result of his own actions.

This is what gives rise to the distinction between two types of natural right: one primary, the other secondary:

BASIC OR PRIMARY NATURAL RIGHT is *the right which emanates directly from the basic constitution of man as God himself has established it, and independently from any human action.*

SECONDARY NATURAL RIGHT is *the right which assumes some human agency, such as the civil state, ownership of property, etc.*

It will be well understood that this secondary natural right simply follows on from the first, or rather it is a just application of the general maxims of natural right to the particular condition of men, and to the different circumstances that they encounter as a result of their own action ... [*Principles*, II, 4]

The civil order

JEAN-JACQUES ROUSSEAU

BIOGRAPHICAL NOTE

Jean-Jacques Rousseau (1712–78) was born in Geneva. From 1728 until 1742 he worked as a servant, engraver, music teacher and tutor, a richly formative period in his life, memorably recorded in his autobiography, the *Confessions*. In 1742 he presented (unsuccessfully) a project for a new system of musical notation to the Academy of Sciences. He stayed in Paris until 1756 teaching, writing, copying and arranging music, a period interrupted only by a brief stay in Venice in 1742–3 as secretary to the French Ambassador. By 1745 he had met Diderot, who invited him to contribute to the *Encyclopedia*. In January 1751 the *Discourse on the sciences and the arts* was published, and the next twelve years were to be the most productive of his life.

His short opera, *The village soothsayer*, was performed at court before Louis XV in 1752, a year which also saw the performance of *Narcissus* at the Comédie-Française. The *Discourse on the origin and the foundations of inequality among men* appeared in 1755, dedicated to the Republic of Geneva. A few months after the appearance of his article on 'Political economy' in the fifth volume of the *Encyclopedia* in November 1755, he left Paris for the Hermitage, a cottage on Mme d'Epinay's estate, where he composed his novel, *Julie, or the new Eloisa*, and soon became embroiled in quarrels with Voltaire.

His interest in political matters was now reaching its peak. In 1761 he issued a sceptical commentary on Saint-Pierre's *A plan for perpetual peace in Europe*, and in 1762 he published the *Social contract*, together with a controversial pedagogical treatise, *Emile, or, on education*. Both works were condemned immediately in Paris and Geneva, and a warrant was issued for Rousseau's arrest. The year 1762 marked the beginning of a painful and dangerous period in Rousseau's life as an outcast moving from refuge to refuge under great mental and physical strain, his condition exacerbated by a brief stay in England in 1766–7 as the guest of David Hume. Disturbing feelings of persecution deepened with the publication in 1764 of a bitingly satirical lampoon by Voltaire. By now Rousseau saw the *philosophes* as his personal enemies.

Political and other writings continued to flow from his pen, however, such as the *Plan for the constitution of Corsica* (1765), the *Considerations on the government of Poland* (1771–2). In his last years he concentrated mainly on autobiographical and personal writings. It was not until 1782, four years after his death, that all of his works became available for the first time with the publication in Geneva of the Dupeyrou-Moultou collective edition of his works.

EDITORIAL NOTE

The extracts from the *Discourse on the origin and the foundations of inequality among men* are taken from the translation by V. Gourevitch.* The base text for the Gourevitch translation is that of the first edition of the *Discours sur l'origine et les fondements de l'inégalité parmi les hommes* (Amsterdam, Marc Michel Rey, 1755). The extract from the *Social contract* is also taken from the Gourevitch translation, for which the base text is the first edition of *Du contrat social* (Amsterdam, Marc Michel Rey, 1762).

FURTHER READING

*Gourevitch, V. (ed.), *Rousseau: 'The discourses' and other early political writings* (Cambridge, Cambridge University Press, 1997). See introduction, pp. ix–xxxi.
Strong, T., *Jean-Jacques Rousseau: the politics of the ordinary* (London, Sage, 1994).
Trachtenberg, Z., *Making citizens* (London and New York, Routledge, 1993).
Wokler, R., *Rousseau* (Oxford, Oxford University Press, 1995).

Discourse on the origin and the foundations of inequality among men (1755)

The first man who, having enclosed a piece of ground, to whom it occurred to say *this is mine*, and found people sufficiently simple to believe him, was the true founder of civil society. How many crimes, wars, murders, how many miseries and horrors Mankind would have been spared by him who, pulling up the stakes or filling in the ditch, had cried out to his kind: Beware of listening to this impostor; You are lost if you forget that the fruits are everyone's and the Earth no one's: But in all likelihood things had by then reached a point where they could not continue as they were; for this idea of property, depending as it does on many prior ideas which could only arise successively, did not take shape all at once in man's mind: Much progress had to have been made, industry and enlightenment acquired, transmitted, and increased from one age to the next, before this last stage of the state of Nature was reached. Let us therefore take up the thread earlier, and try to fit this slow succession of events and of knowledge together from a single point of view, and in their most natural order.

Man's first sentiment was that of his existence, his first care that for his preservation. The Earth's products provided him with all necessary support, instinct moved him to use them. Hunger, other appetites causing him by turns to experience different ways of existing, there was one that prompted him to perpetuate his species; and this blind inclination, devoid of any sentiment of the heart, produced only a purely animal act. The need satisfied, the two sexes no longer recognized one another, and even the child no longer meant anything to the mother as soon as it could do without her.

Such was the condition of nascent man; such was the life of an animal at first restricted to pure sensations, and scarcely profiting from the gifts Nature offered him, let alone dreaming of wresting anything from it; but difficulties soon presented themselves; it became necessary to learn to overcome them: the height of trees which prevented him from reaching their fruits, competition from the animals trying to eat these fruits, the ferociousness of the animals that threatened his very life, everything obliged him to attend to bodily exercise; he had to become agile, run fast, fight vigorously. The natural weapons, branches and stones, were soon at hand. He learned to overcome the obstacles of Nature, fight other animals when necessary, contend even with men for his subsistence, or make up for what had to be yielded to the stronger.

In proportion as mankind spread, difficulties multiplied together with men. Differences of terrain, climate, seasons, could have forced them to introduce differences into their ways of living. Barren years, long and harsh winters, scorching all-consuming summers, required renewed industry on their part. On seashores and riverbanks they invented line and hook; and became fishermen and fish-eaters. In forests they made bows and arrows, and became hunters and warriors; In cold countries they covered themselves with the skins of the beasts they had killed; lightning, a volcano, or some happy accident acquainted them with fire, a new resource against the rigors of winter: They learned to conserve this element, then to reproduce it, and finally to prepare the meats they had previously devoured raw.

This repeated interaction of the various beings with himself as well as with one another must naturally have engendered in man's mind perceptions of certain relations. The relations which we express by the words great, small, strong, weak, fast, slow, fearful, bold, and other such ideas, compared as need required and almost without thinking about it, finally produced in him some sort of reflection, or rather a mechanical prudence that suggested to him the precautions most necessary for his safety.

The new enlightenment that resulted from this development increased his superiority over the other animals by acquainting him with it. He practiced setting traps for them, he tricked them in a thousand ways, and although a number of them might surpass him in strength at fighting, or in speed at running; in time he became the master of those that could be useful, and the scourge of those that could be harmful to him. This is how his first look at himself aroused the first movement of pride in him; this is how, while as yet scarcely able to discriminate ranks, and considering himself in the first rank as a species, he was from afar preparing to claim first rank as an individual.

Although others of his kind were not for him what they are for us, and he had scarcely more dealings with them than with the other animals, they were not neglected in his observations. The conformities which time may have led him to perceive between them, his female, and himself, led him to judge regarding those he did not perceive, and seeing that they all behaved as he would have done in similar circumstances, he concluded that their way of thinking and of feeling fully corresponded to his own, and this important truth, once it was firmly settled in his mind, made him follow, by a premonition as sure as Dialectics and more rapid, the best rules of conduct to observe with them for his advantage and safety.

Taught by experience that love of well-being is the sole spring of human actions, he was in a position to distinguish between the rare occasions when common interest should make him count on the help of his kind, and the even rarer occasions when competition should make him suspicious of them. In the first case he united with them in a herd, or at most in some kind of free association that obligated no one and lasted only as long as the transient need that had formed it. In the second case everyone sought to seize his own advantage, either by open force if he believed that he could do so; or by skill and cunning, if he felt he was the weaker.

This is how men might imperceptibly have acquired some crude idea of mutual engagements and of the advantage of fulfilling them, but only as far as present and perceptible interest could require; for foresight was nothing to them and, far from being concerned with a distant future, they did not even give thought to the next day. If a deer was to be caught, everyone clearly sensed that this required him faithfully to keep his post; but if a hare happened to pass within reach of one of them, he will, without a doubt, have chased after it without a scruple and, after catching his prey, have cared very little about having caused his companions to miss theirs.

It is easy to understand that such dealings did not require a language much more refined than that of crows or of monkeys, which troop together in approximately the same way. Some inarticulate cries, many gestures, and a few imitative noises must, for a long time, have made up the universal language, [and] the addition to it, in every region, of a few articulated and conventional sounds – the institution of which is, as I have already said, none too easy to explain – made for particular languages, crude, imperfect and more or less such as various savage nations have now. I cover multitudes of centuries in a flash, forced by time running out, the abundance of things I have to say, and the almost imperceptible progress of the beginnings; for the more slowly events succeeded one another, the more quickly can they be described.

This initial progress finally enabled man to make more rapid progress. The more the mind became enlightened, the more industry was perfected. Soon ceasing to fall asleep underneath the first tree or to withdraw into caves, they found they could use hard, sharp stones as hatchets to cut wood, dig in the ground, and make huts of branches which it later occurred to them to daub with clay and mud. This was the period of a first revolution which brought about the establishment and the differentiation of families, and introduced a sort of property; from which there perhaps already arose a good many quarrels and fights. However, since the stronger were probably the first to make themselves dwellings they felt they could defend, it seems plausible that the weak found it simpler and safer to imitate them than to try to dislodge them: and as for those who already had huts, a man must rarely have tried to appropriate his neighbor's, not so much because it did not belong to him as because it was of no use to him, and he could not get hold of it without risking a very lively fight with the family that occupied it.

The first developments of the heart were the effect of a new situation that brought husbands and wives, fathers and children together in a common dwelling; the habit of living together gave rise to the sweetest sentiments known to man, conjugal love, and paternal love. Each family became a small society, all the better united as mutual attachment and freedom were its only bonds; and this is when the first difference was established in the ways of living of the two sexes, which until then had had but one. Women became more sedentary and grew accustomed to looking after the hut and children, while the man went in quest of the common subsistence. As a result of their slightly softer life, both sexes also began to lose something of their ferociousness and vigor: but while each separately grew less fit to fight wild beasts, in exchange it became easier to assemble in order to resist them together.

In this new state, with a simple and solitary life, very limited needs, and the implements they had invented to provide for them, men enjoyed a great deal of leisure which they used to acquire several sorts of conveniences unknown to their fathers; and this was the first yoke which, without thinking of it, they imposed on themselves, and the first source of evils they prepared for their descendants; for not only did they, in this way, continue to weaken body and mind, but since these conveniences, by becoming habitual, had almost entirely ceased to be enjoyable, and at the same time had degenerated into true needs, it became much more cruel to be deprived of them than to possess them was sweet, and men were unhappy to lose them without being happy to possess them.

Here one gets a somewhat better view of how the use of speech is imperceptibly established or perfected in the bosom of each family, and one can further conjecture how various particular causes could enlarge language, and accelerate its progress by making it more necessary. Great floods or earthquakes surrounded inhabited areas with waters or precipices; revolutions of the globe broke off portions of the continent and carved them into islands. It seems likely that a common idiom was formed earlier among men brought into closer proximity with one another in this fashion, and forced to live together, than among those who roamed freely through the forests of the mainland. Thus it is very possible that Islanders, after their first attempts at navigation, introduced the use of speech among us; and it is at least very likely that society and languages arose in islands and were perfected there before they were known on the continent.

Everything begins to change in appearance. Men, who until now had roamed in the woods, having become more settled, gradually come together, united in various troops, and finally in every region form a particular nation united in morals and character, not by rules or laws, but by the same kind of life and of foods, and the influence of a shared climate. Permanent proximity cannot fail in the end to give rise to some bond between different families. Young people of the opposite sex live in adjoining huts, the transient dealings demanded by Nature soon lead to others, no less sweet and more permanent as a result of mutual visits. They grow accustomed to attend to different objects and to make comparisons; imperceptibly they acquire ideas of merit and of beauty which produce sentiments of preference. The more they see one another, the less they can do without seeing one another more. A tender and sweet sentiment steals into the soul, and at the least obstacle becomes an impetuous frenzy; jealousy awakens together with love; discord triumphs, and the gentlest of all passions receives sacrifices of human blood.

As ideas and sentiments succeed one another, as the mind and the heart grow active, mankind continues to grow tame, contacts expand and bonds tighten. It became customary to gather in front of the huts or around a large tree: song and dance, true children of love and leisure, became the amusement or rather the occupation of idle men and women gathered together. Everyone began to look at everyone else and to wish to be looked at himself, and public esteem acquired a price. The one who sang or danced best; the handsomest, the strongest, the most skillful, or the most eloquent came to be the most highly regarded, and this was the first step at once towards inequality and vice: from these first preferences arose vanity and contempt on the one hand, shame and envy on the other; and the fermentation caused by these new leavens eventually produced compounds fatal to happiness and innocence.

As soon as men had begun to appreciate one another and the idea of consideration had taken shape in their mind, everyone claimed a right to it, and one could no longer deprive anyone of it with impunity. From here arose the first duties of civility even among savages, and from it any intentional wrong became an affront because, together with the harm resulting from the injury, the offended party saw in it contempt for his person, often more unbearable than the harm itself. Thus everyone punishing the contempt shown him in a manner proportionate to the stock he set by himself, vengeances became terrible, and men bloodthirsty and cruel. This is precisely the stage reached by most of the savage peoples known to us; and it is for want of drawing adequate distinctions between ideas, and noticing how far these peoples already were from the first state of Nature, that many hastened to conclude that man is naturally cruel and that he needs political order in order to be made gentle, whereas nothing is as gentle as he in his primitive state when, placed by Nature at equal distance from the stupidity of the brutes and the fatal enlightenment of civil man, and restricted by instinct and by reason alike to protecting himself against the harm that threatens him, he is restrained by natural pity from doing anyone harm, without being moved to it by anything, even after it has been done to him. For, according to the axiom of the wise Locke, '*Where there is no property, there can be no injury.*'

But it should be noted that beginning society and the already established relations among men required in them qualities different from those they derived from their primitive constitution; that, since morality was beginning to enter into human actions and since, before there were laws, everyone was sole judge and avenger of the offenses he had received, the goodness suited to the pure state of Nature was no longer the goodness suited to nascent society; that punishments had to become more severe in proportion as the opportunities to offend became more frequent, and that the terror of vengeance had to take the place of the laws' restraint. Thus, although men now had less endurance, and natural pity had already undergone some attenuation, this period in the development of human faculties, occupying a just mean between the indolence of the primitive state and the petulant activity of our amour propre, must have been the happiest and the most lasting epoch. The more one reflects on it, the more one finds that this state was the least subject to revolutions, the best for man, and that he must have left it only by some fatal accident which, for the sake of the common utility, should never have occurred. The example of the savages, almost all of whom have been found at this point, seems to confirm that mankind was made always to remain in it, that this state is the genuine youth of the world, and that all subsequent progress has been so many steps in appearance toward the perfection of the individual, and in effect toward the decrepitude of the species.

So long as men were content with their rustic huts, so long as they confined themselves to sewing their clothes of skins with thorns or fish bones, to adorning themselves with feathers and shells, to painting their bodies different colors, to perfecting or embellishing their bows and arrows, to carving a few fishing canoes or a few crude musical instruments with sharp stones; In a word, so long as they applied themselves only to tasks a single individual could perform, and to arts that did not require the collaboration of several hands, they lived free, healthy, good, and happy as far as they could by their nature be, and continued to enjoy the gentleness of independent dealings with one another; but the moment one man needed the help of another; as soon as it was found to be useful for one to have provisions for two, equality disappeared, property appeared, work became necessary, and the vast forests changed into smiling fields that had to be watered with the sweat of men, and where slavery and misery were soon seen to sprout and grow together with the harvests.

Metallurgy and agriculture were the two arts the invention of which brought about this great revolution. For the poet it is gold and silver; but for the philosopher it is iron and wheat that civilized men, and ruined mankind. Indeed, both were unknown to the savages of America who have therefore always remained such; even other peoples seem to have remained barbarians as long as they engaged in one of these arts without the other; and perhaps one of the best reasons why Europe had political order, if not earlier then at least more continuously and better than the other parts of the world, is that it is both the most abundant in iron and the most fertile in wheat.

It is very difficult to conjecture how men came to know and to use iron: for it is not plausible that they imagined on their own extracting ore from the mine and doing what is required to prepare it for smelting, before they knew what the outcome would be. On the other hand, it is even less plausible to attribute this discovery to some accidental fire, as mines are formed only in arid places bare of trees and plants, so that it might seem that Nature had taken precautions to withhold this fatal secret from us. The only remaining alternative, then, is that some extraordinary event, such as a volcano throwing up molten metal, will have given its witnesses the idea of imitating this operation of Nature; even then, they must also be assumed to have had a good deal of courage and foresight to undertake such strenuous labor and to anticipate so far in advance the advantages they might derive from it; which really only accords with minds already more skilled than these must have been.

As for agriculture, its principle was known long before its practice was established, and it is scarcely possible that men constantly engaged in drawing their subsistence from trees and plants would not fairly soon have the idea of how Nature proceeds in the generation of plants; but their industry probably turned in that direction only rather late, either because trees which, together with hunting and fishing, provided their food, did not require their care, or for want of knowing the use of wheat, or for want of implements to cultivate it, or for want of anticipating future need, or, finally, for want of means to prevent others from appropriating the fruit of their labor. Once they had become more industrious, they probably began by cultivating a few vegetables or roots with sharp stones or pointed sticks around their huts, long before they knew how to thresh and grind wheat, and had the implements necessary for large-scale cultivation, to say nothing of the fact that, in order to devote oneself to this occupation and sow fields, one has to decide to take an initial loss for the sake of great future gain; a foresight that is very alien to the turn of mind of savage man who, as I have said, has trouble giving thought in the morning to his needs in the evening.

The Invention of the other arts was therefore necessary to force mankind to attend to the art of agriculture. As soon as men were needed to melt and forge iron, others were needed to feed them. The more the number of workers increased, the fewer hands were engaged in providing for the common subsistence, without there being any fewer mouths to consume it; and as some had to have foods in exchange for their iron, the others finally discovered the secret of using iron to increase foods. Thus arose on the one hand plowing and agriculture, and on the other the art of working metals and multiplying their uses.

From the cultivation of land, its division necessarily followed; and from property, once recognized, the first rules of justice necessarily followed: for in order to render to each his own, each must be able to have something; moreover, as men began to extend their views to the future and all saw that they had some goods to lose, there was no one who did not have to fear reprisals against himself for the wrongs he might do to another. This origin is all the more natural as it is impossible to conceive the idea of nascent property in any other way than in terms of manual labor: for it is not clear what, more than his labor, man can put into things he has not made, in order to appropriate them. Since labor alone gives the cultivator the right to the produce of the land he has tilled, it consequently also gives him a right to the land, at least until the harvest, and thus from one year to the next, which, as it makes for continuous possession, is easily transformed into property. When the Ancients, says Grotius, gave Ceres the title legislatrix and a festival celebrated in her honor the name Thesmophoria, they thereby indicated that the division of land produced a new kind of right. Namely the right of property different from that which follows from natural law.

Things in this state could have remained equal if talents had been equal and if, for example, the use of iron and the consumption of foods had always been exactly balanced; but this proportion, which nothing maintained, was soon upset; the stronger did more work; the more skillful used his work to better advantage; the more ingenious found ways to reduce his labor; the plowman had greater need of iron, or the smith greater need of wheat, and by working equally, the one earned much while the other had trouble staying alive. This is how natural inequality imperceptibly unfolds together with unequal associations, and the differences between men, developed by their different circumstances, become more perceptible, more permanent in their effects, and begin to exercise a corresponding influence on the fate of individuals.

Things having reached this point, it is easy to imagine the rest. I shall not pause to describe the successive invention of the other arts, the progress of languages, the testing and exercise of talents, the inequalities of fortune, the use or abuse of wealth, nor all the details that attend them and which everyone can easily add. I shall limit myself to a brief glance at mankind placed in this new order of things.

Here, then, are all our faculties developed, memory and imagination brought into play, *amour propre* interested, reason become active, and the mind almost at the limit of the perfection of which it is capable. Here are all natural qualities set in action, every man's rank and fate set, not only as to the amount of their goods and the power to help or to hurt, but also as to mind, beauty, strength or skill, as to merit or talents, and, since these are the only qualities that could attract consideration, one soon had to have or to affect them; for one's own advantage one had to seem other than one in fact was. To be and to appear became two entirely different things, and from this distinction arose ostentatious display, deceitful cunning, and all the vices that follow in their wake. Looked at in another way, man, who had previously been free and independent, is now so to speak subjugated by a multitude of new needs to the whole of Nature, and especially to those of his kind, whose slave he in a sense becomes even by becoming their master; rich, he needs their services; poor, he needs their help, and moderate means do not enable him to do without them. He must therefore constantly try to interest them in his fate and to make them really or apparently find their own profit in working for his: which makes him knavish and artful with some, imperious and harsh with the rest, and places him under the necessity of deceiving all those he needs if he cannot get them to fear him and does not find it in his interest to make himself useful to them. Finally, consuming ambition, the ardent desire to raise one's relative fortune less out of genuine need than in order to place oneself above others, instils in all men a black inclination to harm one another, a secret jealousy that is all the more dangerous as it often assumes the mask of benevolence in order to strike its blow in greater safety: in a word, competition and rivalry on the one hand, conflict of interests on the other, and always the hidden desire to profit at another's expense; all these evils are the first effect of property, and the inseparable train of nascent inequality.

Before its representative signs were invented, wealth could scarcely consist in anything but land and livestock, the only real goods that men can possess. Now, once inheritances had increased in number and size to the point where they covered all the land and all adjoined one another, men could no longer aggrandize themselves except at one another's expense, and the supernumeraries whom weakness or indolence had kept from acquiring an inheritance of their own, grown poor without having lost anything because they alone had not changed while everything was changing around them, were obliged to receive or to seize their subsistence from the hands of the rich; and from this began to arise, according to the different characters of the poor and the rich, domination and servitude, or violence and plunder. The rich, for their part, had scarcely become acquainted with the pleasure of dominating than they disdained all other pleasures, and using their old slaves to subject new ones, they thought only of subjugating and enslaving their neighbors; like those ravenous wolves which once they have tasted human flesh scorn all other food, and from then on want to devour only men.

Thus, as the most powerful or the most miserable claimed, on the basis of their strength or of their needs, a kind of right to another person's goods, equivalent, according to them, to the right of property, the breakdown of equality was followed by the most frightful disorder: thus the usurpations of the rich, the banditry of the poor, the unbridled passions of all, stifling natural pity and the still weak voice of justice, made men greedy, ambitious, and wicked. A perpetual conflict arose between the right of the stronger and the right of the first occupant, which only led to fights and murders. Nascent society gave way to the most horrible state of war: humankind, debased and devastated, no longer able to turn back or to renounce its wretched acquisitions, and working only to its shame by the abuse of the faculties that do it honor, brought itself to the brink of ruin.

> *Shocked by the novelty of the evil,*
> *at once rich and miserable,*
> *He seeks to escape his wealth,*
> *and hates what he had just prayed for.*

It is not possible that men should not at last have reflected on such a miserable situation, and on the calamities besetting them. The rich, above all, must soon have sensed how disadvantageous to them was a perpetual war of which they alone bore the full cost, and in which everyone risked his life while only some also risked goods. Besides, regardless of how they painted their usurpations, they realized well enough that they were only based on a precarious and abusive right, and that since they had been acquired solely by force, force could deprive them of them without their having any reason for complaint. Even those whom industriousness alone had enriched could scarcely base their property on better titles. No matter if they said: It is I who built this wall; I earned this plot by my labor. Who set its boundaries for you, they could be answered; and by virtue of what do you lay claim to being paid at our expense for labor we did not impose on you? Do you not know that a great many of your brothers perish or suffer from need of what you have in excess, and that you required the express and unanimous consent of humankind to appropriate for yourself anything from the common subsistence above and beyond your own? Lacking valid reasons to justify and sufficient strength to defend himself; easily crushing an individual, but himself crushed by troops of bandits; alone against all, and unable, because of their mutual jealousies, to unite with his equals against enemies united by the common hope of plunder, the rich, under the pressure of necessity, at last conceived the most well-considered project ever to enter the human mind; to use even his attackers' forces in his favor, to make his adversaries his defenders, to instill in them other maxims and to give them different institutions, as favorable to himself as natural right was contrary to him.

To this end, after exhibiting to his neighbors the horror of a situation that armed all of them against one another, that made their possessions as burdensome to them as their needs, and in which no one found safety in either poverty or wealth, he easily invented specious reasons to bring them around to his goal: 'Let us unite,' he told them, 'to protect the weak from oppression, restrain the ambitious, and secure for everyone the possession of what belongs to him: Let us institute rules of justice and peace to which all are obliged to conform, which favor no one, and which in a way make up for the vagaries of fortune by subjecting the powerful and the weak alike to mutual duties. In a word, instead of turning our forces against one another, let us gather them into a supreme power that might govern us according to wise laws, protect and defend all the members of the association, repulse common enemies, and preserve us in everlasting concord.'

Much less than the equivalent of this Discourse was needed to sway crude, easily seduced men who, in any event, had too much business to sort out among themselves to be able to do without arbiters, and too much greed and ambition to be able to do for long without masters. All ran toward their chains in the belief that they were securing their freedom; for while they had enough reason to sense the advantages of a political establishment, they had not enough experience to foresee its dangers; those most capable of anticipating the abuses were precisely those who counted on profiting from them, and even the wise saw that they had to make up their mind to sacrifice one part of their freedom to preserve the other, as a wounded man has his arm cut off to save the rest of his body.

Such was, or must have been, the origin of society and of laws, which gave the weak new fetters and the rich new forces, irreversibly destroyed natural freedom, forever fixed the law of property and inequality, transformed a skillful usurpation into an irrevocable right, and for the profit of a few ambitious men henceforth subjugated the whole of mankind to labor, servitude and misery. It is easy to see how the establishment of a single society made the establishment of all the others indispensable, and how, in order to stand up to united forces, it became necessary to unite in turn. Societies, multiplying and expanding rapidly, soon covered the entire face of the earth, and it was no longer possible to find a single corner anywhere in the universe where one might cast off the yoke and withdraw one's head out of the way of the often ill-guided sword everyone perpetually saw suspended over it. Civil right having thus become the common rule of the citizens, the law of nature no longer obtained except between different Societies where, under the name of right of nations, it was tempered by a few tacit conventions in order to make commerce possible and to replace natural commiseration which, losing in the relations between one society and another almost all the force it had in the relations between one man and another, lives on only in a few great cosmopolitan souls who cross the imaginary boundaries that separate Peoples and, following the example of the sovereign being that created them, embrace the whole of mankind in their benevolence. [*Discourse*, Part ii]

Social contract (1762)

The most ancient of all societies and the only natural one is that of the family. Even so children remain bound to the father only as long as they need him for their preservation. As soon as that need ceases, the natural bond dissolves. The children, exempt from the obedience they owe the father, the father exempt from the cares he owed the children, all equally return to independence. If they remain united, they are no longer so naturally but voluntarily, and even the family maintains itself only by convention.

This common freedom is a consequence of man's nature. His first law is to attend to his own preservation, his first cares are those he owes himself, and since, as soon as he has reached the age of reason, he is sole judge of the means proper to preserve himself, he becomes his own master.

The family is, then, if you will, the first model of political societies; the chief is the image of the father, the people are the image of the children, and all, being born equal and free, alienate their freedom only for the sake of their utility. The only difference is that in the family the father's love for his children repays him for the cares he bestows on them, and that in the State the pleasure of commanding takes the place of the chief's lack of love for his peoples.

Grotius denies that all human power is established for the sake of the governed: he gives slavery as an example. His most frequent mode of argument is always to establish right by fact. One could use a more consistent method, but not one more favorable to tyrants.

So that, according to Grotius, it is an open question whether humankind belongs to a hundred men, or whether those hundred men belong to humankind, and throughout his book he appears to incline to the first opinion: that is also Hobbes' sentiment. Here, then, is humankind, divided into herds of cattle, each with its chief who tends it to devour it.

As a shepherd is of a nature superior to his flock's, so too are the shepherds of men, who are their chiefs, of a nature superior to their peoples'. This is how, according to Philo, the Emperor Caligula reasoned; concluding rather well from this analogy that kings were Gods, or that peoples were beasts.

Caligula's reasoning amounts to that of Hobbes and of Grotius. Aristotle before all of them had also said that men are not naturally equal, but that some were born for slavery and others for domination.

Aristotle was right, but he mistook the effect for the cause. Any man born in slavery is born for slavery, nothing could be more certain. Slaves lose everything in their chains, even the desire to be rid of them; they love their servitude, as the companions of Ulysses loved their brutishness. Hence, if there are slaves by nature, it is because there were slaves contrary to nature. Force made the first slaves, their cowardice perpetuated them.

I have said nothing about King Adam, or about emperor Noah, father of three great monarchs who among themselves divided the universe, as did the children of Saturn, whom some believed they recognized in them. I hope my moderation will be appreciated; for since I am a direct descendant from one of these princes, and perhaps from the elder branch, for all I know, I might, upon verification of titles, find I am the legitimate King of humankind. Be that as it may, it cannot be denied that Adam was Sovereign of the world as Robinson was of his island, as long as he was its sole inhabitant; and what made this empire convenient was that the monarch, secure on his throne, had neither rebellions, nor wars, nor conspirators to fear. [*Social contract*, i, 2: 'Of the first societies']

I assume men having reached the point where the obstacles that interfere with their preservation in the state of nature prevail by their resistance over the forces which each individual can muster to maintain himself in that state. Then that primitive state can no longer subsist, and humankind would perish if it did not change its way of being.

Now, since men cannot engender new forces, but only unite and direct those that exist, they are left with no other means of self-preservation than to form, by aggregation, a sum of forces that might prevail over those obstacles' resistance, to set them in motion by a single impetus, and make them act in concert.

This sum of forces can only arise from the cooperation of many: but since each man's force and freedom are his primary instruments of self-preservation, how can he commit them without harming himself, and without neglecting the cares he owes himself? This difficulty, in relation to my subject, can be stated in the following terms.

'To find a form of association that will defend and protect the person and goods of each associate with the full common force, and by means of which each, uniting with all, nevertheless obey only himself and remain as free as before.' This is the fundamental problem to which the social contract provides the solution.

The clauses of this contract are so completely determined by the nature of the act that the slightest modification would render them null and void; so that although they may never have been formally stated, they are everywhere the same, everywhere tacitly admitted and recognized; until, the social compact having been violated, everyone is thereupon restored to his original rights and resumes his natural freedom while losing the conventional freedom for which he renounced it.

These clauses, rightly understood, all come down to just one, namely the total alienation of each associate with all of his rights to the whole community: For, in the first place, since each gives himself entirely, the condition is equal for all, and since the condition is equal for all, no one has any interest in making it burdensome to the rest.

Moreover, since the alienation is made without reservation, the union is as perfect as it can be, and no associate has anything further to claim: For if individuals were left some rights, then, since there would be no common superior who might adjudicate between them and the public, each, being judge in his own case on some issue, would soon claim to be so on all, the state of nature would subsist and the association necessarily become tyrannical or empty.

Finally, each, by giving himself to all, gives himself to no one, and since there is no associate over whom one does not acquire the same right as one grants him over oneself, one gains the equivalent of all one loses, and more force to preserve what one has.

If, then, one sets aside everything that is not of the essence of the social compact, one finds that it can be reduced to the following terms: *Each of us puts his person and his full power in common under the supreme direction of the general will; and in a body we receive each member as an indivisible part of the whole.*

At once, in place of the private person of each contracting party, this act of association produces a moral and collective body made up of as many members as the assembly has voices, and which receives by this same act its unity, its common *self*, its life and its will. The public person thus formed by the union of all the others formerly assumed the name *city* and now assumes that of *republic* or of *body politic*, which its members call *state* when it is passive, *sovereign* when active, *power* when comparing it to similar bodies. As for the associates, they collectively assume the name *people* and individually call themselves *citizens* as participants in the sovereign authority, and *subjects* as subjected to the laws of the state. But these terms are often confused and mistaken for one another; it is enough to be able to distinguish them where they are used in their precise sense. [*Social contract,* i, 6: 'Of the social pact']

This formula shows that the act of association involves a reciprocal engagement between the public and private individuals, and that each individual, by contracting, so to speak, with himself, finds himself engaged in a two-fold relation: namely, as member of the Sovereign toward private individuals, and as a member of the state toward the Sovereign. But here the maxim of civil right, that no one is bound by engagements toward himself, does not apply; for there is a great difference between assuming an obligation toward oneself, and assuming a responsibility toward a whole of which one is a part.

It should also be noted that the public deliberation which can obligate all subjects toward the Sovereign because of the two different relations in terms of which each subject is viewed cannot, for the opposite reason, obligate the Sovereign toward itself, and that it is therefore contrary to the nature of the body politic for the Sovereign to impose on itself a law which it cannot break. Since the Sovereign can consider itself only in terms of one and the same relation, it is then in the same situation as a private individual contracting with himself: which shows that there is not, nor can there be, any kind of fundamental law that is obligatory for the body of the people, not even the social contract. This does not mean that this body cannot perfectly well enter into engagements with others about anything that does not detract from this contract; for with regard to foreigners it becomes a simple being, an individual.

But the body politic or Sovereign, since it owes its being solely to the sanctity of the contract, can never obligate itself, even toward another, to anything that detracts from that original act, such as to alienate any part of itself or to subject itself to another Sovereign. To violate the act by which it exists would be to annihilate itself, and what is nothing produces nothing.

As soon as this multitude is thus united in one body, one cannot injure one of the members without attacking the body, and still less can one injure the body without the members being affected. Thus duty and interest alike obligate the contracting parties to help one another, and the same men must strive to combine in this two-fold relation all the advantages attendant on it.

Now the Sovereign, since it is formed entirely of the individuals who make it up, has not and cannot have any interests contrary to theirs; consequently the sovereign power has no need of a guarantor toward the subjects, because it is impossible for the body to want to harm all of its members, and we shall see later that it cannot harm any one of them in particular. The Sovereign, by the mere fact that it is, is always everything it ought to be.

But this is not the case regarding the subjects' relations to the Sovereign, and notwithstanding the common interest, the Sovereign would have no guarantee of the subjects' engagements if it did not find means to ensure their fidelity.

Indeed each individual may, as a man, have a particular will contrary to or different from the general will he has as a citizen. His particular interest may speak to him quite differently from the common interest; his absolute and naturally independent existence may lead him to look upon what he owes to the common cause as a gratuitous contribution, the loss of which will harm others less than its payment burdens him and, by considering the moral person that constitutes the state as a being of reason because it is not a man, he would enjoy the rights of a citizen without being willing to fulfil the duties of a subject; an injustice, the progress of which would cause the ruin of the body politic.

Hence for the social compact not to be an empty formula, it tacitly includes the following engagement which alone can give force to the rest, that whoever refuses to obey the general will shall be constrained to do so by the entire body: which means nothing other than that he shall be forced to be free; for this is the condition which, by giving each citizen to the fatherland, guarantees him against all personal dependence; the condition which is the device and makes for the operation of the political machine, and alone renders legitimate civil engagements which would otherwise be absurd, tyrannical, and liable to the most enormous abuses. [*Social contract*, i, 7: 'Of the Sovereign']

This transition from the state of nature to the civil state produces a most remarkable change in man by substituting justice for instinct in his conduct, and endowing his actions with the morality they previously lacked. Only then, when the voice of duty succeeds physical impulsion and right succeeds appetite, does man, who until then had looked only to himself, see himself forced to act on other principles, and to consult his reason before listening to his inclinations. Although in this state he deprives himself of several advantages he has from nature, he gains such great advantages in return, his faculties are exercised and developed, his ideas enlarged, his sentiments ennobled, his entire soul is elevated to such an extent, that if the abuses of this new condition did not often degrade him to beneath the condition he has left, he should ceaselessly bless the happy moment which wrested him from it forever, and out of a stupid and bounded animal made an intelligent being and a man.

Let us reduce this entire balance to terms easy to compare. What man loses by the social contract is his natural freedom and an unlimited right to everything that tempts him and he can reach; what he gains is civil freedom and property in everything he possesses. In order not to be mistaken about these compensations, one has to distinguish clearly between natural freedom which has no other bounds than the individual's forces, and civil freedom which is limited by the general will, and between possession which is merely the effect of force or the right of the first occupant, and property which can only be founded on a positive title.

To the preceding one might add to the credit of the civil state moral freedom, which alone makes man truly the master of himself; for the impulsion of mere appetite is slavery, and obedience to the law one has prescribed to oneself is freedom. But I have already said too much on this topic, and the philosophical meaning of the word *freedom* is not my subject here. [*Social contract*, I, 8: 'Of the civil state']

The first and the most important consequence of the principles established so far is that the general will alone can direct the forces of the State according to the end of its institution, which is the common good: for while the opposition of particular interests made the establishment of societies necessary, it is the agreement of these same interests which made it possible. What these different interests have in common is what forms the social bond, and if there were not some point on which all interests agree, no society could exist. Now it is solely in terms of this common interest that society ought to be governed.

I say, then, that sovereignty, since it is nothing but the exercise of the general will, can never be alienated, and that the sovereign, which is nothing but a collective being, can only be represented by itself; power can well be transferred, but not will.

Indeed, while it is not impossible that a particular will agree with the general will on some point, it is in any event impossible for this agreement to be lasting and constant; for the particular will tends, by its nature, to partiality, and the general will to equality. It is even more impossible to have a guarantee of this agreement, even if it always obtained; it would be an effect not of art, but of chance. The Sovereign may well say, I currently will what a given man wills or at least what he says he wills; but it cannot say: what this man is going to will tomorrow, I too shall will it; since it is absurd for the will to shackle itself for the future, and since no will can consent to anything contrary to the good of the being that wills. If, then, the people promises simply to obey, it dissolves itself by this very act, it loses its quality of being a people; as soon as there is a master, there is no more sovereign, and the body politic is destroyed forthwith.

This is not to say that the commands of the chiefs may not be taken for general wills as long as the sovereign is free to oppose them and does not do so. In such a case the people's consent has to be presumed from universal silence. This will be explained more fully. [*Social contract*, ii, i: 'That sovereignty is inalienable']

For the same reason that sovereignty is inalienable, it is indivisible. For either the will is general or it is not; it is either the will of the body of the people, or that of only a part. In the first case, the declaration of this will is an act of sovereignty and constitutes law; in the second case it is merely a particular will, or an act of magistracy; at most it is a decree.

But our politicians, unable to divide sovereignty in its principle, divide it in its object; they divide it into force and will, into legislative and executive power, into rights of taxation, justice and war, into domestic administration and the power to conduct foreign affairs: sometimes they mix up all these parts and sometimes they separate them; they turn the Sovereign into a being that is fantastical and formed of disparate pieces; it is as if they were putting together man out of several bodies one of which had eyes, another arms, another feet, and nothing else. Japanese conjurors are said to carve up a child before the spectators' eyes, then, throwing all of its members into the air one after the other, they make the child fall back down alive and all reassembled. That is more or less what our politicians' tricks are like; having dismembered the social body by a sleight-of-hand worthy of the fairground, they put the pieces back together no one knows how.

This error comes from not having framed precise notions of sovereign authority, and from having taken what were mere emanations from this authority for parts of this authority itself. Thus, for example, the act of declaring war and that of making peace have been regarded as acts of sovereignty, which they are not; for neither of these acts is a law but only an application of the law, a particular act which decides a case, as will clearly be seen once the idea that attaches to the word *law* has been fixed.

By examining the other divisions in the same way, one would discover that whenever one believes one sees sovereignty divided, one is mistaken, that the rights which one takes for parts of this sovereignty are all subordinate to it, and always presuppose supreme wills which these rights simply implement.

It would be difficult to exaggerate how much this lack of precision has

clouded the conclusions of writers on matters of political right when they sought
to adjudicate the respective rights of kings and peoples by the principles they had
established. Anyone can see in chapters three and four of the first Book of Grotius
how that learned man and his translator Barbeyrac get entangled and constrained
by their sophisms, fearful of saying too much or not saying enough according to
their views, and of offending the interests they had to reconcile. Grotius, a refugee
in France, discontented with his fatherland, and wanting to pay court to Louis
XIII to whom his book is dedicated, spares nothing to despoil peoples of all their
rights, and to invest kings with them as artfully as possible. This would certainly
also have been to the taste of Barbeyrac, who dedicated his translation to King
George I of England. But unfortunately the expulsion of James II, which he calls
an abdication, forced him to be on his guard, to equivocate, to be evasive, in
order not to make a usurper of William. If these two writers had adopted the two
principles, all their difficulties would have been solved, and they would always
have been consistent; but they would have sadly told the truth and paid court
only to the people. Now, truth does not lead to fortune, and the people confers
no ambassadorships, professorships or pensions. [*Social contract*, ii, 2: 'That sovereignty is indivisible']

If the state or the city is only a moral person whose life consists in the union of
its members, and if the most important of its cares is the care for its self-
preservation, then it has to have some universal and coercive force to move and
arrange each part in the manner most conformable to the whole. Just as nature
gives each man absolute power over his members, the social pact gives the body
politic absolute power over all of its members, and it is this same power which,
directed by the general will, bears, as I have said, the name of sovereignty.

But in addition to the public person, we must consider the private persons who
make it up, and whose life and freedom are naturally independent of it. It is
therefore important to distinguish clearly between the respective rights of the
citizens and of the Sovereign, as well as between duties which the former have to
fulfill as subjects, and the natural right which they must enjoy as men.

It is agreed that each man alienates by the social pact only that portion of his
power, his goods, his freedom, which it is important for the community to be
able to use, but it should also be agreed to that the Sovereign is alone judge of
that importance.

All the services a citizen can render the state, he owes to it as soon as the

Sovereign requires them; but the Sovereign, for its part, cannot burden the subjects with any shackles that are useless to the community; it cannot even will to do so: for under the law of reason nothing is done without cause, any more than under the law of nature.

The commitments which bind us to the social body are obligatory only because they are mutual, and their nature is such that in fulfilling them one cannot work for others without also working for oneself. Why is the general will always upright, and why do all consistently will each one's happiness, if not because there is no one who does not appropriate the word *each* to himself, and think of himself as he votes for all? Which proves that the equality of right and the notion of justice which it produces follows from each one's preference for himself and hence from the nature of man; that the general will, to be truly such, must be so in its object as well as in its essence, that it must issue from all in order to apply to all, and that it loses its natural rectitude when it tends toward some individual and determinate object; for then, judging what is foreign to us, we have no true principle of equity to guide us.

Indeed, whenever what is at issue is a particular fact or right regarding a point not regulated by a general and prior convention, the affair grows contentious. In such a suit, where interested private individuals are one of the parties, and the public the other, I do not see what law should be followed or what judge should pronounce judgment. It would be ridiculous, under these circumstances, to try to invoke an express decision of the general will, which can only be the decision of one of the parties, and is, therefore, as far as the other party is concerned, nothing but a foreign, particular will which on this occasion is inclined to injustice and subject to error. Thus, just as a particular will cannot represent the general will, so the general will changes in nature when it has a particular object, and it cannot, being general, pronounce judgment on a particular man or fact. For example, when the people of Athens appointed or cashiered its chiefs, bestowed honors on one, imposed penalties on another, and by a multitude of particular decrees indiscriminately performed all the acts of government, the people no longer had a general will properly so called; it no longer acted as a Sovereign but as a magistrate. This will appear contrary to the commonly held ideas, but I must be allowed the time to set forth my own.

In view of this, one has to understand that what generalizes the will is not so much the number of voices, as it is the common interest which unites them: for in this institution, everyone necessarily submits to the conditions which he imposes on others; an admirable agreement between interest and justice which confers on common deliberations a character of equity that is seen to vanish in the discussion of any particular affair, for want of a common interest which unites and identifies the rule of the judge with that of the party.

From whatever side one traces one's way back to the principle, one always reaches the same conclusion: namely, that the social pact establishes among the citizens an equality such that all commit themselves under the same conditions and must all enjoy the same rights. Thus by the nature of the pact every act of sovereignty, that is to say every genuine act of the general will, either obligates or favors all citizens equally, so that the Sovereign knows only the body of the nation and does not single out any one of those who make it up. What, then, is, properly, an act of sovereignty? It is not a convention of the superior with the inferior, but a convention of the body with each one of its members: A convention which is legitimate because it is based on the social contract, equitable because it is common to all, and secure because the public force and the supreme power are its guarantors. So long as subjects are subjected only to conventions such as these, they obey no one, but only their own will; and to ask how far the respective rights of Sovereign and citizens extend is to ask how far the citizens can commit themselves to one another, each to all, and all to each.

From this it is apparent that the sovereign power, absolute, sacred, and inviolable though it is, does not and cannot exceed the limits of the general conventions, and that everyone may fully dispose of such of his goods and freedom as are left him by these conventions: so that it is never right for the Sovereign to burden one subject more than another, because it then turns into a particular affair, and its power is no longer competent.

These distinctions once admitted, it is so [evidently] false that the social contract involves any renunciation on the part of individuals, that [rather] as a result of the contract their situation really proves to be preferable to what it had been before, and that instead of an alienation they have only made an advantageous exchange of an uncertain and precarious way of being in favor of a more secure and better one, of natural independence in favor of freedom, of the power to harm others in favor of their own security, and of their force which others could overwhelm in favor of right made invincible by the social union. Their very life which they have dedicated to the state is constantly protected by it, and when they risk it for its defense, what are they doing but returning to it what they have received from it? What are they doing that they would not have done more frequently and at greater peril in the state of nature, when, waging inevitable fights, they would be defending the means of preserving their lives by risking them? All have to fight for the fatherland if need be, it is true, but then no one ever has to fight for himself. Isn't it nevertheless a gain to risk for the sake of what gives us security just a part of what we would have to risk for our own sakes if we were deprived of this security? [*Social contract*, II, 4: 'Of the limits of sovereign power']

To discover the best rules of society suited to each nation would require a superior intelligence who saw all of man's passions and experienced none of them, who had no relation to our nature yet knew it thoroughly, whose happiness was independent of us and who was nevertheless willing to care for ours; finally, one who, preparing his distant glory in the progress of times, could work in one century and enjoy the reward in another. It would require gods to give men laws.

The same reasoning Caligula made as to fact, Plato made as to right in defining the civil or royal man he seeks in his book on ruling; but if it is true that a great prince is a rare man, what of a great lawgiver? The first need only follow the model which the other must propose. He is the mechanic who invents the machine, the first is nothing but the workman who assembles and operates it. At the birth of societies, says Montesquieu, it is the chiefs of republics who make the institution, and after that it is the institutions that form the chiefs of republics.

Anyone who dares to institute a people must feel capable of, so to speak, changing human nature; of transforming each individual who by himself is a perfect and solitary whole into part of a larger whole from which that individual would as it were receive his life and his being; of weakening man's constitution in order to strengthen it; of substituting a partial and moral existence for the independent and physical existence we have all received from nature. In a word, he must take from man his own forces in order to give him forces which are foreign to him and of which he cannot make use without the help of others. The more these natural forces are dead and destroyed, the greater and more lasting are the acquired ones, and the more solid and lasting also is the institution: So that when each citizen is nothing and can do nothing except with all the others, and the force acquired by the whole is equal or superior to the sum of the natural forces of all the individuals, the legislation may be said to be at the highest pitch of perfection it can reach.

The lawgiver is in every respect an extraordinary man in the state. While he must be so by his genius, he is no less so by his office. It is not magistracy, it is not sovereignty. This office which gives the republic its constitution has no place in its constitution: It is a singular and superior function that has nothing in common with human empire; for just as he who has command over men ought not to have command over the laws, so neither should he who has command over the laws have command over men; otherwise the laws, as ministers to his passions, would often only perpetuate his injustices, and he could never avoid having particular views vitiate the sanctity of his work.

When Lycurgus gave his fatherland laws, he began by abdicating the kingship. It was the custom of most Greek cities to entrust the establishment of their laws to foreigners. The modern republics of Italy often imitated this practice: the Republic of Geneva did so as well and to good effect. Rome in its finest period witnessed the rebirth of all the crimes of tyranny in its midst, and found itself on the verge of perishing, for having united the legislative authority and the sovereign power in the same hands.

Yet the Decemvirs themselves never arrogated to themselves the right to have any law passed solely on their authority. *Nothing we propose,* they used to say to the people, *can become law without your consent. Romans, be yourselves the authors of the laws that are to make for your happiness.*

Thus he who drafts the laws has, then, or should have no legislative right, and the people itself cannot divest itself of this non-transferable right, even if it wanted to do so; because according to the fundamental pact only the general will obligates particulars, and there can never be any assurance that a particular will conforms to the general will until it has been submitted to the free suffrage of the people: I have said this already, but it is not useless to repeat it.

So that one finds at one and the same time two apparently incompatible things in the work of legislation: an undertaking beyond human force, and to execute it an authority that is nil.

A further difficulty which deserves attention. The wise who would speak to the vulgar in their own rather than in the vulgar language will not be understood by them. Yet there are a thousand kinds of ideas which it is impossible to translate into the language of the people. Views that are too general and aims that are too remote are equally beyond its reach; each individual, appreciating no other scheme of government than that which bears directly on his particular interest, has difficulty perceiving the advantages he is supposed to derive from the constant privations required by good laws. For a nascent people to be capable of appreciating sound maxims of politics and of following the fundamental rules of reason of state, the effect would have to become the cause, the social spirit which is to be the work of the institution would have to preside over the institution itself, and men would have to be prior to laws what they ought to become by means of them. Thus, since the lawgiver can use neither force nor reasoning, he must of necessity have recourse to an authority of a different order, which might be able to rally without violence and to persuade without convincing.

This is what has at all times forced the fathers of nations to resort to the intervention of heaven and to honor the Gods with their own wisdom, so that peoples, subject to the laws of the state as to those of nature, and recognizing the same power in the formation of man and in that of the city, freely obey the yoke of public felicity, and bear it with docility.

This sublime reason which rises beyond the reach of vulgar men it is whose decisions the lawgiver places in the mouth of the immortals, in order to rally by divine authority those whom human prudence could not move. But it is not up to just anyone to make the Gods speak or to have them believe him when he proclaims himself their interpreter. The great soul of the lawgiver is the true miracle which must prove his mission. Any man can carve tablets of stone, bribe an oracle, feign secret dealings with some divinity, train a bird to speak in his ear, or find other crude ways to impress the people. Someone who can do only that much might even by chance succeed in assembling a flock of fools, but he will never found an empire, and his extravagant work will soon perish together with him. Empty tricks form a passing bond, only wisdom can make it lasting. The Jewish law which still endures, that of Ishmael's child which has ruled half the world for ten centuries, still proclaims today the great men who dictated them; and while prideful philosophy or blind party spirit regards them as nothing but lucky impostors, the true politician admires in their institutions the great and powerful genius which presides over enduring establishments.

One should not from all this conclude with Warburton that among us politics and religion have a common object, but rather that at the origin of nations the one serves as the instrument of the other. [*Social contract*, II, 7: 'Of the law-giver']

Just as an architect, before putting up a large building, observes and tests the ground to see whether it can support the weight, so the wise institutor does not begin by drawing up laws good in themselves, but first examines whether the people for whom he intends them is fit to bear them. That is why Plato refused to give laws to the Arcadians and Cyrenians, since he knew that both peoples were rich and could not tolerate equality: that is why there were good laws and wicked men in Crete, for Minos had done no more than to discipline a vice-ridden people.

A thousand nations on earth have been brilliant which could never have tolerated good laws, and even those which could have tolerated them could have done so only for a very brief period in the course of their entire lifetime. Peoples, like men, are docile only in their youth, with age they grow incorrigible; once customs are established and prejudices rooted, it is a dangerous and futile undertaking to try to reform them; the people cannot tolerate having their evils touched even if only to destroy them, like those stupid and cowardly patients who tremble at the sight of a doctor.

This is not to say that, just as some illnesses overwhelm men's minds and deprive them of the memory of the past, there may not also sometimes occur periods of violence in the lifetime of states when revolutions do to peoples what certain crises do to individuals, when horror of the past takes the place of forgetting, and when the state aflame with civil wars is so to speak reborn from its ashes and recovers the vigor of youth as it escapes death's embrace. Such was Sparta at the time of Lycurgus, such was Rome after the Tarquins; and such, among us, were Holland and Switzerland after the expulsion of the tyrants.

But such events are rare; they are exceptions the reason for which is always found in the particular constitution of the state in question. They could not even happen twice with the same people, for a people can free itself as long as it is merely barbarous, but it can no longer do so once the civil mainspring is worn out. Then troubles may destroy it while revolutions may not be able to restore it, and as soon as its chains are broken, it falls apart and ceases to exist: From then on it needs a master, not a liberator. Free peoples, remember this maxim: Freedom can be gained; but it is never recovered.

For Nations as for men there is a time of maturity for which one has to wait before subjecting them to laws; but the maturity of a people is not always easy to recognize, and if one acts too soon the work is ruined. One people is amenable to discipline at birth, another is not amenable to it after ten centuries. The Russians will never be truly politically organized because they were politically organized too early. Peter's genius was imitative; he did not have true genius, the kind that creates and makes everything out of nothing. Some of the things he did were good, most were misguided. He saw that his people was barbarous, he did not see that it lacked the maturity for political order; he wanted to civilize it when all it needed was to be made warlike. He wanted from the first to make Germans, Englishmen, whereas he should have begun by making Russians; he prevented his subjects from ever becoming what they could be by persuading them that they are what they are not. In the same way a French tutor forms his pupil for a moment's brilliance in childhood, and to be nothing after that. The Russian Empire will try to subjugate Europe, and will itself be subjugated. The Tartars, its subjects or neighbors, will become its masters and ours: This revolution seems to me inevitable. All the Kings of Europe are working in concert to hasten it. [*Social contract*, ii, 8: 'Of the people']

Just as nature has set limits to the stature of a well-formed man, beyond which it makes only giants and dwarfs, so, too, with regard to the best constitution of a state, there are bounds to the size it can have in order not to be either too large to be well governed, or too small to be self-sustaining. In every body politic there is a maximum of force which it cannot exceed, and from which it often strays by dint of growing too large. The more the social bond stretches, the looser it grows, and in general a small state is proportionately stronger than a large one.

A thousand reasons prove this maxim. First, administration grows more diffi-cult at great distances just as a weight grows heavier at the end of a larger lever. It also grows more burdensome as the levels of administration multiply; for, to begin with, each city has its own [administration] for which the people pays, each district has its own for which the people again pays, then each province, then the large governments, the satrapies, the viceregencies, which always have to be paid more the higher up one climbs, and always at the expense of the wretched people; finally comes the supreme administration which crushes everything. All these taxes upon taxes steadily exhaust the subjects; far from being better governed by these various agencies, they are less well governed than if they had just one over them. Yet hardly any resources are left over for emergencies, and when they have to be drawn on, the state is always on the brink of ruin.

Nor is this all; not only is the government less vigorous and less prompt in enforcing the laws, preventing provocations, correcting abuses, thwarting sedi-tious undertakings which may be getting hatched in outlying areas; but also the people has less affection for its chiefs whom it never sees, for a fatherland which in its eyes is as [big as] the world, and for its fellow-citizens most of whom are strangers to it. The same laws cannot suit such a variety of different provinces with different morals, living in widely different climates, unable to tolerate the same form of government. Different laws give rise to nothing but trouble and confusion among peoples who, living under the same chiefs and in constant contact with one another, move back and forth from their own territory to their neighbors', inter-marry, and, since they are then subject to different customs, never quite know whether their patrimony is really theirs. Talents are hidden, virtues unknown, vices unpunished in this multitude of men who do not know one another, and whom the seat of the supreme administration has brought together in one place. The Chiefs, overwhelmed by public affairs, see nothing by themselves, clerks govern the State. In the end the measures which have to be taken to maintain the general authority, an authority which so many distant officials want either to elude or take advantage of, absorb all public attention, there is none left for the people's happiness, and scarcely any left for its defense in an emergency, and that is how a body too large for its constitution collapses and perishes, crushed under its own weight.

Again, a state has to provide itself with some base so as to be solid, so that it can withstand the shocks it is bound to experience and the efforts it will be compelled to make to sustain itself: for all peoples have a kind of centrifugal force by which they constantly act against one another and tend to enlarge themselves at their neighbors' expense, like Descartes's vortices. Thus the weak are in danger of being swallowed up before long, and none can preserve itself except by establishing a kind of equilibrium with all the others, which would more or less equalize the pressure all around.

This shows that there are reasons to expand and reasons to contract, and it is not the least of the politician's talents to find the proportion between these two sets of reasons which most favors the preservation of the state. In general it may be said that the first, since they are merely external and relative, should be subordinated to the others, which are internal and absolute; a healthy and strong constitution is the first thing to strive for, and one should rely more on the vigor born of a good government, than on the resources provided by a large territory.

Still, States have been known which were so constituted that the necessity of conquests entered into their very constitution, and which were forced constantly to expand in order to maintain themselves. They may have been very pleased by this happy necessity which, together with the limitation on their size, however, also showed them the inevitable moment of their fall. [*Social contract*, II, 9]

A body politic can be measured in two ways, by the extent of its territory and by the number of its people, and an appropriate ratio has to obtain between these two measures for the state to be given its genuine [389] size: The men make up the state, and the land feeds the men; thus the ratio requires that there be enough land to support its inhabitants, and as many inhabitants as the land can feed. It is in this proportion that the maximum force of a given number of people consists; for if there is too much land its defense is burdensome, its cultivation deficient, its produce superfluous; this is the proximate cause of defensive wars; if there is not enough land, the state finds itself at its neighbors' discretion for the supplement [it needs]; this is the proximate cause of offensive wars. Any people which, because of its location, has no other alternative than commerce or war is inherently weak; it is dependent on its neighbors; it is dependent on circumstances; it can never have any but a precarious and brief existence. Either it subjugates and changes its situation, or it is subjugated and is nothing. It can preserve its freedom only by being very small or very large.

It is therefore impossible to calculate a fixed ratio between the amount of land and the number of men each requires; because of the differences in properties of the soil, its degrees of fertility, the nature of its products, the influence of climates, as much as because of the differences in temperaments one observes among the men who live in these different climates, some of whom consume little in a fertile country, and others who consume much with a harsh soil. One also has to take into account the greater or lesser fertility of the women, what the country may offer that is more or less favorable to the growth of population, the number of people the lawgiver can hope to contribute to the population by the institutions he establishes; so that he should not base his judgment on what he sees but on what he foresees, nor focus as much on the present state of the population as on the state it should naturally reach. Finally, there are a thousand occasions when particular accidental features of a given place require or permit taking up more land than appears needed. Thus men will spread out a good deal in a mountainous country where the natural produce, namely woods, pastures, require less work, where experience teaches that women are more fertile than in the plains, and where large stretches of sloping terrain leave only a small horizontal band which alone should be counted as land available for vegetation. By contrast, men can draw together at the edge of the sea, even among rocks and sand that are nearly barren; because there fishing can in large measure substitute for products of the earth, because men have to live more closely assembled to repulse pirates, and because, besides, it is easier to rid the country of its excess population by colonies.

To these conditions for the institution of a people, one more has to be added which cannot replace any other, but without which all the rest are useless: the enjoyment of prosperity and peace; for when a state is being organized, like when a battalion is drawing up in formation, is the time when the body is least able to resist and easiest to destroy. One would offer better resistance at a time of absolute disorder than at a time of fermentation when everyone is preoccupied with his rank rather than with the peril. If a war, a famine, a sedition were to arise in such a time of crisis, the state will inevitably be overthrown.

Not that many governments have not been established during such storms; but then it is those governments themselves that destroy the state. Usurpers invariably bring about such times of trouble or choose them and, taking advantage of the public panic, get destructive laws passed which the people would never adopt when calm. The choice of the moment of institution is one of the most reliable features by which to distinguish the work of the lawgiver from the tyrant's.

What people, then, is fit for legislation? One which, while finding itself already bound together by some union of origin, interest, or convention, has not yet borne the true yoke of laws; one with neither deep-rooted customs nor deep-rooted superstitions; one which is not in fear of being overrun by a sudden invasion; which without taking part in its neighbors' quarrels can resist each one of them by itself, or enlist the help of one to repulse the other; one whose every member can be known to all, and where one is not forced to charge a man with a greater burden than a man can bear; one which can do without all other peoples and without which every other people can do; one which is neither rich nor poor, and can be self-sufficient; finally, one which combines the stability of an ancient people with the docility of a new people. What makes the work of legislation difficult is not so much what has to be established as what has to be destroyed; and what makes success so rare is the impossibility of finding the simplicity of nature linked with the needs of society. It is true that it is difficult to find all of these conditions together. This is one reason why one sees few well-constituted states.

There is one country left in Europe capable of receiving legislation; it is the island of Corsica. The valor and steadfastness with which this brave people was able to recover and defend its freedom would amply deserve that some wise man teach it to preserve it. I rather suspect that this small island will one day astound Europe. [*Social contract*, II, 10]

So long as several men united consider themselves a single body, they have but a single will, which is concerned with their common preservation, and the general welfare. Then all of the springs of the state are vigorous and simple, its maxims are clear and perspicuous, it has no confused, contradictory interests, the common good is everywhere fully evident and requires only good sense to be perceived. Peace, union, equality are enemies of political subtleties. Upright and simple men are difficult to deceive because of their simplicity, they are not taken in by sham and special pleading; they are not even clever enough to be dupes. When, among the happiest people in the world, troops of peasants are seen attending to affairs of state under an oak tree and always acting wisely, can one avoid despising the refinements of other nations which make themselves illustrious and miserable with so much art and mystification?

A state thus governed needs very few laws, and as it becomes necessary to promulgate new ones, this necessity is universally seen. The first one to propose them only states what all have already sensed, and there is no need for intrigues or eloquence to secure passage into law of what each has already resolved to do as soon as he is sure that the others will do so as well.

What misleads ratiocinators is that since they only see states which are badly constituted from their origin, they are struck by the impossibility of maintaining such an administration in them. They laugh as they imagine all the nonsense of which a clever knave or an insinuating talker could persuade the people of Paris or London. They do not know that Cromwell would have been condemned to hard labor by the people of Berne, and the Duc de Beaufort to reformatory by the Genevans.

But when the social knot begins to loosen and the state to weaken; when particular interests begin to make themselves felt, and small societies to influence the larger society, the common interest diminishes and meets with opposition, votes are no longer unanimous, the general will is no longer the will of all, contradictions and disagreements arise, and the best opinion no longer carries the day unchallenged.

Finally, when the state close to ruin subsists only in an illusory and vain form, when the social bond is broken in all hearts, when the basest interest brazenly assumes the sacred name of public good; then the general will grows mute, everyone, prompted by secret motives, no more states opinions as a citizen than if the state had never existed, and iniquitous decrees with no other goal than particular interest are falsely passed under the name of laws.

Does it follow that the general will is annihilated or corrupted? No, it remains constant, unalterable, and pure; but it is subordinated to others that prevail over it. Each person, in detaching his interest from the common interest, sees clearly enough that he cannot separate them entirely, but his share of the public evil seems to him as nothing compared to the exclusive good which he seeks to make his own. Except for this particular good, he wills the public good in his own interest just as forcefully as anyone else. Even in selling his vote for money he does not extinguish the general will within himself, he evades it. The mistake he commits is to change the state of the question, and to answer something other than what he is asked: So that instead of saying with his vote, *it is advantageous to the state*, he says, *it is advantageous to this man or to this party that this or that opinion pass.* Thus the law of public order in assemblies consists not so much in upholding the general will in them, as in seeing to it that the general will is always consulted and that it always replies.

I could offer quite a few reflections here on the simple right to vote in every act of sovereignty; a right of which nothing can deprive citizens; and on the right of voicing opinions, proposing, dividing, discussing [motions], which the government always takes great care to allow only to its own members; but this important matter would require a separate treatise, and I cannot say everything in this one. [*Social contract*, IV, 1: 'That the general will is indestructible']

From the preceding chapter it is evident that the way in which general business is conducted provides a fairly reliable indication of the current state of the morals and the health of the body politic. The more concord reigns in assemblies, that is to say the closer opinions come to unanimity, the more the general will also predominates; whereas long debates, dissensions, disturbances, signal the ascendancy of particular interests and the decline of the state.

This seems less obvious when two or more orders enter into its constitution, as did in Rome the Patricians and the Plebeians, whose quarrels often disturbed the comitia even in the finest times of the Republic; but this exception is more apparent than real; for by the vice inherent to the body politic there are then, so to speak, two states in one; [and] what is not true of the two together is true of each separately. And indeed even in the stormiest times the people's plebiscites were always carried quietly and by a large majority, when the Senate did not interfere: The citizens having but a single interest, the people had but a single will.

At the other end of the cycle, unanimity returns. That is when the citizens, fallen into servitude, no longer have freedom or will. Then fear and flattery turn voting into acclamations; they no longer deliberate, they worship or they curse. Such was the vile manner in which the Senate expressed opinions under the Emperors. Sometimes it did so with ridiculous precautions: Tacitus notes that under Otho, the Senators heaping execration on Vitellius took care at the same time to make a frightful noise, so that, if by chance he were to become master, he could not tell what they each had said.

From these various considerations arise the maxims that should regulate the manner in which votes are counted and opinions compared, taking account of whether the general will is more or less easy to know, and the state more or less in decline.

There is only one law which by its nature requires unanimous consent. That is the social pact: for the civil association is the most voluntary act in the world; every man being born free and master of himself, no one may on any pretext whatsoever subject him without his consent. To decide that the son of a slave is born a slave is to decide that he is not born a man.

If, then, at the time of the social pact there are some who oppose it, their opposition does not invalidate the contract, it only keeps them from being included in it; they are foreigners among the citizens. Once the state is instituted, consent consists in residence; to dwell in the territory is to submit to the sovereignty.

Except for this primitive contract, the vote of the majority always obligates all the rest; this is a consequence of the contract itself. Yet the question is raised how a man can be both free and forced to conform to wills which are not his own. How are the opponents both free and subject to laws to which they have not consented?

I answer that the question is badly framed. The citizen consents to all the laws, even to those passed in spite of him, and even to those that punish him when he dares to violate any one of them. The constant will of all the members of the state is the general will; it is through it that they are citizens and free. When a law is proposed in the people's assembly, what they are being asked is not exactly whether they approve the proposal or reject it, but whether it does or does not conform to the general will, which is theirs; everyone states his opinion about this by casting his ballot, and the tally of the votes yields the declaration of the general will. Therefore when the opinion contrary to my own prevails, it proves nothing more than that I made a mistake and that what I took to be the general will was not. If my particular opinion had prevailed, I would have done something other than what I had willed, and it is then that I would not have been free.

This presupposes, it is true, that all the characteristics of the general will are still in the majority: once they no longer are, then regardless of which side one takes there no longer is any freedom.

When earlier I showed how particular wills were substituted for the general will in public deliberations, I indicated clearly enough the practicable ways to prevent this abuse; I shall have more to say on this subject later. As for the proportional number of votes needed to declare the general will, I have also provided the principles by which it can be ascertained. A difference of a single vote breaks a tie, a single opponent destroys unanimity; but between unanimity and a tie there are various uneven divisions, at any one of which this proportion can be fixed, taking the state and the needs of the body politic into account.

Two general maxims can help to regulate these ratios: one, that the more important and serious the deliberations are, the more nearly unanimous should be the opinion that prevails; the other, that the more rapidly the business at hand has to be resolved, the narrower should be the prescribed difference in weighting opinions; in deliberations which have to be concluded straightaway a majority of one should suffice. The first of these maxims appears better suited to laws, the second to business. Be that as it may, it is by a combination of these two maxims that the best ratios for a deciding majority are determined. [*Social contract*, IV, 2: 'Of suffrage']

With regard to the elections of the Prince and the magistrates, which are, as I have said, complex acts, there are two ways to proceed; namely, by choice or by lot. Both have been used in various republics, and a very complicated mixture of the two can still be found at present in the election of the Doge of Venice.

Voting by lot, says Montesquieu, *is in the nature of democracy.* I agree, but why is it? *Drawing lots,* he goes on, *is a way of electing that afflicts no one; it leaves every citizen a reasonable hope of serving the fatherland.* These are not reasons.

If one keeps in mind that the election of chiefs is a function of government and not of sovereignty, one will see why election by lot is more in the nature of democracy, where the administration is all the better in proportion as its acts are fewer.

In every genuine democracy, magistracy is not an advantage but a burdensome charge, which one cannot justly impose on one individual rather than another. Only the law can impose this charge on the one to whom the lot falls. For then, since the condition is equal for all and the choice does not depend on a human will, no particular application can distort the universality of the law.

In Aristocracy the Prince chooses the Prince, the government perpetuates itself by itself, and that is where voting is appropriate.

The example of the election of the Doge of Venice, far from destroying this distinction, confirms it: This composite form suits a mixed government. For it is an error to take the government of Venice for a genuine aristocracy. While the people has no share in the government, the nobility is itself of the people. A multitude of poor Barnabites never came close to any magistracy, and all they get for being noble is the empty title of Excellency and the right to be present at the great Council. Since this great Council is as numerous as our general Council in Geneva, its illustrious members have no more privileges than do our simple citizens. It is certain that, setting aside the extreme disparity between the two republics, the bourgeoisie of Geneva corresponds precisely to the Venetian Patriciate, our natives and inhabitants correspond to the townsmen and the people of Venice, and our peasants correspond to the mainland subjects; in sum, however one considers that Republic, apart from its size, its government is no more aristocratic than is ours. The entire difference is that since we have no chiefs for life, we have not the same need for election by lot.

Elections by lot would entail few inconveniences in a genuine democracy where everything is as equal by virtue of morals and talents as maxims and fortune, because choice would make almost no difference. But I have already said that there is no genuine democracy.

Where election by choice and election by lot are combined, choice should fill the positions that require specific talents, such as military offices; drawing lots is appropriate for the positions for which good sense, justice, integrity suffice, such as judicial responsibilities, because in a well-constituted State these qualities are common to all citizens.

Neither lot nor voting has any place in a monarchical government. Since the Monarch is by right the sole Prince and the only magistrate, the choice of his lieutenants is his alone. When the Abbé de St. Pierre proposed multiplying the Councils of the King of France and electing their members by ballot, he did not realize he was proposing to change the form of the government.

It remains for me to speak about the way votes should be cast and collected in the assembly of the people; but perhaps the historical sketch of Roman adminis- tration in this matter will explain more concretely all the maxims which I might establish. It is not unworthy of a judicious reader to consider in some detail how public and particular business was conducted in a council of two hundred thou- sand men. [*Social contract*, IV, 3: 'Of elections']

JOSEPH PRIESTLEY

BIOGRAPHICAL NOTE

Joseph Priestley (1733–1804) was one of the great experimental scientists in the Baconian–Newtonian empirical tradition of the English Enlightenment, famous for his research in chemistry and electricity, as well as being one of the best-known representatives of English political radicalism. He was born into a family of religious dissenters, and trained for a career in the ministry and in teaching at Daventry Academy. In 1761 he became a Tutor in languages at Warrington Academy. His first published work, the *Rudiments of English grammar* (1761), was followed by *A course of lectures on the theory of language* (1762). In 1767 he became a minister at Mill Hill Chapel in Leeds, publishing in the same year his first scientific treatise.

Priestley became a Socinian and in the 1760s he became deeply involved in the theological and political debate of the period. *An essay on the first principles of government* appeared in 1768. In 1769 he published works on Church authority and Protestant dissent, together with another important political tract, *The present state of liberty in Great Britain and her colonies*. By the 1770s Priestley was part of the circle of dissenters that included Richard Price, Benjamin Franklin and eventually Jeremy Bentham. In 1772 Priestley became librarian and consultant to the Earl of Shelburne, in whose circle he was to meet Bentham. For the next fourteen years Priestley concentrated on the publication of substantial theological and scientific works, together with a number of essays relating to Protestant dissent, and an essay on Hartley's Theory of the human mind (1775). By now he was publishing widely in the areas of politics, history, chemistry, physics, psychology, linguistics, theology and politics. In 1780 he moved to Birmingham, where he became a member of the Lunar Society of Derby, a group of scientists and industrialists that also included Erasmus Darwin, Josiah Wedgwood and Thomas Boulton. By the time of his death he had published more than 150 books, all testifying to his position as one of the Enlightenment's great polymaths.

With the outbreak of the French Revolution, he expressed open support for the Revolutionaries, and attracted controversy and even physical attack for his views. His vindication of the French Revolution was published in his

Letters to Burke: a political dialogue on the general principles of government (1791). In 1793 he published the *Letters to the philosophers and politicians of France*. As a result of the intense hostility to his pro-Revolutionary sympathies, he decided to emigrate to the United States, and in November 1794 the Priestley family, formally welcomed to America by Washington, settled in Northumberland, Pennsylvania. By now Priestley was a Fellow of the Royal Society, and an international celebrity. Two further works of importance were to appear before his death, the *Discourses on the evidences of revealed religion* (1794) and the *Considerations on the doctrine of phlogiston and the decomposition of air* (1796).

EDITORIAL NOTE

The first edition of *An essay on the first principles of government* was followed by a second, enlarged edition in 1771. There was no French translation, and knowledge of Priestley's *Essay* outside Britain in the eighteenth century would not therefore have been wide. The extracts are taken from the edition by P. Miller,* for which the base text is the 'corrected and enlarged' *An essay on the first principles of government, and on the nature of political, civil and religious liberty, including remarks on Dr Brown's code of education, and on Dr Baguley's sermon on church authority* (London, J. Johnson, 1771).

FURTHER READING

Graham, J., 'Revolutionary philosopher: the political ideas of Joseph Priestley (1733–1804)', *Enlightenment and Dissent*, 8 (1989), pp. 43–68; 9 (1990), pp. 14–46.

Hoecker, J., *Joseph Priestley and the idea of progress* (New York and London, Garland, 1987).

*Miller, P. (ed.), *Priestley: political writings* (Cambridge, Cambridge University Press, 1993). See introduction, pp. xi–xxvii.

Thomas, D., 'Progress, liberty and utility: the political philosophy of Joseph Priestley', in *Science, medicine and dissent: Joseph Priestley (1733–1804)*, ed. R. Anderson and C. Lawrence (London, Wellcome Trust, 1987), pp. 73–80.

An essay on the first principles of government, and on the nature of political, civil and religious liberty (1768)

Man derives two capital advantages from the superiority of his intellectual powers. The first is, that, as an individual, he possesses a certain comprehension of mind, whereby he contemplates and enjoys the past and the future, as well as the present. This comprehension is enlarged with the experience of every day; and by this means the happiness of man, as he advances in intellect, is continually less dependent on temporary circumstances and sensations.

The next advantage resulting from the same principle, and which is, in many respects, both the cause and effect of the former, is, that the human species itself is capable of a similar and unbounded improvement; whereby mankind in a later age are greatly superior to mankind in a former age, the individuals being taken at the same time of life. Of this progress of the species, brute animals are more incapable than they are of that relating to individuals. No horse of this age seems to have any advantage over other horses of former ages; and if there be any improvement in the species, it is owing to our manner of breeding and training them. But a man at this time, who has been tolerably well educated, in an improved christian country, is a being possessed of much greater power, to be, and to make happy, than a person of the same age, in the same, or any other country, some centuries ago. And, for this reason, I make no doubt, that a person some centuries hence will, at the same age, be as much superior to us.

The great instrument in the hand of divine providence, of this progress of the species towards perfection, is *society*, and consequently *government*. In a state of nature the powers of any individual are dissipated by an attention to a multiplicity of objects. The employments of all are similar. From generation to generation every man does the same that every other does, or has done, and no person begins where another ends; at least, general improvements are exceedingly slow, and uncertain. This we see exemplified in all barbarous nations, and especially in countries thinly inhabited, where the connections of the people are slight, and consequently society and government very imperfect; and it may be seen more particularly in North America, and Greenland. Whereas a state of more perfect society admits of a proper distribution and division of the objects of human attention. In such a state, men are connected with and subservient to one another; so that, while one man confines himself to one single object, another may give the same undivided attention to another object.

Thus the powers of all have their full effect; and hence arise improvements in all the conveniences of life, and in every branch of knowledge. In this state of things, it requires but a few years to comprehend the whole preceding progress of any one art or science; and the rest of a man's life, in which his faculties are the most perfect, may be given to the extension of it. If, by this means, one art or science should grow too large for an easy comprehension, in a moderate space of time, a commodious subdivision will be made. Thus all knowledge will be subdivided and extended; and *knowledge*, as Lord *Bacon* observes, being *power*, the human powers will, in fact, be enlarged; nature, including both its materials, and its laws, will be more at our command; men will make their situation in this world abundantly more easy and comfortable; they will probably prolong their existence in it, and will grow daily more happy, each in himself, and more able (and, I believe, more disposed) to communicate happiness to others. Thus, whatever was the beginning of this world, the end will be glorious and paradisaical, beyond what our imaginations can now conceive. Extravagant as some may suppose these views to be, I think I could show them to be fairly suggested by the true theory of human nature, and to arise from the natural course of human affairs. But, for the present, I waive this subject, the contemplation of which always makes me happy.

Government being the great instrument of this progress of the human species towards this glorious state, that form of government will have a just claim to our approbation which favours this progress, and that must be condemned in which it is retarded. Let us then, my fellow citizens, consider the business of government with these enlarged views, and trace some of the fundamental principles of it, by an attention to what is most conducive to the happiness of mankind at present, and most favourable to the increase of this happiness in futurity; and, perhaps, we may understand this intricate subject, with some of its most important circumstances, better than we have done; at least we may see some of them in a clearer and stronger point of light.

To begin with first principles, we must, for the sake of gaining clear ideas on the subject, do what almost all political writers have done before us; that is, we must suppose a number of people existing, who experience the inconvenience of living independent and unconnected; who are exposed, without redress, to insults and wrongs of every kind, and are too weak to procure themselves many of the advantages, which they are sensible might easily be compassed by united strength. These people, if they would engage the protection of the whole body, and join their force in enterprizes and undertakings calculated for their common good, must voluntarily resign some part of their natural liberty, and submit their conduct to the direction of the community: for without these concessions, such an alliance, attended with such advantages, could not be formed.

Were these people few in number, and living within a small distance of one another, it might be easy for them to assemble upon every occasion, in which the whole body was concerned; and every thing might be determined by the votes of the majority, provided they had previously agreed that the votes of a majority should be decisive. But were the society numerous, their habitations remote, and the occasions on which the whole body must interpose frequent, it would be absolutely impossible that all the members of the state should assemble, or give their attention to public business. In this case, though, with *Rousseau* it be a giving up of their liberty, there must be deputies, or public officers, appointed to act in the name of the whole body; and, in a state of very great extent, where all the people could never be assembled, the whole power of the community must necessarily, and almost irreversibly, be lodged in the hands of these deputies. In England, the king, the hereditary lords, and the electors of the house of commons, are these *standing* deputies; and the members of the house of commons are, again, the *temporary* deputies of this last order of the state.

In all states, great or small, the sentiments of that body of men in whose hands the supreme power of the society is lodged, must be understood to be the sentiments of the whole body, if there be no other method in which the sentiments of the whole body can be expressed. These deputies, or representatives of the people, will make a wrong judgment, and pursue wrong measures, if they consult not the good of the whole society, whose representatives they are; just as the people themselves would make a wrong judgment, and pursue wrong measures, if they did not consult their own good, provided they could be assembled for that purpose. No maxims or rules of policy can be binding upon them, but such as they themselves shall judge to be conducive to the public good. Their own reason and conscience are their only guide, and the people, in whose name they act, their only judge.

In these circumstances, if I be asked what I mean by *liberty,* I should choose, for the sake of greater clearness, to divide it into two kinds, *political* and *civil;* and the importance of having clear ideas on this subject will be my apology for the innovation. POLITICAL LIBERTY, I would say, *consists in the power, which the members of the state reserve to themselves, of arriving at the public offices, or, at least, of having votes in the nomination of those who fill them*: and I would choose to call CIVIL LIBERTY *that power over their own actions, which the members of the state reserve to themselves, and which their officers must not infringe.*

Political liberty, therefore, is equivalent to the right of magistracy, being the claim that any member of the state hath, to have his private opinion or judgment become that of the public, and thereby control the actions of others; whereas *civil liberty*, extends no farther than to a man's own conduct, and signifies the right he has to be exempt from the control of the society, or its agents; that is, the power he has of providing for his own advantage and happiness. It is a man's civil liberty, which is originally in its full force, and part of which he sacrifices when he enters into a state of society; and political liberty is that which he may, or may not acquire in the compensation he receives for it. For he may either stipulate to have a voice in the public determinations, or, as far as the public determination doth take place, he may submit to be governed wholly by others. Of these two kinds of liberty, which it is of the greatest importance to distinguish, I shall treat in the order in which I have mentioned them. [*Essay*, 1: 'Of the first principles of government and the different kinds of Liberty']

In countries where every member of the society enjoys an equal power of arriving at the supreme offices, and consequently of directing the strength and the sentiments of the whole community, there is a state of the most perfect political liberty. On the other hand, in countries where a man is, by his birth or fortune, excluded from these offices, or from a power of voting for proper persons to fill them; that man, whatever be the form of the government, or whatever civil liberty, or power over his own actions he may have, has no power over those of another; he has no share in the government, and therefore has no political liberty at all. Nay his own conduct, as far as the society does interfere, is, in all cases, directed by others.

It may be said, that no society on earth was ever formed in the manner represented above. I answer, it is true; because all governments whatever have been, in some measure, compulsory, tyrannical, and oppressive in their origin; but the method I have described must be allowed to be the only equitable and fair method of forming a society. And since every man retains, and can never be deprived of his natural right (founded on a regard to the general good) of relieving himself from all oppression, that is, from every thing that has been imposed upon him without his own consent; this must be the only true and proper foundation of all the governments subsisting in the world, and that to which the people who compose them have an unalienable right to bring them back.

It must necessarily be understood, therefore, whether it be expressed or not, that all people live in society for their mutual advantage; so that the good and happiness of the members, that is the majority of the members of any state, is the great standard by which every thing relating to that state must finally be determined. And though it may be supposed, that a body of people may be bound by a voluntary resignation of all their interests to a single person, or to a few, it can never be supposed that the resignation is obligatory on their posterity; because it is manifestly *contrary to the good of the whole that it should be so.*

I own it is rather matter of surprise to me, that this great object of all government should have been so little insisted on by our great writers who have treated of this subject, and that more use hath not been made of it. In treating of particular regulations in states, this principle necessarily obtruded itself; all arguments in favour of any law being always drawn from a consideration of its tendency to promote the public good; and yet it has often escaped the notice of writers in discoursing on the first principles of society, and the subject of civil and religious liberty.

This one general idea, properly pursued, throws the greatest light upon the whole system of policy, morals, and, I may add, theology too. To a mind not warped by theological and metaphysical subtilties, the divine being appears to be actuated by no other views than the noblest we can conceive, the happiness of his creatures. Virtue and right conduct consist in those affections and actions which terminate in the public good; justice and veracity, for instance, having nothing intrinsically excellent in them, separate from their relation to the happiness of mankind; and the whole system of right to power, property, and every thing else in society, must be regulated by the same consideration: the decisive question, when any of these subjects are examined, being, What is it that the good of the community requires?

Let it be observed, in this place, that I by no means assert, that the good of mankind requires a state of the most perfect political liberty. This, indeed, is not possible, except in exceeding small states; in none, perhaps, that are so large as even the republics of ancient Greece; or as Genoa, or Geneva in modern times. Such small republics as these, if they were desirable, would be impracticable; because a state of perfect equality, in communities or individuals, can never be preserved, while some are more powerful, more enterprising, and more successful in their attempts than others. And an ambitious nation could not wish for a fairer opportunity of arriving at extensive empire, than to find the neighbouring countries cantoned out into a number of small governments; which could have no power to withstand it singly, and which could never form sufficiently extensive confederacies, or act with sufficient unanimity, and expedition, to oppose it with success.

Supposing, therefore, that, in order to prevent the greatest of all inconveniences, very extensive, and consequently absolute monarchies, it may be expedient to have such states as England, France, and Spain; political liberty must, in some measure, be restrained; but *in what manner* a restraint should be put upon it, or *how far* it should extend, is not easy to be ascertained. In general, it should seem, that none but persons of considerable fortune should be capable of arriving at the highest offices in the government; not only because, all other circumstances being equal, such persons will generally have had the best education, and consequently be the best qualified to act for the public good; but because also, they will necessarily have the most property at stake, and will, therefore, be most interested in the fate of their country.

Let it be observed, however, that what may be called a *moderate* fortune (though a thing of so variable a nature cannot be defined) should be considered as equivalent in this respect, to the most affluent one. Persons who are born to a moderate fortune, are, indeed, generally better educated, have, consequently, more enlarged minds, and are, in all respects, more truly *independent*, than those who are born to great opulence.

For the same reason, it may, perhaps, be more eligible, that those who are extremely dependent should not be allowed to have votes in the nomination of the chief magistrates; because this might, in some instances, be only throwing more votes into the hands of those persons on whom they depend. But if, in every state of considerable extent, we suppose a *gradation* of elective offices, and if we likewise suppose the lowest classes of the people to have votes in the nomination of the lowest officers, and, as they increase in wealth and importance, to have a share in the choice of persons to fill the higher posts, till they themselves be admitted candidates for places of public trust; we shall, perhaps, form an idea of as much political liberty as is consistent with the state of mankind. And I think experience shows, that the highest offices of all, equivalent to that of *king*, ought to be, in some measure, hereditary, as in England; elective monarchies having generally been the theatres of cabal, confusion, and misery.

[It must be acknowledged, however, to be exceedingly hazardous to the liberties of a people, to have any office of importance frequently filled by the same persons, or their descendants. The boundaries of very great power can never be so exactly defined, but that, when it becomes the interest of men to extend them, and when so flattering an object is kept a long time in view, opportunities will be found for the purpose. What nation would not have been enslaved by the uncontroverted succession of only three such princes as Henry IV. of France, Henry VII. of England, or the present king of Prussia? The more accomplished and glorious they were as warriors, or statesmen, the more dangerous would they be as *princes,* in free states. It is nothing but the continual fear of revolt, in favour of some rival, that could keep such princes within any bounds; i.e. that could make it their interest to court the favour of the people.

Hereditary nobles stand in the same predicament with hereditary princes. The long continuance of the same parliaments have also the same tendency. And had not these things, together with an independent ecclesiastical power, been wonderfully balanced in our constitution, it could never have stood so long. The more complex any machine is, and the more nicely it is fitted to answer its purpose, the more liable it is to disorder. The more avenues there are to arbitrary power, the more attention it requires to guard them; and with all the vigilance of the people of these nations, they have more than once been obliged to have recourse to the sword. The liberties we now enjoy, precarious as they are, have not been purchased without blood.

Though it be very evident that no office of great trust and power should be suffered to continue a long time in the same hands, the succession might be so rapid, that the remedy would be worse than the disease. With respect to this nation, it seems to be agreed, that *septennial parliaments* have brought our liberties into very eminent hazard, and that *triennial,* if not *annual* parliaments would be better. Indeed septennial parliaments were at first a direct usurpation of the rights of the people: for, by the same authority that one parliament prolonged their own power to seven years, they might have continued it to twice seven, or, like the parliament in 1641, have made it perpetual. The bulk of the people never see the most obvious tendencies of things, or so flagrant a violation of the constitution would never have been suffered. But whereas a general *clamour* might have prevented the evil, it may require something more to redress it.]

But though the exact medium of political liberty, [with respect either to the *property* of men in offices of trust, or to their *continuance in power,*] be not easily fixed, it is not of much consequence to do it; since a considerable degree of perfection in government will admit of great varieties in this respect; and the extreme of political slavery, which excludes all persons, except one, or a very few, from having access to the chief magistracy, or from having votes in the choice of magistrates, [and which keeps all the power of the state in the same hands, or the same families,] is easily marked out, and the fatal effects of it are very striking. For such is the state of mankind, that persons possessed of unbounded power will generally act as if they forgot the proper nature and design of their station, and pursue their own interest, though it be opposite to that of the community at large.

[Provided those who make laws submit to them themselves, and, with respect to taxes in particular, so long as those who impose them bear an equal share with the rest of the community, there will be no complaint. But in all cases, when those who lay the tax upon others exempt themselves, there is *tyranny*; and the man who submits to a tax of a penny, levied in this manner, is liable to have the last penny he has extorted from him.

Men of equal rank and fortune with those who usually compose the English house of Commons have nothing to fear from the imposition of taxes, so long as there is any thing like *rotation* in that office; because those who impose them are liable to pay them themselves, and are no better able to bear the burden; but persons of lower rank, and especially those who have no votes in the election of members, may have reason to fear, because an unequal part of the burden may be laid upon them. They are necessarily a *distinct order* in the community, and have no direct method of controlling the measures of the legislature. Our increasing *game-laws* have all the appearance of the haughty decrees of a tyrant, who sacrifices every thing to his own pleasure and caprice.

Upon these principles it is evident, that there must have been a gross inattention to the very first principles of liberty, to say nothing worse, in the first scheme of taxing the inhabitants of America in the British parliament.]

But if there be any truth in the principles above laid down, it must be a fundamental maxim in all governments, that if any man hold what is called a high rank, or enjoy privileges, and prerogatives in a state, it is because the good of the state requires that he should hold that rank, or enjoy those privileges; and such persons, whether they be called kings, senators, or nobles; or by whatever names, or titles, they be distinguished, are, to all intents and purposes, the *servants of the public*, and accountable to the people for the discharge of their respective offices.

If such magistrates abuse their trust, in the people, therefore, lies the right of *deposing*, and consequently of *punishing* them. And the only reason why abuses which have crept into offices have been connived at, is, that the correcting of them, by having recourse to first principles, and the people taking into their own hands their right to appoint or change their officers, and to ascertain the bounds of their authority, is far from being easy, except in small states; so that the remedy would often be worse than the disease.

But, in the largest states, if the abuses of government should, at any time be great and manifest; if the servants of the people, forgetting their *masters*, and their masters' interest, should pursue a separate one of their own; if, instead of considering that they are made for the people, they should consider the people as made for them; if the oppressions and violations of right should be great, flagrant, and universally resented; if the tyrannical governors should have no friends but a few sycophants, who had long preyed upon the vitals of their fellow citizens, and who might be expected to desert a government, whenever their interests should be detached from it: if, in consequence of these circumstances, it should become manifest, that the risk, which would be run in attempting a revolution would be trifling, and the evils which might be apprehended from it, were far less than those which were actually suffered, and which were daily increasing; in the name of God, I ask, what principles are those, which ought to restrain an injured and insulted people from asserting their natural rights, and from changing, or even punishing their governors, that is their *servants*, who had abused their trust; or from altering the whole form of their government, if it appeared to be of a structure so liable to abuse?

To say that these forms of government have been long established, and that these oppressions have been long suffered, without any complaint, is to supply the strongest argument for their abolition. Lawyers, who are governed by rules and precedents, are very apt to fall into mistakes, in determining what is right and lawful, in cases which are, in their own nature, prior to any fixed laws or precedents. The only reason for the authority of precedents and general rules in matters of law and government, is, that all persons may know what *is law*; which they could not do if the administration of it was not uniform, and the same in similar cases. But if the precedents and general rules themselves be a greater grievance than the violation of them, and the establishment of better precedents, and better general rules, what becomes of their obligation? The necessity of the thing, in the changing course of human affairs, obliges all governments to alter their general rules, and to set up new precedents in affairs of less importance; and why may not a proportionably greater necessity plead as strongly for the alteration of the most general rules, and for setting up new precedents in matters of the greatest consequence, affecting the most fundamental principles of any government, and the distribution of power among its several members?

Nothing can more justly excite the indignation of an honest and oppressed citizen, than to hear a prelate, who enjoys a considerable benefice, under a corrupt government, pleading for its support by those abominable perversions of scripture, which have been too common on this occasion; as by urging in its favour that passage of St Paul, *The powers which be are ordained of God*, and others of a similar import. It is a sufficient answer to such an absurd quotation as this, that for the same reason, the powers which *will be* will be ordained of God also.

Something, indeed, might have been said in favour of the doctrines of *passive obedience* and *non-resistance*, at the time when they were first started; but a man must be infatuated who will not renounce them now. The Jesuits, about two centuries ago, in order to vindicate their king-killing principles, happened, among other arguments, to make use of this great and just principle, that *all civil power is ultimately derived from the people*: and their adversaries, in England, and elsewhere, instead of showing how they abused and perverted that fundamental principle of all government in the case in question, did, what disputants warmed with controversy are very apt to do; they denied the principle itself, and maintained that *all civil power is derived from God*, as if the Jewish theocracy had been established throughout the whole world. From this maxim it was a clear consequence, that the governments, which at any time subsist, being *the ordinance of God*, and the kings which are at any time upon the throne, being *the viceregents of God*, must not be opposed.

So long as there were recent examples of good kings deposed, and some of them massacred by wild enthusiasts, some indulgence might be allowed to those warm, but weak friends of society, who would lay hold of any principle, which, however ill founded, would supply an argument for more effectually preserving the public peace; but to maintain the same absurd principles at this day, when the danger from which they served to shelter us is over, and the heat of controversy is abated, shows the strongest and most blameable prepossession. Writers in defence of them do not deserve a serious answer: and to allege those principles in favour of a corrupt government, which nothing can excuse but their being brought in favour of a good one, is unpardonable.

The history of this controversy about the doctrine of passive obedience and non-resistance, affords a striking example of the danger of having recourse to false principles in controversy. They may serve a particular turn, but, in other cases, may be capable of the most dangerous application; whereas universal truth will, in all possible cases, have the best consequences, and be ever favourable to the true interests of mankind.

It will be said, that it is opening a door to *rebellion*, to assert that magistrates, abusing their power, may be set aside by the people, who are of course their own judges when that power is abused. May not the people, it is said, abuse their power, as well as their governors? I answer, it is very possible they may abuse their power: it is possible they may imagine themselves oppressed when they are not: it is possible that their animosity may be artfully and unreasonably inflamed, by ambitious and enterprising men, whose views are often best answered by popular tumults and insurrections; and the people may suffer in consequence of their folly and precipitancy. But what man is there, or what body of men (whose right to direct their own conduct was never called in question) but are liable to be imposed upon, and to suffer in consequence of their mistaken apprehensions and precipitate conduct?

With respect to large societies, it is very improbable, that the people should be too soon alarmed, so as to be driven to these extremities. In such cases, the power of the government, that is, of the governors, must be very extensive and arbitrary; and the power of the people scattered, and difficult to be united; so that, if a man have common sense, he will see it to be madness to propose, or to lay any measures for a general insurrection against the government, except in case of very general and great oppression. Even patriots, in such circumstances, will consider, that present evils always appear greater in consequence of their being present; but that the future evils of a revolt, and a temporary anarchy, may be much greater than are apprehended at a distance. They will, also, consider, that unless their measures be perfectly well laid, and their success decisive, ending in a change, not of *men*, but of *things*; not of governors, but of the rules and administration of government, they will only rivet their chains the faster, and bring upon themselves and their country tenfold ruin.

So obvious are those difficulties, that lie in the way of procuring redress of grievances by force of arms, that I think we may say, without exception, that in all cases of hostile opposition to government, the people must have been in the right; and that nothing but very great oppression could drive them to such desperate measures. The bulk of a people seldom so much as *complain* without reason, because they never think of complaining till they *feel*; so that, in all cases of dissatisfaction with government, it is most probable, that the people are injured.

The case, I own, may be otherwise in states of small extent, where the power of the governors is comparatively small, and the power of the people great, and soon united. These fears, therefore, may be prudent in Venice, in Genoa, or in the small cantons of Switzerland; but it were to the last degree, absurd to extend them to Great-Britain.

The English history will inform us, that the people of this country have always borne extreme oppression, for a long time before there has appeared any danger of a general insurrection against the government. What a series of encroachments upon their rights did even the feudal barons, whose number was not very considerable, and whose power was great, bear from William the Conqueror, and his successors, before they broke out into actual rebellion on that account, as in the reigns of king John, and Henry the third! And how much were the lowest orders of the poor commons trampled upon with impunity by both, till a much later period; when, all the while, they were so far from attempting any resistance, or even complaining of the gross infringements of their rights, that they had not so much as the idea of their having any rights to be trampled upon! After the people had begun to acquire property, independence, and an idea of their natural rights, how long did they bear a load of old and new oppressions under the Tudors, but more especially under the Stuarts, before they broke out into what the friends of arbitrary power affect to call *the grand rebellion*! And how great did that obstinate civil war show the power of the king to be, notwithstanding the most intolerable and wanton abuse of it! At the close of the year 1642, it was more probable that the king would have prevailed than the parliament; and his success would have been certain, if his conduct had not been as weak, as it was wicked.

So great was the power of the crown, that after the restoration, Charles the second was tempted to act the same part with his father, and actually did it, in a great measure, with impunity; till, at last, he was even able to reign without parliaments; and if he had lived much longer, he would, in all probability, have been as arbitrary as the king of France. His brother James the second, had almost subverted both the civil and religious liberties of his country, in the short space of four years, and might have done it completely, if he could have been content to have proceeded with more caution; nay, he might have succeeded notwithstanding his precipitancy, if the divine being had not, at that critical time, raised up William the third, of glorious memory, for our deliverance. But, God be thanked, the government of this country, is now fixed upon so good and firm a basis, and is so generally acquiesced in, that they are only the mere tools of a court party, or the narrow minded bigots among the inferior clergy, who, to serve their own low purposes, do now and then promote the cry, that the church or the state is in danger.

As to what is called the crime of *rebellion*, we have nothing to do either with the name, or the thing, in the case before us. That term, if it admit of any definition, is an attempt to subvert a lawful government; but the question is, whether an oppressive government, though it have been ever so long established, can be a lawful one; or, to cut off all dispute about words, if lawful, legal, and constitutional, be maintained to be the same thing, whether the lawful, legal, and constitutional government be a *good* government, or one in which sufficient provision is made for the happiness of the subjects of it. If it fail in this essential character, respecting the true end and object of all civil government, no other property or title, with which it may be dignified, ought to shelter it from the generous attack of the noble and daring patriot. If the bold attempt be precipitate, and unsuccessful, the tyrannical government, will be sure to term it rebellion, but that censure cannot make the thing itself less glorious. The memory of such brave, though unsuccessful and unfortunate friends of liberty, and of the rights of mankind, as that of Harmodius and Aristogiton among the Athenians, and Russel and Sidney in our own country, – will be had in everlasting honour by their grateful fellow citizens; and history will speak another language than laws.

If it be asked how far a people may lawfully go in punishing their chief magistrates, I answer that, if the enormity of the offence (which is of the same extent as the injury done to the public) be considered, any punishment is justifiable that a man can incur in human society. It may be said, there are no laws to punish those governors, and we must not condemn persons by laws made *ex post facto*; for this conduct will vindicate the most obnoxious measures of the most tyrannical administration. But I answer, that this is a case, in its own nature, prior to the establishment of any laws whatever; as it affects the very being of society, and defeats the principal ends for which recourse was originally had to it. There may be no fixed law against an open invader, who should attempt to seize upon a country, with a view to enslave all its inhabitants; but must not the invader be apprehended, and even put to death, though he have broken no express law then in being, or none of which he was properly apprized? And why should a man, who takes the advantage of his being king, or governor, to subvert the laws and liberties of his country, be considered in any other light than that of a foreign invader? Nay his crime is much more atrocious, as he was appointed the guardian of the laws and liberties, which he subverts, and which he was, therefore, under the strongest obligation to maintain.

In a case, therefore, of this highly criminal nature, *salus populi suprema est lex.*

That must be done which the good of the whole requires; and, generally, kings deposed, banished, or imprisoned, are highly dangerous to a nation; because, let them have governed ever so ill, it will be the interest of some to be their partisans, and to attach themselves to their cause.

It will be supposed, that these observations have a reference to what passed in England in the year 1648. Let it be supposed. Surely a man, and an Englishman, may be at liberty to give his opinion, freely and without disguise, concerning a transaction of so old a date. Charles the first, whatever he was in his private character, which is out of the question here, was certainly a very bad king of England. During a course of many years, and notwithstanding repeated remonstrances, he governed by maxims utterly subversive of the fundamental and free constitution of this country; and, therefore, he deserved the severest punishment. If he was misled by his education, or his friends, he was, like any other criminal, in the same circumstances, to be pitied, but by no means to be spared on that account.

From the nature of things it was necessary that the opposition should begin from a few, who may, therefore, be stiled a *faction*; but after the civil war (which necessarily ensued from the king's obstinacy, and in which he had given repeated instances of dissimulation and treachery) there was evidently no safety, either for the faction or the nation, short of his death. It is to be regretted, that the situation of things was such, that the sentence could not be passed by the whole nation, or their representatives, solemnly assembled for that purpose. I am sensible indeed, that the generality of the nation, at that time, would not have voted the death of their sovereign; but this was not owing to any want of a just sense of the wrongs he had done them, but to an opinion of the *sacredness of kingly power*, from which very few of the friends of liberty in those times, especially among the Presbyterians, who were the majority, could intirely divest themselves. Such a transaction would have been an immortal honour to this country, whenever that superstitious notion shall be obliterated: A notion which has been extremely useful in the infant state of societies; but which, like other superstitions, subsists long after it hath ceased to be of use.

The sum of what hath been advanced upon this head, is a maxim, than which nothing is more true, that *every government, in its original principles, and antecedent to its present form, is an equal republic*; and, consequently, that every man, when he comes to be sensible of his natural rights, and to feel his own importance, will consider himself as fully equal to any other person whatever. The consideration of riches and power, however acquired, must be entirely set aside, when we come to these first principles. The very idea of property, or right of any kind, is founded upon a regard to the general good of the society, under whose protection it is enjoyed; and nothing is properly *a man's own*, but what general rules, which have for their object the good of the whole, give to him. To whomsoever the society delegates its power, it is delegated to them for the more easy management of public affairs, and in order to make the more effectual provision for the happiness of the whole. Whoever enjoys property, or riches in the state, enjoys them for the good of the state, as well as for himself; and whenever those powers, riches, or rights of any kind, are abused, to the injury of the whole, that awful and ultimate tribunal, in which every citizen hath an equal voice, may demand the resignation of them; and in circumstances, where regular commissions from this abused public cannot be had, every man, who has power, and who is actuated with the sentiments of the public, may assume a public character, and bravely redress public wrongs. In such dismal and critical circumstances, the stifled voice of an oppressed country is a loud call upon every man, possessed with a spirit of patriotism, to exert himself; and whenever that voice shall be at liberty, it will ratify and applaud the action, which it could not formally authorize.

In large states, this ultimate seat of power, this tribunal to which lies an appeal from every other, and from which no appeal can even be imagined, is too much hid, and kept out of sight by the present complex forms of government, which derive their authority from it. Hence hath arisen a want of clearness and consistency in the language of the friends of liberty. Hence the preposterous and slavish maxim, that whatever is enacted by that body of men, in whom the supreme power of the state is vested, must, in all cases, be implicitly obeyed; and that no attempt to repeal an unjust law can be vindicated, beyond a simple remonstrance addressed to the legislators. A case, which is very intelligible, but which can never happen, will demonstrate the absurdity of such a maxim.

Suppose the king of England, and the two houses of parliament, should make a law, in all the usual forms, to exempt the members of either house from paying taxes to the government, or to take to themselves the property of their fellow citizens. A law like this would open the eyes of the whole nation, and show them the true principles of government, and the power of governors. The nation would see that the most regular governments may become tyrannical, and their governors oppressive, by separating their interest from that of the people whom they govern. Such a law would show them to be but servants, and servants who had shamefully abused their trust. In such a case, every man for himself would lay his hand upon his sword, and the authority of the supreme power of the state would be annihilated.

So plain are these first principles of all government, and political liberty, that I will take upon me to say, it is impossible a man should not be convinced of them, who brings to the subject a mind free from the grossest and meanest prejudices. Whatever be the form of any government, whoever be the supreme magistrates, or whatever be their number; that is, to whomsoever the power of the society is delegated, their authority is, in its own nature, reversible. No man can be supposed to resign his natural liberty, but on *conditions*. These conditions, whether they be expressed or not, must be violated, whenever the plain and obvious ends of government are not answered; and a delegated power, perverted from the intention for which it was bestowed, expires of course. Magistrates therefore, who consult not the good of the public, and who employ their power to oppress the people, are a public nuisance, and their power is abrogated *ipso facto.*

This, however, can only be the case in extreme oppression; when the blessings of society and civil government, great and important as they are, are bought too dear; when it is better not to be governed at all, than to be governed in such a manner; or, at least, when the hazard of a change of government would be apparently the less evil of the two; and, therefore, these occasions rarely occur in the course of human affairs. It may be asked, what should a people do in case of less general oppression, and only particular grievances; when the deputies of the people make laws which evidently favour themselves, and bear hard upon the body of the people they represent, and such as they would certainly disapprove, could they be assembled for that purpose? I answer, that when this appears to be very clearly the case, as it ought by all means to do (since, in many cases, if the government have not power to enforce a bad law, it will not have power to enforce a good one) the first step which a wise and moderate people will take, is to make a remonstrance to the legislature; and if that be not practicable, or be not heard; still, if the complaints be general, and loud, a wise prince and ministry will pay regard to them; or they will, at length, be weary of enforcing a penal law which is generally abhorred and disregarded; when they see the people will run the risk of the punishment, if it cannot be evaded, rather than quietly submit to the injunction. And a regard to the good of society will certainly justify this conduct of the people.

If an over scrupulous conscience should prevent the people from expressing their sentiments in this manner, there is no method left, until an opportunity offers of choosing honester deputies, in which the voice of the lowest classes can be heard, in order to obtain the repeal of an oppressive law.

Governors will never be awed by the voice of the people, so long as it is a mere voice, without overt-acts. The consequence of these seemingly moderate maxims is, that a door will be left open to all kinds of oppression, without any resource or redress, till the public wrongs be accumulated to the degree above mentioned, when all the world would justify the utter subversion of the government. These maxims, therefore, admit of no remedy but the last, and most hazardous of all. But is not even a mob a less evil than a rebellion, and ought the former to be so severely blamed by writers on this subject, when it may prevent the latter? Of two evils of any kind, political as well as others, it is the dictate of common sense to choose the less. Besides, according to common notions, avowed by writers upon morals on less general principles, and by lawyers too, all penal laws give a man an alternative, either to abstain from the action prohibited, or to take the penalty. [*Essay*, ii: 'Of political liberty']

OF THE NATURE OF CIVIL LIBERTY IN GENERAL

It is a matter of the greatest importance, that we carefully distinguish between the *form* and the *extent of power* in a government; for many maxims in politics depend upon the one, which are too generally ascribed to the other.

It is comparatively of small consequence, *who*, or *how many* be our governors, or *how long* their office continues, provided their power be the same while they are in office, and the administration be uniform and certain. All the difference which can arise to states from diversities, in the number or continuance of governors, can only flow from the motive and opportunities, which those different circumstances may give their deputies, of extending, or making a bad use of their power. But whether a people enjoy more or fewer of their natural rights, under any form of government, is a matter of the last importance; and upon this depends, what, I should choose to call, the *civil liberty* of the state, as distinct from its *political liberty*.

If the power of government be very extensive, and the subjects of it have, consequently, little power over their own actions, that government is tyrannical, and oppressive; whether, with respect to its form, it be a monarchy, an aristocracy, or even a republic. For the government of the temporary magistrates of a democracy, or even the laws themselves may be as tyrannical as the maxims of the most despotic monarchy, and the administration of the government may be as destructive of private happiness. The only consolation that a democracy suggests in those circumstances is, that every member of the state has a chance of arriving at a share in the chief magistracy, and consequently of playing the tyrant in his turn; and as there is no government in the world so perfectly democratical, as that every member of the state, without exception, has a right of being admitted into the administration, great numbers will be in the same condition as if they had lived under the most absolute monarchy; and this is, in fact, almost universally the case with the poor, in all governments.

For the same reason, if there were no fixed laws, but every thing was decided according to the will of the persons in power; who is there that would think it of much consequence, whether his life, his liberty, or his property were at the mercy of one, of a few, or of a great number of people, that is, of a mob, liable to the worst of influences. So far, therefore, we may safely say, with Mr Pope, that *those governments which are best administered are best.* – that is, provided the power of government be moderate, and leave a man the most valuable of his private rights; provided the laws be certainly known to every one, and the administration of them be uniform, it is of no consequence how many, or how few persons are employed in the administration. But it must be allowed, that there is not the same chance for the continuance of such laws, and of such an administration, whether the power be lodged in few, or in more hands.

The governments now subsisting in Europe differ widely in their forms; but it is certain, that the present happiness of the subjects of them can by no means be estimated by a regard to that circumstance only. It depends chiefly upon the power, the extent, and the maxims of government, respecting personal security, private property, &c. and on the certainty and uniformity of the administration.

Civil liberty has been greatly impaired by an abuse of the maxim, that the joint understanding of all the members of a state, properly collected, must be preferable to that of individuals; and consequently that the more the cases are, in which mankind are governed by this united reason of the whole community, so much the better; whereas, in truth, the greater part of human actions are of such a nature, that more inconvenience would follow from their being fixed by laws, than from their being left to every man's arbitrary will.

[We may be assisted in conceiving the nature of this species of liberty, by considering what it is that men propose to gain by entering into society. Now it is evident, that we are not led to wish for a state of society by the want of any thing that we can conveniently procure for ourselves. As a man, and a member of civil society, I am desirous to receive such assistance as *numbers* can give to *individuals*, but by no means that assistance which numbers, as such, cannot give to individuals; and, least of all, such as individuals are better qualified to impart to numbers. There are many things respecting human happiness that properly fall under the two last mentioned classes, and the great difficulty concerning the due extent of civil government lies in distinguishing the objects that belong to these classes. Little difficulty, however, has, in fact, arisen from the nature of the things, in comparison of the difficulties that have been occasioned by its being the interest of men to combine, confound, and perplex them.

As far as mere *strength* can go, it is evident, that *numbers* may assist an individual, and this seems to have been the first, if not the only reason for having recourse to society. If I be injured, and not able to redress my own wrongs, I ask help of my neighbours and acquaintance; and occasions may arise, in which the more assistance I can procure, the better. But I can seldom want the assistance of numbers in managing my domestic affairs, which require nothing but my own constant inspection, and the immediate application of my own faculties. In this case, therefore, any attempt of numbers to assist me, would only occasion embarrassment and distress.

For the purpose of finding out *truth*, individuals are always employed to assist multitudes; for, notwithstanding it be probable, that more discoveries will be made by a number of persons than by one person; and though one person may assist another in suggesting and perfecting any improvements in science; yet still they all act as *independent individuals*, giving voluntary information and advice. For whenever numbers have truth or knowledge for their object, and act as a collective body, i.e. *authoritatively*, so that no single person can have power to determine any thing till the majority have been brought to agree to it, the interests of knowledge will certainly suffer, there is so little prospect of the prejudices of the many giving way to the better judgment of an individual. Here, there is a case, in which society must always be benefited by individuals, as such, and not by numbers, in a collective capacity. It is least of all, therefore, for the advancement of knowledge, that I should be induced to wish for the authoritative interposition of society.

In this manner it might not be a very difficult thing, for candid and impartial persons, to fix reasonable bounds for the interposition of laws and government. They are defective when they leave an individual destitute of that assistance which they could procure for him, and they are burdensome and oppressive; i.e. injurious to the natural rights and civil liberties of mankind, when they lay a man under unnecessary restrictions, by controlling his conduct, and preventing him from serving himself, with respect to those things, in which they can yield him no real assistance, and in providing for which he is in no danger of injuring others.

This question may be farther illustrated by two pretty just comparisons. Magistrates are the *servants* of the public, and therefore the use of them may be illustrated by that of servants. Now let a man's fortune or his incapacity be such that his dependence on servants is ever so great; there must be many things that he will be obliged to do for himself, and in which any attempt to assist him would only embarrass and distress him; and in many cases in which persons *do* make use of servants, they would be much more at their ease, if their situation would allow them to do without their assistance. If magistrates be considered in the more respectable light of *representatives* and *deputies* of the people, it should likewise be considered, that there are many cases, in which it is more convenient for a man to act *in person* than by any deputation whatever.

In some respects, however, it must be acknowledged, that the proper extent of civil government is not easily circumscribed within exact limits. That the happiness of the whole community is the ultimate end of government can never be doubted, and all claims of individuals inconsistent with the public good are absolutely null and void; but there is a real difficulty in determining what general rules, respecting the extent of the power of government, or of governors, are most conducive to the public good.]

Some may think it best, that the legislature should make express provision for every thing which can even indirectly, remotely, and consequentially, affect the public good; while others may think it best, that every thing, which is not properly of a civil nature, should be entirely overlooked by the civil magistrate; that it is for the advantage of the society, upon the whole, that all those things be left to take their own natural course, and that the legislature cannot interfere in them, without defeating its own great object, the public good.

We are so little capable of arguing *a priori* in matters of government, that it should seem, experiments only can determine how far this power of the legislature ought to extend; and it should likewise seem, that, till a sufficient number of experiments have been made, it becomes the wisdom of the civil magistracy to take as little upon its hands as possible, and never to interfere, without the greatest caution, in things that do not immediately affect the lives, liberty, or property of the members of the community; that civil magistrates should hardly ever be moved to exert themselves by the mere *tendencies of things*, those tendencies are generally so vague, and often so imaginary; and that nothing but a manifest and urgent necessity (of which, however, themselves are, to be sure, the only judges) can justify them in extending their authority to whatever has no more than a tendency, though the strongest possible, to disturb the tranquillity and happiness of the state.

There can be no doubt but that any people, forming themselves into a society, may subject themselves to whatever restrictions they please; and consequently, that the supreme civil magistrates, on whom the whole power of the society is devolved, may make what laws they please; but the question is, what restrictions and laws are wise, and calculated to promote the public good; for such only are just, right, and, properly speaking, lawful.

Political and civil liberty, as before explained, though very different, have, however, a very near and manifest connection; and the former is the chief guard of the latter, and on that account, principally, it is valuable, and worth contending for. If all the political power of this country were lodged in the hands of one person, and the government thereby changed into an absolute monarchy, the people would find no difference, provided the same laws, and the same administration, which now subsist, were continued. But then, the people, having no political liberty, would have no *security* for the continuance of the same laws, and the same administration. They would have no guard for their civil liberty. The monarch, having it in his option, might not choose to continue the same laws, and the same administration. He might fancy it to be for his own interest to alter them, and to abridge his subjects in their private rights; and, in general, it may be depended upon, that governors will not consult the interest of the people, except it be their own interest too, because governors are but men. But while a number of the people have a share in the legislature, so as to be able to control the supreme magistrate, there is a great probability that things will continue in a good state. For the more political liberty the people have, the safer is their civil liberty.

[There may, however, be some kind of guard for civil liberty, independent of that which is properly called *political*. For the supreme magistrate, though *nominally*, he have all the power of the state in his hands, and, without violating any of the forms of the constitution, may enact and execute what laws he pleases; yet his circumstances may be such, as shall lay him under what is equivalent to a natural *impossibility* of doing what he would choose. And I do not here mean that kind of restraint, which all arbitrary princes are under, from the fear of a revolt of their subjects; which is often the consequence of great oppression; but from what may be called *the spirit of the times*.

Magistrates, being men, cannot but have, in some measure, the feelings of other men. They could not, therefore, be happy themselves, if they were conscious that their conduct exposed them to universal hatred and contempt. Neither can they be altogether indifferent to the light in which their characters and conduct will appear to posterity. For their own sakes, therefore, they will generally pay some regard to the sentiments of their people.

The more civilized any country is, the more effectual will this kind of guard to political liberty prove; because, in those circumstances, a sense of justice and honour have got firmer hold of the minds of men; so that a violation of them would be more sensibly felt, and more generally and strongly resented. For this reason, a gentleman of fashion and fortune has much less to dread in France, or in Denmark, than in Turkey. The confiscation of an overgrown rich man's effects, without any cause assigned, would make no great noise in the latter; whereas in those countries, in which the *forms* of law and liberty have been long established, they necessarily carry with them more or less of the *substance* also.

There is not, I believe, any country in Europe, in which a man could be condemned, and his effects confiscated, but a crime must be alleged, and a process of law be gone through. The confirmed habit of thinking in these countries is such, that no prince could dispense with these formalities. He would be deemed *insane*, if he should attempt to do otherwise; the succession would be set aside in favour of the next heir, by the general consent of the people, and the revolution would take place without blood shed. No person standing near any European prince would hesitate what to do, if his sovereign should attempt to cut off a man's head, out of mere wantonness and sport, a thing that would only strike the beholders with awe in some foreign courts.

Should the English government become arbitrary, and the people, disgusted with the conduct of their parliaments, do what the people of Denmark have done, choose their sovereign for their perpetual representative, and surrender into his hands all the power of the state; the forms of a free government have been so long established, that the most artful tyrant would be a long time before he could render life and property as precarious as it is even in France. The trial by *juries*, in ordinary cases, would stand a long time; the *habeas corpus* would, generally at least, continue in force, and all executions would be in public.

It may be questioned whether the progress to absolute slavery and insecurity would be more rapid, if the king were *nominally* arbitrary, or only *virtually* so, by uniformly influencing the house of Commons.

In some respects, so large a body of men would venture upon things which no single person would choose to do of his own authority; and so long as they had little intercourse but with one another, they would not be much affected with the sense of fear or shame. One may safely say, that no single member of the house would have had the assurance to decide as the majority have often done, in cases of controverted elections.

But, on the other hand, as the members of the house of Commons necessarily spend a great part of the summer months with their friends in the country, they could not show their faces after passing an act, by which gentlemen like themselves, or even their electors, should be much aggrieved; though they may now and then oppress the poor by unreasonable game acts, &c. because they never converse with any of the poor except their immediate dependants, who would not choose to remonstrate on the subject.

Besides, so long as the members of parliament are *elected*, though only once in seven years, those of them that are really chosen by the people can have no chance of being re-elected but by pleasing the people; and many of them would not choose to reduce themselves and their posterity, out of the house, to a worse condition than they originally were. Let them be ever so obsequious to a court, they will hardly choose to deprive themselves of all power of giving any thing for the future.

Independent, therefore, of all conviction of mind, there must be a *minority* in the house, whose clamour and opposition will impede the progress of tyranny; whereas a king, surrounded by his guards, and a cringing nobility, has no check. If, however, he be a man of sense, and read history, he may comprehend the various causes of the extreme insecurity of despotic princes; many of whom have appeared in all the pomp of power in the morning, and have been in prison, without eyes, or massacred, and dragged about the streets before night.

At all adventures, I should think it more wise to bear with a tyrannical parliament, though a more expensive mode of servitude for the present, than an arbitrary prince. So long as there is a power that can *nominally* put a negative upon the proceedings of the court, there is some chance, that circumstances may arise, in which the prince may not be able to influence them. They may see the *necessity*, if not the *wisdom* of complying with the just desires of the people; and by passing a few fundamentally good laws, true freedom may be established for ages; whereas, were the old forms of constitutional liberty once abolished, as in France, there would be little hope of their revival.

Whenever the house of Commons shall be so abandonedly corrupt, as to join with the court in abolishing any of the *essential forms of the constitution*, or effectually defeating the great purposes of it, let every Englishman, before it be too late, re-peruse the history of his country, and do what Englishmen are renowned for having formerly done in the same circumstances.]

Where civil liberty is intirely divested of its natural guard, political liberty, I should not hesitate to prefer the government of *one*, to that of a *number*, because a sense of shame would have less influence upon them, and they would keep one another in countenance, in cases in which any single person would yield to the sense of the majority.

Political and civil liberty have many things in common, which indeed, is the reason why they have been so often confounded. A sense both of political and civil slavery, makes a man think meanly of himself. The feeling of his insignificance debases his mind, checks every great and enterprising sentiment; and, in fact, renders him that poor abject creature, which he fancies himself to be. Having always some unknown evil to fear, though it should never come, he has no perfect enjoyment of himself, or of any of the blessings of life; and thus, his sentiments and his enjoyments being of a lower kind, the man sinks nearer to the state of the brute creation.

On the other hand, a sense of political and civil liberty, though there should be no great occasion to exert it in the course of a man's life, gives him a constant feeling of his own power and importance; and is the foundation of his indulging a free, bold, and manly turn of thinking, unrestrained by the most distant idea of control. Being free from all fear, he has the most perfect enjoyment of himself, and of all the blessings of life; and his sentiments and enjoyments, being raised, his very *being* is exalted, and the man makes nearer approaches to superior natures.

[Without a spirit of liberty, and a feeling of security and independence, no great improvements in agriculture, or any thing else, will ever be made by men.

A man has but poor encouragement to bestow labour and expense upon a piece of ground, in which he has no secure property; and when neither himself, nor his posterity, will, probably, ever derive any permanent advantage from it. In confirmation of this, I cannot help quoting a few instructive passages from *Mr Du Poivre's Travels of a Philosopher.*

It is his general observation, that 'a country poorly cultivated is always inhabited by men barbarous, or oppressed.' p. 5.

'In a terrestrial paradise, the Siamese are, perhaps, the most wretched people in the world. The government is despotic. The sovereign alone enjoys the true liberty which is natural to all mankind. His subjects are all slaves. Every one of them is annually taxed at six months personal service, without wages, and even without food.' p. 56.

On the other hand, 'The Chinese enjoy, undisturbed, their private possessions, as well as those which, being by their nature indivisible, belong to all; and he who buys a field, or receives it by inheritance from his ancestors, is of course the sole lord or master. The lands are free as the people, without feudal services, or fines of alienation. A tenth part of the produce of the earth is the only tax, or tribute, in the Chinese empire, since the origin of the monarchy. And such is the happy respect which the Chinese have for their ancient customs, that no emperor of China ever entertains the most distant thought of augmenting it, nor his subjects the least apprehension of such augmentation.' p. 78.

In arbitrary governments the *poor* are certainly the most safe, as their condition exhibits nothing that can attract the notice, or tempt the violence of a tyrant. If, therefore, a man aspire to nothing more than to get his bread by the labour of his hands, in some customary employment, he has little to fear, let him live where he will. Like the ass in the fable, he can but bear his burden. No governments can do without labourers and artisans. It is their interest to protect them, and especially those who are dexterous in the more elegant arts, that are subservient to luxury.

But the poorest can hardly be without some degree of ambition, except when that generous principle has been long repressed, and in a manner eradicated by a continual habit of slavery; and the moment that a man thinks of rendering himself in any respect conspicuous, for his wealth, knowledge, or influence of any kind, he begins to be in danger. If he have but a very handsome wife, he must not live near a despotic court, or in the neighbourhood of any great man who is countenanced by it. If he have wealth, he must hide it, and enjoy it in secret, with fear and trembling; and if he have sense, and think differently from his neighbours, he must do the same, or risk the fate of Galileo.]

I shall close this section with a few extracts from travellers, and other writers, which show the importance of political and civil liberty.

'In travelling through Germany,' says Lady M. W. Montague, 'it is impossible not to observe the difference between the free towns, and those under the government of absolute princes, as all the little sovereigns of Germany are. In the first there appears an air of commerce and plenty, the streets are well built, and full of people, the shops are loaded with merchandize, and the commonalty are clean and cheerful. In the other, you see a sort of shabby finery, a number of people of quality tawdried out, narrow nasty streets, out of repair, wretchedly thin of inhabitants, and above half of the common people asking alms.' *Lady M. W. Montague's Letters*, vol. i. page 16.

'Every house in Turkey,' the same excellent writer observes, 'at the death of its master, is at the grand seignior's disposal; and therefore no man cares to make a great expense, which he is not sure his family will be the better for. All their design is to build a house commodious, and that will last their lives, and they are very indifferent if it falls down the next year.' Ib. p. 70.

'The fear of the laws,' says the admirable author of the *Essay on crimes and punishments*, 'is salutary, but the fear of man is a fruitful and fatal source of crimes. Men enslaved are more voluptuous, more debauched, and more cruel than those who are in a state of freedom. These study the sciences, and the interests of nations. They have great objects before their eyes, and imitate them. But those whose views are confined to the present moment, endeavour, amidst the distraction of riot and debauchery, to forget their situation. Accustomed to the uncertainty of all events, the consequences of their crimes become problematical; which gives an additional force to the strength of their passions.' P. 166.

'The Turkish Bashaw once destroyed all the sugar canes in Cyprus, to prevent the people having too much wealth. This island is to this day the clearest proof that can be given, how much a bad government may defeat all the kind intentions of nature: for, in spite of all the advantages a country can possibly have, there never was a more desolate place than this island is at this day.' Thevenot in Knox's collection, vol. 6, p. 71.

There is hardly any greater instance of the wanton abuse of power, in the invasion of the natural rights of mankind, than in the *game laws*, that are in force in different states of Europe. England has just and great complaint to make on this subject; but we are not yet reduced to the deplorable condition of the Saxons, as it is described by Hanway, vol. 1. p. 433.

'Hunting is the ruling passion of the Saxon court, and fatal to the inhabitants. In the hard winter of 1740, it is computed, that above 30,000 deer died in the electorate of Saxony; and yet, in the open lands and forests, there are now reckoned to remain above that number, of which no person dares kill one, under the penalty of being condemned to the gallies. In every town of any note, there are fifty of the inhabitants who watch, five every night, by rotation, and use bells to frighten the deer, and defend their corn. Frequent remonstrances have been made to the court on this subject; but to no other purpose, than to convince the people of their slavery.' – *Felix. quem faciunt, aliena pericula cautum.* [*Essay*, III: 'Of civil liberty', Sect. 1]

The nation state

FRANCOIS-MARIE AROUET DE VOLTAIRE

BIOGRAPHICAL NOTE

François-Marie Arouet de Voltaire (1694–1778), satirist, epic poet, tragedian, scientist, historian, author of many moral, philosophical and political essays, and arguably the most brilliant, witty and influential, though not necessarily the most profound, of the French *philosophes*, was born in Paris to a prosperous middle-class family, and educated at the Jesuit College of Louis-le-Grand. By 1718 he had established himself as a dramatist of repute, but a quarrel with a powerful nobleman, the chevalier de Rohan, led to his exile from Paris, after a brief stay in the Bastille, and his eventual departure for London where he stayed from 1726 to 1728. Voltaire's English experience marked a crucial stage in his intellectual development, and resulted in the publication of the *Letters concerning the English nation* (1733), to be revised and published in 1734 as the *Philosophical letters* (1734). This work was condemned throughout France on publication, and the ensuing controversy obliged Voltaire to spend most of the next decade at Cirey with Mme Du Châtelet working on his translation of Newton's *Principia*. He was appointed Royal Historiographer to Louis XV in 1745, and elected to the French Academy in 1746.

After the death of Mme Du Châtelet in 1750 he accepted Frederick the Great's invitation to join his court at Potsdam. In the course of the next two decades he published many of his most important works, including the *Age of Louis XIV* (1751), the *Essay on the customs and spirit of nations* (1756), *Candide* (1759) and the *History of Russia under Peter the Great* (1759), engaging at the same time in increasingly bitter dispute with church and state authorities. It was during this period that Voltaire assumed leadership of the 'party of humanity', becoming known throughout Europe as 'le roi Voltaire'. By 1754–5 he had broken with Frederick, in whom he once had hopes of seeing Europe's first enlightened 'philosopher-king', and had settled in Geneva. In 1759 he moved to Ferney, situated strategically on the Franco-Swiss border, where he remained until his return to Paris in the last weeks of his life.

Intolerance and religious fanaticism were reaching new heights in France in the years marked by the start of Diderot's great enterprise to publish the

Encyclopedia in 1751, and this intensified after Robert Damiens' attempt on Louis XV's life in 1757. Voltaire's role in defending minority rights, and in holding the *philosophes* together at a time of great danger to their mission, became crucial. In 1762 Jean Calas, a Protestant accused of murdering his Catholic son, was broken on the wheel by order of the Toulouse *parlement*. The case was to be the first of the great public causes, with international reverberations, in which Voltaire challenged openly the power of the state in defence of the individual's rights to justice. The Calas affair was quickly followed by the campaign to rehabilitate Pierre-Paul Sirven, falsely accused in 1764 of murdering his daughter, a sinister echo of the Calas case. The *Treatise on tolerance* was published in 1763, followed in 1764 by the *Philosophical dictionary*.

Voltaire became involved in a third major *cause célèbre* in 1766 with the judicial torture and execution of a young teenager, the chevalier de La Barre, who had been put on trial in Abbeville, along with his companions, and accused of blasphemous behaviour. Voltaire dedicated his *Account of the death of the chevalier de La Barre* to Beccaria.

EDITORIAL NOTE

The texts of 'Homeland' and 'Man' follow the translation by D. Williams.* The base text for the Williams translation of 'Patrie' is the 1769 edition of the *Dictionnaire philosophique, comprenant les 118 articles parus sous ce titre du vivant de Voltaire, avec leurs suppléments parus dans les Questions sur l'Encyclopédie*, ed. J. Benda and R. Naves (Paris, Garnier, 1954), and more recently by C. Mervaud *et al.* in the *Œuvres complètes de Voltaire* (Oxford, The Voltaire Foundation, 1994), vols. xxxv–xxxvi. The base text for the Williams translation of 'Homme' is the *Œuvres complètes de Voltaire*, ed. L. Moland, 52 vols. (Paris, Garnier, 1877–85), xix, pp. 373–85.

FURTHER READING

Gay, P., *Voltaire's politics: the poet as realist* (New Haven/London. Yale University Press, 1988). Reprint.

Perkins, M., *Voltaire's concept of international order*, in *Studies on Voltaire and the Eighteenth Century*, 36 (1965).

Todd, C., *Voltaire: Dictionnaire philosophique* (London, Grant and Cutler, 1980).

*Williams, D. (ed.), *Voltaire: political writings* (Cambridge, Cambridge University Press, 1994). See introduction, pp. xii–xxxiv.

Articles from the *Philosophical Dictionary* and the *Questions on the Encyclopedia*

Homeland (1764)

We shall limit ourselves here, as is our custom, to posing a few questions that we cannot resolve.

Has a Jew got a homeland? If he has been born in Coïmbra it is among a herd of ignorant fools who would argue with him, and to whom, if he dared reply at all, he would give foolish answers. He is watched by inquisitors who will have him burnt if they learn that he does not eat bacon, and all that he owns will belong to them. Is Coïmbra his homeland? Can he love Coïmbra dearly? Can he say, as in Pierre Corneille's *Horace*:

> Alba, my dear country and my first love . . .
> To die for one's country is such a worthy fate
> That crowds would clamour for such a fine death.

Rubbish!

Is his homeland Jerusalem? He has heard vague talk that once upon a time his ancestors, whoever they were, lived in that stony, sterile land, bounded by an awful desert, but that today the Turks are masters of that little country, from which they get almost nothing. Jerusalem is not his homeland. He has none; there is not a square foot of land anywhere on earth that belongs to him.

Can the Ghebr, who is more ancient and a hundred times more respectable than the Jew, a slave of either the Turks or the Persians or the Grand Mogul, count on a few altar-pyres that he raises secretly on mountain-tops as being a sign of his homeland?

Can the Banian and the Armenian, who spend their lives wandering all over the East practising the art of broking, say 'My dear, dear country'? They have no country apart from their stock exchange and their ledgers.

Among our European nations, do all those murderers who hire out their services, and sell their blood to the first king who wants to pay them, have a homeland? They have no more homeland than a bird of prey returning each evening to the craggy hollow where its mother used to nest.

Would monks dare to say that they have a homeland? They say it is in Heaven; good luck to them, but I do not know where their homeland is in this world.

Would this word *homeland* be suitable in the mouth of a Greek, who is unaware that there was ever a Miltiades or an Agesilaus, and who only knows that he is a janissary's slave, who is the slave of an agha, who is the slave of a pasha, who is the slave of a vizir, who is the slave of a Padishah, whom we call in Paris the *Great Turk*?

So what is the homeland? Would it not be by any chance a good field whose owner, comfortably set up in a well-kept house, could say: This field I am cultivating and this house that I have built are mine. I live there under the protection of laws that no tyrant can transgress? When people like me, who own fields and houses, gather together in pursuit of their common interests, I have a vote in that assembly. I am part of the whole, a part of the community, a part of the sovereign power: that is my country. Apart from where men live, is it not the case that everywhere else tends to be a stable run by a groom who whips the horses when he feels like it? You have a country under a good king; you do not have one under a bad king.

A young apprentice pastry-cook, who had been to college, and who still knew a few sentences from Cicero, was preening himself on loving his homeland. 'What do you mean by your homeland?' asked a neighbour, 'is it your oven? Is it the village where you were born, and which you have never seen again since? Is it the street where your mother and father lived, who were ruined and who have reduced you to stuffing little pies for a living? Is it the Town Hall where you will never be a quarter-master's clerk? Is it the church of Our Lady where you have never been able to make it as a choirboy, while a ridiculous fool is archbishop and duke, with an income of twenty thousand gold *louis*?'

The apprentice pastry-cook did not know what to say in reply. A thinker, listening to this conversation, concluded that in a country spread over a fairly large area there were often several million people with no homeland.

You pleasure-loving Parisian, you say you love your homeland! You, who have travelled only as far as Dieppe for fresh fish, who know only your painted town-house, your pretty country house, your box at the Opera, where the rest of Europe persists in getting bored, who speak your mother-tongue so nicely because you don't know any other language, that's what you love, and you love even more the girls you entertain, the champagne you get from Reims, and the pension the Town Hall pays you every six months.

In all conscience, does a financier truly love his homeland?

Do the officer and the soldier, who will lay waste to their winter quarters if they are allowed to, feel a tender love for the peasants they ruin?

Where was the homeland of the Duke of Guise, old scar-face? Was it Nancy, Paris, Madrid, Rome?

What homelands did you have, Cardinals La Balue, Duprat, Lorraine and Mazarin?

Where was Attila's homeland, and that of a hundred heros of that ilk who, always rushing about, never diverged from their path?

I would really like someone to tell me which was Abraham's homeland.

The first to write that the homeland is the place where one feels at home is, I believe, Euripides in his *Phaethon*:

Ὡς πανταχοῦ γε πατρὶς ἡ βόσκουσα γῆ.

But the first man to leave his birthplace to look for somewhere else to feel at home said it before he [did].

A homeland is made up of several families; and just as you normally stand by your family out of pride, when there is no conflicting interest, because of that same pride you support your town or your village, which you call your homeland. The larger that homeland becomes, the less you love it, for a love that is divided is a love that is weakened. It is impossible to love a family dearly that is too large and whom you hardly know.

The man who burns with ambition to be an Aedile, a Tribune, a Praetor, a Consul, a dictator, declares that he loves his country, but he loves only himself. We all want to be sure of being able to sleep in our own beds without someone else arrogating to himself the right to tell us to sleep elsewhere. Everybody wants to be sure of his wealth and his life. With everyone thus having the same desires, it works out that private interest becomes the general interest: when we express our hopes for ourselves, we are expressing them for the Republic.

It is impossible for any state on earth not to have been governed first of all as a republic; it is the natural way forward for human nature. First a few families got together against the bears and the wolves. The family which had grain traded it with the family which had only wood.

When we discovered America, we found all the little tribes there divided into republics. There were only two kingdoms in the whole of that part of the world. Of a thousand nations we found only two that were enslaved.

It was the same with the ancient world. Everything was a republic in Europe before the time of the petty kings of Etruria and Rome. You can still see republics today in Africa. Tripoli, Tunis, Algeria, towards the North where we live, are republics of brigands. The Hottentots in the South still live as we are told people used to live in the earliest ages of man: free, equal, without masters, without subjects, without money, without needs almost. Meat from their sheep fed them, their skins clothed them, huts of wood and earth provided them with shelter. They stink worse than any other men, but are not aware of it; they live and die more peacefully than we [do].

In our Europe there remain eight republics with no monarchs: Venice, Holland, Switzerland, Genoa, Lucca, Ragusa, Geneva and San Marino. Poland, Sweden and England can be considered republics under a king, but Poland is the only one to call itself a republic.

Now, is it better for your homeland to be a monarchical state or a republican state? People have been worrying away at that question for four thousand years. If you ask the rich for a solution, they will all prefer an aristocratic system; ask the people, and they will want democracy. Only kings prefer monarchies. How is it possible, therefore, for almost the entire world to be ruled by monarchs? Ask the rats who proposed to bell the cat. But in truth the real reason is, as has been said before, that men are very rarely fit to rule themselves.

It is sad that in order to be a good patriot one is very often the enemy of the rest of mankind. The elder Cato, that good citizen, always said when speaking in the senate: 'That's what I think, and let Carthage go hang.' To be a good patriot is to want one's city to prosper through trade and be powerful through arms. Clearly, one country cannot win without another losing, and it cannot conquer without making some people unhappy.

So that is the human condition: to want your own country to be great is to wish your neighbours ill. The man who would want his homeland never to be larger, or smaller, or richer or poorer would be a citizen of the world.

Man (1771)

To understand the physical make-up of the human species, you must read works on anatomy, Mr Venel's articles in the *Encyclopaedic dictionary* or, better still, take a course in anatomy.

To understand what is called *moral* man, more than anything else it is necessary to have experienced life and to have reflected on it.

Are not all books on morality summed up in these words of Job: 'Homo natus de muliere, brevi vivens tempore, repletur multis miseriis; qui quasi flos egreditur et conteritur, et fugit velut umbra.' *Man that is born of woman does not live long; he is full of woe; he is like a flower that opens, withers and is crushed; he passes like a shadow.*

We have already seen that mankind has a life-span of only about twenty-two years, including those who die at their wet-nurse's breast and those who drag out what is left of their foolish, miserable lives for anything up to a hundred years.

That old story of the first man, who was destined at first to live a maximum of twenty years, is a fine parable. This came down to five years, taking the average life as the basis to the calculation. Man was in despair; close by was a caterpillar, a butterfly, a peacock, a horse, a fox and a monkey.

'Prolong my life', he said to Jupiter, 'I'm better than all those animals; it's only right that I and my children should live a very long time in order to become the masters of all these beasts.' 'With pleasure', said Jupiter, 'but I've only got a certain number of days to share out among all the beings to whom I've given life. I can only give to you by taking from others. For don't think that just because I'm Jupiter I'm infinite and omnipotent. I've got my own nature and limitations. Now, I'm very willing to give you a few more years, by taking those years from these six creatures you are jealous of, on condition that you take on their life-forms in turn. Man shall first be a caterpillar, crawling around [like a caterpillar] in early childhood. Up to fifteen he will be as fragile as a butterfly; as a youth he will have the vanity of a peacock. In adulthood he will have to work like a horse. In his fifties he will have the cunning of a fox; and in old age he will be as ugly and ridiculous as a monkey.' That just about sums up the destiny of man.

Note also that, in spite of Jupiter's kindness, this animal, even when all the compensations have been made, and with a maximum of twenty-two to twenty-three years of life, taking the human race as a whole, you have to take away a third of that for sleep, during which you are dead; fifteen or so years remain; of those fifteen, take off at least eight for early childhood, which is, as has been said, the hallway to life. The net yield will be seven years; of those seven years at least half will be taken up with various forms of suffering. Assume three and half years for work, boredom and frustration, and how many people have never had any of that! So there we are, poor little animal, are you still able to give yourself airs?

Unfortunately, in that parable, God forgot to dress this animal as he had dressed the monkey, the fox, the horse, the peacock, right down to the caterpillar. The human race only had its bare skin which, being continually exposed to sun, rain and hail, became cracked, burnt and blotchy. On our continent the male was disfigured by sparse body hair that made him hideous, without covering him. His face was hidden under his hair. His chin became a piece of bumpy ground with a forest of tiny stalks with roots on top and branches underneath. It was in this state, and taking his own appearance as the model, that this animal dared to portray God when, in the course of time, he learned to paint.

The female, being weaker, became even more disgusting and horrible in old age; the most hideous thing on earth is a senile old woman. So, without the help of tailors and dressmakers, the human race would never have dared to show itself in public. But before acquiring clothes, before even learning how to speak, many centuries had to pass. That is a proven fact, but it has to be reiterated frequently.

This uncivilised animal, left to himself, must have been the dirtiest and poorest of all the animals.

> Adam, my dear glutton, my good father,
> What did you do in the Garden of Eden?
> Did you work for this foolish human race?
> Did you caress my mother, Mrs Eve?
> Confess to me that both of you had
> Long nails, rather black and dirty,
> Hair that was pretty untidy,
> A dark complexion, your skin ruddy and tanned.
> Without cleanliness, the happiest love
> Is no love at all, just shameful need.
> Soon, weary of their wonderful adventure,
> They dined in fine style beneath an oak
> On water, birdseed and nuts.
> When they had eaten, they slept in the open.
> There is the state of pure nature for you.

It is a little strange that a very respectable contemporary philosopher, the good, innocent Helvétius, has been harassed, reviled, hunted down for having said that if men did not have hands they would not have been able to build houses, or work high-warp tapestry. Apparently, those who condemned this proposition have the secret of how to cut stone and wood, and do needlework with their feet.

I liked the author of the book called *On the mind*. That man is worth more than all his enemies put together; but I have never approved of either the errors in his book or the trivial truths that he utters rather ponderously. I took his side openly when silly people condemned him for those [very same] truths.

I cannot put into words the depth of my contempt for those people who, for example, wanted to legally outlaw this proposition: 'The Turks can be regarded as deists.' Come on, you ill-bred pedants, how do you want us to regard them? As atheists, because they worship only one God?

You also condemn this proposition: 'An intelligent man knows that men are what they must be; that all hatred for them is unjust; that a fool produces foolishness like wild stock produces bitter fruits.'

Oh! You wild stock of the schools, you persecute a man because he does not hate you.

Let us leave the schools there, and continue.

Reason, busy hands, a mind capable of forming ideas, a tongue supple enough to express them: these are the great benefits granted to man by the Supreme Being, to the exclusion of all other animals.

In general, the male lives for a slightly shorter time than the female.

He is always taller, relatively speaking. The tallest man is normally two or three inches taller than the tallest female.

His strength is almost always superior; he is more agile, and because his organs are all stronger, he is more capable of concentration. All the arts were invented by him, and not by woman. It should be noted that it is not the fire of imagination, but perseverance of thought processes and the combination of ideas that caused the arts to be invented, in the same way as machinery, gunpowder, printing, clock-making, etc.

The human species is the only one that knows that it must die, and it knows it only through experience. A child raised in solitude, and transported to a desert island, would have no more certain knowledge of it than a plant or a cat.

A man with a few eccentricities published a book saying that the human body is a fruit that stays green until old age, and that death is the moment of maturity. Rot and dust, that is a strange maturity! It is that philosopher's mind that was not mature. How the mania for saying something new makes people say wild things!

The main preoccupations of our species are shelter, food and clothing; all the rest are incidental, and it is these wretched, incidental things that have produced so much murder and devastation.

ON THE DIFFERENT RACES OF MEN

We have seen elsewhere how this world has in it different races of men, and how surprised the first negro and the first white man must have been when they met each other.

It is even quite probable that several species of men and animals that were too weak have perished. Thus no more murex are to be found; this species was probably devoured by other animals appearing after several centuries on the river banks inhabited by this little shellfish.

Saint Jerome, in his *History of the desert fathers*, speaks of a centaur which had a conversation with Saint Anthony, the hermit. He then gives an account of a conversation that is much longer than [the one that] this same Anthony had with a satyr.

Saint Augustine, in his thirty-third sermon, entitled *To his brothers in the desert*, says things that are just as extraordinary as those that Saint Jerome said: 'I was already the Bishop of Hippo when I went to Ethiopia with a few servants of Christ to preach the Gospel. We saw in that country a lot of men and women without heads, with two big eyes in their chests. In countries even further to the south we saw a people who had only one eye in their foreheads' etc.

It would appear that Augustine and Jerome were speaking at the time in terms of husbandry: they were increasing the works of creation to show to better advantage the works of God. They wished to astonish men with fables so that they could make them more submissive to the yoke of faith.

We can be very good Christians without believing in centaurs, in headless people, in people with only one eye or one leg, etc. But we cannot doubt that the insides of a negro are different to those of a white man, since the network of mucous or fatty membranes is white in one and black in the other. I have already told you that, but you are deaf.

The Albinos and the Darians, the first from Africa, the second from central America, are as different from us as negroes are. There are yellow, red and grey races. We have already seen that all Americans are beardless and have no body hair, except on their eyebrows and their heads. All are equally men, but in the same way as a pine tree, an oak and a pear tree are all equally trees. The pear tree does not come from the pine, and the pine does not come from the oak.

But how is it that in the middle of the Pacific Ocean, on an island called Tahiti, men have beards? That is like asking why we are bearded, while Peruvians, Mexicans and Canadians are not. It is like asking why monkeys have tails, and why nature has refused us this ornament, which is, to say the least, extremely rare among us [humans].

Men's inclinations and natures differ as much as their climates and their governments. It has never been possible to make up a regiment from Laplanders and Samoyeds, whereas their neighbours, the Siberians, make fearless soldiers.

You will have no more success in making a good grenadier out of a poor Darian or an Albino. It is not because they have tawny eyes; it is not because their hair and eyebrows are of the finest, whitest silky texture; but it is because their bodies, and hence their courage, are extremely weak. Only a blind man, and an obstinate blind man at that, could deny the reality of all these different species. It is as great and as varied as the monkeys.

THAT ALL RACES OF MEN HAVE ALWAYS LIVED IN SOCIETY

All people discovered in the most frightful and uncultivated countries live in society, as do beavers, ants, bees and several other animal species.

The country has not been seen where people live separately from one another, where the male mates with the female only by chance, and leaves her out of disgust a moment later; where a mother cannot recognise the children she has reared, where people live without families and without any form of society. A few practical jokers have abused their minds to the point of advancing the astonishing paradox that man was created originally to live alone like a lynx, and that it is society that has depraved his nature. It would be just as valid to say that in the sea herrings were created originally to swim alone, and that it is because of an excess of corruption that they swim in shoals from the polar sea to our coasts; that long ago cranes flew through the air apart from one another, and that through a violation of natural law they decided to travel together.

Each animal has its own instinct; and the instinct of man, strengthened by reason, inclines him towards society, as [it does] towards eating and drinking. The need for society has far from degraded man; it is when he moves away from society that he is degraded. Whoever wants to live completely alone would soon lose his reasoning powers and his ability to express himself; he would be a burden to himself; he would succeed only in changing himself into an animal. Excess of impotent pride, which clashes with the pride of others, can incline a melancholy soul to flee the company of men. In that case, it is that soul that is depraved. It punishes itself for this; its pride becomes its torture; in solitude the secret resentment at being scorned and forgotten gnaws away at it; in order to be free it has enslaved itself in the most horrible way.

Some people have gone so far beyond their normal foolishness as to say that 'it is not natural for a man to stay with a woman during the nine months of her pregnancy. Once their sexual appetite has been satisfied', says the author of these paradoxes, 'the man no longer needs such a woman, nor the woman such a man. The latter has not the slightest concern, nor perhaps the slightest idea, of the consequences of his action. One goes one way, the other goes another, and it would appear that at the end of nine months they have no memory of ever having known each other ... Why should he help her after the birth? Why should he help her raise a child whom he does not even know belongs to him?'

All that is revolting, but fortunately, nothing is more wrong. If this barbaric indifference was a true natural instinct, the human species would have always exhibited it. Instinct is unchangeable; its inconsistencies are very rare. Fathers would have always abandoned mothers, mothers would have abandoned their children, and there would be far less people in the world than there are carnivores; for wild beasts, better equipped and better armed, have a readier instinct, more certain means, and a more certain food-supply, than the human race.

Our nature is very different to the frightful piece of make-believe that this tub-thumper has made out of it. Except for a few barbaric and entirely brutalised souls, or except perhaps for an even more brutalised philosopher, the sternest of men loves, by an overwhelming instinct, the child that has not yet been born, the womb that bears it, and the mother whose love is redoubled for the one from whom she has received in her innermost being the seed of a being similar to herself.

The instinct of the charcoal-burners of the Black Forest speaks to them as loudly, and motivates them as strongly towards their children, as the instinct of pigeons and of nightingales does towards the feeding of their young. People have really wasted their time therefore writing this abominable twaddle.

Is not the great fault of all of these paradoxical books to assume always that human nature is different to what it is? If the satires on men and women that

Boileau wrote were not jokes, they would fall into this basic error of presuming all men to be mad, and all women to be wanton.

The same author, an enemy of society, who is like the fox without a tail, who wants all his fellow foxes to cut their tails off, expresses himself thus in magisterial style: 'The first person who, having enclosed a piece of land, ventured to say: *This is mine*, and found people simple-minded enough to believe him, was the true founder of civil society. What crimes, what wars, what murders, what misery and horror would have been spared the human race if, tearing up the stakes and filling in the ditches, someone had said to his fellow men: Take care not to listen to this imposter; you are lost if you forget that the fruits of the earth are for everyone, and that the earth belongs to no-one.'

Thus, according to this fine philosopher, a thief, a destroyer, would have been the human race's benefactor; and it would have been necessary to punish the honest man who might have said to his children: Let us imitate our neighbour; he has fenced off his field, the animals will no longer come and play havoc with it, his land will become more fertile; let us work ours like he has worked his. He will help us, and we will help him. With every family cultivating their own plot, we will be better fed, healthier, more peaceful, less unhappy. We will try to set up laws of distributive justice for the consolation of our poor species, and we will be worth more than the foxes and the ferrets, which this extremist wishes us to resemble.

Would that speech not be more sensible and honest than that of the wild lunatic who wished to destroy the fellow's orchard?

So what kind of a philosophy is it that makes people say things that common sense rejects from deepest China to Canada? Is it not the philosophy of a tramp who wants all the rich to be robbed by the poor in order to reinforce brotherly union among men?

It is true that if all the hedgerows, all the forests, all the plains, were covered with delicious nourishing fruits, it would be impossible, unjust and ridiculous to keep them for oneself.

If there are some islands where nature makes food, and all that is necessary to life, plentiful without any problem, let us all go and live there, away from the hotchpotch of our laws. But as soon as we have filled them with people, we will have to get back to the law of what is mine and what is yours, to those laws which are often very bad, but which we cannot do without.

WAS MAN BORN WICKED?

Does it not seem to have been proved that man was not born depraved and the child of the Devil? If his nature was like that, he would be committing dark, barbaric deeds as soon as he could walk. He would use the first knife he could find to wound whoever displeased him. He would necessarily resemble little wolf-cubs or foxes, who bite as soon as they are able to.

On the contrary, everywhere in the world his nature is like a lamb's while he is a child. So why and how does he so often turn into a wolf and a fox? Is it not because, having been born neither good nor wicked, education, example, the system of government into which he finds he has been tossed, and ultimately opportunity, determine whether he will follow the path of virtue or crime?

Perhaps human nature could not be otherwise. Man could not always have thoughts that were always wrong, nor thoughts that were always right, feelings that were always tender, nor feelings that were always cruel.

It appears to have been proved that women are better than men; you can see around you a hundred *brotherly enemies* for every one *Clytemnestra*.

There are professions which necessarily make the soul pitiless: that of the soldier, the butcher, the policeman, and jailer and all those jobs based on other people's misery.

The watchman, the henchman, the jailer, for example, are happy only in as much as they make others unhappy. They are, it is true, necessary to combat evil-doers, and in that way are useful to society; but out of a thousand men of that ilk, there is not one whose acts are motivated by the public interest, or who even understands how he serves the public interest.

It is particularly strange to hear them talk about their feats of valour, how they count up their number of victims, the tricks they use to trap them, the pain they make them suffer, and the money they make out of them.

Whoever has got down to examining the minor detail of the business of the bar; whoever has just listened to prosecutors arguing informally among themselves, and congratulating each other on the misfortunes of their clients, might have a very poor opinion of human nature.

There are professions that are even more ghastly, yet which are prized like canonries.

There are some which change an honest man into a rogue, and which accustom him, in spite of himself, to lying and deceiving almost without his noticing it; to putting on blindfolds; to deluding himself by self-interest and by the vanity of status, to plunge without remorse the human race into the depths of blind stupidity.

Women, who are continually occupied with the education of their children, and who are enclosed in [a world of] domestic duties, are excluded from all of these professions which pervert human nature, and make it atrocious. Everywhere they are less barbaric than men.

Physical factors combine with moral factors to distance them from great crimes; their blood is milder; they have less of a liking for strong liquor, which inspires savagery. An obvious proof of this is that out of a thousand victims of the law, a thousand executed murderers, you can scarcely count four women, as we have proved elsewhere. I do not believe that in Asia there are two examples of women being condemned to a public execution.

It appears, therefore, that it is our customs and practices that have made the male species very wicked.

If that was a general truth without any exceptions to it, that species would be more horrible than spiders, wolves and ferrets are to us. But fortunately those professions that harden the heart, and fill it with ugly passions, are few and far between. Note that in a country of about twenty million people, there are at most two hundred thousand soldiers. That is one soldier for every two hundred individuals. Those two hundred thousand soldiers are under the strictest control. Among them are very respectable people who go back to their villages to live out their old age as good fathers and husbands.

Other trades that are dangerous to morality are not numerous.

Ploughmen, artisans, and artists are too busy to get involved in crime very often.

There will always be detestable, wicked men in the world. Books always exaggerate their number which, while it is too big, is less than people say.

If the human race had been under the sway of the devil, there would be nobody left in the world.

Let us take consolation; fine men have been seen, and always will be seen, from Peking to La Rochelle, and whatever the academics and theologians might say, people like Titus, Trajan, the Antonines and Pierre Bayle, were very decent.

ON MAN IN THE STATE OF NATURE

What would man be like in the state of what is called *nature*? An animal far less advanced than the first Iroquois found in North America.

He would be far inferior to those Iroquois, since the latter knew how to ignite fire and to make themselves arrows. Centuries are needed to get to the stage of those two arts.

Man left in the state of nature would have as his only language a few badly articulated sounds; the species would be reduced to very small numbers through food problems and lack of shelter, at least in some of our more desolate parts of the world. There would be no more knowledge of God and of the soul than there would be of mathematics; man's ideas would be focussed on the concern to feed himself. The beavers would be preferable as a species.

That is when man would be just a sturdy child, nothing more nothing less. Many people have been seen in a state not much better than that.

The Laplanders, the Samoyeds, the inhabitants of Kamchatka, the Kaffirs, the Hottentots are to man in the state of nature what the courts of Cyrus and Semiramis once were compared to the inhabitants of the Cevennes Mountains. And yet those inhabitants of Kamchatka and today's Hottentots, who are so superior to true savages, are animals living for six months of the year in caves, where they eat with their bare hands the vermin by which they are themselves eaten.

In general, the human race is only by two or three notches more civilised than the people of Kamchatka. The multitude of dumb animals called *men*, compared to the small number of those who think, is in the ratio of at least a hundred to one in many countries.

It is amusing to consider on one side Father Malebranche, who is on such intimate terms with the Word, and on the other side those millions of animals like him who have never heard of the Word, and who do not have a single metaphysical thought in their heads.

Between men of pure instinct and men of genius float that huge number who are preoccupied exclusively with survival.

That survival costs such an enormously painful effort that often in North America an image of God has to run five or six miles to find something for supper, and in our country the image of God sprinkles the earth with [drops of] his sweat the whole year round to get bread.

If you add to that bread, or its equivalent, a hovel and a wretched garment, there you have man as he is generally throughout the world. And it is only over many, many centuries that he has been able to reach such a high level.

Finally, after a few more centuries, things have reached the stage we see them now. Here a musical tragedy is performed; there in another part of the world people are killing each other at sea with thousands of bits of bronze. An opera and a ship of the line always stretch my imagination. I doubt that one can go further than that on any planet where land is cultivated. Yet more than half of the habitable world is still populated with two-footed animals living in that horrible state near to nature, with barely enough to live on or to clothe themselves, barely enjoying the gift of speech, barely noticing that they are unhappy, living and dying almost without knowing it.

AN EXAMINATION OF ONE OF PASCAL'S THOUGHTS ON MAN

'I can conceive of a man without hands, without feet, and I would conceive of one without a head, if experience did not tell me that it is with this head that he thinks. Thus it is thought that constitutes the essence of man, and without it he could not be conceived of.'

How can you conceive of a man without feet, without hands and without a head? That would be a being as different from a man as from a pumpkin.

If all men were headless, how would your head conceive of the fact that they were animals like you, as they would have nothing of what mainly constitutes your essence? A head counts for something, the five senses are to be found there; thought also. An animal that looked like a man from the nape of the neck downwards, or like one of those monkeys called *orang-utan* or forest-men, would no more resemble a man than a monkey or a bear [would] with its head and tail cut off.

'Thus it is thought that constitutes the essence of man,' etc. In that case, thought would be his essence in the same way that mass and density are the essence of matter. It would be part of the essence of man to be thinking continually, just as matter always has mass and density. He would be thinking when in a deep, dreamless sleep, in a faint, in a state of lethargy, in his mother's womb. I know full well that I have never thought in any of those states. I am often conscious of this, and I suspect that other people are like me.

If thought was of the essence of man, as mass is of matter, it would follow that God was not able to deprive this animal of understanding, since he cannot deprive matter of mass: for then it would no longer be matter. Now, if understanding is of the essence of man, he is therefore a thinking being by virtue of his nature, just like God is God by virtue of *his* nature.

If I wished to try and define God, in as much as feeble creatures like ourselves can define him, I would say that thought is his being, his essence; but man!

We have the faculty of thinking, of walking, of speaking, of eating, of sleeping; but we are not continually making use of these faculties; that is not part of our nature.

Is not thought an attribute with us? And so much of an attribute that it is sometimes weak, sometimes strong, sometimes reasonable, sometimes foolish? It conceals itself, it reveals itself; it goes away, it comes back; it is non-existent; it revives. Essence is something else; it never varies; it does not experience any increase or decrease.

What is this headless animal postulated by Pascal supposed to be? A creature of reason. He might just as well have postulated a tree which God had imbued with thought, like they say the Gods had given a voice to the trees of Dodona.

A GENERAL REFLECTION ON MAN

Twenty years are needed to bring a man from the state of a plant in which he exists in his mother's womb, to the purely animal state, which is the lot of early childhood, to the state at which mature reason dawns. Thirty centuries were needed to gain some understanding of how he is constructed. An eternity would be needed to understand something of his soul. Just an instant is needed to kill him.

JOHANN GOTTFRIED HERDER

BIOGRAPHICAL NOTE

Johann Gottfried Herder (1744–1803) was born in Mohrungen in East Prussia into a poor family of pious Lutherans. After completing his theological studies at the University of Königsberg, he started work as a bookseller's clerk, but he continued to have contact with his former professors, of whom the most influential was Immanuel Kant. Between 1762 and 1764 he came increasingly under Kant's influence, and it was with Kant's help that his interest in philosophy and history developed. It was at this time that Herder also came into contact with Johann Georg Hamann, who opened Herder's eyes to folk poetry and German literature, and also turned Herder against the rationalist ethos of the Enlightenment. The third great influence in Herder's formative years in Königsberg was Rousseau, whose views on nature and natural man intensified his growing antipathy towards Enlightenment values and culture, although he was later to reject Rousseau's views on the conflict between the individual and society. In 1764 Herder moved to Riga where he wrote the *Fragments on German literature* attacking the ways in which German identity had been diluted by imitation of foreign cultures. There, freed from the constraints of Prussian rule, and in a town that still embodied the spirit of the old Hanseatic League, Herder's patriotism was rekindled.

In 1769 he decided to travel to Paris, where he worked for a time as a tutor to a young German Prince with whom he spent three years travelling around France and Europe. These travels resulted in the composition of a travel diary, the *Journal of my voyage in the year 1769*, containing reflections on myth and prejudice, as well as impressions of the various social and political cultures that he had encountered. By 1770 he was in Strasbourg where he underwent painful, and ultimately unsuccessful, eye surgery, and where he also came into contact with Goethe for the first time. In 1771 he moved to Bückerburg, in the principality of Schaumburg-Lippe, where he published his prize-winning essay *On the origin of language* (1772), and completed work on *Yet another philosophy of the history of man* (1774), *On the causes of the decline in taste in various nations* (1775) and *The earliest origins of mankind* (1774–6). In 1776 Goethe persuaded him to accept an ecclesiastical post at the court of the Duke of Weimar, by this time a flourishing centre of cultural and intellectual activity. Herder remained there for the rest of his life, becoming in 1789 Vice-President of the Consistory. He was ennobled by the Elector of Bavaria in 1801.

The Weimar years, during which he composed a voluminous series of treatises on literature, morality, culture and theology, were his most productive. In 1778 the Berlin Academy awarded him its prize for an essay on the influence of governments on the sciences, to be published in 1780 as the *Dissertation on the reciprocal influence of government and the sciences*. The *Ideas for a philosophy of the history of mankind* (1784–91), together with the *Letters for the advancement of humanity* (1793–7), contain some of his most original ideas on the formation of social and political cultures and identities.

Most of Herder's writings are fragmentary, and in many cases unfinished and unpolished. He wrote on a wide range of subjects, but it was his vividly and lucidly formulated thoughts on nationhood and German identity in the *Ideas* and in the *Letters*, writings appearing at a time of unprecedented political upheaval, that caught the attention of late eighteenth-century Europe, and stimulated the study of nationalism as part of the philosophy of history throughout the nineteenth century and beyond.

EDITORIAL NOTE

Extracts from the *Ideas for a philosophy of history* are taken from the translation by F. Barnard.* The base text for the translation of extracts from the *Letters for the advancement of humanity* is that printed in volume v of *Werke*, ed. W. Dobbek (Berlin and Weimar, Bibliothek Deutscher Klassike, 1964), pp. 199–205.

FURTHER READING

*Barnard, F., *J. G. Herder on social and political culture* (Cambridge, Cambridge University Press, 1969). See introduction, pp. 3–60.

Barnard, F., *Herder's social and political thought: from Enlightenment to nationalism* (Oxford, Clarendon Press, 1965).

Berlin, I., 'Herder and the Enlightenment', in *Aspects of the eighteenth century*, ed. E. Wassermann (Baltimore and London: Johns Hopkins Press and Oxford University Press, 1965), pp. 49–53.

Ergang, R., *Herder and the foundations of German nationalism* (New York, Octagon Books, 1966).

Ideas for a philosophy of the history of mankind
(1784–91)

Priestley and others have objected to the spiritualists that no such thing as pure spirit is to be found throughout Nature and that we know far too little about the intrinsic structuring of matter to rule out the possibility of thought or other spiritual powers being material. Both points seem valid to me. We know of no spirit capable of operating apart from, or without, matter. What is more, we observe in matter so many powers of a spirit-like nature, that a complete *opposition* and *contradiction* of these admittedly different elements strikes me as at least unproven if not self-contradictory. For how could we account for the fact that two elements that were fundamentally dissimilar from, and essentially opposed to, each other, would succeed in working together in the closest possible harmony? How, indeed, could we assert that they *are* essentially different or incompatible if we know nothing of the inner nature of either?

Wherever we observe a power in operation, it is inherent in some organ and in harmony with it. For power as such is not open to investigation, at least not by our senses. It only exists for these by its manifestations in and through material forms which, if we may trust the analogy pervading nature as a whole, have been fashioned by it to meet its particular requirements. Seeds *in posse*, lying dormant since Creation, are not evident to our eyes; all that we observe from the first moment of a creature's existence are acting *organic powers*. If an individual being contains these within itself, it propagates its species without assistance. If the sexes are divided, each must contribute to the organization of their progeny, and in different modes according to the diversity of their structure . . . The more complex the organization of a creature, the less recognizable is what we call its seed or genetic origin. It is *organic matter* which, in order to attain the form of the prospective creature, requires the addition of vital powers or life forces. What processes take place in the egg of a bird, before the young acquires and completes its form! The organic powers must destroy while they arrange; they attract parts together and separate them in turn. Indeed it seems as if several powers were in conflict and on the point of causing a miscarriage until an equilibrium is established between them and the creature becomes what it has to become by virtue of its species. Bearing in mind these transformations, these living operations in the egg of the bird or in the womb of the mammal, I feel we speak imprecisely if we talk of seeds that are merely evolving in the manner of an *epigenesis*, according to which limbs are superadded from without. For what really takes place is *creative and total development* or *genesis*, i.e., the operation of internal powers within a mass which Nature supplies and which is being fashioned by these powers in the manner that is manifest to us . . .

The reader would, however, misinterpret my meaning were he to ascribe to me the view that, as some have put it, our *rational mind* forms its structure in the womb by means of its inherent reason. We have noted earlier how late reason develops within us; that, though we are born with a capacity for it, we are not capable of possessing or acquiring it by our own unaided power. How could something which is so highly dependent in its maturation on *conscious* human development possibly come into being at a time when the major part of our vital functions are performed without any conscious volition of our mind, when we are wholly incapable of comprehending any part of its internal or external operations? It was not our reason that fashioned the body, but organic powers, the finger of creative Divinity . . .

If, therefore, we follow the course of Nature, it is evident that:

1. *Powers and organs are indeed intimately connected, but they are not one and the same thing.* The matter of our body existed, but it was shapeless and lifeless until fashioned and vitalized by the organic powers.

2. *Every power operates in harmony with its organ.* For it has fashioned it in such a way as to manifest its essential nature in and through it. It assimilated the parts supplied by the Almighty and used them, as it were, as its husk.

3. When the husk falls off, *the power, which existed before it*, though in an inferior state, *remains*. If it was possible for the power to pass from its original state into a later one, it should not be inconceivable that it might be equally capable of a further transition when it loses its husk. He who has brought it into being originally, albeit in an imperfect form, will take care to provide a medium for its further transformation . . .

Thus, I believe, the fallacy of the arguments by which the materialists imagine they have refuted the notion of immortality becomes evident. Granted that we know nothing of our soul as pure spirit; we even have no wish to know it as such. Granted, too, that it acts only as an organic power; for it is not supposed to act otherwise. Indeed, I would add, our mind only acquired reason and an essentially human character (*Humanität*), by means of organic powers such as the brain and the nerves which enabled it in the first place to learn how to think and feel.

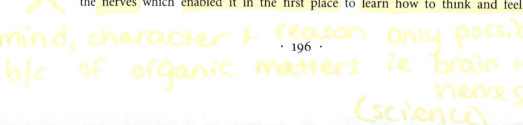

Finally, let us grant also that mind and matter, and all the powers of matter, of attraction and repulsion, of motion, of life, originally form one single entity. Does it, however, follow from this that even such basic powers as attraction and motion are one and the same thing as the material organs through which they manifest themselves? Moreover, is it conceivable that these powers simply vanish or perish? Has anyone ever witnessed the complete destruction of any one single power inherent in nature? Is it not feasible to assume that the combination of matter and power is capable of undergoing a series of mutations from its original state to a more developed and subtle organization? ... [*Ideas*, v, 2: 'No power in nature is without an organ; but the organ is not power itself, but merely its medium']

The principal doubt usually raised against the immortality of organic powers stems from confusing the media through which these powers operate with the powers themselves. I venture to assert that by casting light on this doubt I can not only brighten a hope, but even kindle a certain assurance concerning the efficacy and continuity of their creative propensities. No flower blossoms as a result of the external dust or the mere structure of its material particles. No single activity of so complex an organization of powers as the human mind can be simply resolved into the component parts of the brain. Even physiology bears this out. The external picture that is painted on the eye does not reach the brain; the sound that strikes the ear does not mechanically enter the mind as sound. To imagine the brain, therefore, to be self-cogitative, the neural fluids to be self-sentient, is poor physiology indeed. Surely it is more in keeping with general experience to posit *specific psychological laws* according to which the mind combines ideas and performs its other functions. That it performs these functions in conformity and harmony with its organs is not disputed. If the tools are defective, the greatest artist will fail to produce great works of art. But all this does not in the slightest affect the point I am trying to make here. For I am concerned with the *manner* in which the mind operates and with the *essential nature of its ideas*.

1. It cannot be gainsaid that the *thought* and, indeed, the first perception, by means of which the mind forms an 'image' of an external object is *something totally different from what the sensation itself conveys to the mind*. For what we call an image is not the speck of light which is reflected in the eye and does not even reach the brain. The image in the mind is the product of an intellectual process; it is the creation of the mind itself in response to the stimuli received by the

senses. From the chaos of things that surrounds it, the mind calls forth a configuration (*Gestalt*) on which it focuses its attention and in this manner creates by means of its intrinsic power a unity out of multiplicity, a whole *sui generis*, entirely of its own making. The mind can recall or reconstruct the image, once formed, even when the object to which it refers is no longer present. Dreams and the imagination can and do form it according to laws very different from those underlying normal sense perceptions. The frenzies of disease, which have so often been adduced as proofs of the materiality of the soul, actually attest its immateriality. Listen to the mentally disturbed and observe the progress of his mind. He starts off from the idea which touched him so deeply and as a result deranged his intellectual make-up to such an extent that the connection between the idea and other sensations is broken. Everything is referred by him to the one idea because it dominates him, he is possessed by it and cannot shake it off. In the light of it he creates a world of his own, a concatenation of thoughts of its own peculiar kind, and all the wanderings of his mind and the manner in which it combines ideas is *mental* in the highest degree. It is not the result of a peculiar position of the cells of his brain, nor of the sensations as such, but is wholly determined by the affinity other ideas bear to his *idée fixe* and by the degree the latter warps the former. All the associations of our thought proceed in the same way. They are characteristic of beings capable of recalling past experiences by their own energy and of doing so quite frequently with a particular idiosyncrasy. Ideas are connected, not by some external mechanism, but by feelings of internal affection or repulsion. I wish that ingenious men, especially physicians, would make known the qualities they observe in their patients. If this were done, I am convinced we should have clear evidence of the operations of an admittedly organic, but nonetheless self-powered being, acting in conformity to laws of mental inter-relation.

2. The same thing is demonstrated by the *artificial formation of our ideas from childhood on* and by the slow process through which the mind acquires consciousness of itself and the effort it expends in learning the use of the senses. More than one psychologist has observed the ingeniousness with which a child acquires the idea of colour, figure, magnitude and distance and thus *learns to see.* The sense organ as such learns nothing. For the image is depicted in the eye as faithfully on the first day of life as on the last, but it is the mind which learns to measure, to compare and to absorb the stimuli of the senses. In this the mind is assisted by the ear and by language. That language is an intellectual, and not a material, tool in the formation of ideas seems to me beyond doubt. One must be

wholly devoid of intelligence to regard sounds and words as one and the same thing, for they are as disparate as body and mind, organ and creative power (*Kraft*). A word evokes a corresponding idea and transmits it to our mind from that of another person. But a word by itself is not an idea, any more than a material organ is a thought. As the body gains by taking in food, so our mind is enlarged by absorbing ideas. And we observe in the latter the same laws of *assimilation, growth,* and *production,* only not in a physical manner but in a mode peculiar to itself. Nonetheless, the mind can, like the body, take in food in excess of what it can absorb and convert into nourishment. It must, therefore, preserve a balance of its intellectual powers if it is not to succumb to disease and enfeeblement, i.e., to madness . . . It is not a fanciful exaggeration to say that within every one of us an *inner man of intellect* is continuously taking shape, with a nature of his own, who uses the body only as his implement, and who acts in conformity with this nature even if the bodily organs are seriously impaired. The more the mind gets separated from the body by disease or by violent emotional upsets and is thus forced to move as it were within its own world of ideas, the more we can witness its own power and energy in the creation and connection of ideas. In despair it wanders through the scenes of its earlier life and, unable by its very nature to forgo forming ideas, it creates a new world for itself.

3. That great distinguishing feature of the human mind, clear *consciousness,* has been *acquired by it only gradually in the course of a process of intellectual humanization.* A child possesses little consciousness, even though its mind incessantly attempts to attain it in order to gain awareness of itself and of its sense perceptions. All its endeavours to acquire ideas serve this process, whereby the growing individual strives to ascertain his place in, and relationship to, God's world, so that he can come to enjoy his existence and the use of his human energies. The animal, by contrast, goes through the world as if in a dark dream; its consciousness is diffused through the parts of the body receiving stimuli, and is indeed so powerfully enveloped by these that the progressive emergence of a clearer self-awareness never takes place. Man, too, it is true, is conscious of his sensual nature only by means of his senses; when these suffer injury in any way, his mind may be affected to the extent that one dominant idea can cause his self-awareness to be impaired. In this state he becomes an actor in a drama of his own choosing whether it be a comedy or a tragedy. But even when he is thus transported into a region of phantasy, his consciousness is still operative, his internal power of self-determination is still in evidence in however misguided a

manner ... He may forget himself, become unaware of the lapse of time and indifferent to the promptings of his senses. Yet he is conscious of the high calling of his dominant idea and determined to pursue it. The most dreadful sufferings of the body have often been suppressed by one such vivid idea prevalent in the mind. Men imbued with a strong sentiment, particularly that of the love of God – which may well be the purest and most intense – have shown a complete disregard for life and death. With all their other ideas submerged under one dominant thought, they feel themselves to be in Heaven ... Even the most primitive and the most savage peoples display the power of ideas. Irrespective of what they fight for, they fight under the impulse of ideas. The cannibal, no doubt, expresses his craving for revenge and bravery in an abominable manner, but this does not make his craving any less *spiritual.*

4. Thus, whatever the circumstances, whatever the organic disabilities or peculiarities, it is not they which constitute the *primary* power ... When, one day, the same systematic study that is now devoted to the cure of physical diseases will be applied to disorders of the mind, it will be found that many of the former are in fact attributable to the latter. The realization of this fact will shatter the dogmas of the materialists and cause them to vanish like mists before the sun. Those who are convinced of an *inner life of the self* cannot but regard the external circumstances which continually bring about change in the body, as in all other matter, as secondary and transitory factors that do not affect its essence ...

Of this the Creator has given us ample evidence in our daily experience. We are closest to death when we are asleep, since most of the important functions of life are then in abeyance. Nerves and muscles repose; the senses cease to perceive; yet the mind continues to operate in its own domain. It is no more separated from the body than when it is awake, as the perceptions often interwoven in our dreams bear out. Even in deep sleep – of the dreams of which we have no recollection unless we are suddenly awakened – the mind operates according to laws of its own. Many people have observed that in undisturbed dreams their mind pursues the same series of ideas uninterruptedly, in a manner different from that of waking hours ... The perceptions in a dream are more vivid, the emotions more violent, the connection between a thought and its realization more direct, our sight is keener, and the light surrounding us more brilliant. In healthy sleep we often fly rather than walk, our dimensions are enlarged, our resolutions have more force, our actions are less confined. And though all this depends on the body with which the most minute operation of the mind must necessarily harmonize (in view of their close structural interrelationship), all the phenomena of sleep and dreaming – which would greatly astonish us were we not so accustomed to them – reveal that not every part of our body is equally involved. Certain organs of our machine may be quite inactive, yet this in no way affects the power of our mind to think connectedly, vividly and freely, and to do so, frequently, with greater intensity than when they are active. Now, since all the causes that induce sleep, and all its physical symptoms, are physiologically, and not merely metaphorically, *analogous to those of death*, why should the spiritual symptoms not be likewise? . . . [*Ideas*, v, 4: 'The sphere of human organization is a system of creative mental powers']

Everything in nature is connected: one state strives towards and prepares for the next. If, then, man be the last and highest link, closing as it were the chain of terrestrial organization, he must also begin the chain of a higher order of creatures as its lowest link. He is, therefore, probably, the middle ring between two adjoining systems of Creation. Since no living power can stand still or retreat in the realm of nature, it must push forward, it must progress. This means that for man to progress there must be a further step before him which is at once close to and exalted above him, just as, in the other direction, he is at once bordering on the animal and elevated above it. This view of things, which is supported by all the laws of nature, alone gives us a key to the wonderful phenomenon of man and hence also to a possible *philosophy of human history.*

For if we bear this view in mind, it helps us to throw light on the peculiar contradiction that is inherent in the human condition. Man considered as an animal is a child of the earth and is attached to it as his habitation; but considered as a human being, as a creature of *Humanität*, he has the seeds of immortality within him, and these require planting in another soil. As an animal he can satisfy his wants; there are men who wish for no more and hence can be perfectly happy here below. But those who seek a nobler goal find everything around them imperfect and incomplete, since the most noble has never been accomplished and the most pure has rarely endured on this earth. This is amply illustrated by the history of our species, by the many attempts and enterprises that man has undertaken, and by the events and revolutions that have overtaken him. Now and then a wise man, a good man, emerged to scatter ideas, precepts and deeds onto the flood of time. They caused but ripples on the waters, which the stream soon carried away and obliterated; the jewel of their noble purposes sank to the bottom. Fools overpowered the counsels of the wise and spendthrifts inherited the treasures of wisdom collected by their forefathers . . . An animal lives out its life, and even if its years be too few to attain higher ends, its innermost purpose is accomplished; its skills are what they are and it is what it is meant to be. Man alone of all creatures is in conflict with himself and with the world. Though the most perfect among them, in terms of potentialities, he is also the least successful in developing them to their fullest extent, even at the end of a long and active life. He is the representative of two worlds at once, and from this derives the apparent bipolarity of his nature.

It is not hard to see which part is likely to predominate in most men of this world. The greater part of man is his animal nature. He has brought into the world only a capacity for realizing his human essence (*Humanität*). It requires the utmost effort and diligence to transform this capacity into an operative principle of human behaviour. How few have achieved this, or been helped to achieve it, in the right manner! And how delicate and slender is the divine plant even in the best of us! Throughout life the brute strives to prevail over the man and there are not many who resist the former's dominance. It drags him down when his human spirit and his human heart crave for elevation and a freer sphere. And since the present appears more real and vivid to a sensual creature than the remote, since the visible affects him more powerfully than the invisible, it is not difficult to guess which way the balance tilts. Of how little pure joy, pure knowledge and virtue is man capable! . . . A man who has experienced things deeply, has also learned from them; the careless and indolent learns nothing. He is ignorant of himself and incapable of assessing his actual or potential abilities. Human life, then, is a conflict, and the realization of pure immortal humanity the hard-won crown of a ceaseless struggle .

man is limited

This much is certain: in each of man's powers dwells an infinity which cannot be developed in his present state where it is repressed by other powers, by animal drives and appetites, and weighed down, as it were, by the pulls and pressures of our daily chores . . . The expression of Leibniz, that the mind is a mirror of the universe, contains perhaps a more profound truth than is commonly realized. For the powers of the universe that seem to lie concealed in the mind require only an organization, or a series of organizations, to set them in action . . . To the mind, even in its present fetters, *space* and *time* are empty concepts. They only measure and denote relations of the body and do not bear upon the internal capacity of the mind which transcends time and space ... [*Ideas*, v, 6: 'The present state of man is probably the connecting link of two worlds']

present + the universe

No two leaves of any one tree are exactly alike in nature; still less two human faces or two human constitutions. Of what endless variety is the intricate structure of our body capable! ... 'No man,' says Haller, 'is exactly similar to another in his internal structure; the system of the nerves and blood vessels differs in millions and millions of particulars, so that amidst the variations of these delicate parts, we are scarcely able to discover in what they agree.' If the eye of the anatomist can perceive this infinite variety, what about the possibly even greater variety that may characterize the invisible powers inherent in so intricate an organization? Is not every man, in spite of his external resemblance to other men, in the last analysis (because of this uniquely individual internal structure) a cosmos in himself and, as such, a wholly incomparable being?

Yet man is not an independent entity. All elements of nature are connected with him. He cannot live without air, without nourishment from the many products of the soil, without other diverse foods, and without drink. And whilst he is thus formed and changed with the help of the universe around him, he, in turn, whether he be awake or asleep, at rest or in motion, contributes towards its change. As he makes use of fire, as he absorbs light and contaminates the air he breathes, he continually inter-acts with the elements of his environment. It is scarcely an exaggeration to compare him to an absorbing sponge, or to a glimmering tinder. Man constitutes a multitudinous harmony, a multiplicity and a unity, within his living self, acting, and acted upon, by the harmony of the forces surrounding him.

Man makes use of world

A man's life is one continuous series of change and its phases read like sagas of transformation. The species as a whole goes through a ceaseless metamorphosis. Flowers drop and wither; others sprout and bud. According to calculations based on perspiration, a man of eighty has renovated his whole body at least twenty-four times. If this is so, who can trace the change of matter and its forms through the entire realm of mankind upon earth, by its diverse causes, when not a single point on our diversified globe and not a single wave in the stream of time is like any other? Only a few centuries ago the inhabitants of Germany were giants; but they are so no longer, and their inhabitants in future periods and climates will be equally unlike us ... Thus the history of man is ultimately a theatre of transforma-

Different stages in a man's life

tions which only He, who animates these events and lives and feels Himself in all of them, can review . . .

But since the human understanding seeks unity in diversity, and since its proto-type, the divine mind, has everywhere combined the greatest possible multiplicity with unity, we are brought back to our original proposition which simply asserted that, in spite of the vast realm of change and diversity, *all mankind is one and the same species upon earth.*

I wish the affinity of man to the ape had never been pushed so far as to over-look, while seeking a scale of Being, the actual steps and intervals, without which no scale can exist . . . Most of these apparent resemblances happen to be found in countries where apes never existed, as the reclining skulls of the Kalmucks and Mallicollese, the prominent ears of the Pevas and Amikwa, the small hands of some savages in Carolina, and other instances, show. Moreover, as soon as one has got over first appearances, one finds that the resemblances are quite illusory and actually reveal very little that is of an ape-like nature. Kalmucks and Negroes are entirely human, including the structure of the head and the brain, and the Mallicollese display abilities that many other natives do not possess. It seems quite manifest that apes and men never were one and the same genus. I have yet to come across any evidence that could verify the tiniest remnants of fables which purport that somewhere men and apes have formed sexual relations and lived in joint communities. For each genus Nature has done her share and to each she has given its proper progeny. She has divided the ape into as many species and varieties as possible, and extended these as far as she could. But thou, o man, honour thyself: neither the pongo nor the gibbon is thy brother, but the American [Indian] and the Negro are. These, therefore, thou shouldst not oppress, or murder, or rob; for they are men like thee; with the ape thou canst not enter into fraternity.

Lastly, I should like to express the hope that distinctions that have been made – from a perfectly laudable zeal for scientific exactitude – between different mem-bers of the human species will not be carried beyond bounds. Some, for instance, have thought fit to employ the term *races* for four or five divisions, according to regions of origin or complexion. I see no reason for employing this term. Race refers to a difference of origin, which in this case either does not exist or which comprises in each of these regions or complexions the most diverse 'races'. For every distinct community is a *nation*, having its own national culture as it has its own language. The climate, it is true, may imprint on each its peculiar stamp, or it may spread over it a slight veil, without destroying, however, its original national character. This originality of character extends even to families and its transitions are as variable as they are imperceptible. In short, there are neither four or five races, nor exclusive varieties, on this earth. Complexions run into each other; forms follow the genetic character; and *in toto* they are, in the final analysis, but different shades of the same great picture which extends through all ages and all parts of the earth. Their study, therefore, properly forms no part of biology or systematic natural history but belongs rather to the anthropological history of man. [*Ideas*, VII, 1: 'In spite of considerable differences between men in different parts of the world, there is but one and the same human species']

The natural state of man is society. He is born and brought up in it, and his emerging impulses lead him to it during the years of adolescence. Words which are associated in his mind with the most tender feelings are father, mother, son, brother, sister, lover, and friend; all these entail natural ties which exist in the most primitive societies. The first forms of government arose out of these natural social relationships. They were, essentially, family rules and regulations without which human groupings could not persist; laws formed and limited by nature. We could regard them therefore as representing *natural government of the first order*. It is the most basic political organization, and has proved the most lasting if not the best.

With this stage Nature considered her task accomplished: the foundations of society were laid. It was now up to man to build a higher structure on these foundations if reason or need were to call for it. In all the regions where particular tribes and kinship groups have less need of each other's assistance, they also take less interest in each other's concerns and, as a result, give little thought to the creation of large political systems. This is true of coasts inhabited by fishermen, of pastures and forests and their herdsmen and hunters. Where in these areas paternal and domestic governments cease to be effective, the extension of political organization usually takes the form of *ad hoc* arrangements contractually made for a given task. A nation of hunters, for instance, may feel the need for a leader when embarking on the chase. Such a leader, however, will only be a leader of the hunt. His election as leader will be determined by his reputation as a skilful hunter, and his electors freely choose to obey him because his expertise serves their common interests. For the same reason all gregarious animals elect a leader in such common concerns as migration, attack and defence. A political organiza-

· 205 ·

tion of this type we may classify as *natural government of the second order.* It will be found among those peoples whose chief concerns are common material needs and who are said to live therefore in a state of nature. Even the elected judges of a community come within this category of government; for they are elected to their office by virtue of their wisdom and sense of fairness, and for one specific task only. Their sphere of competence and range of power starts and ends in carrying out this limited task.

Yet how different is the *third type of political order*, hereditary government! For where do the laws of nature begin or cease to operate under such a system? That men in conflict should choose the wisest and most just among their fellows to resolve their disputes for as long as they proved competent was in keeping with the natural order of things. But if the old judge dies, is there any reason why his son should succeed him in office? Surely, the fact that he was begotten by a just and wise father does not constitute such a reason. For neither wisdom nor justice is hereditary. The son is not his father. The nation's recognition of the father's status for purely personal reasons does not commit it to extend the same recognition to his son. Now imagine that a law would be passed that all the descendants of the judge, as yet unborn, should enjoy the same recognition and prestige as he did, merely on account of their birth. Would it not be hard to reconcile such a piece of legislation, enshrining so blatantly the hereditary principle, with the very rudiments of reason and justice? Nature does not distribute her noblest gifts in families. The right of blood, according to which one unborn has a legitimate claim to rule over others yet unborn by right of his birth, is to me one of the most puzzling formulae human language could devise.

There must have been other grounds for the introduction of hereditary government among men, and history is by no means silent about these. What has given Germany, what has given civilized Europe, its governments? The answer is *war.* Hordes of barbarians overran the continent; their leaders and nobles divided the lands and their inhabitants among them. By these means principalities and fiefs arose; serfdom came into being. The conquerors were in possession; any alterations that have occurred since, have been the result of revolutions, wars, and mutual agreements between the powerful, that is to say, by the right of the stronger. This is the royal road of history, and the facts of history speak for themselves. What brought the world under the sway of Rome? What made Greece and the East subservient to Alexander? What has given rise to, or caused the ruin of, all the monarchies since the time of Sesostris and the fabulous Semiramis? The

WAR

answer again is *war*. Forcible conquests assumed the place of law. Only the passage of time or, as our political jurists phrase it, the tacit compact, conferred right upon might, and turned a feat of the sword into an act sanctioned by law. But the tacit compact in this case consists merely in the stronger taking what he wants, and the weaker giving what he cannot keep, or enduring what he cannot change. Thus the right of hereditary government, as that of almost any other hereditary possession, depends on a chain of traditions, the first link of which was forged by force or accident and was followed, occasionally, by wisdom and goodness, but as a rule by more force or further accidents. Heirs and descendants received what the ancestors had taken. That to him who has, more is given in abundance, scarcely needs explaining, for it is the natural corollary of the principle of first possession by the stronger. It applies alike to men and to lands.

As long as a father ruled over his family, he was a *father* (and not a monarch), permitting his sons to become fathers in turn, and seeking no mode of control over them other than that of advice. As long as several tribes chose in free elections their judges and their leaders for any given task, the incumbents of these offices were only servants of the common weal, like chairmen appointed to preside over a meeting. Names such as sovereign, king, absolute prince, arbitrary and hereditary despot, were unknown to these political associations. But if the nations fell asleep and allowed their fathers, leaders and judges to govern over them, in a fit of drowsy gratitude for imagined or real services, or out of fear of their power and wealth, and went so far as to endow them with an hereditary sceptre, they ceased to be adults and turned themselves into children or sheep in need of a tutor or shepherd. The result was utter weakness on the one side and a monopoly of power on the other; in short the right of the stronger. When Nimrod first killed animals and then subjugated men, he acted in both cases as a hunter. The leader of a colony or a clan, whom men followed like animals, soon treated them as such. Whilst they were employed in civilizing the people, they were its fathers and instructors, observing the laws for the general good. But as soon as they became absolute or, indeed, hereditary rulers, they became the personification of power over their powerless subjects. Frequently a fox took the place of the lion, and then the fox was the stronger. For strength does not consist in the force of arms alone. Cunning, trickery, and artful deceit achieve in most cases more than sheer physical power.

In short, the considerable differences in physical and intellectual endowments among men, or sheer accident, has established despotism and servitude on earth, varying in form according to areas, periods and modes of life. In many places change consisted merely in the transition of one form of despotism into another. Warlike mountain peoples, for example, overran the peaceful plains; climate, hardship and want had made them strong and courageous. They spread themselves over the earth as its overlords until they in turn became the victims of luxury in milder climates and then fell under the yoke of others. Our old planet has been a prey to violence and its history presents a melancholy picture of man-hunts and conquests. Almost every little variation of a boundary, every new epoch, is inscribed in the book of Time with the blood of human victims and the tears of the oppressed. The most celebrated names are those of the murderers of mankind, crowned or crown-seeking executioners, and, even more distressingly, the worthiest of men have often been compelled by necessity to help in forging the chains of their brethren. We may well ask why the history of world empires displays such a dearth of rationality in their final achievements. The answer is not hard to find. The majority of history-making events did not spring from rational motives; passions, not humane reason, dominate the world and urge its peoples like wild beasts against each other. Had it pleased Providence to let superior beings govern humanity, its history would, no doubt, have been different. As it was, those who governed humanity have, for the most part, been *heroes*, that is to say, ambitious men, cunning or enterprising seekers of power and glory, who, prompted by passion, spun the thread of events which fate or accident wove into the cloth of history. If nothing else in the history of the world should point to the baseness of our species, the history of government would do so amply. Judging by it, our planet has been mis-named. More appropriately, it should be called Mars or child-devouring Saturn.

. . . The inequality of men is, however, not so great in nature as it has become through education; the nature of the very same people under different political regimes clearly bears this out. Even the noblest nation loses its dignity under the yoke of despotism. The very marrow is crushed in its bones; its finest and most exquisite talents are abused in the service of lies and deceit. Despotism creates slaves, cringing base creatures, shameless flatterers, and dissolute luxury. No wonder that the people eventually accustom themselves to the yoke, that they kiss their chains and decorate them with flowers. From such an abyss of habitual slavery a nation has rarely risen again without the miracle of a complete regeneration.

We may rightly lament this fate of mankind in both history and every-day life;

but we must not delude ourselves into believing that it is the work of nature. Nature extended the bonds of society only to families. Beyond that stage it was left to man how to construct a polity, this most intricate work of art. If he built well, he fared well; if he chose, or endured, tyranny and bad forms of government, he also had to bear their burdens. His good mother, Nature, could do no more than instruct him by means of reason, the tradition of history, or his own perception of pain and misery. Some form of internal human degeneration, therefore, must be the cause of the vices and depravities of political government . . .

But even in man's deepest degeneracy, he is not forsaken by his untiringly beneficent mother Nature. For she contrives at least to mitigate the bitterness of oppression by such palliatives as habit and oblivion. As long as nations retain some vigilance and vigour, or where they are nourished by Nature with the hard bread of industry, no effeminate sultans will stand much chance of success: the rugged land, the hardy way of life, are the pillars of their freedom . . .

Let me, finally, make some general observations.

1. The maxim, that 'man is an animal that needs a lord when he lives with others of his species, so that he may attain happiness and fulfil his destiny on earth', is both facile and noxious as a fundamental principle of a philosophy of history. The proposition, I feel, ought to be reversed. Man is an animal as long as he needs a master to lord over him; as soon as he attains the status of a human being he no longer needs a master in any real sense. Nature has designated no master to the human species; only brutal vices and passions render one necessary. The wife requires a husband; the untutored child requires the instruction of the parents; the sick need the services of a physician; conflicting parties select an umpire, and the herd a leader. These are natural relations; they are inherent in the very notions themselves. The notion of despot, however, is not inherent in the notion of man. It presupposes man to be weak, under age, and hence incapable of managing his own affairs. As a result he needs a protector and guardian. Or, on the other hand, it presupposes man to be a wild, detestable creature, demanding a tamer or a minister of vengeance. Thus all governments of man arose, and continue to exist, because of some human deficiency. A father who brings up his children in a manner which keeps them under age for the rest of their lives and hence in need of a tutor and guardian, is rightly considered a bad father. A physician who contrives to keep his patient in a wretched state to the end of his days so that he will not dispense with his services, is hardly a credit to his profession. Let us apply this line of reasoning to the political teachers of mankind, to the

fathers of nations and their charges. Either the latter are incapable of improvement, or it is odd that the thousands of years that men have been governed should have shown no more perceptible results or even revealed the aims of the educators.

2. It is nature which educates families: the most natural state is, therefore, *one nation*, an extended family with one national character. This it retains for ages and develops most naturally if the leaders come from the people and are wholly dedicated to it. For a nation is as natural a plant as a family, only with more branches. Nothing, therefore, is more manifestly contrary to the purpose of political government than the unnatural enlargement of states, the wild mixing of various races and nationalities under one sceptre. A human sceptre is far too weak and slender for such incongruous parts to be engrafted upon it. Such states are but patched-up contraptions, fragile machines, appropriately called state-*machines*, for they are wholly devoid of inner life, and their component parts are connected through mechanical contrivances instead of bonds of sentiment. Like Trojan horses these machines are pieced together, guaranteeing one another's immortality; yet since they are bereft of national character, it would only be the curse of Fate which would condemn to immortality these forced unions, these lifeless monstrosities. They were contrived by that kind of politics which plays with men and nations as if they were inanimate particles. But history shows sufficiently that these instruments of human pride are formed of clay, and, like all clay, they will dissolve or crumble to pieces.

3. Mutual assistance and protection are the principal ends of all human associations. For a polity, too, this natural order is the best; it should ensure that each of its members be able to become what nature wanted him to become. As soon as the monarch wants to usurp the position of the Creator and bring into being by his own arbitrary will or passion what God had not intended, he becomes the father of misrule and inevitable ruin. The distinctions of social rank, established by tradition, run counter to the forces of nature, which knows no ranks in the distribution of its gifts. Yet since these distinctions persist, it is not surprising that most nations, having tried various forms of government and incurred the inconveniences of each, finally returned in despair to that which wholly made them into machines: despotic hereditary government . . .

O, that another Montesquieu would come and really offer us the spirit of the laws and governments of our globe, instead of a mere classification of governments into three or four empty categories, when in fact no two governments are alike. A classification of states, based on political principles, is also of little avail; for no state is founded on verbal principles, let alone invariably adheres to them at all times or under all circumstances. Least of all are we in need of a scissors and paste approach, where examples are assembled at random from all nations, times, and climates, until we can no longer see the wood for the trees; the genius of our earth as one entity is lost. What we do need is a vivid and philosophical presentation of civil history in which, despite the apparent uniformity, no one scene occurs twice. Not the external constitution as such will reveal the continuous change to which a state and its political institutions are subject, but rather the internal changes in the character and culture of a nation. It is only by tracing the historical process of these inner, and essentially traditional, forces, that we can hope to explain the continuous development of the boldest of man's mechanical works of art.

[*Ideas*, vii, 4: 'Political organization consists of set rules and orders among men, grounded, for the most part, in tradition']

Letters for the advancement of humanity (1793–7)

DEFENCE OF ONE'S OWN NATION

Self-defence is the root of all human and national worth. If a people does not respect itself, how can others respect it, and in turn be respected by it? A nation that cannot defend itself will soon become the mockery and plaything of every other nation, just like worthless Italy.

A few years ago, when the words *coalition powers* were bandied about in newspapers and in conversation, there was much talk in one social gathering about these unusual words. People spoke about that dangerous, much sought-after Brotherhood (Fraternity) of Nations, about the workings of the court of the Amphictionies and their decline among the ancient Greeks, about the Achaean League, the Panaetolium, about the unification of Asia and Europe that Alexander had in mind, and about the principles upon which the unification of the Italian States, the kingdom of Britain, the Swiss Confederation, the seven Belgian Provinces, and the unfortunate Poles were or were not based. The subject of our Germany – so close to the poor Poles – eventually came up, and people spoke of how near the Germans were, in the process of growing together, to [achieving] an internal coalition, or of what hope there was for this. Their song would have dropped down to the level of a tune from Jeremiah's Threnody, or fallen into the rivers of Babylon, if one of the people taking part in the conversation had not livened things up with a reading from a little work called the *Dangers of the age.*[1] When the company, who could not decide on peace or war, got over their shock, they agreed on the following points, tested by time and the world:

1. That a nation that has pride in itself deserves respect; that only a nation with the will and the strength to defend itself, and a constitution suited to the times, is a [true] nation. A constitution, in which individual members fight duels without being punished, bring misfortunes upon others, but neither can nor wish to defend themselves, is no national constitution.

2. A nation, that neither knows nor honours nor loves its own language, has deprived itself of its tongue and its brain, i.e. of its organ [needed] for its own education and for the noblest honour of the nation. If an enemy, whose language it corrupts, whose fashions it follows, whose habits and customs it affects, came with scissors in hand to cut off, like a son of Orcus, its locks of hair, or to cut them in a ridiculous way [as a mark of shame], what would it say?

3. A nation, to which the religion of its forefathers is hateful, is alien or indifferent, has renounced the Palladium of its constitution. In its place there is nothing to be done except to follow the *System of Nature,* or some other miserable piece of foreign superstition that transfixes you with the dazzling words of some fanatic. These wretched gods are the false gods of words and of the arts of deception. From the highest and noblest in the land this contempt for everything sensible and wise (including religion) spreads inexorably to the masses who would like to do without the constraints of positive duties (religion) and morality, for why should they alone wear these shackles? An unavoidable precipice of future immorality and unbound confusion, created by people we will wish were dead and buried! Oh, if only Germany had not come apart in such an unfortunate way in the Reformation! If only the nation had remained like a god and a sacred text, a Christ and a confession. Yet this [Germany] is still there and perhaps, if a new order of things comes about, the German heart and spirit will have a national religion, i.e. the religion of Christ, which assures the heart and spirit of true human freedom.

---

[1] The allusion is to Johannes von Müller's *Anfangs August 1796,* a patriotic, anti-French pamphlet.

4. A nation, whose literature is a tattered coat, from which one province tears the shreds from the hands of another, a nation that shows no participation in the sciences, as though those who work as scientists despise and curse each other in their various countries, a nation that hands out letters of liberty so that in every province a closed-in Pandaemonium of good taste might blossom forth to the honour and slight advantage of that little corner of the world – truly that is a long way from uniting people in salutary exertions of the intellect! A long way from the aims set out by our own Leibniz, who wrote his works near various German Academies of Science, and who wanted to co-ordinate their work.

5. If this disintegration has finally spread to everything in the nation, if arrogance and disputes over ranks and titles (*querelles allemandes*) is the whole story of the nation, ... if the holder of a high Imperial rank knows no greater fame than the servant of the holder of a far lower rank –

Here the conversation became so depressing because of its abject theme, that it just petered out into the sands [of silence]. We were all of the opinion that in Germany, if we do not want to be a second Poland, there could be no task more noble than that of destroying this divisiveness. All weapons of persuasion and irony, of good heart and a sound common sense, must be used to cast down every petty provincial idol to Dan and Bethel, and to brush aside illusion and conceit, and inspire in everyone the great feeling that we are one people, one fatherland, one language. That in all this we must have self-respect, and strive to learn from all nations how to be objective and impartial so that we ourselves can yet learn to be a nation.

The conversation extended to stories of self-defence ranging, I would say, from worms to elephants, from individuals to whole nations. Everyone was agreed on one thing, namely that the most useful example for young people of noble self-defence in the Book of Heroes is that of a man who wishes to keep his honour undamaged, who never wishes to attack the honour of others, and who above all is always ready to help the innocent when they are in danger. Only thoughtless arrogance likes to turn away from the sick, loves wars of aggression, and gambles with its own honour. 'Nine times', says Montesquieu, 'have the French been expelled from Italy for their outrageous treatment of women and young girls. It is asking too much of a nation to put up with a conqueror's pride and malice, even more so to put up with his intemperance, and then even more so again to put up with his thoughtlessness.' What goes for one nation, goes for all (similar) nations and peoples. The surest way to preserve another person's honour is to value one's own honour. The root of all virtue is to keep a careful watch over yourself, and when in danger to defend yourself to the last.

Government

DAVID HUME

BIOGRAPHICAL NOTE

David Hume (1711–76), one of the greatest of Enlightenment philosophers, was born to a well-established rural family in Ninewells, and educated in Edinburgh as a lawyer. A leading economic and political theorist, he was also one of the eighteenth century's most prominent historians, and a close friend of Adam Smith. In addition to his more celebrated treatises, he is also the author of a large number of short political essays on government, freedom of the press, the parliamentary system, civil liberty, balance of power, trade, taxation, contractual theory and cultural and scientific matters.

In 1734 Hume moved to France where he spent three years, during which he completed the first draft of *A Treatise of human nature* (1739–40). He returned to Scotland in 1739, and the *Essays, moral and political* appeared between 1741 and 1742. In 1745 he became a tutor to the Marquess of Annandale, and then spent two years as secretary to General St Clair working on diplomatic and military business. In 1748 he published the *Philosophical essays concerning human understanding*, later to be known as the *Enquiry concerning human understanding*. He had now embarked on the most productive period in his life. The *Enquiry concerning the principles of morals* appeared in 1751, to be followed by the *Political discourse* (1752), the *History of England* (1754–62) and the *Four dissertations* (1757). Hume worked as a secretary to the British ambassador in Paris between 1763 and 1766, and became part of French salon and cultural life at a crucial and intellectually turbulent time. His career as a public servant culminated in 1767 with his two-year appointment as Under-Secretary of State and Minister for Scottish Affairs. His last two works, *My own life* and the controversial *Dialogues concerning natural religion*, were published after his death, in 1777 and 1779 respectively.

Hume's views matured at a time of great uncertainty in British political life during the post-1720 Whig ascendancy, a period marked by threats of invasion from supporters, particularly in France, of the Stuart cause, culminating in the 1745 rebellion. Two major European wars were to take place in his lifetime, the War of the Austrian Succession (1740–8) and the Seven Years War (1756–63), fought largely on issues relating to naval power and international trade. Scotland suffered particularly great economic hardship in this period, the 1707 Union of England and Scotland having illuminated sharply the economic and constitutional discrepancies between the two parts of what was now known as Great Britain. Hume's writings on public issues reflect much of this background of change, insecurity and tension.

EDITORIAL NOTE

The extracts are taken from K. Haakonssen's edition,* for which the base text is taken from the 1772 and 1777 editions of the *Essays and treatises on several subjects* (London: T. Cadell; Edinburgh: A. Kincaid). This was the last edition to be authorised by Hume.

FURTHER READING

Forbes, D., *Hume's philosophical politics* (Cambridge, Cambridge University Press, 1975).
*Haakonssen, K. (ed.), *Hume: political essays* (Cambridge, Cambridge University Press, 1994). See introduction, pp. xi–xxx.
Miller, D., *Hume's political thought* (Oxford, Oxford University Press, 1981).
Stewart, J., *Opinion and reform in Hume's political philosophy* (Princeton, N.J.: Princeton University Press, 1992).

Political essays (1741–77)

That politics may be reduced to a science (1741)

IT is a question with several, whether there be any essential difference between one form of government and another? and, whether every form may not become good or bad, according as it is well or ill administered? Were it once admitted, that all governments are alike, and that the only difference consists in the character and conduct of the governors, most political disputes would be at an end, and all *Zeal* for one constitution above another, must be esteemed mere bigotry and folly. But, though a friend to moderation, I cannot forbear condemning this sentiment, and should be sorry to think, that human affairs admit of no greater stability, than what they receive from the casual humours and characters of particular men.

It is true; those who maintain, that the goodness of all government consists in the goodness of the administration, may cite many particular instances in history, where the very same government, in different hands, has varied suddenly into the two opposite extremes of good and bad. Compare the FRENCH government under HENRY III. and under HENRY IV. Oppression, levity, artifice on the part of the rulers; faction, sedition, treachery, rebellion, disloyalty on the part of the subjects: these compose the character of the former miserable aera. But when the patriot and heroic prince, who succeeded, was once firmly seated on the throne, the government, the people, every thing seemed to be totally changed; and all from the difference of the temper and sentiments of these two sovereigns. Instances of this kind may be multiplied, almost without number, from ancient as well as modern history, foreign as well as domestic.

But here it may be proper to make a distinction. All absolute governments must very much depend on the administration; and this is one of the great inconveniences attending that form of government. But a republican and free government would be an obvious absurdity, if the particular checks and controuls, provided by the constitution, had really no influence, and made it not the interest, even of bad men, to act for the public good. Such is the intention of these forms of government, and such is their real effect, where they are wisely constituted: As on the other hand, they are the source of all disorder, and of the blackest crimes, where either skill or honesty has been wanting in their original frame and institution.

So great is the force of laws, and of particular forms of government, and so little dependence have they on the humours and tempers of men, that consequences almost as general and certain may sometimes be deduced from them, as any which the mathematical sciences afford us.

The constitution of the ROMAN republic gave the whole legislative power to the people, without allowing a negative voice either to the nobility or consuls. This unbounded power they possessed in a collective, not in a representative body. The consequences were: When the people, by success and conquest, had become very numerous, and had spread themselves to a great distance from the capital, the city-tribes, though the most contemptible, carried almost every vote: They were, therefore, most cajoled by every one that affected popularity: They were supported in idleness by the general distribution of corn, and by particular bribes, which they received from almost every candidate: by this means, they became every day more licentious, and the CAMPUS MARTIUS was a perpetual scene of tumult and sedition: Armed slaves were introduced among these rascally citizens;

so that the whole government fell into anarchy, and the greatest happiness, which the ROMANS could look for, was the despotic power of the CAESARS. Such are the effects of democracy without a representative.

A Nobility may possess the whole, or any part of the legislative power of a state, in two different ways. Either every nobleman shares the power as part of the whole body, or the whole body enjoys the power as composed of parts, which have each a distinct power and authority. The VENETIAN aristocracy is an instance of the first kind of government: The POLISH of the second. In the VENETIAN government the whole body of nobility possesses the whole power, and no noble-man has any authority which he receives not from the whole. In the POLISH government every nobleman, by means of his fiefs, has a distinct hereditary authority over his vassals, and the whole body has no authority but what it receives from the concurrence of its parts. The different operations and tendencies of these two species of government might be made apparent even *a priori.* A VENETIAN nobility is preferable to a POLISH, let the humours and education of men be ever so much varied. A nobility, who possess their power in common, will preserve peace and order, both among themselves, and their subjects; and no member can have authority enough to controul the laws for a moment. The nobles will preserve their authority over the people, but without any grievous tyranny, or any breach of private property; because such a tyrannical government promotes not the interest of the whole body, however it may that of some individuals. There will be a distinction of rank between the nobility and people, but this will be the only distinction in the state. The whole nobility will form one body, and the whole people another, without any of those private feuds and animosities, which spread ruin and desolation every where. It is easy to see the disadvantages of a POLISH nobility in every one of these particulars.

It is possible so to constitute a free government, as that a single person, call him doge, prince, or king, shall possess a large share of power, and shall form a proper balance or counterpoise to the other parts of the legislature. This chief magistrate may be either *elective* or *hereditary*; and though the former institution may, to a superficial view, appear the most advantageous; yet a more accurate inspection will discover in it greater inconveniencies than in the latter, and such as are founded on causes and principles eternal and immutable. The filling of the throne, in such a government, is a point of too great and too general interest, not to divide the whole people into factions: Whence a civil war, the greatest of ills, may be apprehended, almost with certainty, upon every vacancy. The prince elected must be either a *Foreigner* or a *Native*: the former will be ignorant of the people whom he is to govern; suspicious of his new subjects, and suspected by them; giving his confidence entirely to strangers, who will have no other care but of enriching themselves in the quickest manner, while their master's favour and authority are able to support them. A native will carry into the throne all his private animosities and friendships, and will never be viewed in his elevation, without exciting the sentiment of envy in those, who formerly considered him as their equal. Not to mention, that a crown is too high a reward ever to be given to merit alone, and will always induce the candidates to employ force, or money, or intrigue, to procure the vote of the electors: So that such an election will give no better chance for superior merit in the prince, than if the state had trusted to birth alone for determining their sovereign.

It may therefore be pronounced as an universal axiom in politics, *That an hereditary prince, a nobility without vassals, and a people voting by their representatives, form the best* MONARCHY, ARISTOCRACY, *and* DEMOCRACY. But in order to prove more fully, that politics admit of general truths, which are invariable by the humour or education either of subject or sovereign, it may not be amiss to observe some other principles of this science, which may seem to deserve that character.

It may easily be observed, that, though free governments have been commonly the most happy for those who partake of their freedom; yet are they the most ruinous and oppressive to their provinces: And this observation may, I believe, be fixed as a maxim of the kind we are here speaking of. When a monarch extends his dominions by conquest, he soon learns to consider his old and his new subjects as on the same footing; because, in reality, all his subjects are to him the same, except the few friends and favourites, with whom he is personally acquainted. He does not, therefore, make any distinction between them in his *general* laws; and, at the same time, is careful to prevent all *particular* acts of oppression on the one as well as on the other. But a free state necessarily makes a great distinction, and must always do so, till men learn to love their neighbours as well as themselves. The conquerors, in such a government, are all legislators, and will be sure to contrive matters, by restrictions of trade, and by taxes, so as to draw some private, as well as public, advantage from their conquests. Provincial governors have also a better chance, in a republic, to escape with their plunder, by means of bribery or intrigue; and their fellow-citizens, who find their own state to be enriched by the spoils of the subject provinces, will be the more inclined to tolerate such abuses. Not to mention, that it is a necessary precaution in a free state to change the governors frequently; which obliges these temporary tyrants to be more expeditious and rapacious, that they may accumulate sufficient wealth before they give place to their successors. What cruel tyrants were the ROMANS over the world during the time of their commonwealth! It is true they had laws to prevent oppression in their provincial magistrates; but CICERO informs us, that the ROMANS could not better consult the interest of the provinces than by repealing these very laws. For, in that case, says he, our magistrates, having entire impunity, would plunder no more than would satisfy their own rapaciousness; whereas, at present, they must also satisfy that of their judges, and of all the great men in ROME, of whose protection they stand in need. Who can read of the cruelties and oppressions of VERRES without horror and astonishment? And who is not touched with indignation to hear, that, after CICERO had exhausted on that abandoned criminal all the thunders of his eloquence, and had prevailed so far as to get him condemned to the utmost extent of the laws; yet that cruel tyrant lived peaceably to old age, in opulence and ease, and, thirty years afterwards, was put into the proscription by MARK ANTHONY, on account of his exorbitant wealth, where he fell with CICERO himself, and all the most virtuous men of ROME? After the dissolution of the commonwealth, the ROMAN yoke became easier upon the provinces, as TACITUS informs us; and it may be observed, that many of the worst emperors, DOMITIAN, for instance, were careful to prevent all oppression on the provinces. In TIBERIUS's time, GAUL was esteemed richer than ITALY itself: Nor, do I find, during the whole time of the ROMAN monarchy, that the empire became less rich or populous in any of its provinces; though indeed its valour and military discipline were always upon the decline. The oppression and tyranny of the CARTHAGINIANS over their subject states in AFRICA went so far, as we learn from POLYBIUS, that, not content with exacting the half of all the produce of the ground, which of itself was a very high rent, they also loaded them with many other taxes. If we pass from ancient to modern times, we shall still find the observation to hold. The provinces of absolute monarchies are always better treated than those of free states. Compare the *Païs conquis* of FRANCE with IRELAND, and you will be convinced of this truth; though this latter kingdom, being, in a good measure, peopled from ENGLAND, possesses so many rights and privileges as should naturally make it challenge better treatment than that of a conquered province. CORSICA is also an obvious instance to the same purpose.

There is an observation in MACHIAVEL, with regard to the conquests of ALEX-ANDER the Great, which I think, may be regarded as one of those eternal political truths, which no time nor accidents can vary. It may seem strange, says that politician, that such sudden conquests, as those of ALEXANDER, should be possessed so peaceably by his successors, and that the PERSIANS, during all the confusions and civil wars among the GREEKS, never made the smallest efforts towards the recovery of their former independent government. To satisfy us concerning the cause of this remarkable event, we may consider, that a monarch may govern his subjects in two different ways. He may either follow the maxims of the eastern princes, and stretch his authority so far as to leave no distinction of rank among his subjects, but what proceeds immediately from himself; no advantages of birth; no hereditary honours and possessions; and, in a word, no credit among the people, except from his commission alone. Or a monarch may exert his power after a milder manner, like our EUROPEAN princes; and leave other sources of honours, beside his smile and favour: Birth, titles, possessions, valour, integrity, knowledge, or great and fortunate achievements. In the former species of government, after a conquest, it is impossible ever to shake off the yoke; since no one possesses, among the people, so much personal credit and authority as to begin such an enterprize: Whereas, in the latter, the least misfortune, or discord among the victors, will encourage the vanquished to take arms, who have leaders ready to prompt and conduct them in every undertaking.

Such is the reasoning of MACHIAVEL, which seems solid and conclusive; though I wish he had not mixed falsehood with truth, in asserting, that monarchies, governed according to eastern policy, though more easily kept when once subdued, yet are the most difficult to subdue; since they cannot contain any powerful subject, whose discontent and faction may facilitate the enterprizes of an enemy. For besides, that such a tyrannical government enervates the courage of men, and renders them indifferent towards the fortunes of their sovereign; besides this, I say, we find by experience, that even the temporary and delegated authority of the generals and magistrates; being always, in such governments, as absolute within its sphere, as that of the prince himself; is able, with barbarians, accustomed to a blind submission, to produce the most dangerous and fatal revolutions. So that, in every respect, a gentle government is preferable, and gives the greatest security to the sovereign as well as to the subject.

Legislators, therefore, ought not to trust the future government of a state entirely to chance, but ought to provide a system of laws to regulate the administration of public affairs to the latest posterity. Effects will always correspond to causes; and wise regulations in any commonwealth are the most valuable legacy that can be left to future ages. In the smallest court or office, the stated forms and methods, by which business must be conducted, are found to be a considerable check on the natural depravity of mankind. Why should not the case be the same in public affairs? Can we ascribe the stability and wisdom of the VENETIAN government, through so many ages, to any thing but the form of government? And is it not easy to point out those defects in the original constitution, which produced the tumultuous governments of ATHENS and ROME, and ended at last in the ruin of these two famous republics? And so little dependence has this affair on the humours and education of particular men, that one part of the same republic may be wisely conducted, and another weakly, by the very same men, merely on account of the difference of the forms and institutions, by which these parts are regulated. Historians inform us that this was actually the case with GENOA. For while the state was always full of sedition, and tumult, and disorder, the bank of St. GEORGE, which had become a considerable part of the people, was conducted, for several ages, with the utmost integrity and wisdom.

The ages of greatest public spirit are not always most eminent for private virtue. Good laws may beget order and moderation in the government, where the manners and customs have instilled little humanity or justice into the tempers of men. The most illustrious period of the ROMAN history, considered in a political view, is that between the beginning of the first and end of the last PUNIC war; the due balance between the nobility and people being then fixed by the contests of the tribunes, and not being yet lost by the extent of conquests. Yet at this very time, the horrid practice of poisoning was so common, that, during part of a season, a Praetor punished capitally for this crime above three thousand persons in a part of ITALY; and found informations of this nature still multiplying upon him. There is a similar, or rather a worse instance, in the more early times of the commonwealth. So depraved in private life were that people, whom in their histories we so much admire. I doubt not but they were really more virtuous during the time of the two *Triumvirates*; when they were tearing their common country to pieces, and spreading slaughter and desolation over the face of the earth, merely for the choice of tyrants.

Here, then, is a sufficient inducement to maintain, with the utmost ZEAL, in every free state, those forms and institutions, by which liberty is secured, the public good consulted, and the avarice or ambition of particular men restrained and punished. Nothing does more honour to human nature, than to see it susceptible of so noble a passion; as nothing can be a greater indication of meanness of heart in any man, than to see him destitute of it. A man who loves only himself, without regard to friendship and desert, merits the severest blame; and a man, who is only susceptible of friendship, without public spirit, or a regard to the community, is deficient in the most material part of virtue.

But this is a subject which needs not be longer insisted on at present. There are enow of zealots on both sides who kindle up the passions of their partizans, and under pretence of public good, pursue the interests and ends of their particular faction. For my part, I shall always be more fond of promoting moderation than zeal; though perhaps the surest way of producing moderation in every party is to increase our zeal for the public. Let us therefore try, if it be possible, from the foregoing doctrine, to draw a lesson of moderation with regard to the parties, into which our country is at present divided; at the same time, that we allow not this moderation to abate the industry and passion, with which every individual is bound to pursue the good of his country.

Those who either attack or defend a minister in such a government as ours, where the utmost liberty is allowed, always carry matters to an extreme, and exaggerate his merit or demerit with regard to the public. His enemies are sure to charge him with the greatest enormities, both in domestic and foreign management; and there is no meanness nor crime, of which, in their account, he is not capable. Unnecessary wars, scandalous treaties, profusion of public treasure, oppressive taxes, every kind of mal-administration is ascribed to him. To aggravate the charge, his pernicious conduct, it is said, will extend its baleful influence even to posterity, by undermining the best constitution in the world, and disordering that wise system of laws, institutions, and customs, by which our ancestors, during so many centuries, have been so happily governed. He is not only a wicked minister in himself, but has removed every security provided against wicked ministers for the future.

On the other hand, the partizans of the minister make his panegyric run as high as the accusation against him, and celebrate his wise, steady and moderate conduct in every part of his administration. The honour and interest of the nation supported abroad, public credit maintained at home, persecution restrained, faction subdued; the merit of all these blessings is ascribed solely to the minister. At the same time, he crowns all his other merits by a religious care of the best constitution in the world, which he has preserved in all its parts, and has transmitted entire, to be the happiness and security of the latest posterity.

When this accusation and panegyric are received by the partizans of each party, no wonder they beget an extraordinary ferment on both sides, and fill the nation with violent animosities. But I would fain persuade these party-zealots, that there is a flat contradiction both in the accusation and panegyric, and that it were impossible for either of them to run so high, were it not for this contradiction. If our constitution be really *that noble fabric, the pride of* BRITAIN, *the envy of our neighbours, raised by the labour of so many centuries, repaired at the expence of so many millions, and cemented by such a profusion of blood;* I say, if our constitution does in any degree deserve these eulogies, it would never have suffered a wicked and weak minister to govern triumphantly for a course of twenty years, when opposed by the greatest geniuses in the nation, who exercised the utmost liberty of tongue and pen, in parliament, and in their frequent appeals to the people. But, if the minister be wicked and weak, to the degree so strenuously insisted on, the constitution must be faulty in its original principles, and he cannot consistently be charged with undermining the best constitution in the world. A constitution is only so far good, as it provides a remedy against mal-administration; and if the BRITISH constitution, when in its greatest vigour, and repaired by two such remarkable events, as the *Revolution* and *Accession,* by which our ancient royal family was sacrificed to it; if our constitution, I say, with so great advantages, does not, in fact, provide any such remedy, we are rather beholden to any minister who undermines it, and affords us an opportunity of erecting in its place a better constitution.

I would employ the same topics to moderate the zeal of those who defend the minister. *Is our constitution so excellent?* Then a change of ministry can be no such dreadful event; since it is essential to such a constitution, in every ministry, both to preserve itself from violation, and to prevent all enormities in the administration. *Is our constitution very bad?* Then so extraordinary a jealousy and apprehension, on account of changes, is ill-placed; and a man should no more be anxious in this case, than a husband, who had married a woman from the stews, should be watchful to prevent her infidelity. Public affairs, in such a constitution, must necessarily go to confusion, by whatever hands they are conducted; and the zeal of *patriots* is in that case much less requisite than the patience and submission of *philosophers.* The virtue and good intentions of CATO and BRUTUS are highly laudable; but, to what purpose did their zeal serve? To nothing, but to hasten the fatal period of the ROMAN government, and render its convulsions and dying agonies more violent and painful.

I would not be understood to mean, that public affairs deserve no care and attention at all. Would men be moderate and consistent, their claims might be admitted; at least might be examined. The *country-party* might still assert, that our constitution, though excellent, will admit of mal-administration to a certain degree; and therefore, if the minister be bad, it is proper to oppose him with a *suitable* degree of zeal. And, on the other hand, the *court-party* may be allowed, upon the supposition that the minister were good, to defend, and with *some* zeal too, his administration. I would only persuade men not to contend, as if they were fighting *pro aris & focis*, and change a good constitution into a bad one, by the violence of their factions.

I have not here considered any thing that is personal in the present controversy. In the best civil constitution, where every man is restrained by the most rigid laws, it is easy to discover either the good or bad intentions of a minister, and to judge, whether his personal character deserve love or hatred. But such questions are of little importance to the public, and lay those, who employ their pens upon them, under a just suspicion either of malevolence or of flattery.

Of the first principles of government (1741)

NOTHING appears more surprizing to those, who consider human affairs with a philosophical eye, than the easiness with which the many are governed by the few; and the implicit submission, with which men resign their own sentiments and passions to those of their rulers. When we enquire by what means this wonder is effected, we shall find, that, as FORCE is always on the side of the governed, the governors have nothing to support them but opinion. It is therefore, on opinion only that government is founded; and this maxim extends to the most despotic and most military governments, as well as to the most free and most popular. The soldan of EGYPT, or the emperor of ROME, might drive his harmless subjects, like brute beasts, against their sentiments and inclination: but he must, at least, have led his *mamalukes*, or *praetorian bands*, like men, by their opinion.

Opinion is of two kinds, to wit, opinion of INTEREST, and opinion of RIGHT. By opinion of interest, I chiefly understand the sense of the general advantage which is reaped from government; together with the persuasion, that the particular government, which is established, is equally advantageous with any other that could easily be settled. When this opinion prevails among the generality of a state, or among those who have the force in their hands, it gives great security to any government.

Right is of two kinds, right to POWER and right to PROPERTY. What prevalence opinion of the first kind has over mankind, may easily be understood, by observing the attachment which all nations have to their ancient government, and even to those names, which have had the sanction of antiquity. Antiquity always begets the opinion of right; and whatever disadvantageous sentiments we may entertain of mankind, they are always found to be prodigal both of blood and treasure in the maintenance of public justice. There is, indeed, no particular, in which, at first sight, there may appear a greater contradiction in the frame of the human mind than the present. When men act in a faction, they are apt, without shame or remorse, to neglect all the ties of honour and morality, in order to serve their party; and yet, when a faction is formed upon a point of right or principle, there is no occasion, where men discover a greater obstinacy, and a more determined sense of justice and equity. The same social disposition of mankind is the cause of these contradictory appearances.

It is sufficiently understood, that the opinion of right to property is of moment in all matters of government. A noted author has made property the foundation of all government; and most of our political writers seem inclined to follow him in that particular. This is carrying the matter too far; but still it must be owned, that the opinion of right to property has a great influence in this subject.

Upon these three opinions, therefore, of public *interest*, of *right to power*, and of *right to property*, are all governments founded, and all authority of the few over the many. There are indeed other principles, which add force to these, and determine, limit, or alter their operation; such as *self-interest, fear,* and *affection:* But still we may assert, that these other principles can have no influence alone, but suppose the antecedent influence of those opinions above-mentioned. They are, therefore, to be esteemed the secondary, not the original principles of government.

For, *first,* as to *self-interest,* by which I mean the expectation of particular rewards, distinct from the general protection which we receive from government, it is evident that the magistrate's authority must be antecedently established, or, at least be hoped for, in order to produce this expectation. The prospect of reward may augment his authority with regard to some particular persons; but can never give birth to it, with regard to the public. Men naturally look for the greatest favours from their friends and acquaintance; and therefore, the hopes of any considerable number of the state would never center in any particular set of men, if these men had no other title to magistracy, and had no separate influence over the opinions of mankind. The same observation may be extended to the other two principles of *fear* and *affection*. No man would have any reason to *fear* the fury of a tyrant, if he had no authority over any but from fear; since, as a single man, his bodily force can reach but a small way, and all the farther power he possesses must be founded either on our own opinion, or on the presumed opinion of others. And though *affection* to wisdom and virtue in a *sovereign* extends very far, and has great influence; yet he must antecedently be supposed invested with a public character, otherwise the public esteem will serve him in no stead, nor will his virtue have any influence beyond a narrow sphere.

A Government may endure for several ages, though the balance of power, and the balance of property do not coincide. This chiefly happens, where any rank or order of the state has acquired a large share in the property; but from the original constitution of the government, has no share in the power. Under what pretence would any individual of that order assume authority in public affairs? As men are commonly much attached to their ancient government, it is not to be expected, that the public would ever favour such usurpations. But where the original constitution allows any share of power, though small, to an order of men, who possess a large share of the property, it is easy for them gradually to stretch their authority, and bring the balance of power to coincide with that of property. This has been the case with the house of commons in ENGLAND.

Most writers, that have treated of the BRITISH government, have supposed, that as the lower house represents all the commons of GREAT BRITAIN, its weight in the scale is proportioned to the property and power of all whom it represents. But this principle must not be received as absolutely true. For though the people are apt to attach themselves more to the house of commons, than to any other member of the constitution; that house being chosen by them as their representatives, and as the public guardians of their liberty; yet are there instances where the house, even when in opposition to the crown, has not been followed by the people; as we may particularly observe of the *tory* house of commons in the reign of king WILLIAM. Were the members obliged to receive instructions from their constituents, like the DUTCH deputies, this would entirely alter the case; and if such immense power and riches, as those of the whole commons of BRITAIN, were brought into the scale, it is not easy to conceive, that the crown could either influence that multitude of people, or withstand that overbalance of property. It is true, the crown has great influence over the collective body of BRITAIN in the elections of members; but were this influence, which at present is only exerted once in seven years, to be employed in bringing over the people to every vote, it would soon be wasted; and no skill, popularity, or revenue, could support it. I must, therefore, be of opinion, that an alteration in this particular would introduce a total alteration in our government, and would soon reduce it to a pure republic; and, perhaps, to a republic of no inconvenient form. For though the people, collected in a body like the ROMAN tribes, be quite unfit for government, yet when dispersed in small bodies, they are more susceptible both of reason and order; the force of popular currents and tides is, in a great measure, broken; and the public interest may be pursued with some method and constancy. But it is needless to reason any farther concerning a form of government, which is never likely to have place in BRITAIN, and which seems not to be the aim of any party amongst us. Let us cherish and improve our ancient government as much as possible, without encouraging a passion for such dangerous novelties.

Idea of a perfect commonwealth (1752)

IT is not with forms of government, as with other artificial contrivances; where an old engine may be rejected, if we can discover another more accurate and commodious, or where trials may safely be made, even though the success be doubtful. An established government has an infinite advantage, by that very circumstance of its being established; the bulk of mankind being governed by authority, not reason, and never attributing authority to any thing that has not the recommendation of antiquity. To tamper, therefore, in this affair, or try experiments merely upon the credit of supposed argument and philosophy, can never be the part of a wise magistrate, who will bear a reverence to what carries the marks of age; and though he may attempt some improvements for the public good, yet will he adjust his innovations, as much as possible, to the ancient fabric, and preserve entire the chief pillars and supports of the constitution.

The mathematicians in EUROPE have been much divided concerning that figure of a ship, which is the most commodious for sailing; and HUYGENS, who at last determined this controversy, is justly thought to have obliged the learned, as well as commercial world; though COLUMBUS had sailed to AMERICA, and Sir FRANCIS DRAKE made the tour of the world, without any such discovery. As one form of government must be allowed more perfect than another, independent of the manners and humours of particular men; why may we not enquire what is the most perfect of all, though the common botched and inaccurate governments seem to serve the purposes of society, and though it be not so easy to establish a new system of government, as to build a vessel upon a new plan? The subject is surely the most worthy curiosity of any the wit of man can possibly devise. And who knows, if this controversy were fixed by the universal consent of the wise and learned, but, in some future age, an opportunity might be afforded of reducing the theory to practice, either by a dissolution of some old government, or by the combination of men to form a new one, in some distant part of the world? In all cases, it must be advantageous to know what is most perfect in the kind, that we may be able to bring any real constitution or form of government as near it as possible, by such gentle alterations and innovations as may not give too great disturbance to society.

All I pretend to in the present essay is to revive this subject of speculation; and therefore I shall deliver my sentiments in as few words as possible. A long dissertation on that head would not, I apprehend, be very acceptable to the public, who will be apt to regard such disquisitions both as useless and chimerical.

All plans of government, which suppose great reformation in the manners of mankind, are plainly imaginary. Of this nature, are the *Republic* of PLATO, and the *Utopia* of Sir THOMAS MORE. The OCEANA is the only valuable model of a commonwealth, that has as yet been offered to the public.

The chief defects of the OCEANA seem to be these. *First*, Its rotation is inconvenient, by throwing men, of whatever ability, by intervals, out of public employments. *Secondly*, Its *Agrarian* is impracticable. Men will soon learn the art, which was practised in ancient ROME, of concealing their possessions under other people's name; till at last, the abuse will become so common, that they will throw off even the appearance of restraint. *Thirdly*, The OCEANA provides not a sufficient security for liberty, or the redress of grievances. The senate must propose, and the people consent; by which means, the senate have not only a negative upon the people, but, what is of much greater consequence, their negative goes before the votes of the people. Were the King's negative of the same nature in the ENGLISH constitution, and could he prevent any bill from coming into parliament, he would be an absolute monarch. As his negative follows the votes of the houses, it is of little consequence: Such a difference is there in the manner of placing the same thing. When a popular bill has been debated in parliament, is brought to maturity, all its conveniencies and inconveniencies weighed and balanced; if afterwards it be presented for the royal assent, few princes will venture to reject the unanimous desire of the people. But could the King crush a disagreeable bill in embrio (as was the case, for some time, in the SCOTCH parliament, by means of the lords of the articles) the BRITISH government would have no balance, nor would grievances ever be redressed: And it is certain, that exorbitant power proceeds not, in any government, from new laws, so much as from neglecting to remedy the abuses, which frequently rise from the old ones. A government, says MACHIAVEL, must often be brought back to its original principles. It appears, then, that, in the OCEANA, the whole legislature may be said to rest in the senate; which HARRINGTON would own to be an inconvenient form of government, especially after the *Agrarian* is abolished.

Here is a form of government, to which I cannot, in theory, discover any considerable objection.

Let GREAT BRITAIN and IRELAND, or any territory of equal extent, be divided into 100 counties, and each county into 100 parishes, making in all 10,000. If the country, proposed to be erected into a commonwealth be of more narrow extent, we may diminish the number of counties; but never bring them below thirty. If it be of greater extent, it were better to enlarge the parishes, or throw more parishes into a county, than increase the number of counties.

Let all the freeholders of twenty pounds a-year in the country, and all the householders worth 500 pounds in the town parishes, meet annually in the parish church, and chuse, by ballot, some freeholder of the county for their member, whom we shall call the county *representative.*

Let the 100 county representatives, two days after their election, meet in the county-town, and chuse by ballot, from their own body, ten county *magistrates,* and one *senator.* There are, therefore, in the whole commonwealth, 100 senators, 1100 county magistrates, and 10,000 county representatives. For we shall bestow on all senators the authority of county magistrates, and on all county magistrates the authority of county representatives.

Let the senators meet in the capital, and be endowed with the whole executive power of the commonwealth; the power of peace and war, of giving orders to generals, admirals, and ambassadors, and, in short, all the prerogatives of a BRITISH King, except his negative.

Let the county representatives meet in their particular counties, and possess the whole legislative power of the commonwealth; the greatest number of counties deciding the question; and where these are equal, let the senate have the casting vote.

Every new law must first be debated in the senate; and though rejected by it, if ten senators insist and protest, it must be sent down to the counties. The senate, if they please, may join to the copy of the law their reasons for receiving or rejecting it.

Because it would be troublesome to assemble all the country representatives for every trivial law, that may be requisite, the senate have their choice of sending down the law either to the county magistrates or county representatives.

The magistrates, though the law be referred to them, may, if they please, call the representatives, and submit the affair to their determination.

Whether the law be referred by the senate to the county magistrates or representatives, a copy of it, and of the senate's reasons, must be sent to every representative eight days before the day appointed for the assembling, in order to deliberate concerning it. And though the determination be, by the senate, referred to the magistrates, if five representatives of the county order the magistrates to assemble the whole court of representatives, and submit the affair to their determination, they must obey.

Either the county magistrates or representatives may give, to the senator of the county, the copy of a law to be proposed to the senate; and if five counties concur in the same order, the law, though refused by the senate, must come either to the county magistrates or representatives, as is contained in the order of the five counties.

Any twenty counties, by a vote either of their magistrates or representatives, may throw any man out of all public offices for a year. Thirty counties for three years.

The senate has a power of throwing out any member or number of members of its own body, not to be re-elected for that year. The senate cannot throw out twice in a year the senator of the same county.

The power of the old senate continues for three weeks after the annual election of the county representatives. Then all the new senators are shut up in a conclave, like the cardinals; and by an intricate ballot, such as that of VENICE or MALTA, they chuse the following magistrates; a protector, who represents the dignity of the commonwealth, and presides in the senate; two secretaries of state; these six councils, a council of state, a council of religion and learning, a council of trade, a council of laws, a council of war, a council of the admiralty, each council consisting of five persons; together with six commissioners of the treasury and a first commissioner. All these must be senators. The senate also names all the ambassadors to foreign courts, who may either be senators or not.

The senate may continue any or all of these, but must re-elect them every year.

The protector and two secretaries have session and suffrage in the council of state. The business of that council is all foreign politics. The council of state has session and suffrage in all the other councils.

The council of religion and learning inspects the universities and clergy. That of trade inspects every thing that may affect commerce. That of laws inspects all the abuses of laws by the inferior magistrates, and examines what improvements may be made of the municipal law. That of war inspects the militia and its discipline, magazines, stores, &c. and when the republic is in war, examines into the proper orders for generals. The council of admiralty has the same power with regard to the navy, together with the nomination of the captains and all inferior officers.

None of these councils can give orders themselves, except where they receive such powers from the senate. In other cases, they must communicate every thing to the senate.

When the senate is under adjournment, any of the councils may assemble it before the day appointed for its meeting.

Besides these councils or courts, there is another called the court of *competitors*; which is thus constituted. If any candidates for the office of senator have more votes than a third of the representatives, that candidate, who has most votes, next to the senator elected, becomes incapable for one year of all public offices, even of being a magistrate or representative: but he takes his seat in the court of competitors. Here then is a court which may sometimes consist of a hundred members, sometimes have no members at all; and by that means, be for a year abolished.

The court of competitors has no power in the commonwealth. It has only the inspection of public accounts and the accusing of any man before the senate. If the senate acquit him, the court of competitors may, if they please, appeal to the people, either magistrates or representatives. Upon that appeal, the magistrates or representatives meet on the day appointed by the court of competitors, and chuse in each county three persons; from which number every senator is excluded. These, to the number of 300, meet in the capital, and bring the person accused to a new trial.

The court of competitors may propose any law to the senate; and if refused, may appeal to the people, that is, to the magistrates or representatives, who examine it in their counties. Every senator, who is thrown out of the senate by a vote of the court, takes his seat in the court of competitors.

The senate possesses all the judicative authority of the house of Lords, that is, all the appeals from the inferior courts. It likewise appoints the Lord Chancellor, and all the officers of the law.

Every county is a kind of republic within itself, and the representatives may make county-laws; which have no authority 'till three months after they are voted. A copy of the law is sent to the senate, and to every other county. The senate, or any single county, may, at any time, annul any law of another county.

The representatives have all the authority of the BRITISH justices of peace in trials, commitments, &c.

The magistrates have the appointment of all the officers of the revenue in each county. All causes with regard to the revenue are carried ultimately by appeal before the magistrates. They pass the accompts of all the officers; but must have all their own accompts examined and passed at the end of the year by the representatives.

The magistrates name rectors or ministers to all the parishes.

The Presbyterian government is established; and the highest ecclesiastical court is an assembly or synod of all the presbyters of the county. The magistrates may take any cause from this court, and determine it themselves.

The magistrates may try, and depose or suspend any presbyter.

The militia is established in imitation of that of SWISSERLAND, which being well known, we shall not insist upon it. It will only be proper to make this addition, that an army of 20,000 men be annually drawn out by rotation, paid and encamped during six weeks in summer; that the duty of a camp may not be altogether unknown.

The magistrates appoint all the colonels and downwards. The senate all upwards. During war, the general appoints the colonel and downwards, and his commission is good for a twelvemonth. But after that, it must be confirmed by the magistrates of the county, to which the regiment belongs. The magistrates may break any officer in the county regiment. And the senate may do the same to any officer in the service. If the magistrates do not think proper to confirm the general's choice, they may appoint another officer in the place of him they reject.

All crimes are tried within the county by the magistrates and a jury. But the senate can stop any trial, and bring it before themselves.

Any county may indict any man before the senate for any crime.

The protector, the two secretaries, the council of state, with any five more that the senate appoints, are possessed, on extraordinary emergencies, of *dictatorial* power for six months.

The protector may pardon any person condemned by the inferior courts.

In time of war, no officer of the army that is in the field can have any civil office in the commonwealth.

The capital, which we shall call LONDON, may be allowed four members in the senate. It may therefore be divided into four counties. The representatives of each of these chuse one senator, and ten magistrates. There are therefore in the city four senators, forty-four magistrates, and four hundred representatives. The magistrates have the same authority as in the counties. The representatives also have the same authority; but they never meet in one general court: They give their votes in their particular county, or division of hundreds.

When they enact any bye-law, the greatest number of counties or divisions determines the matter. And where these are equal, the magistrates have the casting vote.

The magistrates chuse the mayor, sheriff, recorder, and other officers of the city.

In the commonwealth, no representative, magistrate, or senator, as such has any salary. The protector, secretaries, councils, and ambassadors, have salaries.

The first year in every century is set apart for correcting all inequalities, which time may have produced in the representative. This must be done by the legislature.

The following political aphorisms may explain the reason of these orders.

The lower sort of people and small proprietors are good judges enough of one not very distant from them in rank or habitation; and therefore, in their parochial meetings, will probably chuse the best, or nearly the best representative: But they are wholly unfit for county-meetings, and for electing into the higher offices of the republic. Their ignorance gives the grandees an opportunity of deceiving them.

Ten thousand, even though they were not annually elected, are a basis large enough for any free government. It is true, the nobles in POLAND are more than 10,000, and yet these oppress the people. But as power always continues there in the same persons and families, this makes them, in a manner, a different nation from the people. Besides the nobles are there united under a few heads of families.

All free governments must consist of two councils, a less and greater; or, in other words, of a senate and people. The people, as HARRINGTON observes, would want wisdom, without the senate: The senate, without the people, would want honesty.

A large assembly of 1000, for instance, to represent the people, if allowed to debate, would fall into disorder. If not allowed to debate, the senate has a negative upon them, and the worst kind of negative, that before resolution.

Here therefore is an inconvenience, which no government has yet fully remedied, but which is the easiest to be remedied in the world. If the people debate, all is confusion: If they do not debate, they can only resolve; and then the senate carves for them. Divide the people into many separate bodies; and then they may debate with safety, and every inconvenience seems to be prevented.

Cardinal de RETZ says, that all numerous assemblies, however composed, are mere mob, and swayed in their debates by the least motive. This we find confirmed by daily experience. When an absurdity strikes a member, he conveys it to his neighbour, and so on, till the whole be infected. Separate this great body; and though every member be only of middling sense, it is not probable, that anything but reason can prevail over the whole. Influence and example being removed, good sense will always get the better of bad among a number of people.

There are two things to be guarded against in every *senate*: Its combination, and its division. Its combination is most dangerous. And against this inconvenience we have provided the following remedies. 1. The great dependence of the senators on the people by annual election; and that not by an undistinguishing rabble, like the ENGLISH electors, but by men of fortune and education. 2. The small power they are allowed. They have few offices to dispose of. Almost all are given by the magistrates in the counties. 3. The court of competitors, which being composed of men that are their rivals, next to them in interest, and uneasy in their present situation, will be sure to take all advantages against them.

The division of the senate is prevented, 1. By the smallness of their number. 2. As faction supposes a combination in a separate interest, it is prevented by their dependence on the people. 3. They have a power of expelling any factious member. It is true, when another member of the same spirit comes from the county, they have no power of expelling him: Nor is it fit they should; for that shows the humour to be in the people, and may possibly arise from some ill conduct in public affairs. 4. Almost any man, in a senate so regularly chosen by the people, may be supposed fit for any civil office. It would be proper, therefore, for the senate to form some *general* resolutions with regard to the disposing of offices among the members: Which resolutions would not confine them in critical times, when extraordinary parts on the one hand, or extraordinary stupidity on the other, appears in any senator; but they would be sufficient to prevent intrigue and faction, by making the disposal of the offices a thing of course. For instance, let it be a resolution, That no man shall attain the higher offices but through the lower: That no man shall be protector twice, &c. The senate of VENICE govern themselves by such resolutions.

In foreign politics the interest of the senate can scarcely ever be divided from that of the people; and therefore it is fit to make the senate absolute with regard to them; otherwise there could be no secrecy or refined policy. Besides, without money no alliance can be executed; and the senate is still sufficiently dependant. Not to mention, that the legislative power being always superior to the executive, the magistrates or representatives may interpose whenever they think proper.

The chief support of the BRITISH government is the opposition of interests; but that, though in the main serviceable, breeds endless factions. In the foregoing plan, it does all the good without any of the harm. The *competitors* have no power of controlling the senate: They have only the power of accusing, and appealing to the people.

It is necessary, likewise, to prevent both combination and division in the thousand magistrates. This is done sufficiently by the separation of places and interests.

But lest that should not be sufficient, their dependence on the 10,000 for their elections, serves to the same purpose.

Nor is that all: For the 10,000 may resume the power whenever they please; and not only when they all please, but when any five of a hundred please, which will happen upon the very first suspicion of a separate interest.

The 10,000 are too large a body either to unite or divide, except when they meet in one place, and fall under the guidance of ambitious leaders. Not to mention their annual election, by the whole body of the people, that are of any consideration.

A small commonwealth is the happiest government in the world within itself, because every thing lies under the eye of the rulers: But it may be subdued by great force from without. This scheme seems to have all the advantages both of a great and a little commonwealth.

Every county-law may be annulled either by the senate or another county; because that shows an opposition of interest: In which case no part ought to decide for itself. The matter must be referred to the whole, which will best determine what agrees with general interest.

As to the clergy and militia, the reasons of these orders are obvious. Without the dependence of the clergy on the civil magistrates, and without a militia, it is vain to think that any free government will ever have security or stability.

In many governments, the inferior magistrates have no rewards but what arise from their ambition, vanity, or public spirit. The salaries of the FRENCH judges amount not to the interest of the sums they pay for their offices. The DUTCH burgo-masters have little more immediate profit than the ENGLISH justices of peace, or the members of the house of commons formerly. But lest any should suspect, that this would beget negligence in the administration, (which is little to be feared, considering the natural ambition of mankind) let the magistrates have competent salaries. The senators have access to so many honourable and lucrative offices, that their attendance needs not be bought. There is little attendance required of the representatives.

That the foregoing plan of government is practicable, no one can doubt, who considers the resemblance that it bears to the commonwealth of the United Provinces, a wise and renowned government. The alterations in the present scheme seem all evidently for the better. 1. The representation is more equal. 2. The unlimited power of the burgo-masters in the towns, which forms a perfect aristocracy in the DUTCH commonwealth, is corrected by a well-tempered democracy, in giving to the people the annual election of the county representatives. 3. The negative, which every province and town has upon the whole body of the DUTCH republic, with regard to alliances, peace and war, and the imposition of taxes, is here removed. 4. The counties, in the present plan, are not so independent of each other, nor do they form separate bodies so much as the seven provinces; where the jealousy and envy of the smaller provinces and towns against the greater, particularly HOLLAND and AMSTERDAM, have frequently disturbed the government. 5. Larger powers, though of the safest kind, are intrusted to the senate than the States-General possess; by which means, the former may become more expeditious, and secret in their resolutions, than it is possible for the latter.

The chief alterations that could be made on the BRITISH government, in order to bring it to the most perfect model of limited monarchy, seem to be the following. *First*, The plan of CROMWELL's parliament ought to be restored, by making the representation equal, and by allowing none to vote in the county elections who possess not a property of 200 pounds value. *Secondly,* As such a house of Commons would be too weighty for a frail house of Lords, like the present, the Bishops and SCOTCH Peers ought to be removed: The number of the upper house ought to be raised to three or four hundred: Their seats not hereditary, but during life: They ought to have the election of their own members; and no commoner should be allowed to refuse a seat that was offered him. By this means the house of Lords would consist entirely of the men of chief credit, ability, and interest in the nation; and every turbulent leader in the house of Commons might be taken off, and connected in interest with the house of Peers. Such an aristocracy would be an excellent barrier both to the monarchy and against it. At present, the balance of our government depends in some measure on the ability and behaviour of the sovereign; which are variable and uncertain circumstances.

This plan of limited monarchy, however corrected, seems still liable to three great inconveniences. *First,* It removes not entirely, though it may soften the parties of *court* and *country*. *Secondly,* The king's personal character must still have a great influence on the government. *Thirdly,* The sword is in the hands of a single person, who will always neglect to discipline the militia, in order to have a pretence for keeping up a standing army.

We shall conclude this subject, with observing the falsehood of the common opinion, that no large state, such as FRANCE or BRITAIN, could ever be modelled into a commonwealth, but that such a form of government can only take place in a city or small territory. The contrary seems probable. Though it is more difficult to form a republican government in an extensive country than in a city; there is more facility, when once it is formed, of preserving it steady and uniform, without tumult and faction. It is not easy, for the distant parts of a large state to combine in any plan of free government; but they easily conspire in the esteem and reverence for a single person, who, by means of this popular favour, may seize the power, and forcing the more obstinate to submit, may establish a monarchical government. On the other hand, a city readily concurs in the same notions of government, the natural equality of property favours liberty, and the nearness of habitation enables the citizens mutually to assist each other. Even under absolute princes, the subordinate government of cities is commonly republican; while that of counties and provinces is monarchical. But these same circumstances, which facilitate the erection of commonwealths in cities, render their constitution more frail and uncertain. Democracies are turbulent. For however the people may be separated or divided into small parties, either in their votes or elections; their near habitation in a city will always make the force of popular tides and currents very sensible. Aristocracies are better adapted for peace and order, and accordingly were most admired by ancient writers; but they are jealous and oppressive. In a large government, which is modelled with masterly skill, there is compass and room enough to refine the democracy from the lower people, who may be admitted into the first elections or first concoction of the commonwealth, to the higher magistrates, who direct all the movements. At the same time, the parts are so distant and remote, that it is very difficult, either by intrigue, prejudice, or passion, to hurry them into any measures against the public interest.

It is needless to enquire, whether such a government would be immortal. I allow the justness of the poet's exclamation on the endless projects of human race, *Man and for ever!* The world itself probably is not immortal. Such consuming plagues may arise as would leave even a perfect government a weak prey to its neighbours. We know not to what length enthusiasm, or other extraordinary movements of the human mind, may transport men, to the neglect of all order and public good. Where difference of interest is removed, whimsical and unaccountable factions often arise, from personal favour or enmity. Perhaps, rust may grow to the springs of the most accurate political machine, and disorder its motions. Lastly, extensive conquests, when pursued, must be the ruin of every free government; and of the more perfect governments sooner than of the imperfect; because of the very advantages which the former possess above the latter. And though such a state ought to establish a fundamental law against conquest; yet republics have ambition as well as individuals, and present interest makes men forgetful of their posterity. It is a sufficient incitement to human endeavours, that such a government would flourish for many ages; without pretending to bestow, on any work of man, that immortality, which the Almighty seems to have refused to his own productions.

Of the origin of government (1777)

MAN, born in a family, is compelled to maintain society, from necessity, from natural inclination, and from habit. The same creature, in his farther progress, is engaged to establish political society, in order to administer justice; without which there can be no peace among them, nor safety, nor mutual intercourse. We are, therefore, to look upon all the vast apparatus of our government, as having ultimately no other object or purpose but the distribution of justice, or, in other words, the support of the twelve judges. Kings and parliaments, fleets and armies, officers of the court and revenue, ambassadors, ministers, and privy-counsellors, are all subordinate in their end to this part of administration. Even the clergy, as their duty leads them to inculcate morality, may justly be thought, so far as regards this world, to have no other useful object of their institution.

All men are sensible of the necessity of justice to maintain peace and order; and all men are sensible of the necessity of peace and order for the maintenance of society. Yet, notwithstanding this strong and obvious necessity, such is the frailty or perverseness of our nature! it is impossible to keep men, faithfully and unerringly, in the paths of justice. Some extraordinary circumstances may happen, in which a man finds his interests to be more promoted by fraud or rapine, than hurt by the breach which his injustice makes in the social union. But much more frequently, he is seduced from his great and important, but distant interests, by the allurement of present, though often very frivolous temptations. This great weakness is incurable in human nature.

Men must, therefore, endeavour to palliate what they cannot cure. They must institute some persons, under the appellation of magistrates, whose peculiar office it is, to point out the decrees of equity, to punish transgressors, to correct fraud and violence, and to oblige men, however reluctant, to consult their own real and permanent interests. In a word, OBEDIENCE is a new duty which must be invented to support that of JUSTICE; and the tyes of equity must be corroborated by those of allegiance.

But still, viewing matters in an abstract light, it may be thought, that nothing is gained by this alliance, and that the factitious duty of obedience, from its very nature, lays as feeble a hold of the human mind, as the primitive and natural duty of justice. Peculiar interests and present temptations may overcome the one as well as the other. They are equally exposed to the same inconvenience. And the man, who is inclined to be a bad neighbour, must be led by the same motives, well or ill understood, to be a bad citizen and subject. Not to mention, that the magistrate himself may often be negligent, or partial, or unjust in his administration.

Experience, however, proves, that there is a great difference between the cases. Order in society, we find, is much better maintained by means of government; and our duty to the magistrate is more strictly guarded by the principles of human nature, than our duty to our fellow-citizens. The love of dominion is so strong in the breast of man, that many, not only submit to, but court all the dangers, and fatigues, and cares of government; and men, once raised to that station, though often led astray by private passions, find, in ordinary cases, a visible interest in the impartial administration of justice. The persons, who first attain this distinction by the consent, tacit or express, of the people, must be endowed with superior personal qualities of valour, force, integrity, or prudence, which command respect and confidence: and after government is established, a regard to birth, rank, and station has a mighty influence over men, and enforces the decrees of the magistrate. The prince or leader exclaims against every disorder, which disturbs his society. He summons all his partizans and all men of probity to aid him in correcting and redressing it: and he is readily followed by all indifferent persons in the execution of his office. He soon acquires the power of rewarding these services; and in the progress of society, he establishes subordinate ministers and often a military force, who find an immediate and a visible interest, in supporting his authority. Habit soon consolidates what other principles of human nature had imperfectly founded; and men, once accustomed to obedience, never think of departing from that path, in which they and their ancestors have constantly trod, and to which they are confined by so many urgent and visible motives.

But though this progress of human affairs may appear certain and inevitable, and though the support which allegiance brings to justice, be founded on obvious principles of human nature, it cannot be expected that men should beforehand be able to discover them, or foresee their operation. Government commences more casually and more imperfectly. It is probable, that the first ascendant of one man over multitudes began during a state of war; where the superiority of courage and of genius discovers itself most visibly, where unanimity and concert are most requisite, and where the pernicious effects of disorder are most sensibly felt. The long continuance of that state, an incident common among savage tribes, enured the people to submission; and if the chieftain possessed as much equity as prudence and valour, he became, even during peace, the arbiter of all differences, and could gradually, by a mixture of force and consent, establish his authority. The benefit sensibly felt from his influence, made it be cherished by the people, at least by the peaceable and well disposed among them; and if his son enjoyed the same good qualities, government advanced the sooner to maturity and perfection; but was still in a feeble state, till the farther progress of improvement procured the magistrate a revenue, and enabled him to bestow rewards on the several instruments of his administration, and to inflict punishments on the refractory and disobedient. Before that period, each exertion of his influence must have been particular, and founded on the peculiar circumstances of the case. After it, submission was no longer a matter of choice in the bulk of the community, but was rigorously exacted by the authority of the supreme magistrate.

In all governments, there is a perpetual intestine struggle, open or secret, between AUTHORITY and LIBERTY; and neither of them can ever absolutely prevail in the contest. A great sacrifice of liberty must necessarily be made in every government; yet even the authority, which confines liberty, can never, and perhaps ought never, in any constitution, to become quite entire and uncontroulable. The sultan is master of the life and fortune of any individual; but will not be permitted to impose new taxes on his subjects: a French monarch can impose taxes at pleasure; but would find it dangerous to attempt the lives and fortunes of individuals. Religion also, in most countries, is commonly found to be a very intractable principle; and other principles or prejudices frequently resist all the authority of the civil magistrate; whose power, being founded on opinion, can never subvert other opinions, equally rooted with that of his title to dominion. The government, which, in common appellation, receives the appellation of free, is that which admits of a partition of power among several members, whose united authority is no less, or is commonly greater than that of any monarch; but who, in the usual course of administration, must act by general and equal laws, that are previously known to all the members and to all their subjects. In this sense, it must be owned, that liberty is the perfection of civil society; but still authority must be acknowledged essential to its very existence: and in those contests, which so often take place between the one and the other, the latter may, on that account, challenge the preference. Unless perhaps one may say (and it may be said with some reason) that a circumstance, which is essential to the existence of civil society, must always support itself, and needs be guarded with less jealousy, than one that contributes only to its perfection, which the indolence of men is so apt to neglect, or their ignorance to overlook.

CHARLES-LOUIS DE SECONDAT, BARON DE MONTESQUIEU

BIOGRAPHICAL NOTE

Charles-Louis de Secondat, Baron de Montesquieu (1689–1755), was born in Bordeaux, and educated at the Collège de Juilly near Paris. He studied law at the University of Bordeaux, returning to Paris in 1708, where he remained until 1713, collecting material for his novel, the *Lettres persanes* (1721), making contact with thinkers such as Desmolets and Fréret, and gaining experience as a lawyer in the Paris courts. He inherited his estates in 1713, and returned to Bordeaux. In 1715 he was elected to the Bordeaux Academy.

After the publication of the *Lettres persanes* in 1721, Montesquieu became a frequent visitor to Paris over the next seven years, becoming a well-known figure at Louis XV's court. He became an active member of Mme de Lambert's salon circle, and he also frequented the free-thinking Club de l'Entresol. He was elected to the French Academy in 1728. In that year he started to travel widely in Europe, spending time in Germany, Austria and Italy where he met free thinkers and leading scientists, historians and dramatists such as Conti, Muratori, Maffei, Grimaldi and others. Like Voltaire, he spent two years in England, and became acquainted with most of the major English political and literary figures of the time, including Walpole, Bolingbroke, Pope, Defoe and Swift. His celebrated passages on the English constitution, and his advocacy of a system of government based on the separation of powers, almost certainly derive from his observations of the workings of the English Parliament, and of the exercise of the balance of power between the executive and legislative branches of English government.

Montesquieu returned to his estates at La Brède in 1731, at which point he started work on the *Spirit of the laws*. He spent the next seventeen years reading widely. The *Considerations on the causes of the greatness of the Romans, and of their decline* appeared in 1734. In 1748 he published the *Spirit of the laws*, followed two years later by the *Defence of the spirit of the laws*. He also contributed the entry 'On taste' to Diderot's *Encyclopedia*. The publication of the *Spirit of the laws* marked a defining moment in Enlightenment attitudes and approaches to the law, morality, politics and human nature, and its impact on post-Enlightenment political and social science, in particular, has been considerable.

First published in Geneva in 1748, the *Spirit of the laws* was republished in a slightly revised form in 1749, and with further corrections in 1750. After Montesquieu's death in 1755 a revised and expanded edition was published by his son from notes that Montesquieu had left. A third edition with revisions was issued in 1757, two years after Montesquieu's death, using notes that Montesquieu had left to his son. This text was reprinted in the 1758 collective works. The first English translation, by Thomas Nugent, was published in 1750.

EDITORIAL NOTE

The present extracts are taken from the translation of *De l'esprit des lois* by A. Cohler, B. Miller and H. Stone.* The base text for the Cohler–Miller–Stone translation is that of the 1758 edition printed in the first volume of the *Œuvres complètes de Montesquieu*, ed. A. Masson, 9 vols. (Paris, Nagel, 1950–5).

FURTHER READING

*Cohler, A., Miller, S. and Stone, H. (eds.), *Montesquieu: the Spirit of the laws* (Cambridge, Cambridge University Press, 1990). Reprint. See introduction, pp. xxi–xxviii.

Durkheim, E., *Montesquieu and Rousseau: forerunners of sociology* (Ann Arbor, Michigan, University of Michigan Press, 1965).

Shackleton, R., *Montesquieu: a critical biography* (Oxford, Clarendon Press, 1961).

Shklar, J., *Montesquieu* (Oxford, Oxford University Press, 1987).

Spirit of the laws (1748)

Laws, taken in the broadest meaning, are the necessary relations deriving from the nature of things; and in this sense, all beings have their laws: the divinity has its laws, the material world has its laws, the intelligences superior to man have their laws, the beasts have their laws, man has his laws.

Those who have said that *a blind fate has produced all the effects that we see in the world* have said a great absurdity; for what greater absurdity is there than a blind fate that could have produced intelligent beings?

There is, then, a primitive reason; and laws are both the relations that exist between it and the different beings, and the relations of these various beings to each other.

God is related to the universe, as creator and preserver; the laws according to which he created are those according to which he preserves; he acts according to these rules because he knows them; he knows them because he made them; he made them because they are related to his wisdom and his power.

As we see that the world, formed by the motion of matter and devoid of intelligence, still continues to exist, its motions must have invariable laws; and, if one could imagine another world than this, it would have consistent rules or it would be destroyed.

Thus creation, which appears to be an arbitrary act, presupposes rules as invariable as the fate claimed by atheists. It would be absurd to say that the creator, without these rules, could govern the world, since the world would not continue to exist without them.

These rules are a consistently established relation. Between one moving body and another moving body, it is in accord with relations of mass and velocity that all motions are received, increased, diminished, or lost; every diversity is *uniformity*, every change is *consistency*.

Particular intelligent beings can have laws that they have made, but they also have some that they have not made. Before there were intelligent beings, they were possible; therefore, they had possible relations and consequently possible laws. Before laws were made, there were possible relations of justice. To say that there is nothing just or unjust but what positive laws ordain or prohibit is to say that before a circle was drawn, all its radii were not equal.

Therefore, one must admit that there are relations of fairness prior to the positive law that establishes them, so that, for example, assuming that there were societies of men, it would be just to conform to their laws; so that, if there were intelligent beings that had received some kindness from another being, they ought to be grateful for it; so that, if one intelligent being had created another intelligent being, the created one ought to remain in its original dependency; so that one intelligent being who has done harm to another intelligent being deserves the same harm in return, and so forth.

But the intelligent world is far from being as well governed as the physical world. For, though the intelligent world also has laws that are invariable by their nature, unlike the physical world, it does not follow its laws consistently. The reason for this is that particular intelligent beings are limited by their nature and are consequently subject to error; furthermore, it is in their nature to act by themselves. Therefore, they do not consistently follow their primitive laws or even always follow the laws they give themselves.

It is not known whether beasts are governed by the general laws of motion or by a movement particular to themselves. Be that as it may, they do not have a more intimate relation with god than the rest of the material world has, and feeling is useful to them only in their relation to one another, either with other particular beings, or with themselves.

By the attraction of pleasure they preserve their particular being; by the same attraction they preserve their species. They have natural laws because they are united by feeling; they have no positive laws because they are not united by knowledge. Still, they do not invariably follow their natural laws; plants, in which we observe neither knowledge nor feeling, better follow their natural laws.

Beasts do not have the supreme advantages that we have; they have some that we do not have. They do not have our expectations, but they do not have our fears; they suffer death as we do, but without recognizing it; most even preserve themselves better than we do and do not make such bad use of their passions.

Man, as a physical being, is governed by invariable laws like other bodies. As an intelligent being, he constantly violates the laws god has established and changes those he himself establishes; he must guide himself, and yet he is a limited being; he is subject to ignorance and error, as are all finite intelligences; he loses even the imperfect knowledge he has. As a feeling creature, he falls subject to a thousand passions. Such a being could at any moment forget his creator; god has called him back to him by the laws of religion. Such a being could at any moment forget himself; philosophers have reminded him of himself by the laws of morality. Made for living in society, he could forget his fellows; legislators have returned him to his duties by political and civil laws. [*Spirit of the laws*, 1, 1, 1: 'On laws in their relation with the various beings']

Prior to all these laws are the laws of nature, so named because they derive uniquely from the constitution of our being. To know them well, one must consider a man before the establishment of societies. The laws he would receive in such a state will be the laws of nature.

The law that impresses on us the idea of a creator and thereby leads us toward him is the first of the *natural laws* in importance, though not first in the order of these laws. A man in the state of nature would have the faculty of knowing rather than knowledge. It is clear that his first ideas would not be speculative ones; he would think of the preservation of his being before seeking the origin of his being. Such a man would at first feel only his weakness; his timidity would be extreme: and as for evidence, if it is needed on this point, savages have been found in forests; everything makes them tremble, everything makes them flee.

In this state, each feels himself inferior; he scarcely feels himself an equal. Such men would not seek to attack one another, and peace would be the first natural law.

Hobbes gives men first the desire to subjugate one another, but this is not reasonable. The idea of empire and domination is so complex and depends on so many other ideas, that it would not be the one they would first have.

Hobbes asks, *If men are not naturally in a state of war, why do they always carry arms and why do they have keys to lock their doors?* But one feels that what can happen to men only after the establishment of societies, which induced them to find motives for attacking others and for defending themselves, is attributed to them before that establishment.

Man would add the feeling of his needs to the feeling of his weakness. Thus another natural law would be the one inspiring him to seek nourishment.

I have said that fear would lead men to flee one another, but the marks of mutual fear would soon persuade them to approach one another. They would also be so inclined by the pleasure one animal feels at the approach of an animal of its own kind. In addition, the charm that the two sexes inspire in each other by their difference would increase this pleasure, and the natural entreaty they always make to one another would be a third law.

Besides feelings, which belong to men from the outset, they also succeed in gaining knowledge; thus they have a second bond, which other animals do not have. Therefore, they have another motive for uniting, and the desire to live in society is a fourth natural law. [*Spirit of the laws*, I, I, 2: 'On the laws of nature']

As soon as men are in society, they lose their feeling of weakness; the equality that was among them ceases, and the state of war begins.

Each particular society comes to feel its strength, producing a state of war among nations. The individuals within each society begin to feel their strength; they seek to turn to their favor the principal advantages of this society, which brings about a state of war among them.

These two sorts of states of war bring about the establishment of laws among men. Considered as inhabitants of a planet so large that different peoples are necessary, they have laws bearing on the relation that these peoples have with one another, and this is the RIGHT OF NATIONS. Considered as living in a society that must be maintained, they have laws concerning the relation between those who govern and those who are governed, and this is the POLITICAL RIGHT. Further, they have laws concerning the relation that all citizens have with one another, and this is the CIVIL RIGHT.

The *right of nations* is by nature founded on the principle that the various nations should do to one another in times of peace the most good possible, and in times of war the least ill possible, without harming their true interests.

The object of war is victory; of victory, conquest; of conquest, preservation. All the laws that form the *right of nations* should derive from this principle and the preceding one.

All nations have a right of nations; and even the Iroquois, who eat their prisoners, have one. They send and receive embassies; they know rights of war and peace: the trouble is that their right of nations is not founded on true principles.

In addition to the right of nations, which concerns all societies, there is a *political right* for each one. A society could not continue to exist without a government. '*The union of all individual strengths,*' as Gravina aptly says, 'forms what is called the POLITICAL STATE.'

The strength of the whole society may be put in the hands of *one alone* or in the hands of *many*. Since nature has established paternal power, some have thought that government by one alone is most in conformity with nature. But the example of paternal power proves nothing. For, if the power of the father is related to government by one alone, then after the death of the father, the power of the brothers, or after the death of the brothers, the power of the first cousins, is related to government by many. Political power necessarily includes the union of many families.

It is better to say that the government most in conformity with nature is the one whose particular arrangement best relates to the disposition of the people for whom it is established.

Individual strengths cannot be united unless all wills are united. *The union of these wills*, as Gravina again aptly says, *is what is called the* CIVIL STATE.

Law in general is human reason insofar as it governs all the peoples of the earth; and the political and civil laws of each nation should be only the particular cases to which human reason is applied.

Laws should be so appropriate to the people for whom they are made that it is very unlikely that the laws of one nation can suit another.

Laws must relate to the nature and the principle of the government that is established or that one wants to establish, whether those laws form it as do political laws, or maintain it, as do civil laws.

They should be related to the *physical aspect* of the country; to the climate, be it freezing, torrid, or temperate; to the properties of the terrain, its location and extent; to the way of life of the peoples, be they plowmen, hunters, or herdsmen; they should relate to the degree of liberty that the constitution can sustain, to the religion of the inhabitants, their inclinations, their wealth, their number, their commerce, their mores and their manners; finally, the laws are related to one another, to their origin, to the purpose of the legislator, and to the order of things on which they are established. They must be considered from all these points of view.

This is what I undertake to do in this work. I shall examine all these relations; together they form what is called THE SPIRIT OF THE LAWS.

I have made no attempt to separate *political* from *civil* laws, for, as I do not treat laws but the spirit of the laws, and as this spirit consists in the various relations that laws may have with various things, I have had to follow the natural order of laws less than that of these relations and of these things.

I shall first examine the relations that laws have with the nature and the principle of each government, and, as this principle has a supreme influence on the laws, I shall apply myself to understanding it well; and if I can once establish it, the laws will be seen to flow from it as from their source. I shall then proceed to other relations that seem to be more particular. [*Spirit of the laws*, I, I, 3: 'On positive laws']

There are three kinds of government: REPUBLICAN, MONARCHICAL, and DESPOTIC. To discover the nature of each, the idea of them held by the least educated of men is sufficient. I assume three definitions, or rather, three facts: one, *republican government is that in which the people as a body, or only a part of the people, have sovereign power; monarchical government is that in which one alone governs, but by fixed and established laws; whereas, in despotic government, one alone, without law and without rule, draws everything along by his will and his caprices.*

That is what I call the nature of each government. One must see what laws follow directly from this nature and are consequently the first fundamental laws. [*Spirit of the laws*, I, II, I: **'On the nature of the three varieties of governments'**]

In a republic when the people as a body have sovereign power, it is a *democracy*. When the sovereign power is in the hands of a part of the people, it is called an *aristocracy*.

In a democracy the people are, in certain respects, the monarch; in other respects, they are the subjects.

They can be the monarch only through their votes which are their wills. The sovereign's will is the sovereign himself. Therefore, the laws establishing the right to vote are fundamental in this government. Indeed, it is as important in this case to regulate how, by whom, for whom, and on what issues votes should be cast, as it is in a monarchy to know the monarch and how he should govern.

Libanius says that *in Athens a foreigner who mingled in the people's assembly was punished with death*. This is because such a man usurped the right of sovereignty.

It is essential to determine the number of citizens that should form assemblies; unless this is done it cannot be known if the people have spoken or only a part of the people. In Lacedaemonia, there had to be 10,000 citizens. In Rome, which started small and became great, Rome, made to endure all the vicissitudes of fortune, Rome, which sometimes had nearly all its citizens outside its walls and sometimes all Italy and a part of the world within them, the number was not determined; this was one of the great causes of its ruin.

A people having sovereign power should do for itself all it can do well, and what it cannot do well, it must do through its ministers.

Ministers do not belong to the people unless the people name them; therefore it is a fundamental maxim of this government that the people should name their ministers, that is, their magistrates.

The people, like monarchs and even more than monarchs, need to be guided by a council or senate. But in order for the people to trust it, they must elect its members, either choosing the members themselves, as in Athens, or establishing some magistrate to elect them as was occasionally the practice in Rome.

The people are admirable for choosing those to whom they should entrust some part of their authority. They have only to base their decisions on things of which they cannot be unaware and on facts that are evident to the senses. They know very well that a man has often been to war, that he has had such and such successes; they are, then, quite capable of electing a general. They know that a judge is assiduous, that many people leave the tribunal satisfied with him, and that he has not been convicted of corruption; this is enough for them to elect a praetor. They have been struck by the magnificence or wealth of a citizen; that is enough for them to be able to choose an aedile. All these things are facts that they learn better in a public square than a monarch does in his palace. But will the people know how to conduct the public business, will they know the places, the occasions, the moments, and profit from them? No, they will not.

If one were to doubt the people's natural ability to perceive merit, one would have only to cast an eye over that continuous series of astonishing choices made by the Athenians and the Romans; this will doubtless not be ascribed to chance.

It is known that in Rome, though the people had given themselves the right to elevate plebeians to posts, they could not bring themselves to elect them; and in Athens, although, according to the law of Aristides, magistrates could be drawn from any class, Xenophon says that it never happened that the common people turned to those classes that could threaten their well-being or glory.

Just as most citizens, who are competent enough to elect, are not competent enough to be elected, so the people, who are sufficiently capable to call others to account for their management, are not suited to manage by themselves.

Public business must proceed, and proceed at a pace that is neither too slow nor too fast. But the people always act too much or too little. Sometimes with a hundred thousand arms they upset everything; sometimes with a hundred thousand feet they move only like insects.

In the popular state, the people are divided into certain classes. Great legislators have distinguished themselves by the way they have made this division, and upon it the duration and prosperity of democracies have always depended.

Servius Tullius followed the spirit of aristocracy in the composition of his classes. In Livy and Dionysius of Halicarnassus, we see how he put the right to vote into the hands of the principal citizens. He divided the people of Rome into one hundred and ninety-three centuries, forming six classes. He put the rich men, but in smaller numbers, into the first centuries; he put the less rich, but in larger numbers, into the following ones; he put the entire throng of the poor into the last century; and, since each century had only one voice, it was means and wealth that had the vote rather than persons.

Solon divided the people of Athens into four classes. Guided by the spirit of democracy, he made these classes in order to specify not those who were to elect but those who could be elected; and leaving to the citizens the right to elect, he wanted them to be able to elect judges from each of those four classes but magistrates from the first three only, where the well-to-do citizens were found.

Just as the division of those having the right to vote is a fundamental law in the republic, the way of casting the vote is another fundamental law.

Voting by *lot* is in the nature of democracy; voting by *choice* is in the nature of aristocracy.

The casting of lots is a way of electing that distresses no one; it leaves to each citizen a reasonable expectation of serving his country.

But as it is imperfect by itself, the great legislators have outdone each other in regulating and correcting it.

In Athens, Solon established that all military posts would be filled by choice but that senators and judges would be elected by lot.

He wanted the civil magistrates that required great expenditures to be given by choice and the others to be given by lot.

But in order to correct the vote by lot, he ruled that one could elect only from the number of those who presented themselves, that he who had been elected would be examined by judges, and that each judge could accuse him of being unworthy; this derived from both lot and choice. On completing his term, the magistrate had to go through a second judgment regarding the way in which he had conducted himself. People without ability must have been very reluctant to offer their names to be drawn by lot.

The law that determines the way ballots are cast is another fundamental law in democracy. Whether the votes should be public or secret is a great question. Cicero writes that the laws that made them secret in the late period of the Roman republic were one of the major causes of its fall. Given that this practice varies in different republics, here, I believe, is what must be thought about it.

When the people cast votes, their votes should no doubt be public; and this should be regarded as a fundamental law of democracy. The lesser people must be enlightened by the principal people and subdued by the gravity of certain eminent men. Thus in the Roman republic all was destroyed by making the votes secret; it was no longer possible to enlighten a populace on its way to ruin. But votes cannot be too secret in an aristocracy when the body of nobles casts the votes, or in a democracy when the senate does so, for here the only issue is to guard against intrigues.

Intrigue is dangerous in a senate; it is dangerous in a body of nobles; it is not dangerous in the people, whose nature is to act from passion. In states where the people have no part in the government, they become as inflamed for an actor as they would for public affairs. The misfortune of a republic is to be without intrigues, and this happens when the people have been corrupted by silver; they become cool, they grow fond of silver, and they are no longer fond of public affairs; without concern for the government or for what is proposed there, they quietly await their payments.

Yet another fundamental law in democracy is that the people alone should make laws. However, there are a thousand occasions when it is necessary for the senate to be able to enact laws; it is often even appropriate to test a law before establishing it. The constitutions of Rome and Athens were very wise. The decrees of the senate had the force of law for a year; they became permanent only by the will of the people. [*Spirit of the laws*, i, ii, 2: 'On republican government and on laws relative to democracy']

In aristocracy, sovereign power is in the hands of a certain number of persons. They make the laws and see to their execution, and the rest of the people mean at best no more to these persons than the subjects in a monarchy mean to a monarch.

Voting should not be by lot; this would have only drawbacks. Indeed, in a government that has already established the most grievous distinctions, though a man might be chosen by lot, he would be no less odious for it; the noble is envied, not the magistrate.

When there are many nobles, there must be a senate to rule on the affairs that the body of nobles cannot decide and to take the preliminary steps for those on which it decides. In the latter case, it may be said that aristocracy is, in a way, in the senate, that democracy is in the body of nobles, and that the people are nothing.

It is a very fine thing in an aristocracy for the people to be raised from their nothingness in some indirect way; thus, in Genoa, the Bank of St George, administered largely by the principal men among the people, gives the people a certain influence in government, which brings about their whole prosperity.

Senators should not have the right to fill vacancies in the senate; nothing would be more likely to perpetuate abuses. In Rome, which was a kind of aristocracy in its early days, the senate did not name replacements; new senators were named by the censors.

When an exorbitant authority is given suddenly to a citizen in a republic, this forms a monarchy or more than a monarchy. In monarchies, the laws have protected the constitution or have been adapted to it; the principle of the government checks the monarch; but in a republic when a citizen takes exorbitant power, the abuse of this power is greater because the laws, which have not foreseen it, have done nothing to check it.

The exception to this rule occurs when the constitution of the state is such that it needs a magistracy with exorbitant power. Such was Rome with its dictators, such is Venice with its state inquisitors; these are terrible magistracies which violently return the state to liberty. But how does it happen that the magistracies are so different in these two republics? It is because, whereas Venice uses its state inquisitors to maintain its aristocracy against the nobles, Rome was defending the remnants of its aristocracy against the people. From this it followed that the dictator in Rome was installed for only a short time because the people act from impetuosity and not from design. His magistracy was exercised with brilliance, as the issue was to intimidate, not to punish, the people; the dictator was created for but a single affair and had unlimited authority with regard to that affair alone because he was always created for unforeseen cases. In Venice, however, there must be a permanent magistracy: here designs can be laid, followed, suspended, and taken up again; here too, the ambition of one alone becomes that of a family, and the ambition of one family, that of several. A hidden magistracy is needed because the crimes it punishes, always deep-seated, are formed in secrecy and silence. The inquisition of this magistracy has to be general because its aim is not to check known evils but to curb unknown ones. Finally, the Venetian magistracy is established to avenge the crimes it suspects, whereas the Roman magistracy used threats more than punishments, even for those crimes admitted by their instigators.

In every magistracy, the greatness of the power must be offset by the brevity of its duration. Most legislators have fixed the time at a year; a longer term would be dangerous, a shorter one would be contrary to the nature of the thing. Who would want thus to govern his domestic affairs? In Ragusa, the head of the republic changes every month; the other officers, every week; the governor of the castle, every day. This can take place only in a small republic surrounded by formidable powers which could easily corrupt petty magistrates.

The best aristocracy is one in which the part of the people having no share in the power is so small and so poor that the dominant part has no interest in oppressing it. Thus in Athens when Antipater established that those with less than two thousand drachmas would be excluded from the right to vote, he formed the best possible aristocracy, because this census was so low that it excluded only a few people and no one of any consequence in the city.

Therefore, aristocratic families should be of the people as far as possible. The more an aristocracy approaches democracy, the more perfect it will be, and to the degree it approaches monarchy the less perfect it will become.

Most imperfect of all is the aristocracy in which the part of the people that obeys is in civil slavery to the part that commands, as in the Polish aristocracy, where the peasants are slaves of the nobility. [*Spirit of the laws*, I, II, 3: 'On laws relative to the nature of aristocracy']

Intermediate, subordinate, and dependent powers constitute the nature of monarchical government, that is, of the government in which one alone governs by fundamental laws. I have said intermediate, subordinate, and dependent powers; indeed, in a monarchy, the prince is the source of all political and civil power. These fundamental laws necessarily assume mediate channels through which power flows; for, if in the state there is only the momentary and capricious will of one alone, nothing can be fixed and consequently there is no fundamental law.

The most natural intermediate, subordinate power is that of the nobility. In a way, the nobility is of the essence of monarchy, whose fundamental maxim is: *no monarch, no nobility: no nobility, no monarch*; rather, one has a despot.

In a few European states, some people had imagined abolishing all the justices of the lords. They did not see that they wanted to do what the Parliament of England did. If you abolish the prerogatives of the lords, clergy, nobility, and towns in a monarchy, you will soon have a popular state or else a despotic state.

For several centuries the tribunals of a great European state have been constantly striking down the patrimonial jurisdiction of the lords and the ecclesiastical jurisdiction. We do not want to censure such wise magistrates, but we leave it to be decided to what extent the constitution can be changed in this way.

I do not insist on the privileges of the ecclesiastics, but I would like their jurisdiction to be determined once and for all. It is a question of knowing not if one was right in establishing it but rather if it is established, if it is a part of the country's laws, and if it is relative to them throughout; if between two powers recognized as independent, conditions should not be reciprocal; and if it is not all the same to a good subject to defend the prince's justice or the limits that his justice has always prescribed for itself.

To the extent that the power of the clergy is dangerous in republics, it is suitable in monarchies, especially in those tending to despotism. Where would Spain and Portugal have been, after the loss of their laws, without the power that alone checks arbitrary power? Ever a good barrier when no other exists, because, as despotism causes appalling ills to human nature, the very ill that limits it is a good.

Just as the sea, which seems to want to cover the whole earth, is checked by the grasses and the smallest bits of gravel on the shore, so monarchs, whose power seems boundless, are checked by the slightest obstacles and submit their natural pride to supplication and prayer.

In order to favor liberty, the English have removed all the intermediate powers that formed their monarchy. They are quite right to preserve that liberty; if they were to lose it, they would be one of the most enslaved peoples on earth.

Mr. Law, equally ignorant of the republican and of the monarchical constitutions, was one of the greatest promoters of despotism that had until then been seen in Europe. Besides the changes he made, which were so abrupt, so unusual, and so unheard of, he wanted to remove the intermediate ranks and abolish the political bodies; he was dissolving the monarchy by his chimerical repayments and seemed to want to buy back the constitution itself.

It is not enough to have intermediate ranks in a monarchy; there must also be a depository of laws. This depository can only be in the political bodies, which announce the laws when they are made and recall them when they are forgotten. The ignorance natural to the nobility, its laxity, and its scorn for civil government require a body that constantly brings the laws out of the dust in which they would be buried. The prince's council is not a suitable depository. By its nature it is the depository of the momentary will of the prince who executes, and not the depository of the fundamental laws. Moreover, the monarch's council constantly changes; it is not permanent; it cannot be large; it does not sufficiently have the people's trust: therefore, it is not in a position to enlighten them in difficult times or to return them to obedience.

In despotic states, where there are no fundamental laws, neither is there a depository of laws. This is why religion has so much force in these countries; it forms a kind of permanent depository, and if it is not religion, it is customs that are venerated in the place of laws. [*Spirit of the laws,* 1, 11, 4: 'On laws in their **relation to the nature of monarchical government'**]

A result of the nature of despotic power is that the one man who exercises it has it likewise exercised by another. A man whose five senses constantly tell him that he is everything and that others are nothing is naturally lazy, ignorant, and voluptuous. Therefore, he abandons the public business. But, if he entrusted this business to many people, there would be disputes among them; there would be intrigues to be the first slave; the prince would be obliged to return to administration. Therefore it is simpler for him to abandon them to a vizir who will instantly have the same power as he. In this state, the establishment of a vizir is a fundamental law.

It is said that a certain pope, upon his election, overcome with his inadequacy, at first made infinite difficulties. Finally, he agreed to turn all matters of business over to his nephew. He was awestruck and said, 'I would never have believed that it could be so easy.' It is the same for the princes of the East. When, from that prison where eunuchs have weakened their hearts and spirits and have often left them ignorant even of their estate, these princes are withdrawn to be put on the throne, they are stunned at first; but when they have appointed a vizir, when in their seraglio they have given themselves up to the most brutal passions, when in the midst of a downtrodden court they have followed their most foolish caprices, they would never have believed that it could be so easy.

The more extensive the empire, the larger the seraglio, and the more, consequently, the prince is drunk with pleasures. Thus, in these states, the more peoples the prince has to govern, the less he thinks about government; the greater the matters of business, the less deliberation they are given. [*Spirit of the laws,* 1, **11, 5: 'On laws relative to the nature of the despotic state'**]

After having examined the laws relative to the nature of each government, one must look at those that are relative to its principle.

There is this difference between the nature of the government and its principle: its nature is that which makes it what it is, and its principle, that which makes it act. The one is its particular structure, and the other is the human passions that set it in motion.

Now, the laws should be no less relative to the principle of each government than to its nature. Therefore, this principle must be sought. I shall do so in this book. [*Spirit of the laws*, 1, III, 1: 'The difference between the nature of the government and its principle']

I have said that the nature of republican government is that the people as a body, or certain families, have the sovereign power; the nature of monarchical government is that the prince has the sovereign power, but that he exercises it according to established laws; the nature of despotic government is that one alone governs according to his wills and caprices. Nothing more is needed for me to find their three principles; they derive naturally from this. I shall begin with republican government, and I shall first speak of the democratic government. [*Spirit of the laws*, 1, III, 2: 'On the principle of the various governments']

There need not be much integrity for a monarchical or despotic government to maintain or sustain itself. The force of the laws in the one and the prince's ever-raised arm in the other can rule or contain the whole. But in a popular state there must be an additional spring, which is VIRTUE.

What I say is confirmed by the entire body of history and is quite in conformity with the nature of things. For it is clear that less virtue is needed in a monarchy, where the one who sees to the execution of the laws judges himself above the laws, than in a popular government, where the one who sees to the execution of the laws feels that he is subject to them himself and that he will bear their weight.

It is also clear that the monarch who ceases to see to the execution of the laws, through bad counsel or negligence, may easily repair the damage; he has only to change his counsel or correct his own negligence. But in a popular government when the laws have ceased to be executed, as this can come only from the corruption of the republic, the state is already lost.

It was a fine spectacle in the last century to see the impotent attempts of the English to establish democracy among themselves. As those who took part in public affairs had no virtue at all, as their ambition was excited by the success of the most audacious one and the spirit of one faction was repressed only by the spirit of another, the government was constantly changing; the people, stunned, sought democracy and found it nowhere. Finally, after much motion and many shocks and jolts, they had to come to rest on the very government that had been proscribed.

When Sulla wanted to return liberty to Rome, it could no longer be accepted;

Rome had but a weak remnant of virtue, and as it had ever less, instead of reawakening after Caesar, Tiberius, Caius, Claudius, Nero, and Domitian, it became ever more enslaved; all the blows were struck against tyrants, none against tyranny.

The political men of Greece who lived under popular government recognized no other force to sustain it than virtue. Those of today speak to us only of manufacturing, commerce, finance, wealth, and even luxury.

When that virtue ceases, ambition enters those hearts that can admit it, and avarice enters them all. Desires change their objects: that which one used to love, one loves no longer. One was free under the laws, one wants to be free against them. Each citizen is like a slave who has escaped from his master's house. What was a *maxim* is now called *severity*; what was a *rule* is now called *constraint*; what was *vigilance* is now called *fear*. There, frugality, not the desire to possess, is avarice. Formerly the goods of individuals made up the public treasury; the public treasury has now become the patrimony of individuals. The republic is a cast-off husk, and its strength is no more than the power of a few citizens and the license of all.

There were the same forces in Athens when it dominated with so much glory and when it served with so much shame. It had 20,000 citizens when it defended the Greeks against the Persians, when it disputed for empire with Lacedaemonia, and when it attacked Sicily. It had 20,000 when Demetrius of Phalereus enumerated them as one counts slaves in a market. When Philip dared dominate in Greece, when he appeared at the gates of Athens, Athens had as yet lost only time. In Demosthenes one may see how much trouble was required to reawaken it; Philip was feared as the enemy not of liberty but of pleasures. This town, which had resisted in spite of so many defeats, which had been reborn after its destructions, was defeated at Chaeronea and was defeated forever. What does it matter that Philip returns all the prisoners? He does not return men. It was always as easy to triumph over the forces of Athens as it was difficult to triumph over its virtue.

How could Carthage have sustained itself? When Hannibal, as praetor, wanted to keep the magistrates from pillaging the republic, did they not go and accuse him before the Romans? Unhappy men, who wanted to be citizens without a city and to owe their wealth to the hand of their destroyers! Soon Rome asked them to send three hundred of the principal citizens of Carthage as hostages; Rome made them surrender their arms and ships and then declared war on them. Given the things that a disarmed Carthage did from despair, one may judge what it could have done with its virtue when it had its full force. [*Spirit of the laws*, 1, III, 3: 'On the principle of democracy']

Just as there must be virtue in popular government, there must also be virtue in the aristocratic one. It is true that it is not as absolutely required.

The people, who are with respect to the nobles what the subjects are with respect to the monarch, are contained by the nobles' laws. Therefore, they need virtue less than the people of a democracy. But how will the nobles be contained? Those who should see to the execution of the laws against their fellows will instantly feel that they act against themselves. Virtue must, therefore, be in this body by the nature of the constitution.

Aristocratic government has a certain strength in itself that democracy does not have. In aristocratic government, the nobles form a body, which, by its prerogative and for its particular interest, represses the people; having laws is enough to insure that they will be executed.

But it is as easy for this body to repress the others as it is difficult for it to repress itself. Such is the nature of this constitution that it seems to put under the power of the laws the same people it exempts from them.

Now such a body may repress itself in only two ways: either by a great virtue that makes the nobles in some way equal to their people, which may form a great republic; or by a lesser virtue, a certain moderation that renders the nobles at least equal among themselves, which brings about their preservation.

Therefore, *moderation* is the soul of these governments. I mean the moderation founded on virtue, not the one that comes from faintheartedness and from laziness of soul. [*Spirit of the laws*, 1, II, 4: 'On the principle of aristocracy']

In monarchies, politics accomplishes great things with as little virtue as it can, just as in the finest machines art employs as few motions, forces, and wheels as possible.

The state continues to exist independently of love of the homeland, desire for true glory, self-renunciation, sacrifice of one's dearest interests, and all those heroic virtues we find in the ancients and know only by hearsay.

The laws replace all these virtues, for which there is no need; the state excuses you from them: here an action done noiselessly is in a way inconsequential.

Though all crimes are by their nature public, truly public crimes are nevertheless distinguished from private crimes, so called because they offend an individual more than the whole society.

Now, in republics private crimes are more public, that is, they run counter to the constitution of the state more than against individuals; and, in monarchies, public crimes are more private, that is, they run counter to individual fortunes more than against the constitution of the state itself.

I beg that no one be offended by what I have said; I have followed all the histories. I know very well that virtuous princes are not rare, but I say that in a monarchy it is very difficult for the people to be virtuous.

Read what the historians of all times have said about the courts of monarchs; recall the conversations of men from every country about the wretched character of courtiers: these are not matters of speculation but of sad experience.

Ambition in idleness, meanness in arrogance, the desire to enrich oneself without work, aversion to truth, flattery, treachery, perfidy, the abandonment of all one's engagements, the scorn of the duties of citizens, the fear of the prince's virtue, the expectation of his weaknesses, and more than all that, the perpetual ridicule cast upon virtue, these form, I believe, the character of the greater number of courtiers, as observed in all places and at all times. Now, it is very awkward for most of the principal men of a state to be dishonest people and for the inferiors to be good people, for the former to be deceivers and the latter to consent to be no more than dupes.

If there is some unfortunate honest man among the people, hints Cardinal Richelieu in his *Political Testament*, a monarch should be careful not to employ him. So true is it that virtue is not the spring of this government! Certainly, it is not excluded, but it is not its spring. [*Spirit of the laws*, **I, II, 5: 'That virtue is not the principle of monarchical government'**]

I hasten and I lengthen my steps, so that none will believe I satirize monarchical government. No; if one spring is missing, monarchy has another. HONOR, that is, the prejudice of each person and each condition, takes the place of the political virtue of which I have spoken and represents it everywhere. It can inspire the finest actions; joined with the force of the laws, it can lead to the goal of government as does virtue itself.

Thus, in well-regulated monarchies everyone will be almost a good citizen, and one will rarely find someone who is a good man; for, in order to be a good man, one must have the intention of being one and love the state less for oneself than for itself. [*Spirit of the laws*, i, ii, 6: **'How virtue is replaced in monarchical government'**]

Monarchical government assumes, as we have said, preeminences, ranks, and even a hereditary nobility. The nature of *honor* is to demand preferences and distinctions; therefore, honor has, in and of itself, a place in this government.

Ambition is pernicious in a republic. It has good effects in monarchy; it gives life to that government; and it has this advantage, that it is not dangerous because it can constantly be repressed.

You could say that it is like the system of the universe, where there is a force constantly repelling all bodies from the center and a force of gravitation attracting them to it. Honor makes all the parts of the body politic move; its very action binds them, and each person works for the common good, believing he works for his individual interests.

Speaking philosophically, it is true that the honor that guides all the parts of the state is a false honor, but this false honor is as useful to the public as the true one would be to the individuals who could have it.

And is it not impressive that one can oblige men to do all the difficult actions and which require force, with no reward other than the renown of these actions? [*Spirit of the laws*, i, ii, 7: **'On the principle of monarchy'**]

Honor is not the principle of despotic states: as the men in them are all equal, one cannot prefer oneself to others; as men in them are all slaves, one can prefer oneself to nothing.

Moreover, as honor has its laws and rules and is incapable of yielding, as it depends on its own caprice and not on that of another, honor can be found only in states whose constitution is fixed and whose laws are certain.

How could honor be endured by the *despot*? It glories in scorning life, and the despot is strong only because he can take life away. How could honor endure the despot? It has consistent rules and sustains its caprices; the despot has no rule, and his caprices destroy all the others.

Honor, unknown in despotic states where even the word to express it is often lacking, reigns in monarchies; there it gives life to the whole body politic, to the laws, and even to the virtues. [*Spirit of the laws*, i, ii, 8: **'That honor is not the principle of despotic states'**]

put it in this government; those who had enjoyed monarchical government placed it in monarchy. In short, each has given the name of *liberty* to the government that was consistent with his customs or his inclinations; and as, in a republic, one does not always have visible and so present the instruments of the ills of which one complains and as the very laws seem to speak more and the executors of the law to speak less, one ordinarily places liberty in republics and excludes it from monarchies. Finally, as in democracies the people seem very nearly to do what they want, liberty has been placed in this sort of government and the power of the people has been confused with the liberty of the people. [*Spirit of the laws*, II, II, 2: 'The various significations given to the word liberty']

It is true that in democracies the people seem to do what they want, but political liberty in no way consists in doing what one wants. In a state, that is, in a society where there are laws, liberty can consist only in having the power to do what one should want to do and in no way being constrained to do what one should not want to do.

One must put oneself in mind of what independence is and what liberty is. Liberty is the right to do everything the laws permit; and if one citizen could do what they forbid, he would no longer have liberty because the others would likewise have this same power. [*Spirit of the laws*, II, II, 3: 'What liberty is']

In each state there are three sorts of powers: legislative power, executive power over the things depending on the right of nations, and executive power over the things depending on civil right.

By the first, the prince or the magistrate makes laws for a time or for always and corrects or abrogates those that have been made. By the second, he makes peace or war, sends or receives embassies, establishes security, and prevents invasions. By the third, he punishes crimes or judges disputes between individuals. The last will be called the power of judging, and the former simply the executive power of the state.

Political liberty in a citizen is that tranquillity of spirit which comes from the opinion each one has of his security, and in order for him to have this liberty the government must be such that one citizen cannot fear another citizen.

When legislative power is united with executive power in a single person or in a single body of the magistracy, there is no liberty, because one can fear that the same monarch or senate that makes tyrannical laws will execute them tyrannically.

Nor is there liberty if the power of judging is not separate from legislative power and from executive power. If it were joined to legislative power, the power over the life and liberty of the citizens would be arbitrary, for the judge would be the legislator. If it were joined to executive power, the judge could have the force of an oppressor.

All would be lost if the same man or the same body of principal men, either of nobles, or of the people, exercised these three powers: that of making the laws, that of executing public resolutions, and that of judging the crimes or the disputes of individuals.

In most kingdoms in Europe, the government is moderate because the prince, who has the first two powers, leaves the exercise of the third to his subjects. Among the Turks, where the three powers are united in the person of the sultan, an atrocious despotism reigns.

In the Italian republics, where the three powers are united, there is less liberty than in our monarchies. Thus, in order to maintain itself, the government needs means as violent as in the government of the Turks; witness the state inquisitors and the lion's maw into which an informer can, at any moment, throw his note of accusation.

Observe the possible situation of a citizen in these republics. The body of the magistracy, as executor of the laws, retains all the power it has given itself as legislator. It can plunder the state by using its general wills; and, as it also has the power of judging, it can destroy each citizen by using its particular wills.

There, all power is one; and, although there is none of the external pomp that reveals a despotic prince, it is felt at every moment.

Thus princes who have wanted to make themselves despotic have always begun by uniting in their person all the magistracies, and many kings of Europe have begun by uniting all the great posts of their state.

I do believe that the pure hereditary aristocracy of the Italian republics is not precisely like the despotism of Asia. The multitude of magistrates sometimes softens the magistracy; not all the nobles always concur in the same designs; there various tribunals are formed that temper one another. Thus, in Venice, the *Great Council* has legislation; the *Pregadi*, execution; *Quarantia*, the power of judging. But the ill is that these different tribunals are formed of magistrates taken from the same body; this makes them nearly a single power.

The power of judging should not be given to a permanent senate but should be exercised by persons drawn from the body of the people at certain times of the year in the manner prescribed by law to form a tribunal which lasts only as long as necessity requires.

In this fashion the power of judging, so terrible among men, being attached neither to a certain state nor to a certain profession, becomes, so to speak, invisible and null. Judges are not continually in view; one fears the magistracy, not the magistrates.

In important accusations, the criminal in cooperation with the law must choose the judges, or at least he must be able to challenge so many of them that those who remain are considered to be of his choice.

The two other powers may be given instead to magistrates or to permanent bodies because they are exercised upon no individual, the one being only the general will of the state, and the other, the execution of that general will.

But though tribunals should not be fixed, judgments should be fixed to such a degree that they are never anything but a precise text of the law. If judgments were the individual opinion of a judge, one would live in this society without knowing precisely what engagements one has contracted.

Further, the judges must be of the same condition as the accused, or his peers, so that he does not suppose that he has fallen into the hands of people inclined to do him violence.

If the legislative power leaves to the executive power the right to imprison citizens who can post bail for their conduct, there is no longer any liberty, unless the citizens are arrested in order to respond without delay to an accusation of a crime the law has rendered capital; in this case they are really free because they are subject only to the power of the law.

But if the legislative power believed itself endangered by some secret conspiracy against the state or by some correspondence with its enemies on the outside, it could, for a brief and limited time, permit the executive power to arrest suspected citizens who would lose their liberty for a time only so that it would be preserved forever.

And this is the only means consistent with reason of replacing the tyrannical magistracy of the *ephors* and the *state inquisitors* of Venice, who are also despotic.

As, in a free state, every man, considered to have a free soul, should be governed by himself, the people as a body should have legislative power; but, as this is impossible in large states and is subject to many drawbacks in small ones, the people must have their representatives do all that they themselves cannot do.

One knows the needs of one's own town better than those of other towns, and one judges the ability of one's neighbors better than that of one's other compatriots. Therefore, members of the legislative body must not be drawn from the body of the nation at large; it is proper for the inhabitants of each principal town to choose a representative from it.

The great advantage of representatives is that they are able to discuss public business. The people are not at all appropriate for such discussions; this forms one of the great drawbacks of democracy.

It is not necessary that the representatives, who have been generally instructed by those who have chosen them, be instructed about each matter of business in particular, as is the practice in the Diets of Germany. It is true that, in their way, the word of the deputies would better express the voice of the nation; but it would produce infinite delays and make each deputy the master of all the others, and on the most pressing occasions the whole force of the nation could be checked by a caprice.

Mr. Sidney says properly that when the deputies represent a body of people, as in Holland, they should be accountable to those who have commissioned them; it is another thing when they are deputed by boroughs, as in England.

In choosing a representative, all citizens in the various districts should have the right to vote except those whose estate is so humble that they are deemed to have no will of their own.

A great vice in most ancient republics was that the people had the right to make resolutions for action, resolutions which required some execution, which altogether exceeds the people's capacity. The people should not enter the government except to choose their representatives; this is quite within their reach. For if there are few people who know the precise degree of a man's ability, yet every one is able to know, in general, if the one he chooses sees more clearly than most of the others.

Nor should the representative body be chosen in order to make some resolution for action, a thing it would not do well, but in order to make laws or in order to see if those they have made have been well executed; these are things it can do very well and that only it can do well.

In a state there are always some people who are distinguished by birth, wealth, or honors; but if they were mixed among the people and if they had only one voice like the others, the common liberty would be their enslavement and they would have no interest in defending it, because most of the resolutions would be against them. Therefore, the part they have in legislation should be in proportion to the other advantages they have in the state, which will happen if they form a body that has the right to check the enterprises of the people, as the people have the right to check theirs.

Thus, legislative power will be entrusted both to the body of the nobles and to the body that will be chosen to represent the people, each of which will have assemblies and deliberations apart and have separate views and interests.

Among the three powers of which we have spoken, that of judging is in some fashion, null. There remain only two; and, as they need a power whose regulations temper them, that part of the legislative body composed of the nobles is quite appropriate for producing this effect.

The nobility should be hereditary. In the first place, it is so by its nature; and, besides, it must have a great interest in preserving its prerogatives, odious in themselves, and which, in a free state, must always be endangered.

But, as a hereditary power could be induced to follow its particular interests and forget those of the people, in the things about which one has a sovereign interest in corrupting, for instance, in the laws about levying silver coin, it must take part in legislation only through its faculty of vetoing and not through its faculty of enacting.

I call the right to order by oneself, or to correct what has been ordered by another, the *faculty of enacting*. I call the right to render null a resolution taken by another the *faculty of vetoing*, which was the power of the tribunes of Rome. And, although the one who has the faculty of vetoing can also have the right to approve, this approval is no more than a declaration that one does not make use of one's faculty of vetoing, and it derives from that faculty.

The executive power should be in the hands of a monarch, because the part of the government that almost always needs immediate action is better administered by one than by many, whereas what depends on legislative power is often better ordered by many than by one.

If there were no monarch and the executive power were entrusted to a certain number of persons drawn from the legislative body, there would no longer be liberty, because the two powers would be united, the same persons sometimes belonging and always able to belong to both.

If the legislative body were not convened for a considerable time, there would no longer be liberty. For one of two things would happen: either there would no longer be any legislative resolution and the state would fall into anarchy; or these resolutions would be made by the executive power, and it would become absolute.

It would be useless for the legislative body to be convened without interruption. That would inconvenience the representatives and besides would overburden the executive power, which would not think of executing, but of defending its prerogatives and its right to execute.

In addition, if the legislative body were continuously convened, it could happen that one would do nothing but replace the deputies who had died with new deputies; and in this case, if the legislative body were once corrupted, the ill would be without remedy. When various legislative bodies follow each other, the people, holding a poor opinion of the current legislative body, put their hopes, reasonably enough, in the one that will follow; but if the legislative body were always the same, the people, seeing it corrupted, would expect nothing further from its laws; they would become furious or would sink into indolence.

The legislative body should not convene itself. For a body is considered to have a will only when it is convened; and if it were not convened unanimously, one could not identify which part was truly the legislative body, the part that was convened or the one that was not. For if it had the right to prorogue itself, it could happen that it would never prorogue itself; this would be dangerous in the event that it wanted to threaten executive power. Besides, there are some times more suitable than others for convening the legislative body; therefore, it must be the executive power that regulates, in relation to the circumstances it knows, the time of the holding and duration of these assemblies.

If the executive power does not have the right to check the enterprises of the legislative body, the latter will be despotic, for it will wipe out all the other powers, since it will be able to give to itself all the power it can imagine.

But the legislative power must not have the reciprocal faculty of checking the executive power. For, as execution has the limits of its own nature, it is useless to restrict it; besides, executive power is always exercised on immediate things. And the power of the tribunes in Rome was faulty in that it checked not only legislation but even execution; this caused great ills.

But if, in a free state, legislative power should not have the right to check executive power, it has the right and should have the faculty to examine the manner in which the laws it has made have been executed; and this is the advantage of this government over that of Crete and Lacedaemonia, where the *kosmoi* and the *ephors* were not held accountable for their administration.

But, whether or not this examination is made, the legislative body should not have the power to judge the person, and consequently the conduct, of the one who executes. His person should be sacred because, as he is necessary to the state so that the legislative body does not become tyrannical, if he were accused or judged there would no longer be liberty.

In this case, the state would not be a monarchy but an unfree republic. But, as he who executes cannot execute badly without having as ministers wicked counsellors who hate the law although the laws favor them as men, these counsellors can be sought out and punished. And this is the advantage of this government over that of Cnidus, where the people could never get satisfaction for the injustices that had been done to them, as the law did not permit calling the *amymones* to judgment even after their administration.

Although in general the power of judging should not be joined to any part of the legislative power, this is subject to three exceptions founded on the particular interests of the one who is to be judged.

Important men are always exposed to envy; and if they were judged by the people, they could be endangered and would not enjoy the privilege of the last citizen of a free state, of being judged by his peers. Therefore, nobles must not be called before the ordinary tribunals of the nation but before that part of the legislative body composed of nobles.

It could happen that the law, which is simultaneously clairvoyant and blind, might be too rigorous in certain cases. But the judges of the nation are, as we have said, only the mouth that pronounces the words of the law, inanimate beings who can moderate neither its force nor its rigor. Therefore, the part of the legislative body, which we have just said is a necessary tribunal on another occasion, is also one on this occasion; it is for its supreme authority to moderate the law in favor of the law itself by pronouncing less rigorously than the law.

It could also happen that a citizen, in matters of public business, might violate the rights of the people and commit crimes that the established magistrates could not or would not want to punish. But, in general, the legislative power cannot judge, and even less so in this particular case, where it represents the interested party, the people. Therefore, it can be only the accuser. But, before whom will it make its accusation? Will it bow before the tribunals of law, which are lower than it and are, moreover, composed of those who, being also of the people, would be swept along by the authority of such a great accuser? No: in order to preserve the dignity of the people and the security of the individual, that part of the legislature drawn from the people must make its accusation before the part of the legislature drawn from the nobles, which has neither the same interests nor the same passions.

This last is the advantage of this government over most of the ancient republics, where there was the abuse that the people were judge and accuser at the same time.

Executive power, as we have said, should take part in legislation by its faculty of vetoing; otherwise it will soon be stripped of its prerogatives. But if legislative power takes part in execution, executive power will equally be lost.

If the monarch took part in legislation by the faculty of enacting, there would no longer be liberty. But as in spite of this, he must take part in legislation in order to defend himself, he must take part in it by the faculty of vetoing.

The cause of the change in government in Rome was that the senate, which had one part of the executive power, and the magistrates, who had the other, did not have the faculty of vetoing, as the people had.

Here, therefore, is the fundamental constitution of the government of which we are speaking. As its legislative body is composed of two parts, the one will be chained to the other by their reciprocal faculty of vetoing. The two will be bound by the executive power, which will itself be bound by the legislative power.

The form of these three powers should be rest or inaction. But as they are constrained to move by the necessary motion of things, they will be forced to move in concert.

As executive power belongs to the legislative only through its faculty of vetoing, it cannot enter into the discussion of public business. It is not even necessary for it to propose, because, as it can always disapprove of resolutions, it can reject decisions on propositions it would have wanted left unmade.

In some ancient republics, where the people as a body discussed the public business, it was natural for the executive power to propose and discuss with them; otherwise, there would have been a strange confusion in the resolutions.

If the executive power enacts on the raising of public funds without the consent of the legislature, there will no longer be liberty, because the executive power will become the legislator on the most important point of legislation.

If the legislative power enacts, not from year to year, but forever, on the raising of public funds, it runs the risk of losing its liberty, because the executive power will no longer depend upon it; and when one holds such a right forever, it is unimportant whether that right comes from oneself or from another. The same is true if the legislative power enacts, not from year to year, but forever, about the land and sea forces, which it should entrust to the executive power.

So that the one who executes is not able to oppress, the armies entrusted to him must be of the people and have the same spirit as the people, as they were in Rome until the time of Marius. This can be so in only two ways: either those employed in the army must have enough goods to be answerable for their conduct to the other citizens and be enrolled for a year only, as was practiced in Rome; or, if the troops must be a permanent body, whose soldiers come from the meanest parts of the nation, legislative power must be able to disband them as soon as the legislature so desires; the soldiers must live with the citizens, and there must not be a separate camp, a barracks, or a fortified place.

Once the army is established, it should be directly dependent on the executive power, not on the legislative body; and this is in the nature of the thing, as its concern is more with action than with deliberation.

Men's manner of thinking is to make more of courage than of timidity; more of activity than of prudence; more of force than of counsel. The army will always scorn a senate and respect its officers. It will not make much of the orders sent from a body composed of people it believes timid and, therefore, unworthy to command it. Thus, whenever the army depends solely on the legislative body, the government will become military. And if the contrary has ever occurred, it is the effect of some extraordinary circumstances; it is because the army there is always separate, because it is composed of several bodies each of which depends upon its particular province, because the capitals are in excellent locations whose situation alone defends them and which have no troops.

Holland is even more secure than Venice; it could flood rebellious troops; it could leave them to die of hunger; since the troops are not in towns that could give them sustenance, their sustenance is precarious.

For if, in the case of an army governed by the legislative body, particular circumstances keep the government from becoming military, one will encounter other drawbacks; one of these two things must happen, either the army must destroy the government, or the government must weaken the army.

And this weakening will have a fatal cause: it will arise from the very weakness of the government.

If one wants to read the admirable work by Tacitus, *On the Mores of the Germans*, one will see that the English have taken their idea of political government from the Germans. This fine system was found in the forests.

Since all human things have an end, the state of which we are speaking will lose its liberty; it will perish. Rome, Lacedaemonia, and Carthage have surely perished. This state will perish when legislative power is more corrupt than executive power.

It is not for me to examine whether at present the English enjoy this liberty or not. It suffices for me to say that it is established by their laws, and I seek no further.

I do not claim hereby to disparage other governments, or to say that this extreme political liberty should humble those who have only a moderate one. How could I say that, I who believe that the excess even of reason is not always desirable and that men almost always accommodate themselves better to middles than to extremities?

Harrington, in his *Oceana*, has also examined the furthest point of liberty to which the constitution of a state can be carried. But of him it can be said that he sought this liberty only after misunderstanding it, and that he built Chalcedon with the coast of Byzantium before his eyes. [*Spirit of the laws*, II, II, 6: 'On the **constitution of England**']

FRIEDRICH KARL VON MOSER

BIOGRAPHICAL NOTE

Friedrich Karl von Moser (1723–98) came from a family of Württemberg jurists and state officials. He was the son of Johann Jakob von Moser, a professor of law, well-known author of a fifty-volume work on German civil law and a senior civil servant for a number of German states during a long and illustrious career, marred only by his arbitrary imprisonment by the Duke of Württemberg. Friedrich Moser also worked as an itinerant civil servant, spending most of the early years of his career in Hesse-Darmstadt, eventually reaching ministerial level in spite of princely disapproval of his writings. Moser wrote prolifically on religion and morality, as well as politics. In addition to *The master and the servant, or the reciprocal duties of a sovereign and his minister, described with patriotic liberty*, his works include a twelve-volume study of public law, a celebrated essay *On the German national spirit* (1765), a collection of moral and religious apophthegms entitled *Relics* (1776), *Patriotic letters* (1767), *On regents, government and ministers* (1784), *On the administration of ecclesiastical lands in Germany* (1787) and *Patriotic truths* (1796).

Although he believed to some extent in the merits of enlightened absolutism, Moser hated what he called 'the blind and unlimited obedience' demanded by officer-autocrats, who thought they could treat their subjects like soldiers on the parade ground. Unwisely perhaps, he placed his faith in the reformed power of princes rather than in their overthrow, and for many years he defended the imperial ideal and the potential it embodied for creation of a fatherland and the defeat of a particularism that predated the Thirty Years War, a profession of faith that he had first set out in his essay, *On the German national spirit*. Disappointment at the failure of the spirit of national self-renewal to materialise led him to adopt in his last years a deeply pessimistic fatalism with regard to the apparent imperviousness of Germanic political institutions to the pressures for reform and change, even after 1789. *The master and the servant* was published in 1759, reprinted in the same year and again in 1761. It was translated into French in 1760 and 1761.

EDITORIAL NOTE

The base text for the translation of the extracts is that of the first edition of *Der Herr und der Diener, geschildert mit patriotischer Freiheit* (Frankfurt-am-Main, J. Kaspe, 1759).

FURTHER READING

Hertz, F., *The development of the German public mind: a social history of German political sentiments, aspirations and ideas*, II: *The age of Enlightenment* (London, Allen and Unwin, 1962). See especially chapter 19.
Sheehan, J., *German history 1770–1866* (Oxford, Clarendon Press, 1989). See especially chapters 1, 2 and 3.

The master and the servant, or the reciprocal duties of a sovereign and his minister, described with patriotic liberty (1759)

Right thinking, saying what you think and doing as you say, these are what motivate the world, and these are the three qualities essential for a king to run his kingdom.[1]

Just as it is impossible for a father to maintain his household if the general management of his finances is not based on a specific, pre-determined plan, whose minor details can be modified from time to time, so it is impossible, even more so, for a prince to govern his people in a happy, orderly way, even for a short period, if he does not always have before him certain basic maxims as a fixed principle of policy.

Some of these maxims can and must remain forever unchanged; others conversely depend on circumstances; circumstances dictate how long they remain relevant, limit them, extend them, or sometimes even change them completely

. . .

The running of a household or a country, be it good or bad, depends on the master. The most magnificent palace will fall into ruins if the lord who lives there neglects to take care of it, whereas a desert will change into a garden in the hands

---

[1] From Count Tessin to the Crown Prince of Sweden. [*Note by Moser.*]

of a wise and skilful owner. What did Russia not become under Peter the Great! Or Prussia under its current monarch, or his predecessor! Or Austria under the Empress, its finances once in such a crumbling state, and its armies so run down! When, on the other hand, I turn my gaze on certain other countries, so blessed with nature's gifts, when I think of the powerful positions from which they have fallen, and which they could still enjoy, I cannot help groaning at the sight of such a fine and rich heritage being dissipated and reduced to nothing through bad management on the part of an unworthy guardian.

To climb to the top of a mountain you do not go as quickly as you do when you make the descent. In one night a fire can destroy a building on which you have worked for twenty years. You can ruin a country more easily than you can improve it. It must be very hard for a prince who has taken to heart both the honour of his house and the welfare of his subjects, to contemplate [the prospect of] a successor whose birthright will enable him to destroy in one second everything that the prince has nurtured with such wisdom, prudence and care. What sighs must come from a worthy minister who sees his future master associate with people whose advice he knows in advance will lead his future master to do the opposite to what, in his long and wise experience, advances the honour of the royal house and the interests of the country.

The duties of a sovereign are difficult to carry out, and even more so for a bad sovereign. Unhappy is the prince who does not feel their full weight! And unhappier still is the country of a prince who knows what his duties are, but who cannot be bothered to carry them out!

There is an important difference between being the *sovereign* of a country and its *father*. The first title is acquired by right of birth, and the other is his reward for virtue and for carrying out his duties. The one rules over his subjects' possessions, and the other over their hearts ... A prince who has a little intelligence and a good heart is worth infinitely more than a prince who cannot supplement his countless heroic qualities with virtue, who raises statues on the ruins of his subjects' houses, who makes the world tremble in fear and his country in poverty. Sweden will always remember with greater pleasure the gentle, peaceful reign of King Frederick than the great exploits of Charles XII, whose unbreakable courage plunged the country into the utmost misery, from which it will not recover for some time to come ...

If great lords knew how easy it is for them to make themselves loved, they would do much more good. These are people who have the flattering advantage to be in a position to spread joy, gaiety, happiness and prosperity throughout the rest of the world, a world of which they form just a small part.

Yes, in truth, we place in their hands an advantage that for them should be a powerful spur to do good, and to be virtuous. We subjects are too inclined to give our masters the benefit of the doubt; we hasten to cover up and excuse their faults, we value and praise their good qualities to the skies. How easy it is therefore for them to pass as virtuous, just, generous and nice people! Provided a prince is not wicked, vicious, greedy and irritable in public, he is praised. He has to take things to extremes before he falls into bad odour with his people. Does he have a little weakness? Does he sink into the most outrageous debauchery even, something that is only too easy for him to do? No sooner does he express a slight murmur of repentance than everything is forgiven and forgotten. A kind word makes a subject give up his last penny, even money that he has set aside for his widow and children. A smiling face, a gracious tap on the shoulder, will revive an old man whose hair has been turned white by his business worries.

What empire could be more fertile in magnanimous and generous princes than Germany since our [various] constitutions deprive them of no opportunity to do good. Show me any state in Europe where a prince, with only a few miles of territory, can make his subjects so happy, should he wish to. And if you find here and there a sovereign like that living with a small number of subjects like a loving father with his children, it is just as impossible in those circumstances to deny such a kind prince affection, attachment and veneration as it is right conversely to stand in the corner of shame a petty tyrant who, in his rapaciousness, and unable to squeeze anything else out of his subjects, goes as far as to cloak himself in religion in order to cover up his greed.

But as a true patriot I cannot help shedding tears in acknowledging that there are few princes who do not abuse our happy Germanic freedom. The time is fast approaching when it will no longer be permitted to have a choice between what is good and what is bad, but only between what is bad and what is worse. Nothing is less reassuring than a quick glance at the present government. Alas! I am almost ashamed to be a German at the thought of those princes who make up the majority of those destined one day to rule over us ...

Perhaps my distress is the result of my naivety, but may my country hold my name up in horror if any base motive should enter my way of thinking, and seek to move my German heart. Let posterity judge the evidence that reluctantly our century must, alas, confirm.

The education of most princes who are destined one day to rule is as neglected from the standpoint of morality as it is from that of general principles. A young prince has hardly taken leave of his teachers and completed his travels when, the victim of tradition, he is given two choices, either to serve abroad in the army, or to stay at home. Even in the latter case he is entirely isolated from affairs of state; at most he is given a regiment, and made to join the Ministry of Defence. Everything else remains a mystery to him. Also hidden from him are the interests of his household, the strengths and weaknesses of his country, the condition of his subjects, the workings of his courts, the arts of negotiation. He is denied membership of the cabinet. It is even a crime for him to show any desire to learn about the inner workings of government, and people refuse to give him any knowledge of these. The fathers and ancestors of our Sovereigns were initiated into affairs of state at an early age; they were obliged to visit the ministries and work in them; they were members of the Council, and could express their views there once experience and study enabled them to express them judiciously. One can still, to the glory of our times, quote a few such examples, but in truth not very many. The King of Prussia often passes several hours on end with his nephew, and takes pleasure in forming the character of that young prince who, destined one day to succeed him, already provides us with a shining hope that in due course we will see him carry out brilliantly the high destiny to which God and his birth call him. The Crown Prince, at present Landgrave of Hesse-Cassel, was also admitted to his father's Council, and I have even been told that for a time he kept the register.

The reason why few follow the examples I have just quoted is to be found no doubt in the fact that many fathers understand very little themselves about government, have no taste for it, and prefer their pleasures to their duties. We willingly relieve others of something that does not appeal to us. Often jealousy of a son who shows evidence of a lively and enlightened mind contributes much to this. The wickedness and spite of a corrupt minister hasten the isolation of such a witness to their fraudulent activities. Court favourites, those pillars of the ante-chamber and other layabouts maintain as an act of faith that work is not a worthy occupation for a sovereign, that he must make it the responsibility of ministers and dicasteries, thereby defining work in terms of those things that have always delighted princes, without reflecting on the fact that some of the amusements of great lords are really in fact a tiring and much more dangerous form of work.

It is true that a sovereign should not work with the same eye to detail as a royal counsellor, and as soon as I see a prince's office filled from top to bottom with official files, I am immediately as certain that there is no system to his government as I would be if I found the office decorated with hunting whips and antlers. In truth, the architect must have before him the plan of the whole building, and never let go of the set-square, but nevertheless, he is not obliged to turn his head into a well of learned wisdom, or his office into a building site. It is enough for him to see the whole picture, to manage the details in an organised and methodical way only as far as is necessary. But most of our young princes do not understand the one, and could not care less about the other. Would their time not be better used travelling through their lands to learn for themselves some clear notions of rural economy, the true source of wealth, to get acquainted with human realities by a closer contact with the troubles and work of the people, to encourage the enthusiasm of manufacturers and tradespeople, and stimulate their industriousness with a personal visit? By exercising such care, which does a prince so much honour, he will discover his country's internal sources of wealth, he will discover its mines, its salt marshes and other natural blessings; he will learn to understand the genius of his subjects, and their way of thinking, and he will be capable of judging the merits and the faults of his government. How well prepared would a prince with such knowledge be to take up the reins of government! What actually happens, on the other hand? The best years of his life are allowed to trickle away in harmful idleness; his mind is turned away from thoughts of serious work and application in order to be filled at best with just trivialities or things far beneath a person destined one day to rule. And too often those years that a prince should be using exclusively to educate himself for the good of the country are devoted to dissolute living, hunting, gambling, drunken orgies, and to making himself look ridiculous playing soldiers . . .

On succeeding to the throne a prince must not change the system lightly. To do that you have to be very sure of your grounds. But if he finds the old government to be totally bad, if he cannot see how to correct its abuses, then let him work to reform it as soon as he takes power. For with every change of government people are prepared for the bad things that the change brings with it, and consequently the obstacles [to change] are never that big. Nevertheless, one must be careful to present one's plan just as a proposal for fear of just being tempted to follow one's whims, and in order to retain one's freedom to be able honourably to do what is best, and add or take away according to what one thinks is best and most useful.

It is of the utmost importance for a prince to give an advantageous first impression of himself, even if it is not that marked. First impressions are the most vivid and last the longest. If a General has a good first campaign, he can have a set-back subsequently without doing himself any damage. But if he starts off by being beaten, he is an object of contempt until he has re-established his reputation with a brilliant *coup* . . . Public opinion can be changed easily, and one can become a model for others just as easily as before one could become the object of their scorn and criticism.

Courage is needed to set off along such a long and often little-used road. Choosing [wisely] the way to proceed makes it easier, and with time and patience you can succeed in getting to the end.

Many share the same aim, but few succeed. A lengthy book could be written on the fine plans of crown princes. If only a tenth of these plans had been carried out, we would be seeing a new Golden Age in Germany. Must we conclude that they were not serious? Yes, of course they were. But it is one thing to have a plan, and another thing to carry it out. To put a difficult plan into effect, not to lose enthusiasm for it and to complete it, is not within everyone's grasp. They might have the best of intentions, they lack only the means and the manpower, that is to say, skilled people with integrity, without whom everything is but an empty declaration of intent, and they soon revert to the old ways of doing things, often doing them a lot worse.

Even if one assumed that these fine fellows who help to illuminate and expose the faults of the previous government are acting in good faith, they are not always the best people to get rid of the rubble of the old regime, and put up a new building.

Nothing is easier than criticising, and nothing is harder than doing better . . .

The Crown Prince at a certain court had noticed that during the night wine was being quietly removed from the court cellars. He protested in vain against this underhand thieving. His court favourite persuaded him that the whole thing was the result of not having a Master-Butler. Once in power, his first executive decision was to fill this post. After mature reflection, the post was filled by a man who did not like wine. He was given a salary of sixteen hundred florins, a voice at court and enough oats for two horses. Gentlemen rarely refuse to give each other gifts, especially when it is at the prince's expense. It was no longer just at night that people came looking for wine, but in the full light of day, licensed by His Lordship the Master-Butler. This so-called improvement cost the prince five thousand florins a year, whereas what was being stolen from him on the quiet came to scarcely five hundred.

One Crown Prince sighed often at the enormous sums of money that his father spent on his mistresses. He vowed never to cause such a scandal in his own country; but on the other hand he bestows all his favours on a spendthrift who, by governing his heart, soon governed his treasury and the wealth of his subjects. In no time all of this causes more damage than a whole army, and within a year more expense than the sovereign's mistresses. In the end, he reduced his master to utter poverty, exposing him to public ridicule, and his subjects to total misery.

Let a sovereign never treat the love of his people lightly. It is much more effective than force. He will win that love, and retain it, only if he can make his subjects see that he is ruling them not by fear, as if they were slaves, but by good sense, as free people, and if in the management of affairs of state he is guided less by the force of blind whim than by principles, whose unshakeable authority is widely recognised by the wisest heads in his state . . . [*The master and the servant*, 1: 'Maxims and general remarks']

A King's greatness is in proportion to the people of merit around him[2]

The second major point concerns the internal organisation of government.

After the master, everything depends on the sort of people he has in his service.

It is pointless having admirable laws and the best-intentioned of princes, if ministers, counsellors and servants are no good.

A prince is judged by the discernment he shows in his choice of ministers.

An absolute requirement in this choice is that a prince should have an expert eye, for it is always by chance, and by very rare chance, that a prince with moderate intelligence can find and recognise great genius. More commonly what happens is in the story about Cardinal Richelieu. He asked the famous Le Camus, Bishop of Bellay, what he thought about two new works: Balzac's *The prince* and Silhon's *The minister of state*. Whereupon the prelate answered: 'one is not worth very much, and the other nothing at all'.

We are used to seeing princes send experts overseas to find them the best dogs, horses and falcons. Their example tells us that they have no qualms about paying out ten to twelve thousand florins for a top-quality person, even if the search

---

[2] Letter from Count Tessin. [*Note by Moser.*]

extends from Naples to deepest Norway. Would not those same princes take any proposal to spend a few thousand florins to recruit honest, clever people into their service to be the dreams of a spendthrift? And yet the best present that a minister can give to his master is the ability to attract from outside the country good, decent people, and to recruit them to his service ...

I feel delight to the point of ecstasy when I imagine (even just as a theoretical possibility) a prince who is himself a Christian, who would have true Christians as his counsellors and servants, and a large number of true Christians as his subjects. We have had a few in which all that did come together. We still have a few, thank God, but not very many, and such models will always be few and far between.

It is always worth a lot when a sovereign, who follows whatever religion is in fashion, has no problem with having in his cabinet, or in his service, someone professing a positive religious faith.

If great people knew how important true Christians are, they would seek them out with the same sense of urgency and the same care with which they scour the earth for gold and silver mines, and they would regard them as the wealth and backbone of their country. A prince who knows the secret of how to recruit true Christians into his service will work miracles.

Just one single minister who is pious will give a lustre to the whole of his master's government, and if a sovereign has several ministers of this sort, it would be safe to say that when he signifies nothing in himself, apart from his noble birth, he will [still] shine with their brilliance like those glass globes in illuminations held near water reflect the light coming from fires burning nearby, and radiate beams of light, something they would never be able to do by themselves.

How respectfully and appreciatively people still speak about the reign of Duke Ernest the Pious of Saxe-Gotha a hundred years later, not only because he was a great and enlightened prince in his own right, but also because he had Veit Ludwig von Seckendorf as a minister. A certain court, whose justice system was held in the highest esteem, no less, but which nevertheless stood accused of holding some unjust and violent proceedings, recovered its reputation for a while because it engaged a minister whose upright piety and honesty were well known.

If it is a question of posts to do with the country's revenues, you can say frankly that a prince with only true Christians in his Treasury has found the philosopher's stone that so many fools seek in vain. King Frederick William of Prussia preferred pious tax-collectors from his own estates because they did not cheat him, although there is still a tiny amount of it going on there. But what you would call today a good financier is someone who knows how to increase revenues, and there is no surer way for a prince to discover this secret than [by employing] true Christians.

God's blessing is an enormous and inexhaustible source of revenue. If an honest financier gets rid of the curse that had been hanging over his master's house for a long time, if he soothes the lamentations of subjects by relieving their pain and suffering, he will be increasing his prince's revenues in a sure and positive way.

No doubt there are countries where this sort of language will seem fanatical, and people will answer: What we need is money, you can keep your divine blessing. Well, you are not meant to be divinely blessed in that case. To demonstrate what an inexhaustible force for good this blessing is, you only have to look at those countries where the opposite is the case. Take, for example, a country on which God looks down in anger. Money disappears as if blown away by the wind, and as a clear proof of being cursed nobody is very happy living there. People spend a lot without getting much for their money. Other princes with half of those resources have much more to show for it, are happier and are the delight of their subjects.

It could well happen that a Treasury whose members are true Christians would gradually bring a prince, even one who disagreed with them, round to their point of view, if he was not obsessed by [the views of] people whose appalling key principle is that provided the master has enough, provided he has everything he needs, it does not matter where the money comes from, or who groans in pain, who dies as a result, whether the situation ends well or badly, or however long it lasts.

While I praise religion here so strongly, and am right to do so, I do not, however, conclude that a man whom God has blessed with an honest heart is good at everything. Years ago a servant was presented to a person of rank as being an honest man. 'What else?', replied that person, and he was right, for God calls us all to be Christians, but not all of us to be Christian ministers . . .

So for the time being we will take people as they are, and hope that they will become what they should be. There are in consequence three main qualities upon which the work of civil servants should be based, namely that they should be honest, useful and hard-working. These three qualities must be combined, otherwise a master will always be made a fool of.

Ignorant honesty is useless, stupid honesty is often harmful, and misplaced honesty a major liability. To be clever without being honest is to have the nature of a snake. To be talented and lazy is more harmful than stupidity combined with honesty. People who are too clever are sometimes intolerable. People who are hard-working, but who lack honesty, are like spiders drawing out poison from the rose itself. To have a taste for hard work, without the ability to do the work, is just about slaving away in the dark like a mole.

These three qualities are so inseparable and so necessary to a counsellor that it is impossible not to feel sorry for any prince whose so-called counsellors do not possess them.

There are certain posts that just require honesty and nothing more; others require a lot of ability as well.

Minor officials, responsible for the prince's accounts and revenues, fall into the first category. The second category involves the high offices of state.

Ideally, many ministers, whom nobody would deny are honest, should add to their dovish-simplicity a good strong dose of snake-like subtlety, although, given an absolute choice, I would always prefer the dove's heart to the snake's head . . .

The real secret of a good government consists not only in knowing how to deploy the key, cleverest people in accordance with their tastes and abilities, but also in knowing how to allocate to each one duties that fit their knowledge and talents. That is why it is not enough to be clever and virtuous, each one must have the virtues appropriate to his job. Marcellus is a respectable man, but a poor minister. You can spend many an hour chatting with him; there is nothing more agreeable and instructive than his conversation. He is a dynamic, tireless worker when it is a matter of dealing with business in his office. But as soon as it comes to verbal presentation of this business he has neither the quickness nor presence of mind, nor the wisdom to give a measured response to some specious request, and he does not know how to adapt to [new] situations either. His colleague, Altan, gets his affairs in a muddle. Marcellus does not do this, but his affairs get *him* in a muddle, and yet he is the one to whom one is supposed go on matters of policy. As soon as you touch that chord all his nerves are struck, he becomes a different man, he is in torment and he torments other people.

Marcolf is the epitome of honesty, he has got into the cabinet on real merit, but he has the weakness of not being able to conceal anything about what he has been doing from his wife and his friends, something that has already caused him a lot of unpleasantness. He would have all the qualities needed for this post, if only he knew how to keep quiet.

Schlinkschlank was a good man, he would have gone to the stake for his master, he would have had no problem in slapping the prime minister in the face, if the prince had ordered him to do so; he was employed in the least appropriate jobs, and he committed himself to them. At this particular court this is what they called loyalty. Because he had learned to read and write, and knew a bit of Latin, he was made Keeper of the Archives. The story goes that he would never give the royal household's secrets away, and that to avoid even the temptation to do so, he had the shelves of the archives converted into secure cupboards, but had [then] given his wife the key. As he had spent part of his youth riding and hunting, and as it was impossible for him to rest quietly for very long, he had a chair that moved on pulleys set up for himself in the archives. Unfortunately, the rope broke, and the unfortunate Schlinkschank died. He might have lived longer as the King's Messenger ... [*The master and the servant*, 3: 'On the choice of servants and on their qualities']

Civil rights

DENIS DIDEROT

BIOGRAPHICAL NOTE

Denis Diderot (1713–84) was the son of a Langres cutler. He was destined for an ecclesiastical career, but after graduating from the Collège d'Harcourt in 1732, he embarked instead on a somewhat bohemian career in Paris before becoming involved in the controversies of the *philosophes*. His first publication was the *Essay on merit and virtue* (1745), a free translation of Shaftesbury's *Inquiry concerning virtue or merit*. His growing scepticism and inclination towards materialistic atheism were expressed with remarkable audacity in a number of controversial essays in the 1740s, one of which, the *Letter on the blind*, led to a brief period of imprisonment in 1749 at Vincennes.

Diderot's political and moral discourses reflect in different ways his preoccupation with questions relating to human nature, society, morality, freedom and justice, and they testify to the astonishing depth and breadth of his familiarity with the latest scientific and philosophical research. His view of nature and human nature, elaborated in works like the *History of the Two Indies* (1772), the *Supplement to Bougainville's voyage* (1772) and the *Observations on the instruction of the Empress of Russia to the deputies for the making of laws* (1773–4), was shaped as much by his study of chemistry, biology and medicine, as it was by moral and political theorists.

In 1746 Diderot was approached by a publisher named Le Breton to produce a translation of Ephraim Chambers' *Cyclopedia*. This commission was to develop into his most ambitious work, *The Encyclopedia, or rational dictionary of the sciences, arts and crafts*, and in 1750 Diderot and his collaborator, Jean d'Alembert, published the prospectus for this multi-volumed project, destined to become one of the great literary monuments of the Enlightenment. The prospectus attracted more than 2,000 subscribers. The aim was to establish an authoritative 'treasurehouse' of all human knowledge, to set out in secular terms the achievements and glories of man's past, and to chart the course of man's future progress. More than 1,000 entries, the work of numerous contributors, cover a wide range of subjects, including religion, philosophy, literature, morality, politics, economics, medicine, history, law, architecture, metaphysics, mathematics, science, as well as the 'mechanical arts', trades, artisan crafts, industrial and agricultural processes.

The enterprise was weighed down by controversy from the start when in 1752 the abbé Prades, one of Diderot's contributors, and author of the controversial entry, 'Certainty', was accused of heresy, and distribution of the first two volumes of the *Encyclopedia* was banned. The deep hostility of the clergy was deflected by the protection of Mme de Pompadour and Malesherbes (the minister responsible for censorship), and publication of the first eight volumes continued undeterred until 1758 when the privilege to print and sell the *Encyclopedia* was again withdrawn. Work had to continue in secret in a climate of increasing hostility from both Church and Government, inflamed in 1757 with the attempted assassination of Louis XV by Robert Damiens, an event for which the encyclopedists were held morally responsible. Opposition intensified still further in 1758 with the publication of Helvétius' controversial work, *Of the mind*, and again in 1759 with the appearance of d'Alembert's entry, 'Geneva'. Publication proceeded, however, and by 1772 seventeen volumes of double-columned text, together with eleven volumes of superbly engraved plates, had been printed. Seven additional volumes, in which Diderot played no editorial role, appeared between 1776 and 1780.

EDITORIAL NOTE

The *Encyclopedia* entries 'Political authority' (volume I, 1751), 'City' (volume III, 1753), 'Citizen' (volume III, 1753) and 'Natural law' (volume V, 1755) are all by Diderot, or at least bear his asterisk. Extracts are taken from the translation by J. Mason and R. Wokler,* for which the base text is that of the first edition, reprinted in the *Œuvres complètes*, ed. H. Dieckmann, J. Proust and J. Varloot (Paris, Hermann, 1975).

FURTHER READING

*Mason, J. Hope and Wokler, R. (eds.), *Diderot: political writings* (Cambridge, Cambridge University Press, 1992). See introduction, pp. xxxi–xxxv.
Strugnell, A., *Diderot's politics* (The Hague, Nijhoff, 1973).
Wilson, A., 'The development and scope of Diderot's political thought', *Studies on Voltaire and the Eighteenth Century*, 27 (1963), pp. 1871–1900.
Diderot (New York, Oxford University Press, 1973). Reprint.

Articles from *The Encyclopedia, or rational dictionary of the sciences, arts and crafts*

Political authority (1751)

No man has by nature been granted the right to command others. Liberty is a gift from heaven, and every member of the same species has the right to enjoy it as soon as he is in possession of reason. If nature has established any *authority*, it is that of paternal power; but paternal power has its limits, and in the state of nature it would end as soon as children were able to look after themselves. All other *authority* originates outside nature. On close examination, it can always be traced back to one of two sources: either the strength and violence of the person who has got hold of it, or the consent of those who have submitted themselves to it, by virtue of a contract, actual or presumed, with the person on whom they have conferred it.

Power acquired by violence is nothing but usurpation and lasts only as long as the person in command retains greater strength than those who obey, so that if the latter become stronger in their turn and shake off the yoke they do so with as much right and justice as the person who imposed it on them. The same law that bestowed the *authority* thus takes it away: it is the law of the strongest.

Sometimes *authority* established by violence changes its nature, in effect when it endures and is maintained by the express consent of those who have been subjected to it. But in that case it comes under the second category I shall describe, and the person who had once seized it, in becoming a prince, ceases to be a tyrant.

The power which comes from the consent of the people necessarily presupposes conditions which makes its exercise legitimate, useful to society, advantageous to the republic, fixing and restraining it within limits. For a man neither should nor can submit himself entirely without reserve to another man, because he has one supreme master above all to whom he belongs completely. That is God, whose power over His creatures is always direct, who is a master as jealous as He is absolute, who never gives up His rights and never transfers them. For the common good and the maintenance of society, He permits men to establish an order of subordination amongst themselves and to only one of their own number; but He wishes this order to be reasonable and moderate, and not blind and unrestrained, so that no one arrogates the rights of the Creator. Any other form of submission constitutes the veritable crime of idolatry. To bend the knee before a man or a graven image is merely an external ritual for which God, who requires our hearts and minds, cares little. Such ritual He leaves to human fabrication, so that men may make use of it, howsoever they please, as the outward mark of a civil and political cult, or of a religion. It is thus not these ceremonies in themselves but the spirit in which they are established that makes their practice either innocent or criminal. An Englishman has no scruples about serving his king on bended knee; the ceremony signifies no more than what it is designed to do. But to yield up one's heart, mind and principles of conduct without reserve to the will and caprice of just another simple creature, to make him the sole and final motive for one's actions, is undoubtedly a crime of *lèse-majesté* against the Lord. If that were not so, the power of God, about which we hear so much, would be no more than an empty phrase that men would contrive to twist according to their fancy, and which the spirit of irreligion might trifle with in turn, until all our ideas of power and subordination would become confused, with the prince flouting the authority of God, and subjects that of the prince.

True and legitimate power is thus necessarily limited. As Scripture informs us, 'Let your submission be reasonable'; *sit rationabile obsequium vestrum*. 'All power that stems from God is an orderly power'; *omnis potestas a Deo ordinata est*. For that is how we must understand these words, in conformity with right reason and their literal meaning, and not the interpretation that springs from contempt and flattery, according to which all power, of whatever kind, stems from God. Well, then, can there be no unjust powers? Are there no *authorities* which, instead of coming from God, conflict with His orders and oppose His will? Do usurpers have God on their side? Must we pay full allegiance to the persecutors of true faith? . . .

It is from his subjects themselves that the prince derives the *authority* he exercises over them, and this *authority* is limited by the laws of nature and of the state. Maintenance of the laws of nature and of the state are the conditions according to which subjects have submitted themselves, or are deemed to have submitted themselves, to the prince's rule. One of these conditions stipulates that since he has no power or *authority* over them except by their choice and consent, he may never employ his *authority* to breach the act or contract by which it was conferred on him; that would be to act in opposition to himself, since his *authority* can only subsist by virtue of the title which established it. What annuls the one cancels the other. The prince thus cannot dispose of his power or his subjects without the consent of the nation, or independently of the terms stipulated in the contract of submission. If he were to act otherwise, all would be null and void, and the laws would disengage him from any promises and vows he might have made, as in the case of a minor who has acted in ignorance, claiming a right to dispose of something which was his only in trust, substituting an absolute title for his merely conditional power.

The *authority* of government, moreover, while hereditary in one family and placed in the hands of one person, is not a piece of private property but a public good, which consequently can never be taken away from the people, to whom alone full ownership of it essentially belongs. Only the people, therefore, can issue a lease upon its use; they must always take part in any contract which awards the right to exercise it. The state does not belong to the prince, but the prince to the state, though it is for the prince to govern within the state, because the state has chosen him for that task, because he has put himself under an obligation to the people to administer their affairs, and because they, on their side, have undertaken to obey him in conformity with the laws. He who wears the crown may renounce it absolutely if he so wishes, but he may not place it upon the head of another without the consent of the nation which placed it on his. In a word, the Crown, the power of government and public *authority* are all goods of which the nation is proprietor, and of which princes have the usufruct, as its ministers and trustees. Although they are heads of state, they are none the less also members of it, the first members, to be sure, the most venerable and the most powerful, able to do all that is necessary to govern, but unable to act in any legitimate way to change the established government, nor to put another head of state in their place. The sceptre of Louis XV passes of necessity to his eldest son, and there is no power which can oppose this – neither that of the nation, because it is a condition of the contract, nor that of the child's father, for the same reason.

Authority may sometimes be entrusted for a limited period, as in the Roman Republic. It may be conferred for the lifetime of a single man, as in Poland; occasionally for the lifespan of one family, as in England; sometimes for so long as the male line of a family survives, as in France.

This deposition is occasionally entrusted to a particular rank in society; sometimes to several persons selected from all ranks, sometimes to one rank alone.

The conditions of this pact are different in different states. But everywhere the nation has the right to maintain the contract it has made against all opposition; no power may change it; and when it is no longer in force, the nation recovers the right and complete freedom to enter into a new contract with whom and however it pleases. That is what would happen in France if, by the greatest misfortune, the entire ruling family were to die out to the last of its descendants; the sceptre and the Crown would then return to the nation.

Only slaves with minds as narrow as their hearts are vile could think otherwise . . .

The observance of laws, the preservation of liberty and the love of one's country are the fertile sources of all great things and all fine actions. In them can be found the happiness of peoples and the true renown of the princes who govern them. In pursuit of them, obedience is glorious and authority magnificent. On the other hand, flattery, self-interest and a servile mentality give rise to all the evils which overcome a state and the decrepitude which dishonours it. Where they prevail, subjects are wretched and princes hated. With them the monarch never hears himself proclaimed 'beloved'; with them submission is shameful, domination cruel. If I consider France and Turkey together from this point of view, I perceive, on the one hand, a society of men united by reason, inspired by virtue, and governed in accordance with the laws of justice by a leader equally wise and glorious; and, on the other hand, a herd of animals joined only by habit, prodded by the law of the stick, and led by an absolute master according to his whim.

[In support of these claims, Diderot proceeds to cite the authority of King Henri IV, 'one of our greatest kings', in an opening address to the Assembly of Notables in 1596, and, two years later, in exhortations to the bishops and the Parlement of Paris, following the proclamation of the Edict of Nantes. Diderot's citations are drawn from the first volume of Sully's *Mémoires*.]

That is how a monarch should address his subjects when he clearly has justice on his side; and why may he not do what every man can do when equity is on his side? As for his subjects, the first law which religion, reason and nature prescribe to them is to respect the terms of the contract they have made; never to lose sight of the nature of their government; in France, never to forget that so long as the reigning family continues in the male line, they must honour and stand in awe of their master, as the agent through whom they have willed that the image of God should be displayed and made visible on earth; to subscribe to these sentiments in recognition of the tranquillity and benefits which they enjoy on account of the security afforded to them by royalty; to invoke only one remedy against the misfortune, if it should ever befall them, of suffering an unjust, ambitious and violent king – that is, of calming him by their submission and assuaging

God by their prayers; for this is the only legitimate redress, in consequence of the pact of submission sworn of old to the prince regent, and to his descendants in the male line, whoever they may be; and to reflect that all the justifications one imagines for resisting are, on close inspection, only subtly coloured pretexts for disloyalty; and that through such conduct no one ever reformed a prince or abolished taxes but instead only added a new degree of misery to the misfortunes of which he complained already. Such are the foundations upon which peoples and those who govern them may ensure their reciprocal happiness. [*Encyclopedia,* 1]

City (1753)

The first of the major associations of large families, in which expressions of will and the use of force are entrusted to one corporate body or moral being, for reasons of security, internal and external safety, and all the other advantages of life ... The corporate body or moral being entrusted with will and force is said to *command*: the persons who have ceded their will and force are said to *obey*. The concept of *city* thus assumes a connection between a corporate body or moral being with a unique will and physical beings, private individuals, who no longer have a will. Every city has two sources, one philosophical, the other historical. With regard to the first of these sources, it is maintained by some that man is naturally inclined to form *cities* or civil societies, that families tend to assemble with one another, that is, to confer their strength and will on a corporate body or moral being. This may be the case, but it is not easy to prove. Others deduce the *city* from the necessity of a civil society for the establishment and maintenance of the most basic communities, conjugal, paternal and seigneurial – clearly a false deduction, as is demonstrated by the example of patriarchs who live in families which are free and separate. There are some who have recourse either to the defects of human nature, or to its fear of harm, or to its passionate attraction to the comforts of life, or even to debauchery, in order to explain the assembly and survival of families in civil society. The first town or city was formed by Cain. Nimrod, who was evil, and who was one of the earliest men to assume sovereignty, was also a founder of *cities*. With their foundation and growth, we see the birth and increase of corruption and vice. History and philosophy are thus in accord as to the origin of *cities*. Whatever the laws of the *city* in which one resides, they must be known, observed and protected. In forming an impression of families as they come together to create a *city*, we conceive them to be equal. In forming an impression of their assembly, once their separate wills and force have been renounced, we conceive the subordination not only of families, but also of individuals. We must grasp the relation between *cities* in the same way. In forming an impression of *cities* that are isolated, we conceive them only to be equal; in forming an impression of their union, we conceive the establishment of empires and the subordination of *cities*, either amongst themselves, or to a corporate body or some moral being.

If only the same could be said of empires! But just for this reason there has been no association of empires at all, and absolute sovereigns remain equal, living alone and independently of one another in the state of nature. The consent which warrants the subordination to a corporate body or moral being, either of families that form a *city*, or of *cities* that comprise an empire, is evident from the facts; and whoever disturbs the order of families within the *city* is a bad citizen; whoever disturbs the order of *cities* within the empire is a bad subject; and whoever disturbs the order of empires in the world is a bad sovereign. In a well-governed state a *city* may be regarded as a single person, and that person as subject to an authority which resides in the physical form of an individual or in the moral being of a sovereign, whose task it is to attend to the good of *cities* in general and in particular.

The word *city* formerly referred to a state, a nation with all its dependencies, a specific republic. That meaning no longer applies today except to certain German cities and Swiss cantons.

Although the Gauls formed only one nation, they were nevertheless divided into different tribes, which Caesar termed *cities, civitates*. Each *city*, besides having its own assemblies, sent deputies as well to general assemblies, which addressed themselves to the interests of several districts. But the *city* or metropolis or capital in which the assembly met came above all others to be termed *civitas* . . .

Thereafter the word *city* came to apply only to episcopal towns, a terminology which scarcely survives anywhere apart from in England, where the word *city* only achieved currency after the Conquest; before that period all towns had been called boroughs . . . When a town grew over time, the term *city* was applied to the space which it had formerly occupied; in Paris there is thus the *city* and the university; in London the *city* and the suburbs; and in Prague and Cracow, where the town is divided into three parts, the oldest is termed *city*. The word *city* is now hardly used by us except in this last sense; in all other contexts we speak of the *town* (*ville*), or *suburb* (*faubourg*), or *borough* (*bourg*) or *village*. [***Encyclopedia,*** III]

Citizen (1753)

A person who is a member of a free society comprised of several families, who partakes of the rights of that society and enjoys its privileges ... A person who resides in such a society for a particular purpose, and who must depart from it once his business there is concluded, is not a *citizen* of that society but only a temporary subject. A person who makes his home there, but does not partake of its rights and privileges, is similarly not a *citizen*. Someone who has been deprived of the status ceases to be a *citizen*. Women, young children and servants are only granted the title as members of the family of a citizen properly so called; they are not true *citizens* themselves.

Citizens are of two kinds, *original* and *naturalised*. *Original citizens* are native-born. *Naturalised citizens* are those to whom society has granted the rights and privileges of participation, although they were not born in its midst.

Athenians were very cautious about according the title of *citizen* of their state to foreigners; they attached far more importance to it than did the Romans. The title of *citizen* was never debased among them, but neither did they make use of what would perhaps have been the greatest benefit of the esteem in which it was held, that is, of extending it to all who coveted the title. There were scarcely any citizens in Athens apart from those whose parents were themselves *citizens* ...

It was nevertheless possible to become a *citizen* of Athens through adoption by a *citizen*, and with the consent of the people; but this privilege was not frequently extended ...

In order to become a true Roman *citizen*, three things were necessary: to be domiciled in Rome, to be a member of one of the thirty-three tribes, and to be able to hold office in the Republic. Those who possessed certain rights of citizenship by concession and not birth, were only, properly speaking, honorary *citizens* ...

The first privilege of a Roman *citizen* was to be liable only to the judgement of the people. The law of *Portia* prohibited putting a *citizen* to death. Even in the provinces he was not subject to the arbitrary power of a proconsul or praetor . . . At Rome, states M. de Montesquieu, in his book on *The Spirit of the Laws*, Book XI, ch. 19, as well as in Sparta, liberty for *citizens* and servitude for slaves were extremes. Yet despite the privileges, strength and grandeur of these *citizens* . . . it seems to me that the government of the Roman Republic was so composite that a less precise idea of citizenship prevailed there than in the canton of Zurich. To perceive that point clearly, one need only weigh carefully what is discussed in the rest of this article.

Hobbes draws no distinction between subject and *citizen*, correctly so, if one takes the strict meaning of the term *subject*, and the widest sense of the term *citizen*, and if one bears in mind that the latter term pertains only to the laws, while the former is defined in relation to a sovereign. *Citizens* and *subjects* are equally under command, but one by a moral, the other by a physical, force. The word *citizen* is appropriate neither to those who live in servitude nor to those who live in isolation; from which it follows that persons who, like sovereigns, live entirely in the state of nature, and others who, like slaves, have entirely renounced that state, can in no way be regarded as *citizens*; unless one maintains that there can be no reasonable society without an immutable moral being above the physical presence of the sovereign. Pufendorf, showing no regard to that exception, divided his study of duties into two parts, one on the duties of man, the other on the duties of the *citizen*.

Since the laws of free societies of families are not the same everywhere, and since in most such societies there can be found an hierarchical order comprised of ranks, the *citizen* may still be regarded either in relation to the laws of his society, or in relation to the rank he occupies in the hierarchical order. In the second case, there will be a distinction between the magistrate *citizen* and the bourgeois *citizen*; in the first case between the *citizen* of Amsterdam and that of Basel.

Aristotle, in recognising the differences between civil societies and the order of citizens within each society, only acknowledged as real *citizens*, however, those who took part in the administration of justice and who could look forward to passing from the status of commoners to the first ranks of the magistracy – a prospect possible only in pure democracies . . .

Pufendorf, in restricting the name of *citizen* to those who have established the state by a first assembly of families, and to their successors from father to son, introduced a frivolous distinction on which his work sheds little light and which can cause much confusion in a civil society. He differentiates original from naturalised *citizens*, through an ill-conceived idea of nobility. In their own societies, citizens, by virtue of their citizenship, are all equally noble – nobility stemming not from ancestry, but from the common entitlement to occupy the first ranks of the magistracy.

Since the moral being of the sovereign stands in the same relation to the *citizen* as a despotic corporate person with respect to the subject, and since even the most perfect slave does not give up the whole of his being to his sovereign, it must be all the more evident that the *citizen* retains certain rights of which he never divests himself. There are occasions when he finds himself pursuing the same path not merely of his fellow-citizens, but of the moral being which commands them all. That moral being has two dispositions, of which one is private and the other public: in its public face it must never confront resistance; in its private capacity it may suffer such resistance on the part of individuals and may even succumb to it. Because this moral being has estates and responsibilities, and tenancies and tenants, etc., we must, so to speak, distinguish the sovereign from the subject of sovereignty within it. It is thus on occasion both judge and advocate. That is undoubtedly a disadvantage; but it is a feature of all governments in general, and in itself this feature establishes no case either for or against government, except in terms of the frequency of its appearance. It is certainly true that subjects or *citizens* will be less likely to suffer injustice, the less frequently the physical or moral sovereign is both judge and advocate, on those occasions when it is attacked in its private capacity.

When there are disturbances the *citizen* will cling to the party in favour of the established order; when that order is dissolved, he will subscribe to the party of his city, if its judgement is unanimous; and if there is division in the city, he will embrace the party which advocates the equality of its members and the liberty of all.

The closer citizens approach an equality of aspirations and wealth, the more tranquil will the state be: this appears to be an exclusive advantage of pure democracy, in comparison with all other forms of government. But even in the most perfect democracy, complete equality of a state's members is a chimera, and that is perhaps the cause of the dissolution of such a government, unless it is reformed by all the injustices of ostracism. With government in general, as with all animals, each step in life is a step towards death. The best government is not that which is immortal, but that which lasts longest and most peacefully. [*Encyclopedia*, III]

Natural law (1755)

This expression is used so frequently that there is scarcely anyone who is not convinced in his own mind that he knows just what it means. Such an inner conviction is common to the philosopher and the unreflective man alike. The sole difference between them is that in reply to the question, *What is right?*, the latter, bereft of any words and ideas, will refer you to the tribunal of conscience and remain mute, whereas the former will be reduced to silence and deeper reflection only after going round a vicious circle, which either brings him back to his point of departure or hurls him into the midst of another question scarcely less difficult to resolve than the one from which he imagined he had been freed by his definition.

The philosopher, when questioned, replies, *Right is the foundation or principal source of justice.* But what is justice? *It is the obligation to render to each person what is due to him.* But what is it that is due to one person rather than another in a world in which everything belongs to all, and in which the very idea of obligation would perhaps not yet exist? And what would be owed to others by a person who granted them everything and asked nothing of them? It is at this point that the philosopher begins to feel that the idea of *natural right* is, of all our moral concepts, one of the most important and most difficult to specify. We shall therefore be persuaded that we have accomplished much in this article if we succeed in establishing clearly certain principles in the light of which may be resolved the most substantial objections commonly raised against the idea of *natural right*. In order to achieve this, we must take up our discussion once more from the beginning and be mindful to put forward nothing which is not obvious, at least in terms of such evidence as moral questions can admit, and which a reasonable man would find satisfactory.

1.   It is clear that if man is not free, or if his instantaneous decisions, or even his irresolution, spring from some material source external to his character, his choice could not be the pure expression of an immaterial substance and of a simple faculty of that substance. There could thus be neither calculated good nor calculated evil, though instinctual good and evil might exist; there could be no moral good or evil, no justice or injustice, neither obligation nor right. From which can be seen, we may add in passing, how important it is to establish firmly in our minds the reality not merely of free will but of liberty, which is only too often confused with free will. . .

II.   Our existence is mean, contentious, uneasy. We have passions and needs. We wish to be happy, and yet the unjust and impassioned man constantly feels impelled to do unto others what he would not wish them to do unto him. This is a judgement he proclaims in the depths of his soul, and from which he cannot escape. He sees his own nakedness and must either admit it to himself or accord to everyone else the same authority as he assumes.

III.   But what reproaches can we make to the man tormented by such violent passions that life itself becomes burdensome if he does not satisfy them and who, so as to win the right of disposing as he pleases of the existence of others, relinquishes to them the right over himself? What shall we reply to him, if he has the audacity to say, 'I realise that I bring terror and confusion to the human race; but I must either be miserable or create misery for others, and no one is more dear to me than myself. Let no one blame me for this abominable predilection; it is not a matter of free choice. It is the voice of nature, which never speaks more forcefully within me than when it speaks in my favour. But is it only in my own heart that it makes itself heard with such ferocity? Oh, men! I appeal to all of you as my witness! Who, among you, on the verge of death, would not buy back his life at the expense of the majority of the human race, if he could be sure to do so with impunity and in secret?' 'Yet I am fair and honest', he will continue. 'If my happiness demands that I rid myself of all persons who intrude upon my life, then anyone else may equally rid himself of my presence if it offends him. This only stands to reason, and I agree. I am not so unjust as to demand from someone else a sacrifice which I am not myself prepared to make for him.'

IV.   From the outset I perceive one thing which seems to me admitted by the good and the evil man alike, which is that in all things we must exercise our reason, because man is not just an animal but an animal which thinks; that with regard to any subject there are consequently various ways of discovering the truth; that whoever declines to seek that truth forfeits his status as a man and should be treated by the rest of his kind as a wild beast; and that once the truth has been discovered, whoever refuses to accept it is either insane or morally evil by design.

V.   What then shall we reply to this violent interlocutor before smothering him? That everything he says may be reduced to the question of whether he acquires a right over the lives of others in forfeiting control over his own life to them; for he does not wish merely to be happy; he wishes also to be just and by his justice to ward off the ascription of 'evil'; for otherwise we should have to shut him up without any reply. We shall therefore make him see that even if what he repudiates belongs to him so perfectly that he may dispose of it as he likes, and even if the prospect he commends to others were to be truly advantageous to them, he would still have no legitimate authority to make them accept it. We shall point out that whoever says *I wish to live* has as much right on his side as the person who says *I wish to die*; for, as he has only one life, when he abandons it he makes himself master of innumerable other lives. We shall point out that the exchange he proposes would be scarcely just if over the whole earth there were no one else but him and another man just as evil; that it is absurd to wish upon others the same wishes one would entertain for oneself; that it is doubtful whether the hazards he would inflict upon his fellow-man match those to which he would subject himself; that whatever he risks may not be proportionate to what he compels me to put at risk myself; that the question of *natural right* is far more complicated than it appears to him; that he sets himself up as both judge and advocate, and that his tribunal may be incompetent to pronounce on this matter.

vi.   But if we deny the individual the right to determine the nature of justice and injustice, before which bar shall we plead this great question? Where? Before mankind. Mankind alone must settle the matter, because it has no other craving than the good of all. Private wills are suspect; they may be either good or bad. But the general will is always good. It has never beguiled and will never mislead. If the status of animals were roughly equal to our own; if there were reliable means of communication between them and us; if they could transmit their feelings and thoughts to us clearly and come to apprehend our own with equal certainty; if they could, in short, take part in a general assembly, we should have to summon them to it; and the case for *natural right* would no longer be pleaded before the bar of *mankind* but before that of all *animal kind*. But animals are separated from us by fixed and eternal barriers; and we are dealing here with a system of knowledge and ideas peculiar to the human species, arising from and forming its station in the world.

vii.   For an individual to know how far he ought to be a man, a citizen, a subject, a father, or a child, and when it befits him to live or die, he must address himself to the general will. It is for the general will to determine the limits of all duties. You have the most sacred *natural right* to everything that is not resisted by the whole human race. It is the general will which shall enlighten you as to the nature of your thoughts and your desires. Everything you conceive, everything you contemplate, will be good, great, elevated, sublime, if it accords with the general and common interest. There is no quality essential to your species apart from that which you demand from all your fellow-men to ensure your happiness and theirs. It is the measure of your conformity to all of them and of all of them to you which determines when you transgress the boundaries of your species and when you remain within them. Hence do not ever lose sight of it, or else you will find that your comprehension of the notions of goodness, justice, humanity and virtue grows dim. Say to yourself often, 'I am a man, and I have no other truly inalienable *natural rights* except those of humanity.'

VIII.   But, you will ask, in what does this general will reside? Where can I consult it? ... In the principles of prescribed law of all civilised nations; in the social practices of savage and barbarous peoples; in the tacit agreements obtaining amongst the enemies of mankind; and even in those two emotions – indignation and resentment – which nature has extended as far as animals to compensate for social laws and public retribution.

IX.   If you reflect carefully on all the material above, therefore, you will find yourself convinced, (1) that the man who subscribes only to his private will is the enemy of the human race; (2) that the general will is in each person a pure expression of the understanding, which in the silence of the passions calculates what every individual may demand from his fellow-man, and what his fellow-man has a right to demand of him; (3) that this regard for the general will of the species, and for what is the common desire, forms the rule binding the conduct of one individual towards another in the same society, together with the conduct of an individual towards the whole society to which he belongs, and of that society itself towards other societies; (4) that submission to the general will is the bond which holds all societies together, not excluding those formed by crime. Alas, virtue is so attractive that bandits will respect its image even in the depths of their caves!; (5) that laws should be made for all, and not just for one; since otherwise that one solitary being would be just like the violent interlocutor whom we smothered in section v; (6) that since, as between the two wills – one general and the other private – the general will never errs, there can be no difficulty in perceiving to which of them the legislative power should belong so as to ensure the happiness of mankind, nor in establishing what is owed to those august mortals whose private will unites at once the authority and the infallibility of the general; (7) that even if we were to entertain the supposition that species were in perpetual flux, the nature of *natural right* would not change, since it would always correspond to the general will and the common desire of the whole species; (8) that equity relates to justice as cause to its effect, or that justice can never be anything other than equity made plain; (9) that all these consequences, finally, are evident to anyone who uses his reason, and that whoever chooses not to reason, thereby forfeiting his status as a man, ought to be treated as an unnatural being. [*Encyclopedia*, v]

MARIE-JEAN-ANTOINE-NICOLAS DE CARITAT, MARQUIS DE CONDORCET

BIOGRAPHICAL NOTE

Marie-Jean-Antoine-Nicolas de Caritat, Marquis de Condorcet (1743–94), was one of the few eighteenth-century French *philosophes* to have actually taken part in the early phases of the Revolution, and to have had an impact upon its course after 1789 as a legislator. He was trained as a mathematician initially, and published widely on probability theory and its application. A *protégé* of d'Alembert, he was elected Perpetual Secretary of the Academy of Sciences in 1773, becoming a member of the French Academy in 1782. He helped to draft the 'Declaration of the rights of man and of the citizen' in 1789, but fell into disfavour as a result of his Girondist sympathies and died, possibly a suicide, while under sentence of death. He is best known today for his last work, the *Historical sketch of the progress of the human mind* (1795) in which he traced the history of man's progress from the pre-social state of nature to modernity, and offered an interesting vision of the shape of a future predicated upon an assumption of infinite perfectibility. Condorcet's *Sketch*, as well as his numerous treatises on mathematics and the calculus of probabilities, reflects his aim to establish a science of man as precise and systematic as any other science, and he was among the first thinkers to apply mathematics to the study of human behaviour and organisation. He is regarded now as one of the founders of what is now called 'social science', and his thought had a deep influence on the positivism of Saint-Simon and Auguste Comte.

His acceptance of the reality of historical progress and the capacity of man to control the nature of that progress through rational, scientific principles illuminates most of his major publications, including the *Essay on the constitution and functions of provincial assemblies* (1788), *On public education* (1791–2), *On the influence of the American Revolution on Europe* (1786), the *Reflections on criminal jurisprudence* (1775), the *Letters on the grain trade* (1775), the *On the admission of women to the rights of citizenship* (1790) and a substantial body of other writings covering an astonishing range of subjects. He also wrote innumerable pamphlets, drafts of bills and other legislative documents for the National Convention. The *Reflections on black slavery* appeared in 1781, a second edition being published in 1788.

Belief in the objective truths of the moral as well as the physical sciences enabled Condorcet to evolve a methodology that permitted a 'social arithmetic' of man to be calculated in a variety of contexts, and with this he sought to transform the calculus of probabilities into an effective and accurate language of rational decision making and action in ways in which the unpredictable and the contingent could be identified, and minimised. Whether discussing women's rights, taxation, agriculture, education, the salt trade, canal building, the criteria for good legislation, plans for the new constitution, crime or the abolition of slavery, Condorcet offered incisive and original insights based on the empirical observation of data that aimed in all of these contexts at the progressive liberation of man from the darkness of past error and servitude.

EDITORIAL NOTE

The first edition of the *Réflexions sur l'esclavage des nègres* appeared in 1781 (Neuchâtel, Société Typographique). The base text for the translated extracts is that printed in the *Œuvres de Condorcet*, ed. A. Condorcet-O'Connor (Condorcet's son-in-law) and F. Arago, 12 vols. (Paris, Didot, 1847–9), which reprints the second edition (1788). The Arago–O'Connor collective edition is the second, enlarged edition of Condorcet's works, and remains the standard edition despite its many faults and omissions. Condorcet's footnotes have not been included.

FURTHER READING

Stein, R. L., *The French slave trade in the eighteenth century: an old regime business* (Wisconsin, University of Wisconsin Press, 1979).

Williams, D., 'Condorcet and natural rights', *Studies on Voltaire and the Eighteenth Century*, 296 (1992), pp. 103–21.

'Condorcet and the politics of black servitude', in *Making connections*, ed. J. Dolamore (Bern and New York, Peter Lang, 1998), pp. 67–80.

Reflections on black slavery (1781)

To reduce a man to slavery, to buy, sell and keep him enslaved, are real crimes, crimes far worse than robbery. In effect, you are depriving the slave not only of all personal property and wealth, but of the ability ever to acquire ownership of such things, denying him ownership of his own time, of his own strength, of everything that nature has given him to survive and to satisfy his needs. To all this you are adding the further wrong of taking away the slave's right to ownership of his own person.

Either morality does not exist, or [alternatively] you have to accept that public opinion does not attach any stigma to this sort of crime; that the law of the land permits it; and that neither public opinion nor the law can change the way people act. And that all men are presumably in agreement on that! And [yet] presumably the whole human race would also vote unanimously for the law that a crime is always a crime!

In what follows, the act of reducing someone to slavery will often be compared to robbery. These two crimes have much in common, although the latter is much less serious. And as the first has always been a crime of the strong, and theft the crime of the weak, we find that all the issues relating to robbery have been decided in advance by some moralist, and in accordance with grand principles, while the other crime is not even named in their books. An exception must be made, however, for the kind of armed robbery we call *conquest,* and a few other kinds of robbery that also involve the strong stealing from the weak. The moralists are as silent on these crimes as they are on the crime of reducing men to slavery. [*Reflections,* 1: 'On the injustice of black slavery, with reference to slave-masters']

In order to excuse the enslavement of blacks bought in Africa, people say that these wretched people are either criminals who have been condemned to death, or prisoners of war who would be put to death, if they had not been bought by Europeans.

Following this line of argument, some writers present the slave-trade to us almost as a humane act. But we note:

1. That this is not a proven fact, nor even a credible one. What! Before Europeans came along to buy blacks, the Africans used to disembowel all their prisoners! Killing not only married women, as was once, so it is said, the custom with bands of oriental robbers, but even the unmarried girls – something that has never been reported about any people. What! If we did not go off looking for blacks in Africa, the Africans would be killing the slaves that they now intend to sell, both warring parties preferring to club their prisoners to death rather than exchange them! To lend credence to these wild statements, impressive witnesses are needed, and all we have is the testimony of the people employed in the slave-trade. I have never had the chance to move in that circle, but there were some

people engaged in the same trade among the Romans, and their name is still an insult.

2. Suppose that we do save the life of the black we have bought, buying him is just as much a crime if the purpose is to resell him or reduce him to slavery. This is precisely the act of someone who, after saving some poor fellow pursued by murderers, then proceeds to rob him. Or, accepting the theory that Europeans have somehow convinced Africans not to kill their prisoners any more, it is the act of someone who, having succeeded in dissuading bandits from murdering people in the street, then invites the bandits to join him in just robbing them. Could it be said, in one case or the other, that this man is not a thief? A man who, in order to save another man from death, gives from his own pocket, no doubt has the right to demand something in return. He could acquire rights over the property and even the labour of the man he has saved, on condition that he provided the man in his debt with basic subsistence, but he could not reduce him to slavery without creating an injustice. You can acquire rights over the future property of another man, but never over his person. A man can have the right to force another man to work for him, but not to force that man to obey him.

3. On the contrary, this so-called justification is particularly unwarranted because the shameful trade of Europe's bandits is the reason for almost continuous warfare between Africans, caused only by the desire to take prisoners with a view to selling them. The Europeans themselves often ferment these wars with their money or their plotting, so that they are guilty not just of the crime of reducing men to slavery, but also of all murders committed in Africa to prepare the way for this crime. They are skilled in the shameful art of arousing the greed and the passions of the Africans, of getting a father to deliver up his children, of getting brother to betray brother, a prince to sell his subjects. They have given this unhappy people a destructive taste for strong drink. They have infected them with this poison which, [once] hidden away in the forests of America, has now become a world-wide scourge, thanks to the greedy activities of Europeans. And they still have the nerve to talk about humanity!

Even if the excuse that we have just cited exonerates the first buyer, it could exonerate neither the second buyer, nor the colonist in charge of the black, because they do not have the initial justification of rescuing the slave they are buying from death. In the case of the crime of enslavement, they are in exactly the same position as the man involved in a robbery who joins with the robber, or rather as the man who gets someone else to do the robbery and then shares the proceeds with him. There might be reasons in law to treat the robber differently from his accomplice, or from the man behind the crime, but morally the crime is the same.

Finally, this excuse means absolutely nothing to blacks born on the plantation. The owner who brings them up to be slaves is a criminal, because all the care that he might have given them as children cannot give him any semblance of rights over them. Why in fact did they need him? Because, along with their freedom, he stole from their parents the right to raise their own child. So it would be like claiming that committing one crime can legitimise a second. Moreover, let us even assume that the black child had been freely abandoned by its parents. Can the right of a man over an abandoned child he has rescued be the right to keep [that child] enslaved? Could a humane action give anyone the right to commit a crime?

Even the enslavement of criminals, sentenced after due process, is illegal. In fact, one of the necessary conditions for a just punishment is that its nature and duration be determined by the law. Thus the law can condemn [criminals] to hard labour because the duration of the work, the amount of food they get, the punishments for idleness or insubordination, can all be determined by the law. But the law can never sentence a man to be the private slave of another because the sentence is undetermined, and dependent entirely on the whim of the slavemaster. What is more, it is as ridiculous as it is atrocious to advance the view that the majority of wretches bought in Africa are criminals. Are people afraid that we do not despise them enough, that we do not treat them harshly enough? And how can it be assumed that there exists a country where so many crimes are committed, yet where justice is done with such precision? [*Reflections*, 2: 'Reasons used to justify black slavery']

People claim that it is impossible to make the colonies productive without black slaves. We will accept this claim for the sake of argument; we will assume that this absolute impossibility is true: it clearly cannot legitimise slavery. In fact, if the absolute need to survive can authorise us to infringe the rights of another man, violence ceases to be legitimate the moment that absolute need comes to an end. Now here there is no question of this sort of need, but just a question of the colonists losing money. So to ask whether this self-interest legitimises slavery is to ask whether I am permitted to hang on to my wealth by a criminal act. The urgent need I might have for my neighbour's horses to cultivate my field would not give me the right to steal them from him. So why should I have the right to use violence to force him to cultivate them for me? So this need that people assert changes nothing in this case, and does not make slavery any less of a criminal act on the part of the slave-master. [*Reflections*, 3: 'On the so-called need for the **enslavement of blacks, with reference to the rights arising for their masters'**]

A man comes up to me and says; 'Give me some money and I'll be your slave.' I give him the money; he uses it as he wishes (otherwise the deal would be absurd). Have I the right to keep him enslaved? I mean just him, for obviously he does not have the right to sell me his descendants, and whatever the origins of a father's enslavement might be, his children are born free.

I would answer that even in this case I cannot have that right. In fact, if a man hires himself out to another man for a year, for example, either to work in his household, or in his service, he has made a free contract with his master, and each contracting partner has the right to insist that the terms of the contract be honoured. Let us assume that the worker has made a commitment for life. The mutual rights existing between him and the person to whom he is bonded must remain in force, as with a short-term contract. If the fulfilment of the agreement is monitored by law, if the law decides the penalty to be imposed on whoever breaks the agreement, if the blows and insults of the master are punished by financial or physical penalties (and in order for the law to be just, it is necessary to have the same punishment for masters as for employees where the violence or outrage is the same), if the courts cancel the contract in cases where the master is guilty of overworking his servant or contracted worker, or of not providing for his welfare, if, after having profited from the work done by the servant as a young man, his master then abandons him, the law orders the master to pay the man a pension, then this man is not a slave. What in fact is freedom with respect to one man's relationship to another? It is the power to do anything that does not contravene the terms of his contracted agreements and, should he infringe them, the right to be made to fulfil them, or to be punished only by due process for having failed to do so. In short, it is the right to seek the help of the law against any kind of wrong or injury. If a man has renounced these rights, then undoubtedly he becomes a slave, but his agreement intrinsically becomes null and void as if it was the result of endemic madness, or mental derangement caused by passion or extreme poverty. Thus, any man retaining in his contract the natural rights we have just examined is not a slave, and any man who has renounced those rights, and made an invalid agreement, has as much right to reclaim his freedom as the man enslaved through violence. He might remain the debtor, but only a debtor who is free of his master.

There is therefore no case in which slavery, even if arising from a voluntary act, cannot infringe natural law. [*Reflections*, 4: **'On whether a man can buy another man from that man himself'**]

Every legislator, and every single member of a legislative body, is bound by the laws of natural morality. An unjust law that infringes men's rights, whether they be nationals or foreigners, is a crime committed by the legislator in which those members of the legislative body supporting that law are all accomplices. To tolerate an unjust law, when it can be destroyed, is a crime too, but here morality demands nothing from legislators other than what it prescribes for private individuals when it places on them the duty to repair an injustice. This duty is in itself absolute, but there are circumstances when morality only requires people's will to follow it, and leaves the choice of time and means to their judgement. Thus, in repairing an injustice, the legislator may have regard for the interests of the person suffering the injustice, and those interests might require, by way of reparation, precautionary [measures] that involve delay. Attention must also be paid to public order, and measures needed to preserve public order might require the suspension of judicial procedures, even the most useful.

But it will be seen that in this case it can only really be a question of delays and of the slowing down of procedures. In fact, it is impossible for a man, and even more so for an established class of men, to see any useful advantage in being deprived of natural human rights, and a [political] association in which public order required the violation of the rights of citizens and foreigners would no longer be a society of men, but a gang of bandits.

Political society can have no other purpose than the defence of the rights of those who constitute it. Thus any law that infringes the rights of a citizen or a foreigner is an unjust law. It legitimises violence; it is a true crime. Thus police protection afforded to any violation of an individual's rights is a crime on the part of the person in charge of the police. If, however, there is reasonable certainty that a man is incapable of exercising his rights, and that if the exercise of his rights was conferred upon him, he would misuse those rights against other people, or use them to serve his own interests, then society can regard him as having lost his rights, or as having never acquired them. Thus it is that there are some natural rights denied to young children, and which idiots and madmen forfeit. The same principle applies if, because of their upbringing, because of the brutalisation resulting from their enslavement, because of their moral corruption, of the inevitable consequences of vice and of the example of their masters, slaves in Europe's colonies have become incapable of carrying out the responsibilities of free men. Until the experience of freedom has returned to them what slavery has taken from them, you can at least treat them like men deprived of part of their brain by disease or accident, who cannot be allowed fully to exercise their rights without allowing them to harm others, or themselves, and who need not only the protection of the law, but human kindness and care as well.

If a man obtains what he needs from the surrender of his rights, if in giving him his rights you deprive him of what he needs, then common humanity requires the legislator to reconcile that man's safety with his rights. This applies to the case of black slavery as well as to feudal slavery.

In the first instance, the huts of black slaves, their belongings and their food, are all the property of their master. By suddenly restoring to them their freedom, you would reduce them to poverty.

Similarly, in the case of feudal slavery, the labourer, whose field and house belong to his master, could find himself free, but ruined, because the change is too sudden.

Thus in these circumstances, not to allow men to exercise their rights immediately is neither a violation of those rights, nor a perpetuation of protection for those who violate them. It is just a question of applying a necessary measure of wisdom to the process of destroying abuses so that the justice handed out to some miserable wretch can more surely facilitate his happiness.

The right to be protected by the police from violence is one of those rights that man acquires on entry into society. Thus the legislator owes it to society not to admit people who are alien to society, and who might disrupt it. He also owes it to society not to make laws, even the most just of laws, if he thinks that these laws might cause disruption, before assuring himself either of the means to prevent that disruption, and of the force needed to punish those who cause the disruption, with the least possible risk to other citizens. Thus, for example, before raising slaves to the ranks of free men, the law must ensure that with that new status they will not threaten the safety of [other] citizens. In that first moment [of bestowing freedom] we must anticipate all risks to public security arising from the fury of slave-masters, whose two strong passions, greed and pride, have been injured. For a man accustomed to seeing himself surrounded by slaves will not be comforted by the thought of having people who are just of a lower class around him.

These are the only reasons that can permit a legislator to postpone with impunity the destruction of any law depriving a man of his rights.

Commercial prosperity, the nation's wealth, cannot be weighed in the balance against justice. A few men gathered together in an assembly do not have the right to commit what would be, as far as each individual is concerned, an injustice. Thus, those interests relating to a nation's power and wealth must fade before the rights of an individual man, otherwise there is no longer any difference between an ordered society and a band of robbers. If ten thousand, a hundred thousand, men have the right to keep a man in slavery, because their interests require it, why should a strong man like Hercules not be entitled to subject a weaker man to his will? These are the principles of justice that must be our guide when we examine what methods to use in the destruction of slavery. But after having dealt with the issue in the light of principles of justice, it is also useful to look at the question from another angle, and to show that black slavery hurts commercial interests as much as it does justice. It is essential to deprive this crime of the support it gets from politicians who come from the world of finance and business, who do not hear the voice of justice and who, because they are indifferent to injustice, because they tolerate it, authorise it and commit it without any remorse, see themselves as statesmen and deep-thinking politicians ... [*Reflections*, 5: 'On the injustice of black slavery, with reference to the legislator']

It follows from our principles that this inflexible rule of justice, by which kings and nations are as tightly bound as citizens, requires the destruction of slavery.

We have shown that its destruction would harm neither the nation's trade nor its prosperity, since no reduction in production levels would result.

We have shown that the slave-master has no rights over his slave; that the act of keeping him in servitude is not the same as exercising the right to own property, but is a crime; that by freeing a slave, the law is not attacking property, but is no longer tolerating an act that it ought to punish as a capital offence. The sovereign therefore owes no compensation to the slave-master, any more than he does to a thief that a court judgement has deprived of ownership of a stolen object. Public tolerance of a crime absolves people from punishment, but it cannot create an actual right to profit from the crime ... [*Reflections*, 7: 'That black slavery must be abolished and that slave-masters may claim no compensation']

Governments can have no excuse for tolerating either a slave-trade run by traders resident in France, or the importation of slaves. This horrible traffic must therefore be absolutely forbidden. It must be prohibited not in the way smuggling is prohibited, but as a criminal act. It must be punished not by fines but by physical penalties involving public disgrace. Those punishments handed out everywhere for robbery would fit the bill. We are not making any comparison at all between a thief and a man who traffics in other men's freedom, a man who takes men, women and children away from their homeland in a ship, shackled together in twos; who calculates the amount of food they have not on the basis of what they need but according to the dictates of his own greed; who ties their hands together to stop them taking their own lives; who, if the ship is becalmed, coolly throws overboard those for whom he might not get the best price, like people get rid of the shoddiest merchandise first. You can commit a robbery and not have had all human feeling, all natural instinct, crushed out of you; without having lost your nobility of spirit and all notion of virtue; but in a man who trades in blacks there can be no remnant of any feelings, any virtue or honesty even. [*Reflections*, 9: 'On ways of destroying black slavery by degrees']

MARIE OLYMPE AUBRY DE GOUGES [MARIE GOUZE]

BIOGRAPHICAL NOTE

Marie Olympe Aubry de Gouges (1748–93), dramatist, flamboyant revolutionary activist, novelist, journalist and pamphleteer, and a leading champion of women's rights in France, was supposedly the daughter of a Montauban butcher, but claimed to be the illegitimate child of Le Franc de Pompignan. Her illiteracy meant that she had to dictate most of her works to an amenuensis, and her characteristically direct, unpolished style is partly attributable to this, and partly to the fact that as a native of southern (*occitan*) France, French would not have been her first language.

Gouges wrote more than thirty plays, and these reflect many of the themes that also run through her pamphlets and brochures: the iniquities of the slave-trade, divorce, forced vows, marriage, imprisonment for debt, child legislation, government work schemes for the unemployed and other controversial issues. In spite of her radicalism, in the early phases of the Revolution her political position was that of a constitutional monarchist, her distaste for blood-letting, and especially regicide, inclining her towards the Girondin camp. Along with Condorcet, she was one of the earliest public opponents of the slave trade in France with her *Reflections on blacks* (1788).

Gouges' first political brochure, the *Letter to the people, or project for a patriotic fund* appeared on 6 November 1788. A few months later she had completed the *Patriotic remarks* containing prophetic proposals relating to social security, care of the aged, institutions for homeless children, hostels for the unemployed and the introduction of a jury system. In this work she also proclaimed women to be 'ready to shake off the yoke of shameful slavery'. In 1789 she wrote more than a dozen pamphlets on divorce, clerical celibacy, the legalities relating to illegitimate and abandoned children and other issues anticipating many of the concerns of later feminists such as Flora Tristan. In addition to the *Rights of woman*, Gouges wrote a large number of other political essays between 1788 and 1791, including the *Cry of the wise man, by a woman* (1789), written and circulated to deputies after the announcement of Louis XVI's convocation of the Estates-General, the *Letter to the representatives of the nation* (1789), *An allegorical dialogue between*

France and truth (1789), also dedicated to the Estates-General, the *Discourse of a blind man to the French* (1789) and *Will he be king, or will he not?* (1791). *The rights of woman* was published in 1791, a year before the appearance of Mary Wollstonecraft's more celebrated essay, and was dedicated to Marie-Antoinette.

EDITORIAL NOTE

The base text for the present translation of the *Rights*, including Gouges' notes, is that of the copy held by the Bibliothèque Nationale, *Les droits de la femme. A la reine*, printed in Paris in 1791 (Bibliothèque Nationale *E.5568). The British Library also possesses a copy (British Library F.932(14)). There have been several modern editions of the French text, the best of which is to be found in *Olympe de Gouges. Ecrits politiques 1788–1791*, ed. O. Blanc (Paris, Côté-Femmes Editions, 1993), pp. 204–15.

FURTHER READING

Angenot, M., *Les champions de femmes: examen du discours sur la supériorité des femmes 1400–1800* (Montreal, Presses de l'Université du Québec, 1972).

Williams, D., 'The politics of feminism in the French Enlightenment' in *The varied pattern: studies in the eighteenth century*, ed. P. Hughes and D. Williams (Toronto, Hakkert, 1971), pp. 333–51.

The rights of woman (1791)

Man, are you capable of justice? The question is being put to you by a woman; and you will at least not deny her the right to do this. Tell me. What has given you the sovereign right to oppress my sex? Your strength? Your talents? Observe the creator in all his wisdom; look at nature in all its grandeur, to which it seems you want to be close, and give me an example, if you dare, of such tyrannical control as this.[1]

Go back to the animals, consult the elements, study the plants and then cast your eyes over all the different varieties of organised matter; yield to the evidence

---

[1] From Paris to Peru, from Japan to Rome, in my opinion the stupidest animal is Man. [*Note by Gouges.*]

when I give you the means to do so. Seek out, inspect and distinguish, if you can, the sexes in the workings of nature. Everywhere you will find them merged; everywhere they work together as a harmonious whole within this immortal work of art.

Only man has concocted some dreadful principle out of being the exception to this. Bizarre, blind, puffed up by science and, in this century of enlightenment and wisdom, having fallen into the crassest state of ignorance, he wants to rule like a despot over a sex endowed with all the faculties of the intellect. He wants to have the benefits of the Revolution, and demands his rights to equality, at the very least.

DECLARATION OF THE RIGHTS OF WOMAN AND OF THE FEMALE CITIZEN

To be enacted by the National Assembly in its closing sessions, or at a session in the next legislature.

PREAMBLE

Mothers, daughters, sisters, representatives of the nation are [all] demanding to be made part of the National Assembly. Considering ignorance of women's rights, overlooking them or being suspicious of them, to be the sole causes of public misery and government corruption, [they] have resolved to set out in a solemn declaration the natural, inalienable and sacred rights of women so that this declaration, constantly before all members of body politic, always reminds them of their rights and duties, so that the exercise of power by women and the exercise of power by men, will always be consistent with the goal of every political institution, thereby becoming more highly respected, so that the demands of female citizens, based henceforth on clear, incontrovertible principles, centre always on upholding the constitution, sound morality and the happiness of all.

In consequence, the sex as superior in beauty, as it is courageous in the pain of childbirth, recognises and declares in the presence and under the aegis of the Supreme Being, the following rights of woman and of the female citizen:

FIRST ARTICLE

Woman is born free and remains man's equal in the matter of rights. Social distinctions can be based only on usefulness to the community.

II

The goal of all political associations is the preservation of the natural and inalienable rights of woman and man. These are the rights to liberty, property, security and above all the right to resist oppression.

III

The principle of all sovereignty resides essentially in the nation, which is but the coming together of Woman and Man. No body, no person can exercise any authority that does not spring explicitly from this.

IV

Liberty and justice lie in the restoration of everything that belongs to others [as of right]. Thus the exercise of woman's natural rights is limited only by the restrictions that man's perpetual tyranny imposes on it. These restrictions must be reformed by the laws of nature and reason.

V

The laws of nature and reason forbid any action that is harmful to society. Whatever is not forbidden by these wise and holy laws cannot be disallowed, and nobody can be forced to do what [these laws] do not ordain.

VI

The law must be the expression of the general will. All citizens, men as well as women, must concur, personally or through their representatives, in its creation.

It must be the same for everyone: every citizen, man and woman, being equal in its eyes, must be equally eligible for all high honours, public offices and positions, according to their merits and without distinction other than that of their virtues and talents.

VII

No woman is excepted. She is charged, arrested and detained as determined by the law. Women, like men, obey the rigours of this law.

VIII

The law must only prescribe punishments that are strictly and clearly necessary, and nobody may be punished except by virtue of a law decreed and enacted prior to the crime, and applicable legally to women.

IX

Any woman found guilty will be subject to the full rigour of the law.

X

Nobody should be persecuted purely for their deeply held opinions. Woman has the right to mount the scaffold; she must have an equal right to mount the tribune, provided that what she says does not disturb public order as established by the law.

XI

The free communication of thoughts and opinions is one of the most precious rights that woman has, since this freedom ensures the legitimacy of fathers towards their children. Any female citizen may therefore say freely: *I am the mother of a child who belongs to you*, without being forced by some barbaric prejudice to hide the truth. The exception to this would be in cases determined by the law where it is necessary to counter abuse of this freedom.

XII

The guarantee of woman's rights and of those of the female citizen entails service. This guarantee must be established for the advantage of all, and not just for those to whom it is specifically granted.

XIII

The contributions of men and women towards the upkeep of the forces of law and order and towards the cost of government administration are equal. Woman participates in the compulsory labour of the *corvée*, and in all the other tough jobs; so she ought to be included in the distribution of appointments, posts, public offices, as well as [posts in] trade and industry.

XIV

Citizens, men and women, have the right to ascertain directly, or through their representatives, what is necessary for public taxation. Female citizens can only support [such decisions] by being given an equal share not only in matters of finance but also in public administration, and in the right to determine the level of taxes, their basis, collection and duration.

XV

All women, joined together with men with regard to taxation, have the right to call any public servant to account for his administrative decisions.

XVI

Any society in which rights are not guaranteed, or the separation of powers not determined, has no constitution. The constitution is void if the majority of individuals who make up the nation have not played a role in drafting it.

XVII

Properties are shared or divided by both sexes. They are for each person an inviolable and sacred right. Nobody can be deprived of their true and natural heritage, unless public need, legally ascertained, clearly demands it, and then only on condition of just, pre-determined compensation.

POSTSCRIPT

Women, wake up! The alarm-bells of reason can be heard all over the world. Recognise your rights. The powerful rule of nature is no longer hemmed in by prejudices, fanaticism, superstition and lies. The torch of truth has dispelled the clouds of foolishness and usurpation. Man enslaved has doubled his efforts, and [still] needed yours to break his chains. Now that he is free, he has become unjust towards his companion. Oh Women! Women! When will your blindness end? What advantages have you gained from the Revolution? A more marked distrust, a more obvious contempt. In the centuries of corruption you have reigned only over man's weakness. Your little empire has been destroyed; so what do you have left? The proof of man's injustices. Your claims to a heritage based on Nature's wise decrees. What would you have to fear from such a fine enterprise? The fine words of the Legislator [Christ] at the marriage-feast at Canaa? Are you afraid that our own French legislators, the correctors of a morality long entangled in the branches of politics, and which has now had its day, might ask: Women, what do you have in common with us? Everything, you will answer. If they persist, in their weakness, in contradicting their principles with this absurdity, be courageous enough to oppose these vain claims to superiority with the force of reason. Unite beneath the banners of philosophy. Bring to bear all the energy of your nature, and you will soon see these arrogant men crawling at your feet in servile adoration, but proud to share with you the precious gifts of the Supreme Being. Whatever obstacles are put in your way, you have the power to surmount them; you just have to have the will to do so.

Let us move on now to the appalling sight of what you have been in society and, since there is some question at the moment of a national education [system], let us see whether our wise legislators will have sensible thoughts on the education of women.

Women have done more harm than good. Constraint and dissimulation have been their lot. What force has stolen from them, guile has returned to them. They have played on their charms for all that they are worth, and the most irreproachable of men could not resist them. Poison and cold steel were placed at their disposal; they reigned over crime as they did virtue. The French government, especially, has depended for ages on the way women managed things in the dark of night. The cabinet held no secrets from their indiscretions. The world of ambassadors, commanders, ministers, presidents, pontiffs,[2] cardinals, in short everything that characterises men's stupidity in profane and sacred affairs, has served the greed and ambition of the sex that was once despised but respectable and which, since the Revolution, has become respectable but despised.

I could say so much more about these contradictions! I have just one moment to make them, but that moment will capture the attention of the most remote posterity. In the *ancien régime* it was all vice and guilt; but couldn't people see a potential for improvement within the very nature of the vices [involved]? A woman had only to be beautiful or likeable; if she had these two assets she would see a hundred fortunes laid at her feet. Not to take advantage of them [meant that] she was an odd character, or [subscribed to] an unusual philosophy leading her to disparage wealth. She would then be just considered wrong-headed. Gold made the most indecent women respectable. The trade in women, henceforth to be discredited, was a kind of commerce accepted by the upper classes. If it still was, the Revolution would be lost, and in a different set-up we would be forever corrupt. But reason may hide the fact that any other road to fortune is closed to the women men buy, as it is to the slaves [they buy] on the coast of Africa. There is a big difference, I know. The slave is the property of a master; but if the master gives her liberty without compensation at an age when she has lost all her charms, what will become of the poor woman? A plaything of suspicion. The doors of

---

[2] M. de Bernis, in the style of Mme de Pompadour. [*Note by Gouges.*]

charity itself are closed to her. They will say that she is poor and old; why did she not manage to make her fortune? Other, even more touching examples can be considered. A young, inexperienced girl, seduced by a man she loves, leaves her parents to follow him. After a few years this heartless man will abandon her, and the longer they have been together, the more inhuman his unfaithfulness will be. If she has children, he will still abandon her. If he is rich, he will think himself exempt from sharing his wealth with his noble victims. If some commitment binds him to his responsibilities, he will use the law to break its power over him. If he is married, all other rights are lost. So what laws are still to be enacted to root out vice? Those relating to the division of wealth between men and women, and to public [assistance]. You can easily understand that a woman born into a rich family stands to gain a lot from an equal division of wealth. But what of a deserving and virtuous woman born into a poor family, what is her lot? Poverty and shame. If she does not excel specifically in painting or in music, she cannot be appointed to any public office, however capable she might be of filling them. I just want to give you a general idea of how things are. I shall go into them in more detail in a new annotated edition of my political works that I propose to offer to the public in a few days time.

I go back to morality. Marriage is the tomb of trust and love. A married woman can present her husband with bastards with impunity, and give them a fortune that does not belong to them. An unmarried woman's rights are feeble. Ancient, inhuman laws refuse her children any right to their father's name and property, and no new laws on this subject have been made. If trying to give my sex honour and justice is now seen as a paradox on my part, as aiming for the impossible, I leave to the men of the future the glory of dealing with this issue. But in the meantime we can pave the way towards [that future] through a national [system of] education, through moral renewal and marriage contracts.

FORM OF THE SOCIAL CONTRACT BETWEEN MAN AND WOMAN

We, *name* and *name*, of our own free will, come together for as long as we live, and for as long as our mutual feelings for each other last, on the following conditions: It is our wish and intention to put our wealth into common ownership, reserving the right to divide that wealth up for the benefit of our own children, and of those born of other liaisons, each of us recognising that our property belongs directly to our children, from whatever bed they might have come, and that they all have the right, without distinction, to bear *the names of the fathers and mothers* who acknowledge them as theirs. We undertake to subscribe to any law punishing the denial of one's own flesh and blood. We also make a commitment, should we separate, to divide our wealth, and to set aside our children's share, as prescribed by the law. In a perfect union, the first to die would leave half his property to his children or, if without issue, would leave everything to the surviving partner, unless the deceased had bequeathed his half to whomever he thought fit.

This is more or less the form of the marriage contract that I propose. I can already see all the Tartuffes, the straitlaced prudes, the clergy, and the whole infernal gang, rising up against me after reading this strange document. But think how this will provide the wise with the moral means to achieve a happy, perfectible government! I am going to offer you some brief, concrete evidence. The rich childless pleasure-seeker thinks it a good idea to pay a visit to his poor neighbour to extend his family. When there is a law allowing the poor man's wife to make the rich man adopt her children then the ties binding us together in society will be tighter, and morality purer.[3] Perhaps this law will preserve the goodness of the community, and rein back the disorder which drives so many victims into those asylums of shame, depravity and degeneration of human principles against which Nature has so long cried out. So let the detractors of this sane philosophy stop expostulating against basic morals, or let them go to the source of their quotations and find their defeat there.

I would also like to see a law that would benefit widows and young girls deceived by the false promises of men with whom they might have got involved. I want this law to force an unfaithful man to honour his commitments, or pay a proportion of his wealth as compensation. In addition, I want this law to be applied rigorously to women, or at least to those impudent enough to resort to a law they have themselves infringed through their loose behaviour, should this be proved. At the same time, as I said in *The primitive happiness of man* in 1788, I would like prostitutes to be placed in specially designated districts. It is not prostitutes who contribute most to the corruption of morals, but society women. By making new women of the latter, you will

---

[3] Thus Abraham had very legitimate children with Agar, his wife's servant. [*Note by Gouges.*]

change the former. This chain of fraternal links will cause disorder at first, but in time will create perfect unity.

I am offering a sure way to raise women's spirits: let them join in all of men's activities. If men persist in finding this impractical, let them share their wealth with their wives, not according to their whims but according to the wisdom of the laws. Prejudice will fall, morals will be purified, and all the rights of Nature will be restored. Add to all this married priests, a King safely ensconced on his throne, and the French government will never perish.

It is essential for me to say a few words about the trouble supposedly caused by a decree that was to benefit the blacks in our island [colonies]. These are the places where Nature shudders with horror; where reason and humanity has not yet touched hardened hearts; where the inhabitants are torn by division and discord. It is not difficult to guess who the instigators of this inflammatory unrest are. Some of them are right in the bosom of the National Assembly. They are lighting in Europe the fire that was to set America alight. Colonists claim [the right] to rule as despots over men whose fathers and brothers they are. They fail to recognise natural rights, even for those with the tiniest drop of their own blood in their veins. These inhuman colonists say: our blood runs in their veins, but we will spill it all, if necessary, to satisfy our greed and our blind ambition. It is in these places, closest to Nature, where father fails to recognise son. Deaf to the call of blood, he destroys its hold over him. What can we expect from the resistance to all this? Using violence against it will turn it into something terrible, leave those who resist still in chains, and channel every calamity in the direction of America. A divine hand seems to extend man's prerogative everywhere: *Liberty.* Only the law has the right to curb this liberty if it degenerates into licence. But Liberty must apply equally to all. It is Liberty above all, dictated by wisdom and justice, that must be embodied in the National Assembly's decree. May it be applied equally to the [whole] French state, and be as responsive to the new abuses as it has been to the old abuses which grow more appalling by the day! My own view would still be to reconcile the executive with the legislative, for it seems to me that one is everything and the other nothing, resulting possibly in the unfortunate loss of the French empire. I consider that these two powers, like man and woman[4]

---

[4] At Monsieur de Merville's magical supper-party, Ninon asked what the name was of Louis XVI's mistress. The reply was: the nation. This mistress will corrupt the government if she gets too much power. [*Note by Gouges.*]

must be joined together, but equal in strength and virtue, to form a good marriage . . .

(14 September 1791)

MARY WOLLSTONECRAFT

BIOGRAPHICAL NOTE

Mary Wollstonecraft (1759–97) was born in Spitalfields in London to a family that had made its fortune in silk. However, family money was inherited only by her father, whom she hated for his brutality, and her brother, and after 1778 Wollstonecroft was obliged to earn her own living, working for a time as a paid companion to an elderly lady in Bath. Her writings were eventually to become her sole source of income. The Wollstonecrafts fragmented as a family after the death of her mother in 1782, and she went to live with the family of Fanny Blood, whom she had met some years previously. In 1783, and for most of 1784, Wollstonecraft was preoccupied with the welfare of her sister, with whom she founded a school, together with Fanny Blood, in Islington and, later, in Newington Green. It was at Newington that she met Richard Price, gaining through Price an entry into dissenting circles.

In 1785 her close friend, Fanny Blood, died in childbirth in Lisbon. Returning from Lisbon to London in 1786, Wollstonecraft became governess to the daughters of Viscount Kingsborough, and moved to Dublin. By then she had written her *Thoughts on the education of daughters* (1787). For a time, after her dismissal by the Kingsborough family, she worked as a translator for, and contributor to, the *Analytical review*. By 1790 she had assumed the role of editorial assistant, and her reputation had been growing since 1788 with the publication in that year of *Mary, a fiction*, and *Original stories from real life*, as well as several translations such as that of Necker's *Of the importance of religious opinions*.

On 1 November 1790 Burke's *Reflections on the Revolution in France* appeared, and Wollstonecraft published anonymously in the same year her riposte, *A vindication of the rights of man*, of which a second edition quickly followed under her name. In the following year work started on *A vindication of the rights of woman*. These years marked a period in her life when she met Talleyrand, William Godwin and, a year after her arrival in Paris in December 1792, Gilbert Imlay, by whom she conceived a child. Imlay registered her at the American Embassy in Paris as his wife, and in January 1794 Wollstonecraft moved to Le Havre, where her daughter, Fanny Imlay, was born in May. *An historical and moral view of the origin and progress of the French Revolution, and the effect it has produced in Europe* was published later in the same year, an account of the French Revolution in which she seemed to renounce her earlier criticisms of Burke.

She returned to London in 1795 suffering from depression, probably as a result of her failing relationship with Imlay, and twice attempted suicide. A visit to Scandinavia bore fruit as *Letters written during a short residence in Sweden, Norway and Denmark* (1796). Friendship with Godwin was resumed, and their marriage took place in March 1797. Wollstonecraft was now working on *The wrongs of woman: or Maria* (1798). On 30 August her second daughter was born and named Mary Wollstonecraft Godwin, the future wife of Shelley, and later to gain literary immortality in her own right as the author of *Frankenstein.* Mary Wollstonecraft died of septicaemia on 10 September 1797. *A vindication of the rights of woman: with strictures on political and moral subjects* was published in January 1792, and reprinted in the same year.

EDITORIAL NOTE

The selected extracts are taken from S. Tomaselli's edition* of *A vindication,* for which the base text is the second 1792 edition.

FURTHER READING

Kelly, G., *Revolutionary feminism: the mind and career of Mary Wollstonecraft* (Basingstoke, Macmillan, 1992).

Sapiro, V., *Vindication of political virtue: the political theory of Mary Wollstonecraft* (Chicago/London, University of Chicago Press, 1992).

Todd, J., (ed.), *Mary Wollstonecraft: political writings* (London, William Pickering, 1993). See introduction, pp. vii–xxvi.

Tomalin, C., *The life and death of Mary Wollstonecraft* (London, Penguin, 1992).

*Tomaselli, S. (ed.), *Mary Wollstonecraft: a vindication of the rights of man and A vindication of the rights of woman and hints* (Cambridge, Cambridge University Press, 1995). See introduction, pp. ix–xxix.

A vindication of the rights of woman: with strictures on political and moral subjects (1792)

To account for, and excuse the tyranny of man, many ingenious arguments have been brought forward to prove, that the two sexes, in the acquirement of virtue, ought to aim at attaining a very different character: or, to speak explicitly, women are not allowed to have sufficient strength of mind to acquire what really deserves the name of virtue. Yet it should seem, allowing them to have souls, that there is but one way appointed by Providence to lead *mankind* to either virtue or happiness.

If then women are not a swarm of ephemeron triflers, why should they be kept in ignorance under the specious name of innocence? Men complain, and with reason, of the follies and caprices of our sex, when they do not keenly satirize our headstrong passions and groveling vices. – Behold, I should answer, the natural effect of ignorance! The mind will ever be unstable that has only prejudices to rest on, and the current will run with destructive fury when there are no barriers to break its force. Women are told from their infancy, and taught by the example of their mothers, that a little knowledge of human weakness, justly termed cunning, softness of temper, *outward* obedience, and a scrupulous attention to a puerile kind of propriety, will obtain for them the protection of man; and should they be beautiful, every thing else is needless, for, at least, twenty years of their lives.

Thus Milton describes our first frail mother; though when he tells us that women are formed for softness and sweet attractive grace, I cannot comprehend his meaning, unless, in the true Mahometan strain, he meant to deprive us of souls, and insinuate that we were beings only designed by sweet attractive grace, and docile blind obedience, to gratify the senses of man when he can no longer soar on the wing of contemplation.

How grossly do they insult us who thus advise us only to render ourselves gentle, domestic brutes! For instance, the winning softness so warmly, and frequently, recommended, that governs by obeying. What childish expressions, and how insignificant is the being – can it be an immortal one? who will condescend to govern by such sinister methods! 'Certainly,' says Lord Bacon, 'man is of kin to the beasts by his body; and if he be not of kin to God by his spirit, he is a base and ignoble creature!' Men, indeed, appear to me to act in a very unphilosophical manner when they try to secure the good conduct of women by attempting to keep them always in a state of childhood. Rousseau was more consistent when he wished to stop the progress of reason in both sexes, for if men eat of the tree of knowledge, women will come in for a taste; but, from the imperfect cultivation which their understandings now receive, they only attain a knowledge of evil.

Children, I grant, should be innocent; but when the epithet is applied to men, or women, it is but a civil term for weakness. For if it be allowed that women were destined by Providence to acquire human virtues, and by the exercise of their understandings, that stability of character which is the firmest ground to rest our future hopes upon, they must be permitted to turn to the fountain of light, and not forced to shape their course by the twinkling of a mere satellite. Milton, I grant, was of a very different opinion; for he only bends to the indefeasible right of beauty, though it would be difficult to render two passages which I now mean to contrast, consistent. But into similar inconsistencies are great men often led by their senses . . .

By individual education, I mean, for the sense of the word is not precisely defined, such an attention to a child as will slowly sharpen the senses, form the temper, regulate the passions as they begin to ferment, and set the understanding to work before the body arrives at maturity; so that the man may only have to proceed, not to begin, the important task of learning to think and reason.

To prevent any misconstruction, I must add, that I do not believe that a private education can work the wonders which some sanguine writers have attributed to it. Men and women must be educated, in a great degree, by the opinions and manners of the society they live in. In every age there has been a stream of popular opinion that has carried all before it, and given a family character, as it were, to the century. It may then fairly be inferred, that, till society be differently constituted, much cannot be expected from education. It is, however, sufficient for my present purpose to assert, that, whatever effect circumstances have on the abilities, every being may become virtuous by the exercise of its own reason; for if but one being was created with vicious inclinations, that is positively bad, what can save us from atheism? or if we worship a God, is not that God a devil?

Consequently, the most perfect education, in my opinion, is such an exercise of the understanding as is best calculated to strengthen the body and form the heart. Or, in other words, to enable the individual to attain such habits of virtue as will render it independent. In fact, it is a farce to call any being virtuous whose virtues do not result from the exercise of its own reason. This was Rousseau's opinion respecting men: I extend it to women, and confidently assert that they have been drawn out of their sphere by false refinement, and not by an endeavour to acquire masculine qualities. Still the regal homage which they receive is so intoxicating, that till the manners of the times are changed, and formed on more reasonable principles, it may be impossible to convince them that the illegitimate power which they obtain, by degrading themselves, is a curse, and that they must return to nature and equality, if they wish to secure the placid satisfaction that unsophisticated affections impart. But for this epoch we must wait – wait, perhaps, till kings and nobles, enlightened by reason, and, preferring the real dignity of man to childish state, throw off their gaudy hereditary trappings: and if then women do not resign the arbitrary power of beauty – they will prove that they have *less* mind than man.

I may be accused of arrogance; still I must declare what I firmly believe, that all the writers who have written on the subject of female education and manners from Rousseau to Dr. Gregory, have contributed to render women more artificial, weak characters, than they would otherwise have been; and, consequently, more useless members of society. I might have expressed this conviction in a lower key; but I am afraid it would have been the whine of affectation, and not the faithful expression of my feelings, of the clear result, which experience and reflection have led me to draw. When I come to that division of the subject, I shall advert to the passages that I more particularly disapprove of, in the works of the authors I have just alluded to; but it is first necessary to observe, that my objection extends to the whole purport of those books, which tend, in my opinion, to degrade one half of the human species, and render women pleasing at the expence of every solid virtue.

Though, to reason on Rousseau's ground, if man did attain a degree of perfection of mind when his body arrived at maturity, it might be proper, in order to make a man and his wife *one*, that she should rely entirely on his understanding; and the graceful ivy, clasping the oak that supported it, would form a whole in which strength and beauty would be equally conspicuous. But, alas! husbands, as well as their helpmates, are often only overgrown children; nay, thanks to early debauchery, scarcely men in their outward form – and if the blind lead the blind, one need not come from heaven to tell us the consequence.

Many are the causes that, in the present corrupt state of society, contribute to enslave women by cramping their understandings and sharpening their senses. One, perhaps, that silently does more mischief than all the rest, is their disregard of order.

To do every thing in an orderly manner, is a most important precept, which women, who, generally speaking, receive only a disorderly kind of education, seldom attend to with that degree of exactness that men, who from their infancy are broken into method, observe. This negligent kind of guess-work, for what other epithet can be used to point out the random exertions of a sort of instinctive common sense, never brought to the test of reason? prevents their generalizing matters of fact – so they do to-day, what they did yesterday, merely because they did it yesterday.

This contempt of the understanding in early life has more baneful consequences than is commonly supposed; for the little knowledge which women of strong minds attain, is, from various circumstances, of a more desultory kind than the knowledge of men, and it is acquired more by sheer observations on real life, than from comparing what has been individually observed with the results of experience generalized by speculation. Led by their dependent situation and domestic employments more into society, what they learn is rather by snatches; and as learning is with them, in general, only a secondary thing, they do not pursue any one branch with that persevering ardour necessary to give vigour to the faculties, and clearness to the judgement. In the present state of society, a little learning is required to support the character of a gentleman; and boys are obliged to submit to a few years of discipline. But in the education of women, the cultivation of the understanding is always subordinate to the acquirement of some corporeal accomplishment; even while enervated by confinement and false notions of modesty, the body is prevented from attaining that grace and beauty which relaxed half-formed limbs never exhibit. Besides, in youth their faculties are not brought forward by emulation; and having no serious scientific study, if they have natural sagacity it is turned too soon on life and manners. They dwell on effects, and modifications, without tracing them back to causes; and complicated rules to adjust behaviour are a weak substitute for simple principles.

As a proof that education gives this appearance of weakness to females, we may instance the example of military men, who are, like them, sent into the world before their minds have been stored with knowledge or fortified by principles. The consequences are similar; soldiers acquire a little superficial knowledge, snatched from the muddy current of conversation, and, from continually mixing with society, they gain, what is termed a knowledge of the world; and this acquaintance with manners and customs has frequently been confounded with a knowledge of the human heart. But can the crude fruit of casual observation, never brought to the test of judgement, formed by comparing speculation and experience, deserve such a distinction? Soldiers, as well as women, practise the minor virtues with punctilious politeness. Where is then the sexual difference, when the education has been the same? All the difference that I can discern, arises from the superior advantage of liberty, which enables the former to see more of life.

It is wandering from the present subject, perhaps, to make a political remark; but, as it was produced naturally by the train of my reflections, I shall not pass it silently over.

Standing armies can never consist of resolute, robust men; they may be well disciplined machines, but they will seldom contain men under the influence of strong passions, or with very vigorous faculties. And as for any depth of under-standing, I will venture to affirm, that it is as rarely to be found in the army as amongst women; and the cause, I maintain, is the same. It may be further observed, that officers are also particularly attentive to their persons, fond of dancing, crowded rooms, adventures, and ridicule. Like the *fair* sex, the business of their lives is gallantry. – They were taught to please, and they only live to please. Yet they do not lose their rank in the distinction of sexes, for they are still reckoned superior to women, though in what their superiority consists, beyond what I have just mentioned, it is difficult to discover.

The great misfortune is this, that they both acquire manners before morals, and a knowledge of life before they have, from reflection, any acquaintance with the grand ideal outline of human nature. The consequence is natural; satisfied with common nature, they become a prey to prejudices, and taking all their opin-ions on credit, they blindly submit to authority. So that, if they have any sense, it is a kind of instinctive glance, that catches proportions, and decides with respect to manners; but fails when arguments are to be pursued below the surface, or opinions analyzed.

May not the same remark be applied to women? Nay, the argument may be carried still further, for they are both thrown out of a useful station by the unnatural distinctions established in civilized life. Riches and hereditary honours have made cyphers of women to give consequence to the numerical figure; and idleness has produced a mixture of gallantry and despotism into society, which leads the very men who are the slaves of their mistresses to tyrannize over their sisters, wives, and daughters. This is only keeping them in rank and file, it is true. Strengthen the female mind by enlarging it, and there will be an end to blind obedience; but, as blind obedience is ever sought for by power, tyrants and sensualists are in the right when they endeavour to keep women in the dark, because the former only want slaves, and the latter a play-thing. The sensualist, indeed, has been the most dangerous of tyrants, and women have been duped by their lovers, as princes by their ministers, whilst dreaming that they reigned over them ...

Women are, therefore, to be considered either as moral beings, or so weak that they must be entirely subjected to the superior faculties of men.

Let us examine this question. Rousseau declares that a woman should never, for a moment, feel herself independent, that she should be governed by fear to exercise her *natural* cunning, and made a coquettish slave in order to render her a more alluring object of desire, a *sweeter* companion to man, whenever he chooses to relax himself. He carries the arguments, which he pretends to draw from the indications of nature, still further, and insinuates that truth and fortitude, the cornerstones of all human virtue, should be cultivated with certain restrictions, because, with respect to the female character, obedience is the grand lesson which ought to be impressed with unrelenting rigour.

What nonsense! when will a great man arise with sufficient strength of mind to puff away the fumes which pride and sensuality have thus spread over the subject! If women are by nature inferior to men, their virtues must be the same in quality, if not in degree, or virtue is a relative idea; consequently, their conduct should be founded on the same principles, and have the same aim.

Connected with man as daughters, wives, and mothers, their moral character may be estimated by their manner of fulfilling those simple duties; but the end, the grand end of their exertions should be to unfold their own faculties and acquire the dignity of conscious virtue. They may try to render their road pleasant; but ought never to forget, in common with man, that life yields not the felicity which can satisfy an immortal soul. I do not mean to insinuate, that either sex should be so lost in abstract reflections or distant views, as to forget the affections and duties that lie before them, and are, in truth, the means appointed to produce the fruit of life; on the contrary, I would warmly recommend them, even while I assert, that they afford most satisfaction when they are considered in their true, sober light.

Probably the prevailing opinion, that woman was created for man, may have taken its rise from Moses's poetical story; yet, as very few, it is presumed, who have bestowed any serious thought on the subject, ever supposed that Eve was, literally speaking, one of Adam's ribs, the deduction must be allowed to fall to the ground; or, only be so far admitted as it proves that man, from the remotest antiquity, found it convenient to exert his strength to subjugate his companion, and his invention to shew that she ought to have her neck bent under the yoke, because the whole creation was only created for his convenience or pleasure.

Let it not be concluded that I wish to invert the order of things; I have already granted, that, from the constitution of their bodies, men seem to be designed by Providence to attain a greater degree of virtue. I speak collectively of the whole sex; but I see not the shadow of a reason to conclude that their virtues should differ in respect to their nature. In fact, how can they, if virtue has only one eternal standard? I must therefore, if I reason consequentially, as strenuously maintain that they have the same simple direction, as that there is a God.

It follows then that cunning should not be opposed to wisdom, little cares to great exertions, or insipid softness, varnished over with the name of gentleness, to that fortitude which grand views alone can inspire.

I shall be told that woman would then lose many of her peculiar graces, and the opinion of a well known poet might be quoted to refute my unqualified assertion. For Pope has said, in the name of the whole male sex,

> Yet ne'er so sure our passion to create,
> As when she touch'd the brink of all we hate.

In what light this sally places men and women, I shall leave to the judicious to determine; meanwhile I shall content myself with observing, that I cannot discover why, unless they are mortal, females should always be degraded by being made subservient to love or lust.

To speak disrespectfully of love is, I know, high treason against sentiment and fine feelings; but I wish to speak the simple language of truth, and rather to address the head than the heart. To endeavour to reason love out of the world, would be to out Quixote Cervantes, and equally offend against common sense; but an endeavour to restrain this tumultuous passion, and to prove that it should not be allowed to dethrone superior powers, or to usurp the sceptre which the understanding should ever coolly wield, appears less wild.

Youth is the season of love in both sexes; but in those days of thoughtless enjoyment provision should be made for the more important years of life, when reflection takes place of sensation. But Rousseau, and most of the male writers who have followed his steps, have warmly inculcated that the whole tendency of female education ought to be directed to one point: – to render them pleasing.

Let me reason with the supporters of this opinion who have any knowledge of human nature, do they imagine that marriage can eradicate the habitude of life? The woman who has only been taught to please will soon find that her charms are oblique sunbeams, and that they cannot have much effect on her husband's heart when they are seen every day, when the summer is passed and gone. Will she then have sufficient native energy to look into herself for comfort, and cultivate her dormant faculties? or, is it not more rational to expect that she will try to please other men; and, in the emotions raised by the expectation of new conquests, endeavour to forget the mortification her love or pride has received? When the husband ceases to be a lover – and the time will inevitably come, her desire of pleasing will then grow languid, or become a spring of bitterness; and love, perhaps, the most evanescent of all passions, gives place to jealousy or vanity.

I now speak of women who are restrained by principle or prejudice; such women, though they would shrink from an intrigue with real abhorrence, yet, nevertheless, wish to be convinced by the homage of gallantry that they are cruelly neglected by their husbands; or, days and weeks are spent in dreaming of the happiness enjoyed by congenial souls till their health is undermined and their spirits broken by discontent. How then can the great art of pleasing be such a necessary study? it is only useful to a mistress; the chaste wife, and serious mother, should only consider her power to please as the polish of her virtues, and the affection of her husband as one of the comforts that render her task less difficult and her life happier. – But, whether she be loved or neglected, her first wish should be to make herself respectable, and not to rely for all her happiness on a being subject to like infirmities with herself. [*A **vindication**, 2: **'The prevailing opinion of a sexual character discussed'**]

That woman is naturally weak, or degraded by a concurrence of circumstances, is, I think, clear. But this position I shall simply contrast with a conclusion, which I have frequently heard fall from sensible men in favour of an aristocracy: that the mass of mankind cannot be any thing, or the obsequious slaves, who patiently allow themselves to be driven forward, would feel their own consequence, and spurn their chains. Men, they further observe, submit every where to oppression, when they have only to lift up their heads to throw off the yoke; yet, instead of asserting their birthright, they quietly lick the dust, and say, let us eat and drink, for to-morrow we die. Women, I argue from analogy, are degraded by the same propensity to enjoy the present moment; and, at last, despise the freedom which they have not sufficient virtue to struggle to attain. But I must be more explicit.

With respect to the culture of the heart, it is unanimously allowed that sex is out of the question; but the line of subordination in the mental powers is never to be passed over. Only 'absolute in loveliness,' the portion of rationality granted to woman, is, indeed, very scanty; for, denying her genius and judgment, it is scarcely possible to divine what remains to characterize intellect.

The stamen of immortality, if I may be allowed the phrase, is the perfectibility of human reason; for, were man created perfect, or did a flood of knowledge break in upon him, when he arrived at maturity, that precluded error, I should doubt whether his existence would be continued after the dissolution of the body. But, in the present state of things, every difficulty in morals that escapes from human discussion, and equally baffles the investigation of profound thinking, and the lightning glance of genius, is an argument on which I build my belief of the immortality of the soul. Reason is, consequentially, the simple power of improvement; or, more properly speaking, of discerning truth. Every individual is in this respect a world in itself. More or less may be conspicuous in one being than another; but the nature of reason must be the same in all, if it be an emanation of divinity, the tie that connects the creature with the Creator; for, can that soul be stamped with the heavenly image, that is not perfected by the exercise of its own reason? Yet outwardly ornamented with elaborate care, and so adorned to delight man, 'that with honour he may love,' the soul of woman is not allowed to have this distinction, and man, ever placed between her and reason, she is always represented as only created to see through a gross medium, and to take things on trust. But dismissing these fanciful theories, and considering woman as a whole, let it be what it will, instead of a part of man, the inquiry is whether she have reason or not. If she have, which, for a moment, I will take for granted, she was not created merely to be the solace of man, and the sexual should not destroy the human character.

Into this error men have, probably, been led by viewing education in a false light; not considering it as the first step to form a being advancing gradually towards perfection; but only as a preparation for life. On this sensual error, for I must call it so, has the false system of female manners been reared, which robs the whole sex of its dignity, and classes the brown and fair with the smiling flowers that only adorn the land. This has ever been the language of men, and the fear of departing from a supposed sexual character, has made even women of superior sense adopt the same sentiments. Thus understanding, strictly speaking, has been denied to woman; and instinct, sublimated into wit and cunning, for the purposes of life, has been submitted in its stead.

The power of generalizing ideas, of drawing comprehensive conclusions from individual observations, is the only acquirement, for an immortal being, that really deserves the name of knowledge. Merely to observe, without endeavouring to account for any thing, may (in a very incomplete manner) serve as the common sense of life; but where is the store laid up that is to clothe the soul when it leaves the body?

This power has not only been denied to women; but writers have insisted that it is inconsistent, with a few exceptions, with their sexual character. Let men prove this, and I shall grant that woman only exists for man. I must, however, previously remark, that the power of generalizing ideas, to any great extent, is not very common amongst men or women. But this exercise is the true cultivation of the understanding; and every thing conspires to render the cultivation of the understanding more difficult in the female than the male world . . .

I lament that women are systematically degraded by receiving the trivial attentions, which men think it manly to pay to the sex, when, in fact, they are insultingly supporting their own superiority. It is not condescension to bow to an inferior. So ludicrous, in fact, do these ceremonies appear to me, that I scarcely am able to govern my muscles, when I see a man start with eager, and serious solicitude, to lift a handkerchief, or shut a door, when the *lady* could have done it herself, had she only moved a pace or two.

A wild wish has just flown from my heart to my head, and I will not stifle it though it may excite a horse-laugh. – I do earnestly wish to see the distinction of sex confounded in society, unless where love animates the behaviour. For this distinction is, I am firmly persuaded, the foundation of the weakness of character ascribed to woman; is the cause why the understanding is neglected, while accomplishments are acquired with sedulous care: and the same cause accounts for their preferring the graceful before the heroic virtues.

Mankind, including every description, wish to be loved and respected by *something*; and the common herd will always take the nearest road to the completion of their wishes. The respect paid to wealth and beauty is the most certain, and unequivocal; and, of course, will always attract the vulgar eye of common minds. Abilities and virtues are absolutely necessary to raise men from the middle rank of life into notice; and the natural consequence is notorious, the middle rank contains most virtue and abilities. Men have thus, in one station, at least an opportunity of exerting themselves with dignity, and of rising by the exertions which really improve a rational creature; but the whole female sex are, till their character is formed, in the same condition as the rich: for they are born, I now speak of a state of civilization, with certain sexual privileges, and whilst they are gratuitously granted them, few will ever think of works of supererogation, to obtain the esteem of a small number of superiour people.

When do we hear of women who, starting out of obscurity, boldly claim respect on account of their great abilities or daring virtues? Where are they to be found? – 'To be observed, to be attended to, to be taken notice of with sympathy, complacency, and approbation, are all the advantages which they seek.' – True! my male readers will probably exclaim; but let them, before they draw any conclusion, recollect that this was not written originally as descriptive of women, but of the rich. In Dr. Smith's Theory of Moral Sentiments, I have found a general character of people of rank and fortune, that, in my opinion, might with the greatest propriety be applied to the female sex. I refer the sagacious reader to the whole comparison; but must be allowed to quote a passage to enforce an argument that I mean to insist on, as the one most conclusive against a sexual character. For if, excepting warriors, no great men, of any denomination, have ever appeared amongst the nobility, may it not be fairly inferred that their local situation swallowed up the man, and produced a character similar to that of women, who are *localized*, if I may be allowed the word, by the rank they are placed in, by *courtesy*? Women, commonly called Ladies, are not to be contradicted in company, are not allowed to exert any manual strength; and from them the negative virtues only are expected, when any virtues are expected, patience, docility, good-humour, and flexibility; virtues incompatible with any vigorous exertion of intellect. Besides, by living more with each other, and being seldom absolutely alone, they are more under the influence of sentiments than passions. Solitude and reflection are necessary to give to wishes the force of passions, and to enable the imagination to enlarge the object, and make it the most desirable. The same may be said of the rich; they do not sufficiently deal in general ideas, collected by impassioned thinking, or calm investigation, to acquire that strength of character on which great resolves are built. But hear what an acute observer says of the great.

'Do the great seem insensible of the easy price at which they acquire the publick admiration; or do they seem to imagine that to them, as to other men, it must be the purchase either of sweat or of blood? By what important accomplishments is the young nobleman instructed to support the dignity of his rank, and to render himself worthy of that superiority over his fellow-citizens, to which the virtue of his ancestors had raised them? Is it by knowledge, by industry, by patience, by self-denial, or by virtue of any kind? As all his words, as all his motions are attended to, he learns an habitual regard to every circumstance of ordinary behaviour, and studies to perform all those small duties with the most exact propriety. As he is conscious how much he is observed, and how much mankind are disposed to favour all his inclinations, he acts, upon the most indifferent occasions, with that freedom and elevation which the thought of this naturally inspires. His air, his manner, his deportment, all mark that elegant and graceful sense of his own superiority, which those who are born to inferior station can hardly ever arrive at. These are the arts by which he proposes to make mankind more easily submit to his authority, and to govern their inclinations according to his own pleasure: and in this he is seldom disappointed. These arts, supported by rank and preeminence, are, upon ordinary occasions, sufficient to govern the world. Lewis XIV. during the greater part of his reign, was regarded, not only in France, but over all Europe, as the most perfect model of a great prince. But what were the talents and virtues by which he acquired this great reputation? Was it by the scrupulous and inflexible justice of all his undertakings, by the immense dangers and difficulties with which they were attended, or by the unwearied and unrelenting application with which he pursued them? Was it by his extensive knowledge, by his exquisite judgment, or by his heroic valour? It was by none of these qualities. But he was, first of all, the most powerful prince in Europe, and consequently held the highest rank among kings; and then, says his historian, 'he surpassed all his courtiers in the gracefulness of his shape, and the majestic beauty of his features. The sound of his voice, noble and affecting, gained those hearts which his presence intimidated. He had a step and a deportment which could suit only him and his rank, and which would have been ridiculous in any other person. The embarrassment which he occasioned to those who spoke to him, flattered that secret satisfaction with which he felt his own superiority.' These frivolous accomplishments, supported by his rank, and, no doubt too, by a degree of other talents and virtues, which seems, however, not to have been much above mediocrity, established this prince in the esteem of his own age, and have drawn, even from posterity, a good deal of respect for his memory. Compared with these, in his own times, and in his own presence, no other virtue, it seems, appeared to have any merit. Knowledge, industry, valour, and beneficence, trembled, were abashed, and lost all dignity before them.'

Woman also thus 'in herself complete,' by possessing all these *frivolous* accomplishments, so changes the nature of things

———That what she wills to do or say
Seems wisest, virtuousest, discreetest, best;
All higher knowledge in *her presence* falls
Degraded. Wisdom in discourse with her
Loses discountenanc'd, and, like Folly, shows;
Authority and Reason on her wait.' –

And all this is built on her loveliness!

In the middle rank of life, to continue the comparison, men, in their youth, are prepared for professions, and marriage is not considered as the grand feature in their lives; whilst women, on the contrary, have no other scheme to sharpen their faculties. It is not business, extensive plans, or any of the excursive flights of ambition, that engross their attention; no, their thoughts are not employed in rearing such noble structures. To rise in the world, and have the liberty of running from pleasure to pleasure, they must marry advantageously, and to this object their time is sacrificed, and their persons often legally prostituted. A man when he enters any profession has his eye steadily fixed on some future advantage (and the mind gains great strength by having all its efforts directed to one point), and, full of his business, pleasure is considered as mere relaxation; whilst women seek for pleasure as the main purpose of existence. In fact, from the education, which they receive from society, the love of pleasure may be said to govern them all; but does this prove that there is a sex in souls? It would be just as rational to declare that the courtiers in France, when a destructive system of despotism had formed their character, were not men, because liberty, virtue, and humanity, were sacrificed to pleasure and vanity. – Fatal passions, which ever domineered over the *whole* race!

The same love of pleasure, fostered by the whole tendency of their education, gives a trifling turn to the conduct of women in most circumstances: for instance, they are ever anxious about secondary things; and on the watch for adventures, instead of being occupied by duties.

A man, when he undertakes a journey, has, in general, the end in view; a woman thinks more of the incidental occurrences, the strange things that may possibly occur on the road; the impression that she may make on her fellow-travellers; and, above all, she is anxiously intent on the care of the finery that she carries with her, which is more than ever a part of herself, when going to figure on a new scene; when, to use an apt French turn of expression, she is going to produce a sensation. – Can dignity of mind exist with such trivial cares?

In short, women, in general, as well as the rich of both sexes, have acquired all the follies and vices of civilization, and missed the useful fruit. It is not necessary for me always to premise, that I speak of the condition of the whole sex, leaving exceptions out of the question. Their senses are inflamed, and their understandings neglected, consequently they become the prey of their senses, delicately termed sensibility, and are blown about by every momentary gust of feeling. Civilized women are, therefore, so weakened by false refinement, that, respecting morals, their condition is much below what it would be were they left in a state nearer to nature. Ever restless and anxious, their over exercised sensibility not only renders them uncomfortable themselves, but troublesome, to use a soft phrase, to others. All their thoughts turn on things calculated to excite emotion; and feeling, when they should reason, their conduct is unstable, and their opinions are wavering – not the wavering produced by deliberation or progressive views, but by contradictory emotions. By fits and starts they are warm in many pursuits; yet this warmth, never concentrated into perseverance, soon exhausts itself; exhaled by its own heat, or meeting with some other fleeting passion, to which reason has never given any specific gravity, neutrality ensues. Miserable, indeed, must be that being whose cultivation of mind has only tended to inflame its passions! A distinction should be made between inflaming and strengthening them. The passions thus pampered, whilst the judgment is left unformed, what can be expected to ensue? – Undoubtedly, a mixture of madness and folly! . . .

Another argument that has had great weight with me, must, I think, have some force with every considerate benevolent heart. Girls who have been thus weakly educated, are often cruelly left by their parents without any provision; and, of course, are dependent on, not only the reason, but the bounty of their brothers. These brothers are, to view the fairest side of the question, good sort of men, and give as a favour, what children of the same parents had an equal right to. In this equivocal humiliating situation, a docile female may remain some time, with a tolerable degree of comfort. But, when the brother marries, a probable circumstance, from being considered as the mistress of the family, she is viewed with averted looks as an intruder, an unnecessary burden on the benevolence of the master of the house, and his new partner.

Who can recount the misery, which many unfortunate beings, whose minds and bodies are equally weak, suffer in such situations – unable to work, and ashamed to beg? The wife, a cold-hearted, narrow-minded, woman, and this is not an unfair supposition; for the present mode of education does not tend to enlarge the heart any more than the understanding, is jealous of the little kindness which her husband shews to his relations; and her sensibility not rising to humanity, she is displeased at seeing the property of *her* children lavished on a helpless sister.

These are matters of fact, which have come under my eye again and again. The consequence is obvious, the wife has recourse to cunning to undermine the habitual affection, which she is afraid openly to oppose; and neither tears nor caresses are spared till the spy is worked out of her home, and thrown on the world, unprepared for its difficulties; or sent, as a great effort of generosity, or from some regard to propriety, with a small stipend, and an uncultivated mind, into joyless solitude.

These two women may be much upon a par, with respect to reason and humanity; and changing situations, might have acted just the same selfish part; but had they been differently educated, the case would also have been very different. The wife would not have had that sensibility, of which self is the centre, and reason might have taught her not to expect, and not even to be flattered by, the affection of her husband, if it led him to violate prior duties. She would wish not to love him merely because he loved her, but on account of his virtues; and the sister might have been able to struggle for herself instead of eating the bitter bread of dependence.

I am, indeed, persuaded that the heart, as well as the understanding, is opened by cultivation; and by, which may not appear so clear, strengthening the organs; I am not now talking of momentary flashes of sensibility, but of affections. And, perhaps, in the education of both sexes, the most difficult task is so to adjust instruction as not to narrow the understanding, whilst the heart is warmed by the generous juices of spring, just raised by the electric fermentation of the season; nor to dry up the feelings by employing the mind in investigations remote from life.

With respect to women, when they receive a careful education, they are either made fine ladies, brimful of sensibility, and teeming with capricious fancies; or mere notable women. The latter are often friendly, honest creatures, and have a shrewd kind of good sense joined with worldly prudence, that often render them more useful members of society than the fine sentimental lady, though they possess neither greatness of mind nor taste. The intellectual world is shut against them; take them out of their family or neighbourhood, and they stand still; the mind finding no employment, for literature affords a fund of amusement which they have never sought to relish, but frequently to despise. The sentiments and taste of more cultivated minds appear ridiculous, even in those whom chance and family connections have led them to love; but in mere acquaintance they think it all affectation.

A man of sense can only love such a woman on account of her sex, and respect her, because she is a trusty servant. He lets her, to preserve his own peace, scold the servants, and go to church in clothes made of the very best materials. A man of her own size of understanding would, probably, not agree so well with her; for he might wish to encroach on her prerogative, and manage some domestic concerns himself. Yet women, whose minds are not enlarged by cultivation, or the natural selfishness of sensibility expanded by reflection, are very unfit to manage a family; for, by an undue stretch of power, they are always tyrannizing to support a superiority that only rests on the arbitrary distinction of fortune. The evil is sometimes more serious, and domestics are deprived of innocent indulgences, and made to work beyond their strength, in order to enable the notable woman to keep a better table, and outshine her neighbours in finery and parade. If she attend to her children, it is, in general, to dress them in a costly manner – and, whether this attention arise from vanity or fondness, it is equally pernicious.

Besides, how many women of this description pass their days; or, at least, their evenings, discontentedly. Their husbands acknowledge that they are good managers, and chaste wives; but leave home to seek for more agreeable, may I be allowed to use a significant French word, *piquant* society; and the patient drudge, who fulfils her task, like a blind horse in a mill, is defrauded of her just reward; for the wages due to her are the caresses of her husband; and women who have so few resources in themselves, do not very patiently bear this privation of a natural right.

A fine lady, on the contrary, has been taught to look down with contempt on the vulgar employments of life; though she has only been incited to acquire accomplishments that rise a degree above sense; for even corporeal accomplishments cannot be acquired with any degree of precision unless the understanding has been strengthened by exercise. Without a foundation of principles taste is superficial, grace must arise from something deeper than imitation. The imagination, however, is heated, and the feelings rendered fastidious, if not sophisticated; or, a counterpoise of judgment is not acquired, when the heart still remains artless, though it becomes too tender.

These women are often amiable; and their hearts are really more sensible to general benevolence, more alive to the sentiments that civilize life, than the square-elbowed family drudge; but, wanting a due proportion of reflection and self-government, they only inspire love; and are the mistresses of their husbands, whilst they have any hold on their affections; and the platonic friends of his male acquaintance. These are the fair defects in nature; the women who appear to be created not to enjoy the fellowship of man, but to save him from sinking into absolute brutality, by rubbing off the rough angles of his character; and by playful dalliance to give some dignity to the appetite that draws him to them. – Gracious Creator of the whole human race! hast thou created such a being as woman, who can trace thy wisdom in thy works, and feel that thou alone art by thy nature exalted above her, – for no better purpose? – Can she believe that she was only made to submit to man, her equal, a being, who, like her, was sent into the world to acquire virtue? – Can she consent to be occupied merely to please him; merely to adorn the earth, when her soul is capable of rising to thee? – And can she rest supinely dependent on man for reason, when she ought to mount with him the arduous steeps of knowledge? –

Yet, if love be the supreme good, let women be only educated to inspire it, and let every charm be polished to intoxicate the senses; but, if they be moral beings, let them have a chance to become intelligent; and let love to man be only a part of that glowing flame of universal love, which, after encircling humanity, mounts in grateful incense to God . . .

It would almost provoke a smile of contempt, if the vain absurdities of man did not strike us on all sides, to observe, how eager men are to degrade the sex from whom they pretend to receive the chief pleasure of life; and I have frequently with full conviction retorted Pope's sarcasm on them; or, to speak explicitly, it has appeared to me applicable to the whole human race. A love of pleasure or sway seems to divide mankind, and the husband who lords it in his little haram thinks only of his pleasure or his convenience. To such lengths, indeed, does an intemperate love of pleasure carry some prudent men, or worn out libertines, who marry to have a safe bed-fellow, that they seduce their own wives. – Hymen banishes modesty, and chaste love takes its flight.

Love, considered as an animal appetite, cannot long feed on itself without expiring. And this extinction in its own flame, may be termed the violent death of love. But the wife who has thus been rendered licentious, will probably endeavour to fill the void left by the loss of her husband's attentions; for she cannot contentedly become merely an upper servant after having been treated like a goddess.

She is still handsome, and, instead of transferring her fondness to her children, she only dreams of enjoying the sunshine of life. Besides, there are many husbands so devoid of sense and parental affection, that during the first effervescence of voluptuous fondness they refuse to let their wives suckle their children. They are only to dress and live to please them: and love – even innocent love, soon sinks into lasciviousness when the exercise of a duty is sacrificed to its indulgence.

Personal attachment is a very happy foundation for friendship; yet, when even two virtuous young people marry, it would, perhaps, be happy if some circumstances checked their passion; if the recollection of some prior attachment, or disappointed affection, made it on one side, at least, rather a match founded on esteem. In that case they would look beyond the present moment, and try to render the whole of life respectable, by forming a plan to regulate a friendship which only death ought to dissolve.

Friendship is a serious affection; the most sublime of all affections, because it is founded on principle, and cemented by time. The very reverse may be said of love. In a great degree, love and friendship cannot subsist in the same bosom; even when inspired by different objects they weaken or destroy each other, and for the same object can only be felt in succession. The vain fears and fond jealousies, the winds which fan the flame of love, when judiciously or artfully tempered, are both incompatible with the tender confidence and sincere respect of friendship.

Love, such as the glowing pen of genius has traced, exists not on earth, or only resides in those exalted, fervid imaginations that have sketched such dangerous pictures. Dangerous, because they not only afford a plausible excuse, to the voluptuary who disguises sheer sensuality under a sentimental veil; but as they spread affectation, and take from the dignity of virtue. Virtue, as the very word imports, should have an appearance of seriousness, if not of austerity; and to endeavour to trick her out in the garb of pleasure, because the epithet has been used as another name for beauty, is to exalt her on a quicksand; a most insidious attempt to hasten her fall by apparent respect. Virtue and pleasure are not, in fact, so nearly allied in this life as some eloquent writers have laboured to prove. Pleasure prepares the fading wreath, and mixes the intoxicating cup; but the fruit which virtue gives, is the recompence of toil: and, gradually seen as it ripens, only affords calm satisfaction; nay, appearing to be the result of the natural tendency of things, it is scarcely observed. Bread, the common food of life, seldom thought of as a blessing, supports the constitution and preserves health; still feasts delight the heart of man, though disease and even death lurk in the cup or dainty that elevates the spirits or tickles the palate. The lively heated imagination likewise, to apply the comparison, draws the picture of love, as it draws every other picture, with those glowing colours, which the daring hand will steal from the rainbow that is directed by a mind, condemned in a world like this, to prove its noble origin by panting after unattainable perfection; ever pursuing what it acknowledges to be a fleeting dream. An imagination of this vigorous cast can give existence to insubstantial forms, and stability to the shadowy reveries which the mind naturally falls into when realities are found vapid. It can then depict love with celestial charms, and dote on the grand ideal object – it can imagine a degree of mutual affection that shall refine the soul, and not expire when it has served as a 'scale to heavenly'; and, like devotion, make it absorb every meaner affection and desire. In each others arms, as in a temple, with its summit lost in the clouds, the world is to be shut out, and every thought and wish, that do not nurture pure affection and permanent virtue. – Permanent virtue! alas! Rousseau, respectable visionary! thy paradise would soon be violated by the entrance of some unexpected guest. Like Milton's it would only contain angels, or men sunk below the dignity of rational creatures. Happiness is not material, it cannot be seen or felt! Yet the eager pursuit of the good which every one shapes to his own fancy, proclaims man the lord of this lower world, and to be an intelligential creature, who is not to receive, but acquire happiness. They, therefore, who complain of the delusions of passion, do not recollect that they are exclaiming against a strong proof of the immortality of the soul.

But leaving superior minds to correct themselves, and pay dearly for their experience, it is necessary to observe, that it is not against strong, persevering passions; but romantic wavering feelings that I wish to guard the female heart by exercising the understanding: for these paradisiacal reveries are oftener the effect of idleness than of a lively fancy.

Women have seldom sufficient serious employment to silence their feelings; a round of little cares, or vain pursuits frittering away all strength of mind and organs, they become naturally only objects of sense. – In short, the whole tenour of female education (the education of society) tends to render the best disposed romantic and inconstant; and the remainder vain and mean. In the present state of society this evil can scarcely be remedied, I am afraid, in the slightest degree;

should a more laudable ambition ever gain ground they may be brought nearer to nature and reason, and become more virtuous and useful as they grow more respectable.

But, I will venture to assert that their reason will never acquire sufficient strength to enable it to regulate their conduct, whilst the making an appearance in the world is the first wish of the majority of mankind. To this weak wish the natural affections, and the most useful virtues are sacrificed. Girls marry merely to *better themselves*, to borrow a significant vulgar phrase, and have such perfect power over their hearts as not to permit themselves to *fall in love* till a man with a superiour fortune offers. On this subject I mean to enlarge in a future chapter; it is only necessary to drop a hint at present, because women are so often degraded by suffering the selfish prudence of age to chill the ardour of youth.

From the same source flows an opinion that young girls ought to dedicate great part of their time to needle-work; yet, this employment contracts their faculties more than any other that could have been chosen for them, by confining their thoughts to their persons. Men order their clothes to be made, and have done with the subject; women make their own clothes, necessary or ornamental, and are continually talking about them; and their thoughts follow their hands. It is not indeed the making of necessaries that weakens the mind; but the frippery of dress. For when a woman in the lower rank of life makes her husband's and children's clothes, she does her duty, this is her part of the family business; but when women work only to dress better than they could otherwise afford, it is worse than sheer loss of time. To render the poor virtuous they must be employed, and women in the middle rank of life, did they not ape the fashions of the nobility, without catching their ease, might employ them, whilst they themselves managed their families, instructed their children, and exercised their own minds. Gardening, experimental philosophy, and literature, would afford them subjects to think of and matter for conversation, that in some degree would exercise their understandings. The conversation of French women, who are not so rigidly nailed to their chairs to twist lappets, and knot ribands, is frequently superficial; but, I contend, that it is not half so insipid as that of those English women whose time is spent in making caps, bonnets, and the whole mischief of trimmings, not to mention shopping, bargain-hunting, &c. &c.: and it is the decent, prudent women, who are most degraded by these practices; for their motive is simply vanity. The wanton who exercises her taste to render her passion alluring, has something more in view.

These observations all branch out of a general one, which I have before made, and which cannot be too often insisted upon, for, speaking of men, women, or professions, it will be found that the employment of the thoughts shapes the character both generally and individually. The thoughts of women ever hover round their persons, and is it surprising that their persons are reckoned most valuable? Yet some degree of liberty of mind is necessary even to form the person; and this may be one reason why some gentle wives have so few attractions beside that of sex. Add to this, sedentary employments render the majority of women sickly – and false notions of female excellence make them proud of this delicacy, though it be another fetter, that by calling the attention continually to the body, cramps the activity of the mind.

Women of quality seldom do any of the manual part of their dress, consequently only their taste is exercised, and they acquire, by thinking less of the finery, when the business of their toilet is over, that ease, which seldom appears in the deportment of women, who dress merely for the sake of dressing. In fact, the observation with respect to the middle rank, the one in which talents thrive best, extends not to women; for those of the superior class, by catching, at least, a smattering of literature, and conversing more with men, on general topics, acquire more knowledge than the women who ape their fashions and faults without sharing their advantages. With respect to virtue, to use the word in a comprehensive sense, I have seen most in low life. Many poor women maintain their childen by the sweat of their brow, and keep together families that the vices of the fathers would have scattered abroad; but gentlewomen are too indolent to be actively virtuous, and are softened rather than refined by civilization. Indeed, the good sense which I have met with, among the poor women who have had few advantages of education, and yet have acted heroically, strongly confirmed me in the opinion that trifling employments have rendered woman a trifler. Man, taking her body, the mind is left to rust; so that while physical love enervates man, as being his favourite recreation, he will endeavour to enslave woman: – and, who can tell, how many generations may be necessary to give vigour to the virtue and talents of the freed posterity of abject slaves?

In tracing the causes that, in my opinion, have degraded woman, I have confined my observations to such as universally act upon the morals and manners of the whole sex, and to me it appears clear that they all spring from want of understanding. Whether this arise from a physical or accidental weakness of faculties, time alone can determine; for I shall not lay any great stress on the example of a few women who, from having received a masculine education, have acquired courage and resolution; I only contend that the men who have been placed in similar situations, have acquired a similar character – I speak of bodies of men, and that men of genius and talents have started out of a class, in which women have never yet been placed. [*A vindication*, 4: 'Observations on the state of degradation to which woman is reduced by various causes']

War and international relations

CHARLES-IRENEE CASTEL DE SAINT-PIERRE

BIOGRAPHICAL NOTE

Charles-Irénée Castel de Saint-Pierre (1658–1743) was born into a noble family near Barfleur in Normandy. He was educated at the Jesuit Collège de Caen. Never either professionally or spiritually a committed churchman (he called religion 'small-pox of the mind'), by 1686 he was in Paris just at the point when Louis XIV's reign was starting to lose its glitter, and opposition, with which Saint-Pierre was soon associated, was growing. His interests in economics, politics and moral philosophy developed quickly in Paris, where he was soon an active participant in the free-thinking circles that heralded the dawn of the French Enlightenment. Influenced by representatives of the new scepticism such as Fontenelle, Varignon and scientists such as Du Vernay, Huygens and Cassini, Saint-Pierre became part of the great intellectual reorientation of the period towards empirical observation and experimentation, in which the values of tradition and authority had little role to play. A worldly and well-liked figure, who moved at the highest levels of society, he purchased a position at court in 1692, and took his seat in the Academy in 1694.

It was during this period that he started to assemble material for his *Political annals* (1757), and immersed himself in politics and international law. In 1702 he became first chaplain to the Duchesse d'Orléans, who subsequently made him abbé of Tiron. Between 1708 and 1730 Saint-Pierre published an astonishing number of pamphlets on a wide variety of subjects: on the repair of the highways (1708), on the policing of the highways (1715), on duelling (1715), on the Bull Unigenitus (1718), on education (1728), the reform of spelling (1730) and many other subjects.

In 1712 Polignac took him as a secretary to Utrecht for the peace negotiations that were to bring the War of the Spanish Succession to an end. From this experience, enabling him to witness at first hand the complexities of international diplomacy (Utrecht involved eleven separate treaties), and offering him the chance to study Dutch culture and institutions, he conceived the project to draft a set of articles, proposals and reflections in the form of his best-known work, *A plan for perpetual peace in Europe*. In 1716 he published a *Memoir on the establishment of proportional taxation*. This was followed in 1718 by the *Discourse on polysynody*, a treatise on the use of councils in government, and containing open criticism of the new regent's policies of centralisation, as well as an attack on Louis XIV's record. The ensuing scandal resulted in Saint-Pierre's expulsion from the Academy. Together with d'Argenson and Alary, he became a founder-member of a circle of freethinkers, the *Club de l'entresol*.

    A plan for perpetual peace in Europe was published in 1712, the first edition being a heavily annotated volume with no title page, signed and dated in the author's hand, and dedicated to the Marquis de Torey. Thirty-six copies were printed to distribute to friends for their comments. The *Plan* was then published in Cologne by 'J. Le Pacifique' later in the same year as the *Memoir for perpetual peace in Europe*. Another edition was brought out in Utrecht in 1713 and 1717, and it was reprinted in 1747 and 1761.

EDITORIAL NOTE

The base text for the translated extracts is the annotated copy of the first edition of the *Plan*, the *Mémoire pour rendre la paix perpétuelle en Europe*, printed without title page, and signed and dated by the author '1 septembre 1712' (Bibliothèque Nationale E. 2232). The recent edition of the *Projet*, edited by S. Goyard-Fabre (Paris, Garnier, 1981), has also been consulted.

FURTHER READING

Perkins, M., *The moral and political philosophy of the abbé de Saint-Pierre* (Paris and Geneva, Droz, 1959).
  'Six French *philosophes* on human rights, international rivalry, and war: their message today', *Studies on Voltaire and the Eighteenth Century*, 260 (1989), pp. 1–158. See section 1 ('Saint-Pierre: violence and its control'), pp. 3–22.

A plan for perpetual peace in Europe (1712)

About four years ago, after completing the first draft of some regulations relating to the kingdom's internal trade, having seen with my own eyes the utter poverty to which nations are reduced by heavy taxes, and informed by various personal accounts of excessive levies, pillaging, fires, violence, cruelty and murder suffered every day by those unfortunates living on the frontiers of Christian states, in short, moved deeply by all the evils that war causes for Europe's rulers, and for their subjects, I resolved to investigate the original sources of the evil, and deduce from my own reflections whether this evil really was linked to the nature of sovereign states, or rulers, and whether it was absolutely incurable. I started digging into the subject by ascertaining whether or not it was possible to find practical ways to end all their future disputes *without declaring war*, and thereby establishing permanent peace between them . . .

1. *The present constitution of Europe can only ever result in continuous warfare because it could never provide a sufficient guarantee of the implementation of treaties.*

2. *The balance of power between the House of France and the House of Austria could not provide sufficient guarantee either against foreign wars or against civil wars, and in consequence could not provide sufficient guarantee either against the preservation of states or trade.*

The first step needed to be taken to find a definite cure for a great, deeply rooted evil, to which so far only completely ineffective remedies have been applied, is to analyse all the various causes of the evil on the one hand, and on the other the inappropriate nature of these remedies in relation to the evil itself.

I then sought to discover whether or not rulers could find some form of *sufficient guarantee* that the commitments they gave each other would be carried out through the creation of a permanent machinery for arbitration between them. I found that if, in order to preserve their present forms of government, avoid war between themselves, and secure all the advantages of continuous trade between one nation and another, the eighteen major sovereign powers of Europe were willing to sign a treaty of union, and set up a permanent congress more or less on the same model as either that of the seven sovereign Dutch states, or that of the thirteen sovereign Swiss states, or the sovereign states of Germany, and found the European Union on what was good about these unions, and especially the *Germanic Union.* [This European Union would be] made up of more than two hundred sovereign states, of which the weakest would have *sufficient guarantee* that the great power of the strongest could not harm them, that each would keep exactly to their mutual agreements, that trade would never be disrupted, and that all future disputes would be ended *without declaring war* through arbitration, without which such a guarantee could never be achieved.

Here are the major sovereign Christian powers who would each have a voice in the General Diet of Europe: (1) France; (2) Spain; (3) England; (4) Holland; (5) Portugal; (6) Switzerland and its associated territories; (7) Florence and its associated territories; (8) Genoa and its associated territories; (9) the Vatican State;

(10) Venice; (11) Savoy; (12) Lorraine; (13) Denmark; (14) Courlande with Danzig, etc.; (15) The Emperor and the Holy Roman Empire; (16) Poland; (17) Sweden; (18) Moscow . . .

RECAPITULATION

(1) This is a project of the greatest importance for the peace and happiness of Europe; therefore no effort should be spared to make it succeed. (2) It has the disadvantage of new ideas, or of ideas that seem new, and with which the reader might not be accustomed, so he must be helped to remember the judgements he might have made on each section [of the treatise]. (3) To be in a position to judge a work rich in [detailed] argument, it is necessary not only to have examined each discourse separately, but if possible to see them in closer order and proximity to each other in order to better appreciate their combined impact. (4) If this is necessary just to make a good judgement on a purely speculative system, it is even more necessary when it is a question of prevailing upon the reader to act in the light of what he reads. Now this work will have two types of reader: those very important ones, few in number, either sovereign rulers or ministers of European states, or those around ministers with most influence over their thinking.

It is a matter of prevailing upon rulers to form a committee, a junta, a board, a congregation, or a council specifically to examine whether or not something useful, both for rulers and the ruled, can be extracted from this essay, and to turn it into something appropriate enough to be the subject of negotiation between a few neighbouring sovereigns. The other type is the ordinary reader who can only get hold of accurate translations and new editions, but who, by speaking with one voice, can put pressure on government officials to examine the work more promptly and with greater attention. This is still about prevailing upon people to act. Now in every case it seems to me that it is up to the author to help the reader's memory, and his duty to present them with this eight- or nine-page summary. This might make more of an impression on them than the eight or nine hundred pages of details they have seen.

In every century, the most powerful of rulers have felt like the least powerful, and those coming to the end of their reign who are ready to leave their lands to regents, would be very glad to assure their successors of a peace that would be unchangeable inside and outside their country, and would be a vital, powerful protection against internal plots. There is not one who has not felt personally the damage incurred by the disruption of trade and by the weight of prodigious expenditure. All of them have wished, not for a truce, but for a true peace, a peace that would last for ever, and this has always included the most foolish along with the most powerful, as well as all republics and republican states.

But what preventative measures have they taken so far to avoid war? Only treaties, that is to say, futile and ineffective treaties by which they make promises to each other. Experience has demonstrated the ineffectiveness of this only too well:

1. Among the signatories to such treaties, a number have signed unwillingly, forced into doing so by great fear. This is a case of the weakest deferring against his will to the strongest, and then waiting for the first opportunity to break the treaty, and get out of keeping his promise.

2. Even when promises might have been made without any pressure, one of the parties is often aggrieved and regrets making them, and as it can refuse to execute the terms of the treaty on the slightest pretext *with impunity*, the treaty is no longer operative.

3. In vain have rulers passed laws relating to their treaties to take account of particular issues arising. Further issues crop up every day that they have not fore-seen, and that would have been impossible for them to foresee. And that is a great pretext for whoever believes himself to be the strongest to make unfair demands, and to start the war up again because he can do so *with impunity*.

We have noticed that individuals, living as members of a permanently estab-lished association, are not in such an unsatisfactory position. Their disputes are resolved either by mutual promises written down in contracts, or by judges appointed by society to settle any issues for which provision has not been made in their contracts, and without anyone having recourse to arms. The reason why they keep strictly to their mutual promises is that these promises have the backing of a permanent association which is ready to use force to restrain the party wishing to renege on his promise. Why do they obey punctiliously the decisions of soci-ety's representatives, or rather society's judges? Because they cannot resist *with impunity*. Why does the strongest, the most violent, the most hot-headed among them not have recourse to arms? Because he knows without a moment's doubt that he cannot commit any act of violence *with impunity*, and that, not only is his wealth at stake, but also his life if he was to cause someone's death, either directly or indirectly. So [there will be] no war between members of a permanently established association. There are disputes, but they are all ended *without declaring war*, and it is business as usual.

Europe's rulers, having no *permanently established form of association*, have felt inescapably exposed to the miseries of almost continuous warfare. In this situation they have been concerned only with protecting themselves from the worst of misfortunes, that is to say, of being thrown off their thrones by the victors:

1. During truces they have kept on guard against each other for fear of surprise attacks, fortifications, munitions, arsenals, troops – all the things that involve high expenditure, but an expenditure that is absolutely necessary until a permanent association is set up.

2. The weakest have sought to make out of their confederations defensive and offensive treaties against the strongest, but these were treaties that did not last long, and were more or less useless because any of the members of the confederacy could *with impunity* withdraw from being bound by them. So no *sufficient guarantee* in that quarter.

3. When the weaker states saw two sovereign rulers in Germany with formidable power, they tried to keep them divided fearing that they might be over-run by one of them. When the rulers of Europe saw the House of France and the House of Austria becoming much more powerful than the rest of them, they put all their efforts into keeping them divided, establishing what amounted to a balance of power. Given the need to wage continuous warfare, that is all that the most skilful politicians have been able to come up with so far to stop the strongest from destroying the weakest, and give mutual protection to their territory, religion and laws.

We have seen how fragile this notion of balance is, and how many advantages the establishment of a *permanent association* between Europe's princes would have over the theory of balance. We have seen that this association would ensure the meticulous implementation of promises, that is to say, of the laws that rulers would impose on themselves through their treaties, that none of them would be able to get out of [these commitments] *with impunity* just because of disputes that might arise, or because of issues that were ill-defined in the treaties, or which might not have been foreseen. Such disputes would be settled by the rulers themselves through their representatives. We have seen that nobody could *with impunity* avoid implementing these decisions, that nobody could *with impunity* take up arms to resist the Association, and that therefore there would be no more fear of war, either inside or outside the state. [We have seen that] there would be no more disruption to trade, that each ruler would be spared the enormous expense involved in either maintaining vigilance during truces, or defending themselves in time of war, and that no system of balance could ever secure such advantages. We have seen that the Germans, having learned from sad experience that this system of balance was inadequate as a protection, have gone as far as to create a *permanent form of association* between themselves.

I offered some reflections on the unhappy life of savages. In truth, they depend on no ruler, no laws, no society; but because of the need to survive they are very dependent on the seasons. They even depend on wild animals, and what is even more terrible about their state of dependency is that they are dependent on their neighbours, who are no better than wild animals themselves, and could rob them with impunity of their property, and even their lives. They are not supported by the arts and by trade because they have no laws or any form of permanent association that could *punish* those who break the laws. In vain have they entered into treaties between families and between villages. In vain have they given each other promises to enjoy in peace what they have. They have no guarantee that these promises will be kept. In vain have the weakest set up confederations to protect themselves from the violence of the strongest. In vain have they tried to keep the latter divided, and to maintain a sort of balance between them. All of these precautions are useless as long as they have no *permanent form of association strong enough and determined enough to punish infringements.* We have been able to note easily the difference between our lives and theirs. We do in truth depend on laws, and on a society that protects those laws; but we are no longer dependent on each other. We are no longer each other's mortal enemy. Unlike them, we no longer behave like wild animals towards each other. Our conventions are observed because they cannot be transgressed *with impunity.* Thus we have the arts and trade, and with the help of the arts and trade we have all the guarantees, all the security, all the comforts and all the pleasures of life. Who would be so eccentric as to prefer the life of savages, with their independence of all laws combined with their difficult continual dependence on each other, to the lives that we lead quite independently of each other in conjunction with our dependency on the law? Who would be so foolish as to prefer their misery to our happiness, the life of their richest to that of our richest? . . .

I have examined the motives that the German rulers might have had in those early days for agreeing to a treaty of *permanent association*, and I have not discovered any that our rulers do not have for signing a similar treaty. Each ruler wanted to keep his territory intact as it stood; each wanted to acquire through the Association sure and sufficient protection for himself and his descendants from all plots, rebellions, civil wars and foreign wars. Each wanted to get from this Association a sufficient guarantee that future treaties would be implemented. Each wanted to be spared the expense and misery of war. Each wanted to maintain trade between their subjects. Now, do our current sovereign rulers not have the same motives? And have we not seen that as the European Association will be much more powerful than the Germanic Association, we will never have to fear that any member might ever wish to disturb the peace, as had happened often in Germany, that there will never be any ruler in Europe in a position to support a rebel member? Now, since permanent peace will be immeasurably more certain in the European Association, the motives for wanting it to come into existence will be immeasurably stronger than those that sufficed to create the Germanic Association . . .

After surveying the motives and the obstacles, I examined the means used by the German rulers to make their treaty and set up this Association, and it so happens that they did not have any that we do not have, and that we even have some that they did not have:

(1) They agreed to be satisfied with what they possessed currently. (2) They agreed to take the path of arbitration to settle their future differences. (3) They agreed that anyone who refused to implement his promises or the decision of the arbitrators would be banished from Europe. (4) They agreed to find money for the establishment of circles so that they could vote and have their votes counted. Now, would our twenty-four rulers, each with a vote, not be like the twenty-four circles of Europe? And who can say that we could not agree to a roughly similar and equivalent arrangement just as easily as they did? (5) They had no model in front of them, but we have one in front of us. (6) They made the error of electing a permanent Head, and as they have felt through experience how harmful this article in their treaty is to their liberty, what we still have, that they did not have, is their unhappy experience of the article relating to the position of the Head. For being able to profit, not only from what is good in a model, but also from what turns out to be defective in it, is a way of creating something better and more solid . . .

Until someone shows me in detail why the project is impossible, and why it is irremediably so, is it not obvious that the European Union seems to be so viable, so practical, so desirable to everyone that those with the most to gain would be making a big mistake not to make the attempt to set it up by putting the project up for discussion in their own countries, and then holding negotiations about it with some of their neighbours and, if a General Congress of Europe already existed, to have the project discussed by authorised representatives in the very place where the Congress is being held? Thus it remains a demonstrated fact that the Germanic Union is really a model for a much greater Union, and that this model can be developed, gradually and painlessly, and to a greater degree of perfection, into the *European Union.*

JEAN BARBEYRAC

BIOGRAPHICAL NOTE

Jean Barbeyrac (1674–1744) was born into a family of Huguenots in Béziers, and he was educated at the Calvinist Collège de Montagnac, and subsequently at the Lausanne Academy. In 1693 he was sent to Geneva to study theology with a view to following an ecclesiastical career. By 1697 Barbeyrac was in Berlin studying law. He became an associate member of the Berlin Academy of Sciences in 1713, and Rector at Lausanne in the following year, a post from which he resigned when requested to sign the profession of faith required of all public servants in that city. After completing his doctorate in law at Basel, he was appointed to the chair of Natural Law at Groningen, where he remained for the rest of his life.

Barbeyrac is the author of numerous articles and books on the philosophy of law, but his reputation and importance are based on his well-annotated and very free translations of the work of Hugo Grotius, widely recognised as the founder of the modern school of natural law philosophy, and of his successor, Pufendorf. Their classic formulations of natural law theory became familiar to many eighteenth-century readers as a consequence of Barbeyrac's propagation and development of their principles. His translation of Pufendorf's *On the duties of man and citizen according to natural law* is a very free and expanded version of the original, accompanied by notes that were reprinted in many subsequent editions of Pufendorf's works in the eighteenth century. Barbeyrac also translated in the same year Noodt's *On the power of sovereigns and on freedom of conscience*. His *Treatise on gambling, in which the main questions of natural law and morality relating to this matter are examined* (1709) is one of his few completely original works. Barbeyrac is also the translator of Richard Cumberland's *Philosophical treatise on natural law* (1744).

EDITORIAL NOTE

Barbeyrac's translation of Grotius' treatise on war and peace was first published in 1724. The notes were first translated into English in 1738. The base text for the extracts is the second edition of Barbeyrac's translation of *Le droit de la guerre et de la paix. Par Hugues Grotius. Nouvelle Traduction. Par Jean Barbeyrac. Professeur en droit à Groningue, et membre de la Société Royale des Sciences à Berlin. Avec les notes de l'auteur même qui n'avaient point encore parues en français, et de nouvelles notes du traducteur* (Amsterdam, P. de Coup, 1729). Each extract in the present translation is preceded by the relevant passage from Grotius' text to which Barbeyrac's commentary is keyed. Grotius' text has been italicised.

FURTHER READING

Haakonssen, K., 'Hugo Grotius and the history of political thought', *Political Theory*, 13 (1985), pp. 239–65.

Hochstrasser, T., 'Conscience and reason: the natural law theory of Jean Barbeyrac', *Historical Journal*, 36 (1993), pp. 289–308.

Rosenblatt, H., *Rousseau and Geneva: from the First discourse to the Social contract 1749–1762* (Cambridge, Cambridge University Press, 1997). See pp. 90–9.

Notes on Grotius' *On the law of war and peace* (1724)

The reasons put forward by all who share these views [on embassies and ambassadors] do not lead to any precise conclusion because the rules of the law of nations, which is what this is about, are not the logically demonstrable outcome of fixed, invariable principles, like those of natural law, but of factors that depend on the will of nations. [*Notes*, ii, 18: 'On the law relating to embassies']

In truth, if the consent of nations was the only foundation for ambassadors' rights, it would be very difficult to prove the truth of the maxim in question, and to define the degree to which it is valid. But our author has not studied natural law closely enough, which would have provided him with clear and certain reasons ... There is no difficulty with regard to ambassadors from a friendly country, with whom we are at peace, who have harmed nobody. The most widely accepted and obvious maxims of natural law require an absolute guarantee of their safety, so that if an ambassador is somehow insulted or offended, his master is given a just cause for war.

As far as ambassadors representing an enemy are concerned, and who have done no harm before their arrival, their safety depends entirely on the laws of humanity. For an enemy has the right to harm his enemy. So, leaving aside agreements through which people become in a sense temporary friends, one is only obliged to spare the life of an enemy's ambassador because of humanitarian feelings, which one must never cast aside, and which persuade us to respect everything that encourages peace. Thus when one commits some hostile act against an enemy's ambassador before receiving him, one does not thereby provide a new pretext for war; one is simply confirming the cause for war that the enemy already had, assuming it was legitimate. I say *assuming it was legitimate*, for if the war was unjust, that is to say, that if the person sending the ambassador had actually committed some wrong against the person receiving the ambassador, thereby authorising that person to have recourse to arms, hostile acts committed by the latter against the ambassador do not transfer right to the other side, unless the offender has sent the ambassador to offer his enemy reasonable satisfaction. For that should then be seen as a matter of necessity which changes a perfect obligation into an imperfect one.

But once an enemy's ambassador has been received, one has clearly then committed oneself, albeit generally speaking implicitly, to ensuring his complete safety as long as he does no evil himself. So that if one fails to fulfil this commitment, one thereby furnishes an unjust cause for war, or at the very least one transfers right to the other side, because every agreement provides a perfect right. We need not even make an exception for the *heralds* who are sent to declare war, provided they do it in a way that has nothing offensive about it. For, according to the custom of civilised peoples, this declaration implies a proclamation that one wishes to use force of arms in accordance with true reason, and with the intention of achieving a good peace. So much for innocent ambassadors.

With respect to ambassadors who have incurred guilt in some way, they have done evil either *of their own accord*, or *on their master's orders*. If it is *of their own accord*, they lose the right to safety, when the crime is horrible and clear-cut. For an ambassador, whoever he might be, can never be in a more privileged position than his master. Now the master himself would never be forgiven such a crime. By *horrible crime* we must understand in this context those crimes which tend either to disrupt the state, or to cause the death of the subjects of the prince to whom the ambassador has been sent, or to cause serious harm to their honour or their property, particularly in the case of people close to the prince. When the crime offends the state, or the head of state, directly, whether the ambassador has actually used violence or not, that is to say, incited subjects to some act of sedition, or plotted against the state, or supported a plot, or taken up arms with the rebels or with the enemy, or incited the enemy's supporters to take up arms, vengeance can be taken on him; he can even be killed, not as a subject, but as an enemy. For even his master could not have expected better treatment.

If he is spared, his master is obliged to surrender him, when requested to do so. But when the crime, however horrible and clear-cut, hurts only a private individual, the ambassador must not for that reason be seen as an enemy of the state, or of the prince. But since, if his master had committed this kind of crime, one would ask him for compensation, and not take up arms against him unless he refused to give it, the same principle of equity requires the person in whose state the crime had been committed to send the ambassador back to his master with a request to surrender him, or punish him. For to keep him in prison until his master either recalls him for punishment, or announces that he is abandoning him, would be to show a mistrust of the master's system of justice, and thus in a way insult him, for the ambassador still represents him. What is more, when one does not have the right to punish a person, one does not normally have the right to seize his person either.

It is another matter when the crime has been committed on the orders of his master, for in that case it would be unwise to return the ambassador to him, as one would have every reason to believe that the person who had ordered the crime to be carried out would take care neither to give up the culprit, nor to punish him. Thus one can keep the person of the ambassador under lock and key until his master has made up for the offence committed, whether by his ambassador or by himself. As far as people who do not represent the person of the prince are concerned, such as simple messengers or envoys, these can be killed on the spot if, for example, they have come to insult another prince on their master's orders. Nothing is more absurd than the claim that every evil deed that ambassadors do on the orders of their master should be solely the responsibility of that master. If that was the case, ambassadors would have more privileges abroad than their master would have, if he were to come himself; and the country's sovereign conversely would have less power in his own land than a father has in his own household.

Moreover, even when the justice of a war is as clear as day, it does not seem right to force Christians to bear arms. [*Notes*, **ii**, **24**: 'How persons of lower rank can legitimately bear arms for persons of higher rank']

In truth, it is good not to force anyone, as long as enough homegrown or foreign soldiers can be found, and as long as they join up on a voluntary basis. But as a shortage of troops could happen, the state would find itself defenceless if the sovereign was never allowed to force his subjects to bear arms for any just cause he might have. Mr Buddeus who thinks, along with our author, that a subject should not take up arms to serve his prince if he has any doubts about it, maintains, nevertheless, that when the just nature of a war is clear, a prince can oblige his subjects to march off to war ... Regarding that, I am not sure whether the principles of this clever author are sufficiently coherent. For however well founded a prince believes his justifications to be, and although they might actually be well founded, as soon as his subjects say that they do not find them to be so, and that they have doubts about their soundness, as each man is the sole judge of what goes on in his own conscience, they will never be persuaded of the justice of their cause, and consequently they should never be forced. The truth is that, as a necessary consequence of the very constitution of civil societies, a sovereign has the complete right to force his subjects to bear arms when he determines to fight a war for reasons that can be justified and substantiated, and when an insufficient number of people are joining up voluntarily, without having to take into consideration the scruples of those whose strong arms he urgently needs. But I believe that it is quite rare for subjects to be utterly convinced that a cause is unjust, provided that it is quite clear why it is right. In those circumstances even the simplest of men could scarcely have any doubts, and in my view a doubt does not relieve anyone of the duty of obedience. After all, the conflict between the rights of conscience of a few individuals and the rights of the sovereign might well authorise those individuals to refuse to obey, but would not prevent the sovereign retaining his authority. The good of the state must never be sacrificed to vain scruples.

It is thus permissible to do harm to the person or property of an enemy when you have a just cause for war, and when hostile acts do not go beyond the limits that we have said are prescribed by nature. This applies equally to both parties to the conflict, so that nobody on either side, when captured outside the war-zone, can be treated as a murderer or thief, and no other state can declare war on one of the two enemies for reasons related to that. In a word, the laws of war allow the victor . . . to do anything.

It is not necessary to assume the existence in all this of either a people's tacit consent or an arbitrary right of individuals, the reality of which is unprovable. We can bring forward very good reasons, based on the law of nature itself, relevant to wars of a different kind to the open, formally declared wars to which our author wrongly restricts the [law of] impunity to which he is referring.

Let us suppose that in the independent conditions of the state of nature thirty family chieftains, living together in the same land, but having no other links with each other apart from a sense of neighbourliness and friendship that living near to each other can produce, formed an alliance to attack or repel an army of other family chieftains. I say that neither during nor after this war, could those living in the same land, or elsewhere, who were not in any way part of the alliance, punish as a murderer or thief any member of either of the two sides who happened to fall into their hands, nor should they. They could not do such a thing during the course of the war because that would have meant embracing the cause of one side, and also because, by reason of the fact that they had stayed initially neutral, they had clearly, albeit tacitly, given up the right to involve themselves. They would have even less justification for doing such a thing after the war was over, because as the war could not have ended without some sort of agreement or peace treaty, the interested parties themselves must have given each other a mutual pardon for the evils that each had inflicted on the other.

This is also what it is in the interests of human society to require. For if those who had stayed neutral had nevertheless been authorised to acknowledge acts of hostility committed in other people's wars, and to punish those they deemed to have committed acts that were unjustified, or to take up arms over the issue, then instead of one war, two would have broken out, or more, and that would have been a [further] source of dispute and disorder. The more frequent wars became between human beings, the more it became necessary, for the sake of peace, not to take up lightly the quarrels of others and, when it was judged inappropriate to take sides in a war, to regard everything that happened in that war as having been legitimised by the laws of warfare. The foundation of civil societies only made this impunity all the more necessary, because wars then became, if not more frequent, then at least more prolonged, and accompanied by a larger number of evils.

Thus there is nothing here that requires either the general consent of nations, or anything that is peculiar to formally declared wars fought between two sover-eigns. The issue in question is based on one of the clearest and most general of natural laws, and the custom that most nations have found to be in accordance with this law has only made its practice increasingly the rule because, as I have noted on several occasions, you are assumed to have agreed to a custom when, in the event, you have shown no sign of wishing to be excused from it.

Our author makes an exception for brigands and pirates . . . with respect to the right to possession of material captured in war. Now if those robbers do not have the privilege of impunity, this is because they are robbers, and consequently people whose every act of hostility is clearly unjust, and because they are declared enemies of the human race. Whereas in other types of warfare, it is often quite difficult to judge where right lies with the result that the matter remains, and must remain, unsettled as far as those who are not participants are concerned. As far as civil wars are concerned, for which our author also makes an exception, the reasons I have put forward have even more strength with regard to that sort of warfare than to a war between two kings or two peoples, because the constitu-tion of civil societies, and peace between human beings, places an even greater requirement on foreigners not to involve themselves easily in events happening in [another] state. And moreover, we need to know whether the law of impunity and the right to possession of material captured in war is, or is not, valid between members of the same civil society, either in wars between one part of a republican state and another, or in wars between a king and his subjects. The resolution of this issue depends on other principles.

In conclusion, I cannot see that a declaration of war affects one way or the other the issues in question. Such a declaration is often just a question of ceremony. But whether war is formally declared or not, the reasons that I have set out still apply in all their force.

That if there have been people who, having found a way to have their enemy killed, did not wish to take advantage of this, and even regretted the offers they received to execute the deed, this was either because of their generosity of spirit or because of the confidence they had in their armies, and not because they thought it unjust to use such methods.

But it is not the same thing when we come to murderers who by killing someone commit a perfidious act. They are contravening the law of nations, and at the same time so are their employers. In truth, when it comes to other things, when you use the Ministry of the Wicked against an enemy, however guilty you might be before God, before men you are regarded as being innocent ... But the privilege of this custom has not been extended so far as to allow you, in order to take the life of an enemy, to use the hand of a person who betrays him. Thus those who take such a path are deemed to have violated both the law of nature and the law of nations. [*Notes*, III, 4: 'On the right to kill enemies']

And it must be added that from the way in which our author expresses himself here, he seems to imply that either it is always unlawful, according to natural law, to make use of a traitor to gain some advantage over, or take hostile action against, an enemy, all of which contradicts what he says in the passage I am annotating, or that the law of nations he refers to, which in forbidding the murder of an enemy by the hand of a traitor, applies only to those who have incited him to treason, and not to those profiting from the willingness of a traitor offering his services of his own free will. All of this is indefensible, for those nations who hold the first proposition to be unlawful have also condemned the second.

I do not think, however, that our author has had a change of heart about his distinction, which he discusses again elsewhere, nor that he wishes to restrict his arbitrary rule of the law of nations. But this is the point at which he has let slip an inaccurate expression, and one which, I do not know how, he did not pick up even in his corrections to the work. So when he says here that we *sin against God* and *violate natural law* when we *make use of the Ministry of the Wicked against an enemy and use a traitor's hand to get rid of an enemy*, this must be taken to relate, following the distinction to which I have referred, only to those who seek out this path of action themselves, and incite to treason people to whom the idea would never perhaps have occurred without the bait of the rewards they are promised, or even given in advance. As for the thing itself, here, in my view, is what can be said about it:

1. We must distinguish here between two different types of question: one being whether one is behaving wrongly towards the enemy himself against whom one is using traitors, and the other being whether, although one is doing him no wrong, one is nevertheless committing something bad. It seems to me that, on the assumption that the war is a just one, one is doing no wrong to the enemy, whether one is taking advantage of the opportunity to use a traitor who volunteers his services, or whether one seeks him out and persuades him oneself. The state of war into which the enemy has entered, and into which it is up to him not to enter, in itself authorises any action against him, so that he has no grounds

for complaint, whatever one does. Moreover, one is no more bound to respect the rights he has over his subjects, and the loyalty they owe him because of his position, than their lives and property which one can deprive them of by the laws of war.

2. However, I think that a sovereign with the slightest conscience, utterly convinced of the justice of his cause, will not seek out treasonable acts in order to defeat his enemy, and will not welcome with open arms those offers to commit treason that are volunteered freely. His justified confidence in Heaven's protection, his abhorrence of the perfidy of others, his fear of becoming their accomplice and providing a bad example that might backfire on him, and on others who did not deserve it, will make him either disdain, or accept only with great reluctance, any advantage that he might derive from such a method.

3. This method could not even be regarded as something whose use is always innocent as far as the user is concerned. The state of war, which deprives trade of favourable conditions in which to operate, and which legitimises harm, does not mean, on the other hand, that we have to sever all links with humanity, and does not prevent us from meeting, as far as possible, the obligation to avoid being the cause of some bad act against the enemy, or his family. This is especially relevant to those who have nothing to do with the cause of the war. Now it is an undeniable fact that every traitor commits a deed that is both shameful and criminal, for to say that when just cause is with the other side then the person who betrays his prince is not guilty of a truly perfidious act simply because the person for whose benefit he is committing murder had the right to kill that prince. That, I repeat, is indefensible for in truth a subject must excuse himself from serving his prince in a war that is clearly unjust, but he is not by that same token authorised to take sides with the enemy. And the injustice with which the prince is treating foreigners does not release subjects from the loyalty they owe him. Thus, I agree with our author that we must never consciously persuade or incite an enemy's subjects to act treasonably, because that would be leading them positively and directly into committing an abominable crime which they would not otherwise have been inclined to commit.

4. It is a different matter when one simply takes advantage of the opportunity and of the willingness that one detects in someone who has no need of persuasion. Here the stain of perfidy does not spread to the person who discovers perfidy already in existence in the traitor's heart. That traitor, from the moment he crystallises within himself the will to betray, can be regarded as being as guilty as

when he actually commits the act . . . What all this amounts to is that, for reasons already established, one must only avail oneself of an act of treachery in order to gain some major advantage, or to avoid some great peril. In a word, through a kind of necessity.

5. So much for the law of nature. With regard to the law of nations, to which our author refers, basically just a custom observed by a number of nations, although there is no element of obligation *per se* in this custom, as soon as those nations with which one has an issue to resolve regard even the acceptance of offers to commit certain kinds of perfidy as being unlawful, such as the murder of a prince or a general, then you must submit tacitly to this in ways, and for the reasons, that I state below.

According to the law of nations, which is relevant here, the establishment of a condition of enslavement extends a little further both with regard to people and possessions. For in respect of people, those classed as slaves are not only those who surrender, or who submit voluntarily to slavery on the basis of their word but also, generally speaking, everyone taken prisoner in an open and formally declared war. [**Notes, III, 7: 'On rights over prisoners of war'**]

That is to say, when the custom is to enslave prisoners of war, for our author says later on that this no longer happens today among *Christians*, and that even in days gone by the custom was not accepted by every nation. But here, as with other things that our author links to his arbitrary law of nations, the power of a master over slaves taken in this way does not originate only in custom. If a prisoner of war found that his conditions as a slave were too harsh, it was up to him to avoid them by indicating that he did not wish to recognise as his master the person who had captured him. In so doing he was not in the wrong; he was violating no law to which he could be held subject. All that this amounted to was that he was courting the consequences of exposing himself to the fury of the enemy, and of losing his life for fear of losing his freedom. But if the prisoner made no declaration of intent contrary to the accepted custom between enemy peoples, he was thereby deemed to have submitted to it tacitly, upon which the victor indicated for his part that he wished to spare his life on condition that the prisoner acknowledged him as his master, which he did by not keeping the prisoner in chains or closely guarded, for he was not strictly bound by custom to give the prisoner his life, even if the latter was willing on those terms to submit to slavery. He needed only to let his will be known that he did not wish to accept the prisoner's concessions. Thus the strength of accepted custom was founded only on mutual consent, explicit or implicit, of the victor and the prisoner, from which resulted an assumed contract, easily assumed because of the strong reasons why the custom had been introduced, and which our author will discuss later.

IMMANUEL KANT

BIOGRAPHICAL NOTE

Immanuel Kant (1724–1804), arguably the most celebrated philosopher of the Enlightenment, was born into a poor family of peasants and devoted pietists in Königsberg in East Prussia, one of Frederick the Great's more important garrison towns. Pietism, a fundamentalist reformist tradition within the Lutheran Church with a strong emphasis on duty and conscience, exerted a powerful sway over Kant's early childhood, and also over his later development as a moral philosopher. Although Kant was later to comment disparagingly on his early education at the pietist Collegium Fredericianum, the religious impact that it made on him proved to be tenacious, and is reflected in many aspects of his thought, including his views on universal moral codes. Kant entered the University of Königsberg, at the age of sixteen, to study initially mathematics and physics. He worked as a tutor in Königsberg until 1755 when, after the publication in that year of the *General history of nature and theory of the heavens*, he was given his first appointment at the University. In 1770 he was elected to the chair of metaphysics and logic, and he remained in Königsberg for the rest of his life.

Kant was in every way a product of the Enlightenment, and its leading exponent in eighteenth-century Germany. His international reputation started to grow with the publication of the *Observations on the sentiment of the beautiful and the sublime* (1764), an essay on the nature of man that reflected the influence of Rousseau, 'the Newton of the moral world'. The *Critique of pure reason*, Kant's most celebrated, and for modern philosophers in many ways one of the most important and difficult works of all time, was not published until 1781. This seminal Kantian treatise, dealing with issues relating to metaphysics and epistemology, and containing in the section entitled 'Transcendental dialectic I' the essence of his general political vision, was followed by a shorter, complementary work, the *Prolegomena to any future metaphysic which shall lay claim to being a science* (1783), designed to illuminate the more densely written areas of the *Critique*.

Explicitly political ideas are not to be found in any single essay, and there is no single comprehensive Kantian work on politics. His political thoughts are scattered across a number of essays, two of which appeared in 1784. The first, *An answer to the question: what is Enlightenment?*, reviewed what Kant saw as the dynamic and on-going processes of intellectual liberation that had been unleashed in the Age of Reason (not yet for Kant the Age of Enlightenment), and their implications for German intellectual and political life. The second was the *Idea for a universal history with a cosmopolitan purpose*. These works were then followed by publications reflecting Kant's deep and long-standing interests in ethics and moral theory: the *Foundations of the metaphysic of morals* (1785), and also in his second *Critique*, the *Critique of practical reason* (1788). The trilogy of Kantian *Critiques* was completed with a treatise on aesthetics, the *Critique of judgement* (1790). He did not return to specific political issues until after the outbreak of the French Revolution and Germany's subsequent awakening from its long political sleep. The most notable of these post-Revolution writings are *On the common saying: 'This may be true in theory, but it does not apply in practice'* (1792), *Perpetual peace: a philosophical sketch* (1795), *The metaphysics of morals* (1797) and *The contest of faculties* (1798).

Kant's one brush with the Prussian authorities arose with the accession to the throne of Frederick William II, and as a consequence of the new regime's attempts to end religious toleration in Germany. His opposition resulted in *Religion within the limits of reason alone* (1793), which incurred official displeasure. In addition to these publications, Kant was the author of many other, shorter treatises and essays.

EDITORIAL NOTE

The extracts from *Perpetual peace* are taken from the translation by B. Nisbet,* for which the base text is the first edition of *Zum ewigen Frieden: ein philosophischer Entwurf* (Königsberg, Friedrich Nicolovius, 1795). Kant's text has lengthy annotations which have been omitted.

FURTHER READING

*Reiss, H. (ed.) and Nisbet, B. (trans.), *Kant: political writings* (Cambridge, Cambridge University Press, 1991). See introduction, pp. i–xl.

Riley, P., *Kant's political philosophy* (New Jersey, Rowman and Littlefield, 1983). See particularly chapter 6.

Sullivan, R., *Introduction to Kant's ethics* (Cambridge, Cambridge University Press, 1994).

Williams, H., *Kant's political philosophy* (Oxford, Blackwell, 1983). See chapter 10.

Perpetual peace: a philosophical sketch (1795)

PERPETUAL PEACE

A Dutch innkeeper once put this satirical inscription on his signboard, along with the picture of a graveyard. We shall not trouble to ask whether it applies to men in general, or particularly to heads of state (who can never have enough of war), or only to the philosophers who blissfully dream of perpetual peace. The author of the present essay does, however, make one reservation in advance. The practical politician tends to look down with great complacency upon the political theorist as a mere academic. The theorist's abstract ideas, the practitioner believes, cannot endanger the state, since the state must be founded upon principles of experience; it thus seems safe to let him fire off his whole broadside, and the *worldly-wise* statesman need not turn a hair. It thus follows that if the practical politician is to be consistent, he must not claim, in the event of a dispute with the theorist, to scent any danger to the state in the opinions which the theorist has randomly uttered in public. By this saving clause, the author of this essay will consider himself expressly safeguarded, in correct and proper style, against all malicious interpretation.

FIRST SECTION
WHICH CONTAINS THE PRELIMINARY ARTICLES OF A PERPETUAL PEACE BETWEEN STATES

1. 'No conclusion of peace shall be considered valid as such if it was made with a secret reservation of the material for a future war.'

For if this were the case, it would be a mere truce, a suspension of hostilities, not a *peace*. Peace means an end to all hostilities, and to attach the adjective 'perpetual' to it is already suspiciously close to pleonasm. A conclusion of peace nullifies all existing reasons for a future war, even if these are not yet known to the contracting parties, and no matter how acutely and carefully they may later be pieced together out of old documents. It is possible that either party may make a mental reservation with a view to reviving its old pretensions in the future. Such reservations will not be mentioned explicitly, since both parties may simply be too exhausted to continue the war, although they may nonetheless possess sufficient ill will to seize the first favourable opportunity of attaining their end. But if we consider such reservations in themselves, they soon appear as Jesuitical casuistry; they are beneath the dignity of a ruler, just as it is beneath the dignity of a minister of state to comply with any reasoning of this kind.

But if, in accordance with 'enlightened' notions of political expediency, we believe that the true glory of a state consists in the constant increase of its power by any means whatsoever, the above judgement will certainly appear academic and pedantic.

2. 'No independently existing state, whether it be large or small, may be acquired by another state by inheritance, exchange, purchase or gift.'

For a state, unlike the ground on which it is based, is not a possession (*patrimonium*). It is a society of men, which no-one other than itself can command or dispose of. Like a tree, it has its own roots, and to graft it on to another state as if it were a shoot is to terminate its existence as a moral personality and make it into a commodity. This contradicts the idea of the original contract, without which the rights of a people are unthinkable. Everyone knows what danger the supposed right of acquiring states in this way, even in our own times, has brought upon Europe (for this practice is unknown in other continents). It has been thought that states can marry one another, and this has provided a new kind of industry by which power can be increased through family alliances, without expenditure of energy, while landed property can be extended at the same time. It is the same thing when the troops of one state are hired to another to fight an enemy who is not common to both; for the subjects are thereby used and misused as objects to be manipulated at will.

3. 'Standing armies (*miles perpetuus*) will gradually be abolished altogether.'

For they constantly threaten other states with war by the very fact that they are always prepared for it. They spur on the states to outdo one another in arming unlimited numbers of soldiers, and since the resultant costs eventually make peace more oppressive than a short war, the armies are themselves the cause of wars of aggression which set out to end burdensome military expenditure. Furthermore, the hiring of men to kill or to be killed seems to mean using them as mere machines and instruments in the hands of someone else (the state), which cannot easily be reconciled with the rights of man in one's own person. It is quite a different matter if the citizens undertake voluntary military training from time to time in order to secure themselves and their fatherland against attacks from outside. But it would be just the same if wealth rather than soldiers were accumulated, for it would be seen by other states as a military threat; it might compel them to mount preventive attacks, for of the three powers within a state – the *power of the army*, the *power of alliance* and the *power of money* – the third is probably the most reliable instrument of war. It would lead more often to wars if it were not so difficult to discover the amount of wealth which another state possesses.

4. 'No national debt shall be contracted in connection with the external affairs of the state.'

There is no cause for suspicion if help for the national economy is sought inside or outside the state (e.g. for improvements to roads, new settlements, storage of foodstuffs for years of famine, etc.). But a credit system, if used by the powers as an instrument of aggression against one another, shows the power of money in its most dangerous form. For while the debts thereby incurred are always secure against present demands (because not all the creditors will demand payment at the same time), these debts go on growing indefinitely. This ingenious system, invented by a commercial people in the present century, provides a military fund which may exceed the resources of all the other states put together. It can only be exhausted by an eventual tax-deficit, which may be postponed for a considerable time by the commercial stimulus which industry and trade receive through the credit system. This ease in making war, coupled with the warlike inclination of those in power (which seems to be an integral feature of human nature), is thus a great obstacle in the way of perpetual peace. Foreign debts must therefore be prohibited by a preliminary article of such a peace, otherwise national bankruptcy, inevitable in the long run, would necessarily involve various other states in the resultant loss without their having deserved it, thus inflicting upon them a public injury. Other states are therefore justified in allying themselves against such a state and its pretensions.

5. 'No state shall forcibly interfere in the constitution and government of another state.'

For what could justify such interference? Surely not any sense of scandal or offence which a state arouses in the subjects of another state. It should rather serve as a warning to others, as an example of the great evils which a people has incurred by its lawlessness. And a bad example which one free person gives to another (as a *scandalum acceptum*) is not the same as an injury to the latter. But it would be a different matter if a state, through internal discord, were to split into two parts, each of which set itself up as a separate state and claimed authority over the whole. For it could not be reckoned as interference in another state's constitution if an external state were to lend support to one of them, because their condition is one of anarchy. But as long as this internal conflict is not yet decided, the interference of external powers would be a violation of the rights of an independent people which is merely struggling with its internal ills. Such interference would be an active offence and would make the autonomy of all other states insecure.

6. 'No state at war with another shall permit such acts of hostility as would make mutual confidence impossible during a future time of peace. Such acts would include the employment of *assassins* (*percussores*) or *poisoners* (*venefici*), *breach of agreements, the instigation of treason* (*perduellio*) within the enemy state, etc.'

These are dishonourable stratagems. For it must still remain possible, even in wartime, to have some sort of trust in the attitude of the enemy, otherwise peace could not be concluded and the hostilities would turn into a war of extermination (*bellum internecinum*). After all, war is only a regrettable expedient for asserting one's rights by force within a state of nature, where no court of justice is available to judge with legal authority. In such cases, neither party can be declared an unjust enemy, for this would already presuppose a judge's decision; only the *outcome* of the conflict, as in the case of a so-called 'judgement of God', can decide who is in the right. A war of punishment (*bellum punitivum*) between states is inconceivable, since there can be no relationship of superior to inferior among them. It thus follows that a war of extermination, in which both parties and right itself might all be simultaneously annihilated, would allow perpetual peace only on the vast graveyard of the human race. A war of this kind and the employment of all means which might bring it about must thus be absolutely prohibited. But the means listed above would inevitably lead to such a war, because these diabolical arts, besides being intrinsically despicable, would not long be confined to war alone if they were brought into use. This applies, for example, to the employment of spies (*uti exploratoribus*), for it exploits only the dishonesty of others (which can never be completely eliminated). Such practices will be carried over into peacetime and will thus completely vitiate its purpose.

All of the articles listed above, when regarded objectively or in relation to the intentions of those in power, are *prohibitive laws* (*leges prohibitivae*). Yet some of them are of the *strictest* sort (*leges strictae*), being valid irrespective of differing circumstances, and they require that the abuses they prohibit should be abolished *immediately* (Nos. 1, 5, and 6). Others (Nos. 2, 3, and 4), although they are not exceptions to the rule of justice, allow some *subjective* latitude according to the circumstances in which they are applied (*leges latae*). The latter need not necessarily be executed at once, so long as their ultimate purpose (e.g. the *restoration* of freedom to certain states in accordance with the second article) is not lost sight of. But their execution may not be *put off* to a non-existent date (*ad calendas graecas*, as Augustus used to promise), for any delay is permitted only as a means of avoiding a premature implementation which might frustrate the whole purpose of the article. For in the case of the second article, the prohibition relates only to the *mode of acquisition*, which is to be forbidden henceforth, but not to the present *state of political possessions*. For although this present state is not backed up by the requisite legal authority, it was considered lawful in the public opinion of every state at the time of the putative acquisition.

FIRST DEFINITIVE ARTICLE OF A PERPETUAL PEACE:
THE CIVIL CONSTITUTION OF EVERY STATE SHALL BE REPUBLICAN

A *republican constitution* is founded upon three principles: firstly, the principle of *freedom* for all members of a society (as men); secondly, the principle of the *dependence* of everyone upon a single common legislation (as subjects); and thirdly, the principle of legal *equality* for everyone (as citizens). It is the only constitution which can be derived from the idea of an original contract, upon which all rightful legislation of a people must be founded. Thus as far as right is concerned, republicanism is in itself the original basis of every kind of civil constitution, and it only remains to ask whether it is the only constitution which can lead to a perpetual peace.

The republican constitution is not only pure in its origin (since it springs from the pure concept of right); it also offers a prospect of attaining the desired result, i.e. a perpetual peace, and the reason for this is as follows. – If, as is inevitably the case under this constitution, the consent of the citizens is required to decide whether or not war is to be declared, it is very natural that they will have great hesitation in embarking on so dangerous an enterprise. For this would mean calling down on themselves all the miseries of war, such as doing the fighting themselves, supplying the costs of the war from their own resources, painfully making good the ensuing devastation, and, as the crowning evil, having to take upon themselves a burden of debt which will embitter peace itself and which can never be paid off on account of the constant threat of new wars. But under a constitution where the subject is not a citizen, and which is therefore not republican, it is the simplest thing in the world to go to war. For the head of state is not a fellow citizen, but the owner of the state, and a war will not force him to make the slightest sacrifice so far as his banquets, hunts, pleasure palaces and court festivals are concerned. He can thus decide on war, without any significant reason, as a kind of amusement, and unconcernedly leave it to the diplomatic corps (who are always ready for such purposes) to justify the war for the sake of propriety.

The following remarks are necessary to prevent the republican constitution from being confused with the democratic one, as commonly happens. The various forms of state (*civitas*) may be classified either according to the different persons who exercise supreme authority, or according to the way in which the nation is governed by its ruler, whoever he may be. The first classification goes by the form of sovereignty (*forma imperii*), and only three such forms are possible, depending on whether the ruling power is in the hands of an *individual*, of *several persons* in association, or of *all* those who together constitute civil society (i.e. *autocracy*, *aristocracy* and *democracy* – the power of a prince, the power of a nobility, and the power of the people). The second classification depends on the form of government (*forma regiminis*), and relates to the way in which the state, setting out from its constitution (i.e. an act of the general will whereby the mass becomes a people), makes use of its plenary power. The form of government, in this case, will be either *republican* or *despotic*. *Republicanism* is that political principle whereby the executive power (the government) is separated from the legislative power. Despotism prevails in a state if the laws are made and arbitrarily executed by one and the same power, and it reflects the will of the people only in so far as the ruler treats the will of the people as his own private will. Of the three forms of sovereignty, *democracy*, in the truest sense of the word, is necessarily a *despotism*, because it establishes an executive power through which all the citizens may make decisions about (and indeed against) the single individual without his consent, so that decisions are made by all the people and yet not by all the people;

and this means that the general will is in contradiction with itself, and thus also with freedom.

For any form of government which is not *representative* is essentially an *anomaly*, because one and the same person cannot at the same time be both the legislator and the executor of his own will, just as the general proposition in logical reasoning cannot at the same time be a secondary proposition subsuming the particular within the general. And even if the other two political constitutions (i.e. autocracy and aristocracy) are always defective in as much as they leave room for a despotic form of government, it is at least possible that they will be associated with a form of government which accords with the *spirit* of a representative system. Thus Frederick II at least *said* that he was merely the highest servant of the state, while a democratic constitution makes this attitude impossible, because everyone under it wants to be a ruler. We can therefore say that the smaller the number of ruling persons in a state and the greater their powers of representation, the more the constitution will approximate to its republican potentiality, which it may hope to realise eventually by gradual reforms. For this reason, it is more difficult in an aristocracy than in a monarchy to reach this one and only perfectly lawful kind of constitution, while it is possible in a democracy only by means of violent revolution. But the people are immensely more concerned with the mode of government than with the form of the constitution, although a great deal also depends on the degree to which the constitution fits the purpose of the government. But if the mode of government is to accord with the concept of right, it must be based on the representative system. This system alone makes possible a republican state, and without it, despotism and violence will result, no matter what kind of constitution is in force. None of the so-called 'republics' of antiquity employed such a system, and they thus inevitably ended in despotism, although this is still relatively bearable under the rule of a single individual.

SECOND DEFINITIVE ARTICLE OF A PERPETUAL PEACE:
THE RIGHT OF NATIONS SHALL BE BASED ON A FEDERATION OF FREE STATES

Peoples who have grouped themselves into nation states may be judged in the same way as individual men living in a state of nature, independent of external laws; for they are a standing offence to one another by the very fact that they are neighbours. Each nation, for the sake of its own security, can and ought to demand of the others that they should enter along with it into a constitution, similar to the civil one, within which the rights of each could be secured. This would mean establishing a *federation of peoples*. But a federation of this sort would not be the same thing as an international state. For the idea of an international state is contradictory, since every state involves a relationship between a superior (the legislator) and an inferior (the people obeying the laws), whereas a number of nations forming one state would constitute a single nation. And this contradicts our initial assumption, as we are here considering the right of nations in relation to one another in so far as they are a group of separate states which are not to be welded together as a unit.

We look with profound contempt upon the way in which savages cling to their lawless freedom. They would rather engage in incessant strife than submit to a legal constraint which they might impose upon themselves, for they prefer the freedom of folly to the freedom of reason. We regard this as barbarism, coarseness, and brutish debasement of humanity. We might thus expect that civilised peoples, each united within itself as a state, would hasten to abandon so degrading a condition as soon as possible. But instead of doing so, each *state* sees its own majesty (for it would be absurd to speak of the majesty of a *people*) precisely in not having to submit to any external legal constraint, and the glory of its ruler consists in his power to order thousands of people to immolate themselves for a cause which does not truly concern them, while he need not himself incur any danger whatsoever. And the main difference between the savage nations of Europe and those of America is that while some American tribes have been entirely eaten up by their enemies, the Europeans know how to make better use of those they have defeated than merely by making a meal of them. They would rather use them to increase the number of their own subjects, thereby augmenting their stock of instruments for conducting even more extensive wars.

Although it is largely concealed by governmental constraints in law-governed civil society, the depravity of human nature is displayed without disguise in the unrestricted relations which obtain between the various nations. It is therefore to be wondered at that the word *right* has not been completely banished from military politics as superfluous pedantry, and that no state has been bold enough to declare itself publicly in favour of doing so. For Hugo Grotius, Pufendorf, Vattel and the rest (sorry comforters as they are) are still dutifully quoted in *justification* of military aggression, although their philosophically or diplomatically formulated codes do not and cannot have the slightest *legal* force, since states as such are not subject to a common external constraint. Yet there is no instance of a state ever having been moved to desist from its purpose by arguments supported by the testimonies of such notable men. This homage which every state pays (in words at least) to the concept of right proves that man possesses a greater moral capacity, still dormant at present, to overcome eventually the evil principle within him (for he cannot deny that it exists), and to hope that others will do likewise. Otherwise the word *right* would never be used by states which intend to make war on one another, unless in a derisory sense, as when a certain Gallic prince declared: 'Nature has given to the strong the prerogative of making the weak obey them.' The way in which states seek their rights can only be by war, since there is no external tribunal to put their claims to trial. But rights cannot be decided by military victory, and a *peace treaty* may put an end to the current war, but not to that general warlike condition within which pretexts can always be found for a new war. And indeed, such a state of affairs cannot be pronounced completely unjust, since it allows each party to act as judge in its own cause. Yet while natural right allows us to say of men living in a lawless condition that they ought to abandon it, the right of nations does not allow us to say the same of states. For as states, they already have a lawful internal constitution in accordance with their conception of right. On the other hand, reason, as the highest legislative moral power, absolutely condemns war as a test of rights and sets up peace as an immediate duty. But peace can neither be inaugurated nor secured without a general agreement between the nations; thus a particular kind of league, which we might call a *pacific federation* (*foedus pacificum*) is required. It would differ from *peace treaty* (*pactum pacis*) in that the latter terminates *one* war, whereas the former would seek to end *all* wars for good. This federation does not aim to acquire any power like that of a state, but merely to preserve and secure the *freedom* of each state in itself, along with that of the other confederated states, although this does not mean that they need to submit to public laws and to a coercive power which enforces them, as do men in a state of nature. It can be shown that this idea of *federalism*, extending gradually to encompass all states and thus leading to perpetual peace, is practicable and has objective reality. For if by good fortune one powerful and enlightened nation can form a republic (which is by its nature inclined to seek perpetual peace), this will provide a focal point for federal association among other states. These will join up with the first one, thus securing the freedom of each state in accordance with the idea of international right, and the whole will gradually spread further and further by a series of alliances of this kind.

It would be understandable for a people to say: 'There shall be no war among us; for we will form ourselves into a state, appointing for ourselves a supreme legislative, executive and juridical power to resolve our conflicts by peaceful means.' But if this state says: 'There shall be no war between myself and other states, although I do not recognise any supreme legislative power which could secure my rights and whose rights I should in turn secure', it is impossible to understand what justification I can have for placing any confidence in my rights, unless I can rely on some substitute for the union of civil society, i.e. on a free federation. If the concept of international right is to retain any meaning at all, reason must necessarily couple it with a federation of this kind.

The concept of international right becomes meaningless if interpreted as a right to go to war. For this would make it a right to determine what is lawful not by means of universally valid external laws, but by means of one-sided maxims backed up by physical force. It could be taken to mean that it is perfectly just for men who adopt this attitude to destroy one another, and thus to find perpetual peace in the vast grave where all the horrors of violence and those responsible for them would be buried. There is only one rational way in which states coexisting with other states can emerge from the lawless condition of pure warfare. Just like individual men, they must renounce their savage and lawless freedom, adapt themselves to public coercive laws, and thus form an *international state* (*civitas gentium*), which would necessarily continue to grow until it embraced all the peoples of the earth. But since this is not the will of the nations, according to their present conception of international right (so that they reject *in hypothesi* what is true *in thesi*), the positive idea of a *world republic* cannot be realised. If all is not to be lost, this can at best find a negative substitute in the shape of an enduring and gradually expanding *federation* likely to prevent war. The latter may check the current of man's inclination to defy the law and antagonise his fellows, although there will always be a risk of it bursting forth anew. *Furor impius intus – fremit horridus ore cruento* (Virgil).

THIRD DEFINITIVE ARTICLE OF A PERPETUAL PEACE:
COSMOPOLITAN RIGHT SHALL BE LIMITED TO CONDITIONS OF
UNIVERSAL HOSPITALITY

As in the foregoing articles, we are here concerned not with philanthropy, but with *right*. In this context, *hospitality* means the right of a stranger not to be treated with hostility when he arrives on someone else's territory. He can indeed be turned away, if this can be done without causing his death, but he must not be treated with hostility, so long as he behaves in a peaceable manner in the place he happens to be in. The stranger cannot claim the *right of a guest* to be enter-tained, for this would require a special friendly agreement whereby he might become a member of the native household for a certain time. He may only claim a *right of resort*, for all men are entitled to present themselves in the society of others by virtue of their right to communal possession of the earth's surface. Since the earth is a globe, they cannot disperse over an infinite area, but must necessarily tolerate one another's company. And no-one originally has any greater right than anyone else to occupy any particular portion of the earth. The community of man is divided by uninhabitable parts of the earth's surface such as oceans and deserts, but even then, the *ship* or the *camel* (the ship of the desert) make it possible for them to approach their fellows over these ownerless tracts, and to utilise as a means of social intercourse that *right to the earth's surface* which the human race shares in common. The inhospitable behaviour of coastal dwellers (as on the Barbary coast) in plundering ships on the adjoining seas or enslaving stranded seafarers, or that of inhabitants of the desert (as with the Arab Bedouins), who regard their proximity to nomadic tribes as a justification for plundering them, is contrary to natural right. But this natural right of hospitality, i.e. the right of strangers, does not extend beyond those conditions which make it possible for them to *attempt* to enter into relations with the native inhabitants. In this way, continents distant from each other can enter into peaceful mutual relations which may eventually be regulated by public laws, thus bringing the human race nearer and nearer to a cosmopolitan constitution.

If we compare with this ultimate end the *inhospitable* conduct of the civilised states of our continent, especially the commercial states, the injustice which they display in *visiting* foreign countries and peoples (which in their case is the same as *conquering* them) seems appallingly great. America, the negro countries, the Spice Islands, the Cape, etc. were looked upon at the time of their discovery as ownerless territories; for the native inhabitants were counted as nothing. In East India (Hindustan), foreign troops were brought in under the pretext of merely setting up trading posts. This led to oppression of the natives, incitement of the various Indian states to widespread wars, famine, insurrection, treachery and the whole litany of evils which can afflict the human race.

China and Japan (Nippon), having had experience of such guests, have wisely placed restrictions on them. China permits contact with her territories, but not entrance into them, while Japan only allows contact with a single European people, the Dutch, although they are still segregated from the native community like prisoners. The worst (or from the point of view of moral judgements, the best) thing about all this is that the commercial states do not even benefit by their violence, for all their trading companies are on the point of collapse. The Sugar Islands, that stronghold of the cruellest and most calculated slavery, do not yield any real profit; they serve only the indirect (and not entirely laudable) purpose of training sailors for warships, thereby aiding the prosecution of wars in Europe. And all this is the work of powers who make endless ado about their piety, and who wish to be considered as chosen believers while they live on the fruits of iniquity.

The peoples of the earth have thus entered in varying degrees into a universal community, and it has developed to the point where a violation of rights in *one* part of the world is felt *everywhere*. The idea of a cosmopolitan right is therefore not fantastic and overstrained; it is a necessary complement to the unwritten code of political and international right, transforming it into a universal right of humanity. Only under this condition can we flatter ourselves that we are continually advancing towards a perpetual peace.

FIRST SUPPLEMENT: ON THE GUARANTEE OF A PERPETUAL PEACE

Perpetual peace is *guaranteed* by no less an authority than the great artist *Nature* herself (*natura daedala rerum*). The mechanical process of nature visibly exhibits the purposive plan of producing concord among men, even against their will and indeed by means of their very discord. This design, if we regard it as a compelling cause whose laws of operation are unknown to us, is called *fate*. But if we consider its purposive function within the world's development, whereby it appears as the underlying wisdom of a higher cause, showing the way towards the objective goal of the human race and predetermining the world's evolution, we call it *providence*. We cannot actually observe such an agency in the artifices of nature, nor can we even *infer* its existence from them. But as with all relations between the form of things and their ultimate purposes, we can and must *supply it mentally* in order to conceive of its possibility by analogy with human artifices. Its relationship to and conformity with the end which reason directly prescribes to us (i.e. the end of morality) can only be conceived of as an idea. Yet while this idea is indeed far-fetched in *theory*, it does possess dogmatic validity and has a very real foundation in *practice*, as with the concept of *perpetual peace*, which makes it our duty to promote it by using the natural mechanism described above. But in contexts such as this, where we are concerned purely with theory and not with religion, we should also note that it is more in keeping with the limitations of human reason to speak of *nature* and not of *providence*, for reason, in dealing with cause and effect relationships, must keep within the bounds of possible experience. *Modesty* forbids us to speak of providence as something we can recognise, for this would mean donning the wings of Icarus and presuming to approach the mystery of its inscrutable intentions.

But before we define this guarantee more precisely, we must first examine the situation in which nature has placed the actors in her great spectacle, for it is this situation which ultimately demands the guarantee of peace. We may next enquire in what manner the guarantee is provided.

Nature's provisional arrangement is as follows. Firstly, she has taken care that human beings are able to live in all the areas where they are settled. Secondly, she has driven them in all directions by means of *war*, so that they inhabit even the most inhospitable regions. And thirdly, she has compelled them by the same means to enter into more or less legal relationships. It is in itself wonderful that moss can still grow in the cold wastes around the Arctic Ocean; the *reindeer* can scrape it out from beneath the snow, and can thus itself serve as nourishment or as a draft animal for the Ostiaks or Samoyeds. Similarly, the sandy salt deserts contain the *camel*, which seems as if it had been created for travelling over them in order that they might not be left unutilised. But evidence of design in nature emerges even more clearly when we realise that the shores of the Arctic Ocean are inhabited not only by fur-bearing animals, but also by seals, walruses and whales, whose flesh provides food and whose fat provides warmth for the native inhabitants. Nature's care arouses most admiration, however, by carrying drift-wood to these treeless regions, without anyone knowing exactly where it comes from. For if they did not have this material, the natives would not be able to construct either boats or weapons, or dwellings in which to live. And they have enough to do making war on the animals to be able to live in peace among themselves. But it was probably nothing but war which *drove* them into these regions. And the first *instrument of war* among all the animals which man learned to domesticate in the course of peopling the earth was the *horse*. For the elephant belongs to that later age of luxury which began after states had been established. The same applies to the art of cultivating certain kinds of grasses known as *cereals*, whose original nature is now unknown to us, and to the production and refinement of various *fruits* by transplanting and grafting (in Europe, perhaps only two species were involved, the crab-apple and the wild pear). Such arts could arise only within established states in which landed property was secure, after men had made the transition to an *agricultural* way of life, abandoning the lawless freedom they had enjoyed in their previous existence as hunters, fishers and shepherds. *Salt* and *iron* were next discovered, and were perhaps the first articles of trade between nations to be in demand everywhere. In this way, nations first entered into *peaceful relations* with one another, and thus achieved mutual understanding, community of interests and peaceful relations, even with the most distant of their fellows.

In seeing to it that men *could* live everywhere on earth, nature has at the same time despotically willed that they *should* live everywhere, even against their own inclinations. And this obligation does not rest upon any concept of duty which might bind them to fulfil it in accordance with a moral law; on the contrary, nature has chosen war as a means of attaining this end.

We can observe nations which reveal the unity of their descent by the unity of their language. This is the case with the *Samoyeds* on the Arctic Ocean and another people with a similar language living two hundred miles away in the Altai Mountains; another people of Mongol extraction, given to horsemanship and hence to warlike pursuits, has pushed its way between them, thus driving the one part of the tribe far away from the other into the most inhospitable Arctic regions, where it would certainly not have gone by its own inclinations. In the same way, the Finns in the northernmost region of Europe (where they are known as Lapps) are now far separated from the Hungarians, to whom they are linguistically related, by Gothic and Sarmatian peoples who have pushed their way in between them. And what else but war, nature's means of peopling the whole earth, can have driven the Eskimos so far North – for they are quite distinct from all other American races, and are perhaps descended from European adventurers of ancient times; the Pesherae have been driven South into Tierra del Fuego in the same manner. War itself, however, does not require any particular kind of motivation, for it seems to be ingrained in human nature, and even to be regarded as something noble to which man is inspired by his love of honour, without selfish motives. Thus warlike courage, with the American savages as with their European counterparts in medieval times, is held to be of great and immediate value – and not just *in times of* war (as might be expected), but also *in order that* there may be war. Thus wars are often started merely to display this quality, so that war itself is invested with an inherent *dignity*, for even philosophers have eulogised it as a kind of ennobling influence on man, forgetting the Greek saying that 'war is bad in that it produces more evil people than it destroys'. So much, then, for what nature does to further *her own end* with respect to the human race as an animal species.

We now come to the essential question regarding the prospect of perpetual peace. What does nature do in relation to the end which man's own reason prescribes to him as a duty, i.e. how does nature help to promote his *moral purpose*? And how does nature guarantee that what man *ought* to do by the laws of his freedom (but does not do) will in fact be done through nature's compulsion, without prejudice to the free agency of man? This question arises, moreover, in all three areas of public right – in *political, international* and *cosmopolitan right.* For if I say that nature *wills* that this or that should happen, this does not mean that nature imposes on us a *duty* to do it, for duties can only be imposed by practical reason, acting without any external constraint. On the contrary, nature does it herself, whether we are willing or not: *fata volentem ducunt, nolentem trahunt.*

1. Even if people were not compelled by internal dissent to submit to the coercion of public laws, war would produce the same effect from outside. For in accordance with the natural arrangement described above, each people would find itself confronted by another neighbouring people pressing in upon it, thus forcing it to form itself internally into a *state* in order to encounter the other as an *armed power.* Now the *republican* constitution is the only one which does complete justice to the rights of man. But it is also the most difficult to establish, and even more so to preserve, so that many maintain that it would only be possible within a state of *angels*, since men, with their self-seeking inclinations, would be incapable of adhering to a constitution of so sublime a nature. But in fact, nature comes to the aid of the universal and rational human will, so admirable in itself but so impotent in practice, and makes use of precisely those self-seeking inclinations in order to do so. It only remains for men to create a good organisation for the state, a task which is well within their capability, and to arrange it in such a way that their self-seeking energies are opposed to one another, each thereby neutralising or eliminating the destructive effects of the rest. And as far as reason is concerned, the result is the same as if man's selfish tendencies were non-existent, so that man, even if he is not morally good in himself, is nevertheless compelled to

be a good citizen. As hard as it may sound, the problem of setting up a state can be solved even by a nation of devils (so long as they possess understanding). It may be stated as follows: 'In order to organise a group of rational beings who together require universal laws for their survival, but of whom each separate individual is secretly inclined to exempt himself from them, the constitution must be so designed that, although the citizens are opposed to one another in their private attitudes, these opposing views may inhibit one another in such a way that the public conduct of the citizens will be the same as if they did not have such evil attitudes.' A problem of this kind must be soluble. For such a task does not involve the moral improvement of man; it only means finding out how the mechanism of nature can be applied to men in such a manner that the antagonism of their hostile attitudes will make them compel one another to submit to coercive laws, thereby producing a condition of peace within which the laws can be enforced. We can even see this principle at work among the actually existing (although as yet very imperfectly organised) states. For in their external relations, they have already approached what the idea of right prescribes, although the reason for this is certainly not their internal moral attitudes. In the same way, we cannot expect their moral attitudes to produce a good political constitution; on the contrary, it is only through the latter that the people can be expected to attain a good level of moral culture. Thus that mechanism of nature by which selfish inclinations are naturally opposed to one another in their external relations can be used by reason to facilitate the attainment of its own end, the reign of established right. Internal and external peace are thereby furthered and assured, so far as it lies within the power of the state itself to do so. We may therefore say that nature *irresistibly wills* that right should eventually gain the upper hand. What men have neglected to do will ultimately happen of its own accord, albeit with much inconvenience. As Bouterwek puts it: 'If the reed is bent too far, it breaks; and he who wants too much gets nothing.'

2. The idea of international right presupposes the separate existence of many independent adjoining states. And such a state of affairs is essentially a state of war, unless there is a federal union to prevent hostilities breaking out. But in the light of the idea of reason, this state is still to be preferred to an amalgamation of the separate nations under a single power which has overruled the rest and created a universal monarchy. For the laws progressively lose their impact as the government increases its range, and a soulless despotism, after crushing the germs of goodness, will finally lapse into anarchy. It is nonetheless the desire of every

state (or its ruler) to achieve lasting peace by thus dominating the whole world, if at all possible. But *nature* wills it otherwise, and uses two means to separate the nations and prevent them from intermingling – *linguistic* and religious differences. These may certainly occasion mutual hatred and provide pretexts for wars, but as culture grows and men gradually move towards greater agreement over their principles, they lead to mutual understanding and peace. And unlike that universal despotism which saps all man's energies and ends in the graveyard of freedom, this peace is created and guaranteed by an equilibrium of forces and a most vigorous rivalry.

3. Thus nature wisely separates the nations, although the will of each individual state, even basing its arguments on international right, would gladly unite them under its own sway by force or by cunning. On the other hand, nature also unites nations which the concept of cosmopolitan right would not have protected from violence and war, and does so by means of their mutual self-interest. For the *spirit of commerce* sooner or later takes hold of every people, and it cannot exist side by side with war. And of all the powers (or means) at the disposal of the power of the state, *financial power* can probably be relied on most. Thus states find themselves compelled to promote the noble cause of peace, though not exactly from motives of morality. And wherever in the world there is a threat of war breaking out, they will try to prevent it by mediation, just as if they had entered into a permanent league for this purpose; for by the very nature of things, large military alliances can only rarely be formed, and will even more rarely be successful.

In this way, nature guarantees perpetual peace by the actual mechanism of human inclinations. And while the likelihood of its being attained is not sufficient to enable us to *prophesy* the future theoretically, it is enough for practical purposes. It makes it our duty to work our way towards this goal, which is more than an empty chimera.

Trade and economics

BERNARD MANDEVILLE

BIOGRAPHICAL NOTE

Bernard Mandeville (1670–1733) was born in Rotterdam, and educated at the University of Leyden, where he studied philosophy and medicine. He continued with his philosophical studies until 1691 when he decided to follow the family tradition and enter the medical profession. Soon afterwards, possibly after touring Europe, he went to England and by 1699 he was settled in London where he remained as a respected medical practitioner until his death. Little more of substance is known about his life, in spite of the international notoriety that his free-thinking works were soon to attract, although anecdotal evidence about his character and activities is plentiful.

In 1703 Mandeville published a translation in verse of twenty-seven of La Fontaine's fables, and this was followed in 1704 with further translations of La Fontaine, and also of Scarron's satirical verse. Modelling himself on La Fontaine, he published anonymously in 1705 a brief poem entitled *The grumbling hive: or, knaves turn'd honest*, the seed from which was to grow *The fable of the bees*. He continued to concern himself mainly with medical matters for the next few years, but in 1714 the poem was re-issued, again anonymously, along with a corpus of *Remarks*, as part of a book entitled *The fable of the bees: or, private vices, publick benefits*. Other works by Mandeville include *The virgin unmask'd: or, female dialogues betwixt an elderly maiden lady, and her niece* (1709), *A treatise of the hypochondriack and hysterick passions* (1711), *Free thoughts on religion, the church, and national happiness* (1720), *A modest defence of publick stews* (1724), *An enquiry into the causes of the frequent executions at Tyburn* (1725) and *An enquiry into the origin of honour, and the usefulness of Christianity in war* (1732).

The *Fable* was to preoccupy Mandeville for more than twenty-four years. With the appearance of the first 1714 edition of the *Fable*, containing twenty *Remarks* and *An enquiry into the origin of moral virtue*, Mandeville began to attract public attention, although at this stage the work was still only half as long as it was eventually to be. The original poem was now overshadowed by the accompanying commentaries which he continued to expand over the years, combining prose commentary with anecdote, fables and parables. A new, expanded edition appeared in 1723 containing, in addition to two new *Remarks*, two additional essays, *An essay on charity and charity-schools* and *A search into the nature of society*. By now the *Fable* was causing controversy, and a particularly venomous attack was printed in the *London Journal* by 'Theophilus Philo-Britannus', prompting Mandeville to defend himself in August 1723, also in the *London Journal*, in a defence that he printed with the 1723 and all subsequent editions. This defence was re-issued as a pamphlet, along with the texts of the attacks, and added to the 1724 edition of the *Fable* as *A vindication of the book*.

Attacks on Mandeville continued to be mounted by philosophers and theologians, and his views on human nature and human folly were to fuel controversy for many years. Between 1724 and 1729 three further editions appeared. In 1728, Mandeville published *The fable of the bees, Part II*, consisting of a preface and six dialogues. Bishop George Berkeley issued a powerful attack on Mandeville's ethical position in the second dialogue of *Alciphron: or, the minute philosopher* (1732), and just before his death Mandeville published his rebuttal in *A letter to Dion, occasioned by his book call'd Alciphron* (1732). The scandalous reception given to the 'licentious doctrine' ensured that the *Fable* became an international best-seller, much translated and much condemned, throughout the eighteenth century, and most of the nineteenth.

EDITORIAL NOTE

The base text of *The moral* and *Remark L* from *An enquiry into the origin of moral virtue* is that of the last edition issued during Mandeville's lifetime, *The fable of the bees: or, private vices, publick benefits* (Oxford, Clarendon Press, 1732). This is the text printed by F. Kaye* in what is still the best modern edition. On the variants relating to all components of the *Fable*, see Harth 1970, pp. 47–50.

FURTHER READING

Dickenson, H., 'The politics of Bernard Mandeville', in *Mandeville studies: new explorations in the art and thought of Dr Bernard Mandeville (1670– 1733)*, ed. I. Primer (The Hague, Martinus Nijhoff, 1975), pp. 80–97.

*Kaye, F. (ed.), *The fable of the bees, or, private vices, publick benefits*, 2 vols. (Oxford, Oxford University Press, 1966). Reprint. See introduction, pp. vii–cxlvi.

Speck, W., 'Mandeville and the eutopia seated in the brain', in *Mandeville studies: new explorations in the art and thought of Dr Bernard Mandeville (1670–1733)*, ed. I. Primer (The Hague, Martinus Nijhoff, 1975), pp. 66–79.

The fable of the bees: or, private vices, publick benefits (1714)

The moral

Then leave Complaints: Fools only strive	
To make a great an honest Hive	
T'enjoy the World's Conveniences,	
Be fam'd in War, yet live in Ease,	
Without great Vices, is a vain	5
EUTOPIA seated in the Brain.	
Fraud, Luxury and Pride must live,	
While we the Benefits receive:	
Hunger's a dreadful Plague, no doubt,	
Yet who digests or thrives without?	10
Do we not owe the Growth of Wine	
To the dry shabby crooked Vine?	
Which, while its Shoots neglected stood,	
Chok'd other Plants, and ran to Wood;	
But blest us with its noble Fruit,	15
As soon as it was ty'd and cut:	
So Vice is beneficial found,	
When it's by Justice lopt and bound;	
Nay, where the People would be great,	
As necessary to the State,	20
As Hunger is to make 'em eat.	
Bare Virtue can't make Nations live	
In Splendor; they, that would revive	
A Golden Age, must be as free	
For Acorns, as for Honesty.	25

Remark L

Whilst Luxury
Employ'd a Million of the Poor, etc.[1]

If every Thing is to be Luxury (as in strictness it ought) that is not immediately necessary to make Man subsist as he is a living Creature, there is nothing else to be found in the World, no not even among the naked Savages, of which it is not probable that there are any but what by this time have made some Improvements upon their former manner of Living; and either in the Preparation of their Eatables, the ordering of their Huts, or otherwise, adding something to what once sufficed them. This Definition every body will say is too rigorous; I am of the same Opinion; but if we are to abate one Inch of this Severity, I am afraid we shan't know where to stop. When People tell us they only desire to keep themselves sweet and clean, there is no understanding what they would be at; if they made use of these Words in their genuine proper literal Sense, they might soon be satisfy'd without much cost or trouble, if they did not want Water: But these two little Adjectives are so comprehensive, especially in the Dialect of some Ladies, that no body can guess how far they may be stretcht. The Comforts of Life are likewise so various and extensive, that no body can tell what People mean by them, except he knows what sort of Life they lead. The same obscurity I observe in the words Decency and Conveniency, and I never understand them unless I am acquainted with the Quality of the Persons that make use of them. People may go to Church together, and be all of one Mind as much as they please, I am apt to believe that when they pray for their daily Bread, the Bishop includes several things in that Petition which the Sexton does not think on.

By what I have said hitherto I would only shew, that if once we depart from calling every thing Luxury that is not absolutely necessary to keep a Man alive, that then there is no Luxury at all; for if the wants of Men are innumerable, then what ought to supply them has no bounds; what is call'd superfluous to some Degree of People will be thought requisite to those of higher Quality; and neither the World nor the Skill of Man can produce any thing so curious or extravagant, but some most Gracious Sovereign or other, if it either eases or diverts him, will

---

[1] *The grumbling hive: or, knaves turn'd honest,* lines 180–1.

reckon it among the Necessaries of Life; not meaning every body's Life, but that of his Sacred Person.

It is a receiv'd Notion, that Luxury is as destructive to the Wealth of the whole Body Politick, as it is to that of every individual Person who is guilty of it, and that a National Frugality enriches a Country in the same manner as that which is less general increases the Estates of Private Families. I confess, that tho' I have found Men of much better Understanding than my self of this Opinion, I cannot help dissenting from them in this Point. They argue thus: We send, say they, for Example to *Turkey* of Woollen Manufactury, and other things of our own Growth, a Million's worth every Year; for this we bring back Silk, Mohair, Drugs, etc. to the value of Twelve Hundred Thousand Pounds, that are all spent in our own Country. By this, say they, we get nothing; but if most of us would be content with our own Growth, and so consume but half the quantity of those Foreign Commodities, then those in *Turkey*, who would still want the same quantity of our Manufactures, would be forc'd to pay ready Money for the rest, and so by the Balance of that Trade only, the Nation should get Six Hundred Thousand pounds *per Annum*.

To examine the force of this Argument, we'll suppose (what they would have) that but half the Silk, etc. shall be consumed in *England* of what there is now; we'll suppose likewise, that those in *Turkey*, tho' we refuse to buy above half as much of their Commodities as we used to do, either can or will not be without the same quantity of our Manufactures they had before, and that they'll pay the Balance in Money; that is to say, that they shall give us as much Gold or Silver, as the value of what they buy from us exceeds the value of what we buy from them. Tho' what we suppose might perhaps be done for one Year, it is impossible it should last: Buying is Bartering, and no Nation can buy Goods of others that has none of her own to purchase them with. *Spain* and *Portugal*, that are yearly supply'd with new Gold and Silver from their Mines, may for ever buy for ready Money as long as their yearly increase of Gold or Silver continues, but then Money is their Growth and the Commodity of the Country. We know that we could not continue long to purchase the Goods of other Nations, if they would not take our Manufactures in Payment for them; and why should we judge otherwise of other Nations? If those in *Turkey* then had no more Money fall from the Skies than we, let us see what would be the consequence of what we supposed. The Six Hundred Thousand Pounds in Silk, Mohair, etc. that are left upon their Hands the first Year, must make those Commodities fall considerably: Of this the *Dutch* and the

French will reap the Benefit as much as our selves; and if we continue to refuse taking their Commodities in Payment for our Manufactures, they can trade no longer with us, but must content themselves with buying what they want of such Nations as are willing to take what we refuse, tho' their Goods are much worse than ours, and thus our Commerce with *Turkey* must in few Years be infallibly lost.

But they'll say, perhaps, that to prevent the ill consequence I have shew'd, we shall take the *Turkish* Merchandizes as formerly, and only be so frugal as to consume but half the quantity of them our selves, and send the rest Abroad to be sold to others. Let us see what this will do, and whether it will enrich the Nation by the balance of that Trade with Six Hundred Thousand Pounds. In the first Place, I'll grant them that our People at Home, making use of so much more of our own Manufactures, those who were employ'd in Silk, Mohair, etc. will get a living by the various Preparations of Woollen Goods. But in the second, I cannot allow that the Goods can be sold as formerly; for suppose the Half that is wore at Home to be sold at the same Rate as before, certainly the other Half that is sent Abroad will want very much of it: For we must send those Goods to Markets already supply'd; and besides that there must be Freight, Insurance, Provision, and all other Charges deducted, and the Merchants in general must lose much more by this Half that is re-shipp'd, than they got by the Half that is consumed here. For tho' the Woollen Manufactures are our own Product, yet they stand the Merchant that ships them off to Foreign Countries, in as much as they do the Shopkeeper here that retails them: so that if the Returns for what he sends Abroad repay him not what his Goods cost him here, with all other Charges, till he has the Money and a good Interest for it in Cash, the Merchant must run out, and the Upshot would be, that the Merchants in general finding they lost by the *Turkish* Commodities they sent Abroad, would ship no more of our Manufactures than what would pay for as much Silk, Mohair, etc., as would be consumed here. Other Nations would soon find Ways to supply them with as much as we should send short, and some where or other to dispose of the Goods we should refuse: So that all we should get by this Frugality would be, that those in *Turkey* would take but half the Quantity of our Manufactures of what they do now, while we encourage and wear their Merchandizes, without which they are not able to purchase ours.

As I have had the Mortification for several Years to meet with Abundance of sensible People against this Opinion, and who always thought me wrong in this

Calculation, so I had the pleasure at last to see the Wisdom of the Nation fall into the same Sentiments, as is so manifest from an Act of Parliament made in the year 1721, where the Legislature disobliges a powerful and valuable Company, and overlooks very weighty Inconveniences at Home, to promote the Interest of the *Turkey* Trade, and not only encourages the Consumption of Silk and Mohair, but forces the Subjects on Penalties to make use of them whether they will or not.

What is laid to the Charge of Luxury besides, is that it increases Avarice and Rapine: And where they are reigning Vices, Offices of the greatest Trust are bought and sold; the Ministers that should serve the Publick, both great and small, corrupted, and the Countries every Moment in danger of being betray'd to the highest Bidders: And lastly, that it effeminates and enervates the People, by which the Nations become an easy Prey to the first Invaders. These are indeed terrible Things; but what is put to the Account of Luxury belongs to Male-Administration, and it is the Fault of bad Politicks. Every Government ought to be thoroughly acquainted with, and stedfastly to pursue the Interest of the Country. Good Politicians by dextrous Management, laying heavy Impositions on some Goods, or totally prohibiting them, and lowering the Duties on others, may always turn and divert the Course of Trade which way they please; and as they'll ever prefer, if it be equally considerable, the Commerce with such Countries as can pay with Money as well as Goods, to those that can make no Returns for what they buy, but in the Commodities of their own Growth and Manufactures, so they will always carefully prevent the Traffick with such Nations as refuse the Goods of others, and will take nothing but Money for their own. But above all, they'll keep a watchful Eye over the Balance of Trade in general, and never suffer that all the Foreign Commodities together, that are imported in one Year, shall exceed in Value what of their own Growth or Manufacture is in the same exported to others. Note, that I speak now of the Interest of those Nations that have no Gold or Silver in their Growth, otherwise this Maxim need not to be so much insisted on.

If what I urg'd last be but diligently look'd after, and the Imports are never allow'd to be superior to the Exports, no Nation can ever be impoverish'd by Foreign Luxury; and they may improve it as much as they please, if they can but in proportion raise the Fund of their own that is to purchase it.

Trade is the Principal, but not the only Requisite, to aggrandize a Nation: there are other Things to be taken care of besides. The *Meum* and *Tuum* must be secur'd, Crimes punish'd, and all other Laws concerning the Administration of

Justice, wisely contriv'd, and strictly executed. Foreign Affairs must be likewise prudently manag'd, and the Ministry of every Nation ought to have a good Intelligence abroad, and be well acquainted with the Publick Transactions of all those Countries, that either by their Neighbourhood Strength or Interest, may be hurtful or beneficial to them, to take the necessary Measures accordingly, of crossing some and assisting others, as Policy and the Balance of Power direct. The Multitude must be aw'd, no Man's Conscience forced, and the Clergy allow'd no greater Share in State Affairs than our Saviour has bequeathed them in his Testament. These are the Arts that lead to worldly Greatness: what Sovereign Power soever makes a good use of them, that has any considerable Nation to govern, whether it be a Monarchy, a Commonwealth, or a Mixture of both, can never fail of making it flourish in spight of all the other Powers upon Earth, and no Luxury or other Vice is ever able to shake their Constitution. But here I expect a full-mouth'd Cry against me; What! has God never punish'd and destroy'd great Nations for their Sins? Yes, but not without Means, by infatuating their Governors, and suffering them to depart from either all or some of those general Maxims I have mentioned; and of all the famous States and Empires the World has had to boast of hitherto, none ever came to Ruin whose Destruction was not principally owing to the bad Politicks, Neglects, or Mismanagements of the Rulers.

There is no doubt but more Health and Vigour is to be expected among a People, and their Offspring, from Temperance and Sobriety, than there is from Gluttony and Drunkenness; yet I confess, that as to Luxury's effeminating and enervating a Nation, I have not such frightful Notions now as I have had formerly. When we hear or read of Things which we are altogether Strangers to, they commonly bring to our Imagination such Ideas of what we have seen, as (according to our Apprehension) must come the nearest to them: And I remember, that when I have read of the Luxury of *Persia, Egypt,* and other Countries where it has been a reigning Vice, and that were effeminated and enervated by it, it has sometimes put me in mind of the cramming and swilling of ordinary Tradesmen at a City Feast, and the Beastliness their over-gorging themselves is often attended with; at other Times it has made me think on the Distraction of dissolute Sailors, as I had seen them in Company of half a dozen lewd Women roaring along with Fiddles before them; and was I to have been carried into any of their great Cities, I would have expected to have found one Third of the People sick a-bed with Surfeits; another laid up with the Gout, or crippled by a more ignominious Distemper; and the rest, that could go without leading, walk along the Streets in Pettycoats.

It is happy for us to have Fear as a Keeper, as long as our Reason is not strong enough to govern our Appetites: And I believe that the great Dread I had more particularly against the Word, *to enervate*, and some consequent Thoughts on the Etymology of it, did me Abundance of Good when I was a Schoolboy: But since I have seen something of the World, the Consequences of Luxury to a Nation seem not so dreadful to me as they did. As long as Men have the same Appetites, the same Vices will remain. In all large Societies, some will love Whoring and others Drinking. The Lustful that can get no handsome clean Women, will content themselves with dirty Drabs; and those that cannot purchase *Hermitage* or *Pontack*, will be glad of more ordinary *French* claret. Those that can't reach Wine, take up with worse Liquors, and a Foot Soldier or a Beggar may make himself as drunk with Stale-Beer or Malt-Spirits, as a Lord with *Burgundy*, *Champaign* or *Tokay*. The cheapest and most slovenly way of indulging our Passions, does as much Mischief to a Man's Constitution, as the most elegant and expensive.

The greatest Excesses of Luxury are shewn in Buildings, Furniture, Equipages and Clothes: Clean Linen weakens a Man no more than Flannel; Tapistry, fine Painting or good Wainscot are no more unwholesom than bare Walls; and a rich Couch, or a gilt Chariot are no more enervating than the cold Floor or a Country Cart. The refin'd Pleasures of Men of Sense are seldom injurious to their Constitution, and there are many great Epicures that will refuse to eat or drink more than their Heads or Stomachs can bear. Sensual People may take as great Care of themselves as any: and the Errors of the most viciously luxurious, don't so much consist in the frequent Repetitions of their Lewdness, and their Eating and Drinking too much (which are Things which would most enervate them) as they do in the operose [elaborate] Contrivances, the Profuseness and Nicety they are serv'd with, and the vast Expence they are at in their Tables and Amours.

But let us once suppose that the Ease and Pleasures the Grandees and the rich People of every great Nation live in, render them unfit to endure Hardships, and undergo the Toils of War. I'll show that most of the common Council of the City would make but very indifferent Foot-Soldiers; and I believe heartily, that if your Horse was to be compos'd of Aldermen, and such as most of them are, a small Artillery of Squibs would be sufficient to rout them. But what have the Aldermen, the Common-Council, or indeed all People of any Substance, to do with the War, but to pay Taxes? The Hardships and Fatigues of War that are personally suffer'd, fall upon them that bear the Brunt of every Thing, the meanest Indigent Part of the Nation, the working slaving People: For how excessive soever the Plenty and Luxury of a Nation may be, some Body must do the Work, Houses and Ships must be built, Merchandizes must be remov'd, and the Ground till'd. Such a Variety of Labours in every great Nation require a vast Multitude, in which there are always loose, idle, extravagant Fellows enough to spare for an Army; and those that are robust enough to Hedge and Ditch, Plow and Thrash, or else not too much enervated to be Smiths, Carpenters, Sawyers, Clothworkers, Porters or Carmen, will always be strong and hardy enough in a Campaign or two to make good Soldiers, who, where good Orders are kept, have seldom so much Plenty and Superfluity come to their Share as to do them any hurt.

The Mischief then to be fear'd from Luxury among the People of War, cannot extend it self beyond the Officers. The greatest of them are either Men of very high Birth and Princely Education, or else extraordinary Parts, and no less Experience; and whoever is made choice of by a wise Government to command an Army *en chef*, should have a consummate Knowledge in Martial Affairs, Intrepidity to keep him calm in the midst of Danger, and many other Qualifications that must be the Work of Time and Application, on Men of quick Penetration, a distinguish'd Genius and a World of Honour. Strong Sinews and supple Joints are trifling Advantages not regarded in Persons of their Reach and Grandeur, that can destroy Cities a-bed, and can ruin whole Countries while they are at Dinner. As they are most commonly Men of great Age, it would be ridiculous to expect a hale Constitution and Agility of Limbs from them: So their Heads be but active and well-furnished, 'tis no great Matter what the rest of their Bodies are. If they cannot bear the Fatigue of being on Horseback, they may ride in Coaches, or be carried in Litters. Mens Conduct and Sagacity are never the less for their being Cripples, and the best General the King of *France* has now, can hardly crawl along. Those that are immediately under the chief Commanders must be very nigh of the same Abilities, and are generally Men that have rais'd themselves to those Posts by their Merit. The other Officers are all of them in their several Stations obliged to lay out so large a Share of their Pay in fine Clothes, Accoutrements, and other things by the Luxury of the Times call'd necessary, that they can spare but little Money for Debauches; for as they are advanc'd and their Salaries rais'd, so they are likewise forced to increase their Expenses and their Equipages, which as well as every thing else, must still be proportionable to their Quality: By which means the greatest Part of them are in a manner hindred from those Excesses that might be destructive to Health; while their Luxury thus turn'd another way serves moreover to heighten their Pride and Vanity, the greatest Motives to make them behave themselves like what they would be thought to be.

There is nothing refines Mankind more than Love and Honour. Those two Passions are equivalent to many Virtues, and therefore the greatest Schools of Breeding and good Manners are Courts and Armies; the first to accomplish the Women, the other to polish the Men. What the generality of Officers among civiliz'd Nations affect is a perfect Knowledge of the World and the Rules of Honour; an Air of Frankness, and Humanity peculiar to Military Men of Experi-ence, and such a mixture of Modesty and Undauntedness, as may bespeak them both Courteous and Valiant. Where good Sense is fashionable, and a genteel Beha-viour is in Esteem, Gluttony and Drunkenness can be no reigning Vices. What Officers of Distinction chiefly aim at is not a Beastly, but a Splendid Way of Living, and the Wishes of the most Luxurious in their several degrees of Quality, are to appear handsomely, and excel each other in Finery of Equipage, Politeness of Entertainments, and the Reputation of a judicious Fancy in every thing about them.

But if there should be more dissolute Reprobates among Officers than there are among Men of other Professions, which is not true, yet the most debauch'd of them may be very serviceable, if they have but a great Share of Honour. It is this that covers and makes up for a multitude of Defects in them, and it is this that none (how abandon'd soever they are to Pleasure) dare pretend to be without. But as there is no Argument so convincing as Matter of Fact, let us look back on what so lately happen'd in our two last Wars with *France*. How many puny young Striplings have we had in our Armies, tenderly Educated, nice in their Dress, and curious in their Diet, that underwent all manner of Duties with Gallantry and Chearfulness?

Those that have such dismal Apprehensions of Luxury's enervating and effemi-nating People, might in *Flanders* and *Spain* have seen embroider'd Beaux with fine lac'd Shirts and powder'd Wigs stand as much Fire, and lead up to the Mouth of a Cannon, with as little Concern as it was possible for the most stinking Slovens to have done in their own Hair, tho' it had not been comb'd in a Month; and met with Abundance of wild Rakes, who had actually impair'd their Healths, and broke their Constitutions with Excesses of Wine and Women, that yet behav'd themselves with Conduct and Bravery against their Enemies. Robustness is the least Thing requir'd in an Officer, and if sometimes Strength is of Use, a firm Resolution of Mind, which the Hopes of Preferment, Emulation, and the Love of Glory inspire them with, will at a Push supply the Place of bodily Force.

Those that understand their Business, and have a sufficient Sense of Honour, as soon as they are used to Danger will always be capable Officers: And their Luxury, as long as they spend no body's Money but their own, will never be prejudicial to a Nation.

By all which I think I have proved what I design'd in this Remark on Luxury. First, That in one Sense every Thing may be call'd so, and in another there is no such Thing. Secondly, That with a wise Administration all People may swim in as much Foreign Luxury as their Product can purchase, without being impoverish'd by it. And Lastly, That where Military Affairs are taken care of as they ought, and the Soldiers well paid and kept in good Discipline, a wealthy Nation may live in all the Ease and Plenty imaginable; and in many Parts of it, shew as much Pomp and Delicacy, as Human Wit can invent, and at the same Time be formidable to their Neighbours, and come up to the Character of the Bees in the Fable, of which I said, That

> *Flatter'd in Peace, and fear'd in Wars,*
> *They were th'Esteem of Foreigners,*
> *And lavish of their Wealth and Lives,*
> *The Balance of all other Hives.*[2]

---

[2] *The grumbling hive: or, knaves turn'd honest,* lines 157–60.

FRANÇOIS QUESNAY

BIOGRAPHICAL NOTE

François Quesnay (1694–1774), demographer, *philosophe* and one of the most controversial economic theorists of the French Enlightenment, trained first as a surgeon and gynaecologist in Paris, where until 1716 he combined his medical studies with an apprenticeship to an engraver. His first published work was the *Observations on the effect of bleeding* (1730), in which he contested successfully the theories of Jean-Baptiste Silva, the leading contemporary authority on the subject. His reputation as a doctor was officially recognised in 1749 when he was appointed as Mme de Pompadour's personal physician. In 1752 he was appointed physician to Louis XV, and ennobled.

In the 1750s Quesnay turned from medicine to politics and economics, and became a close associate of the *philosophes*, providing two potentially controversial entries on 'Evidence' and 'Function of the soul' for Diderot's *Encyclopedia*. In the same volume of the *Encyclopedia* (vol. VI) Quesnay also published his first major statement on economic issues, the entry 'Farmers (political economy)'. This was followed in 1757 by the appearance in the next volume of the *Encyclopedia* (vol. VII) of his second celebrated entry on political economy, 'Grain'. Their contents, together with that of another entry written in the same period, but not published until later, 'Tax', and a third essay, *Interest on money* (published under a different title in 1766, not as part of the *Encyclopedia*), encapsulate the basic principles of Quesnay's economic analysis. He had not yet developed a fully coherent system, but these early essays bear the signs of his conversion from a mercantilist to a physiocratic philosophy, and are relevant to an understanding of *The economic tableau.*

As the physiocrats consolidated, their enemies increased. Louis-François Graslin denounced the new economic thinking as fantasy in his *Analytical essay on wealth and tax* (1767), and Forbonnais sought to undermine Quesnay's reputation in 1767 in the *Journal of Agriculture*, as well as in his *Economic principles and observations*, in which he concentrated on attacking the 'obscure metaphysics' of the *Tableau* itself. Quesnay then issued, under the aegis of Dupont de Nemours, a collection of essays entitled *Physiocracy, or the natural constitution of the government most advantageous to the human species* (1767), in which the neologism, 'physiocracy', was used in print for the first time.

Opposition to Quesnay came from Voltaire, Rousseau, Mably, Linguet, Grimm, Galiani and others, and spread eventually to government circles and the general public, the decline of physiocracy in France in the 1770s coinciding ironically with the growth in its popularity abroad. After 1769 Quesnay's interest in physiocratic theory waned, and for the remaining part of his life he turned his attention increasingly to mathematics. With Louis XV's death in 1774, the year in which Turgot came to power and re-established the free trade in grain, Quesnay fell from royal favour. His death was announced to the Academy of Surgery on 22 December of that year.

The publishing history of the *Tableau* is complex and still somewhat mysterious, but modern scholarship indicates that the earliest appearance of a manuscript version was December 1758 (Kuczynski and Meek 1972). This 'first edition' was sent to Mirabeau, and was probably little more than a hand-drawn diagram, without the maxims and notes. A printed version of this diagrammatic formulation (the 'zig-zag'), together with other documentation, the 'second edition', appeared a few months later, but again was given only to Mirabeau. A 'third edition', revised and expanded, and containing the full set of maxims and notes, probably appeared sometime in 1759 (Kuczynski 1965). Quesnay circulated this version to a wider circle of friends, but it was not put on sale to the public, and most contemporaries knew the *Tableau* only in forms printed in the sixth part of Mirabeau's *Friend of man* (1760) and in his *Rural philosophy* (1763), and in Quesnay's *Analysis*, and *First economic problem* (1766) and his *Second economic problem* (1767).

EDITORIAL NOTE

The base text for the present translation is the 'third edition' of the *Tableau économique* (1759), edited in facsimile reproduction by M. Kuczynski and R. Meek, and interleaved with an English translation. The present translation owes much to the Kuczynski–Meek English text.* Twenty-four maxims have been translated in their entirety, but only extracts from the last two of Quesnay's twenty lengthy annotations have been included.

FURTHER READING

Fox-Genovese, E., *The origins of physiocracy: economic revolution and social order in eighteenth-century France* (Ithaca and London, Cornell University Press, 1976).

*Kuczynski, M. and Meek, R., *Quesnay's Tableau économique*, edited with new material, translations and notes (London, Macmillan; New York, Augustus M. Kelley, 1972). See introduction.

Lough, J., *The Encyclopédie* (Geneva, Slatkine, 1989). Reprint. See particularly pp. 39–50.

The economic tableau (1758)

EXTRACT FROM M. DE SULLY'S ROYAL MAXIMS ON ECONOMIC GOVERNMENT

In the preceding *Tableau* you can see that in regard to the 600 million of annual revenue in regular circulation, these 600 million are obtained by means of 900 million of annual advances, and are distributed annually to four million heads of families. There are one million proprietors, whose average expenditure is estimated to be 600 *livres* each and three million heads of families in paid work or jobs, each of whom takes 300 *livres* in all for his expenses.

But we assume in this distribution:

1. That the whole revenue of 600 million goes into annual circulation, and is fully deployed, that it does not create monetary fortunes, or that at least there is a balance between the fortunes that are created and those entering into general circulation again. For otherwise these monetary fortunes would stop the flow of part of this annual national revenue, and constrain the kingdom's stock of wealth, or financial holdings, in a way that would be detrimental to the repayment of advances, to the payment of artisans' wages, to the reproduction of revenue, and to taxation.

2. That no part of the total sum of revenues should go to foreign countries without a return in the form of money and commodities.

3. That the nation suffers no loss in its mutual trading activities with other countries, even if these activities are highly profitable to merchants through the profits they make from their fellow-citizens on the sale of the goods they import. For then the increase in these merchants' fortunes represents a reduction in the circulation of revenue, which is detrimental to distribution and reproduction.

4. That people are not deceived by an apparent advantage in mutual trade with other countries through judging things simply by balancing sums of money, [and] without examining the greater or lesser profit resulting from the commodities

themselves that have been bought and sold; for a loss is often incurred by the nation receiving a money surplus, and this loss damages the distribution and reproduction of revenue. In the mutual trade in raw materials purchased from abroad, and manufactured commodities sold abroad, the disadvantage usually lies with the latter because the sale of raw materials yields much greater profits.

5. That proprietors, and those engaged in the paid professions, are not persuaded by any worry, unforeseen by the government, to go in for sterile savings, which would remove a proportion of their revenues or gains from circulation and distribution.

6. That the administration of [public] finances, whether in the form of tax collection or government expenditure, does not generate monetary fortunes, which take a slice of revenue out of circulation, distribution and reproduction.

7. That taxes should not be destructive or disproportionate to the nation's total revenue; that tax increases follow increases in revenue; that taxation is based directly on the net product of landed property, and not on produce, where it would escalate the costs of collection, and be detrimental to trade. That tax is not raised from the advances made to farmers of landed property either; for the advances made to the kingdom's agricultural sector should be seen as a piece of property that must be very carefully preserved [to ensure] the production of the nation's taxes and revenues. Otherwise taxation degenerates into plunder, and causes a deterioration that quickly leads to a state's ruination.

8. That the farmers' advances be sufficient for the expenses of cultivation to reproduce by at least a hundred per cent, for if the advances are not sufficient then the expenses of cultivation are proportionately higher, and generate less net product.

9. That the children of farmers settle in the countryside in order to keep up the supply of farm managers, for if harassment makes them abandon the land and persuades them to return to the cities, they will take with them their fathers' wealth which used to be invested in cultivation. It is not so much men as wealth that must be attracted to the land, for the more that people use wealth to grow corn, the fewer the men needed, the more the cultivation of corn prospers, and the more net profit it yields. This is the case with the large-scale cultivation that rich farmers engage in, compared to the small-scale cultivation of poor tenant farmers who plough [their fields] using oxen or cows.

10. That the desertion of the kingdom by inhabitants taking their money with them be avoided.

11. That barriers are not raised against the external trade in raw produce, *for reproduction follows market demand.*

12. That the price of produce and commodities in the kingdom is not made to fall, for mutual foreign trade would then not be to the nation's advantage. MARKET VALUE REFLECTS REVENUE. *Abundance and worthlessness do not mean wealth. Shortages and high prices mean poverty. Abundance and high prices mean affluence.*

13. That no one should think that cheap produce profits the common people, for the low price of produce makes their wages fall, diminishes their sense of well-being, provides them with less work or paid jobs, and reduces the nation's revenue.

14. That the well-being of the common people not be reduced, for they would not then be able to contribute enough to the consumption of produce that can only be consumed inside the country, and the nation's reproduction and revenue would fall.

15. That the breeding of livestock be encouraged, for livestock provides the land with the manure that ensures rich harvests.

16. That luxury in the form of ornamentation not be encouraged because it is sustained only at the expense of the luxury of subsistence. It is the latter that maintains the market and good prices for raw produce, and the reproduction of the nation's revenue.

17. That economic government concerns itself only with the encouragement of productive expenditure and the external trade in raw produce, and that it leaves sterile expenditure alone.

18. That resources for the extraordinary needs of the state can be expected to come only from the nation's prosperity, and not out of credit from financiers; for *monetary fortunes are clandestine wealth that knows neither King nor country.*

19. That the state avoids loans which generate private incomes, which burden the state with ruinous debt, and which cause a traffic or trade in finance through the medium of negotiable bills, on which the discount increases sterile monetary fortunes more and more, distancing finance from agriculture, and depriving [agriculture] of the wealth necessary for the improvement of landed property, and the cultivation of the land.

20. That a nation with a large territory to cultivate, and the means to carry on a large trade in raw produce, does not extend its use of money and men too far into the manufacture and trade in luxury goods to the detriment of the labour and expenditure [allocated to] agriculture; for above all else the kingdom must be well provided with rich cultivators.

21. That land used for the cultivation of corn be concentrated as far as possible on large farms worked by prosperous farm-managers; for the upkeep and maintenance of buildings in large agricultural businesses is much less costly, relatively speaking, and yields much more net produce than small ones do, because the latter employ a larger number of farmers' families to no good purpose, paid for out of the revenue from the land, the extent of whose activities and means leaves them too inadequately provided for to carry on a prosperous cultivation of the land. This proliferation of farmers is less advantageous to the [whole] people than is the increase in revenues, for the most secure kind of people, the people readiest to undertake the various occupations and various jobs that divide men up into different classes, is the one that is supported by the net product. All forms of savings employed profitably in the form of work that can be done by animals, machines, rivers, etc., brings benefits to the people and to the state, more net product assures men of a higher reward for other sorts of services, or other kinds of work.

22. That each man is free to cultivate in his field whatever products are suggested to him by his interests, his means, and the nature of the land, so that he may extract from it the greatest possible yield. A monopoly in the cultivation of landed property must not be encouraged, because it has a detrimental effect on the nation's general income. The prejudice that leads to the encouragement of an abundance of basic, primary produce at the expense of produce that is less necessary, [and] to the detriment of the market value of one or the other, is inspired by a short-sighted view that masks the effects of mutual external trade which provides for everything, and determines the price of the produce that each nation can cultivate most profitably. Revenue and taxes are the basic, primary wealth of a state; they are needed to defend its subjects against shortages and enemies, to maintain the glory and power of the monarch, and the prosperity of the nation.[1]

23. That the government be less concerned with making economies than with the transactions needed for the kingdom's prosperity, for an expenditure that is too high can cease to be excessive through an increase in wealth. But abuses must not be confused with simple expenditure, for abuses could swallow up the whole of the nation's, and the sovereign's, wealth.

24. That less attention be paid to increasing the population than to increasing revenue, for the greater well-being procured through higher revenues is to be preferred to the greater need for urgent subsistence required by a population that

is too large for the nation's revenue. When the people feel well-off there are more resources to meet the needs of the state, and more means to make agriculture prosper as well.[2]

Without these conditions, the agricultural [system] assumed in the *Tableau*, producing a hundred per cent [yield], as it does in England, would be a fiction, but the principles behind it would be no less certain for all that, nor would the true principles of the science of economic government be confused here with the trivial and specious financial transactions whose only concern is the nation's stock of money and the movement of currency arising from the traffic in money where credit, the attraction of interest rates, etc., only produce, as in the case of gambling, a sterile circulation. This can only be advantageous in exceptional circumstances. The science of a kingdom's economic government lies in a knowledge of the true sources of wealth, and of the means of increasing and preserving them.

Economic government opens up the sources of wealth. Wealth attracts men. Men and wealth make agriculture prosper, expand trade, stimulate industry, increase and preserve wealth. Economic government averts any decline in the affluence and strength of the nation. The success of other parts of the kingdom's administration depends on the abundance of resources [it creates]. Economic government strengthens the power of the state, attracts the respect of other nations, guarantees the glory of the monarch and the happiness of the people. It includes in its purview all the essential principles of perfect government, in which authority is always protective, benevolent, a well-loved guardian, not open to anything that might divert it from its [true] path, its influence never too extreme, incapable of causing anxiety, protecting the nation's interests in every way: good order, public rights, [and] the power and dominion of the Sovereign.

---

[1] What does the prosperity of an agricultural nation consist of? IN LARGE ADVANCES TO PERPETUATE AND INCREASE REVENUES AND TAXES; IN A FREE AND UNRESTRICTED INTERNAL AND EXTERNAL TRADE; IN THE ENJOYMENT OF THE ANNUAL WEALTH OF LANDED PROPERTY; IN SUBSTANTIAL CASH PAYMENTS OF REVENUE AND TAXES. Abundant productivity comes from large advances. Consumption and trade sustain the sales and market value of products. Market value is the measure of the nation's wealth. Wealth regulates the level of taxes that can be imposed, and provides the money that pays for them. This money must circulate in trading [activities], but there must not be so much of it around that it affects adversely the country's use and consumption of the annual product, which ought to perpetuate real wealth through reproduction and mutual trade.

Money in the form of coinage is wealth paid for by other kinds of wealth, which is for nations *a token of mediation between sales and purchases.* It no longer contributes towards the perpetuation of wealth in any country where it is kept out of circulation, and no longer returns wealth for wealth. Thus the more it is accumulated, the more it costs in terms of wealth that is not renewed, and the more it impoverishes the nation. Money is therefore an active and truly profitable sort of wealth for a country only in so far as it continually returns wealth for wealth, because by itself money is only sterile wealth with no value apart from its usefulness for selling and buying [things], and for the payment of revenues and taxes which recirculate it so that the same money is continually meeting these payments in turn, and for its use in trade.

Thus the total stock of money of an agricultural nation turns out to be only equal approximately to the net product, or annual revenue of its landed property, for when it stands in this proportion it is more than sufficient for the nation's use. A greater quantity of money would not be a useful form of wealth for the state. For although taxes are paid with money, it is not money which provides for them, it is the wealth from the land, regenerated each year. It is in this regenerated wealth and not, as the vulgar think, in the nation's cash reserves that the prosperity and strength of a state consists. You could never provide the means for the successive renewal of this wealth from cash reserves, but in trade money is easily taken care of with written pledges, guaranteed by a country's wealth, which is transferable abroad. Greed for money is a lively passion in individuals because they are greedy for a wealth that represents other forms of wealth, but this kind of greed, divorced from its object, should not be a passion with the state. A great stock of money is desirable in a state only in so far as it is in proportion to revenue, and denotes in this way an affluence that is perpetually regenerated, and whose enjoyment is effective and fully assured. The abundance of money in the reign of Charles V, known as the Wise, was of this variety, reflecting other forms of wealth in the kingdom. You can judge this from the categories of wealth listed in that prince's huge inventory, apart from a reserve in his treasury of 27 million (almost 200 million in today's currency). This great amount of wealth is all the more remarkable when you think that the domains of the Kings of France at that time did not include a third of the [present] kingdom.

Money is therefore not the real wealth of a state, the wealth that is continually consumed and regenerated, for money does not create money. It is true that an *écu*, well invested, can generate a wealth of two *écus*, but then this is wealth that has increased, not money. Thus money should not remain in sterile hands. Therefore, whether money goes into Peter's or into Paul's pocket is not such a matter of indifference to the state as people think, for it is essential that it is not taken out of the pocket of the one who will use it for the benefit of the state. But strictly speaking, money that is used in this way in a nation is not owned by anyone; it belongs to the state's needs, which cause it to circulate for the reproduction of the wealth for the nation's subsistence, and for the contribution to the Sovereign.

This money must not be confused with those funds that are the subject of the ruinous traffic in loans and interest, and which escape the contributions that all annual revenue should pay to the state. This money, for use in times of need, has with all individuals a destination to which it definitely belongs. That which is destined for the payment of current taxes belongs to the taxes; that which is destined to meet the need for some purchase belongs to that need; that which stimulates agriculture, trade and industry belongs to that usage; and that which is destined to pay a debt that has fallen due, or a loan which is about to expire, belongs to that debt, etc., and not to the man who possesses it. It is the nation's money. No one can lend it, because it belongs to no one. Yet it is money dispersed [like this] that forms the main part of a really wealthy kingdom's treasure, where it is always being used for the benefit of the state. People do not even hesitate to sell it at a higher price than it cost, that is, to allow it to go abroad to purchase goods whenever there is a sure profit [to be made]. And foreign countries are not unaware either of the advantages of this trade, in which profit determines the exchange of money for goods. Money and goods everywhere represent wealth only in relation to their market value.

Money which lies idle, and which cannot be regenerated, is small change that is soon exhausted whenever there is a slight increase in borrowing. However, it is this idle money that gives the common people illusions. This is what the vulgar see as the nation's wealth, and as an important resource to meet the nation's needs, even those of a great state which can really only be rich by means of the net product of the wealth generated each year on its territory, and which, as it were, causes money to be regenerated by renewing it, and continually accelerating its circulation.

Moreover, when a kingdom is rich and flourishing because of the trade in its products, it has, as a result of its trading links, wealth in other countries, and paper is substituted for money. The abundance and sale of the kingdom's products therefore ensures that it has the use of the cash reserves of every other nation. And money is never in short supply either in a kingdom that is properly cultivated in ways that pay the Sovereign and the proprietors the revenue from the net product of the exchangeable produce, which the soil regenerates annually. But although money is not lacking for the payment of these revenues, we must not deceive ourselves into thinking that money can bear the burden of providing revenue for the state.

Money is a kind of wealth that disappears before your eyes. The raising of taxes can only be based on tangible wealth, wealth that is always being regenerated, and is exchangeable. This provides revenue for the Sovereign who will, moreover, find in it assured resources to meet the urgent needs of the state. The net product of landed property is distributed to three proprietors: the state, landowners and owners of tithes. It is only that part of the property belonging to the owner that is transferable, and its selling price is related only to the revenue it produces, for this is the product that governs the purchase price. The owner's property does not therefore extend any further than that. Thus he is not the one who pays the other proprietors who have shares in the property, since their shares do not belong to him, he has not acquired them, and they are not transferable. Thus the owner of the property should not regard ordinary taxes as a charge levied on his share, for he is not the one paying for this revenue. It is the part of the property that he has not acquired, and which does not belong to him, which pays it to the person to whom it is due. But whenever it is necessary all proprietors should make contributions, based on their share of the property, to the temporary subsidy that urgent needs of state might require. Thus, in agricultural nations, where agriculture is rich and flourishing, there are guaranteed resources for the state in the revenue from landed property.

The government's field of vision should not therefore stop at money, but should extend further, and focus on the abundance and market value of products that come from the land in order to increase revenue. The affluence and power of the monarch, and the prosperity of the nation, consists of this area of visible, annual wealth, and it is this that binds and attaches [the Sovereign's] subjects to the land. Money, industry, mercantile trade and traffic form only an artificial and independent sector which, without the wealth that comes from the land, would be nothing more than a republican state. Constantinople itself, which has no control over wealth of this nature, but is reduced to the mobile wealth of the re-export trade, acquires, in the midst of its despotism, something of the flair and independence of [the former] in its international links, and in the free condition of its commercial wealth. [Note by Quesnay.]

² The predominant notion that nations have of war makes people think that the strength of states consists in large populations, but the military part of a nation can only survive and operate thanks to the tax-paying part. Could it be assumed that the great wealth of a state comes about through a plentiful supply of men? But men can obtain and perpetuate wealth only by means of wealth, and only in so far as men and wealth are in a proper ratio to each other.

Nations never believe that they have enough men, but it escapes people's notice that there are not enough wages to maintain a larger population, and that destitute men are of no benefit to a country, unless they can find assured earnings there to get a living from their work. In the absence of earnings or wages, common people in rural areas may in truth generate, in order to feed themselves, certain low-priced products requiring no expenditure and no prolonged labour, and for which they do not have to wait long to reap the rewards. But these men, these products, and the soil that generates them, are worth nothing to the state. In order to extract revenue from the land, work on the land must yield a net product beyond that of the wages paid to the workers, for it is this net product which enables the other classes of men necessary to the state to subsist. You cannot expect to get this from poor men working the land with their hands, or in other inadequate ways, because they can only procure for themselves alone enough to live on by giving up the cultivation of corn. The cultivation of corn requires too much time, too much work and too much expenditure to be done by men who are destitute, and reduced to extracting their food from the earth just through their physical labour alone.

Thus you should not entrust the cultivation of your land to poor peasants. Animals should plough and fertilise your fields; consumption, sales, free, unrestricted internal and external trade are what guarantee the market value that constitutes your revenue. So responsibility for the cultivation of land, and for the management of rural businesses, should be given to rich men in order to enrich yourself, enrich the state, and to enable inexhaustible wealth to be regenerated. By these means you will be able to enjoy abundantly the products of the land, the arts, maintain a strong defence against your enemies, provide ample subsidies for the costs of the public works needed for the nation's comfort, facilitate trade in what you produce, fortify your frontiers, maintain a formidable navy, beautify the kingdom, and provide working people with the earnings and wages to attract them, and keep them in the kingdom. Thus the political management of agriculture, and of the trade in its produce, is the basic role of the Treasury, and of all the other administrative arms of government in an agricultural nation.

Large armies are not enough to constitute a strong defensive force. The soldier must be well paid so that he can be well disciplined, well trained, energetic, happy and brave. Land and sea wars use other resources apart from men's strength, and require other forms of expenditure much greater than that needed for soldiers' subsistence. Thus wealth, much more than men, is what sustains a war, for as long as one has the wealth to pay men well, there will be no shortage of recruits. The more wealth a nation has to enable it to regenerate wealth annually, the fewer men it needs for this annual reproduction, the more net product it yields, the more men the government has at its disposal for public service and public works. And the more wages there are for their subsistence, the more useful these men are to the state by virtue of the work they do, and by virtue of what they spend, which causes their pay to be recirculated.

Battles won simply by killing men, without causing any other damage, do little to weaken the enemy if he still has the wages [at his disposal] of the men he has lost, and if those are high enough to attract other men. An army of a hundred thousand well-paid men is an army of a million men, for no army to which men are attracted because of the pay can ever be destroyed. It is then up to the soldiers to defend themselves bravely; they have the most to lose, for there is no shortage of people to replace them who are quite prepared to face the dangers of war. Thus it is wealth that maintains the honour of the profession of arms. The hero who wins the battles, gains the glory, and is the first to be exhausted, is not the victor. A historian who confines himself to wonderful events in his account of military exploits offers posterity little insight into the successes [resulting from] the decisive events of the war if he allows posterity to remain unaware of the situation with regard to basic strengths, and to the policies of the nations whose history he is writing, for it is in the permanent well-being of the tax-paying part of the nation, and in the patriotic virtues, that the permanent power of a state resides.

We must think in the same way about public works which facilitate an increase in wealth, such as the construction of canals, the upkeep of roads, rivers, etc. These things can only be undertaken as a result of the well-being of tax-payers in a position to subsidise this expenditure, without harming the annual reproduction of the nation's wealth. Otherwise such expensive public works, although very desirable, would become ruinous undertakings through unregulated taxes or continual *corvées*. The consequences of this would not be repaired by the usefulness of this enforced and exhausting work. For it is difficult to halt the decline of a state. Destructive causes, which proliferate, reduce all the caution and efforts of the Treasury to nothing when we focus only on keeping the effects under control instead of returning to basic principles . . . [Note by Quesnay.]

ADAM SMITH

BIOGRAPHICAL NOTE

Adam Smith (1723–90) was born in Kirkcaldy to a prosperous middle-class family, where his father, another Adam Smith, was a public official, and was educated at the Burgh School in Kirkcaldy. In 1737 he attended Glasgow College, later to become the University of Glasgow, where the chair of moral philosophy was held by Francis Hutcheson. Hutcheson made a deep impression on the young Smith, and it was through Hutcheson that Smith first became acquainted with the work of Quesnay, Cantillon and the physiocratic school. Smith was destined for an ecclesiastical career, but he left Glasgow for Oxford in 1740 to study ancient classical literature instead. In 1750 he was appointed to the chair of logic in Glasgow (a post in which Hume and also Burke had expressed interest), and subsequently to Hutcheson's chair of moral philosophy. He lectured on theology, ethics and jurisprudence, but it was in the early 1750s that he also laid the foundations of his famous doctrine of free trade, and formulated the key concepts later to be developed in *An inquiry into the nature and causes of the wealth of nations*.

By the mid-1750s, when Cantillon and Quesnay were starting to publish the economic treatises that were to underpin the French physiocratic movement, Smith was developing his own economic philosophy. In 1759 he published the *Theory of moral sentiments*, a book that brought him widespread recognition at home and abroad (six editions were printed in his lifetime). The moral and philosophical position adopted by Smith in this work differs in a number of ways from the position he was to take up in the *Wealth*, but it contains elements of his later thinking on questions relating to political economy.

The *Theory*, much admired by Burke, attracted the attention of Charles Towns(h)end, the guardian of the young Duke of Buccleuch, whom Smith was persuaded to accompany as tutor on his travels in Switzerland and France. This post brought Smith into contact with intellectual circles in London for the first time, and enabled him to travel widely in Europe and, towards the end of 1765, to live in Paris for a few months. It was in Paris that he met many of the leading *philosophes*, and also the influential economist, André Morellet, who was later to translate the *Wealth* into French.

Smith was back in London by 1766, and in the following year he returned home to Kirkcaldy. In 1773, armed with the completed manuscript of the *Wealth*, he returned to London for a brief period to find a publisher. His most celebrated treatise was published in March 1776, fulfilling a promise made in 1759 in the concluding paragraph of the *Theory*. In December 1777, following the publication of the second edition of the *Wealth*, Smith was appointed Commissioner of Customs in Scotland, a post which also included the Commissionership of the Salt Duties. His new responsibilities required him to live in Edinburgh where he soon became involved in the North government's policies relating to the question of Irish free trade. By 1789 the fifth edition of the *Wealth* had appeared, and Smith had started work on revisions to the *Theory*. The new edition of the *Theory*, published in the early part of 1790, was the last work that he published before his death.

EDITORIAL NOTE

The *Wealth* was first published in 1776. The base text for the present extracts is the fifth edition, *An inquiry into the nature and causes of the wealth of nations* (London, A. Strahan and T. Cadell, 1789). This is the last edition printed in Smith's lifetime.

FURTHER READING

Cropsey, J., *Polity and economy. An interpretation of the principles of Adam Smith* (The Hague, Martinus Nijhoff, 1957).

Lindgren, J., *The social philosophy of Adam Smith* (The Hague, Martinus Nijhoff, 1973).

Morrow, G., *The ethical and economic theories of Adam Smith* (Clifton, N.J., Augustus M. Kelly, 1973). Reprint.

An inquiry into the nature and causes of the wealth of nations (1776)

INTRODUCTION AND PLAN OF THE WORK

The annual labour of every nation is the fund which originally supplies it with all the necessaries and conveniences of life which it annually consumes, and which consist always in the immediate produce of that labour, or in what is purchased with that produce from other nations.

According, therefore, as this produce, or what is purchased with it, bears a greater or smaller proportion to the number of those who are to consume it, the nation will be better or worse supplied with all the necessaries and conveniences for which it has occasion.

But this proportion must in every nation be regulated by two different circumstances; first by the skill, dexterity and judgment with which its labour is generally applied; and secondly, by the proportion between the number of those who are employed in useful labour, and that of those who are not so employed. Whatever be the soil, climate or extent of territory of any particular nation, the abundance or scantiness of its annual supply must, in that particular situation, depend upon those two circumstances.

The abundance or scantiness of this supply too seems to depend more upon the former of those two circumstances than upon the latter. Among the savage nations of hunters and fishers, every individual who is able to work is more or less employed in useful labour, and endeavours to provide as well as he can the necessaries and conveniences of life for himself, or such as his family or tribe as are either too old, or too young, or too infirm to go a-hunting and fishing. Such nations, however, are so miserably poor that from mere want they are frequently reduced, or at least think themselves reduced, to the necessity sometimes of directly destroying, and sometimes of abandoning their infants, their old people, and those afflicted with lingering diseases, to perish with hunger, or be devoured by wild beasts. Among civilised and thriving nations, on the contrary, though a great number of people do not labour at all, many of whom consume the produce of ten times, frequently of a hundred times more labour than the greater part of those who work; yet the produce of the whole labour of the society is so great that all are often abundantly supplied, and a workman, even of the lowest and poorest order, if he is frugal and industrious, may enjoy a greater share of the necessaries and conveniences of life than it is possible for any savage to acquire.

The causes of this improvement in the productive powers of labour, and the order according to which its produce is naturally distributed among the different ranks and conditions of men in the society, make the subject of the First Book of this inquiry.

Whatever be the actual state of the skill, dexterity and judgment with which labour is applied in any nation, the abundance or scantiness of its annual supply must depend, during the continuance of the state, upon the proportion between the number of those who are annually employed in useful labour, and that of those who are not so employed. The number of useful and productive labourers, it will hereafter appear, is everywhere in proportion to the quantity of capital stock which is employed in setting them to work, and to the particular way in which it is so employed. The Second Book, therefore, treats of the nature of capital stock, of the manner of which it is gradually accumulated, and of the different quantities in labour which it puts into motion, according to the different ways in which it is employed.

Nations tolerably well advanced as to skill, dexterity and judgment in the application of labour have followed very different plans in the general conduct or direction of it; and those plans have not all been equally favourable to the greatness of its produce. The policy of some nations has given extraordinary encouragement to the industry of the country; that of others to the industry of towns. Scarce any nation has dealt equally and impartially with every sort of industry. Since the downfall of the Roman empire, the policy of Europe has been more favourable to arts, manufactures and commerce, the industry of towns, than to agriculture, the industry of the country. The circumstances which seem to have introduced and established this policy are explained in the Third Book.

Though those different plans were perhaps first introduced by the private interests and prejudices of particular orders of men without any regard to, or foresight of, their consequences upon the general welfare of the society, yet they have given occasion to very different theories of political oeconomy; of which some magnify the importance of that industry which is carried on in towns, others of that which is carried on in the country. Those theories have had a considerable influence, not only upon the opinions of men of learning, but upon the public conduct of princes and sovereign states. I have endeavoured, in the Fourth Book, to explain, as fully and distinctly as I can, those different theories, and the principal effects which they have produced in different ages and nations.

To explain in what has consisted the revenue of the great body of the people, or what has been the nature of those funds, which in different ages and nations have supplied their annual consumption, is the object of these four first books. The Fifth and last Book treats of the revenue of the sovereign, or commonwealth. In this book I have endeavoured to show: first, what are the necessary expenses of the sovereign, or commonwealth; which of those expenses ought to be defrayed by the general contribution of the whole society, and what are the principal advantages and inconveniences of each of those methods; and thirdly, and lastly, what are the reasons and causes which have induced almost all modern governments to mortgage some part of this revenue, or to contract debts, and what have been the effects of those debts upon the real wealth, the annual produce of the land and labour of the society.

The greatest improvement in the productive powers of labour, and the greater part of the skill, dexterity and judgment with which it is anywhere directed or applied, seem to have been the effects of the division of labour.

The effects of the division of labour, in the general business of society, will be more easily understood by considering in what manner it operates in some particular manufactures. It is commonly supposed to be carried furthest in some very trifling ones; not perhaps that it really is carried further in them than in others of more importance; but in those trifling manufactures, which are destined to supply the small wants of but a small number of people, the whole number of workmen must necessarily be small; and those employed in every different branch of the work can often be collected into the same workhouse, and placed at once under the view of the spectator. In those great manufactures, on the contrary, which are destined to supply the great wants of the great body of the people, every different branch of the work employs so great a number of workmen that it is impossible to collect them all into the same workhouse. We can seldom see more, at one time, than those employed in one single branch. Though in such manufactures, therefore, the work may really be divided into a much greater number of parts than in those of a more trifling nature; the division is not near so obvious, and has accordingly been much less observed.

To take an example, therefore, from a very trifling manufacture, but one in which the division of labour has been very often taken notice of, the trade of the pin-maker; a workman not educated to this business (which the division of labour has rendered a distinct trade), nor acquainted with the use of the machinery employed in it (to the invention of which the same division of labour has probably given occasion), could scarce perhaps with his utmost industry make one pin in a day, and certainly could not make twenty. But in the way in which this business is now carried on, not only the whole work is a peculiar trade, but it is divided into a number of branches, of which the greater part are likewise peculiar trades. One man draws out the wire, another straights it, a third cuts it, a fourth points it, a fifth grinds it at the top for receiving the head; to make the head requires two or three distinct operations; to put it on is a peculiar business, to whiten the pin is another; it is even a trade by itself to put them into the paper; and the important business of making a pin is, in this manner, divided into about eighteen distinct operations which, in some manufactories, are all performed by distinct hands, though in others the same man will sometimes perform two or three of them. I have seen a small manufactory of this kind where ten men only were employed, and where some of them consequently performed two or three distinct operations. But though they were very poor, and therefore but indifferently accommodated with the necessary machinery, they could, when they exerted themselves, make among them about twelve pounds of pins in a day. There are in a pound upwards of four thousand pins of a middling size. Those ten persons, therefore, could make among them upwards of forty-eight thousand pins in a day. Each person, therefore, making a tenth part of forty-eight thousand pins, might be considered as making four thousand eight hundred pins in a day. But if they had all wrought separately and independently, and without any of them having been educated to this peculiar business, they certainly could not each of them have made twenty, perhaps not one pin in a day; that is, certainly, not the two hundred and fortieth, perhaps not the four thousand eight hundredth part of what they are at present capable of performing in consequence of a proper division and combination of their different operations.

In every other art and manufacture, the effects of the division of labour are similar to what they are in this very trifling one; though in many of them the labour can neither be so much subdivided, nor reduced to so great a simplicity of operation. The division of labour, however, so far as it can be introduced, occasions in every art a proportionable increase of the productive powers of labour. The separation of different trades and employments from one another seems to have taken place in consequence of this advantage. This separation too is generally carried furthest in those countries which enjoy the highest degree of industry and improvement; what is the work of one man in a rude state of society being generally that of several in an improved one. In every improved society, the farmer is generally nothing but a farmer; the manufacturer nothing but a manufacturer. The labour too which is necessary to produce any one complete manufacture is almost always divided among a great number of hands. How many different trades are employed in each branch of the linen and woollen manufac-tures, from the growers of the flax and the wool, to the bleachers and smoothers of the linen, or to the dyers and dressers of the cloth! The nature of agriculture, indeed, does not admit of so many subdivisions of labour, nor of so complete a separation of one business from another, as manufactures. It is impossible to separate so entirely the business of the grazier from that of the corn-farmer, as the trade of the carpenter is commonly separated from that of the smith. The spinner is almost always a distinct person from the weaver; but the ploughman, the harrower, the sower of the seed, and the reaper of the corn, are often the same. The occasions for those different sorts of labour returning with the different seasons of the year, it is impossible that one man should be constantly employed in any one of them. This impossibility of making so complete and entire a separation of all the different branches of labour employed in agriculture is perhaps the reason why the improvement of the productive powers of labour in this art does not always keep pace with their improvement in manufactures. The most opulent nations, indeed, generally excel all their neighbours in agriculture as well as in manufactures; but they are commonly more distinguished by their superiority in the latter than in the former. Their lands are in general better cultivated and, having more labour and expense bestowed upon them, produce more in proportion to the extent and natural fertility of the ground. But this superiority of produce is seldom much more than in proportion to the superiority of labour and expense. In agriculture the labour of the rich country is not always much more productive than that of the poor; or, at least, it is never so much more productive as it commonly is in manufactures. The corn of the rich country, therefore, will not always, in the same degree of goodness, come cheaper to market than that of the poor. The corn of Poland, in the same degree of goodness, is as cheap as that of France, notwithstanding the superior opulence and improvement of the latter country. The corn of France is, in the corn provinces, fully as good, and in most years nearly about the same price with the corn of England, though in opulence and improvement France is perhaps inferior to England. The corn-lands of England, however, are better cultivated than those of France, and the corn-lands of France are said to be much better cultivated than those of Poland. But though the poor country, notwithstanding the inferiority of its cultivation, can in some measure rival the rich in the cheapness and goodness of its corn, it can pretend to no such competition in its manufactures, at least if those manufactures suit the soil, climate and situation of the rich country. The silks of France are better and cheaper than those of England, because the silk manufacture, at least under the present high duties upon the importation of raw silk, does not so well suit the climate of England as that of France. But the hard-ware and coarse woollens of England are beyond all comparison superior to those of France, and much cheaper too in the same degree of goodness. In Poland there are said to be scarce any manufactures of any kind, a few of those coarser household manufactures excepted, without which no country can well subsist.

This great increase of the quantity of work which, in consequence of the division of labour, the same number of people are capable of performing, is owing to three different circumstances; first to the increase of dexterity in every particular workman; secondly, to the saving of the time which is commonly lost in passing from one species of work to another; and lastly, to the invention of a great number of machines which facilitate and abridge labour, and enable one man to do the work of many . . . [**Wealth of nations, I, 1: 'Of the division of labour'**]

The great commerce of every civilised society is that carried on between the inhabitants of the town and those of the country. It consists in the exchange of rude for manufactured produce, either immediately, or by the intervention of money, or of some sort of paper which represents money. The country supplies the town with the means of subsistence and the materials of manufacture. The town repays this supply by sending back a part of the manufactured produce to the inhabitants of the country. The town, in which there neither is nor can be any reproduction of substances, may very properly be said to gain its whole wealth and subsistence from the country. We must not, however, upon this account imagine that the gain of the town is the loss of the country. The gains of both are mutual and reciprocal, and the division of labour is in this, as in all other cases, advantageous to all the different persons employed in the various occupations into which it is subdivided. The inhabitants of the country purchase of the town a greater quantity of manufactured goods with the produce of a much smaller quantity of their own labour than they must have employed had they attempted to prepare them themselves. The town affords a market for the surplus produce of the country, or what is over and above the maintenance of the cultivators, and it is there that the inhabitants of the country exchange it for something else which is in demand among them. The greater the number and revenue of the inhabitants of the town, the more extensive is the market which it affords to those of the country; and the more extensive that market, it is always the more advantageous to a great number. The corn which grows within a mile of the town sells there for the same price with that which comes from twenty miles distance. But the price of the latter must generally not only pay the expense of raising and bringing it to market, but afford too the ordinary profits of agriculture to the farmer. The proprietors and cultivators of the country, therefore, which lies in the neighbourhood of the town, over and above the ordinary profits of agriculture, gain in the price of what they sell the whole value of the carriage of the like produce that is brought from more distant parts, and they save, besides, the whole value of this carriage in the price of what they buy. Compare the cultivation of the lands in the neighbourhood of any considerable town with that of those which lie at some distance from it, and you will easily satisfy yourself how much the country is benefited by the commerce of the town. Among all the absurd speculations that have been propagated concerning the balance of trade, it has never been pretended that either the country loses by its commerce with the town, or the town by that with the country which maintains it.

As subsistence is, in the nature of things, prior to conveniency and luxury, so the industry which procures the former must necessarily be prior to that which ministers to the latter. The cultivation and improvement of the country, therefore, which affords subsistence, must necessarily be prior to the increase of the town, which furnishes only the means of conveniency and luxury. It is the surplus produce of the country only, or what is over and above the maintenance of the cultivators, that constitutes the subsistence of the town, which can therefore increase only with the increase of this surplus produce. The town, indeed, may not always derive its whole subsistence from the country in its neighbourhood, or even from the territory to which it belongs, but from very distant countries, and this, though it forms no exception from the general rule, has occasioned considerable variations in the progress of opulence in different ages and nations.

That order of things which necessity imposes in general, though not in every particular country, is in every particular country promoted by the natural inclinations of man. If human institutions had never thwarted those natural inclinations, the towns could nowhere have improved beyond what the improvement and cultivation of the territory in which they were situated could support; till such time, at least, as the whole of that territory was completely cultivated and improved. Upon equal, or nearly equal profits, most men will choose to employ their capital rather in the improvement and cultivation of land than either in manufactures or in foreign trade. The man who employs his capital in land has it more under his view and command, and his fortune is much less liable to accidents than that of the trader who is obliged frequently to commit it, not only to the winds and the waves, but to the more uncertain elements of human folly and injustice, by giving great credits in distant countries to men with whose character and situation he can seldom be thoroughly acquainted. The capital of the landlord, on the contrary, which is fixed in the improvement of his land, seems to be as well secured as the nature of human affairs can admit of. The beauty of the country besides, the pleasures of a country life, the tranquillity of mind which it promises, and wherever the injustice of human laws does not disturb it, the independency which it really affords, have charms that more or less attract everybody; and as to cultivate the ground was the original destination of man, so in every stage of his existence he seems to retain a predilection for this primitive employment.

Without the assistance of some artificers, indeed, the cultivation of land cannot be carried on but with great inconveniency and continual interruption. Smiths, carpenters, wheelwrights and ploughwrights, masons and bricklayers, tanners, shoemakers, and taylors are people whose service the farmer has frequent occasion for. Such artificers too stand occasionally in need of the assistance of one another; and as their residence is not, like that of the farmer, necessarily tied down to a precise spot, they naturally settle in the neighbourhood of one another, and thus form a small town or village. The butcher, the brewer and the baker soon join them, together with many other artificers and retailers necessary or useful for supplying their occasional wants, and who contribute still further to augment the town. The inhabitants of the town and those of the country are mutually the servants of one another. The town is a continual fair or market to which the inhabitants of the country resort in order to exchange their rude for manufactured produce. It is this commerce which supplies the inhabitants of the town both with the materials of their work and the means of their subsistence. The quantity of the finished work which they sell to the inhabitants of the country necessarily regulates the quantity of the materials and provisions which they buy. Neither their employment nor subsistence, therefore, can augment but in proportion to the augmentation of the demand from the country for finished work; and thus demands can augment only in proportion to the extension of improvement and cultivation. Had human institutions, therefore, never disturbed the natural course of things, the progressive wealth and increase of the towns would, in every political society, be consequential, and in proportion to the improvement and cultivation of the territory or country.

In our North American colonies, where uncultivated land is still to be had on easy terms, no manufactures for distant sale have ever yet been established in any of their towns. When an artificer has acquired a little more stock than is necessary for carrying on his own business in supplying the neighbouring country, he does not, in North America, attempt to establish with it a manufacture for more distant sale, but employs it in the purchase and improvement of uncultivated land. From artificer he becomes planter, and neither the large wages nor the easy subsistence which that country affords to artificers can bribe him rather to work for other people than for himself. He feels that an artificer is the servant of his customers, from whom he derives his subsistence; but that a planter who cultivates his own land, and derives his necessary subsistence from the labour of his own family, is really a master, and independent of all the world.

In countries, on the contrary, where there is either no uncultivated land, or none that can be had upon easy terms, every artificer who has acquired more stock than he can employ in the occasional jobs of the neighbourhood endeavours to prepare work for more distant sale. The smith erects some sort of iron, the weaver some sort of linen or woollen manufactury. Those different manufactures come, in process of time, to be gradually subdivided, and thereby improved and refined in a great variety of ways, which may easily be conceived, and which it is therefore unnecessary to explain any further.

In seeking for employment to a capital, manufactures are, upon equal or nearly equal profits, naturally preferred to foreign commerce, for the same reason that agriculture is naturally preferred to manufactures. As the capital of the landlord or farmer is more secure than that of the manufacturer, so the capital of the manufacturer, being at all times within his view and command, is more secure than that of the foreign merchant. In every period, indeed, of every society the surplus part both of the rude and manufactured produce, or that for which there is no demand at home, must be sent abroad in order to be exchanged for something for which there is some demand at home. But whether the capital, which carries this surplus produce abroad, be a foreign or a domestic one, is of very little importance. If the society has not acquired sufficient capital both to cultivate all its lands and to manufacture in the completest manner the whole of its rude produce, there is even a considerable advantage that that rude produce should be exported by a foreign capital in order that the whole stock of the society may be employed in more useful purposes. The wealth of ancient Egypt, that of China and Indostan, sufficiently demonstrate that a nation may attain a very high degree of opulence, though the greater part of its exportation trade be carried on by foreigners. The progress of our North American and West Indian colonies would have been much less rapid had no capital but what belonged to themselves been employed in exporting their surplus produce.

According to the natural course of things, therefore, the greater part of the capital of every growing society is first directed to agriculture, afterwards to manufactures, and last of all to foreign commerce. This order of things is so very natural that in every society that had any territory it has always, I believe, been in some degree observed. Some of their lands must have been cultivated before any considerable towns could be established, and some sort of coarse industry of the manufacturing kind must have been carried on in those towns before they could well think of employing themselves in foreign commerce.

But though this natural order of things must have taken place in some degree in every such society, it has, in all the modern states of Europe, been in many respects entirely inverted. The foreign commerce of some of their cities has introduced all their finer manufactures, or such as were fit for distant sale; and manufactures and foreign commerce together have given birth to the principal improvements of agriculture. The manners and customs which the nature of their original government introduced, and which remained after that government was greatly altered, necessarily forced them into this unnatural and retrograde order. [*Wealth of nations*, III, 1: 'On the natural progress of opulence']

That wealth consists in money, or in gold and silver, is a popular notion which naturally arises from the double function of money as the instrument of commerce and as the measure of value. In consequence of its being the instrument of commerce, when we have money we can more readily obtain whatever else we have occasion for than by means of any other commodity. The great affair, we always find, is to get money. When that is obtained, there is no difficulty in making any subsequent purchase. In consequence of its being the measure of value, we estimate that of all other commodities by the quantity of money which they will exchange for we say of a rich man that he is worth a great deal, and of a poor man that he is worth very little money. A frugal man, or a man eager to be rich, is said to love money; and a careless, a generous or a profuse man is said to be indifferent about it. To grow rich is to get money; and wealth and money, in short, are in common language considered as in every respect synonymous.

A rich country, in the same manner as a rich man, is supposed to be a country abounding in money; and to heap up gold and silver in any country is supposed to be the readiest way to enrich it . . .

It would be too ridiculous to go about seriously to prove that wealth does not consist in money, or in gold and silver, but in what money purchases, and is valuable only for purchasing. Money, no doubt, makes always a part of the national capital, but it has already been shown[1] that it generally makes but a small part, and always the most unprofitable part of it.

It is not because wealth consists more essentially in money than in goods that the merchant finds it generally more easy to buy goods with money than to buy money with goods; but because money is the known and established instrument of commerce, for which everything is readily given in exchange, but which is not always with equal readiness to be got in exchange for everything. The greater part of goods besides are more perishable than money, and he may frequently sustain a much greater loss by keeping them. When his goods are upon hand too, he is more liable to such demands for money as he may not be able to answer than when he has got their price in his coffers. Over and above all this, his profit arises more directly from selling than from buying, and he is upon all these accounts generally much more anxious to exchange his goods for money than his money for goods. But though a particular merchant, with abundance of goods in his warehouse, may sometimes be ruined by not being able to sell them in time, a nation or country is not liable to the same accident. The whole capital of a merchant frequently consists in perishable goods destined for purchasing money. But it is but a very small part of the annual produce of the land and labour of a country which can ever be destined for purchasing gold and silver from their neighbours. The far greater part is circulated and consumed among themselves; and even of the surplus which is sent abroad, the greater part is generally destined for the purchase of other foreign goods. Though gold and silver, therefore, could not be had in exchange for the goods destined to purchase them, the nation would not be ruined. It might, indeed, suffer some loss or inconveniency, and be forced upon some of those expedients which are necessary for supplying the place of money. The annual produce of its land and labour, however, would be the same, or very nearly the same, as usual, because the same, or very nearly the same, consumable capital would be employed in maintaining it. And though goods do not always draw money so readily as money draws goods, in the long run they draw it more necessarily than even it draws them. Goods can serve many other purposes besides purchasing money, but money can serve no other purpose besides purchasing goods. Money, therefore, necessarily runs after goods, but

[1] *Wealth of nations*, II, 2: 'Of money considered as a particular branch of the general stock of the society, or Of the expense of maintaining the national capital.'

goods do not always or necessarily run after money. The man who buys does not always mean to sell again, but frequently to use or to consume; whereas he who sells always means to buy again. The one may frequently have done the whole, but the other can never have done more than the one-half of his business. It is not for its own sake that men desire money, but for the sake of what they can purchase with it . . .

The importation of gold and silver is not the principal, much less the sole benefit which a nation derives from its foreign trade. Between whatever places foreign trade is carried on, they all of them derive two distinct benefits from it. It carries out that surplus part of the produce of their land and labour for which there is no demand among them, and brings back in return for it something else for which there is a demand. It gives a value to their superfluities by exchanging them for something else which may satisfy a part of their wants, and increase their enjoyments. By means of it the narrowness of the home market does not hinder the division of labour in any particular branch of art or manufacture from being carried to the highest perfection. By opening a more extensive market for whatever part of the produce of their labour may exceed the home consumption, it encourages them to improve its productive powers, and augment its annual produce to the utmost, and thereby to increase the real revenue and wealth of the society. These great and important services foreign trade is continually occupied in performing to all the different countries between which it is carried on. They all derive great benefit from it, though that in which the merchant resides generally derives the greatest, as he is generally more employed in supplying the wants, and carrying out the superfluities of his own than of any other particular country. To import the gold and silver which may be wanted into countries which have no mines is no doubt a part of the business of foreign commerce. It is, however, a most insignificant part of it. A country which carried on foreign trade merely upon this account could scarce have occasion to freight a ship in a century.

It is not by the importation of gold and silver that the discovery of America has enriched Europe. By the abundance of the American mines, those metals have become cheaper. A service of plate can now be purchased for about a third part of the corn, or a third part of the labour, which it would have cost in the fifteenth century. With the same annual expense of labour and commodities, Europe can annually purchase about three times the quantity of plate which it could have purchased at that time. But when a commodity comes to be sold for a third part of what had been its usual price, not only those who purchased it before can purchase three times their former quantity, but it is brought down to the level of a much greater number of purchasers, perhaps to more than ten, perhaps to more than twenty times the former number. So that there may be in Europe at present not only more than three times, but more than twenty or thirty times the quantity of plate which would have been in it, even in its present state of improvement, had the discovery of the American mines never been made. So far Europe has, no doubt, gained a real conveniency, though surely a very trifling one. The cheapness of gold and silver renders those metals rather less fit for the purposes of money than they were before. In order to make the same purchases, we must load ourselves with a greater quantity of them, and carry about a shilling in our pocket where a groat would have done before. It is difficult to say which is most trifling, this inconveniency or the opposite conveniency. Neither the one or the other could have made any very essential change in the state of Europe. The discovery of America, however, certainly made a most essential one. By opening a new and inexhaustible market to all the commodities of Europe, it gave occasion to new divisions of labour and improvements of art which, in the narrow circle of the ancient commerce, could never have taken place for want of a market to take off the greater part of their produce. The productive powers of labour were improved, and its produce increased in all the different countries of Europe, and together with it the real revenue and wealth of the inhabitants. The commodities of Europe were almost all new to America, and many of those of America were new to Europe. A new set of exchanges, therefore, began to take place which had never been thought of before, and which should naturally have proved as advantageous to the new as it certainly did to the old continent. The savage injustice of the Europeans rendered an event, which ought to have been beneficial to all, ruinous and destructive to several of those unfortunate countries. . . [***Wealth of nations***, IV, I: **'Of the principle of the commercial or mercantile system'**]

Crime and punishment

CESARE BONESANA BECCARIA

BIOGRAPHICAL NOTE

Cesare Bonesana, Marquis of Beccaria (1738–94), studied law at the University of Pavia, and as a young man came under the formative influence of a group of young, aristocratic, but dissident, thinkers under the leadership of Pietro Verri who met regularly in the early 1760s to discuss radical ideas. The activities of the Verri circle, and in particular the close friendship between Beccaria and Verri, played an important role in the composition of *On crimes and punishments*, and indeed provided much of the intellectual vitality for the Italian Enlightenment in general. Verri helped to shape much of Beccaria's thinking on morality, secular values, political economy, happiness, justice and virtue, and an early example of his impact can be seen in the *Meditations on happiness* (1763). Verri's role was to be crucial in persuading Beccaria, some time between March 1763 and January 1764, to start writing *On crimes and punishments*, the first draft of which he was to improve stylistically and structurally.

Beccaria was also greatly influenced by the *philosophes*, having been first attracted to French critical thinking after reading Montesquieu's *Persian letters* (1721). With its radical criticism of contemporary, still largely feudal, Italian institutions, his work reflects the impression made upon him, not only by Montesquieu, but also Rousseau, Hume, d'Alembert, Melon, Forbonnais, Locke, Helvétius, Condillac and Voltaire. In return, Beccaria's impact on the European Enlightenment, especially after the publication of *On crimes and punishments*, was to be equally significant.

Beccaria's first published work was concerned with the state finances of Milan, and appeared in 1762. From 1764 to 1766 he contributed several important articles to the Verri circle's periodical, *Il caffè*. His great treatise on crimes and punishments was published in April 1764, and was acclaimed throughout Europe, although it encountered fierce criticism in 1765 from Ferdinando Facchinei in his *Notes and observations on the book Crimes and punishments*. However, it found much favour in France, and as a result Beccaria was invited to Paris in October 1766. Morellet translated *On crimes and punishments* in 1765, and in 1766 Voltaire published his *Commentary on*

the book *On crimes and punishments,* by a provincial lawyer. Despite his welcome, Beccaria did not feel comfortable in French philosophical circles, and
left Paris after a month, an abrupt departure that led to his break with Verri.
Catherine the Great then invited him to Russia to advise on penal reform,
an invitation which, although declined, added to his growing reputation.
Between 1768 and 1769 he held the chair of cameral sciences in Milan.

In 1771 Beccaria was appointed to the Supreme Economic Council of Lombardy, and made responsible for monetary reform. He rose steadily through
the ranks of Lombardy's bureaucracy, becoming in 1778 provincial magistrate
for the Mint. From 1778 until his sudden death in 1794, he was responsible
for the administration of schools, trade, industry and agriculture. He was
also entrusted with a review of the penal code, and in 1792 famously proposed
the abolition of the death penalty. His later career is dominated by his activities as an official working in Lombardy for the Habsburgs, and his later contributions as a reformer tended to be of a practical rather than theoretical
nature.

EDITORIAL NOTE

On crimes and punishments was written between March 1763 and January
1764. It was revised by Verri, who sent the revised copy to a publisher at
Livorno, and the treatise was published in July 1764. Verri was for a time
suspected of being the author, a confusion in which he willingly collaborated.
A pirated second edition appeared in Florence in 1764, and a third, revised
edition was published in March 1765. Excluding pirated versions and
reprintings, seven editions had appeared in Italy by 1774. *Dei delitti e delle
pene* was first translated into English in 1767. In 1774 an Italian version of the
Morellet translation appeared, and this served as the standard Italian text
until 1958, when Franco Venturi established the fifth edition (March 1766) as
the authorised standard version.

The present extracts are taken from the translation by Richard Davies* for
which the base text is the fifth edition of *Dei delitti e delle pene* (1766). The
text of this edition is also printed in the *Edizione nazionale,* ed. G. Francioni
(Milan, Mediobanca, 1984).

FURTHER READING

*Bellamy, R. (ed.) and Davies, R. (trans.), *Beccaria: 'On crimes and punish-
    ments' and other writings* (Cambridge, Cambridge University Press,
    1995). See introduction, pp. ix–xxx.
Heath, J., *Eighteenth-century penal theory* (Oxford, Oxford University Press,
    1963).

Maestro, M., *Cesare Beccaria and the origins of penal reform* (Philadelphia, Temple University Press, 1973).

Ten, C., *Crime, guilt and punishment* (Oxford, Clarendon Press, 1987).

On crimes and punishments (1764)

For the most part, men leave the care of the most important regulations either to common sense or to the discretion of individuals whose interests are opposed to those most foresighted laws which distribute benefits to all and resist the pressures to concentrate those benefits in the hands of a few, raising those few to the heights of power and happiness, and sinking everyone else in feebleness and poverty. It is, therefore, only after they have experienced thousands of miscarriages in matters essential to life and liberty, and have grown weary of suffering the most extreme ills, that men set themselves to right the evils that beset them and to grasp the most palpable truths which, by virtue of their simplicity, escape the minds of the common run of men who are not used to analysing things, but instead passively take on a whole set of second-hand impressions of them derived more from tradition than from enquiry.

If we open our history books we shall see that the laws, for all that they are or should be contracts amongst free men, have rarely been anything but the tools of the passions of a few men or the offspring of a fleeting and haphazard necessity. They have not been dictated by a cool observer of human nature, who has brought the actions of many men under a single gaze and has evaluated them from the point of view of whether or not they conduce to *the greatest happiness shared among the greater number*. Blessed are those very few nations which have not waited for the slow succession of coincidence and contingencies to bring about some tentative movement towards the good from out of the extremities of evil, but which have sped with good laws through the intervening stages. And that philosopher who had the courage to scatter out among the multitudes from his humble, despised study the first seeds of those beneficial truths that would be so long in bearing fruit, deserves the gratitude of all humanity.

We have discovered the true relations between sovereign and subjects and between nation and nation. Commerce has been stimulated by philosophic truths disseminated by the press, and there is waged among nations a silent war by trade, which is the most humane sort of war and more worthy of reasonable men. Such is the progress we owe to the present enlightened century. But there are very few who have scrutinised and fought against the savagery and the disorderliness of the procedures of criminal justice, a part of legislation which is so prominent and so neglected in almost the whole of Europe. How few have ascended to general principles to expose and root out the errors that have built up over the centuries, so curbing, as far as it is within the power of disseminated truths to do, the all too free rein that has been given to misdirected force, which has, up to now, provided an entrenched and legitimised example of cold-blooded atrocity. And yet, the groans of the weak, sacrificed to cruel indifference and to wealthy idleness, the barbarous tortures that have been elaborated with prodigal and useless severity, to punish crimes unproven or illusory, the horrors of prison, compounded by that cruellest tormentor of the wretched, uncertainty, ought to have shaken into action that rank of magistrates who guide the opinions and minds of men.

The immortal president Montesquieu glossed over this subject. Indivisible truth has set me to follow in the enlightened footsteps of that great man, but the thinking men for whom I write will know how to distinguish my steps from his. I shall be happy if, like him, I can deserve the private thanks of humble and peaceable lovers of reason and if I can arouse that sweet stirring of sympathy with which sensitive souls respond to whoever upholds the interests of humanity. [*On crimes and punishments*, 'Introduction']

Laws are the terms under which independent and isolated men come together in society. Wearied by living in an unending state of war and by a freedom rendered useless by the uncertainty of retaining it, they sacrifice a part of that freedom in order to enjoy what remains in security and calm. The sum of these portions of freedom sacrificed to the good of all makes up the sovereignty of the nation, and the sovereign is the legitimate repository and administrator of these freedoms. But it was insufficient to create this repository; it was also necessary to protect it from the private usurpations of each individual, who is always seeking to extract from the repository not only his own due but also the portions which are owing to others. What were wanted were sufficiently tangible motives to prevent the despotic spirit of every man from resubmerging society's laws into the ancient chaos. These tangible motives are the punishments enacted against law-breakers. I say *tangible motives* because experience shows that the common run of men do not accept stable principles of conduct. Nor will they depart from the universal principle of anarchy which we see in the physical as well as in the moral realm, unless they are given motives which impress themselves directly on the senses and which, by dint of repetition, are constantly present in the mind as a counterbalance to the strong impressions of those self-interested passions which are ranged against the universal good. Neither eloquence, nor exhortations, not even the most sublime truths have been enough to hold back for long the passions aroused by the immediate impact made by objects which are close at hand. [*On crimes and punishments*, 1: 'The origin of punishment']

Every punishment which is not derived from absolute necessity is tyrannous, says the great Montesquieu, a proposition which may be generalised as follows: every act of authority between one man and another which is not derived from absolute necessity is tyrannous. Here, then, is the foundation of the sovereign's right to punish crimes: the necessity of defending the repository of the public well-being from the usurpations of individuals. The juster the punishments, the more sacred and inviolable is the security and the greater the freedom which the sovereign preserves for his subjects. If we consult the human heart, we find in it the fundamental principles of the sovereign's true right to punish crimes, for it is vain to hope that any lasting advantage will accrue from public morality if it be not founded on ineradicable human sentiments. Any law which differs from them will always meet with a resistance that will overcome it in the end, in the same way that a force, however small, applied continuously, will always overcome a sudden shock applied to a body.

No man has made a gift of part of his freedom with the common good in mind; that kind of fantasy exists only in novels. If it were possible, each one of us would wish that the contracts which bind others did not bind us. Every man makes himself the centre of all the world's affairs.

The multiplication of the human race, however gradual, greatly exceeded the means that a sterile and untended nature provides for the satisfaction of man's ever-evolving needs, and brought primitive men together. The first unions inescapably gave rise to others to resist them, and so the state of war was translated from individuals to nations.

Thus it was necessity which compelled men to give up a part of their freedom; and it is therefore certain that none wished to surrender to the public repository more than the smallest possible portion consistent with persuading others to defend him. The sum of these smallest possible portions constitutes the right to punish; everything more than that is no longer justice, but an abuse; it is a matter of fact not of right. Note that the word 'right' is not opposed to the word 'power', but the former is rather a modification of the latter, that is to say, the species which is of the greatest utility to the greatest number. And by 'justice' I mean nothing other than the restraint necessary to hold particular interests together, without which they would collapse into the old state of unsociability. Any punishment that goes beyond the need to preserve this bond is unjust by its very nature. We must be careful not to attach any notion of something real to this word 'justice', such as a physical force or an actual entity. It is simply a way whereby humans conceive of things, a way which influences beyond measure the happiness of all. Nor do I speak here of that justice which flows from God and whose direct bearing is on the punishments and rewards of the after-life. [*On crimes and punishments*, 2: **'The right to punish'**]

The first consequence of these principles is that laws alone can decree punishments for crimes, and that this authority resides only with the legislator, who represents the whole of society united by the social contract. No magistrate (who is a member of society) can justly establish of his own accord any punishment for any member of the same society. A punishment which exceeds the limit laid down by law is the just punishment with another punishment superadded. Therefore, a magistrate may not, on any pretext of zeal or concern for the public good whatsoever, increase the punishment laid down by law for a miscreant citizen.

The second consequence is that whilst every individual is bound to society, society is likewise bound to every individual member of it by a pact which, by its very nature, places obligations on both parties. These obligations, which descend from the palace to the hovel, bind equally the most elevated and the humblest of men, mean nothing other than that it is in the interests of all that the pacts useful to the greatest number be observed. Violation by even one man begins to legitimate anarchy. The sovereign, as the representative of society, may only frame laws in general terms which are binding on all members. He may not rule on whether an individual has violated the social pact, because that would divide the nation into two parts: one, represented by the sovereign, who asserts the violation of the contract, and the other, represented by the accused, who denies it. There is, therefore, need of a third party to judge the truth of the matter. Herein lies the need for the magistrate, whose sentences admit of no appeal and consist in simply confirming or denying particular facts.

The third consequence is that, even if it could be shown that the extreme severity of some punishments, even if not directly contrary to the public good and the aim of discouraging crimes, is merely useless, even then, it will be contrary not only to those beneficent virtues which arise from an enlightened reason which prefers to govern happy men than a herd of slaves among whom timorous cruelty is rife, but also be contrary to justice and to the very nature of the social contract. [*On crimes and punishments*, 3: 'Consequences']

It is in the common interest not only that crimes not be committed, but that they be rarer in proportion to the harm they do to society. Hence the obstacles which repel men from committing crimes ought to be made stronger the more those crimes are against the public good and the more inducements there are for committing them. Hence, there must be a proportion between crimes and punishments.

It is impossible to foresee all the mischiefs which arise from the universal struggle of the human emotions. They multiply at a compound rate with the growth of population and with the criss-crossing of private interests, which cannot be geometrically directed towards the public utility. In political arithmetic, we must substitute the calculus of probabilities for mathematical exactitude. Even a cursory look at history shows that disorder grows as the boundaries of empires expand. As patriotic sentiment correspondingly wanes, there is a growth in the motives for crime insofar as each individual has an interest in that very disorder: therefore, the need to stiffen the punishments continually increases.

That force which attracts us, like gravity, to our own good can be controlled only by equal and opposite obstacles. The effects of this force are the whole confused gamut of human actions: if these interfere with and obstruct one another, then the punishments, which we may call *political obstacles*, eliminate their evil effects, without destroying the moving cause, which is the very sensibility inalienable from man's nature. And the legislator behaves like the skilled architect, whose task is to counteract the destructive forces of gravity and to exploit those forces that contribute to the strengthening of the building.

Given men's need to come together, and given the compacts which necessarily arise from the very opposition of private interests, we can make out a scale of wrong actions, of which the highest grade consists in those which spell the immediate destruction of society, and the lowest those which involve the smallest possible injustice to its private participants. Between these two extremes are distributed in imperceptible gradations from the highest to the lowest, all the actions which are inimical to the public good and which can be called crimes. If it were possible to measure all the infinite and untoward combinations of human actions geometrically, then there should be a corresponding scale of punishments running from the harshest to the mildest. But it is enough that the wise lawgiver signposts the main stages, without confusing the order and not reserving for the crimes of the highest grade the punishments of the lowest. If there were an exact and universal scale of crimes and punishments, we should have an approximate and common measure of the gradations of tyranny and liberty, and of the basic humanity and evil of the different nations.

Any action which does not fall between the two limits noted above cannot be called a *crime*, nor be punished as such, unless by those who find it in their own interest so to call it. Uncertainty about where the limits lie has produced in nations a morality which is at odds with the law, enactments which are at odds with each other, and a mass of laws which expose the most sterling men to the most severe punishments, but which leave the words *vice* and *virtue* vague and afloat, raising those doubts about one's very existence which lead to the drowsiness and torpor fatal to the body politic. Anyone who reads the laws and histories of nations with a philosophical eye will see the changes which have always occurred over the centuries in the words *vice* and *virtue, good citizen* and *bad*, not as a result of changes in the countries' circumstances and so in the common interest, but as a result of the passions and false beliefs which at various times have motivated the different lawgivers. The reader will see often enough that the passions of one century are the basis of the morals of later centuries, that strong emotions, the offspring of fanaticism and enthusiasm, are weakened and, so to speak, gnawed away by time, which returns all physical and moral phenomena to equilibrium, and they become the common sense of the day and a powerful tool in the hands of the strong and astute. In this way, the very obscure notions of virtue and honour were born, and they are so obscure because they change with the passage of time which preserves words rather than things, and they change with the rivers and mountains which so often form the boundaries not only of physical but also of moral geography.

If pleasure and pain are the motive forces of all sentient beings, and if the invisible legislator has decreed rewards and punishments as one of the motives that spur men even to the most sublime deeds, then the inappropriate distribution of punishments will give rise to that paradox, as little recognised as it is common, that punishments punish the crimes they have caused. If an equal punishment is laid down for two crimes which damage society unequally, men will not have a stronger deterrent against committing the greater crime if they find it more advantageous to do so. [*On crimes and punishments*, 6: 'The proportion between crimes and punishments']

We have seen what the true measure of crimes is, namely, *harm to society*. This is one of those palpable truths which, though they call for neither quadrants nor telescopes to be discovered, but are within the grasp of the average intelligence, nevertheless have, by a curious conjunction of circumstances, only been firmly recognised by a few thinkers in every nation and in every century. But opinions worthy only of Asiatic despots and emotions robed in authority and power have blotted out, mainly by unfelt pressures but sometimes by violent impressions affecting the timid credulity of men, the simple ideas, which perhaps shaped the first philosophy of those youthful societies, and to which the enlightenment of the present century seems to be leading us back, with that greater conviction that results from a rigorous analysis, from a thousand unhappy experiences and the very obstacles themselves.

It would now seem appropriate to examine and to distinguish all the various sorts of crimes and the ways of punishing them, if it were not for the fact that this would demand immense and tedious detail because of the variations caused by the differing circumstances of differing times and places. But it will be enough to point out the most general principles and the most baneful and common mistakes to correct both those who, from a misguided love of freedom, would wish to introduce anarchy, and those who would like to reduce men's lives to monastic regularity.

Some crimes directly destroy society or its representative. Some undermine the personal security of a citizen by attacking his life, goods or honour. Others still are actions contrary to what each citizen, in view of the public good, is obliged by law to do or not do. The first, which are the greatest crimes, because the most damaging, are those which are called *lèse-majesté* or sedition. Only tyranny and ignorance, which can confuse even the clearest of words and ideas, could apply this term – and a correspondingly severe punishment – to crimes of a different nature, thus making men the victims of a word, as on countless other occasions. Every crime, even a private one, offends against society, but not all aim at its immediate destruction. Like physical actions, moral actions have their own limited sphere of action and, like any other movement in nature, are located differently in time and space; so that only a captious understanding, which is the standard philosophy of slavery, can confuse what eternal truth has separated by immutable relations.

After these, there are the crimes which run counter to the security of individuals. Since this is the main purpose of every legitimate association, the violation of the right to security which each citizen has earned must be assigned one of the heavier punishments contemplated by the laws.

Every citizen ought to believe himself able to do anything which is not against the law without fearing any other consequence than what follows from the action itself. This is the political creed which ought to be received by the people and preached by magistrates scrupulously upholding the law. This is a sacred creed, without which there cannot be a legitimate society; a just recompense for men's sacrifice of that universal power over all things common to all sentient creatures, and limited only by their own strength. This creed liberates and invigorates the spirit and enlightens the mind, making men virtuous with that virtue which knows no fear and not with that pliant prudence which is fitting only to those who have to live a precarious and uncertain existence. Therefore, attacks on citizens' security and freedom are among the greatest crimes, and into this class fall not only the murders and thefts practised by common people, but also those of the nobility and magistrates, whose influence is wider and has a greater effect, destroying the subjects' faith in the ideas of justice and duty, and replacing it with the notion that might is right, which is as dangerous in him who adopts it as it is in him who suffers from it. [*On crimes and punishments*, 8: 'The classification of crimes']

It is evident from the simple considerations already set out that the purpose of punishment is not that of tormenting or afflicting any sentient creature, nor of undoing a crime already committed. How can a political body, which as the calm modifier of individual passions should not itself be swayed by passion, harbour this useless cruelty which is the instrument of rage, of fanaticism or of weak tyrants? Can the wailings of a wretch, perhaps, undo what has been done and turn back the clock? The purpose, therefore, is nothing other than to prevent the offender from doing fresh harm to his fellows and to deter others from doing likewise. Therefore, punishments and the means adopted for inflicting them should, consistent with proportionality, be so selected as to make the most efficacious and lasting impression on the minds of men with the least torment to the body of the condemned. [*On crimes and punishments*, 12: '**The purpose of punishment**']

The torture of a criminal while his trial is being put together is a cruelty accepted by most nations, whether to compel him to confess a crime, to exploit the contradictions he runs into, to uncover his accomplices, to carry out some mysterious and incomprehensible metaphysical purging of his infamy, or, lastly, to expose other crimes of which he is guilty but with which he has not been charged.

No man may be called guilty before the judge has reached his verdict; nor may society withdraw its protection from him until it has been determined that he has broken the terms of the compact by which that protection was extended to him. By what right, then, except that of force, does the judge have the authority to inflict punishment on a citizen while there is doubt about whether he is guilty or innocent? This dilemma is not a novelty: either the crime is certain or it is not; if it is certain, then no other punishment is called for than what is established by law and other torments are superfluous because the criminal's confession is superfluous; if it is not certain, then an innocent man should not be made to suffer, because, in law, such a man's crimes have not been proven. Furthermore, I believe it is a wilful confusion of the proper procedure to require a man to be at once accuser and accused, in such a way that physical suffering comes to be the crucible in which truth is assayed, as if such a test could be carried out in the sufferer's muscles and sinews. This is a sure route for the acquittal of robust ruffians and the conviction of weak innocents. Such are the evil consequences of adopting this spurious test of truth, but a test worthy of a cannibal, that the ancient Romans, for all their barbarity on many other counts, reserved only for their slaves, the victims of a fierce and overrated virtue.

What is the political purpose of punishment? The instilling of terror in other men. But how shall we judge the secret and secluded torture which the tyranny of custom visits on guilty and innocent alike? It is important that no established crime go unpunished; but it is superfluous to discover who committed a crime which is buried in shadows. A misdeed already committed, and for which there can be no redress, need be punished by a political society only when it influences other people by holding out the lure of impunity. If it is true that, from fear or from virtue, more men observe the laws that break them, the risk of torturing an innocent ought to be accounted all the greater, since it is more likely that any given man has observed the laws than that he has flouted them.

Another absurd ground for torture is the purging of infamy, that is, when a man who has been attainted by the law has to confirm his own testimony by the dislocation of his bones. This abuse should not be tolerated in the eighteenth century. It presupposes that pain, which is a sensation, can purge infamy, which is a mere moral relation. Is torture perhaps a crucible and the infamy some impurity? It is not hard to reach back in time to the source of this absurd law, because even the illogicalities which a whole nation adopts always have some connection with its other respected commonplaces. It seems that this practice derives from religious and spiritual ideas, which have had so much influence on the ideas of men in all nations and at all times. An infallible dogma tells us that the stains springing from human weakness, but which have not earned the eternal anger of the great Being, have to be purged by an incomprehensible fire. Now, infamy is a civil stain and, since pain and fire cleanse spiritual and incorporeal stains, why should the spasms of torture not cleanse the civil stain of infamy? I believe that the confession of guilt, which in some courts is a prerequisite for conviction, has a similar origin, for, before the mysterious court of penitence, the confession of sin is an essential part of the sacrament. It is thus that men abuse the clearest illuminations of revealed truth; and, since these are the only enlightenment to be found in times of ignorance, it is to them that credulous mankind will always turn and of them that it will make the most absurd and far-fetched use. But infamy is a sentiment which is subject neither to the law nor to reason, but to common opinion. Torture itself causes real infamy to its victims. Therefore, by this means, infamy is purged by the infliction of infamy.

The third ground for torture concerns that inflicted on suspected criminals who fall into inconsistency while being investigated, as if both the innocent man who goes in fear and the criminal who wishes to cover himself would not be made to fall into contradiction by fear of punishment, the uncertainty of the verdict, the apparel and magnificence of the judge, and by their own ignorance, which is the common lot both of most knaves and of the innocent; as if the inconsistencies into which men normally fall even when they are calm would not burgeon in the agitation of a mind wholly concentrated on saving itself from a pressing danger.

This shameful crucible of the truth is a standing monument to the law of ancient and savage times, when ordeal by fire, by boiling water and the lottery of armed combat were called the *judgements* of God, as if the links in the eternal chain which originates from the breast of the First Mover could be continually disrupted and uncoupled at the behest of frivolous human institutions. The only difference which there might seem to be between torture and ordeal by fire or boiling water is that the result of the former seems to depend on the will of the criminal, and that of the latter on purely physical and external factors; but this difference is only apparent and not real. Telling the truth in the midst of spasms and beatings is as little subject to our will as is preventing without fraud the effects of fire and boiling water. Every act of our will is always proportional to the force of the sensory impression which gives rise to it; and the sensibility of every man is limited. Therefore, the impression made by pain may grow to such an extent that, having filled the whole of the sensory field, it leaves the torture victim no freedom to do anything but choose the quickest route to relieving himself of the immediate pain. Thus the criminal's replies are as necessitated as are the effects of fire and boiling water. And thus the sensitive but guiltless man will admit guilt if he believes that, in that way, he can make the pain stop. All distinctions between the guilty and the innocent disappear as a consequence of the use of the very means which was meant to discover them.

It would be redundant to make this point twice as clear by citing the numerous cases of innocent men who have confessed their guilt as a result of the convulsions of torture. There is no nation nor age which cannot cite its own cases, but men do not change nor do they think out the consequences of their practices. No man who has pushed his ideas beyond what is necessary for life, has not sometimes headed towards nature, obeying her hidden and indistinct calls; but custom, that tyrant of the mind, repulses and frightens him.

The result, therefore, of torture depends on a man's predisposition and on calculation, which vary from man to man according to their hardihood and sensibility, so that, with this method, a mathematician would settle problems better than a judge. Given the strength of an innocent man's muscles and the sensitivity of his sinews, one need only find the right level of pain to make him admit his guilt of a given crime.

A guilty man is interrogated in order to know the truth, but if this truth is hard to discover from the bearing, the gestures and the expression of a man at rest, it will be much the harder to discover it from a man in whom every feature, by which men's faces sometimes betray the truth against their will, has been altered by spasms of pain. Every violent action confuses and clouds the tiny differences in things which sometimes serve to distinguish truth from falsehood.

These truths were known to the ancient Roman legislators, who only allowed the torture of slaves, who were denied the status of persons. They are also evident in England, a nation the glory of whose letters, the superiority of whose trade and wealth, and hence power, and whose examples of virtue and courage leave us in no doubt about the goodness of her laws. Torture has been abolished in Sweden and by one of the wisest monarchs of Europe who, bringing philosophy to the throne and legislating as the friend of his subjects, has set them equal and free under the law, which is the only equality and freedom which reasonable men could demand in the present state of things. Martial law does not believe torture necessary for armies, which are made up for the most part of the scum of society whom you might have thought more in need of it than any other class of person. How strange it must seem to anyone who does not take account of how great the tyranny of habit is, that peaceful laws should have to learn a more humane system of justice from souls inured to massacre and blood.

This truth is also felt, albeit indistinctly, by those very people who apparently deny it. No confession made under torture can be valid if it is not given sworn confirmation when it is over; but if the criminal does not confirm his crime, he is tortured afresh. Some learned men and some nations do not allow this vicious circle to be gone round more than three times; other nations and other learned men leave it to the choice of the judge, in such a way that, of two men equally innocent or equally guilty, the hardy and enduring will be acquitted and the feeble and timid will be convicted by virtue of the following strict line of reasoning: *I, the judge, had to find you guilty of such and such a crime; you, hardy fellow, could put up with the pain, so I acquit you; you, feeble fellow, gave in, so I convict you. I know that the confession extorted from you in the midst of your agonies would carry no weight, but I shall torture you afresh if you do not confirm what you have confessed.*

A strange consequence which necessarily follows from the use of torture is that the innocent are put in a worse position than the guilty. For, if both are tortured, the former has everything against him. Either he confesses to the crime and is convicted, or he is acquitted and has suffered an unwarranted punishment. The criminal, in contrast, finds himself in a favourable position, because if he staunchly withstands the torture he must be acquitted and so has commuted a heavier sentence into a lighter one. Therefore, the innocent man cannot but lose and the guilty man may gain.

The law which calls for torture is a law which says: *Men, withstand pain, and if nature has placed in you an inextinguishable self-love, if she has given you an inalienable right to self-defence, I create in you an entirely opposite propensity, which is a heroic self-hatred, and I order you to denounce yourselves, telling the truth even when your muscles are being torn and your bones dislocated.*

Torture is given to discover if a guilty man has also committed other crimes to those with which he is charged. The underlying reasoning here is as follows: *You are guilty of one crime, therefore you may be of a hundred others; this doubt weighs on me and I want to decide the matter with my test of the truth; the laws torture you because you are guilty, because you may be guilty, or because I want you to be guilty.*

Finally, torture is applied to a suspect in order to discover his accomplices in crime. But if it has been proven that torture is not a fit means of discovering the truth, how can it be of any use in unmasking the accomplices, which is one of the truths to be discovered? As if a man who accuses himself would not more readily accuse others. And can it be right to torture a man for the crimes of others? Will the accomplices not be discovered by the examination of witnesses, the interrogation of the criminal, the evidence and the *corpus delicti*, in short, by the very means which ought to be used to establish the suspect's guilt? Generally, the accomplices flee as soon as their partner is captured; the uncertainty of their fate condemns them to exile and frees the nation of the danger of further offences, while the punishment of the criminal in custody serves its sole purpose, which is that of discouraging with fear other men from perpetrating a similar crime. [*On crimes and punishments*, 16: 'Of torture']

The swifter and closer to the crime a punishment is, the juster and more useful it will be. I say juster, because it spares the criminal the useless and fierce torments of uncertainty which grow in proportion to the liveliness of one's imagination and one's sense of one's own impotence. Juster because, loss of freedom being a punishment, a man should suffer it no longer than necessary before being sentenced. Remand in custody, therefore, is the simple safe-keeping of a citizen until he may be judged guilty, and since this custody is intrinsically of the nature of a punishment, it should last the minimum possible time and should be as lacking in severity as can be arranged. The minimum time should be calculated taking into account both the length of time needed for the trial and the right of those who have been held the longest to be tried first. The stringency of the detention ought not to be greater than what is necessary to prevent escape or to save evidence from being covered up. The trial itself ought to be brought to a conclusion in the shortest possible time. What crueller contrast could there be than that between the procrastination of the judge and the anguish of the accused? On the one hand, the callous magistrate thinking of his comforts and pleasures, on the other, the prisoner languishing in tears and dejection. In general, the severity of a punishment and the consequence of crime ought to be as effective as possible on others and as lenient as possible on him who undergoes it, because a society cannot be called legitimate where it is not an unfailing principle that men should be subjected to the fewest possible ills.

I have said that promptness of punishment is more useful because the smaller the lapse of time between the misdeed and the punishment, the stronger and more lasting the association in the human mind between the two ideas *crime* and *punishment*. The former will come to be sensed as the cause and the latter as the necessary, inexorable effect. It is proven that the compounding of ideas is the cement which holds together the fabric of the human intellect, and without it pleasure and pain would be unconnected feelings and of no effect. The further men move away from general ideas and universal principles, that is, the less refined they are, the more they act on immediate associations that are closer to home, ignoring the more remote and complicated ones which are of use only to men strongly impassioned by the object of their desire, the light of whose attention illuminates a single object, leaving everything else in the dark. The more remote and complicated associations are also of use to more sophisticated minds, which have become accustomed to passing many objects in review at one time, and are able to compare many fragmentary feelings with each other, in such a way that the resulting action is less risky and uncertain.

Therefore, the contiguity of crime and punishment is of the highest importance if we want the idea of punishment to be immediately associated in unsophisticated minds with the enticing picture of some lucrative crime. A long delay only serves to separate these two ideas further. Whatever impression the punishment of a crime may make, {it makes less as punishment than as spectacle, and} it will be felt only after the spectators have half-forgotten their horror at the crime in question, which would have served to reinforce their sense of what punishment is.

There is another principle which serves admirably to draw even closer the important connection between a misdeed and its punishment. And that is that the punishment should, as far as possible, fit the nature of the crime. This sort of fit greatly eases the comparison which ought to exist between the incentive to crime and the retribution of punishment, so that the latter removes and redirects the mind to ends other than those which the enticing idea of breaking the law would wish to point it. [*On crimes and punishments*, 19: 'Of prompt punishments']

But my thoughts have carried me away from my topic, which I must now waste no time in returning to. One of the most effective brakes on crime is not the harshness of its punishment, but the unerringness of punishment. This calls for vigilance in the magistrates, and that kind of unswerving judicial severity which, to be useful to the cause of virtue, must be accompanied by a lenient code of laws. The certainty of even a mild punishment will make a bigger impression than the fear of a more awful one which is united to a hope of not being punished at all. For, even the smallest harms, when they are certain, always frighten human souls, whereas hope, that heavenly gift which often displaces every other sentiment, holds at bay the idea of larger harms, especially when it is reinforced by frequent examples of the impunity accorded by weak and corrupt judges. The harsher the punishment and the worse the evil he faces, the more anxious the criminal is to avoid it, and it makes him commit other crimes to escape the punishment of the first. The times and places in which the penalties have been fiercest have been those of the bloodiest and most inhuman actions. Because the same brutal spirit which guided the hand of the lawgiver, also moved the parricide's and the assassin's. He decreed iron laws from the throne for the savage souls of slaves, who duly obeyed them; and in secluded darkness he urged men to murder tyrants only to create new ones.

As punishments became harsher, human souls which, like fluids, find their level from their surroundings, become hardened and the ever lively power of the emotions brings it about that, after a hundred years of cruel tortures, the wheel only causes as much fear as prison previously did. If a punishment is to serve its purpose, it is enough that the harm of punishment should outweigh the good which the criminal can derive from the crime, and into the calculation of this balance, we must add the unerringness of the punishment and the loss of the good produced by the crime. Anything more than this is superfluous and, therefore, tyrannous. Men are guided by the repeated action on them of the harms they know and not by those they do not. Imagine two states, in which the scales of punishment are proportionate to the crimes and that in one the worst punishment is perpetual slavery, and that in the other it is breaking on the wheel. I maintain that there would be as much fear of the worst punishment in the first as in the second; and if there were cause to introduce in the first the worst punishments of the second, the same cause would produce an increase in the punishments of the second, which would gradually move from the wheel via slower and more elaborate torments to reach the ultimate refinements of that science which tyrants know all too well.

Two other disastrous consequences contrary to the very purpose of preventing crime follow from having harsh punishments. One is that it is not easy to sustain the necessary proportion between crime and punishment because, despite all the efforts of cruelty to devise all manner of punishments, they still cannot go beyond the limits of endurance of the human organism and feeling. Once this point has been reached, no correspondingly greater punishments necessary to prevent the more damaging and atrocious crimes can be found. The other consequence is that the harshness of punishments gives rise to impunity. Men's capacity for good or evil is confined within certain bounds, and a spectacle which is too awful for humanity cannot be more than a temporary upset, and can never become a fixed system of the sort proper to the law. If the laws are truly cruel, they must either be changed or they will occasion a fatal impunity.

What reader of history does not shudder with horror at the barbaric and useless tortures that so-called wise men have cold-bloodedly invented and put into operation? Who can fail to feel himself shaken to the core by the sight of thousands of wretches whom poverty, either willed or tolerated by the laws, which have always favoured the few and abused the masses, has dragged back to the primitive state of nature, and either accused of impossible crimes invented out of a cringing ignorance or found guilty of nothing but being faithful to their own principles, and who are then torn apart with premeditated pomp and slow tortures by men with the same faculties and emotions, becoming the entertainment of a fanatical mob? [*On crimes and punishments*, 27: 'Lenience in punishing']

I am prompted by this futile excess of punishments, which have never made men better, to enquire whether the death penalty is really useful and just in a well-organised state. By what right can men presume to slaughter their fellows? Certainly not that right which is the foundation of sovereignty and the laws. For these are nothing but the sum of the smallest portions of each man's own freedom; they represent the general will which is the aggregate of the individual wills. Who has ever willingly given up to others the authority to kill him? How on earth can the minimum sacrifice of each individual's freedom involve handing over the greatest of all goods, life itself? And even if that were so, how can it be reconciled with the other principle which denies that a man is free to commit suicide, which he must be, if he is able to transfer that right to others or to society as a whole?

Thus, the death penalty is not a matter of *right*, as I have just shown, but is an act of war on the part of society against the citizen that comes about when it is deemed necessary or useful to destroy his existence. But if I can go on to prove that such a death is neither necessary nor useful, I shall have won the cause of humanity.

There are only two grounds on which the death of a citizen might be held to be necessary. First, when it is evident that even if deprived of his freedom, he retains such connections and such power as to endanger the security of the nation, when, that is, his existence may threaten a dangerous revolution in the established form of government. The death of a citizen becomes necessary, therefore, when the nation stands to gain or lose its freedom, or in periods of anarchy, when disorder replaces the laws. But when the rule of law calmly prevails, under a form of government behind which the people are united, which is secured from without and from within, both by its strength and, perhaps more efficacious than force itself, by public opinion, in which the control of power is in the hands of the true sovereign, in which wealth buys pleasures and not influence, then I do not see any need to destroy a citizen, unless his death is the true and only brake to prevent others from committing crimes, which is the second ground for thinking the death penalty just and necessary.

Although men, who always suspect the voice of reason and respect that of authority, have not been persuaded by the experience of centuries, during which the ultimate penalty has never dissuaded men from offending against society, nor by the example of the citizens of Rome, nor by the twenty years of the reign of the Empress Elizabeth of Muscovy, in which she set the leaders of all peoples an outstanding precedent, worth at least as much as many victories bought with the blood of her motherland's sons, it will suffice to consult human nature to be convinced of the truth of my claim.

It is not the intensity, but the extent of a punishment which makes the greatest impression on the human soul. For our sensibility is more easily and lastingly moved by minute but repeated impressions than by a sharp but fleeting shock. Habit has universal power over every sentient creature. Just as a man speaks and walks and goes about his business with its help, so moral ideas are only impressed on his mind by lasting and repeated blows. It is not the terrible but fleeting sight of a felon's death which is the most powerful brake on crime, but the long-drawn-out example of a man deprived of freedom, who having become a beast of burden, repays the society which he has offended with his labour. Much more potent than the idea of death, which men always regard as vague and distant, is the efficacious because often repeated reflection that *I too shall be reduced to so dreary and so pitiable a state if I commit similar crimes.*

For all its vividness, the impression made by the death penalty cannot compensate for the forgetfulness of men, even in the most important matters, which is natural and speeded by the passions. As a general rule, violent passions take hold of men but not for long; thus they are suited to producing those revolutions which make normal men into Persians or Spartans; whereas the impressions made in a free and peaceful state should be frequent rather than strong.

For most people, the death penalty becomes a spectacle and for the few an object of compassion mixed with scorn. Both these feelings occupy the minds of the spectators more than the salutary fear which the law claims to inspire. But with moderate and continuous punishments it is this last which is the dominant feeling, because it is the only one. The limit which the lawgiver should set to the harshness of punishments seems to depend on when the feeling of compassion at a punishment, meant more for the spectators than for the convict, begins to dominate every other in their souls.

If a punishment is to be just, it must be pitched at just that level of intensity which suffices to deter men from crime. Now there is no-one who, after considering the matter, could choose the total and permanent loss of his own freedom, however profitable the crime might be. Therefore, permanent penal servitude in place of the death penalty would be enough to deter even the most resolute soul: indeed, I would say that it is more likely to. Very many people look on death with a calm and steadfast gaze, some from fanaticism, some from vanity, a sentiment that almost always accompanies a man to the grave and beyond, and some from a last desperate effort either to live no more or to escape from poverty. However, neither fanaticism nor vanity survives in manacles and chains, under the rod and the yoke or in an iron cage; and the ills of the desperate man are not over, but are just beginning. Our spirit withstands violence and extreme but fleeting pains better than time and endless fatigue. For it can, so to speak, condense itself to repel the former, but its tenacious elasticity is insufficient to resist the latter.

With the death penalty, every lesson which is given to the nation requires a new crime; with permanent penal servitude, a single crime gives very many lasting lessons. And, if it is important that men often see the power of the law, executions ought not to be too infrequent: they therefore require there to be frequent crimes; so that, if this punishment is to be effective, it is necessary that it not make the impression that it should make. That is, it must be both useful and useless at the same time. If it be said that permanent penal servitude is as grievous as death, and therefore as cruel, I reply that, if we add up all the unhappy moments of slavery, perhaps it is even more so, but the latter are spread out over an entire life, whereas the former exerts its force only at a single moment. And this is an advantage of penal servitude, because it frightens those who see it more than those who undergo it. For the former thinks about the sum of unhappy moments, whereas the latter is distracted from present unhappiness by the prospect of future pain. All harms are magnified in the imagination, and the sufferer finds resources and consolations unknown and unsuspected by the spectators, who put their own sensibility in the place of the hardened soul of the wretch.

A thief or murderer who has nothing to weigh against breaking the law except the gallows or the wheel reasons pretty much along the following lines. (I know that self-analysis is a skill which we acquire with education; but just because a thief would not express his principles well, it does not mean that he lacks them.) *What are these laws which I have to obey, which leave such a gulf between me and the rich man? He denies me the penny I beg of him, brushing me off with the demand that I should work, something he knows nothing about. Who made these laws? Rich and powerful men, who have never condescended to visit the filthy hovels of the poor, who have never broken mouldy bread among the innocent cries of starving children and a wife's tears. Let us break these ties, which are pernicious to most people and only useful to a few and idle tyrants; let us attack injustice at its source. I shall return to my natural state of independence; for a while I shall live free and happy on the fruits of my courage and industry; perhaps the day for suffering and repentance will come, but it will be brief, and I shall have one day of pain for many years of freedom and pleasure. King of a small band of men, I shall put to rights the iniquities of fortune, and I shall see these tyrants blanch and cower at one whom they considered, with insulting ostentation, lower than their horses and dogs.* Then, religion comes into the mind of the ruffian, who makes ill-use of everything, and, offering an easy repentance and near-certainty of eternal bliss, considerably diminishes for him the horror of the last tragedy.

But a man who sees ahead of him many years, or even the remainder of his life, passed in slavery and suffering before the eyes of his fellow citizens, with whom he currently lives freely and sociably, the slave of those laws by which he was protected, will make a salutary calculation, balancing all of that against the uncertainty of the outcome of his crimes, and the shortness of the time in which he could enjoy their fruit. The continued example of those whom he now sees as the victims of their own lack of foresight will make a stronger impression on him than would a spectacle which hardens more than it reforms him.

The death penalty is not useful because of the example of savagery it gives to men. If our passions or the necessity of war have taught us how to spill human blood, laws, which exercise a moderating influence on human conduct, ought not to add to that cruel example, which is all the more grievous the more a legal killing is carried out with care and pomp. It seems absurd to me that the laws, which are the expression of the public will, and which hate and punish murder, should themselves commit one, and that to deter citizens from murder, they should decree a public murder. What are the true and most useful laws? Those contracts and terms that everyone would want to obey and to propose so long as the voice of private interest, which is always listened to, is silent or in agreement with the public interest. What are everyone's feelings about the death penalty? We can read them in the indignation and contempt everyone feels for the hangman, who is after all the innocent executor of the public will, a good citizen who contributes to the public good, as necessary an instrument of public security within the state as the valiant soldier is without. What, then, is the root of this conflict? And why is this feeling ineradicable in men, in spite of reason? It is because, deep within their souls, that part which still retains elements of their primitive nature, men have always believed that no-one and nothing should hold the power of life and death over them but necessity, which rules the universe with its iron rod.

What are men to think when they see the wise magistrates and the solemn ministers of justice order a convict to be dragged to his death with slow ceremony, or when a judge, with cold equanimity and even with a secret complacency in his own authority, can pass by a wretch convulsed in his last agonies, awaiting the *coup de grâce*, to savour the comforts and pleasures of life? *Ah!*, they will say, *these laws are nothing but pretexts for power and for the calculated and cruel formalities of justice; they are nothing but a conventional language for killing us all the more surely, like the preselected victims of a sacrifice to the insatiable god of despotism. Murder, which we have preached to us as a terrible crime, we see instituted without disgust and without anger. Let us profit from this example. From the descriptions we have been given of it, violent death seemed to be a terrible thing, but we see it to be the work of a minute. How much the less it will be for him who, unaware of its coming, is spared almost everything about it which is most painful!* This is the horrific casuistry which, if not clearly, at least confusedly, leads men – in whom, as we have seen, the abuse of religion can be more powerful than religion itself – to commit crimes.

If it is objected that almost all times and almost all places have used the death penalty for some crimes, I reply that the objection collapses before the truth, against which there is no appeal, that the history of mankind gives the impression of a vast sea of errors, among which a few confused truths float at great distances from each other. Human sacrifices were common to almost all nations; but who would dare to justify them? That only a few societies have given up inflicting the death penalty, and only for a brief time, is actually favourable to my argument, because it is what one would expect to be the career of the great truths, which last but a flash compared with the long and dark night which engulfs mankind. The happy time has not yet begun in which the truth, like error hitherto, is the property of the many. Up until now, the only truths which have been excepted from this universal rule have been those which the infinite Wisdom wished to distinguish from the others by revealing them.

The voice of a philosopher is too weak against the uproar and the shouting of those who are guided by blind habit. But what I say will find an echo in the hearts of the few wise men who are scattered across the face of the earth. And if truth, in the face of the thousand obstacles which, against his wishes, keep it far from the monarch, should arrive at his throne, let him know that it arrives with the secret support of all men, and let him know that its glory will silence the blood-stained reputation of conquerors and that the justice of future ages will award him peaceful trophies above those of the Tituses, the Antonines and the Trajans.

How happy humanity would be if laws were being decreed for the first time, now that we see seated on the thrones of Europe benevolent monarchs, inspirers of the virtues of peace, of the sciences, of the arts, fathers of their peoples, crowned citizens. Their increased power serves the happiness of their subjects because it removes that crueller, because more capricious intermediary despotism, which choked the always sincere desires of the people which are always beneficial when they may approach the throne! If they leave the ancient laws in place, I say, it is because of the endless difficulty of removing the venerated and centuries-old rust.

That is a reason for enlightened citizens to wish all the more fervently for their authority to continue to increase. [*On crimes and punishments*, 28: 'The death penalty']

Once the evidence has been collected and the crime established, it is necessary to allow the accused time and the means to clear himself. But the time should be brief so as not to compromise the promptness of punishment, which we have seen to be one of the main brakes on crime. Some have opposed such brevity out of a misguided love of humanity, but all doubts will vanish once it is recognised that it is the defects in the laws that increase the dangers to the innocent.

But the laws ought to establish a certain amount of time for preparing both the defence and the prosecution, and the judge would become a lawmaker if it fell to him to decide how much time was to be set aside for trying a given crime. However, those crimes that are so awful that they linger in men's memories, once proven, admit of no limitation on the period within which a prosecution must be brought in the case of a criminal who has sought to flee his punishment. But in lesser and insignificant crimes a time-limit ought to be set to save a citizen from uncertainty, because the long obscurity of the crime prevents its being an example of impunity to others, and the possibility remains of the guilty party's reforming in the interim. It is enough to point out these principles, because a limit can only be fixed with precision in relation to a particular code of laws and the given circumstances of a society. I shall merely add that, in a nation which has discovered the usefulness of moderate punishments, laws which extend or shorten the period available for prosecution in proportion to the gravity of the crime, using remand and voluntary exile as part of the punishment, will be able to provide a simple and restricted class of lenient punishments for a wide range of crimes.

But the periods in question shall not increase in direct proportion to the seriousness of the crime, since the likelihood of a crime is in inverse proportion to its seriousness. The period of investigation ought to diminish accordingly, therefore, and the time within which a prosecution must occur increase, which may seem to be in conflict with what I have said about equal punishments being given for unequal crimes if we count the period of remand or period of limitation before the verdict as part of the punishment. To clarify my idea for the reader, I distinguish two classes of crime: the first consists of serious crimes beginning with murder and including all the worst villainies; the second consists of minor crimes.

This distinction has its foundation in human nature. The safety of one's own life is a natural right, the protection of property is a social right. The number of motives which impel men to overstep the natural feelings of pity is far fewer than the number of motives which impel them by the natural desire to be happy to violate a right which they do not find in their hearts but in social conventions. The vastness of the difference in probability of these two classes of crimes requires them to be regulated by different principles. In the most serious crimes, because they are the rarest, the period of enquiry should be decreased because of the greater likelihood that the accused is innocent, and the time set aside for preparation of the case ought to be increased, because the removal of the seductive prospect of impunity, which is the more harmful the more serious the crime, depends on a definitive verdict of innocence or guilt. But in minor crimes, since the accused's innocence is less likely, the time set aside for investigation should increase, and, since the harm caused by impunity is the less, the period for preparing the trial should decrease. Dividing crimes into two classes in this way would not be acceptable if the harm caused by crimes going unpunished decreased as the likelihood of guilt increased. It might be recalled that an accused, who is found neither innocent nor guilty but who is discharged for lack of evidence, can be re-imprisoned and undergo a fresh investigation for the same crime if new and legally relevant evidence should turn up before the period of limitations for the crime has elapsed. At least this seems to me to be the proper attitude for the defence of both the subjects' security and their liberty. For it is too easy to favour either one of them at the expense of the other, so that each of these inalienable and equal prerogatives of every citizen goes unprotected and uncared for, the former in the face of overt or covert despotism and the latter in the face of turbulent popular anarchy. [*On crimes and punishments*, 30: 'Trials and prescriptions']

Suicide is a crime which seems not to allow of being punished strictly speaking, since such a thing can only be visited either on the innocent or on a cold and insensible corpse. In the latter case, punishment would make no more impression on the living than whipping a statue. In the former case, it is unjust and tyrannical because man's political freedom presupposes that punishment be directed only at the actual culprit of a crime. Men love life too much and everything around them confirms them in this love. The enticing image of pleasure and hope, that sweetest snare of mortals, for which they will gulp down great draughts of evil if it is mixed with a few drops of delight, is too alluring for there to be any need to fear that the necessary impossibility of punishing such a crime will have any influence on men. He who fears pain obeys the law; but death extinguishes all the bodily sources of pain. What motive, then, can stay the desperate man's hand from suicide?

One who kills himself does less harm to society than one who leaves its borders forever; for the former leaves all his belongings, whilst the latter takes with him some part of what he owns. Indeed, if the strength of a nation consists in the number of its citizens, one who leaves a society to join a neighbouring nation does twice the harm of one who simply removes himself by death. The question then boils down to knowing whether it is useful or damaging to a country to allow its members a standing freedom to remove themselves beyond its borders.

No law should be issued which cannot be enforced or which the nature of the circumstances makes unenforceable. Since men are ruled by opinion, which obeys the slow and indirect pressure of the lawgiver, but resists measures which are abrupt or direct, so laws which are useless and scorned by men will bring into disrepute even the most salutary laws, which will come to be viewed as obstacles to be overcome rather than as the repository of the public good. Indeed, if, as we have said, our feelings are limited, the greater esteem men have for objects other than the laws, the less they will have for the laws themselves. From this principle the wise arranger of the public happiness can draw several useful conclusions, but setting them out would take us too far from our main topic, which is to show the pointlessness of turning a state into a prison. Such a law is pointless because, unless unscalable cliffs or impassable seas separate a country from all others, how can every point on its border be closed and how is one to guard the guards? Someone who takes everything with him cannot be punished. Once such a crime has been committed, it can no longer be punished; and punishing it beforehand is to punish men's will and not their actions, which would be to control the intentions, a part of a man utterly free from the reign of human laws. To punish the truant through the property he has left behind, even omitting the ease and inevitability of collusion, which could not be avoided without a tyrannical interference with contracts, would bog down all trade between nations. Punishing the criminal when he returns would prevent him from undoing the harm done to society by making all truancies permanent. The very ban on leaving a country breeds in the residents a desire to leave it, and is a warning to foreigners not to enter.

What should we think of a government which has no means but fear to prevent from leaving men who are naturally attached to their country since the earliest impressions of childhood? The surest way to bind men to their homeland is to raise the relative well-being of every one of them. Just as every effort ought to be made to keep the balance of trade in our favour, so the sovereign's and the nation's highest interest lies in ensuring that, compared with neighbouring countries, the total amount of happiness in the nation be greater than elsewhere. The pleasures of luxury are not the principal elements of this happiness, though they are a necessary remedy for inequality, which grows as the nation advances, as, without them, all the wealth would be concentrated in a single pair of hands. Where the borders of a country are extended more quickly than the population grows, luxury favours despotism. One reason for this is because, where there are fewer inhabitants, there is less industry, and where there is less industry, the poor are more dependent on the pomp of the rich, and the union of the oppressed against their oppressors is harder to organise and less to be feared. Another reason is because the homage, public offices, distinctions and deference which make the differences between the strong and the weak more obvious can be more easily exacted from a few people than from many, since men are more independent when less observed and less observed when they are in larger numbers. But where the population grows more quickly than the borders do, luxury is opposed to the growth of despotism. For it stimulates men's industry and activity, and the accruing needs offer too many pleasures and comforts to rich men for them to be overly concerned with display, which is something that strengthens the sentiment of dependence, to play the major role in the economy. Therefore, we see that, unless some other factor is operative, in large, weak and underpopulated states the luxury of ostentation prevails over that of comfort; but in countries which are more populous than extensive, the luxury of comfort always diminishes ostentation. But commerce and the circulation of luxury goods has the unfortunate side-effect that, although it is carried out by the many, it arises from and ends up satisfying the pleasures of a few and the great majority of those involved enjoy only the smallest part of it. As a result, this trade does not choke off the feeling of poverty, which is caused more by relative differences than by real ones. But security and a freedom which is limited only by the laws are the main foundation of a nation's happiness; with them the pleasures of luxury benefit the people; without them they become instruments of tyranny. Just as the noblest animals and the freest birds flee to lonely places and impenetrable woods, and abandon the fertile and joyful fields where the huntsman lays his snares, so men refrain from pleasures themselves when tyranny offers them.

It is therefore established that the law which makes of its subjects prisoners in their own land is useless and unjust. Hence, so too will be any punishment for suicide; for even if it is a sin which God will punish, because only He can punish after death, it is not a crime before men, since the punishment, instead of falling on the malefactor, falls on his family. If it should be urged against me that such a punishment may nevertheless draw a man back from killing himself, I reply that one who calmly gives up the benefits of life, who so hates life here below as to prefer an eternity of sorrow, could hardly be prevailed upon by the less powerful and more distant thought of his children or relatives. [*On crimes and punishments*, 32: 'Suicide']

It is better to prevent crimes than to punish them. This is the principal goal of all good legislation, which is the art of guiding men to their greatest happiness, or the least unhappiness possible, taking into account all the blessings and evils of life. But the means hitherto employed have been mistaken or opposed to the proposed goal. The chaos of men's activities cannot be reduced to a geometric order devoid of irregularity and confusion. Just as the constant and very simple laws of nature do not prevent the planets being disturbed in their orbits, so human laws cannot prevent disturbances and disorders among the infinite and very opposite motive forces of pleasure and pain. Yet this is the fantasy of limited men when they have power in their hands. To forbid a large number of trivial acts is not to prevent the crimes they may occasion. It is to create new crimes, wilfully to redefine virtue and vice, which we are exhorted to regard as eternal and immutable. What a state would we be reduced to if we were forbidden everything which might tempt us to crime? It would be necessary to deprive a man of the use of his senses. For every motive which urges a man to commit a real crime, there are a thousand which urge him to perform those trivial actions which bad laws call crimes. And if the likelihood of crimes is proportional to the number of motives a man might have for them, broadening the range of crimes only increases the likelihood of their being committed. The majority of the laws are mere privileges, that is to say, a tribute from everyone for the comfort of the few.

Do you want to prevent crimes? Then make sure that the laws are clear and simple and that the whole strength of the nation is concentrated on defending them, and that no part of it is used to destroy them. Make sure that the laws favour individual men more than classes of men. Make sure that men fear the laws and only the laws. Fear of the law is salutary; but man's fear of his fellows is fatal and productive of crimes. Slavish men are more debauched, more sybaritic and crueller than free men. The latter ponder the sciences and the interests of the nation, they envisage and aspire to great things; but the former are content with the present moment and seek amid the din of depravity a distraction from the emptiness of their everyday lives. Accustomed to uncertainty about the result of everything, the result of their crimes becomes doubtful to them, reinforcing the emotions by which they are driven. In a country which is idle by virtue of its climate, uncertainty in its laws maintains and increases the country's idleness and stupidity. If a country is debauched but energetic, uncertainty in its laws will waste the country's energy in the formation of numberless little cabals and intrigues, which spread suspicion in every heart and make betrayal and pretence the basis of good sense. If a country is brave and strong, uncertainty eventually will be removed, though only after the nation has passed through many fluctuations from freedom to slavery and from slavery to freedom. [*On crimes and punishments*, **41: 'How to prevent crimes'**]

Revolution

THOMAS PAINE

BIOGRAPHICAL NOTE

Surprisingly, not a great deal is known about the life of Thomas Paine (1737–1809), widely acknowledged as one of the most radically subversive writers of the Enlightenment. Outspoken advocate of revolution, an active participant in the two great revolutionary events of the century, the American War of Independence and the French Revolution, the fine detail of his life remains nevertheless elusive, due to the loss of many of his papers, and the lack of contemporary documentation about his private affairs.

The author of the *Rights of man*, a work that was possibly the most keenly read political tract of the eighteenth century, was born into a Quaker family in Thetford, and started his working life as a corset-maker. Between 1750 and 1774 he worked as a shopkeeper, excise official and schoolteacher before emigrating to America (with the support of Benjamin Franklin) to escape imprisonment for debt. Soon after his arrival in America, he became editor of the *Pennsylvania Magazine*. After the publication of *Common sense: addressed to the inhabitants of America* in January 1776 he enlisted in the American army, and in December of that year the first of a series of sixteen essays on *The crisis* (1776–83) appeared, composed as a defence of, and an inspiration to, the rebels fighting against the British crown. Paine was now entering that remarkable period in his life which would see his metamorphosis from a poor, uneducated British artisan into the leading ideologue of the American Revolution.

In 1777–9 he served as Secretary to the Committee of Foreign Affairs, becoming in 1779 Clerk of the Pennsylvania Assembly. In 1786 he published various essays on political and economic matters, including the *Dissertations on government*. He went to France in 1787 to promote his bridge-building projects, and by 1791 he was back in England. The first part of the *Rights* appeared in February 1791, written in response to Edmund Burke's *Reflections on the Revolution in France* (1790). The second part followed in 1792. Paine was subsequently charged with sedition, but avoided trial by escaping to France, where he became a member of the National Convention. The Revolution brought the guillotine very close when he was imprisoned during the

Terror. His release in 1794 coincided with the publication of the first part of the *Age of reason* (Part II was published in 1796). He regained his seat in the National Convention, but by 1802 he was back in America, a much hated and vilified figure in many quarters. He lived for another seven years, but his tumultuous career, though not his reputation, as a firebrand revolutionary was over, and he died in penury and disgrace.

EDITORIAL NOTE

The selected extracts from *Common sense* are taken from the edition by B. Kuklick,* *Thomas Paine: political writings*, pp. 3–38. Paine's pamphlet first appeared in January 1776. Between 1776 and 1793 the pamphlet went through ten editions. It was translated into French in 1791 by A. Griffet de La Baume.

FURTHER READING

Ayer, A. *Thomas Paine* (Chicago, Chicago University Press, 1988).
Butler, M. (ed.), *Burke, Paine, Godwin, and the Revolution controversy* (Cambridge, Cambridge University Press, 1984).
Keane, J., *Tom Paine: a political life* (London, Bloomsbury, 1996).
*Kuklick, B. (ed.), *Paine: political writings* (Cambridge, Cambridge University Press, 1989). See introduction, pp. vii–xvii.

Common sense: addressed to the inhabitants of America (1776)

Some writers have so confounded society with government as to leave little or no distinction between them; whereas they are not only different, but have different origins. Society is produced by our wants and government by our wickedness; the former promotes our happiness *positively* by uniting our affections, the latter *negatively* by restraining our vices. The one encourages intercourse, the other creates distinctions. The first is a patron, the last a punisher.

Society in every state is a blessing, but government, even in its best state, is but a necessary evil; in its worst state an intolerable one; for when we suffer or are exposed to the same miseries *by a government*, which we might expect in a country *without government*, our calamity is heightened by reflecting that we furnish the means by which we suffer. Government, like dress, is the badge of lost innocence;

the palaces of kings are built upon the ruins of the bowers of paradise. For were the impulses of conscience clear, uniform, and irresistibly obeyed, man would need no other lawgiver; but that not being the case, he finds it necessary to surrender up a part of his property to furnish means for the protection of the rest; and this he is induced to do by the same prudence which in every other case advises him out of two evils to choose the least. *Wherefore,* security being the true design and end of government, it unanswerably follows that whatever *form* thereof appears most likely to ensure it to us, with the least expense and greatest benefit, is preferable to all others.

In order to gain a clear and just idea of the design and end of government, let us suppose a small number of persons settled in some sequestered part of the earth, unconnected with the rest; they will then represent the first peopling of any country, or of the world. In this state of natural liberty, society will be their first thought. A thousand motives will excite them thereto; the strength of one man is so unequal to his wants, and his mind so unfitted for perpetual solitude, that he is soon obliged to seek assistance and relief of another, who in his turn requires the same. Four or five united would be able to raise a tolerable dwelling in the midst of a wilderness, but *one* man might labor out the common period of life without accomplishing anything; when he had felled his timber he could not remove it, nor erect it after it was removed; hunger in the meantime would urge him to quit his work, and every different want would call him a different way. Disease, nay even misfortune, would be death; for though neither might be mortal, yet either would disable him from living, and reduce him to a state in which he might rather be said to perish than to die.

Thus necessity, like a gravitating power, would soon form our newly arrived emigrants into society, the reciprocal blessings of which would supersede and render the obligations of law and government unnecessary while they remained perfectly just to each other; but as nothing but heaven is impregnable to vice, it will unavoidably happen that in proportion as they surmount the first difficulties of emigration, which bound them together in a common cause, they will begin to relax in their duty and attachment to each other; and this remissness will point out the necessity of establishing some form of government to supply the defect of moral virtue.

Some convenient tree will afford them a statehouse, under the branches of which the whole colony may assemble to deliberate on public matters. It is more than probable that their first laws will have the title only of REGULATIONS and be enforced by no other penalty than public disesteem. In this first parliament every man by natural right will have a seat.

But as the colony increases, the public concerns will increase likewise, and the distance at which the members may be separated will render it too inconvenient for all of them to meet on every occasion as at first, when their number was small, their habitations near, and the public concerns few and trifling. This will point out the convenience of their consenting to leave the legislative part to be managed by a select number chosen from the whole body, who are supposed to have the same concerns at stake which those have who appointed them, and who will act in the same manner as the whole body would act were they present. If the colony continue increasing, it will become necessary to augment the number of represent-atives, and that the interest of every part of the colony may be attended to, it will be found best to divide the whole into convenient parts, each part sending its proper number; and that the *elected* might never form to themselves an interest separate from the *electors*, prudence will point out the propriety of having elec-tions often, because as the *elected* might by that means return and mix again with the general body of the *electors* in a few months, their fidelity to the public will be secured by the prudent reflection of not making a rod for themselves. And as this frequent interchange will establish a common interest with every part of the community, they will mutually and naturally support each other, and on this (not in the unmeaning name of king) depends the *strength of government and the happiness of the governed.*

Here then is the origin and rise of government; namely, a mode rendered neces-sary by the inability of moral virtue to govern the world; here too is the design and end of government, viz., freedom and security. And however our eyes may be dazzled with show or our ears deceived by sound; however prejudice may warp our wills or interest darken our understanding, the simple voice of nature and reason will say, it is right.

I draw my idea of the form of government from a principle in nature which no art can overturn, viz. that the more simple anything is, the less liable it is to be disordered, and the easier repaired when disordered; and with this maxim in view, I offer a few remarks on the so much boasted constitution of England. That it was noble for the dark and slavish times in which it was erected, is granted. When the world was overrun with tyranny, the least remove therefrom was a glorious rescue. But that it is imperfect, subject to convulsions, and incapable of producing what it seems to promise, is easily demonstrated.

Absolute governments (though the disgrace of human nature) have this advantage with them, they are simple; if the people suffer, they know the head from which their suffering springs; know likewise the remedy; and are not bewildered by a variety of causes and cures. But the constitution of England is so exceedingly complex that the nation may suffer for years together without being able to discover in which part the fault lies; some will say in one and some in another, and every political physician will advise a different medicine.

I know it is difficult to get over local or long standing prejudices, yet if we will suffer ourselves to examine the component parts of the English constitution, we shall find them to be the base remains of two ancient tyrannies, compounded with some new republican materials.

First. – The remains of monarchical tyranny in the person of the King.

Secondly. – The remains of aristocratical tyranny in the persons of the Peers.

Thirdly. – The new republican materials, in the persons of the Commons, on whose virtue depends the freedom of England.

The two first, by being hereditary, are independent of the people; wherefore in a *constitutional sense* they contribute nothing towards the freedom of the state.

To say that the constitution of England is a *union* of three powers, reciprocally *checking* each other, is farcical; either the words have no meaning, or they are flat contradictions.

To say that the commons is a check upon the king, presupposes two things.

First. – That the king is not to be trusted without being looked after; or in other words, that a thirst for absolute power is the natural disease of monarchy.

Secondly. – That the commons, by being appointed for that purpose, are either wiser or more worthy of confidence than the crown.

But as the same constitution which gives the commons a power to check the king by withholding the supplies, gives afterwards the king a power to check the commons, by empowering him to reject their other bills; it again supposes that the king is wiser than those whom it has already supposed to be wiser than him. A mere absurdity!

There is something exceedingly ridiculous in the composition of monarchy; it first excludes a man from the means of information, yet empowers him to act in cases where the highest judgment is required. The state of a king shuts him from the world, yet the business of a king requires him to know it thoroughly; wherefore the different parts, by unnaturally opposing and destroying each other, prove the whole character to be absurd and useless.

Some writers have explained the English constitution thus: the king, say they, is one, the people another; the peers are a house in behalf of the king, the commons in behalf of the people; but this hath all the distinctions of a house divided against itself; and though the expressions be pleasantly arranged, yet when examined they appear idle and ambiguous; and it will always happen that the nicest construction that words are capable of, when applied to the description of something which either cannot exist or is too incomprehensible to be within the compass of description, will be words of sound only, and though they may amuse the ear, they cannot inform the mind; for this explanation includes a previous question, viz. *how came the king by a power which the people are afraid to trust, and always obliged to check?* Such a power could not be the gift of a wise people, neither can any power, *which needs checking,* be from God; yet the provision which the constitution makes supposes such a power to exist.

But the provision is unequal to the task; the means either cannot or will not accomplish the end, and the whole affair is a *felo de se*; for as the greater weight will always carry up the less, and as all the wheels of a machine are put in motion by one, it only remains to know which power in the constitution has the most weight, for that will govern; and though the others, or a part of them, may clog, or check the rapidity of its motion, yet so long as they cannot stop it, their endeavours will be ineffectual; the first moving power will at last have its way, and what it wants in speed is supplied by time.

That the crown is this overbearing part in the English constitution needs not be mentioned, and that it derives its whole consequence merely from being the giver of places and pensions is self-evident; wherefore, though we have been wise enough to shut and lock a door against absolute monarchy, we at the same time have been foolish enough to put the crown in possession of the key.

The prejudice of Englishmen in favor of their own government by king, lords, and commons, arises as much or more from national pride than reason. Individuals are undoubtedly safer in England than in some other countries: but the *will* of the king is as much the *law* of the land in Britain as in France, with this difference, that instead of proceeding directly from his mouth, it is handed to the people under the formidable shape of an act of parliament. For the fate of Charles the First hath only made kings more subtle – not more just.

Wherefore, laying aside all national pride and prejudice in favor of modes and forms, the plain truth is that *it is wholly to the constitution of the people, and not to the constitution of the government* that the crown is not as oppressive in England as in Turkey.

An inquiry into the *constitutional errors* in the English form of government is at this time highly necessary; for as we are never in a proper condition of doing justice to others while we continue under the influence of some leading partiality, so neither are we capable of doing it to ourselves while we remain fettered by any obstinate prejudice. And as a man who is attached to a prostitute is unfitted to choose or judge of a wife, so any prepossession in favor of a rotten constitution of government will disable us from discerning a good one. [*Common sense*, I: 'On the origin and design of government in general, with concise remarks on the English constitution']

Mankind being originally equals in the order of creation, the equality could only be destroyed by some subsequent circumstance: the distinctions of rich and poor may in a great measure be accounted for, and that without having recourse to the harsh ill-sounding names of oppression and avarice. Oppression is often the *consequence*, but seldom or never the *means* of riches; and though avarice will preserve a man from being necessitously poor, it generally makes him too timorous to be wealthy.

But there is another and greater distinction for which no truly natural or religious reason can be assigned, and that is the distinction of men into *kings* and *subjects*. Male and female are the distinctions of nature, good and bad the distinctions of heaven; but how a race of men came into the world so exalted above the rest, and distinguished like some new species, is worth inquiring into, and whether they are the means of happiness or of misery to mankind.

In the early ages of the world, according to the Scripture chronology there were no kings; the consequence of which was there were no wars; it is the pride of kings which throws mankind into confusion. Holland without a king hath enjoyed more peace for this last century than any of the monarchical governments in Europe. Antiquity favors the same remark; for the quiet and rural lives of the first patriarchs have a happy something in them, which vanishes when we come to the history of Jewish royalty.

Government by kings was first introduced into the world by the heathens, from whom the children of Israel copied the custom. It was the most prosperous invention the Devil ever set on foot for the promotion of idolatry. The heathens paid divine honors to their deceased kings, and the Christian world has improved on the plan by doing the same to their living ones. How impious is the title of sacred Majesty applied to a worm, who in the midst of his splendor is crumbling into dust!

As the exalting one man so greatly above the rest cannot be justified on the equal rights of nature, so neither can it be defended on the authority of Scripture; for the will of the Almighty, as declared by Gideon and the prophet Samuel, expressly disapproves of government by kings. All anti-monarchical parts of Scripture have been very smoothly glossed over in monarchical governments, but they undoubtedly merit the attention of countries which have their governments yet to form. '*Render unto Cæsar the things which are Cæsar's,*' is the scripture doctrine of courts, yet it is no support of monarchical government, for the Jews at that time were without a king, and in a state of vassalage to the Romans.

Near three thousand years passed away, from the Mosaic account of the creation, till the Jews under a national delusion requested a king. Till then their form of government (except in extraordinary cases where the Almighty interposed) was a kind of republic, administered by a judge and the elders of the tribes. Kings they had none, and it was held sinful to acknowledge any being under that title but the Lord of Hosts. And when a man seriously reflects on the idolatrous homage which is paid to the persons of kings, he need not wonder that the Almighty, ever jealous of his honour, should disapprove a form of government which so impiously invades the prerogative of heaven.

Monarchy is ranked in scripture as one of the sins of the Jews, for which a course in reserve is denounced against them. The history of that transaction is worth attending to.

The children of Israel being oppressed by the Midianites, Gideon marched against them with a small army, and victory through the Divine interposition decided in his favor. The Jews elate with success and attributing it to the generalship of Gideon, proposed making him a king, saying, *Rule thou over us, thou and thy son, and thy son's son.* Here was temptation in its fullest extent; not a kingdom only, but an hereditary one; but Gideon in the piety of his soul replied, *I will not rule over you, neither shall my son rule over you.* THE LORD SHALL RULE OVER YOU. Words need not be more explicit; Gideon doth not *decline* the honor, but denieth their right to give it; neither doth he compliment them with invented declarations of his thanks, but in the positive style of a prophet charges them with disaffection to their proper sovereign, the King of Heaven.

About one hundred and thirty years after this, they fell again into the same error. The hankering which the Jews had for the idolatrous customs of the heathens is something exceedingly unaccountable; but so it was that laying hold of the misconduct of Samuel's two sons who were intrusted with some secular concerns, they came in an abrupt and clamorous manner to Samuel, saying, *Behold thou art old, and thy sons walk not in thy ways, now make us a king to judge us like all the other nations.* And here we cannot but observe that their motives were bad, viz. that they might be *like* unto other nations, i.e. the heathens, whereas their true glory lay in being as much *unlike* them as possible. *But the thing displeased Samuel when they said, give us a king to judge us; and Samuel prayed unto the Lord, and the Lord said unto Samuel, hearken unto the voice of the people in all that they say unto thee, for they have not rejected thee, but they have rejected me,* THAT I SHOULD NOT REIGN OVER THEM. *According to all the works which they have done since the day that I brought them up out of Egypt even unto this day, wherewith they have forsaken me, and served other Gods: so do they also unto thee. Now therefore hearken unto their voice, howbeit, protest solemnly unto them and show them the manner of the king that shall reign over them,* i.e. not of any particular king, but the general manner of the kings of the earth whom Israel was so eagerly copying after. And notwithstanding the great distance of time and difference of manners, the character is still in fashion. *And Samuel told all the words of the Lord unto the people, that asked of him a king. And he said, This shall be the manner of the king that shall reign over you. He will take your sons and appoint them for himself for his chariots and to be his horsemen, and some shall run before his chariots* (this description agrees with the present mode of impressing men) *and he will appoint him captains over thousands and captains over fifties, will set them to ear his ground and to reap his harvest, and to make his instruments of war, and instruments of his chariots. And he will take your daughters to be confectionaries, and to be cooks, and to be bakers* (this describes the expense and luxury as well as the oppression of kings) *and he will take your fields and your vineyards, and your olive yards, even the best of them, and give them to his servants. And he will take the tenth of your seed, and of your vineyards, and give them to his officers and to his servants* (by which we see that bribery, corruption, and favoritism are the standing vices of kings) *and he will take the tenth of your men servants, and your maid servants, and your goodliest young men, and your asses, and put them to his work: and he will take the tenth of your sheep, and ye shall be his servants, and ye shall cry out in that day because of your king which ye shall have chosen,* AND THE LORD

WILL NOT HEAR YOU IN THAT DAY. This accounts for the continuation of monarchy; neither do the characters of the few good kings which have lived since, either sanctify the title, or blot out the sinfulness of the origin; the high encomium given of David takes no notice of him *officially as a king*, but only as a *man* after God's own heart. *Nevertheless the People refused to obey the voice of Samuel, and they said, Nay but we will have a king over us, that we may be like all the nations, and that our king may judge us, and go out before us and fight our battles.* Samuel continued to reason with them, but to no purpose; he set before them their ingratitude, but all would not avail; and seeing them fully bent on their folly, he cried out, *I will call unto the Lord, and he shall send thunder and rain* (which was then a punishment, being in the time of wheat harvest) *that ye may perceive and see that your wickedness is great which ye have done in the sight of the Lord,* IN ASKING YOU A KING. *So Samuel called unto the Lord, and the Lord sent thunder and rain that day, and all the people greatly feared the Lord and Samuel. And all the people said unto Samuel, Pray for thy servants unto the Lord thy God that we die not, for* WE HAVE ADDED UNTO OUR SINS THIS EVIL, TO ASK A KING. These portions of scripture are direct and positive. They admit of no equivocal construction. That the Almighty hath here entered his protest against monarchical government is true, or the scripture is false. And a man hath good reason to believe that there is as much of kingcraft as priestcraft in withholding the scripture from the public in popish countries. For monarchy in every instance is the popery of government.

To the evil of monarchy we have added that of hereditary succession; and as the first is a degradation and lessening of ourselves, so the second, claimed as a matter of right, is an insult and imposition on posterity. For all men being originally equals, no *one* by *birth* could have a right to set up his own family in perpetual preference to all others forever, and though himself might deserve *some* decent degree of honors of his contemporaries, yet his descendants might be far too unworthy to inherit them. One of the strongest *natural* proofs of the folly of hereditary right in kings, is that nature disapproves it, otherwise she would not so frequently turn it into ridicule by giving mankind an *ass for a lion*.

Secondly, as no man at first could possess any other public honors than were bestowed upon him, so the givers of those honors could have no power to give away the right of posterity, and though they might say 'we choose you for our head,' they could not without manifest injustice to their children say 'that your children and your children's children shall reign over our's forever.' Because such an unwise, unjust, unnatural compact might (perhaps) in the next succession put them under the government of a rogue or a fool. Most wise men in their private sentiments have ever treated hereditary right with contempt; yet it is one of those evils which when once established is not easily removed; many submit from fear, others from superstition, and the more powerful part shares with the king the plunder of the rest.

This is supposing the present race of kings in the world to have had an honorable origin; whereas it is more than probable that, could we take off the dark covering of antiquity and trace them to their first rise, we should find the first of them nothing better than the principal ruffian of some restless gang, whose savage manners of pre-eminence in subtility obtained him the title of chief among plunderers; and who by increasing in power, and extending his depredations, overawed the quiet and defenseless to purchase their safety by frequent contributions. Yet his electors could have no idea of giving hereditary right to his descendants, because such a perpetual exclusion of themselves was incompatible with the free and unrestrained principles they professed to live by. Wherefore, hereditary succession in the early ages of monarchy could not take place as a matter of claim, but as something casual or complemental; but as few or no records were extant in those days, and traditionary history stuffed with fables, it was very easy, after the lapse of a few generations, to trump up some superstitious tale conveniently timed, Mahomet-like, to cram hereditary right down the throats of the vulgar. Perhaps the disorders which threatened, or seemed to threaten, on the decease of a leader and the choice of a new one (for elections among ruffians could not be very orderly) induced many at first to favor hereditary pretensions; by which means it happened, as it hath happened since, that what at first was submitted to as a convenience was afterwards claimed as a right.

England, since the conquest, hath known some few good monarchs, but groaned beneath a much larger number of bad ones; yet no man in his senses can say that their claim under William the Conqueror is a very honorable one. A French bastard, landing with an armed banditti and establishing himself king of England against the consent of the natives, is in plain terms a very paltry rascally original. It certainly hath no divinity in it. However it is needless to spend much time in exposing the folly of hereditary right; if there are any so weak as to believe it, let them promiscuously worship the Ass and the Lion, and welcome. I shall neither copy their humility, nor disturb their devotion.

Yet I should be glad to ask how they suppose kings came at first? The question admits but of three answers, viz., either by lot, by election, or by usurpation. If the first king was taken by lot, it establishes a precedent for the next, which excludes hereditary succession. Saul was by lot, yet the succession was not hereditary, neither does it appear from that transaction that there was any intention it ever should. If the first king of any country was by election that likewise establishes a precedent for the next; for to say that the right of all future generations is taken away by the act of the first electors in their choice not only of a king, but of a family of kings forever, hath no parallel in or out of scripture but the doctrine of original sin, which supposes the free will of all men lost in Adam; and from such comparison, and it will admit of no other, hereditary succession can derive no glory. For as in Adam all sinned, and as in the first electors all men obeyed; as in the one all mankind were subjected to Satan, and in the other to sovereignty; as our innocence was lost in the first, and our authority in the last; and as both disable us from reassuming some former state and privilege, it unanswerably follows that original sin and hereditary succession are parallels. Dishonorable rank! inglorious connection! yet the most subtle sophist cannot produce a juster simile.

As to usurpation, no man will be so hardy as to defend it; and that William the Conqueror was a usurper is a fact not to be contradicted. The plain truth is, that the antiquity of English monarchy will not bear looking into.

But it is not so much the absurdity as the evil of hereditary succession which concerns mankind. Did it insure a race of good and wise men it would have the seal of divine authority, but as it opens a door to the *foolish*, the *wicked*, and the *improper*, it hath in it the nature of oppression. Men who look upon themselves born to reign, and others to obey, soon grow insolent. Selected from the rest of mankind, their minds are early poisoned by importance; and the world they act in differs so materially from the world at large that they have but little opportunity of knowing its true interest, and when they succeed to the government are frequently the most ignorant and unfit of any throughout the dominions.

Another evil which attends hereditary succession is, that the throne is subject to be possessed by a minor at any age; all which time the regency, acting under the cover of a king, have every opportunity and inducement to betray their trust. The same national misfortune happens when a king, worn out with age and infirmity, enters the last stage of human weakness. In both these cases the public becomes a prey to every miscreant who can temper successfully with the follies either of age or infancy.

The most plausible plea which hath ever been offered in favor of hereditary succession is that it preserves a nation from civil wars; and were this true, it would be weighty; whereas, it is the most barefaced falsity ever imposed upon mankind. The whole history of England disowns the fact. Thirty kings and two minors have reigned in that distracted kingdom since the conquest, in which time there have been (including the Revolution) no less than eight civil wars and nineteen rebellions. Wherefore instead of making for peace, it makes against it, and destroys the very foundation it seems to stand upon.

The contest for monarchy and succession between the houses of York and Lancaster laid England in a scene of blood for many years. Twelve pitched battles, besides skirmishes and sieges, were fought between Henry and Edward. Twice was Henry prisoner to Edward, who in his turn was prisoner to Henry. And so uncertain is the fate of war and the temper of a nation, when nothing but personal matters are the ground of a quarrel, that Henry was taken in triumph from a prison to a palace, and Edward obliged to fly from a palace to a foreign land; yet, as sudden transitions of temper are seldom lasting, Henry in his turn was driven from the throne, and Edward recalled to succeed him. The parliament always following the strongest side.

This contest began in the reign of Henry the Sixth, and was not entirely extinguished till Henry the Seventh, in whom the families were united. Including a period of sixty-seven years, viz., from 1422 to 1489.

In short, monarchy and succession have laid (not this or that kingdom only) but the world in blood and ashes. 'Tis a form of government which the word of God bears testimony against, and blood will attend it.

If we inquire into the business of a king, we shall find (in some countries they may have none) that after sauntering away their lives without pleasure to themselves or advantages to the nation, they withdraw from the scene, and leave their successors to tread the same idle round. In absolute monarchies the whole weight of business, civil and military, lies on the king; the children of Israel in their request for a king urged this plea, 'that he may judge us, and go out before us and fight our battles.' But in countries where he is neither a judge nor a general, as in England, a man would be puzzled to know what *is* his business.

The nearer any government approaches to a republic, the less business there is for a king. It is somewhat difficult to find a proper name for the government of England. Sir William Meredith calls it a republic; but in its present state it is unworthy of the name, because the corrupt influence of the crown, by having all the places in its disposal, hath so effectually swallowed up the power, and eaten out the virtue of the House of Commons (the republican part in the constitution) that the government of England is nearly as monarchical as that of France or Spain. Men fall out with names without understanding them. For 'tis the republican and not the monarchical part of the constitution of England which Englishmen glory in, viz. the liberty of choosing a house of commons from out of their own body – and it is easy to see that when republican virtues fail, slavery ensues. Why is the constitution of England sickly but because monarchy hath poisoned the republic, the crown has engrossed the commons?

In England a king hath little more to do than to make war and give away places; which in plain terms is to impoverish the nation and set it together by the ears. A pretty business indeed for a man to be allowed eight hundred thousand sterling a year for, and worshipped into the bargain! Of more worth is one honest man to society, and in the sight of God, than all the crowned ruffians that ever lived.
[*Common sense*, ii: **'Of monarchy and hereditary succession'**]

. . . Thousands are already ruined by British barbarity; (thousands more will probably suffer the same fate). Those men have other feelings than us who have nothing suffered. All they *now* possess is liberty; what they before enjoyed is sacrificed to its service, and having nothing more to lose they disdain submission. Besides, the general temper of the colonies towards a British government will be like that of a youth who is nearly out of his time; they will care very little about her. And a government which cannot preserve the peace is no government at all, and in that case we pay our money for nothing; and pray what is it that Britain can do, whose power will be wholly on paper, should a civil tumult break out the very day after reconciliation? I have heard some men say, many of whom I believe spoke without thinking, that they dreaded an independence, fearing that it would produce civil wars. It is but seldom that our first thoughts are truly correct, and that is the case here; for there is ten times more to dread from a patched up connection than from independence. I make the sufferer's case my own, and I protest, that were I driven from house and home, my property destroyed, and my circumstances ruined, that as a man, sensible of injuries, I could never relish the doctrine of reconciliation, or consider myself bound thereby.

The colonies have manifested such a spirit of good order and obedience to continental government as is sufficient to make every reasonable person easy and happy on that head. No man can assign the least pretense for his fears on any other grounds than such as are truly childish and ridiculous, viz., that one colony will be striving for superiority over another.

Where there are no distinctions there can be no superiority; perfect equality affords no temptation. The republics of Europe are all (and we may say always) in peace. Holland and Switzerland are without wars, foreign or domestic. Monarchical governments, it is true, are never long at rest: the crown itself is a temptation to enterprising ruffians at *home*; and that degree of pride and insolence ever attendant on regal authority, swells into a rupture with foreign powers in instances where a republican government, by being formed on more natural principles, would negotiate the mistake.

If there is any true cause of fear respecting independence, it is because no plan is yet laid down. Men do not see their way out. Wherefore, as an opening into that business I offer the following hints; at the same time modestly affirming that I have no other opinion of them myself than that they may be the means of giving rise to something better. Could the straggling thoughts of individuals be collected, they would frequently form materials for wise and able men to improve into useful matter.

Let the assemblies be annual, with a president only. The representation more equal, their business wholly domestic, and subject to the authority of a continental congress.

Let each colony be divided into six, eight, or ten, convenient districts, each district to send a proper number of delegates to congress, so that each colony send at least thirty. The whole number in congress will be at least 390. Each congress to sit and to choose a president by the following method. When the delegates are met, let a colony be taken from the whole thirteen colonies by lot, after which let the congress choose (by ballot) a president from out of the delegates of that province. In the next congress, let a colony be taken by lot from twelve only, omitting that colony from which the president was taken in the former congress, and so proceeding on till the whole thirteen shall have had their proper rotation. And in order that nothing may pass into a law but what is satisfactorily just, not less than three fifths of the congress to be called a majority. He that will promote discord, under a government so equally formed as this, would have joined Lucifer in his revolt.

But as there is a peculiar delicacy from whom, or in what manner, this business must first arise, and as it seems most agreeable and consistent that it should come from some intermediate body between the governed and the governors, that is, between the congress and the people, let a CONTINENTAL CONFERENCE be held in the following manner, and for the following purpose:

A committee of twenty-six members of congress, viz., two for each colony. Two members from each house of assembly, or provincial convention; and five representatives of the people at large, to be chosen in the capital city or town of each province, for, and in behalf of the whole province, by as many qualified voters as shall think proper to attend from all parts of the province for that purpose; or, if more convenient, the representatives may be chosen in two or three of the most populous parts thereof. In this CONFERENCE, thus assembled, will be united the two grand principles of business, *knowledge* and *power*. The members of congress, assemblies, or conventions, by having had experience in national concerns, will be able and useful counsellors, and the whole being empowered by the people, will have a truly legal authority.

The conferring members being met, let their business be to frame a CONTINENTAL CHARTER, or Charter of the United Colonies (answering to what is called the Magna Charta of England); fixing the number and manner of choosing members of congress, members of assembly, with their date of sitting, and drawing the line of business and jurisdiction between them (always remembering, that our strength is continental, not provincial); securing freedom and property to all men, and above all things the free exercise of religion, according to the dictates of conscience; with such other matter as it is necessary for a charter to contain. Immediately after which, the said conference to dissolve, and the bodies which shall be chosen conformable to the said charter, to be the legislators and governors of this continent for the time being: Whose peace and happiness, may God preserve. AMEN.

Should any body of men be hereafter delegated for this or some similar purpose, I offer them the following extracts from that wise observer on governments, Dragonetti. 'The science,' says he, 'of the politician consists in fixing the true point of happiness and freedom. Those men would deserve the gratitude of ages, who should discover a mode of government that contained the greatest sum of individual happiness, with the least national expense.'

But where, say some, is the king of America? I'll tell you, friend, he reigns above, and doth not make a havoc of mankind like the Royal Brute of Great Britain. Yet that we may not appear to be defective even in earthly honors, let a day be solemnly set apart for proclaiming the charter; let it be brought forth placed on the divine law, the Word of God; let a crown be placed thereon, by which the world may know, that so far as we approve of monarchy, that in America THE LAW IS KING. For as in absolute governments the king is law, so in free countries the law *ought* to BE king, and there ought to be no other. But lest any ill use should afterwards arise, let the crown at the conclusion of the ceremony be demolished, and scattered among the people whose right it is.

A government of our own is our natural right; and when a man seriously reflects on the precariousness of human affairs, he will become convinced, that it is infinitely wiser and safer to form a constitution of our own in a cool deliberate manner, while we have it in our power, than to trust such an interesting event to time and chance. If we omit it now, some Massanello may hereafter arise, who, laying hold of popular disquietudes, may collect together the desperate and the discontented, and by assuming to themselves the powers of government, finally sweep away the liberties of the continent like a deluge. Should the government of America return again into the hands of Britain, the tottering situation of things will be a temptation for some desperate adventurer to try his fortune; and in such a case, what relief can Britain give? Ere she could hear the news, the fatal business might be done; and ourselves suffering like the wretched Britons under the oppression of the conqueror. Ye that oppose independence now, ye know not what ye do; ye are opening a door to eternal tyranny by keeping vacant the seat of government. There are thousands and tens of thousands who would think it glorious to expel from the continent that barbarous and hellish power which hath stirred up the Indians and the Negroes to destroy us; the cruelty hath a double guilt, it is dealing brutally by us, and treacherously by them.

To talk of friendship with those in whom our reason forbids us to have faith, and our affections wounded through a thousand pores instruct us to detest, is madness and folly. Every day wears out the little remains of kindred between us and them; and can there be any reason to hope that as the relationship expires the affection will increase, or that we shall agree better when we have ten times more and greater concerns to quarrel over than ever?

Ye that tell us of harmony and reconciliation, can ye restore to us the time that is past? Can ye give to prostitution its former innocence? Neither can ye reconcile Britain and America. The last cord now is broken, the people of England are presenting addresses against us. There are injuries which nature cannot forgive; she would cease to be nature if she did. As well can the lover forgive the ravisher of his mistress, as the continent forgive the murders of Britain. The Almighty hath implanted in us these inextinguishable feelings for good and wise purposes. They are the guardians of his image in our hearts. They distinguish us from the herd of common animals. The social compact would dissolve, and justice be extirpated from the earth, or have only a casual existence, were we callous to the touches of affection. The robber and the murderer would often escape unpunished, did not the injuries which our tempers sustain, provoke us into justice.

O ye that love mankind! Ye that dare oppose not only the tyranny but the tyrant, stand forth! Every spot of the old world is overrun with oppression. Freedom hath been hunted round the globe. Asia and Africa have long expelled her. Europe regards her like a stranger, and England hath given her warning to depart. O receive the fugitive, and prepare in time an asylum for mankind. [*Common sense*, III: 'Thoughts on the present state of American affairs']

... The infant state of the colonies, as it is called, so far from being against, is an argument in favor of independence. We are sufficiently numerous, and were we more so we might be less united. It is a matter worthy of observation that the more a country is peopled the smaller their armies are. In military numbers, the ancients far exceeded the moderns; and the reason is evident, for trade being the consequence of population men became too much absorbed thereby to attend to anything else. Commerce diminishes the spirit both of patriotism and military defense. And history sufficiently informs us that the bravest achievements were always accomplished in the nonage of a nation. With the increase of commerce England hath lost its spirit. The city of London, notwithstanding its numbers, submits to continued insults with the patience of a coward. The more men have to lose, the less willing are they to venture. The rich are in general slaves to fear, and submit to courtly power with the trembling duplicity of a spaniel.

Youth is the seedtime of good habits, as well in nations as in individuals. It might be difficult, if not impossible, to form the continent into one government half a century hence. The vast variety of interests, occasioned by an increase of trade and population, would create confusion. Colony would be against colony. Each, being able, would scorn each other's assistance; and while the proud and foolish gloried in their little distinctions, the wise would lament that the union had not been formed before. Wherefore the present time is the true time for establishing it. The intimacy which is contracted in infancy and the friendship which is formed in misfortune are of all others the most lasting and unalterable.

Our present union is marked with both these characters; we are young, and we have been distressed; but our concord hath withstood our troubles, and fixes a memorable era for posterity to glory in.

The present time, likewise, is that peculiar time which never happens to a nation but once, viz. the time of forming itself into a government. Most nations have let slip the opportunity, and by that means have been compelled to receive laws from their conquerors instead of making laws for themselves. First they had a king, and then a form of government; whereas the articles or charter of government should be formed first, and men delegated to execute them afterwards: but from the errors of other nations let us learn wisdom and lay hold of the present opportunity – *to begin government at the right end.*

When William the Conqueror subdued England, he gave them law at the point of the sword; and until we consent that the seat of government in America be legally and authoritatively occupied, we shall be in danger of having it filled by some fortunate ruffian who may treat us in the same manner, and then where will be our freedom? where our property?

As to religion, I hold it to be the indispensable duty of government to protect all conscientious professors thereof, and I know of no other business which government has to do therewith. Let a man throw aside that narrowness of soul, that selfishness of principle, which the niggards of all professions are so unwilling to part with, and he will be at once delivered of his fears on that head. Suspicion is the companion of mean souls and the bane of all good society. For myself, I fully and conscientiously believe that it is the will of the Almighty that there should be a diversity of religious opinions among us. It affords a larger field for our Christian kindness. Were we all of one way of thinking, our religious dispositions would want matter for probation; and on this liberal principle I look on the various denominations among us to be like children of the same family, differing only in what is called their Christian names.

. . . I threw out a few thoughts on the propriety of a continental charter (for I only presume to offer hints, not plans) and in this place I take the liberty of re-mentioning the subject by observing that a charter is to be understood as a bond of solemn obligation, which the whole enters into, to support the right of every separate part, whether of religion, professional freedom, or property. A right reckoning makes long friends.

I have heretofore, likewise, mentioned the necessity of a large and equal representation; and there is no political matter which more deserves our attention. A small number of electors, or a small number of representatives, are equally dangerous. But if the number of the representatives be not only small, but unequal, the danger is increased. As an instance of this I mention the following; when the petition of the associates was before the house of assembly of Pennsylvania, twenty-eight members only were present; all the Bucks county members, being eight, voted against it, and had seven of the Chester members done the same, this whole province had been governed by two counties only; and this danger it is always exposed to. The unwarrantable stretch, likewise, which the house made in their last sitting to gain an undue authority over the delegates of that province, ought to warn the people at large, how they trust power out of their hands. A set of instructions for their delegates were put together, which in point of sense and business would have dishonored a schoolboy, and after being approved by a few, a very few, without doors, were carried into the house, and there passed in behalf of the whole colony; whereas, did the whole colony know with what ill-will that house had entered on some necessary public measures, they would not hesitate a moment to think them unworthy of such a trust.

Immediate necessity makes many things convenient, which if continued would grow into oppressions. Expedience and right are different things. When the calamities of America required a consultation, there was no method so ready, or at that time so proper, as to appoint persons from the several houses of assembly for that purpose; and the wisdom with which they have proceeded hath preserved this continent from ruin. But as it is more than probable that we shall never be without a CONGRESS, every well-wisher to good order must own that the mode for choosing members of that body deserves consideration. And I put it as a question to those who make a study of mankind, whether representation and election is not too great a power for one and the same body of men to possess? When we are planning for posterity, we ought to remember that virtue is not hereditary.

It is from our enemies that we often gain excellent maxims, and are frequently surprised into reason by their mistakes. Mr. Cornwall (one of the lords of the treasury) treated the petition of the New York assembly with contempt, because *that* house, he said, consisted but of twenty-six members, which trifling number, he argued, could not with decency be put for the whole. We thank him for his involuntary honesty.

TO CONCLUDE. However strange it may appear to some, or however unwilling they may be to think so, matters not, but many strong and striking reasons may be given to show that nothing can settle our affairs so expeditiously as an open and determined DECLARATION FOR INDEPENDENCE. Some of which are:

First. It is the custom of nations, when any two are at war, for some other powers not engaged in the quarrel to step in as mediators, and bring about the preliminaries of a peace; but while America calls herself the Subject of Great Britain, no power, however well disposed she may be, can offer her mediation. Wherefore, in our present state we may quarrel on forever.

Secondly. It is unreasonable to suppose that France or Spain will give us any kind of assistance if we mean only to make use of that assistance for the purpose of repairing the breach and strengthening the connection between Britain and America; because those powers would be sufferers by the consequences.

Thirdly. While we profess ourselves the subjects of Britain, we must, in the eyes of foreign nations, be considered as rebels. The precedent is somewhat dangerous to *their peace,* for men to be in arms under the name of subjects: we, on the spot, can solve the paradox; but to unite resistance and subjection requires an idea much too refined for common understanding.

Fourthly. Were a manifesto to be published and despatched to foreign courts, setting forth the miseries we have endured and the peaceful methods which we have ineffectually used for redress; declaring at the same time that, not being able any longer to live happily or safely under the cruel disposition of the British court, we have been driven to the necessity of breaking off all connections with her; at the same time assuring all such courts of our peaceable disposition towards them, and of our desire of entering into trade with them: such a memorial would produce more good effects to this continent, than if a ship were freighted with petitions to Britain.

Under our present denomination of British subjects, we can neither be received nor heard abroad: the custom of all courts is against us, and will be so until by an independence we take rank with other nations.

These proceedings may at first seem strange and difficult, but like all other steps which we have already passed over, will in a little time become familiar and agreeable; and until an Independence is declared, the continent will feel itself like a man who continues putting off some unpleasant business from day to day, yet knows it must be done, hates to set about it, wishes it over, and is continually haunted with the thoughts of its necessity. [**Common sense, IV: 'Of the present ability of America, with some miscellaneous reflections'**]

EMMANUEL-JOSEPH SIEYES

BIOGRAPHICAL NOTE

Emmanuel-Joseph Siéyès (1748–1836) was an ordained priest and church administrator who first rose to prominence in Parisian political circles in 1788 as a writer of uncompromisingly radical revolutionary tracts. His writings crystallise the political ideology of the first, pre-Terror stage of the French Revolution, and provide a luminous exposition of the theoretical case for representative government and democratically organised state institutions. Strongly influenced by Bonnet's views on natural harmony and the 'order of things', and by the thought of Condillac and Locke on inequality and sovereignty, Siéyès' work signals a significant turning-point in political thought with regard to the basic aims and organisation of modern nation states. Siéyès' fame as a political polemicist led to his election in May 1789 as a deputy in the Estates-General, in which capacity, in effect, he inaugurated the Revolution with his appeal to the representatives of the Third Estate on 17 June 1789 to transform the Estates-General into a National Assembly with integrated orders, possibly his most important, single political achievement.

A founder-member with Condorcet of the 1789 Society, he remained at the centre of revolutionary developments, helping to draft the new constitution, devising the Tennis Court Oath with Mounier, supporting the nationalisation of church property and joining forces with Mirabeau against the attempted *coup* by the Court against the Assembly. Robespierre's triumph over the Girondins led to his withdrawal from active politics for a time, and it was not until March 1795 that he re-entered the political arena as a member of the Committee of Public Safety to support legislation against further insurrection, and help prepare the 1795 constitution.

Having inaugurated the Revolution, Siéyès was to be a key player in its termination. By May 1799 he was a member of the precarious Directory. Convinced of the need for further constitutional reform in the face of continuing instability and resurgent Jacobinism, he collaborated with Napoleon in the *coup* of 9–10 November 1799 (18–19 Brumaire, Year VIII), and joined Napoleon as one of the three members of the provisional Consulate. After the defeat of Napoleon and the restoration of the Bourbons, Siéyès, accused of regicide, went into a long exile in Brussels, not returning to France until 1830. His shadow thus falls across most of the events that destroyed the *ancien régime*, and his political writings and activities reflect France's transition from absolute monarchy to a republic.

Despite his remarkable career, relatively little is known about Siéyès. An archetypal grey eminence, he remains a deeply ambiguous, mysterious and still controversial figure, masked rather than illuminated by his centre-stage public role. During the Revolution he enjoyed enormous prestige and a towering reputation as the incarnation of victory over France's feudal past. By substituting the sovereignty of the nation for that of the King, and by equating the nation's cause with that of the third estate, Siéyès in a sense *made* the Revolution. *What is the third estate?* was written in November–December 1788, and published in January 1789.

EDITORIAL NOTE

The base text for the present translation is that of the third edition of *Qu'est-ce que le tiers état?* (1789). This is the text printed in Jean-Denis Bredin's edition of *Qu'est-ce que le tiers état?* (Paris, Flammarion, 1988). Siéyès' annotations have not been included in the extract.

FURTHER READING

Campbell, P., 'Siéyès and *What is the third estate?*', in *What is the third estate?*, ed. and trans. by M. Blondel and S. Finer (London, Pall Mall Press, 1963), pp. 3–31.

Forsyth, M., *Reason and Revolution: the political thought of the abbé Siéyès* (New York, Leicester University Press, 1987).

Sewell, W., *A rhetoric of bourgeois revolution: the abbé Siéyès and What is the third estate?* (Durham, N.C., Duke University Press, 1994).

What is the third estate? (1789)

'*As long as the philosopher does not go beyond the bounds of truth, do not accuse him of going too far. His function is to show us the goal; so he must [first] reach it. If he stopped and dared to raise his signpost half way there, it might mislead us. The duty of the administrator, in contrast, is to think out the path ahead and inch forward with due regard to the nature of the difficulties . . . If the philosopher has reached the goal, he does not know where he is. If the administrator cannot see the goal, he does not know where he is going.'*

The plan of this work is quite simple. We have three questions to ask ourselves.

1. What is the Third Estate? – *Everything.*
2. What has it been so far in the political order? – *Nothing.*
3. What does it ask to be? – *Something.*

We shall see if these are the right answers. Meanwhile, it would be wrong to say that these truths have been exaggerated when you have not yet seen the supporting evidence. Next we shall examine the measures that have been tried, and those that must [still] be taken, for the Third Estate to actually become *something.*
Thus we shall state:

4. What ministers have tried to do in the interests of the Third Estate, and what the privileged themselves propose to do for it;
5. What should have been done;
6. And finally, what remains to be done for the Third Estate so that it can take up the place that is its due ...

What is a nation? A body of people who join together to live under *common* laws and be represented by the same *legislative assembly.* It is only too clear, isn't it, that the nobility has privileges and exemptions it dares to call its rights that are separate from the rights of the main body of citizens. As a consequence of these special rights, it does not belong to the common order, [nor is it subject to] the common law. Thus its private rights already make the nobility into a separate people, a nation within a nation. It really is a case of *imperium in imperio.*

With regard to its *political* rights, these also it exercises separately. It has its own representatives without any mandate from the people. Its corps of deputies sits separately, and even if it should sit in the same chamber as the deputies of ordinary citizens, its representative function would still be fundamentally distinct and separate. The nobility is alien to the nation, firstly from the standpoint of *principle,* since it does not derive its powers from the people; secondly from the standpoint of its objectives since these involve defending, not the general interest, but the private one.

The Third Estate thus contains everything proper to the nation; and those who do not belong to the Third Estate cannot be seen as part of the nation. What is the Third Estate? *Everything.* [***What is the third estate?*** 1: 'The Third Estate is the complete nation']

We shall examine neither the servitude in which the people have suffered for so long, nor the restrictions and humiliations which still constrain it. Its civil status has changed; it must change still more. It is absolutely impossible for the nation as a whole, or even for any separate order, to be free, if the Third Estate is not. We do not get our freedom from privileges, but from our rights as citizens, rights which belong to everyone.

If the aristocrats seek to keep the people in a state of oppression at the expense of that very freedom of which they have proved themselves to be unworthy, the people may well ask on what grounds. If the answer is 'by right of conquest', you will agree that this means going back in time a bit. Yet the Third Estate need not fear going back to the past. It will take itself back to the year preceding the 'conquest', and as it is strong enough nowadays not to allow itself to be conquered, its powers of resistance will no doubt be more effective. Why should it not send all those families with a wild claim to be descendants of a race of conquerors, and to have inherited *the right of conquest*, back to the forests of Franconia?

The nation, then purged, will, I think, be able to live with the thought that henceforth it was just composed of descendants of the Gauls and the Romans. Actually, if people insist on distinguishing between one lineage and another, could we not reveal to our poor fellow citizens that a lineage going back to the Gauls and the Romans is worth no more than one going back to the Sicambrians, the Welches and other savages from the woods and bogs of Old Germania? Yes, you might say, but conquest has upset all the old relationships, and hereditary noble status is now passed on down the line of conquerors. Very well, arrangements must be made for it to descend down the other line. The Third Estate will become noble again by being a conqueror in its turn.

But if all the races are mixed up, if the blood of the Franks, which has no more value in itself than any other, mingles with the blood of the Gauls, if the fathers of the Third Estate are the fathers of the whole nation, can we not hope one day to see an end to this prolonged parricide that one class prides itself on committing day after day on everybody else? Why should not reason and justice, which one day will be as strong a force as vanity, press the privileged to seek their *rehabilitation* within the order of the Third Estate by means of a new, but truer, more social sense of self-interest?

Let us pursue our theme. We must take the Third Estate to mean all citizens belonging to the common order. All those holding legal privileges, of whatever kind, are outside the common order; [they] are an exception to the common law, and in consequence do not belong to the Third Estate. As we have said already, a common system of laws and a common form of representation is what makes *one* nation. No doubt it is only too true that in France you are *nothing* if you are protected only by common law. If you do not have some sort of privilege to cling to you must resign yourself to enduring all manner of contempt, insult and humiliation. What is an unprivileged wretch to do to avoid being completely crushed? His only recourse is to attach himself in various contemptible ways to some great man. He sells his morals and his dignity as a human being in order to buy the possibility of protection from a *somebody*, should the need arise.

But here we need to consider the order of the Third Estate more from the standpoint of its relationship to the constitution than from that of its civil status. Let us see what the Third Estate amounts to in the Estates-General.

Who have been its so-called representatives? Those raised to the nobility or those with temporary privileges. These false deputies have not always even resulted from a free election by the people. Sometimes in the Estates-General, and almost always in the provincial assemblies, representation of the people is considered to be a right enjoyed by [the holder of] certain positions or offices.

The old aristocracy cannot stand the new; they do not let the new nobility sit with them unless they can prove, as the saying goes, 'four generations plus a hundred years'. So the new nobility are relegated to the Third Estate, to which they clearly no longer belong.

However, in the eyes of the law, all nobles are equal, yesterday's nobility just as much as those who succeed for better or for worse in concealing where they come from and what they have usurped. They all have the same privileges. Only opinion distinguishes them one from another. But if the Third Estate is forced to put up with a prejudice sanctioned by the law, there is no reason why it should submit to a prejudice that runs counter to the law.

Let them create as many new nobles as they like. What is for sure is that from the moment a citizen acquires privileges contrary to common law, he is no longer part of the common order. His new interest is opposed to the general interest. He is unfit to vote in the name of the people.

This incontrovertible principle similarly prevents those with temporary privileges from representing the Third Estate. Their interest is also more or less contrary to the common interest; and although the general view is to rank them within the Third Estate, and the law has nothing to say about them, the nature of things, which is stronger than both opinion and the law, sets them indubitably apart from the common order.

Will it be said that the wish to exclude from the Third Estate, not only those with hereditary privileges, but also those with merely temporary ones, amounts to a thoughtless attempt to weaken that order by depriving it of its most enlightened, courageous and respected members?

Far be it from me to want to diminish the strength or dignity of the Third Estate, since it is always associated in my mind with [my] idea of a nation. But whatever our motives, can we turn what is true into what is not true? Just because an army has been unfortunate enough to be deserted by its best troops, should it still entrust to these troops the defence of its camp? All privilege, it cannot be overstated, is contrary to the common law. Thus all privilege, without exception, creates a class that is different from, and opposed to, the Third Estate. At the same time, I would point out that there is nothing in this truth to alarm the friends of the people. On the contrary, it takes us back to the higher national interest by making us feel strongly the need to suppress immediately all temporary privileges which divide the Third Estate, and which would appear to force the Third Estate to hand its destiny over to its enemies. Besides, this observation should not be separated from the following one: the abolition of privileges within the Third Estate does not mean the loss of those immunities that some of its members enjoy as rewards. These immunities are nothing but common rights. It was grossly unjust to deprive the greater part of the people of them. So I am not calling for the loss of a right, but its restitution; and if the objection is made that making certain privileges available to all – for example, not balloting for militia service – would affect our ability to satisfy a public requirement, I would answer that any public requirement is necessarily the responsibility of everyone, not just of a separate class of citizens, and that you must be deaf to all reason as well as justice not to be able to find a more nationally based way of achieving and maintaining whatever level of military capability you might wish to have.

Thus, either because they were never elected at all, or because they were not elected by the whole of the Third Estate in the towns and rural areas entitled to representation, or because of the fact that as privileged persons they were not even eligible [to stand], these so-called deputies of the Third Estate, who until now have been sitting in the Estates-General, have never really had a mandate from the people.

Sometimes, people seem surprised to hear complaints about the triple *aristocracy* of Church, Army and Law. They like to think that this is just a manner of speaking; but the phrase must be taken literally. If the Estates-General is the interpreter of the general will, and has legislative power in that capacity, then surely it is precisely this that makes the Estates-General, in as much as it is just a *clerical-noble-judicial* assembly, into a true aristocracy.

Add to this awful truth the fact that, in one way or another, every branch of the executive has fallen into the hands of the caste that supplies the Church, the Law and the Army with their members. Feelings of brotherhood or *comradeship* of some sort make nobles always prefer each other to the rest of the nation. The usurpation is total; they reign over us in every sense.

Read your history to check whether or not this statement fits the facts, and you will see, as I have seen, that it is a great mistake to think that France is governed as a monarchy. In the annals of our history, if you make an exception for a few years during the reign of Louis XI, and of Richelieu, and a few moments during Louis XIV's reign, when it was a matter of despotism pure and simple, you will think you are reading the history of a *palace* autocracy. It is the court that reigns, not the monarch. The court has made and the court has unmade, has appointed ministers and dismissed them, has created posts and filled them, and so on. And what is the court but the head of this vast aristocracy overrunning the whole of France, which through its members seizes on everything and exercises total control over every essential aspect of public life. So in their muted complaints, the people has become used to distinguishing the monarch from those who exercise power. It has always looked upon the King as a man so thoroughly deceived and so defenceless in the midst of an active, all-powerful court that it has never thought of blaming him for all the evil that is done in his name. Finally, is it not enough to open people's eyes to what is happening around us at this very moment? What do you see? The aristocracy, isolated, fighting simultaneously against reason, justice, the people, the minister and the King. The outcome of this terrible struggle is still unclear; and to think that people say the aristocracy is just an illusion!

To sum up, so far the Third Estate has not had any true representatives in the Estates-General. Thus its political rights have been non-existent. [*What is the third estate?* 2: 'What has the Third Estate been until now? Nothing']

The demands of the Third Estate must not be judged from the isolated observations of certain writers with some inklings of the rights of man. The Third Estate is still very backward in this respect, not only, I would say, by comparison with the enlightened views of students of the social order, but also with that mass of common ideas that forms public opinion. You can only make a judgment on the authentic petitions of the Third Estate through the formal demands which the great municipalities of the kingdom have addressed to the government. What do we see in these demands? That the people want to be *something* – to be honest, the least thing possible. First, it wants to have genuine representatives in the Estates-General, that is to say deputies *drawn from its own order*, able to interpret its wishes and defend its interests. But what would be the use of [the Third Estate] participating in the Estates-General if interests hostile to its own were to predominate? All it would do is sanction by its presence an oppression of which it would be the eternal victim. So it certainly cannot go and cast its vote in the Estates-General unless it exerted *an influence at least equal to that of the privileged orders*. Secondly, it demands that the number of its representatives be equal to that of the two other orders put together. However, this equality of representation would become a complete illusion if each chamber had its own separate vote. The Third Estate demands thirdly therefore that votes be counted *by heads and not by orders*. This is what these demands that have apparently set off alarm bells among the privileged orders boil down to. They thought that for this reason alone the reform of abuses was becoming indispensable.

The modest objective of the Third Estate is to have an influence in the Estates-General equal to that of the privileged orders. I repeat, could it ask for less? And is it not clear that if its influence is less than equal, it has no hope of emerging from its state of political non-existence, and of becoming *something*?

The unhappy truth of the matter is that the three articles constituting the Third Estate's demand are not in fact enough to give it that essential equality of influence. True, it will gain an equal number of representatives drawn from within its own ranks, but the influence of the privileged orders will continue to dominate in the Third Estate's own inner sanctum. Who has the offices, the posts and livings to hand out? Which side needs protection? And which side has the power to protect? In that thought alone there is something to make the friends of the people tremble.

As for those unprivileged [citizens] who seem by their talents to be best fitted to uphold the interests of their order, are they not brought up with a superstitious, obligatory respect for the nobility? We know how easily men generally adapt to whatever form of behaviour might be useful to them. Men are constantly preoccupied with the improvement of their fortunes, and when personal effort cannot advance them by honest means, they set off down false paths. We read that among ancient peoples children were trained to expect their food only after they had performed some strenuous or skilful exercise. It was a way of making them excel in such matters. With us, the cleverest people in the Third Estate are obliged to practise flattery and devote themselves to the service of the powerful to get what they need, a less honourable, less social kind of education, but just as effective. This unhappy part of the nation has come to resemble a huge antechamber which, constantly preoccupied with what its masters are saying or doing, is always ready to sacrifice everything to the fruits it imagines it will gain from being lucky enough to find favour. When we witness such conduct, how can we fail to fear that those qualities most suited to the defence of the national interest are being prostituted in defence of prejudices? The boldest champions of the aristocracy are to be found within the Third Estate, among those endowed at birth with plenty of intelligence but very little soul, who are as greedy for money, power and pats on the back from the great as they are incapable of understanding the value of freedom.

Over and above the empire of the aristocracy, which controls everything in France, and of the feudal superstition still debasing most minds, there is the influence of property. This [influence] is a natural thing, and I do not condemn it; but you will agree that this is yet another advantage to the privileged, and that the fear that it lends powerful support to the privileged against the Third Estate is justified. Municipalities have been too ready to believe that they could be sheltered from the influence of the privilege by just precluding privileged people from representing the people. In rural communities, and everywhere else in fact, is there any reasonably popular lord who does not have at his beck and call, if he so wishes, as large a crowd of commoners as he wants? Work out the consequences and repercussions of this primary influence, and then keep calm, if you can, about the effect on voting in an assembly that to your eyes is far removed from those first electoral colleges [*comitias*], but which for all that is still just a combination of those early forms. The more you consider this issue, the more you perceive the inadequacy of the Third Estate's three demands. In fact, however, even as they stand, they have been strongly attacked. But let us examine the pretexts for such odious hostility.

FIRST DEMAND

That the representatives of the Third Estate be chosen only from among those citizens who really belong to the Third Estate.

We have already explained that, in order to belong genuinely to the Third Estate, either you must be untainted by privileges of any sort, or you must completely and immediately relinquish them.

Lawyers, who have attained noble status through a door that for some reason they have decided to close behind them, insist in the teeth of all opposition on being part of the Estates-General. They tell themselves: 'The nobility wants nothing to do with us; we want nothing to do with the Third Estate; if only we could form a separate order, that would be wonderful; but we cannot. What shall we do? There is nothing for it but to maintain the old abuse by which the Third Estate elected nobles as deputies. By this means, we shall satisfy our desires without undermining our pretensions.' All new nobles, whatever their origins, fell over themselves to repeat in the same spirit that the Third Estate must be able to elect noblemen as deputies. The old nobility, which calls itself the true nobility, does not have the same stake in the preservation of this abuse; but it knows how to do its sums. It said: 'We shall put our sons in the Commons, so on the whole it is an excellent idea to charge us with representing the Third Estate.'

Once the mind is made up, reasons, as you well know, are always forthcoming. 'The old *custom* must be maintained', people said . . . An excellent custom which, intended to ensure representation for the Third Estate, has so far positively precluded it from being represented! The order of the Third Estate has its political rights as it has its civil rights; it must exercise the one, as it must the other, by itself. What a good idea – to make a *distinction* between the orders when it is to the advantage of the two first orders and bad luck on the third, and to bring them *together* as soon as it becomes even more useful to the first two and harmful to the nation! What a good custom it is to preserve that which allows clerics and nobles to take over the Chamber of Deputies! In all good faith, would [the privileged] think themselves well represented if the Third Estate could invade their corps of deputies?

To demonstrate the flaw in a principle, it is legitimate to push its consequences to the limit. Using this method, my argument goes like this: If the members of the three orders are prepared to elect whomsoever they wish, the possibility arises of having an assembly consisting of members drawn from one order only. Would you accept, for example, that the clergy alone could represent the whole nation?

I go further: after having just worked on the assumption that all three estates chose deputies from a single order, let us now assume that all of the citizens elect a single individual to represent them? Will you maintain that a single individual could replace the Estates-General? Whenever the consequences of a principle lead to absurdities, it is because it is a bad principle.

It is also said that if the choice before electors was limited, this would compromise their freedom. I have two answers to that so-called difficulty. First, those who raise it, do so in bad faith, and I can prove it. We all know about the sovereignty of lords over peasants and other country people; we all know about the usual scheming, or potential for it, of their numerous agents, including their law officers. Thus any lord wanting to influence the first round of elections can generally get himself sent as a deputy to a bailiwick where it just remains to choose [a candidate] from among the lords themselves, or from among those in their closest confidence. Is it then for the sake of the people's freedom that you make it possible to violate and betray its trust? It is appalling to hear the sacred name of freedom being defiled in order to conceal those designs most hostile to it. Of course electors must be left completely free, and this is precisely why all those privileged orders, too accustomed to ruling imperiously over the people, must be precluded from representing them.

My second answer is blunt. In no circumstances can a freedom or a right be unlimited. In every country the law has prescribed certain conditions which qualify people to be either electors, or to be eligible for election. So, for example, the law must determine the age below which one would not be competent to represent one's fellow citizens. Thus, rightly or wrongly, women are everywhere excluded from powers of representation of this kind. It is an unquestioned fact that a tramp or a beggar cannot be charged with the political trust of nations. Would a servant, or anyone dependent upon a master, or a non-naturalised foreigner be admitted to the ranks of the nation's representatives? Political liberty, therefore, has its limits, as does individual civil liberty. The only question is whether the regulation relating to non-eligibility of members of the privileged orders demanded by the Third Estate has as much priority as any of the others I have mentioned. Now, any comparison works in the Third Estate's favour; for a beggar or a foreigner might not have interests contrary to those of the Third Estate; whereas nobles and clerics are, by their very status, well disposed towards the privileges from which they profit. So the restriction demanded by the Third Estate is the most important of all the conditions which the law, in accordance with fair play and the nature of things, must prescribe for the selection of deputies.

To make my line of reasoning clearer, I offer this hypothesis. Suppose that France is at war with England, and that everything to do with the conduct of the war is controlled by a Directory made up of national representatives. In these circumstances, I ask you this: would we let the provinces, on the grounds of not infringing their freedom, choose as their deputies to the Directory members of the English cabinet? The privileged orders certainly seem to be no less the enemies of the common order than the English of the French in time of war. From among the illustrations that proliferate and swirl around in my head, I select another. If the question arose of [establishing] a general diet of maritime peoples to regulate the freedom and safety of the seas, do you think that Genoa, Leghorn, Venice and others would choose their plenipotentiaries from among the Barbary pirates? Or that a law allowing rich pirates to buy or bribe voters in Genoa would be a good one? I do not know if that comparison is an exaggeration or not, but to my mind it clarifies what I have to say. Besides, like anyone else, I am hoping that since enlightenment must eventually have an effect, aristocrats will one day cease to resemble France's [own] Algerian pirates.

Following on from these principles, we must not allow those members of the Third Estate who are under the exclusive domination of the first two orders to be charged with the trust of the commons. Because of their dependency the feeling is that they are not trustworthy; unless there is a formal exclusion, the lords will surely use the influence they can no longer use directly themselves, to the advantage of those in their service. I draw your attention in particular to the many agents of feudal power. It is to the odious remnants of this barbarous regime that we still owe the division [of France] into three orders, each the enemy of the other, that still survives to France's misfortune. All would be lost if the representatives of feudalism managed to usurp the right to serve as deputies representing the common order. We all know that servants seem to be more ruthless and bold in [pursuing] the interests of their masters than the masters are themselves. I know that this proscription would cover a lot of people, since it affects in particular officers of all feudal courts, but here necessity has priority over all else ...

SECOND DEMAND OF THE THIRD ESTATE

That the number of its deputies be equal to that of the two privileged orders.

I must repeat once more: the feeble inadequacy of this demand is still redolent of the old days. Towns in this kingdom have not taken the progress of enlightenment, and even of public opinion, sufficiently into account. They would have encountered less difficulties by asking for two votes to one, and perhaps then people would have rushed to offer them the very equality over which people are fighting so noisily today.

What's more, when you want to decide a question like this, you must not, as happens so often, just pass your wishes, your will or custom off as reasons. You must go back to first principles. Political rights, like civil rights, must derive from the status of being a citizen. This legal property is the same for everyone regardless of the amount of real property making up the wealth or income enjoyed by each individual. Any citizen fulfilling the conditions prescribed for becoming an elector has the right to be represented, and his representation cannot be a fraction of someone else's representation. This right is indivisible; everyone exercises it equally, just as everyone has equal protection under the law that they have agreed to make. How can you argue on the one hand that the law is the expression of the general will, that is to say of the plurality, and claim on the other that ten individual wills can cancel out a thousand other individual wills? Do we not then run the risk of having the law made by a minority? This is obviously contrary to the nature of things.

If these principles, certain as they are, seem to be derived too much from common ideas, I bring the reader back to a comparison right in front of his nose. Is it not true that everyone finds it fair for the huge bailiwick of Poitou to have more representatives in the Estates-General than the tiny bailiwick of Gex? Why is that? Because, they say, the population and tax revenue of Poitou are much higher than that of Gex. Thus principles are being accepted which permit you to determine the ratio of representatives. Do you want taxation to be the basis? Although we do not know precisely what the respective tax contribution of the different orders is, the Third Estate obviously bears more than half of the burden
. . .

As far as population is concerned, the vast [numerical] superiority of the third order over the first two is well known. Like everybody else, I do not know what the real proportion is, but like anybody else I can do my sums . . . In total, there are less than two hundred thousand privileged persons in the first two orders. Compare that figure with a twenty-five to twenty-six million total population, and draw your own conclusions.

To get the same answer on the basis of different, but equally incontrovertible, principles, let us take the view that the privileged orders are to the great mass of citizens what exceptions are to the law. Every society must be regulated by common laws and be subject to a common order. If you make exceptions to that, they ought at the very least to be rare ones, and there can never be any question of the exception having the same weight and influence in public life as the norm. It is really insane to treat the interests of these exceptions as somehow balancing out those of the great mass of the people . . . In a few years time, when people come to look back on all the obstacles blocking this all too modest demand of the Third Estate, they will be surprised at the lack of substance in the arguments used against it, and even more surprised by the brazen effrontery of those who were bold enough to dig those excuses up.

The very people who invoke the authority of facts against the Third Estate could read in those facts a rule for their own conduct, if they were honest with themselves. The existence of a few loyal cities was enough to form a Chamber of Commons in the Estates-General under Philip the Fair.

Since then, feudal servitude has disappeared, and rural areas have presented us with a large population of *new citizens*. Towns have multiplied and grown. Commerce and the arts have created, as it were, a multitude of new classes with large numbers of prosperous families full of well-educated, public-spirited men. Why has this dual growth, so much greater than that of those loyal cities of earlier times, not encouraged this same authority to create two new chambers in favour of the Third Estate? Justice and sound politics alike require it.

Nobody has dared be so unreasonable in respect of another sort of increase that has taken place in France; I refer to the new provinces united with France since the last session of the Estates-General. Nobody would dare to claim that these new provinces should have no representatives over and above those already in the Estates-General of 1614. But don't manufactures and the arts create new riches, new sources of tax revenue and a new population just as much as new territory does? So why, when this kind of increase is easily compared to that of territory, why, I repeat, do people refuse to accord it extra representatives in addition to those in the 1614 Estates-General?

But I am using reason against people who can listen only to the voice of their own self-interest. Let us give them something to think about that might touch them more closely. Is it appropriate for today's nobility to hang on to the language and attitudes of the gothic age? Is it appropriate for the Third Estate, at the end of the eighteenth century, to stagnate in the sad, cowardly habits of the old servitude? If the Third Estate recognised and respected itself, then others would surely respect it too! People should note that the old relationship between the orders has been changed simultaneously on both sides. The Third Estate, which had been reduced to nothing, has regained, through its industry, part of what had been stolen from it by the offence [committed] against it by those who were stronger. Instead of demanding its rights back, it has consented to pay for them; they have not been restored to the Third Estate but sold back to it; and it has acquiesced in their purchase. But in the end, in one way or another, it can take possession of them. It must not forget that today it constitutes a reality in the nation, whereas before it was a shadow, [and] that, in the course of this long process of change, the nobility has ceased to be the monstrous feudal power that could oppress with impunity. It is the nobility that is now no more than the shadow of what it was, and this shadow is still trying to terrify a whole nation, but in vain – unless this nation wants to be regarded as the vilest on earth.

THIRD AND FINAL DEMAND OF THE THIRD ESTATE

That the Estates-General should vote, not by orders, but by heads.

This question can be approached in three ways: from the standpoint of the Third Estate, in accordance with the interests of the privileged, and lastly in the light of sound principles. As far as the first is concerned, there is no point in adding anything to what has already been said; clearly the Third Estate thinks that this demand follows on as the logical consequence of the other two.

The privileged orders fear the third order having equality of influence, and so they declare it to be unconstitutional. This behaviour is all the more remarkable for the fact that until now they have been two against one without finding anything unconstitutional in that unjust advantage. They feel very deeply the need to retain the veto over anything that could be against their interest. I will not repeat the reasons used by a score of writers to combat this pretentious argument in support of the old way of doing things. I have just one observation to make. There are certainly abuses in France. These abuses profit someone; they are hardly advantageous to the Third Estate, but they are particularly harmful to it. Now, I ask whether in this situation it is possible to end any abuse while those who profit from it are allowed to retain the veto. Justice would be completely powerless; we would have to be entirely dependent on the sheer generosity of the privileged. Is that what our idea of social order should be?

If we now want to look at the same question independently of all special interests, and in accordance with principles designed to illuminate it, that is to say in accordance with those principles that form the science of social order, we shall see this question in a new light. I maintain that the demand of the Third Estate, or the defence put forward by the privileged orders, cannot be accepted without turning the most firmly held ideas on their head. I am certainly not accusing the loyal towns of the kingdom of having had that intention. They wished simply to get within striking distance of their rights by asking for at least a balance between the two factions with influence. Moreover, they professed some excellent truths, for it is quite clear that one order's right of veto over the others amounts to the right to bring everything to a standstill in a country where interests are so different and so opposed. Certainly, unless votes are counted by heads, the true majority could not be recognised, and that would be the worst thing to go wrong, because the law would be completely nullified. These truths are indisputable. But, given the way in which they are constituted, will the three orders be able to unite to vote by heads? That is the real point. No. If we keep to true principles, they cannot vote *together* at all, either by heads or by orders. In whatever ratio you divide them up, it cannot achieve the intended aim – that is, to bind the whole body of representatives together by a *single* common will. This statement no doubt needs [further] elaboration and proof . . . I have no wish to displease those moderates who always fear that the truth should come out at the wrong moment. First of all, we must get them to admit that the current situation has come about only because of the privilged orders [and nobody else], that it is time to stand up and take a decision, and say loudly and clearly what is true and just. [*What is the third estate?* 3: 'What does the Third Estate ask to be? Something']

EDMUND BURKE

BIOGRAPHICAL NOTE

Edmund Burke (1729/30–97) was born in Dublin, and educated at Trinity College where, between 1743 and 1748, he studied law. He moved to London in 1750, and began to make a name for himself in London literary circles with the publication of the *Vindication of natural society* (1756). The *Vindication* offers early intimations of the way in which Burke was to link morality and civil government closely to the divine order, and to the providential authority of God. The Rousseauist rejection of inequality meant for Burke nothing less than the rejection of the civil order and God-given natural law, and he pursued the point in *A philosophical enquiry into the origin of our ideas of the sublime and beautiful* (1757) in which he defended inequality and the consequent generation of the aristocratic order as natural and progressive concepts that guaranteed the civil order. The year 1757 also saw the start of historical projects such as the *Abridgement of English history* (not published until 1812) and the *Account of the European settlements in America.* His editorial association with the *Annual register* began in 1758. In 1761 he returned to Ireland where he remained until 1764 as a secretary to the Chief Secretary to Lord Halifax, the Lord Lieutenant of Ireland. Returning to London in 1765, he was appointed as Rockingham's secretary, and became MP for Wendover. In 1766 Burke joined Rockingham on the Opposition benches.

The *Observations on a late pamphlet entitled A state of the nation* appeared in 1769, to be followed in 1770 with the better known *Thoughts on the cause of the present discontents.* In the latter essay, composed in the light of rapidly changing, unstable and unpopular governments, and the decline of the party system, he saw court cabals as a major threat to liberty and political harmony, and sought to reassert Whig principles with a redefinition of the whole nature and purpose of party. In 1771 he became an agent for New York Province, and American problems began to replace English preoccupations. His *Speech on American taxation* (1774) appeared in the year following the Boston Tea Party, and by then Burke was MP for Bristol. The outbreak of war with the American colonies prompted the *Speech on conciliation with America* (1775).

In 1780, the year of the Gordon Riots, Burke became MP for Malton, and subsequently Paymaster-General of the Forces in Rockingham's second ministry. He continued in this post after Rockingham's death, and in 1783 the main focus of his political attention was India. Between 1786 and 1795 Burke was closely involved in the impeachment, trial and eventual acquittal of Warren Hastings. In 1789 France moved centre stage in the increasingly volatile theatre of European politics, and the French crisis prompted Burke to publish a number of celebrated works and speeches relating to the causes and, above all, the effects of the Revolution, including the *Speech ... in the debate on the army estimates ... comprehending a discussion of the present situation of affairs in France* (1790), the *Letter to a member of the National Assembly*, the *Appeal from the old to the new Whigs*, and the *Thoughts on French affairs*, all appearing in 1791. Burke retired from Parliament, isolated and unpopular, in 1794. His last published work was the *Letters on a regicide peace* (1796). The *Reflections on the Revolution in France, and on the proceedings in certain societies in London relative to that event: in a letter intended to have been sent to a gentleman in Paris* were first published on 1 November 1790.

EDITORIAL NOTE

The base text for the selected extracts is that of the second edition of the *Reflections* (1796). This is the text printed in volume IV of the eight-volume collective edition of *The works and correspondence of the Right Honourable Edmund Burke* (London, Francis and John Rivington, 1852).

FURTHER READING

Butler, M. (ed.), *Burke, Paine, Godwin and the Revolution controversy* (Cambridge, Cambridge University Press, 1984).

Dreyer, F., 'The genesis of Burke's *Reflections*', *Journal of Modern History*, 50 (1978), pp. 462–79.

Harris, I., *Burke: pre-revolutionary writings* (Cambridge, Cambridge University Press, 1993). See introduction, pp. xvi–xxxiii.

Lock, F., *Burke's reflections on the Revolution in France* (London, Allen and Unwin, 1985).

O'Gorman, F., *Edmund Burke: his political philosophy* (London, Allen and Unwin, 1973)

Reflections on the Revolution in France, and on the proceedings in certain societies in London relative to that event: in a letter intended to have been sent to a gentleman in Paris (1790)

Dear Sir,

You are pleased to call again, and with some earnestness, for my thoughts on the late proceedings in France . . .

Solicitous chiefly for the peace of my own country, but by no means unconcerned for yours, I wish to communicate more largely what was at first intended only for your private satisfaction. I shall still keep your affairs in my eye, and continue to address myself to you. Indulging myself in the freedom of epistolary intercourse, I beg leave to throw out my thoughts, and express my feelings just as they arise in my mind, with very little attention to formal method. I set out with the proceedings of the Revolution Society, but I shall not confine myself to them. Is it possible I should? It appears to me as if I were in a great crisis, not of the affairs of France alone, but of all Europe, perhaps of more than Europe. All circumstances taken together, the French Revolution is the most astonishing that has hitherto happened in the world. The most wonderful things are brought about in many instances by means the most absurd and ridiculous, in the most ridiculous modes and apparently by the most contemptible instruments. Everything seems out of nature in this strange chaos of levity and ferocity, and of all sorts of crimes jumbled together with all sorts of follies. In viewing this monstrous, tragicomic scene, the most opposite passions necessarily succeed, and sometimes mix with each other in the mind: alternate contempts and indignation, alternate laughter and tears, alternate scorn and horror.

It cannot however be denied that to some this strange scene appeared in quite another point of view. Into them it inspired no other sentiments than those of exultation and rapture. They saw nothing in what has been done in France but a firm and temperate exertion of freedom; so consistent, on the whole, with morals and with piety as to make it deserving not only of the secular applause of dashing Machiavellian politicians, but to render it a fit scheme for all the devout effusions of sacred eloquence.

On the forenoon of the 4th of November last, Doctor Richard Price, a nonconforming minister of eminence, preached at the dissenting meeting-house of the Old Jewry to his club or society a very extraordinary, miscellaneous sermon in which there are some good and moral sentiments, and not ill expressed, mixed up with a sort of porridge of various political opinions and reflections. But the Revolution in France is the grand ingredient in the cauldron. I consider the address transmitted by the Revolution Society to the National Assembly through Earl Stanhope as originating in the principles of the sermon, and as a corollary from them. It was moved by the preacher of that discourse. It was passed by those who came reeking from the effect of the sermon, without any censure or qualification, expressed or implied. If, however, any of the gentlemen concerned shall wish to separate the sermon from the resolution, they know how to acknowledge the one, and to disavow the other. They may do it: I cannot.

For my part, I looked on that sermon as the public declaration of a man much connected with literary caballers, and intriguing philosophers, with political theologians and theological politicians both at home and abroad. I know they set him up as a sort of oracle, because, with the best intentions in the world, he naturally *philippizes*, and chants his prophetic song in exact unison with their designs.

That sermon is in a strain which I believe has not been heard in this kingdom, in any of the pulpits which are tolerated or encouraged in it, since the year 1648, when a predecessor of Dr Price, the Reverend Hugh Peters, made the vault of the King's own chapel at St James's ring with the honours and privilege of the saints who, with the 'high praises of God in their mouths, and a *two*-edged sword in their hands, were to execute judgment on the heathen, and punishments upon the *people*, to bind their *kings* with chains, and their *nobles* with fetters of iron'. Few harangues from the pulpit, except in the days of your league in France, or in the days of our solemn league and covenant in England, have ever breathed less of the spirit of moderation than this lecture in the Old Jewry. Supposing, however, that something like moderation were visible in this political sermon; yet politics and the pulpit are terms that have little agreement. No sound ought to be heard in the church but the healing voice of Christian charity. The cause of civil liberty and civil government gains as little as that of religion by this confusion of duties. Those who quit their proper character to assume what does not belong to them are, for the greater part, ignorant both of the character they leave and of the character they assume. Wholly unacquainted with the world in which they are so fond of meddling, and inexperienced in all its affairs, on which they pronounce with so much confidence, they have nothing of politics but the passions they excite. Surely the church is a place where one day's truce ought to be allowed to the dissensions and animosities of mankind . . .

But I may say of our preacher *utinam nugis tota illa dedisset tempora saevitiae.* All things in this, his fulminating bull, are not of so innoxious a tendency. His doctrines affect our constitution in its vital parts. He tells the Revolution Society in this political sermon that His Majesty 'is almost the *only* lawful king in the world, because the *only* one who owes his crown to *the choice of his people*'. As to the kings of *the world*, all of whom (except one) this arch pontiff of the *rights of men*, with all the plenitude, and with more than the boldness of the papal deposing power in its meridian fervour of the twelfth century, puts into one sweeping clause of ban and anathema, and proclaims usurpers by circles of longitude and latitude over the whole globe, it behoves them to consider how they admit into their territories these apostolic missionaries who are to tell their subjects they are not lawful kings. That is their concern. It is ours, as a domestic interest of some moment, seriously to consider the solidity of the *only* principle upon which these gentlemen acknowledge a King of Great Britain to be entitled to their allegiance.

This doctrine, as applied now to the prince on the British throne, either is nonsense, and therefore neither true nor false, or it affirms a most unfounded, dangerous, illegal and unconstitutional position. According to this spiritual doctor of politics, if His Majesty does not owe his crown to the choice of his people, he is no *lawful king.* Now nothing can be more untrue than that the crown of this kingdom is so held by His Majesty. Therefore, if you follow their rule, the King of Great Britain, who most certainly does not owe his high office to any form of popular election, is in no respect better than the rest of the gang of usurpers who reign, or rather rob, all over the face of this our miserable world without any sort of right or title to the allegiance of their people. The policy of this general doctrine, so qualified, is evident enough. The propagators of this political gospel are in hopes that their abstract principle (their principle that a popular choice is necessary to the legal existence of the sovereign magistracy) would be overlooked, whilst the King of Great Britain was not affected by it. In the meantime, the ears of their congregations would be gradually habituated to it, as if it were a first principle admitted without dispute. For the present, it would only operate as a theory, pickled in the preserving juices of pulpit eloquence, and laid by for future use. *Condo et compono quae mox depromere possim.* By this policy, whilst our government is soothed with a reservation in its favour, to which it has no claim, the

security, which it has in common with all governments, so far as opinion is security, is taken away.

Thus these politicians proceed, whilst little notice is taken of their doctrines;
but when they come to be examined upon the plain meaning of their words, and
the direct tendency of their doctrines, then equivocations and slippery construc-
tions come into play. When they say the King owes his crown to the choice of
his people, and is therefore the only lawful sovereign in the world, they will perhaps tell us they mean to say no more than that some of the King's predecessors
have been called to the throne by some sort of choice, and therefore he owes his
crown to the choice of his people. Thus, by a miserable subterfuge, they hope to
render their proposition safe by rendering it nugatory. They are welcome to the
asylum they seek for their offence, since they take refuge in their folly. For if you
admit this interpretation, how does their idea of election differ from our idea of
inheritance? And how does the settlement of the crown in the Brunswick line,
derived from James I, come to legalise our monarchy, rather than that of any of
the neighbouring countries? At some time or other, to be sure, all the beginners
of dynasties were chosen by those who called them to govern. There is ground
enough for the opinion that all the kingdoms of Europe were, at a remote period,
elective, with more or fewer limitations in the objects of choice. But whatever
kings might have been here, or elsewhere, a thousand years ago, or in whatever
manner the ruling dynasties of England or France may have begun, the King of
Great Britain is at this day King by a fixed rule of succession according to the
laws of his country; and whilst the legal conditions of the compact of sovereignty
are performed by him (as they are performed), he holds his crown in contempt
of the choice of the Revolution Society, who have not a single vote for a King
amongst them, either individually or collectively, though I make no doubt they
would soon erect themselves into an electoral college, if things were ripe enough
to give effect to their claim. His Majesty's heirs and successors, each in his time
and order, will come to the crown with the same contempt of their choice with
which His Majesty has succeeded to that he wears.

Whatever may be the success of evasion in explaining away the gross error of
fact, which supposes that His Majesty (though he holds it in concurrence with
the wishes) owes his crown to the choice of his people, yet nothing can evade
their full explicit declaration concerning the principle of a right in the people to
choose, which right is directly maintained, and tenaciously adhered to. All the
oblique insinuations concerning election bottom in this proposition, and are

referable to it. Lest the foundation of the King's exclusive legal title should pass for a mere rant of adulatory freedom, the political divine proceeds dogmatically to assert that by the principles of the Revolution the people of England have acquired three fundamental rights, all of which with him compose one system, and lie together in one short sentence, namely that we have acquired a right

1. 'To choose our own governors.'
2. 'To cashier them for misconduct.'
3. 'To frame a government for ourselves.'

This new, and hitherto unheard of, bill of rights, though made in the name of the whole people, belongs to those gentlemen and their faction only. The body of the people of England have no share in it. They utterly disclaim it. They will resist the practical assertion of it with their lives and fortunes. They are bound to do so by the laws of their country, made at the time of that very Revolution which is appealed to in favour of the fictitious rights claimed by the society which abuses its name.

These gentlemen of the Old Jewry, in all their reasonings on the Revolution of 1688, have a revolution, which happened in England about forty years before, and the late French Revolution so much before their eyes, and in their hearts, that they are constantly confounding all the three together. It is necessary that we should separate what they confound. We must recall their erring fancies to the *acts* of the Revolution which we revere for the discovery of its true *principles*. If the *principles* of the Revolution of 1688 are anywhere to be found, it is in the statute called the *Declaration of Right*. In that most wise, sober, and considerate declaration, drawn up by great lawyers and great statesmen, and not by warm and inexperienced enthusiasts, not one word is said, nor one suggestion made, of a general right 'to choose our own *governors*, to cashier them for misconduct, and to *form* a government for *ourselves*'.

This Declaration of Right (the act of the 1st of William and Mary, sess. 2, ch. 2) is the cornerstone of our constitution, as reinforced, explained, improved and in its fundamental principles forever settled. It is called 'An Act for declaring the rights and liberties of the subject, and for *settling* the *succession* of the crown.' You will observe that these rights and this succession are declared in one body, and bound indissolubly together . . .

You had all these advantages in your ancient states; but you chose to act as if you had never been moulded into civil society, and had everything to begin anew ...

Compute your gains; see what is got by those extravagant and presumptuous speculations which have taught your leaders to despise all their predecessors and all their contemporaries, and even to despise themselves until the moment in which they became truly despicable. By following those false lights France has bought undisguised calamities at a higher price than any nation has purchased the most unequivocal blessings! France has bought poverty by crime! France has not sacrificed her virtue to her interest, but she has abandoned her interest, that she might prostitute her virtue. All other nations have begun the fabric of a new government, or the reformation of an old, by establishing originally, or by enforcing with greater exactness, some rites or other of religion. All other people have laid the foundations of civil freedom in severer manners, and a system of a more austere and masculine morality. France, when she let loose the reins of regal authority, doubled the licence of a ferocious dissoluteness in manners, and of an insolent irreligion in opinions and practices; and has extended through all ranks of life, as if she were communicating some privilege, or laying open some secluded benefit, all the unhappy corruptions that usually were the disease of wealth and power. This is one of the new principles of equality in France.

France, by the perfidy of her leaders, has utterly disgraced the tone of lenient counsel in the cabinets of princes, and disarmed it of its most potent topics. She has sanctified the dark, suspicious maxims of tyrannous distrust, and taught kings to tremble at (what will hereafter be called) the delusive plausibilities of moral politicians. Sovereigns will consider those who advise them to place an unlimited confidence in their people as subverters of their thrones; as traitors who aim at their destruction by leading their easy good nature under specious pretences to admit combinations of bold and faithless men into a participation of their power. This alone (if there were nothing else) is an irreparable calamity to you and to mankind. Remember that your parliament of Paris told your King that, in calling the states together, he had nothing to fear but the prodigal excess of their zeal in providing for the support of the throne. It is right that these men should hide their heads. It is right that they should bear their part in the ruin which their counsel has brought on their sovereign and their country. Such sanguine declarations tend to lull authority asleep, to encourage it rashly to engage in perilous adventures of untried policy, to neglect those provisions, preparations and precautions which distinguish benevolence from imbecility, and without which no man can answer for the salutary effect of any abstract plan of government or of freedom. For want of these, they have seen the medicine of the state corrupted into its poison. They have seen the French rebel against a mild and lawful monarch with more fury, outrage and insult than ever any people has been known to rise against the most illegal usurper, or the most sanguinary tyrant. Their resistance was made to concession; their revolt was from protection; their blow was aimed at a hand holding out graces, favours and immunities.

This was unnatural. The rest is in order. They have found their punishment in their success. Laws overturned; tribunals subverted; industry without vigour; commerce expiring; the revenue unpaid, yet the people impoverished; a church pillaged, and a state not relieved; civil and military anarchy made the constitution of the kingdom; everything human and divine sacrificed to the idol of public credit, and national bankruptcy the consequence; and, to crown all, the paper securities of new, precarious, tottering power, the discredited paper securities of impoverished fraud and beggared rapine, held out as the currency for the support of an empire in lieu of the two great recognised species that represent the lasting, conventional credit of mankind, which disappeared and hid themselves in the earth from whence they came when the principle of property, whose creatures and representatives they are, was systematically subverted.

Were all these dreadful things necessary? Were they the inevitable results of the desperate struggle of determined patriots, compelled to wade through blood and tumult to the quiet shore of a tranquil and prosperous liberty? No! Nothing like it. The fresh ruins of France, which shock our feelings wherever we can turn our eyes, are not the devastation of civil war; they are the sad but instructive monuments of rash and ignorant counsel in time of profound peace. They are the display of inconsiderate and presumptuous, because unresisted and irresistible, authority. The persons who have thus squandered away the precious treasure of their crimes, the persons who have made this prodigal and wild waste of public evils (the last stake reserved for the ultimate ransom of the state) have met in their progress with little, or rather with no, opposition at all. Their whole march was more like a triumphal procession than the progress of a war. Their pioneers have gone before them, and demolished and laid everything level at their feet. Not one drop of *their* blood have they shed in the cause of the country they have ruined. They have made no sacrifices to their projects of greater consequence than their shoebuckles, whilst they were imprisoning their King, murdering their fellow-citizens, and bathing in tears and plunging in poverty and distress thousands of worthy men and worthy families. Their cruelty has not even been the base result of fear. It has been the effect of their sense of perfect safety in authorising treasons, robberies, rapes, assassinations, slaughters and burnings throughout their harassed land. But the cause of all was plain from the beginning.

This unforced choice, this fond election of evil, would appear perfectly accountable if we did not consider the composition of the National Assembly; I do not mean its formal constitution which, as it now stands, is exceptionable enough, but the materials of which in great measure it is composed, which is of ten thousand times greater consequence than all the formalities in the world. If we were to know nothing of this assembly but by its title and function, no colours could paint to the imagination anything more venerable. In that light the mind of an enquirer, subdued by such an awful image as that of the virtue and wisdom of a whole people collected into one focus, would pause and hesitate in condemning things even of the very worst aspect. Instead of blamable, they would appear only mysterious. But no name, no power, no function, no artificial institution whatsoever can make the men of whom any system of authority is composed any other than God and nature, and education and their habits of life have made them. Capacities beyond these the people have not to give. Virtue and wisdom may be the objects of their choice, but their choice confirms neither the one nor the other on those upon whom they lay their ordaining hands. They have not the engagement of nature, they have not the promise of revelation for any such powers . . .

Government is not made in virtue of natural rights, which may and do exist in total independence of it, and exist in much greater clearness, and in a much greater degree of abstract perfection, but their abstract perfection is their practical defect. By having a right to everything, they want everything. Government is a contrivance of human wisdom to provide for human *wants*. Men have a right that these wants should be provided for by this wisdom. Among those wants is to be reckoned the want, out of civil society, of a sufficient restraint upon their passions. Society requires not only that the passions of individuals should be subjected, but that even in the mass and body, as well as in the individuals, the inclinations of men should be frequently thwarted, their will controlled, and their passions brought into subjection. This can only be done *by a power out of themselves*, and not, in the exercise of its function, subject to that will and to those passions which it is its office to bridle and subdue. In this sense the restraints on men, as well as their liberties, are to be reckoned among their rights. But as the liberties and the restrictions vary with times and circumstances, and admit of infinite modifications, they cannot be settled upon any abstract rule, and nothing is so foolish as to discuss them upon that principle.

The moment you abate anything from the full rights of men, each to govern himself and suffer any artificial, positive limitation upon those rights, from that moment the whole organisation of government becomes a consideration of convenience. This it is which makes the constitution of a state, and the due distribution of its powers, a matter of the most delicate and complicated skill. It requires a deep knowledge of human nature and human necessities, and of the things which facilitate or obstruct the various ends which are to be pursued by the mechanism of civil institutions. The state is to have recruits to its strength, and remedies to its distempers. What is the use of discussing a man's abstract right to food or medicine? The question is upon the method of procuring and administering them. In that deliberation I shall always advise to call in the aid of the farmer and the physician, rather than the professor of metaphysics.

The pretended rights of these theorists are all extremes; and in proportion as they are metaphysically true, they are morally and politically false. The rights of men are in a sort of *middle*, incapable of definition, but not impossible to be discerned. The rights of men in governments are their advantages, and these are often in balances between differences of good, in compromises sometimes between good and evil, and sometimes between evil and evil. Political reason is a computing principle: adding, subtracting, multiplying and dividing morally, and not metaphysically or mathematically, true moral denominations . . .

These professors, finding their extreme principles not applicable to cases which call only for a qualified or, as I may say, civil and legal resistance, in such cases apply no resistance at all. It is with them a war or a revolution, or it is nothing. Finding their schemes of politics not adapted to the state of the world in which they live, they often come to think lightly of all public principle, and are ready, on their part, to abandon for a very trivial interest what they find of very trivial value. Some, indeed, are of more steady and persevering natures, but these are eager politicians out of parliament, who have little to tempt them to abandon their favourite projects. They have some change in the church or state, or both, constantly in their view. When that is the case, they are always bad citizens, and perfectly unsure connections. For, considering their speculative designs as of infinite value, and the actual arrangement of the state as of no estimation, they are at best indifferent about it. They see no merit in the good, and no fault in the vicious management of public affairs; they rather rejoice in the latter, as more propitious to revolution. They see no merit or demerit in any man, or any action, or any political principle, any further than as they may forward or retard their design of change; they therefore take up one day the most violent and stretched prerogative, and another time the wildest democratic ideas of freedom, and pass from the one to the other without any sort of regard to cause, to person, or to party.

In France you are now in the crisis of a revolution, and in the transit from one form of government to another – you cannot see that character of men exactly in the same situation in which we see it in this country. With us it is militant; with you it is triumphant; and you know how it can act when its power is commensurate to its will. I would not be supposed to confine those observations to any description of men, or to comprehend all men of any description within them – No! far from it. I am as incapable of that injustice as I am of keeping terms with those who profess principles of extremes, and who under the name of religion teach little else than wild and dangerous politics. The worst of these politics of revolution is this: they temper and harden the breast in order to prepare it for the desperate strokes which are sometimes used in extreme occasions. But as these occasions may never arrive, the mind receives a gratuitous taint, and the moral sentiments suffer not a little when no political purpose is served by the depravation. This sort of people are so taken up with their theories about the rights of man that they have totally forgotten his nature. Without opening one new avenue to the understanding, they have succeeded in stopping up those that lead to the heart. They have perverted in themselves, and in those that attend to them, all the well-placed sympathies of the human breast . . .

To avoid therefore the evils of inconstancy and versatility, ten thousand times worse than those of obstinacy and the blindest prejudice, we have consecrated the state, that no man should approach to look into its defects or corruptions but with due caution; that he should never dream of beginning its reformation by its subversion; that he should approach to the faults of the state as to the wounds of a father, with pious awe and trembling solicitude. By this wise prejudice we are taught to look with horror on those children of their country who are prompt rashly to hack that aged parent in pieces, and put him into the kettle of magicians in hopes that by their poisonous weeds and wild incantations they may regenerate the paternal constitution, and renovate their father's life.

Society is indeed a contract. Subordinate contracts for objects of mere occasional interest may be dissolved at pleasure – but the state ought not to be considered nothing better than a partnership agreement in a trade of pepper and coffee, calico or tobacco, or some other such low concern, to be taken up for a little temporary interest, and to be dissolved by the fancy of the parties. It is to be looked on with other reverence, because it is not a partnership in things subservient only to the gross animal existence of a temporary and perishable nature. It is a partnership in all science; a partnership in all art; a partnership in every virtue, and in all perfection. As the ends of such a partnership cannot be obtained in many generations, it becomes a partnership not only between those who are living, but between those who are living, those who are dead, and those who are to be born. Each contract of each particular state is but a clause in the great primeval contract of eternal society, linking the lower with the higher natures, connecting the visible and the invisible world, according to a fixed compact sanctioned by the inviolable oath which holds all physical and all moral natures each in their appointed place. This law is not subject to the will of those who, by an obligation above them, and infinitely superior, are bound to submit their will to that law. The municipal corporations of that universal kingdom are not morally at liberty at their pleasure, and on their speculations of a contingent improvement, wholly to separate and tear asunder the bands of their subordinate community, and to dissolve it into an unsocial, uncivil, unconnected chaos of elementary principles. It is the first and supreme necessity only, a necessity that is not chosen, but chooses, a necessity paramount to deliberation that admits no discussion, and demands no evidence, which alone can justify a resort to anarchy. This necessity is no exception to the rule, because this necessity itself is a part too of that moral and physical disposition of things to which man must be obedient by consent of force; but if that which is only submission to necessity should be made the object of choice, the law is broken, nature is disobeyed, and the rebellious are outlawed, cast forth, and exiled from this world of reason and order, and peace and virtue, and fruitful penitence, into the antagonist world of madness, discord, vice, confusion and unavailing sorrow . . .

Our people will find employment enough for a truly patriotic, free and independent spirit in guarding what they possess from violation. I would not exclude alteration neither; but even when I changed, it should be to preserve. I should be led to my remedy by a great grievance. In what I did, I should follow the example of our ancestors. I would make the reparation as nearly as possible in the style of the building. A politic caution, a guarded circumspection, a moral rather than a complexional timidity were among the ruling principles of our forefathers in their most decided conduct. Not being illuminated with the light of which the gentlemen of France tell us they have got so abundant a share, they acted under a strong impression of the ignorance and fallibility of mankind. He that had made them thus fallible, rewarded them for having in their conduct attended to their nature. Let us imitate their caution, if we wish to deserve their fortune, or to retain their bequests. Let us add, if we please, but let us preserve what they have left; and, standing on the firm ground of the British constitution, let us be satisfied to admire, rather than attempt to follow in their desperate flights the aeronauts of France . . .

PRIMARY TEXTS CONSULTED

Barbeyrac, J., *Le droit de la guerre et de la paix. Par Hugues Grotius* (Amsterdam, P. de Coup, 1729).

Beccaria, C., *Dei delitti e delle pene* (Paris, Molini, 1766).

    Dei Delitti e delle pene, ed. G. Franconi, *Edizione nationale* (Milan, Mediobanca, 1984), I.

Burke, E., *Reflections on the Revolution in France, and on the proceedings in certain societies in London relative to that event: in a letter intended to have been sent to a gentleman in Paris* (London, J. Dodsley, 1790).

    The works and correspondence of the Right Honourable Edmund Burke, IV (London, Francis and John Rivington, 1852).

Burlamaqui, J.-J., *Principles of natural right [and natural law]*, trans. Thomas Nugent (London, J. Nourse, 1748).

    Principes du droit naturel . . . Nouvelle édition revue et corrigée (Geneva and Copenhagen, C. and A. Philibert, 1762).

Condorcet, M.-J.-A.-N., de Caritat, Marquis de, *Réflexions sur l'esclavage des nègres* (Neuchâtel, Société Typographique, 1781).

    Œuvres de Condorcet, ed. A. Condorcet-O'Connor and F. Arago, 12 vols. (Paris, Didot, 1847–9).

Diderot, D., *L'Encyclopédie ou dictionnaire raisonné des sciences, des arts et des métiers* (Paris, Briasson, 1751–2), I, III, V.

    Œuvres complètes, ed. H. Dieckmann, J. Proust and J. Varloot (Paris, Hermann, 1975).

Gouges, M. Olympe Aubry de, *Les droits de la femme. A la reine* ([Paris], 1791).

    Œuvres, ed. B. Groult (Paris, Mercure de France, 1986).

    Olympes de Gouges. Ecrits politiques 1788–1791, ed. O. Blanc (Paris, Côté-Femmes Editions, 1993).

Herder, J. G., *Ideen zur Geschichte der Menschheit* (Riga and Leipzig, Hartknock, 1784–91).

    Briefe zur Beförderung der Humanität, ed. W. Dobbek, *Herders Werke* (Berlin and Weimar, Bibliothek Deutscher Klassiker, 1964), V, pp. 202–5.

Hobbes, T., *Leviathan, or the matter of forme and power of a commonwealth ecclesiasticall and civil* (London, Crooke, 1651).
Leviathan, or the matter of forme and power of a commonwealth ecclesiasticall and civil, ed. M. Oakshott (Oxford, Blackwell, 1960).
Hume, D., *Essays and treatises on several subjects* (London, T. Cadell, 1972; Edinburgh, A. Kincaid, 1777).
A treatise of human nature, ed. L. Selby Biggs (Oxford, Clarendon Press, 1968). Reprint.
Kant, I., *Zum ewigen Frieden: ein philosophischer Entwurf* (Königsberg, Friedrich Nicolovius, 1795).
Mandeville, B., *The fable of the bees: or, private vices, publick benefits* (Oxford, Clarendon Press, 1732).
Montesquieu, C.-L. de Secondat, Baron de, *De l'esprit des lois ou du rapport que les lois doivent avoir avec la constitution de chaque gouvernement . . .* , 2 vols. (Geneva, Barrillon, 1748).
Œuvres complètes de Montesquieu, ed. A. Masson, 9 vols. (Paris, Nagel, 1950–5).
Moser, F. K. von, *Der Herr und der Diener, geschildert mit patriotischer Freiheit* (Frankfurt-am-Main, J. Kaspe, 1759).
Paine, T., *Common sense: addressed to the inhabitants of America . . .* (London, Jordan, 1791).
Rights of man: being an answer to Mr Burke's attack on the French Revolution (London, Johnson, 1791).
Price, R., *A discourse on the love of our country* (London, 1789).
Priestley, J., *An essay on the first principles of government, and on the nature of political, civil and religious liberty, including remarks on Dr Brown's code of education, and on Dr Baguley's sermon on church authority* (London, 1771).
Quesnay, F., *Tableau économique, von François Quesnay*, ed. M. Kuczynski (Berlin, Akademie-Verlag, 1965).
Rousseau, J.-J., *Discours sur l'origine et les fondements de l'inégalité parmi les hommes* (Amsterdam, Marc Michel Rey, 1755).
Du contrat social (Amsterdam, Marc Michel Rey, 1762).
Du contrat social (Paris, Garnier, 1952).
Emile, ou de l'éducation (Paris, Garnier, 1964).
Saint-Pierre, C.-I., Castel de, *Mémoire pour rendre la paix perpétuelle en Europe* ([Paris], Bibliothèque Nationale E.2232, 1712).
Projet pour rendre la paix perpétuelle en Europe, ed. S. Goyard-Fabre (Paris, Garnier, 1981).

Siéyès, E.-J., *Qu'est-ce que le tiers état?* ([Paris], 1789).

    Qu'est-ce-que le tiers état?, ed. J.-D. Bredin (Paris, Flammarion, 1988).

Smith, A., *An inquiry into the nature and causes of the wealth of nations* (London, A. Strahan and T. Cadell, 1789). Fifth edition.

Voltaire, F.-M., Arouet de, *Dictionnaire philosophique* ([Geneva, Cramer], 1764).

    Questions sur l'Encyclopédie (Geneva, Bardini, 1775).

    Œuvres complètes de Voltaire, ed. L. Moland, 52 vols. (Paris, Garnier, 1877–85).

    Dictionnaire philosophique, ed. J. Benda and R. Naves (Paris, Garnier, 1954).

    Letters concerning the English nation, ed. N. Cronk (Oxford and New York, Oxford University Press, 1994).

    Œuvres complètes de Voltaire, xxxv–xxxvi, ed. C. Mervaud *et al.* (Oxford, The Voltaire Foundation, 1994).

Wollstonecraft, M., *A vindication of the rights of woman: with strictures on political and moral subjects* (London, 1792).

    Mary Wollstonecraft: political writings, ed. J. Todd (London, William Pickering, 1993).

    Mary Wollstonecraft: A vindication of the rights of men and A vindication of the rights of woman, ed. S. Tomaselli (Cambridge, Cambridge University Press, 1995).

INDEX

abolitionism *see* slavery

Adams, John 61

agriculture 52, 57, 113–14, 412–17, 430–2

Alembert, Jean le Rond d' 2, 32

America 1, 20, 484–91

Antraigues, Emmanuel-Henri Louis Alexandre de Launay, comte d' 19

Aquinas, St Thomas 11; *Summa* 8

aristocracy 24, 27, 67–8, 220–1, 255–7, 262, 495–8

Aristotle 8

balance of power 29; *see also* Saint-Pierre

Barbeyrac, Jean 3, 6, 9, 13, 14, 15, 33, 44, 54–5, 364; ambassadors 365–8; right to kill enemies 368–71; treatment of prisoners 371–3

Bayle, Pierre 2, 3, 7; *Thoughts on the comet* 2

Beccaria, Cesare Bonesana 439–40; death penalty 456–62; definition of crime 447–8, 462–3; justice 453–5; leniency 455–6; *On crimes and punishments* 58–61; prevention 466–7; purpose of punishment 448; relationship between crime and punishment 445–7; suicide 463–6; theory of punishment 442–4; torture 449–53

Bentham, Jeremy 58

Bolingbroke, Henry St John, Lord 13

Boufflers, Stanislas-Jean 35

Boyle, Robert 3, 8

Brissot, Jean-Pierre Warville de 35

Brown, Dr John 20

Brucker, Johann Jakob 6

Buhle, Johann 6

Burke, Edmund 3, 67–8, 508–9; defence of monarchy 512–14; illegitimacy of French Revolution 515–17, 519; natural rights 517–19; *Reflections* 39, 47, 67–9; Revolution Society 510–15; social contract 519–20

Burlamaqui, Jean-Jacques 6, 9, 85; man's law 92–3; natural law 93–102; natural right 86–90, 102; *Principles* 10–14; sociability 99–102

Calas, Jean 57, 58, 60

Calonne, Charles-Alexandre de 64, 65

Cantillon, Richard 54

Charles I 5

Charron, Pierre 3

Claumette, Pierre-Gaspard 38

Cicero 8

civil order 14–22, 205–11, 242–4, 297–9

Clarke, Samuel 19, 20

climate 28, 29, 110

colonies: British 484–91; French 311–16

Condillac, Etienne de 58

Condorcet, Marie-Jean-Antoine-Nicolas de Caritat, Marquis de 3, 19, 20, 36, 52, 61, 63, 307–8; abolition 316; *Historical sketch* 7; injustice of slave trade 308–15; slavery and natural law 312–13; *Réflexions* 34–6

contract 4, 11, 15, 21, 296–7, 519–20; origins 17–18, 33, 118–42; sexual contract 325–8

Court de Gébelin 51

crime 49, 57–8; *see also* Beccaria

Cumberland, Richard 4, 8, 9

Declaration of Independence 1, 28, 32, 64

Declaration of rights 1, 32, 34, 35, 36

decline, causes 28–9

democracy 28, 260–2

Descartes, René 3

despotisms 29, 31, 264–6

Diderot, Denis 2, 32–4, 60, 291–2; authority and power 293–6; 'Citizen' 33, 299–301; 'City' 33, 297–9; contract 296–7; *Encyclopedia* 2, 33, 48, 52, 56; 'Natural law' 33, 34, 302–4;

62157504R10300

Made in the USA
Middletown, DE
19 January 2018